# ᴛʜᴇ BARBOUR
# COLLECTION
## ᴏғ CONNECTICUT TOWN
# VITAL RECORDS

# ≡ BARBOUR COLLECTION
# OF CONNECTICUT TOWN
# VITAL RECORDS

EAST HARTFORD 1783–1853

EAST HAVEN 1700–1852

EAST LYME 1839–1853

*Compiled by*

Christina Bailey

# INTRODUCTION

As early as 1640 the Connecticut Court of Election ordered all magistrates to keep a record of the marriages they performed. In 1644 the registration of births and marriages became the official responsibility of town clerks and registrars, with deaths added to their duties in 1650. From 1660 until the close of the Revolutionary War these vital records of birth, marriage, and death were generally well kept, but then for a period of about two generations, until the mid-nineteenth century, the faithful recording of vital records declined in some towns.

General Lucius Barnes Barbour was the Connecticut Examiner of Public Records from 1911 to 1934 and, in that capacity, directed a project in which the vital records kept by the towns up to about 1850 were copied and abstracted. Barbour previously had directed the publication of the Bolton and Vernon vital records for the Connecticut Historical Society. For this new project he hired several individuals who were experienced in copying old records and familiar with the old script.

Barbour presented the completed transcriptions of town vital records to the Connecticut State Library where the information was typed onto printed forms. The form sheets were then cut, producing twelve small slips from each sheet. The slips for most towns were the alphabetized and the information was then typed a second time on large sheet of rag paper, which were subsequently bound into separate volumes for each town. The lists for all towns were then interfiled, forming a statewide alphabetized slip index for most surviving town vital records.

The dates of coverage vary from town to town and, of course, the records of some towns are more complete than others. Altogether the entire Barbour Collection -- one of the great genealogical manuscript collections and one of the last to be published -- covers 137 towns and comprises 14, 333 typed pages.

# TABLE OF CONTENTS

# ABBREVIATIONS

ae ------- age
b. ------- born
bd. ----- buried or baptized
bp. ----- baptized
d. ------- daughter or died or day
h. ------- hour
J. P. ---- Justice of the Peace
m. ------ married or month
res. ----- resident
s. ------- son
s.b. ----- stillborn
w. ------ week
wid. ---- widow
wk. ----- week
y. ------- year

# THE BARBOUR COLLECTION
# OF CONNECTICUT TOWN
# VITAL RECORDS

# EAST HARTFORD VITAL RECORDS
# 1783 - 1853

|  | Vol. | Page |
|---|---|---|
| [ABBE], ABBEY, ABBY, Abigail, m. Harry ENSIGN, Apr. 8, 1821, | | |
| by Joy H. Fairchild | 1 | 95 |
| Ann, m. Edward GILMAN, Sept. 25, 1817 | 1 | 68 |
| Betsey, d. Jan. 12, 1829, ae 68 | 1 | 74 |
| Betsy, bd. by Samuel COX, Jan. 17, 1829, ae 69 | 1 | 75 |
| Caty, m. Eligah VIBBERT, [          ] | 1 | 31 |
| Daniel, d. [May] [  ], 1827 | 1 | 168 |
| David, his child d. [          ], 1814 | 1 | 67 |
| David, d. Apr. [  ], [1827] | 1 | 74 |
| Edmund, m. Harriot GAINES, Aug. 2, 1821, by Joy H. | | |
| Fairchild | 1 | 96 |
| Frank, d. July 9, 1831, ae 35 | 1 | 74 |
| Frank, bd. July 10, 1831, ae 35 | 1 | 76 |
| Harriet, of East Hartford, m. Russell HOLLISTER, of Berlin, | | |
| June 26, 1837, by Samuel Spring | 1 | 123 |
| Harriet, of East Hartford, m. William T. HOLLISTER, of | | |
| Glastenbury, Dec. 24, 1848, by Rev. J. O. | | |
| Goodridge | 1 | 155 |
| Harriet, ae 23, of East Hartford, m. W[illia]m T. HOLLISTER, | | |
| mason, ae 24, b. Glastonbury, res. Windsor Locks, | | |
| Dec. 28, 1848, by [          ] Goodrich | 1 | 52 |
| Harriet, d. Sept. 24, 1850, ae 51 | 1 | 60 |
| Henry, of East Windsor, m. Lucretia L. PORTER, of East | | |
| Hartford, May 5, 1830, by Rev. Samuel H. Biddle | 1 | 112 |
| Jane, d. John, farmer & Sarah, b. Sept. 17, 1848 | 1 | 51 |
| Joel, bd. Jan. 11, 1839, ae 34, by his sister Mrs. Edward | | |
| GILMAN | 1 | 78 |
| Lois, d. Sept. 15, 1822 | 1 | 74 |
| Lucretia, m. George ROBERTS, Mar. 19, 1822, by Joy H. | | |
| Fairchild | 1 | 98 |
| Martha, b. Aug. 19, 1759; m. Jesse VIBBERT, Aug. 7, 1783 | 1 | 26 |
| Mary, wid., d. [          ], 1809, ae 82 | 1 | 66 |
| Miles M., of East Windsor, m. Lucretia COWLES, of East | | |
| Hartford, May 2, 1821, by Rev. Elisha B. Cook | 1 | 96 |
| Roswell, of Enfield, m. Sarah KILLAM, of East Hartford, Nov. | | |
| 15, 1836, by Samiel Spring | 1 | 121 |
| Russell, d. July 7, 1828, ae 59 | 1 | 74 |
| Ruth, m. John RISLEY, Sept. [  ], 1793* *(Probably "1773") | 1 | 16 |
| Stephen, his d. [          ], b. Jan. [  ], 1798 | 1 | 63 |
| Stephen, d. May 29, 1823, ae 69 | 1 | 74 |
| Thankful, m. W[illia]m W. LARRABEE, May 4, 1819 | 1 | 69 |
| ——, Mrs., d. Jan. [  ], 1798 | 1 | 63 |
| ——, Mrs., d. Jan. [  ], 1804 | 1 | 64 |
| ——, Mr., d. [          ], 1805 | 1 | 65 |
| ——, his child d. [          ], 1806 | 1 | 65 |

| | Vol. | Page |
|---|---|---|
| **ANDERSON**, (cont.), | | |
| Ira, painter, ae 27, m. Jennette **ENSIGN**, ae 24, b. of East Hartford, Mar. 12, 1850, by S. Spring | 1 | 56 |
| Ira, m. Jenette **ENSIGN**, b. of East Hartford, Mar. 12, 1850, by Samuel Spring | 1 | 158 |
| Lusina, [d. Timothy], b. Mar. 14, 1782 | 1 | 41 |
| Mary, [d. Timothy], b. Oct. 28, 1786 | 1 | 41 |
| Norman, [s. Timothy], b. July 8, 1799 | 1 | 41 |
| Norman, m. Emeline **CULVER**, Nov. 16, 1826, by Joy H. Fairchild | 1 | 107 |
| Russell, [s. Timothy], b. Oct. [23]*, 1796 *[may be 26, typewriter strike over is unclear] | 1 | 41 |
| Sallay, [d. Timothy], b. Apr. 19, 1784 | 1 | 41 |
| Sarah C., m. Elisha B. **BREWER**, b. of East Hartford, Apr. 3, 1850, by Samuel Spring | 1 | 158 |
| Sarah C., ae 22, m. Elisha C. **BREWER**, machinist, ae 28, b. of East Hartford, Apr. 23, 1850, by S. Spring | 1 | 56 |
| Timothy, b. Aug. 6, 1762; m. 1st w. [        ] **BURNHAM**, [        ]; m. 2nd w. Lewis **GUERNSEY**, [        ] | 1 | 41 |
| Timothy, [s. Timothy], b. Nov. 22, 1788 | 1 | 41 |
| ------, Mrs., d. [        ], 1802 | 1 | 64 |
| **ANDREWS**, [see also **ANDROSS**], Abner B., of South Windsor, m. Mary S. **COWLES**, of East Hartford, Aug. 22, 1849, by Samuel Spring | 1 | 157 |
| Betsy, [d. Urial & Lucina], b. Apr. 16, 1801 | 1 | 16 |
| George, [s. Urial & Lucina], b. Nov. 27, 1798 | 1 | 16 |
| George H., s. Henry P., weaver, ae 45 & Francis C., ae 39, b. Jan. 15, 1850 | 1 | 54 |
| Henry R., of Ashford, m. Francis C. **WILLIAMS**, of East Hartford, Oct. 26, 1845, by Samuel Spring | 1 | 150 |
| Nancy, [d. Urial & Lucina], b. Oct. 7, 1796 | 1 | 16 |
| Urial, m. Lucina **BARRET**, Mar. 20, 1794 | 1 | 16 |
| Urial, [s. Urial & Lucina], b. Feb. 2, 1795 | 1 | 16 |
| **ANDROSS, ANDROS, ANDRUS**,[see also, **ANDREWS**], A. B., merchant, ae 24, b. S. Windsor, res. East Hartford, m. M. S. **COWLES**, ae 24, res. East Hartford, res. same, Aug. 22, 1849, by Rev. S. Spring | 1 | 55 |
| Caroline, m. Ambrose **CASE**, Jan. 1, 1822, by Elisha Cushman | 1 | 97 |
| Electa, m. Simond **LANDFEAR**, b. of East Hartford, Oct.3, 1822, by Rev. Elisha B. Cook | 1 | 99 |
| Parmelia, m. Anson **HILLS**, Oct. 12, 1820, by Joy H. Fairchild | 1 | 94 |
| William, of East Hartford, m. Lucy Ann **SLOANE**, of Hartford, Apr. 1, 1834, by Samuel Spring | 1 | 116 |
| William F., s. Abner B., merchant, ae 25, & Mary L., ae 25, b. June 21, 1850 | 1 | 55 |
| **ANTRIM**, Eliza A., of South Windsor, m. Albert B. **GILMAN**, of East Hartford, Oct. 29, 1848, by Samuel Spring | 1 | 155 |
| **ARCHER**, ------, his child bd., Sept. 1, 1832 | 1 | 76 |
| **ARMSTRONG**, Catherine, m. John **PARKER**, b. of East Hartford, Mar. 29, 1840, by Samuel Spring | 1 | 132 |

| ARMSTRONG, (cont.), | Vol. | Page |
|---|---|---|
| Cornelia C., of East Hartford, m. Charles SMITH, of Ellington, | | |
| May 15, 1850, at Colchester, by Rev. George W. | | |
| Pendleton | 1 | 159 |
| ARNERIUS, [see also ARNOVINA], Augustus, gunsmith, ae 25, b. | | |
| Berlin, Pa., res. Hartford, m. Francisha SOHALY*, | | |
| ae 20, July 13, 1851, by S. Spring *(Probably | | |
| "SCHULTZ") | 1 | 59 |
| ARNOLD, Almira, m. Jabez WATERMAN, Nov. 28, 1822, by Joy H. | | |
| Fairchild | 1 | 100 |
| Anne, m. Julius GRISWOLD, Jan. 3, 1822, by Joy H. Fairchild | 1 | 97 |
| Betsy, [d. Samuel & Lucy], b. Feb. 19, 1781*      *(1787?) | 1 | 29 |
| Charlotte, of East Hartford, m. Estis H. SMITH, of Sag Harbor, | | |
| L. I., May 13, 1840, by Samuel Spring | 1 | 132 |
| Clarissa R., of East Hartford, m. Charles KNOX, of Hartford, | | |
| Nov. 12, 1843, by B. R. Northrop | 1 | 144 |
| Doris, [d. Samuel & Lucy], b. Jan. 17, 1773 | 1 | 29 |
| Elisha, [s. Samuel & Lucy], b. Jan. 25, 1778 | 1 | 29 |
| Elisha, farmer, d. Sept. 8, 1848, ae 70 | 1 | 53 |
| Elizabeth, of East Hartford, m. Ebenezer P. KIMBALL, of | | |
| Petersborega, N. H., Dec. 9, 1834, by Samuel Spring | 1 | 118 |
| Ethan, [s. Samuel & Lucy], b. Aug. 21, 1784 | 1 | 29 |
| George, [s. Samuel & Lucy], b. Sept. 23, 1782 | 1 | 29 |
| George, d. Sept. 30, 1849, ae 5 | 1 | 56 |
| George W., bd. Oct. 14, 1838, ae 57 | 1 | 78 |
| Harriet, of East Hartford, m. Joseph HOLLISTER, of | | |
| Glastenbury, July 12, 1841, by Samuel Spring | 1 | 135 |
| Jo, his s. [      ], d. May [ ], 1798 | 1 | 63 |
| John, [s. Samuel & Lucy], b. Mar. 28, 1771 | 1 | 29 |
| John, m. Mary BURNHAM, Feb. 7, 1828, by Enoch Brent | 1 | 109 |
| John, his child bd. June 7, 1836, ae 9 m. | 1 | 77 |
| Joseph, m. wid. Sarah SMITH, Dec. 30, 1784, by Rev. Dr. | | |
| Williams | 1 | 61 |
| Lucretia, [d. Samuel & Lucy], b. Aug. 9, 1778*      *(1776?) | 1 | 29 |
| Lucretia, m. Jared SPENCER, May 10, 1795 | 1 | 26 |
| Lucy, [d. Samuel & Lucy], b. June 2, 1767 | 1 | 29 |
| Lucy, m. David JONES, b. of East Hartford, Sept.12, 1852(?), | | |
| by Rev. Benjamin C. Phelps | 1 | 163 |
| Mary, m. Noah RISLEY, Nov. 2, 1786, by Rev. Dr. Williams | 1 | 61 |
| Mary, m. William WATERMAN, Dec. 22, 1825, by Joy H. | | |
| Fairchild | 1 | 105 |
| Ruth, d. Sept. 29, 1849, ae 69 y. | 1 | 56 |
| Samuel, m. Lucy PRAT, Dec. 25, 1766 | 1 | 29 |
| Samuel, [s. Samuel & Lucy], b. Nov. 21, 1768 | 1 | 29 |
| Samuel, his s. [      ], d. [        ], 1799 | 1 | 63 |
| Sarah, m. Ashbel EASTON, Aug. 22, 1784, by Rev. Dr. | | |
| Williams | 1 | 61 |
| Sarah, m. John F. COWLES, b. of East Hartford, Dec. 25, | | |
| 1851, by Samuel Spring | 1 | 161 |
| Sarah A., m. John F. COWLES, Dec. 25, 1851, by Rev. | | |
| Samuel Spring | 1 | 60 |
| Sophia, m. John B. SCOTT, b. of East Hartford, July 16, 1849, | | |
| by Rev. Benjamin C. Phelps | 1 | 158 |

| | Vol. | Page |
|---|---|---|
| **ARNOLD**, (cont.). | | |
| Susan, d. Elisha & Abigail, m. Orrin **SELLEW**, s. George & | | |
|    Dorothy, Oct. 19, 1830, by Asa Mead | 1 | 70 |
| Susan, m. Orrin **SELLEW**, Oct. 19, 1830, by Rev. Asa Mead | 1 | 112 |
| Susan, her child, bd. Sept. 4, 1842, ae 2 m. | 1 | 79 |
| Susan, of East Hartford, m. Jedediah **SMITH**, of Glastenbury, | | |
|    July 17, 1845, by Levi Daggett, Jr. | 1 | 149 |
| Wait, [child of Samuel & Lucy], b. Jan. 9, 1775 | 1 | 29 |
| Wait, m. Susan **CULLIVER**, Apr. 5, 1820, by [      ] | 1 | 69 |
| -----, Mrs., d. Nov. [ ], 1806 | 1 | 65 |
| **ARNOVINA**, [see also **ARNERIUS**], Gustavus, m. Franzisku | | |
|    **SCHULTZ**, b. of Berlin, Prussia, July 13, 1851, by | | |
|    Samuel Spring | 1 | 160 |
| **ASHLEY**, Charles N., b. Oct. 31, 1843 | 1 | 41 |
| Jane L., d. Charles, farmer & Jane, b. Apr. 2, 1849 | 1 | 51 |
| Jedediah, d. [    ], 1814 | 1 | 67 |
| **ATHERTON**, Laomi, m. Royal **GURLEY**, [    ] | 1 | 1 |
| **AUSTIN**, George C., of Wethersfield, m. Margaret **CAMP**, of East | | |
|    Hartford, July 5, 1846, by Samuel Spring | 1 | 152 |
| Harriet, of East Hartford, m. James **WOODBRIDGE**, of | | |
|    Hartford, Nov. 11, 1840, by Samuel Spring | 1 | 134 |
| Julia S., of East Hartford, m. William H. **DRAKE**, of New | | |
|    York City, June 1, 1836, by Samuel Spring | 1 | 121 |
| Mary C., of East Hartford, m. Philip Melancthon **HUDSON**, of | | |
|    Hartford, Jan. 3, 1837, by Samuel Spring | 1 | 122 |
| **AVERY**, Ephraim K., m. Sophia **HILLS**, Sept. 25, 1822, by Rev. Elisha | | |
|    Blake | 1 | 99 |
| W[illia]m L., of Willimantic, m. Caroline **BREWER**, of East | | |
|    Hartford, Dec. 24, 1845, by Samuel Spring | 1 | 150 |
| **AYRES, AYERS**, Ann L., of Willimantic, N.J., m. Thaddeus | | |
|    **PRENTICE**, Jr., of Willimantic, Mar. 30, 1846, by | | |
|    Samuel Spring | 1 | 151 |
| Fredrick Howard, s. Jared A., teacher, ae 35, b. June 19, 1851 | 1 | 58 |
| Henry Wilcox, [s. Jared, teacher, ae 35 & Sarah L. , ae 30, b. | | |
|    May 9, 1848 | 1 | 46 |
| Jared, his w. [    ], bd. Mar. 14, 1844, ae 71 | 1 | 80 |
| **BABCOCK**, Charles B., teacher, ae 29, b. Coventry, res. East Hartford, m. | | |
|    Delia P. **BLISS**, ae 20, b. East Hartford, res. same, | | |
|    Dec. 5, 1847, by Samuel Springs | 1 | 48 |
| Charles I., of South Coventry, m. Delia P. **BLISS**, of East | | |
|    Hartford, Dec. 5, 1847, by Samuel Spring | 1 | 154 |
| Leonard, m. Sally **LUTHUR**, July 4, 1826, by Joy H. Fairchild | 1 | 106 |
| Mary, m. Josiah **OLCOTT**, Jr., May 27, 1778 | 1 | 72 |
| **BACON**, Stiles, m. Mary Ann **CLARK**, May 2, 1849, by Rev. S. Spring | 1 | 52 |
| Styles, m. Mary Ann **CLARK**, b. of East Hartford, June 20, | | |
|    1849, by Rev. Benjamin O. Phelps | 1 | 157 |
| **BAGG**, Nelson, m. Julia **HOUSE**, b. of East Hartford, May 2, 1849, by | | |
|    Rev. S. Spring | 1 | 52 |
| Nelson P., of East Hartford, m. Julia L. **HOUSE**, of East | | |
|    Hartford, May 22, 1849, by Rev. Benjamin O. | | |
|    Phelps | 1 | 156 |

|  | Vol. | Page |
|---|---|---|
| **BAILEY, BAYLEY**, Jared C., d. at Dudley Hills Tavern, parents lived in Columbia Coos Cty. of New Hampshire, bd. Jan. 22, 1841, ae 26 | 1 | 79 |
| V. A., of Hartford, m. Mary C. **WILLIAMS**, of East Hartford, Nov. 10, 1840, by Samuel Spring | 1 | 134 |
| **BAIRTH**, Francis, of Germany, m. George **SEITZ**, of Glastenbury, May 24, 1852, by Charles C. Ashley, J. P. | 1 | 163 |
| **BAKER**, Harriet A., m. Charles **DEMING**, b. of East Hartford, Jan. 4, 1848, by Samuel Spring | 1 | 154 |
| Harriet A., ae 19, b. Glastenbury, res. East Hartford, m. Charles **DEMMING**, sadler, ae 21, b. East Hartford, res. same, Jan. [ ], 1848, by Samuel Springs | 1 | 48 |
| **BALDWIN**, George, of Washington, Conn., m. Fidelia **BURNHAM**, of East Hartford, May 21, 1837, by Samuel Spring | 1 | 123 |
| Ja[me]s F., m. Sarah **PITKIN**, July 30, 1818 | 1 | 68 |
| **BALL**, Daniel A., of Springfield, Mass., m. Polly **CASE**, of East Hartford, Oct. 3, 1820, by Rev. Elisha B. Cook | 1 | 95 |
| **BANCROFT**, Thomas L., m. Clarrisa Ann **PORTER**, June 6, 1826, by Joy H. Fairchild | 1 | 106 |
| **BANNING**, Erastus M., had d. [ ], b. [ ] | 1 | 55 |
| **BARBER**, Eli, m. Anne **BIDWELL**, Nov. 18, 1818 | 1 | 68 |
| Elizabeth, of Hebron, m. Amos **ROBBINS**, of Hartford, June 23, 1844, by Samuel Spring | 1 | 145 |
| George, m. Emily **FORBES**, b. of East Hartford, June 17, 1829, by Rev. Samuel Spring, of Hartford | 1 | 110 |
| Joshua, m. Jane **KENNEDY**, May 7, 1823, by Joy H. Fairchild | 1 | 101 |
| Mary, m. Saley Jones **RATHBUM**, Nov. 15, 1818 | 1 | 68 |
| **BARKER**, Delia, d. J. W., tailor, ae 26, & Francis, ae 19, b. Feb. 26, 1850 | 1 | 55 |
| John, tailor, [ ] 27, had d. [ ], b. Mar. [ ], 1851 | 1 | 58 |
| **BARNARD**, Edwin, of Rochester, N. Y., m. Henrietta **RIPLEY**, of Hartford, Mar. 7, 1831, by Rev. Asa Mead | 1 | 112 |
| Edwin W., of Rochester, N. Y., s. Cyprian, m. Henrietta **RIPLEY**, d. John & Elizabeth, late of Hartford, Mar. 7, 1831, by Asa Mead | 1 | 70 |
| Louisa, m. John **VIBBERT**, b. of East Hartford, May 11, 1846, by Samuel Spring | 1 | 151 |
| **BARNES**, Franklin, m. Ann **HILLS**, Apr. 13, 1836, by Samuel Spring | 1 | 120 |
| Franklin, m. Jane A. **COWLES**, b. of East Hartford, Jan. 1, 1846, by Samuel Spring | 1 | 150 |
| **BARNUM, BARNAM**, Eli, m. Tirzah **WELLS**, b. of East Hartford, Dec. 16, 1832, by Rev. Gustavus F. Davis, of Hartford | 1 | 113 |
| Eli, m. Almira **HALL**, b. of East Hartford, Apr. 17, 1834, by Rev. Gustavus F. Davis, of Hartford | 1 | 116 |
| Eliza H., b. New York City, res. same, d. Sept. 9, 1849, ae 31 | 1 | 56 |
| Henry C., b. New York City, res. same, d. Sept.11, 1849, ae 5 m. | 1 | 56 |
| Levi P., m. Julia **CAMP**, b. of East Hartford, Sept. 5, 1836, by Rev. Asher Moore, of Hartford | 1 | 119 |
| Monroe, d. Nov. 20, 1848, ae 10 | 1 | 53 |
| **BARRET**, Lucina, m. Urial **ANDREWS**, Mar. 20, 1794 | 1 | 16 |
| **BARROWS**, Andrew L., of Hartford, m. Elizabeth P. **RISLEY**, of East Hartford, Dec. 20, 1840, by Samuel Spring | 1 | 134 |

| | Vol. | Page |
|---|---|---|
| BATES, Mary, d. Hibbard, ae 30, & Are(?), ae 30, b. July 10, 1851 | 1 | 57 |
| [BEAMON], BEAMONT, BEMONT, [see also BEAUMONT], | | |
| Abigail, Mrs., d. Apr. [ ], 1806, ae 84 | 1 | 65 |
| Delia, of East Hartford, m. Seth W. JOHNSON, of Vernon, | | |
| May 4, 1836, by Samuel Spring | 1 | 120 |
| Elisa, m. Gideon M. MURPHY, b. of East Hartford, Jan.15, | | |
| 1829, by Rev. Timothy Benedict | 1 | 110 |
| Ira, bd. Apr. 16, 1842, ae 56 | 1 | 79 |
| Leonard, d. [ ], 1799, ae 20 | 1 | 63 |
| Martha, m. Nehemiah RISLEY, June 3, 1784, by Rev. Dr. | | |
| Williams | 1 | 61 |
| Mary, m. Andrew H. DEWER*, Mar. 1, 1826, by Joy H. | | |
| Fairchild *("BREWER?") | 1 | 105 |
| T.O., bd. Mar. 12, 1841, ae 3 | 1 | 79 |
| BEAUMONT, [see also BEAMON], Eliza, m. Joseph MERRIMAN, b. | | |
| of East Hartford, Sept. 26, 1838, at her father's | | |
| house, by Rev. Henry Jackson, of Hartford | 1 | 126 |
| BEAUREL, Rosella, milliner, ae 26, b. New Hampshire, res. East Hartford, | | |
| m. W[illia]m CULVER, bricklayer, ae 33, b. | | |
| Norwich, res. same, Jan. 8, 1848, by Rev. S. Spring | 1 | 52 |
| BECKET, ——, Mrs., d. [ ], 1826 | 1 | 168 |
| BEEBE, Edmond M., m. Lucinda BIDWELL, July 7, 1824, by Rev. | | |
| Lewis Pease | 1 | 102 |
| Robert, m. Olive SPENCER, b. of East Hartford, Nov. 27, | | |
| 1828, by Rev. Timothy Benedict | 1 | 110 |
| BELDEN, David L., m. Polly HILLS, b. of East Hartford, Apr. 9, 1828, | | |
| by Rev. Samuel H. Puddle | 1 | 109 |
| Delia, m. Ashbel OLMSTED, Mar. 9, 1825, by Joy H. | | |
| Fairchild | 1 | 103 |
| Mary A., m. Ranson RILEY, May 4, 1843, by Cephas Brainard | 1 | 151 |
| Russell, d. [ ], 1804, at Sea | 1 | 64 |
| Sarah, m. Elam GLEASON, Jan. 17, 1821, by Joy H. Fairchild | 1 | 95 |
| ——, his child d. [ ], 1809 | 1 | 66 |
| BELL, George E., m. Sarah E. PERSENS, b. of East Hartford, Mar. 30, | | |
| 1851, by S. Spring | 1 | 59 |
| George E., m. Sarah H. PERSONS, b. of East Hartford, Mar. | | |
| 30, 1851, by Samuel Spring | 1 | 160 |
| BELLOWS, Alonzo, mechanic, ae 30, b. Wethersfield, res. Hartford, m. | | |
| 2nd w. Dorcinda R. CLARK, ae 28, b. East | | |
| Hartford, res. same, Dec. 31, 1849, by H. Bushnell | 1 | 56 |
| BEMIS, BEMISS, Mary L., ae 20, b. East Hartford, res. same, m. James | | |
| G. FITCH, ae 34, b. Hartford, res. East Hartford, | | |
| Oct. 20, 1847, by Jos. Harrington | 1 | 48 |
| Mary Lamb, m. James Goodwin FITCH, b. of East Hartford, | | |
| Oct. 20, 1847, by Rev. Joseph Harrington, of | | |
| Hartford | 1 | 154 |
| BEMONT, [see under BEAMON] | | |
| BENJAMIN, Daniel, d. [ ], 1807 | 1 | 65 |
| Rebecca, m. Benjamin HOWELL, Nov. 20, 1823, by Joy H. | | |
| Fairchild | 1 | 102 |
| Sarah M., m. Avery JACKSON, b. of Pittsfield, Mass., Nov. | | |
| 25, [1847], by Samuel Springs | 1 | 48 |

8 BARBOUR COLLECTION

| | Vol. | Page |
|---|---|---|
| **BENJAMIN,** (cont.), | | |
| Sarah M., m. Avery **JACKSON,** b. of Pitttsfield, Mass., Nov. | | |
| 25, 1847, by Samuel Spring | 1 | 154 |
| -----, Mrs., bd. Sept. 22, 1829, by Osymon Pitkin | 1 | 75 |
| **BENT,** Lovina, m. Richard **JOHNSON,** Nov. 11, 1821, by Rev. Isaac | | |
| Divinel | 1 | 97 |
| **BENTON,** *Clarisa, m. Elisha **TREAT,** b. of Glastonbury, Oct. 19, 1820, | | |
| by Joy W. Fairchild *(In red ink "d. of Joseph") | 1 | 94 |
| **BIDWELL,** Alford, [s. Ozias P. & Mary], b. Oct. 12, 1800 | 1 | 27 |
| Anne, m. Eli **BARBER,** Nov. 18, 1818 | 1 | 68 |
| Ashbel, d. [          ], 1807 | 1 | 65 |
| Ashbel, d. Dec. 21, 1830, ae 79 | 1 | 74 |
| Ashbel, f. of Lewis, bd. Dec. 30, 1830, ae 79 | 1 | 76 |
| Austin, of Manchester, m. Caroline **JUDSON,** of East Hartford, | | |
| Oct. 26, 1836, by S. L. Tracy | 1 | 119 |
| Benjamin F., s. Benson, stuff(?) collars, ae 26, & Mary, ae 21, | | |
| b. Oct. 29, 1849 | 1 | 54 |
| Betsy, [d. Ozias P. & Mary], b. Oct. 4, 1798 | 1 | 27 |
| Betsy, m. Sylvester **ROBERTS,** Dec. 12, 1819 | 1 | 69 |
| Betsy, m. Horace **STARKS,** Apr. 2, 1828, by Rev. Samuel | | |
| Spring, of Hartford | 1 | 109 |
| Chester, [s. Stephen & Hannah], b. Sept. 14, 1792 | 1 | 24 |
| Chester, [s. Ozias P. & Mary], b. Nov. 26, 1796 | 1 | 27 |
| Frank L., s. S.O., painter, ae 26, & Mary E., ae 22, b. Nov. 2, | | |
| 1848 | 1 | 50 |
| Hannah, [d. Stephen & Hannah], b. Nov. 17, 1784 | 1 | 24 |
| Hannah, d. Jan. 13, 1806, ae 89 | 1 | 65 |
| Henry, of Manchester, m. Cornelia J. **WILLIAMS,** of East | | |
| Hartford, Apr. 17, 1850, by Samuel Spring | 1 | 158 |
| Heppy, m. Asahel **JONES,** Mar. 4, 1819 | 1 | 69 |
| Hepsba, d. June 6, 1851, ae 87 | 1 | 60 |
| Jameson S., s. Sidney, farmer, ae 31 & Elizabeth, ae 29, b. Dec. | | |
| 13, 1847 | 1 | 46 |
| Jerusha, m. Allen **WADSWORTH,** b. of East Hartford, July | | |
| 11, 1820, by Joy H. Fairchild | 1 | 94 |
| Jesse, s. Rodolphus, d. [          ], 1806, ae 10 | 1 | 65 |
| John, d. [          ], 1804 | 1 | 64 |
| John N., s. Samuel C., painter, ae 28, b. Sept. 5, 1850 | 1 | 58 |
| Joseph, Dr., d. [          ], 1798, ae 89 | 1 | 63 |
| Julius, s. Moses & Lucy, m. Rhoda **COOK,** d. [    ] & Sally, | | |
| Feb. 23, 1831, by Asa Mead | 1 | 70 |
| Julius, m. Rhoda **COOK,** Feb. 23, 1831, by Rev. Asa Mead | 1 | 112 |
| Leonard, m. Abbey **COMSTOCK,** May 25, 1819 | 1 | 69 |
| Lewis, m. Cynthia **ROBERTS,** Dec. 31, 1816 | 1 | 68 |
| Lucinda, m. Edmond M. **BEEBE,** July 7, 1824, by Rev. Lewis | | |
| Pease | 1 | 102 |
| Martin, m. Malinda **KEENY,** b. of East Hartford, Oct.10, | | |
| 1822, by Rev. Elisha B. Cook | 1 | 99 |
| Mary, of East Hartford, m. Daniel **DEMING,** of Wethersfield, | | |
| Nov. 16, 1822, by Joy H. Fairchild | 1 | 100 |
| Mary, of East Hartford, m. Eldad **WEBSTER,** of Casenovia, | | |
| N. Y., Oct. 28, 1832, by Rev. Samuel Spring, of | | |
| Hartford | 1 | 115 |

| | Vol. | Page |
|---|---|---|
| **BIDWELL**, (cont.), | | |
| Mary, d. Oct. 9, 1849, ae 63 | 1 | 56 |
| Mima, [d. Stephen & Hannah], b. Feb. 6, 1799 | 1 | 24 |
| Mirna, [d. Stephen & Hannah], b. Mar. 18, 1788; d. May 14, | | |
| 1789 | 1 | 24 |
| Morton, d. Apr. [ ], 1826 | 1 | 167 |
| Ostin, his w. [ ], d. June [ ], 1826 | 1 | 168 |
| Ozias P., m Mary **WITHEREL**, Sept. 26, 1793 | 1 | 27 |
| Polly, [d. Ozias P. & Mary], b. Oct. 1, 1794 | 1 | 27 |
| Rinda, d. Apr. 17, 1851, ae 73 | 1 | 59 |
| Rodolphus, his child d. [ ], 1800 | 1 | 63 |
| Ruhannah W., of East Hartford, m. Moses **ELMER**, Jr., of East | | |
| Windsor, Apr. 20, 1836, by Samuel Spring | 1 | 120 |
| Sally, m. Nathaniel **WARREN**, Aug. 24, 1820, by Joy H. | | |
| Fairchild | 1 | 94 |
| Samuel, his w. [ ], d. [ ], 1800 | 1 | 63 |
| Samuel, m. Dorinda **CASE**, Oct. 26, 1822, by Joy H. Fairchild | 1 | 99 |
| Sarah, m. Charles **BUNCE**, Dec. 31, 1789 | 1 | 30 |
| Solomon, m. Caroline **SKINNER**, Aug. 5, 1818 | 1 | 68 |
| Stephen, m. Hannah **WHITE**, June 26, 1783 | 1 | 24 |
| Timothy, his child d. [ ], 1803 | 1 | 64 |
| Timothy, his child d. [ ], 1814 | 1 | 67 |
| Tracy, m. Nancy **GRISWOLD**, b. of East Hartford, Dec. 25, | | |
| 1822, by Rev. Elisha B. Cook | 1 | 101 |
| Warren, of Manchester, m. Ann P. **WILLIAMS**, of East | | |
| Hartford, Sept. 19, 1841, by Rev. B. M. Walker | 1 | 136 |
| ——, wid., d. [ ], 1800 | 1 | 63 |
| ——, Mrs., bd. July 3, 1830, ae 77 | 1 | 76 |
| **BIGELOW**, W[illia]m, farmer, b. Ashford, res. East Hartford, d. Feb. 17, | | |
| 1851, ae 78 | 1 | 59 |
| **BILL**, Frank W., Rev. of Glastenbury, m. Rowena **CLEVELAND**, of | | |
| Wethersfield, Mar. 14, 1843, by Rev. B. M. Walker | 1 | 142 |
| Sarah, of Glastenbury, m. Lyman **TREAT**, of East Hartford, | | |
| Jan. 2, 1843, by Samuel Spring | 1 | 141 |
| **BILLINGS**, Henry E., miller, ae 24, b. Chatham, res. [ ], m. | | |
| Celestia **BREWER**, ae 19, b. East Hartford, res. | | |
| same, Jan. 5, 1848, by Samuel Springs | 1 | 48 |
| Henry E., of Glastenbury, m. Celesta P. **BREWER**, of East | | |
| Hartford, Jan. 5, 1848, by Samuel Spring | 1 | 154 |
| **BINDLE**, Rosina, of Werlemberel, Germany, m. Phillip **HIEM**, of | | |
| Glastenbury, July 16, [probably 1854], by C. C. | | |
| Ashley, J. P. | 1 | 166 |
| **BINGHAM**, Alexander H., of Rockville, m. Ella L. **ALLEN**, of East | | |
| Hartford, Mar. 26, 1854, by Rev. B. C. Phelps | 1 | 166 |
| Ira, of Whiting, O., m. Adeline **WARREN**, of East Hartford, | | |
| Oct. 14, 1833, by Samuel Spring | 1 | 114 |
| **BIRGE**, Daniel, m. Mira(?) **WADSWORTH**, Nov. 5, 1801, by Rev. Dr. | | |
| Williams | 1 | 62 |
| Edwin, m. Naomi **OLMSTED**, b. of East Hartford, Aug. 9, | | |
| 1837, by Samuel Spring | 1 | 123 |
| Simeon, m. Electa **PITKIN**, Sept. 22, 1819 | 1 | 38 |
| Simeon Pitkin, [s. Simeon & Electa], b. July 9, 1820 | 1 | 38 |

|  | Vol. | Page |
|---|---|---|
| **BISHOP**, Nancy, of Bolton, m. Daniel **COLBOURN**, of Windham, Sept. 28, 1820, by Rev. Elisha B. Cook | 1 | 95 |
| **BISSELL, BISSEL,** Doshe, b. Aug. 14, 1769; m. David **LANDFEAR,** Mar. 26, 1801 | 1 | 5 |
| Elizabeth B., of East Hartford, m. Royal **ROBBINS,** of Berlin, Oct. 17, 1839, by Samuel Spring | 1 | 130 |
| Harriet, of Manchester, m. Jared W. **HOLLISTER,** of Glastonbury, Dec. 1, 1847, by Samuel Spring | 1 | 48 |
| Harriet, of Manchester, m. Jared W. **HOLLISTER,** of Glastenbury , Dec. 1, 1847, by Samuel Spring | 1 | 154 |
| Sarah, of East Hartford, m. Harvey **WRIGHT,** of Coventry, June 15, 1820, by Rev. Elisha B. Cook | 1 | 94 |
| **BLISS,** Delia P., ae 20, b. East Hartford, res. same, m. Charles B. **BABCOCK,** teacher, ae 29, b. Coventry, res. East Hartford, Dec. 5, 1847, by Samuel Springs | 1 | 48 |
| Delia P., of East Hartford, m. Charles I. **BABCOCK,** of South Coventry, Dec. 5, 1847, by Samuel Spring | 1 | 154 |
| Edmund A., of Manchester, m. Delia C. **SPENCER,** of East Hartford, May 12, 1841, by Samuel Spring | 1 | 135 |
| Ira, m. Paulina **ROWELL,** Aug. 24, 1826, by Joy H. Fairchild | 1 | 106 |
| Joseph J., m. Lois **ROWELL,** b. of East Hartford, Aug. 13, 1834, by Samuel Spring | 1 | 116 |
| Sarah Ann, m. Benjamin W. **RISLEY,** b. of East Hartford, Sept. 6, 1842, by Samuel Spring | 1 | 139 |
| **BLUMENTHAL,** Albert, of Hartford, m. Mary J. **GAINES,** of East Hartford, Aug. 12, 1846, by Samuel Spring | 1 | 152 |
| **BOAGE,** S., of New Haven, m. Martha G. **PRATT,** of East Hartford, May 13, 1827, by Rev. Joel H. Linsley | 1 | 108 |
| **BOUCH,** Samuel H., m. Sophia **BURNHAM,** July 30, 1824, by Joy H. Fairchild | 1 | 102 |
| **BOW,** Jonathan, of Litchfield, m. Lucy **ROWELL,** of East Hartford, Jan. 1, 1822, by Joy H. Fairchild | 1 | 97 |
| Mary H., m. Samuel **ALEXANDER,** b. of East Hartford, Feb. 3, 1841, by Samuel Spring | 1 | 134 |
| **BOWLES,** I. I., his child bd. May 10, 1835 | 1 | 77 |
| **BRACE,** John, m. Sally **BROWN,** Dec. 19, 1822, by Joy H. Fairchild | 1 | 100 |
| **BRADFORD, BRADSFORD,** Charles H., of Great Falls, N. H., m. Miranda **SKINNER,** of East Hartford, Sept. 28, 1846, by Rev. H. B. Soule, of Hartford | 1 | 152 |
| Hiram S., d. [        ], 1848, ae 8 m. | 1 | 49 |
| **BRAGG,** Delia, d. Sidney, farmer, ae 27, b. June 9, 1851 | 1 | 58 |
| Nelson P., cordwainer, b. W. Springfield, res. East Hartford, d. Feb. 28, 1851, ae 36 | 1 | 59 |
| **BRAINARD, BRAINERD,** Allen, m. Sabrina **WING,** Sept. 17, 1822, by Elisha Cushman | 1 | 99 |
| Charlotte, [d. Ezra & Mabel], b. July 17, 1786 | 1 | 11 |
| Emmaley, [d. Ezra & Mabel], b. June 1, 1789 | 1 | 11 |
| Emily, m. Adoniram **FOOT,** Jan. 29, 1817 | 1 | 68 |
| Erastus, [s. Ezra & Mabel], b. Mar. 7, 1792 | 1 | 11 |
| Ezra, m. Mabel **PORTER,** Mar. 9, 1786 | 1 | 11 |
| Ezra, m. Mabel **PORTER,** Mar. 9, 1786, by Rev. Dr. Williams | 1 | 61 |
| Ezra, [s. Ezra & Mabel], b. Oct. 15, 1787 | 1 | 11 |

| BRAINARD, BRAINERD, (cont.), | Vol. | Page |
|---|---|---|
| Lawrence, [s. Ezra & Mabel], b. Mar. 16, 1794 | 1 | 11 |
| Lyman, [s. Ezra & Mabel], b. July 28, 1796 | 1 | 11 |
| Lyman, m. Sally HALL, Nov. 29, 1820, by Joy H. Fairchild | 1 | 95 |
| Naomy, m. George SPENCER, [ ] | 1 | 18 |
| Norman, [s. Ezra & Mabel], b. Mar. 2, 1799 | 1 | 11 |
| Otis, [s. Ezra & Mabel], b. June 12, 1801 | 1 | 11 |
| BRAUNSON, [see under BRONSON] | | |
| BRENT, Henry, s. Royal, farmer & Hebsibah, b. Dec. 30, 1848 | 1 | 51 |
| BREWER, Abbott, s. Reuben, farmer, ae 43 & Jane, ae 36, b. Sept. 15, 1847 | 1 | 47 |
| Abigail, d. Jan. 3, 1819, ae 64 | 1 | 73 |
| Adelia, of Bolton, m. Stephen CONE, of East Hartford, May 1, 1822, by Rev. Elisha B. Cook | 1 | 98 |
| Adeline, of East Hartford, m. Nathaniel K. CONE, of Batavia, N. Y., Nov. 9, 1840, by Samuel Spring | 1 | 133 |
| Albert, wagon maker, ae 22, b. East Hartford, res. same, m. Emma EGLISTON, ae 20, b. Bloomfield, res. East Hartford, Oct. 31, 1847, by Rev. Whiting | 1 | 48 |
| Alice R., d. Sherman, farmer, ae 30, & Deantha, ae 29, b. Mar. 12, 1848 | 1 | 46 |
| Andrew H.*, m. Mary BEMONT, Mar. 1, 1826, by Joy H. Fairchild    *(written "Andrew H. DEWER") | 1 | 105 |
| Angeline S., d. Ashbel H., marriner, b. Sept. 24, 1850 | 1 | 57 |
| Caroline, m. Jesse GAINES, Feb. 26, 1823, by Joy H. Fairchild | 1 | 101 |
| Caroline, of East Hartford, m. W[illia]m L. AVERY, of Willimantic, Dec. 24, 1845, by Samuel Spring | 1 | 150 |
| Celestia, ae 19, b. East Hartford, res. same, m. Henry E. BILLINGS, miller, ae 24, b. Chatham, res. [ ], Jan. 5, 1848, by Samuel Springs | 1 | 48 |
| Celesta P., of East Hartford, m. Henry E. BILLINGS, of Glastenbury, Jan. 5, 1848, by Samuel Spring | 1 | 154 |
| Charlotte, of East Hartford, m. Edward D. HOWLETT, of Hartford, Mar. 10, 1853, by Rufus Smith | 1 | 166 |
| Chauncy, m. Samantha TREAT, Feb. 10, 1825, by Joy H. Fairchild | 1 | 103 |
| Cynthia, m. Andrew VIBBERT, b. of East Hartford, Oct. 25, 1846, by Samuel Spring | 1 | 152 |
| Daniel, his child d. [ ], 1798 | 1 | 63 |
| Daniel, d. Nov. 4, 1823, ae 85 (Revolutionary Pensioner) | 1 | 73 |
| Daniel, d. Dec. 21, 1830, ae 80 | 1 | 74 |
| Delia, ae 19, m. Elizur R. ENSIGN, ae 25, b. of East Hartford, May 24, 1849, by Rev. S. Spring | 1 | 52 |
| Delia, m. Elisur R. ENSIGN, b. of East Hartford, May 24, 1849, by Samuel Spring | 1 | 157 |
| Edward, m. Lydia L. KIMBALL, b. of East Hartford, Jan. 1, 1846, by Levi Daggett, Jr. | 1 | 150 |
| Edward, s. M. or I. JANEWAY, carpenter, b. Sept. 16, 1849 | 1 | 54 |
| Electa, of East Hartford, m. J. Milton SMITH, of New York City, Nov. 25, 1845, by Samuel Spring | 1 | 150 |
| Eli, d. Feb. 14, 1802 | 1 | 64 |
| Elisha B., m. Sarah C. ANDERSON, b. of East Hartford, Apr. 3, 1850, by Samuel Spring | 1 | 158 |

**BREWER**, (cont.),                                                      Vol.      Page
Elisha C., machinist, ae 28, m. Sarah C. **ANDERSON**, ae 22, b.
  of East Hartford, Apr. 23, 1850, by S. Spring          1         56
Eliza, d. Daniel & Mary, m. Hiram **GOODALE**, s. Daniel &
  Rachael, Nov. 17, 1830, by Asa Mead                    1         70
Eliza, m. Hiram **GOODALE**, Nov. 17, 1830, by Rev. Asa
  Mead                                                   1         112
Ellen E., d. Sept. 28, 1849, ae 6                        1         56
Emeline, of East Hartford, m. Ralph **WILLIAMS**, of
  Willington, Jan. 1, 1838, by Samuel Spring             1         125
Ellsworth, of East Hartford, m. Mary Ann **PIBBLES**, of
  Glastenbury, Oct. 9, 1842, by Rev. B. M. Walker        1         140
Emely, m. John **VIBBERT**, Nov. 29, 1820, by Joy H. Fairchild   1    95
Esther, d. Royal H., farmer, ae 25 & Esther, ae 21, b. June 14,
  1848                                                   1         46
Eunice, of East Hartford, m. Palmer **SESSIONS**, of
  Willimantic, May 8, 1847, by Samuel Spring             1         153
Eveline, d. Royal H., farmer, b. Oct. 27, 1850          1         57
Francis Elliett, child of Francis, shoemaker, b. Mar. 15, 1851   1    57
Francis F., m. Theodocia **GROSEMAN**, b. of East Hartford,
  May [   ], 1839, by Samuel Spring                      1         129
George P., ae 21, of East Hartford, m. Julia, A. **HULBERT**, ae
  18, b. Glastonbury, res. same, May 1, 1849, by Rev.
  Smith                                                  1         52
Hansey L., m. William **JONES**, b. of East Hartford, Nov. 25,
  1846, by Samuel Spring                                 1         153
Henrietta, m. Alonso **EDWARDS**, b. of East Hartford, Dec. 31,
  1846, by Samuel Spring                                 1         153
Henry C., m. Susan **HILLS**, b. of East Hartford, Nov. 24, 1836,
  by Samuel Spring                                       1         121
Jane, m. Ralph **HILLS**, b. of East Hartford, Mar. 20, 1834, by
  Rev. Samuel Spring                                     1         115
Janeway, m. Sarah **MARBLE**, b. of East Hartford, Feb. 7,
  1833, by Rev. Samuel Spring                            1         113
Joel, s. Henry, farmer, b. Apr. 19, 1851                1         57
John C., m. Amanda **BURNHAM**, b. of East Hartford, Apr. 19,
  1840, by Samuel Spring                                 1         132
Julia Ann, of East Hartford, m. John H. **CHAFFEE**, of Ashford,
  Nov. 6, 1839, by Samuel Spring                         1         131
Julius, m. Rachel **GOODALE**, Dec. 31, 1826, by Joy H.
  Fairchild                                              1         107
Laura, m. Talcott **HILLS**, Aug. 15, 1826, by Joy H. Fairchild  1    106
Loiza, twin with Lowell H., d. Ashbel, farmer, ae 38 & Mary, ae
  42, b. Nov. 27, 1848                                   1         46
Lowell H., twin with Loiza, s. Ashbel, farmer, ae 38 & Mary, ae
  42, b. Nov. 27, 1848                                   1         46
Lucretia, m. Elisha **WARREN**, Dec. 28, 1786, by Rev. Dr.
  Williams                                               1         61
Mary, of East Hartford, m. Edwin **STEVENS**, of Hartford, Apr.
  8, 1840, by Samuel Spring                              1         132
Mary E., d. Sherman A., farmer, b. Oct. 25, 1850        1         57
Mary Velina, d. Francis, [   ] & Theodosia, b. Mar. 8, 1849   1    51

|                                                                                           | Vol. | Page |
|-------------------------------------------------------------------------------------------|------|------|
| **BREWER**, (cont.),                                                                       |      |      |
| Reuben, m. Jane M. **HILLS**, b. of East Hartford, Sept. 10,                               |      |      |
| 1834, by Samuel Spring                                                                     | 1    | 117  |
| Roselle, m. James M. **WARNER**, b. of East Hartford, Aug. 15,                             |      |      |
| 1852, by B. C. Phelps                                                                      | 1    | 162  |
| Royal H., of East Hartford, m. Esther **FORBES**, of Manchester,                           |      |      |
| Nov. 27, 1844, by Samuel Spring                                                            | 1    | 148  |
| Samuel, b. Feb. 18, 1776; m. Prudence **DEMMING**, Oct. 5,                                 |      |      |
| 1797; d. [    ], 1847                                                                      | 1    | 25   |
| Samuel, [s. Samuel & Prudence], b. Oct. 4, 1798                                            | 1    | 25   |
| Samuel, m. Elizabeth **ROBERTS**, b. of East Hartford, Sept. 2,                            |      |      |
| 1839, by Samuel Spring                                                                     | 1    | 129  |
| Selden, [s. Samuel & Prudence], b. Sept. 14, 1800                                          | 1    | 25   |
| Sophia, m. Epaphras **GAINES**, Nov. 27, 1816                                              | 1    | 68   |
| Sophia, of East Hartford, m. Chauncy **RISLEY**, of Glastenbury,                           |      |      |
| Sept. 8, 1833, by Rev. Samuel Spring                                                       | 1    | 114  |
| Velina, d. Nov. 18, 1848, ae [  ]                                                          | 1    | 53   |
| ----, Capt , his children drowned [          ], 1807                                       | 1    | 66   |
| **BREWSTER**, Liddia Martha, m. Daniel **LYAMAN**, Jan. 16, 1794                           | 1    | 6    |
| **BROCKWAY**, David, of Lime, m. Eliza G. **GOODALE**, of East Hartford,                   |      |      |
| Dec. 1, 1833, by G. A. Calhoue                                                             | 1    | 115  |
| **BRONSON, BRAUNSON**, Willis L., of Hartford, m. Sarah A.                                 |      |      |
| **WINSLOW**, of East Hartford, Nov. 20, 1845, by                                           |      |      |
| Rev. Gurdon Robins, of Hartford                                                            | 1    | 152  |
| Wyllys, of Vernon, m. Lucy M. **WINCHELL**, of Berlin, May                                 |      |      |
| 19, 1829, by Rev. Thomas Robbins                                                           | 1    | 110  |
| **BROOKS**, Peter, m. Emily I. **WOODWARD**, Nov. 28, 1827, by Rev. Joel                   |      |      |
| Hawes, of Hartford                                                                         | 1    | 109  |
| Richard, of South Windsor, m. Augusta **McGILL**, of                                       |      |      |
| Manchester, June 17, 1853, by Samuel Spring                                                | 1    | 164  |
| **BROWN**, Abigail, [d. Benjamin & Sarah], b. Aug. 17, 1769                                | 1    | 8    |
| Achsah, [child of Benjamin & Sarah], b. Aug. 23, 1778; d. May                             |      |      |
| 24, 1795                                                                                   | 1    | 8    |
| Benjamin, m. Sarah **KEENY**, Sept. 4, 1763                                                | 1    | 8    |
| Benjamin, [s. Benjamin & Sarah], b. Aug. 20, 1767                                          | 1    | 8    |
| Betsy, [d. James Sheffield & Elizabeth], b. July 11, 1794                                  | 1    | 28   |
| Betsy, m. Abner **MASON**, Nov. 5, 1818                                                    | 1    | 68   |
| David L., of New Marlboro, Mass., m. Louisa J. **STEDMAN**,                                |      |      |
| of Manchester, May 15, 1831, by Asa Mead                                                   | 1    | 70   |
| David L., of New Marlborough, Mass., m. Louisa J.                                          |      |      |
| **STEDMAN**, of Manchester, May 15, 1831, by                                               |      |      |
| Rev. Asa Mead                                                                              | 1    | 112  |
| Edmond, [s. Benjamin & Sarah], b. Mar. 2, 1792 [1772?]                                     | 1    | 8    |
| Eliza L., ae 15, b. East Hartford, res. same, m. John A. **LADD**,                         |      |      |
| wagonmaker, ae 21, b. Haverhill, N. H., res. East                                          |      |      |
| Hartford, May 1, 1850, by S. Spring                                                        | 1    | 56   |
| Elizabeth, of East Hartford, m. John G. **MALONEY**, of R. I.,                             |      |      |
| July 29, 1849, by Samuel Spring                                                            | 1    | 157  |
| Elizabeth L., of East Hartford, m. John A. **LADD**, of Haverhill,                         |      |      |
| N. H., May 1, 1850, by Samuel Spring                                                       | 1    | 158  |
| Emily, m. Sylvester **TREAT**, May 9, 1822, by Joy H. Fairchild                            | 1    | 98   |
| Emily, of East Hartford, m. Elery **CHAMPLAIN**, of Hartford,                              |      |      |
| July 12, 1835, by Charles Remington, Elder                                                 | 1    | 118  |

| | Vol. | Page |
|---|---|---|
| **BROWN**, (cont.), | | |
| Esther, [d. Benjamin & Sarah], b. June 6, 1774 | 1 | 8 |
| Ireanus, [s. Benjamin & Sarah], b. Oct. 23, 1780 | 1 | 8 |
| Irenus, his s. [       ], d. Mar. [ ], 1826 | 1 | 167 |
| James, [s. Benjamin & Sarah], b. Apr. 5, 1783 | 1 | 8 |
| James, [s. James Sheffield & Elizabeth], b. Jan. 16, 1796 | 1 | 28 |
| James, his child d. Nov. [ ], 1826 | 1 | 168 |
| James, m. Elizabeth A. **BURNHAM**, b. of East Hartford, Nov. 7, 1833/4, by Jeremiah Brown, J. P. | 1 | 115 |
| Jas., his child bd. Sept. 19, 1840, ae 7 m. | 1 | 78 |
| Ja[me]s, his child bd. June 21, 1841, ae 2 wks. | 1 | 79 |
| James, farmer, d. Oct. 27, 1847, ae 53 | 1 | 49 |
| James Sheffield, m. Elizabeth **FORBS**, July 4, 1793 | 1 | 28 |
| Sally, [d. James Sheffield & Elizabeth], b. Nov. 16, 1800 | 1 | 28 |
| Sally, m. John **BRACE**, Dec. 19, 1822, by Joy H. Fairchild | 1 | 100 |
| Sarah, [d. Benjamin & Sarah], b. Aug. 13, 1764; d. Sept. 17, 1785 | 1 | 8 |
| Sarah, [d. Benjamin & Sarah], b. Dec. 26, 1784 | 1 | 8 |
| Stanton, [s. James Sheffield & Elizabeth], b. Mar. 10, 1798 | 1 | 28 |
| **BROWNELL**, Clarence Melville, [s. Dr. [      ], b. May 2, 1828 | 1 | 39 |
| Edward Rogerson, [s. Dr. [      ], b. Oct. 2, 1825 | 1 | 39 |
| **BRYANT**, Bettie, [d. Timothy & Sarah], b. Sept. 30, 1787 | 1 | 167 |
| Ebenezer, [s. Timothy & Sarah], b. June 1, 1794 | 1 | 167 |
| Hannah W., of East Hartford, m. William **SPENCER**, of Hartford, Nov. 27, 1839, by Samuel Spring | 1 | 131 |
| Janette, of East Hartford, m. William **SPENCER**, of Hartford, Sept. 6, 1842, by Samuel Spring | 1 | 139 |
| Juliany, [d. Timothy & Sarah], b. Apr. 17, 1776 | 1 | 167 |
| Mary E., m. Ezra E. **SMITH**, b. of East Hartford, May 4, 1847, by Samuel Spring | 1 | 153 |
| Mary Josephine, d. W[illia]m B., painter, ae 23, b. June 2, 1851 | 1 | 58 |
| Nehemiah, [s. Timothy & Sarah], b. Feb. 16, 1792 | 1 | 167 |
| Phile (Fila?), d. [Timothy & Sarah], b. Apr. 4, 1785 | 1 | 167 |
| Sally, m. Martin **HILLS**, Mar. 9, 1798 | 1 | 14 |
| Sarah, [d. Timothy & Sarah], b. Nov. 21, 1779 | 1 | 167 |
| Sarah, [d. Timothy & Sarah], b. Mar. 29, 1809 | 1 | 167 |
| Susanah, [d. Timothy & Sarah], b. Nov. 26, 1781 | 1 | 167 |
| Timothy, m. Sarah **FLINT**, May 7, 1775 | 1 | 167 |
| Timothy, & Sarah, had 2nd child b. Aug. 11, 1778; d. same day | 1 | 167 |
| Timothy, [s. Timothy & Sarah], b. Mar. 1, 1784; d. Mar. 4, 1784 | 1 | 167 |
| Timothy, [s. Timothy & Sarah], b. Jan. 13, 1790 | 1 | 167 |
| Timothy, [s. Timothy & Sarah], d. Feb. 17, 1794 | 1 | 167 |
| W[illia]m, painter, ae 23, m. Sarah **HARDING**, ae 21, b. of East Hartford, May 10, 1850, by S. Spring | 1 | 56 |
| William B., m. Sarah B. **HARDING**, b. of East Hartford, May 14, 1850, by Samuel Spring | 1 | 159 |
| ----, wid., d. [         ], 1797 | 1 | 63 |
| **BUCKLAND**, Akcy*, d. [         ], 1826          *(Achsa?) | 1 | 168 |
| Chester, m. Esther **McKEE**, Oct. 13, 1802 | 1 | 22 |
| Esther, w. Chester, d. Dec. 9, 1802 | 1 | 22 |
| Francis, of East Hartford, m. W[illia]m **SHELDON**, of Huntington, Oct. 16, 1827, by Rev. Samuel Spring | 1 | 109 |

| | Vol. | Page |
|---|---|---|
| **BUCKLAND**, (cont.), | | |
| Jno, d. [ ], 1801 | 1 | 63 |
| Orrin, bd. Feb. 6, 1834, ae 35 | 1 | 76 |
| Susan, m. Eleazar **FOX**, May 17, 1821, by Joy H. Fairchild | 1 | 96 |
| Timothy, m. Tryphena **HILLS**, Oct. 12, 1820, by Joy H. Fairchild | 1 | 94 |
| ----, wid., d.[ ], 1798 | 1 | 63 |
| **BUCKLEY**, Orrin, his child, bd. Oct. 21, 1832 | 1 | 76 |
| ----, Mr., d. [ ], 1805 | 1 | 65 |
| ----*, Miss, bd. Mar. 4, 1842, ae 78 *(**BUCKLAND**?) | 1 | 79 |
| **BUEL**, Harvey, m. Harriet E. **PARSONS**, Dec. 17, 1836, by Samuel Spring | 1 | 121 |
| **BUGBY**, Apollos S., m. Martha **COOK**, b. of Hartford, July 17, 1854, by Rev. Benjamin C. Phelps | 1 | 166 |
| **BULL**, Charlott A., d. Horace, machinist, b. Apr. 7, 1850 | 1 | 55 |
| **BUNCE**, Charles, m. Sarah **BIDWELL**, Dec. 31, 1789 | 1 | 30 |
| Charles, [s. Charles & Sarah], b. Feb. 1, 1800 | 1 | 30 |
| George, [s. Charles & Sarah], b. Apr. 1, 1790 | 1 | 30 |
| Harriot, [d. Charles & Sarah], b. Jan. 20, 1798 | 1 | 30 |
| Harriot, m. Matthew **CADWELL**, Dec. 21, 1820, by Rev. Elisha B. Cook | 1 | 95 |
| Heman, [s. Charles & Sarah], b. Jan. 12, 1792 | 1 | 30 |
| Isreal, his w. [ ], d. [May] [ ], 1827 | 1 | 168 |
| Marvin, [s. Charles & Sarah], b. Jan. 26, 1794 | 1 | 30 |
| Sally, [d. Charles & Sarah], b. Jan. 10, 1796 | 1 | 30 |
| Sally, m. John **McLEAN**, b. of East Hartford, July 19, 1821, by Rev. Elisha B. Cook | 1 | 96 |
| Walter, of Manchester, m. Catherine **KENNEDY**, of East Hartford, Nov. 27, 1834, by Samuel Spring | 1 | 118 |
| **BURBAKS**, Emeline, bd. Sept. 27, 1832, ae 30 | 1 | 76 |
| **BURKE**, Andrew, of Glastenbury, m. Clarissa R. **HILLS**, of East Hartford, Feb. 13, 1853, by Rev. George W. Brewster | 1 | 164 |
| **BURNHAM, BURNAM**, Aaron, Jr., d. [ ], 1797 | 1 | 63 |
| Aaron, his wid. [ ], bd. July 18, 1840, ae 70 | 1 | 78 |
| Albert, d. July 1, 1850, ae 4 | 1 | 57 |
| Almira, m. David **DELIVER**, Jan. 3, 1822, by Joy H. Fairchild | 1 | 97 |
| Amanda, m. John C. **BREWER**, b. of East Hartford, Apr. 19, 1840, by Samuel Spring | 1 | 132 |
| Amariah, s. Austin, farmer, ae 30 & Francis, ae 32, b. Aug. 24, 1849 | 1 | 54 |
| Ann, m. Horace **HUBBARD**, May 6, 1827, by Joy H. Fairchild | 1 | 108 |
| Anna Porter, mother of Joshua, bd. May 24, 1834, ae 83 | 1 | 76 |
| Austin, m. Mary F. **OLMSTED**, b. of East Hartford, Nov. 27, 1844, by Samuel Spring | 1 | 148 |
| Betsy, m. James M. **GATES**, of Windham, Sept. 28, 1831, by Rev. Gurdon Robins, of East Windsor | 1 | 113 |
| Cornelia L., of East Hartford, m. Aaron G. **WILLIAMS**, of East Windsor, Feb. 26, 1840, by Samuel Spring | 1 | 132 |
| Cornelius, his child, d. [ ], 1806 | 1 | 65 |
| Cornelius, his child d. [ ], 1809, ae 6 m. | 1 | 66 |
| David, d. Mar. 3, 1835 | 1 | 74 |
| David, bd. Mar. 5, 1835, ae 62 | 1 | 77 |
| Eleazer, his child d. [ ], 1806 | 1 | 65 |

| BURNHAM, BURNAM, (cont.), | Vol. | Page |
|---|---|---|
| Eleazer, m. Jane Ann HALE, b. of East Hartford, Nov. 6, 1838, | | |
| by Samuel Spring | 1 | 127 |
| Elizabeth A., m. James BROWN, b. of East Hartford, Nov. 7, | | |
| 1833/4, by Jeremiah Brown, J. P. | 1 | 115 |
| Elizabeth M., ae 23, b. East Hartford, res. same, m. Levi C. | | |
| YATES, joiner, ae 32, b. Haddam, res. Hartford, | | |
| Nov. 12, 1850, by W. Clark | 1 | 59 |
| Emeline, of East Hartford, m. Andrew H. WING, of St. Louis, | | |
| Mo., Sept. 30, 1841, by Samuel Spring | 1 | 136 |
| Erastus W., m. Emeline PARSONS, b. of East Hartford, Feb. 8, | | |
| 1833, by Rev. Samuel Spring | 1 | 117 |
| Eunice, w. Sellah, d. June [ ], 1807, ae 33 | 1 | 66 |
| F., Jr., d. May [ ], 1798 | 1 | 63 |
| Fidelia, of East Hartford, m. George BALDWIN, of | | |
| Washington, Conn., May 21, 1837, by Samuel | | |
| Spring | 1 | 123 |
| George, d. [ ], 1806 | 1 | 65 |
| George D., s. Anthony, farmer, ae 26 & Ann Marie, ae 22, b. | | |
| Apr. 2, 1849 | 1 | 50 |
| Gilbert, his child of Hartford, bd. May 17, 1842 | 1 | 79 |
| Harriet R., m. George S. PHELPS, b. of East Hartford, July 1, | | |
| 1847, by Samuel Spring | 1 | 153 |
| J. P., farmer, d. Mar. 29, 1849, ae 73 | 1 | 53 |
| Ja[me]s, his child bd. Apr. 8, 1836, ae 6 m. | 1 | 78 |
| Jemima, m. Daniel ABEL, Nov. 1, 1820, by Joy H. Fairchild | 1 | 95 |
| John, m. Wealthy RISLEY, Mar. 29, 1820 | 1 | 69 |
| John, his wid. bd. Nov. 6, 1835, ae 44 | 1 | 77 |
| Julia, of East Hartford, m. George W. KING, of Hartford, Oct. | | |
| 5, 1842, by Samuel Spring | 1 | 140 |
| Julia L., m. Nathan C. GEER, b. of East Hartford, Oct. 12, | | |
| 1842, by Samuel Spring | 1 | 140 |
| Julius, of East Windsor, m. Laura HILLS, of East Hartford, | | |
| Dec. 15, 1841, by Rev. Cephas Brainard | 1 | 137 |
| Levi, his child bd. Apr. 9, 1838, ae 6 m. | 1 | 78 |
| Levi, m. Fanny CULVER, Apr. 25, 1841, by Abner Hale, J. P. | 1 | 135 |
| Lucinda, m. Lewis E. GUERNSEY, Apr. 19, 1835, by Charles | | |
| Remington, Elder | 1 | 118 |
| Lucy, d. Aaron, bd. July 21, 1828, ae 36 | 1 | 75 |
| Mary, m. Stephen ROBERTS, Jan. 6, 1785, by Rev. Dr. | | |
| Williams | 1 | 61 |
| Mary, m. John ARNOLD, Feb. 7, 1828, by Enoch Brent | 1 | 109 |
| Mary, m. James BURNS, b. of East Hartford, May 7, 1829, by | | |
| Rev. Thomas Robbins | 1 | 110 |
| Michael, m. Hepsibeth HURLBURT, Sept. 21, 1819 | 1 | 69 |
| Moses, d. [ ], 1798 | 1 | 63 |
| Moulton, his child bd. Apr. 21, 1838, ae 7 m. | 1 | 78 |
| Moulton, his child bd. Dec. 25, 1840, ae 5 | 1 | 79 |
| Olive, m. Roswell ROCKWELL, Dec. 25, 1817 | 1 | 68 |
| Philo*, bd. Mar. 30, 1836    *(Philo BURNAM) | 1 | 77 |
| Philo, see Philo BURNHAM | 1 | 77 |
| Phineas, Jr., bd. Dec. 12, 1840, ae 33 | 1 | 78 |
| Phineas, his wid. & mother of William, bd. Sept. 12, 1841, ae 58 | 1 | 79 |

| | Vol. | Page |
|---|---|---|
| **BURNHAM**, (cont.), | | |
| Roger, see under C. **HEATH** | 1 | 76 |
| Russell (?), d. [ ], 1801 | 1 | 63 |
| Ruth, of East Hartford, m. Lewis **ROWELL**, of Hartford, Dec. | | |
| 7, 1831, by Rev. G. F. Davis | 1 | 113 |
| Sarah L., d. Zenas, Jr. & Sarah, of East Windsor, m. Abraham | | |
| **WILLIAMS**, s. David & Rachael, of East Hartford, | | |
| Apr. 7, 1831, at East Windsor, by Asa Mead | 1 | 70 |
| Seth, his child d. [ ], 1801 | 1 | 63 |
| Seth, his child d. [ ], 1803 | 1 | 64 |
| Sophia, m. Samuel H. **BOUCH**, July 30, 1824, by Joy H. | | |
| Fairchild | 1 | 102 |
| Sophia, of East Hartford, m. Joseph E. **FISH**, of East Windsor, | | |
| Mar. 2, 1837, by Charles Remington | 1 | 122 |
| Stephen, his child d. [ ], 1799 | 1 | 63 |
| Stephen, his child d. Aug. 8, 1802 | 1 | 64 |
| Stephen, d. Apr. [ ], 1826, ae 85 | 1 | 74 |
| Theodore, saddler, d. Aug. 25, 1849, ae 59 | 1 | 56 |
| Thomas, his child bd. June 20, 1840, ae 10 | 1 | 78 |
| Timothy, m. Roxey E. **GILLETT**, b. of South Windsor, Oct. | | |
| 13, 1846, by Samuel Spring | 1 | 152 |
| Tryphena, m. John **WRIGHT**, June 3, 1823, by Joy H. | | |
| Fairchild | 1 | 101 |
| W[illia]m, d. Dec. [ ], 1824 | 1 | 74 |
| ----, wid., d. [ ], 1800 | 1 | 63 |
| ----, Mrs., d. Aug. [ ], 1804 | 1 | 64 |
| ----, Mrs., d. [ ], 1805 | 1 | 65 |
| ----, his child d. [ ], 1805 | 1 | 65 |
| ----, Mr., d. [ ], 1806 | 1 | 65 |
| ----, Mr., d. [ ], 1806 | 1 | 65 |
| ----, Mr., d. [ ], 1814 | 1 | 66 |
| ----, wid. bd. Apr. 21, 1831, ae 68 | 1 | 76 |
| ----, m. Timothy **ANDERSON**, [ ] | 1 | 41 |
| **BURNS**, James, m. Mary **BURNHAM**, b. of East Hartford, May 7, 1829, | | |
| by Rev. Thomas Robbins | 1 | 110 |
| James, m. Elizabeth **NORTON**, b. of East Hartford, Oct. 3, | | |
| 1837, by Samuel Spring | 1 | 124 |
| ----, his w. [ ], bd. Mar. 25, 1830, ae 29 | 1 | 76 |
| **BURR**, Edward, m. Jane E. **GREENLEAF**, b. of Hartford, June 14, 1846, | | |
| by Samuel Spring | 1 | 152 |
| **BUTLER**, Betsy, m. Asa **MANNING**, Nov. 27, 1817 | 1 | 68 |
| Caroline, of East Hartford, m. William L. **CARPENTER**, of | | |
| Philadelphia, Pa., June 16, 1852, by Samuel Spring | 1 | 162 |
| Caroline Matilda, [d. James & Esther], b. Feb. 27, 1798 | 1 | 12 |
| Edwin, [s. James & Esther], b. [ ] | 1 | 12 |
| Eliza, [d. James & Esther], b. Aug. 24, 1800 | 1 | 12 |
| James, m. Esther **SMITH**, Feb. 22, 1796 | 1 | 12 |
| James, of Hartford, m. Anna **ROBERTS**, of East Hartford, Dec. | | |
| 28, 1843, by Samuel Spring | 1 | 144 |
| ----, his child, d. [ ], 1803 | 1 | 64 |
| ----, his child, d. [ ], 1805 | 1 | 65 |
| ----, Mrs., d. June [ ], 1806 | 1 | 65 |

|                                                                                                          | Vol. | Page |
|----------------------------------------------------------------------------------------------------------|------|------|
| **BUTZELL**, William, of Glastenbury, m. Mary **LIGHTFAIRTH**, of                                         |      |      |
| Germany, Apr. 20, 1852, by Charles C. Ashley, J. P.                                                       | 1    | 163  |
| **CABLES**, Jane R., d. Thomas, hatter, ae 52 & Martha A., ae 40, b. Dec.                                 |      |      |
| 10, 1849                                                                                                  | 1    | 54   |
| **CADWELL**, Ben, [s. Matthew & Mary], b. Nov. [ ], 1779; d. July [ ],                                    |      |      |
| 1780                                                                                                      | 1    | 17   |
| Bissell W., s. David & Caroline, of Hartford, m. Emiline R.                                               |      |      |
| **SPENCER**, d. Solomon & Phebe, June 7, 1831, by                                                         |      |      |
| Asa Mead                                                                                                  | 1    | 70   |
| Bissell W., see also Russell W. **CADWELL**                                                               | 1    | 70   |
| David, m. Mindwell **JUDSON**, Nov. 12, 1783, by Rev. Dr.                                                 |      |      |
| Williams                                                                                                  | 1    | 61   |
| David, d. [          ], 1807                                                                              | 1    | 65   |
| Harriet, of Manchester, m. Giles M. **HILLS**, of East Hartford,                                          |      |      |
| Nov. 28, 1847, by Francis Robins                                                                          | 1    | 48   |
| Harriet, of Manchester, m. Giles M. **HILLS**, of East Hartford,                                          |      |      |
| Nov. 28, 1847, by Rev. Francis L. Robins, of Enfield                                                      | 1    | 154  |
| Henrietta, m. Sylvester **SMITH**, Jan. 21, 1827, by Joy H.                                               |      |      |
| Fairchild                                                                                                 | 1    | 107  |
| Jimme, [s. Matthew & Mary], b. Dec. 8, 1768; d. Jan. [ ], 1771                                            | 1    | 17   |
| Jimme, [s. Matthew & Mary], b. Oct. 11, 1772; d. Nov. 2, 1778                                             | 1    | 17   |
| Lucy, [d. Matthew & Mary], b. Jan. 4, 1771                                                                | 1    | 17   |
| Lucy, [d. Matthew & Mary], b. Aug. 24, 1774; d. Sept. [ ],                                                |      |      |
| 1778                                                                                                      | 1    | 17   |
| Mary, [d. Matthew & Mary], b. Dec. 28, 1761                                                               | 1    | 17   |
| Matthew, m. Mary **VANSANT**, May [ ], 1761                                                               | 1    | 17   |
| Matthew, m. Harriot **BUNCE**, Dec. 21, 1820, by Rev. Elisha B.                                           |      |      |
| Cook                                                                                                      | 1    | 95   |
| Matthew Champlin, s. Tempy **NOYES** & adopted s. Matthew                                                 |      |      |
| **CADWELL**, b. Dec. 5, 1786; d. July [ ], 1847                                                           | 1    | 17   |
| Prudence, [d. Matthew & Mary], b. Sept. 10, 1777; d. Sept [ ],                                            |      |      |
| 1779                                                                                                      | 1    | 17   |
| Reuben, [s. Matthew & Mary], b. June 28, 1763                                                             | 1    | 17   |
| Russel W., m. Emiline B. **SPENCER**, June 7, 1831, by Rev.                                               |      |      |
| Asa Mead                                                                                                  | 1    | 112  |
| Russell W., see also Bissell W. **CADWELL**                                                               | 1    | 70   |
| Sarah, [d. Matthew & Mary], b. Feb. 15, 1765                                                              | 1    | 17   |
| Simeon, [s. Matthew & Mary], b. Oct. 8, 1766                                                              | 1    | 17   |
| Susanna, m. Nathaniel **RISLEY**, [          ]                                                            | 1    | 35   |
| **CAMP**, Emeline, m. Orrin **FORBES**, 3rd, b. of East Hartford, Nov. 13,                                |      |      |
| 1839, by Samuel Spring                                                                                    | 1    | 131  |
| Julia, m. Levi P. **BARNUM**, b. of East Hartford, Sept. 5, 1836,                                         |      |      |
| by Rev. Asher Moore, of Hartford                                                                          | 1    | 119  |
| Lucy Ann, of East Hartford, m. Norris W. **TAYLOR**, of                                                   |      |      |
| Glastenbury, May 19, 1844, by Rev. Warren G.                                                              |      |      |
| Jones, of So. Glastenbury                                                                                 | 1    | 145  |
| Margaret, of East Hartford, m. George C. **AUSTIN**, of                                                   |      |      |
| Wethersfield, July 5, 1846, by Samuel Spring                                                              | 1    | 152  |
| Sarah, m. George **RISLEY**, b. of East Hartford, Jan. 12, 1843,                                          |      |      |
| by Samuel Spring                                                                                          | 1    | 142  |
| **CAMPBELL**, Thomas, m. Eden **LESTER**, Oct. 27, 1832/3, by Rev.                                        |      |      |
| Reuben Ranson                                                                                             | 1    | 114  |

|  | Vol. | Page |
|---|---|---|
| **CAREY, CARY**, G. Washington, of Hartford, m. Martha W. **HILLS**, of East Hartford, June 28, 1849, by Samuel Spring | 1 | 157 |
| George W., boat maker, ae 21, b. Mansfield, res. Hartford, m. Martha W. **HILLS**, ae 20, b. Hartford, June 28, 1849, by Rev. S. Spring | 1 | 52 |
| **CARPENTER**, Elizabeth, b. Glastonbury, res. East Hartford, d. Feb. 13, 1848, ae 56 | 1 | 53 |
| William L., of Philadelphia, Pa., m. Caroline **BUTLER**, of East Hartford, June 16, 1852, by Samuel Spring | 1 | 162 |
| **CARROLL**, Joseph, white paper maker, ae 39 & Mary, ae 35, had d. [      ], b. Feb. 11, 1850 | 1 | 55 |
| Mary A., ae 22, b. Ireland, res. East Hartford, m. Charles **GOODALE**, harness maker, ae 22, b. East Hartford, res. same, July 21, 1850, by Rev. Alderman | 1 | 56 |
| Thomas, s. Joseph, paper maker, ae 38, b. Oct. 18, 1848 | 1 | 51 |
| Thomas, d. Oct. 21, 1849, ae 2 d. | 1 | 53 |
| **CASE**, Ambrose, m. Caroline **ANDRUS**, Jan. 1, 1822, by Elisha Cushman | 1 | 97 |
| Betsy, of East Hartford, m. Eli **McKEE**, of Glastenbury, Nov. 19, 1821, by Rev. Elisha B. Cook | 1 | 97 |
| Dorinda, m. Samuel **BIDWELL**, Oct. 26, 1822, by Joy H. Fairchild | 1 | 99 |
| Hannah, of East Hartford, m. George W. **SMITH**, of Suffield, Jan. 26, 1841, by Samuel Spring | 1 | 134 |
| Osmon, m. Ann Pane **WALLACE**, Aug. 21, 1842, by Cephas Brainard | 1 | 139 |
| Polly, of East Hartford, m. Daniel A. **BALL**, of Springfield, Mass., Oct. 3, 1820, by Rev. Elisha B. Cook | 1 | 95 |
| Richard, d. Jan. 3, 1827, ae 86 | 1 | 74 |
| Richard, brother of Thomas, bd. Jan. 5, 1827, ae 86 | 1 | 75 |
| Sarah, d. [      ], 1799, ae 48 | 1 | 63 |
| **CHADWICK**, Hannah, m. Jason **MULLER**, Jan. 1, 1784, by Rev. Dr. Williams | 1 | 61 |
| **CHAFFEE**, John H., of Ashford, m. Julia Ann **BREWER**, of East Hartford, Nov. 6, 1839, by Samuel Spring | 1 | 131 |
| Reuben, shoemaker, b. R. I., res. East Hartford, d. Sept. 6, 1849, ae 57 | 1 | 56 |
| **CHALKER**, Elizabeth B., of East Hartford, m. John **RUSSELL**, of Wethersfield, Dec. 11, 1845, by Rev. W[illia]m Bentley | 1 | 150 |
| Maria, seamstress, ae 19, b. East Hartford, res. same, m. Reuben **HUNT**, s. b. agent, b. Vernon, res. Hartford, May 3, 1848, by Rev. Turnbull | 1 | 48 |
| ----, neice of Capt. W. S. **CHALKER**, bd. Oct. 4, 1842, ae 20 y. | 1 | 79 |
| **CHAMBERLAIN, CHAMBERLIN**, [see also **CHARMBLIN**], Harrison, m. Eveline **JONES**, Nov. 15, 1837, by Samuel Spring | 1 | 124 |
| Harrison, his w. [      ] & d. of Joseph P. **JONES**, bd. Apr. 3, 1841, ae 29 | 1 | 79 |
| **CHAMPLIN, CHAMPLAIN**, (see also **CHARMBLIN**), Christopher, m. Electa **HILLS**, Apr. 10, 1827, by Joy H. Fairchild | 1 | 107 |

| | Vol. | Page |
|---|---|---|
| **CHAMPLIN, CHAMPLAIN,** (see also, **CHARMBLIN**), (cont.), | | |
| Elery, of Hartford, m. Emily **BROWN**, of East Hartford, July | | |
| 12, 1835, by Charles Remington, Elder | 1 | 118 |
| Mary E., m. Jason **ROBERTS**, b. of East Hartford, Apr. 27, | | |
| 1841, by Rev. John Moore, of Hartford | 1 | 136 |
| **CHANDLER,** Charles M., of Franklin, N. H., m. Mary **VIBBERT**, of East | | |
| Hartford, Oct. 4, 1837, by Samuel Spring | 1 | 124 |
| Elizabeth, m. Solomon **ENSIGN**, Oct. 11, 1792, by Rev. Dr. | | |
| Williams | 1 | 62 |
| Hannah, m. Elijah **FULLER**, Sept. 21, 1794, by Rev. Dr. | | |
| Williams | 1 | 62 |
| Mary Jane, of East Hartford, m. Edwin W. **DIMOCK**, of | | |
| Coventry, Feb. 7, 1838, by Samuel Spring | 1 | 125 |
| -----, his child d. [          ], 1801 | 1 | 63 |
| **CHAPIN,** Elam, m. Leonora **COOK**, of East Hartford, Apr. 9, 1837, by | | |
| Rev. George May | 1 | 122 |
| Elam, of Vernon, m. Harriet M. **OLMSTED**, of East Hartford, | | |
| Jan. 1, 1840, by Samuel Spring | 1 | 131 |
| Elam, his w. [          ], bd. Sept. 24, 1843, ae 24 | 1 | 80 |
| Wight, d. [          ], 1803, at Sea | 1 | 64 |
| **CHAPMAN,** Caroline, d. R. A., merchant, ae 41 & Caroline, ae 40, b. | | |
| Sept. 27, 1848 | 1 | 50 |
| Erastus, blacksmith, b. Glastenbury, d. Nov. 5, 1849, ae 25 | 1 | 56 |
| John, his child bd. June 8, 1829, ae 4 d. | 1 | 75 |
| John M., m. Ann **GULLIVER**, Jan. 11, 1827, by Joy H. | | |
| Fairchild | 1 | 107 |
| Peleg, m. Mary **ROBERTS**, Apr. 1, 1819 | 1 | 69 |
| Samuel E., of Hartford, m. Adeline **HASKELL**, of East | | |
| Hartford, Dec. 26, 1836, by Samuel Spring | 1 | 121 |
| Silas, bd. May 4, [1827], ae 8 (?) | 1 | 75 |
| Susan C., of East Hartford, m. Alonzo **RISLEY**, of | | |
| Glastenbury, June 3, 1847, by Samuel Spring | 1 | 153 |
| T. P., of Glastenbury, m. Emily **HILLS**, of East Hartford, Mar. | | |
| 30, 1851, by Rev. B. C. Phelps | 1 | 160 |
| **CHARMBLIN,** [see also **CHAMBERLAIN & CHAMPLIN**], -----, his | | |
| child d. [          ], 1826 | 1 | 168 |
| **CHENEY, CHEENEY, CHEENY,** Betsy, [d. Timothy & Rhoda], b. Sept. | | |
| 23, 1791 | 1 | 5 |
| Cyrus, of Hartford, m. Clarissa Ann **HUBBARD**, of East | | |
| Hartford, Oct. 30, 1837, by Rev. Elias C. Scott | 1 | 124 |
| Daniel, [s. Timothy & Rhoda], b. Apr. 19, 1789 | 1 | 5 |
| George, b. Dec. 20, 1771; m. Electa **WOODBRIDGE**, Oct. 18, | | |
| 1798 | 1 | 4 |
| George Wells, [s. George & Electa], b. Oct. 22, 1799 | 1 | 4 |
| Halsey, [s. Timothy & Rhoda], b. June 30, 1799 | 1 | 5 |
| Harriott, [d. Timothy & Rhoda], b. Jan. 12, 1801 | 1 | 5 |
| Horris, m. Ruth **HILLS**, Jan. 22, 1822, by Rev. Ebenezer Blake | 1 | 98 |
| Joel, [s. Timothy & Rhoda], b. Nov. 9, 1787 | 1 | 5 |
| John, [s. George & Electa], b. Oct. 20, 1801 | 1 | 4 |
| Martha, wid. Timothy, formerly wid. of Lemual **WHITE**, d. | | |
| Jan. 28, 1803 | 1 | 64 |
| Mary, m. Roswell **PITKIN**, Oct. [ ], 1806; d. Sept. 12, 1813 | 1 | 37 |

| | Vol. | Page |
|---|---|---|
| CHENEY, CHEENEY, CHEENY, (cont.), | | |
| Mary Ann, of East Hartford, m. Waterman CUMMINGS, of | | |
| Mansfield, Sept. 9, 1844, by Rev. C. W. Turner | 1 | 145 |
| Rodah, [d. Timothy & Rhoda], b. Dec. 5, 1794 | 1 | 5 |
| Timothy, Sergt., m. Martha WHITE, May 17, 1787, by Rev. | | |
| Dr. Williams | 1 | 61 |
| Timothy, m. Rhoda SKINNER, July 11, 1787, by B. Philps | 1 | 5 |
| Timothy, [s. Timothy & Rhoda], b. Feb. 1, 1797 | 1 | 5 |
| ----, wid., d. Jan. 28, 1803 | 1 | 64 |
| CHILDS, CHILDE, Frank Russel, s. Seth L., physician, ae 38 & Juliett, | | |
| ae 31, b. Apr. 19, 1849 | 1 | 50 |
| James Little, d. Mar. [ ], 1826 | 1 | 167 |
| CHITMAN, ----, Capt., d. [ ], 1814 | 1 | 66 |
| CHRISTA, Henry, manufacturer, ae 22, b. Pawtucket, R. I., res. Rockville, | | |
| m. Mary DANIELS, ae 22, b. Hartford, May 23, | | |
| 1850, by D. Bradbury | 1 | 56 |
| CHURCH, Samuell, m. Dorothy OLMSTED, Mar. 11, 1784, by Rev. Dr. | | |
| Williams | 1 | 61 |
| Samuel O., of Meriden, m. Eliza A. COWDERY, of East | | |
| Hartford, Oct. 18, 1852, by Samuel Spring | 1 | 163 |
| CLAPP, ----, his child bd. Nov. 30, 1844, ae 2 m. | 1 | 80 |
| CLARK, CLARKE, Alice, b. Hartford, res. East Hartford, d. Aug. 27, | | |
| 1847, ae 5 m. | 1 | 49 |
| Charles E., m. Dorinda R. HALE, b. of East Hartford, June 25, | | |
| 1846, by Samuel Spring | 1 | 152 |
| Chester, m. Nancy WILLIAMS, Jan. 28, 1819 | 1 | 69 |
| David, m. Lucy M. GAINES, Dec. 9, 1824, by Joy H. Fairchild | 1 | 103 |
| Dorcinda R., ae 28, b. East Hartford, res. same, m. 2nd h. | | |
| Alonzo BELLOWS, mechanic, ae 30, b. | | |
| Wethersfield, res. Hartford, Dec. 31, 1849, by H. | | |
| Bushnell | 1 | 56 |
| Edward P., of Galena, Ill., m. Eliza E. GOODWIN, of East | | |
| Hartford, Mar. 16, 1852, by Samuel Spring | 1 | 162 |
| Harriet, m. Henry F. FORD, Mar. 30, 1817 | 1 | 68 |
| Hiram, m. Emeline HAYES, May 2, 1826, by Joy H. Fairchild | 1 | 105 |
| Lucy, m. Alvan FLINT, Mar. 24, 1834, by Rev. Samuel Spring | 1 | 115 |
| Mary Ann, m. Stiles BACON, May 2, 1849, by Rev. S. Spring | 1 | 52 |
| Mary Ann, m. Styles BACON, b. of East Hartford, June 20, | | |
| 1849, by Rev. Benjamin O. Phelps | 1 | 157 |
| Sarah, of East Hartford, m. George N. CUMMINGS , of | | |
| Hartford, June 10, 1844, by Rev. C. W. Turner | 1 | 145 |
| Sophia, of East Hartford, m. John N. WARREN, of | | |
| Glastenbury, Sept. 21, 1834, by Samuel Spring | 1 | 118 |
| Sylvester, m. Emma HILLS, Nov. 3, 1819 | 1 | 69 |
| Sylvester, m. Jerusha HILLS, May 1, 1822, by Joy H. Fairchild | 1 | 98 |
| William, m. Lucy HAYES, Feb. 3, 1824, by Joy H. Fairchild | 1 | 102 |
| ----, Mrs., bd. May 21, 1842, ae 77 | 1 | 79 |
| CLEAVES, Erastus, of Glastenbury, m. Angeline WELLS, of | | |
| Wethersfield, Feb. 8, 1852, by Benjamin C. Phelps | 1 | 162 |
| CLEVELAND, Olive, of Hartford, m. Lucius RISLEY, of East Hartford, | | |
| Nov. 5, 1846, by Levi Daggett, Jr. | 1 | 153 |
| Rowena, of Wethersfield, m. Frank W. BILL (Rev.), of | | |
| Glastenbury, Mar. 14, 1843, by Rev. B. M. Walker | 1 | 142 |

| CONE, (cont.), | Vol. | Page |
|---|---|---|
| Nathaniel K., of Batavia, N. Y., m. Adeline **BREWER**, of East | | |
| Hartford, Nov. 9, 1840, by Samuel Spring | 1 | 133 |
| Ralph, [s. Marion], b. Aug. 20, 1818 | 1 | 38 |
| Russell, m. Mary **PITKIN**, Dec. 13, 1787 | 1 | 3 |
| Stephen, of East Hartford, m. Adelia **BREWER**, of Bolton, May | | |
| 1, 1822, by Rev. Elisha B. Cook | 1 | 98 |
| Stephen, d. Mar. [ ], 1827 | 1 | 168 |
| **CONWAY**, Thomas, d. Nov. 18, 1835 | 1 | 77 |
| **COOK**, Angeline, of Bristol, m. Henry B. **WILSON**, of Torringford, Aug. | | |
| 31, 1841, by Samuel Spring | 1 | 136 |
| Elisha, of Branford, m. Martha M. **CRANE**, of East Hartford, | | |
| Apr. 29, 1849, by Samuel Spring | 1 | 156 |
| Elisha B., s. Elisha B. & Esther H., b. July 28, 1816 | 1 | 38 |
| Esther H., w. Elisha B., d. Dec. 21, 1816 | 1 | 38 |
| Harriet, m. Lorin **HILLS**, b. of East Hartford, Aug. 21, 1839, | | |
| by Samuel Spring | 1 | 129 |
| Harriot S., d. Elisha B., b. Oct. 4, 1822 | 1 | 38 |
| Leonora, m. Elam **CHAPIN**, Apr. 9, 1837 by Rev. George May | 1 | 122 |
| Martha, m. Apollos S. **BUGBY**, b. of Hartford, July 17, 1854, | | |
| by Rev. Benjamin C. Phelps | 1 | 166 |
| Mary, m. Gardiner **FORD**, Feb. 2, 1817, b. of Hadley, Mass. | 1 | 68 |
| Rhoda, d. [ ] & Sally, m. Julius **BIDWELL**, s. Moses | | |
| & Lucy, Feb. 23, 1831, by Asa Mead | 1 | 70 |
| Rhoda, m. Julius **BIDWELL**, Feb. 23, 1831, by Rev. Asa Mead | 1 | 112 |
| **COOLEY**, Abril (?), m. Lucretia **HURLBERT**, July 15, 1821, by Isaac | | |
| Divinel | 1 | 96 |
| Andrew, m. Maria I. **COOLEY**, b. of East Hartford, May 12, | | |
| 1850, by Rev. W. Clark | 1 | 159 |
| Charlie, s. Andrew, beer maker, ae 21, b. Nov. 9, 1850 | 1 | 58 |
| Charles E., s. Francis, farmer, ae 31 & Laury Ann, ae 29, b. | | |
| Mar. 16, 1848 | 1 | 46 |
| Charles W., d. Aug. 20, 1849, ae 15 m. | 1 | 56 |
| Francis, of Hartford, m. Laura Ann **PALMER**, of East Hartford, | | |
| Apr. 3, 1840, by Rev. O. E. Daggett, of Hartford | 1 | 133 |
| Maria I., m. Andrew **COOLEY**, b. of East Hartford, May 12, | | |
| 1850, by Rev. W. Clark | 1 | 159 |
| Thomas, m. Ann **KENNEDY**, Sept. 25, 1817 | 1 | 68 |
| William, Dr. of East Hartford, m. Jerusha **PITKIN**, of | | |
| Ellington, Oct. 14, 1821, by Daniel Dorchester. | | |
| Witnesses John H. **MACK** & Betsy E. **MACK** | 1 | 96 |
| William, Dr., bd. Jan. 14, 1839, ae 57 | 1 | 78 |
| -----, Dr., m. Lucretia **ROBERTS**, May 8, 1820 | 1 | 69 |
| **COOPER**, Pervis, b. July 12, 1770; m. Alexander **McKEE**, July 27, 1788 | 1 | 37 |
| **COOZINS**, -----, Mr., d. [ ], 1814 | 1 | 67 |
| **CORNING**, -----, Mr., d. [ ], 1814 | 1 | 67 |
| **CORNWALL**, **CORNWELL**, Horace D., s. Horace, lawyer, ae 30 & | | |
| Lucy Ann, ae 29, b. Nov. 26, 1847 | 1 | 47 |
| Horace D., d. Mar. 24, 1848, ae 4 m. | 1 | 49 |
| Katie D., twin with Willie D., d. Horrace, lawyer, ae 32, b. Sept. | | |
| 25, 1851 | 1 | 58 |
| Willie D., twin with Katie D., s. Horrace, lawyer, ae 32, b. Sept. | | |
| 25, 1851 | 1 | 58 |

|                                                                                                                                                | Vol. | Page |
|------------------------------------------------------------------------------------------------------------------------------------------------|------|------|
| **CORSACK**, Catherine, b. Russell, Mass., res. East Hartford, d. Apr. 13,                                                                      |      |      |
| 1849, ae 2                                                                                                                                      | 1    | 53   |
| Thomas, master, had d. [          ], b. Apr. 10, 1848                                                                                           | 1    | 51   |
| **COTE**, Maria, of East Hartford, m. Joseph L. **STEDMAN**, of                                                                                 |      |      |
| Southampton, Mass., Feb. 19, 1834, by Samuel                                                                                                    |      |      |
| Spring                                                                                                                                          | 1    | 115  |
| **COTENEY**, Barkes, of Collinsville, m. Jane A. **PITKIN**, of East Hartford,                                                                  |      |      |
| May 3, 1837, by Samuel Spring                                                                                                                   | 1    | 123  |
| **COTTON**, Albert H., see James W. **COTTON**                                                                                                  | 1    | 41   |
| Allen, his w. [          ], d. [          ], 1806                                                                                               | 1    | 65   |
| Christina (?), m. Edward **WILLIAMS**, Jan. 18, 1801, by Rev.                                                                                   |      |      |
| Dr. Williams                                                                                                                                    | 1    | 62   |
| David, his child d. [          ], 1799                                                                                                          | 1    | 63   |
| David, d. [          ], 1799(?), ae 37                                                                                                          | 1    | 63   |
| Deborah, m. Eldridge **FOSTER**, Oct. 18, 1820, by Joy H.                                                                                       |      |      |
| Fairchild                                                                                                                                       | 1    | 94   |
| Isadora, d. Aug. 25, 1849, ae 2 y.                                                                                                              | 1    | 56   |
| James W., s. George, joiner & Esther (**KILBOURN**), b. Nov.                                                                                    |      |      |
| 15, 1832. This affidavit made by Albert H.                                                                                                      |      |      |
| **COTTON**, of Middletown, Feb. 15, 1908, before                                                                                               |      |      |
| Jos. O. Goodwin                                                                                                                                 | 1    | 41   |
| John, m. Eunice **WARREN**, Apr. 4, 1790, by Rev. Dr.                                                                                           |      |      |
| Williams                                                                                                                                        | 1    | 61   |
| ----, Mrs., d. May [  ], 1798                                                                                                                   | 1    | 63   |
| ----, m. Eli **PRATT**, Apr. 21, 1819                                                                                                           | 1    | 69   |
| **COUCH**, Chester, [s. John & Susannah], b. Dec. 19, 1783                                                                                      | TR2  | 1    |
| Chester, [s. John & Susanna], b. Dec. 19, 1783                                                                                                  | 1    | 71   |
| Elijah, [s. John & Susannah], b. Jan. 25, 1777                                                                                                  | TR2  | 1    |
| Elijah, [s. John & Susanna], b. Jan. 25, 1777                                                                                                   | 1    | 71   |
| George, [s. John & Susannah], b. Jan. 21, 1789                                                                                                  | TR2  | 1    |
| George, [s. John & Susanna], b. Jan. 21, 1789                                                                                                   | 1    | 71   |
| John, m. Susanah **WEBSTER**, Jan. 25, 1774                                                                                                     | TR2  | 1    |
| John, m. Susanna **WEBSTER**, Jan. 25, 1774                                                                                                     | 1    | 71   |
| John, Jr., [s. John & Susannah], b. Sept. 6, 1775                                                                                               | TR2  | 1    |
| John, Jr., [s. John & Susanna], b. Sept. 6, 1775                                                                                                | 1    | 71   |
| Russell, [s. John & Susannah], b. Sept. 2 or 7, 1779                                                                                            | TR2  | 1    |
| Russell, [s. John & Susanna], b. Sept. 2, 1779                                                                                                  | 1    | 71   |
| Susanah, [d. John & Susannah], b. Sept. 10, 1781                                                                                                | TR2  | 1    |
| Susanna, [d. John & Susanna], b. Sept. 10, 1781                                                                                                 | 1    | 71   |
| **COVELL**, **COVIL**, S., of Sandwich, Mass., m. Dorithy **FOX**, of East                                                                      |      |      |
| Hartford, July 8, 1833, by Rev. Samuel Spring                                                                                                   | 1    | 117  |
| Wells, m. Elizabeth **HOUSE**, b. of East Hartford, Dec. 31,                                                                                    |      |      |
| 1846, by Samuel Spring                                                                                                                          | 1    | 153  |
| **COWDERY**, Eliza A., of East Hartford, m. Samuel O. **CHURCH**, of                                                                            |      |      |
| Meriden, Oct. 18, 1852, by Samuel Spring                                                                                                        | 1    | 163  |
| Laura, m. Isaac **ROBERTS**, b. of East Hartford, Feb. 24, 1847,                                                                                |      |      |
| by Samuel Spring                                                                                                                                | 1    | 153  |
| **COWLES**, Abigail, m. John **WILLIAMS**, Apr. 26, 1824, by Joy H.                                                                             |      |      |
| Fairchild                                                                                                                                       | 1    | 102  |
| Anna, w. George, d. Mar. 31, 1814, ae 34                                                                                                        | 1    | 66   |
| Anna, m. Elizar **ANDERSON**, Nov. 14, 1820, by Joy H.                                                                                          |      |      |
| Fairchild                                                                                                                                       | 1    | 95   |

| | Vol. | Page |
|---|---|---|
| **COWLES**, (cont.), | | |
| Aurilia A., of East Hartford, m. Henry H. **DICKINSON**, of | | |
| Hartford, May 2, 1838, by Samuel Spring | 1 | 125 |
| Calesta, of East Hartford, m. Joseph **ELMORE**, of East | | |
| Windsor, Sept. 11, 1839, by Samuel Spring | 1 | 129 |
| Charlotte C., m. Ira T. **ROBERTS**, Apr. 10, 1839, by Samuel | | |
| Spring | 1 | 128 |
| Clarissa, of East Hartford, m. James A. **MOORE**, of Tolland, | | |
| Dec. 11, 1845, by Samuel Spring | 1 | 150 |
| Cornelia, m. Ralph A. **OLMSTED**, b. of East Hartford, Nov. 6, | | |
| 1838, by Samuel Spring | 1 | 127 |
| Ebenezer, d. [          ], 1801 | 1 | 63 |
| Edwin K., s. W[illia]m C., farmer, b. Nov. 30, 1850 | 1 | 59 |
| Elianer, m. Israiel **LOMIS**, Feb. 2, 1800 | 1 | 28 |
| Francis A., illeg. s. Almira **RISLEY**, ae 26, res. Manchester, b. | | |
| Jan. 15, 1849 | 1 | 54 |
| Francis W., of Manchester, m. Harriet **WING**, of East Hartford, | | |
| Nov. 13, 1834, by Samuel Spring | 1 | 118 |
| George, s. G[          ], d. May [   ], 1798, ac 2 d. | 1 | 63 |
| Ira(?) Chester, d. [          ], 1804, at Sea | 1 | 64 |
| Jane A., m. Franklin **BARNES**, b. of East Hartford, Jan. 1, | | |
| 1846, by Samuel Spring | 1 | 150 |
| John F., m. Sarah A. **ARNOLD**, Dec. 25, 1851, by Rev. | | |
| Samuel Spring | 1 | 60 |
| John F., m. Sarah **ARNOLD**, b. of East Hartford, Dec. 25, | | |
| 1851, by Samuel Spring | 1 | 161 |
| Lucretia, of East Hartford, m. Miles M. **ABBY**, of East | | |
| Windsor, May 2, 1821, by Rev. Elisha B. Cook | 1 | 96 |
| M. S., ae 24, res. East Hartford, res. same, m. A. B. **ANDROSS**, | | |
| merchant, ae 24, b. S. Windsor, res. East Hartford, | | |
| Aug. 22, 1849, by Rev. S. Spring | 1 | 55 |
| Maria, of East Hartford, m. Orrin F. **INGRAM**, of | | |
| Middleburgh, N. Y., Dec. 11, 1852, by Samuel | | |
| Spring | 1 | 164 |
| Martha, wid., d. [          ], 1814 | 1 | 66 |
| Mary Ann, of Rathway, N. J., m. Edwin M. **ROBERTS**, of East | | |
| Hartford, Sept. 17, 1844, by Samuel Spring | 1 | 145 |
| Mary S., of East Hartford, m. Abner B. **ANDREWS**, of South | | |
| Windsor, Aug. 22, 1849, by Samuel Spring | 1 | 157 |
| Romanda, m. Cornelia **HILLS**, b. of East Hartford, May 5, | | |
| 1830, by V. R. Osbourn, V. D. M. | 1 | 111 |
| Ruth, d. [          ], 1798 | 1 | 63 |
| Samuel Albert, s. William C., farmer, ae 42 & Jane, ae 37, b. | | |
| June 29, 1848 | 1 | 46 |
| Sarah, d. John, of Hadley, Mass., m. Nathaniel **GOODWIN**, | | |
| [          ], 1664; d. [          ], 1676, ae 30 | 1 | 43 |
| Sarah A., ae 20, b. East Windsor, res. same, m. Lee W. | | |
| **ELMER**, farmer, ae 26, b. East Windsor, res. S. | | |
| Windsor, Nov. 3, 1847, by Samuel Springs | 1 | 48 |
| Sarah A., of East Hartford, m. Lee W. **ELMER**, of South | | |
| Windsor, Nov. 3, 1847, by Samuel Spring | 1 | 154 |
| Timothy, m. Eliza **OLMSTED**, Apr. 26, 1787, by Rev. Dr. | | |
| Williams | 1 | 61 |

| | Vol. | Page |
|---|---|---|
| **COWLES**, (cont.), | | |
| Timothy, Dea., d. [      ], 1809, ae 89 | 1 | 66 |
| William Chester, of East Hartford, m. Jane E. **KILBOURN**, of | | |
| East Windsor, Mar. 18, 1829, by Otto S. Hoyt | 1 | 110 |
| ----, Mrs., d. Apr. [ ], 1809 | 1 | 66 |
| **COX**, Samuel, m. Ruhanna **ALLEN**, b. of East Hartford, Feb. 8, 1852, by | | |
| Samuel Spring | 1 | 161 |
| **CRANE**, Dutey Saunders, [child of John], b. Feb. 28, 1808 | 1 | 39 |
| Elizabeth, m. Samuel **OLMSTED**, Mar. 13, 1825, by Joy H. | | |
| Fairchild | 1 | 104 |
| Elizabeth Pitkin, [d. John], b. Nov. 19, 1811 | 1 | 39 |
| Joel Ward, [s. John], b. Feb. 12, 1816 | 1 | 39 |
| John Nelson, [s. John], b. Sept. 18, 1813 | 1 | 39 |
| John W., M. D., of New York, m. Mary **PITKIN**, of East | | |
| Hartford, July 15, 1839, by Rev. John A. Hempsted | 1 | 128 |
| Martha M., of East Hartford, m. Elisha **COOK**, of Branford, | | |
| Apr. 29, 1849, by Samuel Spring | 1 | 156 |
| ----, Mr., d. [      ], 1805 | 1 | 65 |
| **CROMWELL**, James, d. [      ], 1809 | 1 | 66 |
| **CROSBY**, Anne, m. Philemon **STEDMON**, June 2, 1785, by Rev. Dr. | | |
| Williams | 1 | 61 |
| **CROWELL**, ----, Capt., his child bd. Feb. 27, 1845, ae 9 m. | 1 | 80 |
| **CULIVER**, [see under **CULVER**] | | |
| **CULVER, CULIVER, CULLIVER**, Abigal, m. Elisha **KEENY**, Apr. 9, | | |
| 1795 | 1 | 33 |
| Ben, joiner, d. Apr. 20, 1849, ae 60 | 1 | 53 |
| Clarissa A., of East Hartford, m. Leonard **GOWDY**, of Enfield, | | |
| Nov. 30, 1843, by Daniel Pitkin, J. P. | 1 | 144 |
| Emeline, m. Norman **ANDERSON**, Nov. 16, 1826, by Joy H. | | |
| Fairchild | 1 | 107 |
| Fanny, m. Levi **BURNHAM**, Apr. 25, 1841, by Abner | | |
| Hale, J. P. | 1 | 135 |
| Susan, m. Wait **ARNOLD**, Apr.5, 1820 | 1 | 69 |
| W[illia]m, brick layer, ae 33, b. Norwich, res. same, m. Rosella | | |
| **BEAUREL**, milliner, ae 26, b. New Hampshire, res. | | |
| East Hartford, Jan. 8, 1848, by Rev. S. Spring | 1 | 52 |
| ----, Mrs., d. Feb. [ ], 1826 | 1 | 167 |
| **CUMMINGS**, Betsey, m. Jonathan **PITKIN**, Mar. 28, 1802, by Mr. Yates | 1 | 67 |
| Eugene D., s. George N., silversmith, ae 25 & Sarah, b. Sept. 21, | | |
| 1847 | 1 | 46 |
| George N., of Hartford, m. Sarah **CLARK**, of East Hartford, | | |
| June 10, 1844, by Rev. C. W. Turner | 1 | 145 |
| Waterman, of Mansfield, m. Mary Ann **CHEENEY**, of East | | |
| Hartford, Sept. 9, 1844, by Rev. C. W. Turner | 1 | 145 |
| **CURTIS**, George R., m. Elizabeth R. **FORBES**, b. of East Hartford, Jan. 1, | | |
| 1845, by Samuel Spring | 1 | 147 |
| Louisa P., of Glastenbury, m. Peter V. **HALL**, of East Hartford, | | |
| Apr. 11, 1849, by Samuel Spring | 1 | 156 |
| ----, Miss, bd. May or June, 1843 | 1 | 79 |
| **CUSHING, CUSHINGS**, Charles H., s. H. W., carpenter, b. Sept. 28, | | |
| 1849 | 1 | 54 |
| Francis, of East Hartford, m. Alexander **STUDLEY**, of Boston, | | |
| Mass., May 11, 1846, by Samuel Spring | 1 | 151 |

| | Vol. | Page |
|---|---|---|
| **CUSHING, CUSHINGS**, (cont.), | | |
| Henry W., of Hanover, Mass., m. Maria A. **HILLS**, of East | | |
| Hartford, Dec. 20, 1837, by Samuel Spring | 1 | 125 |
| Henry W., m. Mary C. **SPENCER**, b. of East Hartford, Jan. 1, | | |
| 1845, by Samuel Spring | 1 | 147 |
| **DAGGETT**, William H. H., of Andover, m. Lucy A. **PRATT**, of East | | |
| Hartford, Nov. 21, 1844, by Samuel Spring | 1 | 148 |
| **DANIELS**, Charles S., s. Charles, joiner, ae 32 & Emily G., ae 32, b. Feb. | | |
| 13, 1848 | 1 | 51 |
| Elizabeth, ae 17, b. Conn., m. W[illia]m H. **SPENCER**, joiner, | | |
| ae 27, b. Mass., res. same, Sept. 5, 1850, by D. | | |
| Bradbury | 1 | 59 |
| Elizabeth D., of East Hartford, m. William H. **SPENCER**, of | | |
| Warehouse Point, Sept. 5, 1850, by David Bradbury | 1 | 159 |
| James, m. Julia Ann **PHELPS**, b. of East Hartford, July 28, | | |
| 1846, by Samuel Spring | 1 | 152 |
| Joseph R., of East Hartford, m. Eliza W. **FAY**, of Otis, Mass., | | |
| Dec. 28, 1851, by Samuel Spring | 1 | 161 |
| Mary, ae 22, b. Hartford, m. Henry **CHRISTA**, manufacturer, | | |
| ae 22, b. Pawtucket, R. I., res. Rockville, May 23, | | |
| 1850, by D. Bradbury | 1 | 56 |
| Stephen, s. Henry, shoemaker, ae 24, b. Aug. 10, 1850 | 1 | 58 |
| Ward, m. Sophia **SWEETLAND**, Feb. 13, 1823, by Isaac | | |
| Devinel | 1 | 101 |
| **DART**, Jerusha, m. Russell **KEENY**, [ ], 1796 | 1 | 12 |
| Joseph, d. Oct. [ ], 1826 | 1 | 168 |
| Lyddia, m. Edmond **HALE**, Dec. 26, 1785 | 1 | 9 |
| Sally, m. John **YANCE**, b. of East Hartford, Jan. 7, 1823, by | | |
| Rev. Elisha B. Cook | 1 | 101 |
| **DAVIS**, Clarissa, of Vernon, m. W[illia]m **KEENEY**, of East Hartford, | | |
| June 24, 1821, by Rev. Isaac Divinel | 1 | 96 |
| Joseph, m. Emely **PERRY**, b. of Hartford, Nov. 20, 1836, by | | |
| S. L. Tracy | 1 | 119 |
| **DeDION**, Elizabeth Philippina, m. Charles Lewis **DESPENVILLE**, Sept. | | |
| 6, 1796, in Hispaniola | 1 | 37 |
| **DELIVER**, David, m. Almira **BURNHAM**, Jan. 3, 1822, by Joy H. | | |
| Fairchild | 1 | 97 |
| **DELLIBER**, ----, his s. [ ], d. Jan. [ ], 1798 | 1 | 63 |
| **DEMING, DEMMING**, Charles, sadler, ae 21, b. East Hartford, res. same, | | |
| m. Harriet A. **BAKER**, ae 19, b. Glastenbury, res. | | |
| East Hartford, Jan. [ ], [1848], by Samuel Springs | 1 | 48 |
| Charles, m. Harriet A. **BAKER**, b. of East Hartford, Jan. 4, | | |
| 1848, by Samuel Spring | 1 | 154 |
| Charles, harness maker, ae 22 & Harriet B., ae 22, had | | |
| s. [ ], b. Nov. [ ], 1848 | 1 | 50 |
| Charles, his child s.b. Dec. [ ], 1848 | 1 | 53 |
| Charles E., s. Charles, harness maker, ae 23 & Harriet A., ae 21, | | |
| b. Apr. 22, 1850 | 1 | 55 |
| Daniel, of Wethersfield, m. Mary **BIDWELL**, of East Hartford, | | |
| Nov. 16, 1822, by Joy H. Fairchild | 1 | 100 |
| Edwin, m. Ann **SAGE**, b. of East Hartford, Oct. 15, 1838, by | | |
| Samuel Spring | 1 | 126 |
| Elizah, m. Lucy **RISLEY**, Apr. 8, 1784 | 1 | 23 |

| | Vol. | Page |
|---|---|---|
| **DEMING, DEMMING,** (cont.), | | |
| Elizah, m. Lucy **RISLEY**, Apr. 8, 1784, by Rev. Dr. Williams | 1 | 61 |
| Eliza, m. Eleazer P. **HOWLETT**, b. of East Hartford, Oct. 23, | | |
| 1833, by Samuel Spring | 1 | 114 |
| Eunice, m. John **RODERSON**, Mar. 21, 1802, by Mr. Yates | 1 | 67 |
| Hannah, wid. Lemuel, d. Nov. 8, 1822, ae 85 | 1 | 73 |
| Julia, d. Oct. 19, 1849, ae 45 | 1 | 56 |
| Lemuel, m. Thankful **ROBERTS**, Apr. 1, 1784, by Rev. Dr. | | |
| William | 1 | 61 |
| Lemuel, d. [          ], 1801 | 1 | 63 |
| Mary, bd. by Jas. Hart, Nov. 21, 1839, ae 68 | 1 | 78 |
| Olive, m. Elisha E. **SAGE**, b. of East Hartford, Sept. 7, 1841, by | | |
| Samuel Spring | 1 | 136 |
| Phebe, m. Russel **HILLS**, [          ], 1783 | 1 | 21 |
| Prudence, b. May 15, 1778; m. Samuel **BREWER**, Oct. 5, | | |
| 1797 | 1 | 25 |
| Prudence, of East Hartford, m. Joseph **SAWYER**, of | | |
| Windham, Oct. 1, 1843, by Samuel Spring | 1 | 143 |
| Ruth, m. Ebenezer **HILLS**, Nov. 16, 1775 | 1 | 1 |
| Ruth, m. Jno(?) **FARRINGTON**, Dec. 29, 1792, by Rev. Dr. | | |
| Williams | 1 | 62 |
| Sarah, of East Hartford, m. Griswold **WRIGHT**, of Hartford, | | |
| Sept. 8, 1834, by Samuel Spring | 1 | 116 |
| Seth, [s. Elizah & Lucy], b. Apr. 26, 1786 | 1 | 23 |
| Timothy, m. Eliza **WING**, Nov. 22, 1825, by Joy H. Fairchild | 1 | 104 |
| Wealthy, m. William R. **WILBER**, b. of Hartford, May 29, | | |
| 1836, by Samuel Spring | 1 | 121 |
| ----, Mrs., d. [          ], 1805, at Sea | 1 | 65 |
| **DERBY, DURBY,** Adaline, of Glastenbury, m. Morgan **HOLLISTER,** | | |
| July 4, 1841, in Wethersfield | 1 | 40 |
| Eliza C., m. Lester **RISLEY**, b. of East Hartford, Aug. 7, 1840, | | |
| by Samuel Spring | 1 | 133 |
| **DESPENVILLE,** Charles Lewis, m. Elizabeth Philippina **DeDION**, Sept. | | |
| 6, 1796, in Hispaniola | 1 | 37 |
| Charles Lewis Amedee, [s. Charles Lewis & Elizabeth | | |
| Philippina], b. Dec. 23, 1798. Witnesses Charles | | |
| **DESPENVILLE**, Timothy **PITKIN**, John | | |
| **WYLES**, Jerusha **PITKIN** | 1 | 37 |
| **DEVINEL,** Lucius, s. Isaac **DEVINEL**, b. Dec. 10, 1821 | 1 | 98 |
| **DEWER\*,** Andrew H., m. Mary **BEMONT**, Mar. 1, 1826, by Joy H. | | |
| Fairchild    \*(**BREWER**?) | 1 | 105 |
| **DEWEY,** ----, wid., d. June [ ], 1827 | 1 | 168 |
| **DICKENSON, DICKINSON,** Abner W., of Glastenbury, m. Fedelia L. | | |
| **HALL**, of East Hartford, Feb. 28, 1844, by Samuel | | |
| Spring | 1 | 145 |
| Ann Eliza, of Haddam, m. John L. **HALE**, of Portland, June 11, | | |
| 1854, by Rev. B. C. Phelps | 1 | 166 |
| Henry H., of Hartford, m. Aurilia A. **COWLES**, of East | | |
| Hartford, May 2, 1838, by Samuel Spring | 1 | 125 |
| **DICKEY, DICKIE,** Christopher, m. Jane **GRAHAM**, b. of Glastenbury, | | |
| Oct. 3, 1853, by Rev. B. C. Phelps | 1 | 166 |
| John, m. Maria Francis **ROBERTS**, b. of East Hartford, Sept. | | |
| 18, 1834, by Samuel Spring | 1 | 117 |

|  | Vol. | Page |
|---|---|---|
| **DIMOCK**, Edwin W., of Coventry, m. Mary Jane **CHANDLER**, of East Hartford, Feb. 7, 1838 by Samuel Spring | 1 | 125 |
| **DOANE**, Nancy, m. George **WELLS**, Oct. 17, 1821, by Joy H. Fairchild | 1 | 96 |
| **DORMAN**, D. W., of Trenton, N. J., m. Albina **WADSWORTH**, of East Hartford, Dec. 29, 1851, by Rev. Benjamin C. Phelps | 1 | 162 |
| **DOWD, DOWDS, DOUDE**, Lester, m. Pamelia **TREET**, Feb. 9, 1823, by Joy H. Fairchild | 1 | 101 |
| Milley, d. [      ], 1805 | 1 | 65 |
| Thomas, of Hartford, m. Nancy **WILLIAMS**, of East Hartford, June 5, 1839, by Samuel Spring | 1 | 129 |
| Thomas W. *, s. Thomas, merchant, ae 32 & Nancy, ae 34, b. Jan. 16, 1850      *(Written "Thomas W. **DOWE**") | 1 | 54 |
| **DRAKE**, Esther, m. Chester **TREAT**, Feb. 20, 1822, by Rev. Isaac Divinel | 1 | 98 |
| Jerusha, of East Windsor, m. Levi **GOODWIN**, [           ] | 1 | 43 |
| Shuball, m. Bathsheba **WILLIAM**, Dec. 8, 1785, by Rev Dr Williams | 1 | 61 |
| William H., of New York City, m. Julia S. **AUSTIN**, of East Hartford, June 1, 1836, by Samuel Spring | 1 | 121 |
| **DUFFEY, DUFFY**, Elizabeth, d. John, blacksmith, ae 20, b. Aug. 2, 1850 | 1 | 57 |
| John, s. John, blacksmith, ae 39 & Maria, ae 38, b. Oct. 8, 1848 | 1 | 51 |
| **DUNHAM**, Allison W., child of Levi A., farmer, ae 30 & Amy, ae 21, b. Mar. 20, 1848 | 1 | 46 |
| Elizabeth, m. Andrew H. **WING**, June 6, 1836, by Samuel Spring | 1 | 121 |
| **DUNTON**, Henry, m. Ann **MATTHEWS**, b. of East Hartford, June 27, 1841, by Samuel Spring | 1 | 135 |
| **DURBY**, [see under **DERBY**] | | |
| **DYAR**, -----, his s. [           ], d. [           ], 1800 | 1 | 63 |
| **EASTON**, [see also **EATON**], Adeliza, of East Hartford, m. Sidney **SPENCER**, of Springfield, Mass., Sept. 27, 1837, by Samuel Spring | 1 | 123 |
| Agis, his child bd. May 27, 1832, ae 6 d. | 1 | 76 |
| Ages, farmer, ae 42, m. 2nd w. Harriet **SYMONDS**, ae 26, b. of East Hartford, Sept. 21, 1848, by Rev. S. Spring | 1 | 52 |
| Agis, m. Harriet **SIMONDS**, b. of East Hartford, Sept. 21, 1848, by Samuel Spring | 1 | 155 |
| Ashbel, m. Sarah **ARNOLD**, Aug. 22, 1784, by Rev. Dr. Williams | 1 | 61 |
| Chauncey, m. Fanny **SHEPHERD**, Aug. 20, 1819 | 1 | 69 |
| Clarissa, m. Silas **HILLS**, Nov. 7, 1799 | 1 | 29 |
| Elizabeth, m. George **FORBES**, b. of East Hartford, Aug. 19, 1851, by Samuel Spring | 1 | 160 |
| Harriet, d. Agis, farmer, ae 44 & Harriet, ae 27, b. Sept. [ ], 1849 | 1 | 54 |
| Harriet, d. Sept. [ ], 1849, ae 3 wks. | 1 | 56 |
| Mabel, m. Daniel **ROBERTS**, July 8, 1794, by Rev. Dr. Williams | 1 | 62 |
| Margaret, d. July 22, 1849, ae 61 | 1 | 53 |
| Mary, b. Middletown, res. East Hartford, d. Oct. 7, 1847, ae 35 y. | 1 | 49 |

| | Vol. | Page |
|---|---|---|
| **EASTON**, [see also **EATON**], (cont.), | | |
| Nancy, m. Henry **HOUSE**, b. of East Hartford, Oct. 4, 1829, by | | |
| Herman Perry | 1 | 111 |
| Prudence, wid. Timothy, d. Oct. 2, 1797, ae 98 | 1 | 63 |
| Samuel, d. [        ], 1800 | 1 | 63 |
| -----, his child d. Mar. [  ], 1806 | 1 | 65 |
| **EATON**, [see also, **EASTON**], Justice*, his d. [        ] & wid. of Harry | | |
| **HOUSE**, bd. Dec. 20, 1836, ae 27 y.    *("Justice | | |
| **EASTON**?") | 1 | 78 |
| **EDWARDS**, Alonso, m. Henrietta **BREWER**, b. of East Hartford, Dec. | | |
| 31, 1846, by Samuel Spring | 1 | 153 |
| Benjamin, his w. [        ], d. [        ], 1800 | 1 | 63 |
| Esther A., d. Alonzo, joiner, b. Oct. 22, 1850 | 1 | 58 |
| **EGBERT**, Tunis, his child bd. Nov. 8, 1839, ae 10 m. | 1 | 78 |
| **EGLISTON**, Emma, ae 20, b. Bloomfield, res. East Hartford, m. Albert | | |
| **BREWER**, wagon maker, ae 22, b. East Hartford, | | |
| res. same, Oct. 31, 1847, by Rev. Whiting | 1 | 48 |
| **ELI**, Henry, R. R. overseer, ae 34, b. Ireland, had s. [        ], b. Feb. [  ], | | |
| 1848 | 1 | 50 |
| Henry, his child s.b. Feb. [  ], 1849 | 1 | 53 |
| **ELLIS**, Matilda, of Enfield, m. Edward **HOUSE**, of Glastenbury, Apr. 17, | | |
| 1840, by Samuel Spring | 1 | 132 |
| Oliver J., m. Harriet **WARNER**, Oct. 25, 1818 | 1 | 68 |
| **ELMER**, **ELMORE**, Anna, m. John **MAGILL**, Feb. 1, 1801 | 1 | 40 |
| Ellen, d. Sept. 5, 1849, ae 4 | 1 | 56 |
| Joseph, of East Windsor, m. Calesta **COWLES**, of East | | |
| Hartford, Sept. 11, 1839, by Samuel Spring | 1 | 129 |
| Laury, child of Moses, farmer, ae 38 & [        ], ae 41, b. | | |
| July 9, 1847 | 1 | 47 |
| Laura, d. Aug. 13, 1847, ae 35 days | 1 | 49 |
| Lee W., farmer, ae 26, b. East Windsor, res. S. Windsor, m. | | |
| Sarah A. **COWLES**, ae 20, b. East Hartford, res. | | |
| same, Nov. 3, 1847, by Samuel Springs | 1 | 48 |
| Lee W., of South Windsor, m. Sarah A. **COWLES**, of East | | |
| Hartford, Nov. 3, 1847, by Samuel Spring | 1 | 154 |
| Mary A., d. Moses, farmer, ae 40 & Ruhama, ae 43, b. Mar. 21, | | |
| 1850 | 1 | 55 |
| Moses, Jr., of East Windsor, m. Ruhannah W. **BIDWELL**, of | | |
| East Hartford, Apr. 20, 1836, by Samuel Spring | 1 | 120 |
| Naomi, bd. by Elijah **FORBES**, Mar. 12, 1826, ae 60 | 1 | 75 |
| Samuel, of East Windsor, m. Dorcas **PRATT**, of East Hartford, | | |
| Dec. 13, 1836, by Samuel Spring | 1 | 121 |
| **ELTON**, Harriet E., of Hartford, m. Orville H. **STEVENS**, of Waterbury, | | |
| May 5, 1853, by Samuel Spring | 1 | 164 |
| **EMMERSON**, Daniel, m. Betsy **JEFFORDS**, b. of Coventry, June 28, | | |
| 1820, by Rev. Elisha B. Cook | 1 | 94 |
| **ENGLISH**, John, bd. Oct. 27, 1828, ae 28 | 1 | 75 |
| **ENSIGN**, Albert, s. Ralph, blacksmith, ae 53, b. Nov. 6, 1851 | 1 | 58 |
| Anna, m. Isaac **ROBERTS**, Apr. 2, 1817 | 1 | 68 |
| Anne, [d. Moses & Jennet], b. Sept. 21, 1796 | 1 | 21 |
| Betsey, [d. Moses & Jennet], b. July 10, 1794 | 1 | 21 |
| Charles A., m. Cornelia H. **STEVENS**, b. of East Hartford, | | |
| Nov. 12, 1844, by Samuel Spring | 1 | 147 |

| | Vol. | Page |
|---|---|---|
| **ENSIGN**, (cont.), | | |
| Charles Henry, s. Charles A., shoemaker, ae 26 & Cornelia H., | | |
| ae 25, b. Feb. 28, 1848 | 1 | 47 |
| Cornelia H., b. Glastonbury, res. East Hartford, d. Nov. 15, | | |
| 1848, ae 26 | 1 | 53 |
| David Forbs, [s. Moses & Jennet], b. Dec. 30, 1786; d. Feb. 25, | | |
| 1787 | 1 | 21 |
| Elizur R., ae 25, m. Delia **BREWER**, ae 19, b. of East Hartford, | | |
| May 24, 1849, by Rev. S. Spring | 1 | 52 |
| Elisur R., m. Delia **BREWER**, b. of East Hartford, May 24, | | |
| 1849, by Samuel Spring | 1 | 157 |
| Fanny, d. Ralph, blacksmith, ae 47 & Laura, ae 37, b. May 4, | | |
| 1848 | 1 | 47 |
| Harry, m. Abigail **ABBY**, Apr. 8, 1821, by Joy H. Fairchild | 1 | 95 |
| Henry, tailor, ae 22, b. East Hartford, res. Hartford, m. Lucy | | |
| H. A. **ENSIGN**, ae 21, b. Andover, res. Hartford, | | |
| Oct. 20, [1847], by James Eli | 1 | 48 |
| Jennette, ae 24, m. Ira **ANDERSON**, painter, ae 27, b. of East | | |
| Hartford, Mar. 12, 1850, by S. Spring | 1 | 56 |
| Jenette, m. Ira **ANDERSON**, b. of East Hartford, Mar. 12, | | |
| 1850, by Samuel Spring | 1 | 158 |
| Lucy H. A., ae 21, b. Andover, res. Hartford, m. Henry | | |
| **ENSIGN**, tailor, ae 22, b. East Hartford, res. | | |
| Hartford, Oct. 20, [1847], by James Eli | 1 | 48 |
| Mary*, [child of Moses & Jennet], b. Nov. 4, 1798 | | |
| *(In pencil "Harry") | 1 | 21 |
| Mary, m. Joseph H. **PORTER**, b. of East Hartford, Oct. 31, | | |
| 1844, by Samuel Spring | 1 | 146 |
| Moses, m. Jennet **FORBS**, Feb. 16, 1786 | 1 | 21 |
| Moses, m. Jennie **FORBES**, Feb. 16, 1786, by Rev. Dr. | | |
| Williams | 1 | 61 |
| Moses, [s. Moses & Jennet], b. July 21, 1790; d. Sept. 16, 1790 | 1 | 21 |
| Moses, [s. Moses & Jennet], b. Sept. 6, 1791 | 1 | 21 |
| Moses, Jr., m. Patty **RISLEY**, May 23, 1820 | 1 | 69 |
| Ralph, [s. Moses & Jennet], b. Dec. 21, 1800 | 1 | 21 |
| Ralph, m. Ruth Williams **HOTTEN***, Oct. 14, 1824, by Joy H. | | |
| Fairchild      *("HOLTON"?) | 1 | 102 |
| Ralph, m. Laura **HILLS**, b. of East Hartford, Sept. 14, 1845, by | | |
| Samuel Spring | 1 | 149 |
| Rosanna, of East Hartford, m. Lorin **HALE**, of So. Glastenbury, | | |
| Dec. 31, 1844, by Samuel Spring | 1 | 146 |
| Solomon, m. Elizabeth **CHANDLER**, Oct. 11, 1792, by Rev. | | |
| Dr. Williams | 1 | 62 |
| **ENSWORTH**, John, m. Eliza **KENNEDY**, Nov. 26, 1818 | 1 | 69 |
| **ERVIN**, Elizabeth, d. George G., laborer, b. May 14, 1851 | 1 | 58 |
| **ERWIN**, Joseph, m. Sally **TREAT**, b. of East Hartford, Nov. 5, 1843, by | | |
| Rev. C. W. Turner | 1 | 144 |
| **EVANS**, Benjamin, d. Apr. [ ], 1809 | 1 | 66 |
| Demy*, m. McKee **McKEE**, s. Nat & Sally, Sept. 6, 1801 | | |
| *("Dency?") | 1 | 2 |
| J. W., joiner, ae 35 & Mary J., ae 22, had d. [        ], b. May | | |
| 22, 1850 | 1 | 55 |
| Theosy, m. Oliver **GRAY**, Dec. 17, 1821, by Isaac Divinel | 1 | 97 |

32        BARBOUR COLLECTION

EVANS, (cont.),                                                         Vol.   Page
----, Mrs., d. [          ], 1809, ae 83                                 1      66
----, Mrs., d. [          ], 1814                                        1      66
F[      ], Polly, of Newport & John KELSEY, of East Hartford, Int. Pub.,
          Mar. 9, 1806                                                   1      67
FAIRCHILD, Harriet, m. George Olcott GOODWIN, s. Joseph, 2nd &
          Eleanor, [          ]                                          1      44
FARMER, Fanny, m. George PHILLIPS, b. of Bolton, Nov. 27, 1820, by
          Rev. Isaac Divinnell                                           1      95
FARNHAM, Augustus, his child bd. Jan. 9, 1843, ae 3 m.                   1      79
          Augustus, s. Augustus, joiner, ae 32 & Persis S., ae 30, b. June
          10, 1848                                                       1      46
          Elias, m. Fanny HURLBERT, Sept. 16, 1824, by Joy H.
          Fairchild                                                      1     103
          Frank W., [s. Sylvester G. & Mary], b. Jan. 12, 1852           1      39
          Marcus A., s. Augustus, joiner, ae 35, b. Mar. 23, 1851        1      58
          Mary, [d. Sylvester G. & Mary], b. Apr. 6, 1833                1      39
          Sylvester G., b. Sept. 13, 1795, at Ashford, Conn.; m. Mary
          WHITON, Mar. 1, 1827, at Ashford, Conn.                        1      39
          Sylvester G., [s. Sylvester G. & Mary], b. Apr. 11, 1828       1      39
FARRINGTON, Jno (?), m. Ruth DEMING, Dec. 29, 1792, by Rev. Dr.
          Williams                                                       1      62
FAY, Eliza W., of Otis, Mass., m. Joseph R. DANIELS, of East Hartford,
          Dec. 28, 1851, by Samuel Spring                                1     161
FENDRICK, Joseph, of Baltimore, Md., m. Lucy Ann WELLS, of East
          Hartford, Apr. 30, 1848, by Samuel Spring                      1     155
FILLAINE, Lyman, m. Mary Ann SHOFFORD, b. of Bolton, Sept. 6,
          1842, by Samuel Spring                                         1     140
FILLASER, Jacob, m. Sophia RISLEY, b. of Glastenbury, Nov. 23, 1851,
          by Rev. B. C. Phelps                                           1     161
FILLEY, Barnaby, m. Elizabeth HILLS, Nov. 18, 1818                       1      68
FISH, Joseph E., of East Windsor, m. Sophia BURNHAM, of East
          Hartford, Mar. 2, 1837, by Charles Remington                   1     122
          Lydia, m. Hubbard KEENEY, b. of Manchester, Dec. 15, 1841,
          by Rev. B. M. Walker                                           1     137
FITCH, Eunice, m. Jonathan THOMPSON, Apr. 24, 1789, by Rev. Dr.
          Williams                                                       1      61
          James G., ae 34, b. Hartford, res. East Hartford, m. Mary L.
          BEMISS, ae 20, b. East Hartford, res. same, Oct.
          20, 1847, by Jos. Harrington                                   1      48
          James Goodwin, m. Mary Lamb BEMIS, b. of East Hartford,
          Oct. 20, 1847, by Rev. Joseph Harrington of
          Hartford                                                       1     154
          Warren, m. Mrs. Catherine STEWART, b. of Tolland, Sept. 26,
          1844, by Samuel Spring                                         1    145-6
FLAGG, Saffa, m. Shuball GRISWOLD, May 25, 1786, by Rev. Dr.
          Williams                                                       1      61
          Samuel, m. Polly WYLES, Nov. 28, 1790, by Rev. Dr.
          Williams                                                       1      61
          Samuel, Dr., d. [          ], 1814, ae 79                      1      67
          W[illia]m, his child d. [          ], 1801                     1      63
FLANNIGAN, Margaret, d. Tho[ma]s, laborer, b. May 19, 1851             1      58

| FORBES, FORBS, (cont.), | Vol. | Page |
|---|---|---|
| Elizabeth R., m. George R. CURTIS, b. of East Hartford, Jan. 1, 1845, by Samuel Spring | 1 | 147 |
| Ellen, m. Frank AMADON, b. of East Hartford, Oct. 19, 1851, by Rev. Royal Robins | 1 | 161 |
| Emely, [d. Aaron & Lois], b. Apr. 23, 1788 | 1 | 15 |
| Emily, m. George BARBER, b. of East Hartford, June 17, 1829, by Rev. Samuel Spring, of Hartford | 1 | 110 |
| Esther, [d. Aaron & Lois], b. Feb. 26, 1777; d. Jan. 19, 1797 | 1 | 15 |
| Esther, of Manchester, m. Royal H. BREWER, of East Hartford, Nov. 27, 1844, by Samuel Spring | 1 | 148 |
| Eunice, of East Hartford, m. Leveritt MELLORD, of Vernon, May 27, 1822, by Rev. Elisha B. Cook | 1 | 99 |
| Francis, ae 26, b. East Hartford, res. same, m. Henry KING, farmer, ae 32, b. S. Windsor, res. same, Dec. 25, 1849, by S. Spring | 1 | 56 |
| Francis M., of East Hartford, m. Henry M. KING, of South Windsor, Dec. 25, 1849, by Samuel Spring | 1 | 157 |
| George, m. Elizabeth EASTON, b. of East Hartford, Aug. 19, 1851, by Samuel Spring | 1 | 160 |
| George D., s. Henry, blacksmith, ae 36, b. Nov. 19, 1850 | 1 | 59 |
| George D., d. Jan. 7, 1851, ae 6 wks. | 1 | 60 |
| Giles, m. Sarah P. STANLEY, b. of East Hartford, Mar. 26, 1839, by Samuel Spring | 1 | 127 |
| Hannah, of East Hartford, m. Henry H. TREAT, of Glastenbury, Mar. 19, 1845, by Samuel Spring | 1 | 148 |
| Harriet, of East Hartford, m. Alniarin (?) HOUSE, of Glastenbury, Oct. 19, 1842, by Samuel Spring | 1 | 140 |
| Harriet, d. Henry, blacksmith, b. May 1, 1848 | 1 | 47 |
| Harriet E., m. Henry H. SPAFFORD, Nov. 25, 1852, by Rev. John F. Sheffield | 1 | 163 |
| Harriet H., of East Hartford, m. Fredus H. GRISWOLD, of Barton, Miss., Jan. 11, 1854, by Samuel Spring | 1 | 165 |
| Heppy, m. Hezekiah WADSWORTH, b. of East Hartford, Apr. 9, 1837, by Samuel Spring | 1 | 122 |
| Ichabod, his w. [        ], d. Feb. 21, 1805 | 1 | 65 |
| Ichabod, d. Jan. 15, 1825 | 1 | 73 |
| Jared, [s. Eiligah & Rebeckah], b. May 16, 1784 | 1 | 22 |
| Jennet, m. Moses ENSIGN, Feb. 16, 1786 | 1 | 21 |
| Jennie, m. Moses ENSIGN, Feb. 16, 1786, by Rev. Mr. Williams | 1 | 61 |
| Jerusha, m. Howell HILLS, Jan. 1, 1829, by Enoch Brent | 1 | 110 |
| Joel, of East Hartford, m. Almira SPAFFORD, of Coventry, Apr. 5, 1846, by Samuel Spring | 1 | 151 |
| Joseph, [s. Eligah & Rebeckah], b. Aug. 28, 1775; d. Oct. 31, 1776 | 1 | 22 |
| Joseph, [s. Eligah & Rebeckah], b. Aug. 27, 1779 | 1 | 22 |
| Julia F., [d. Giles, farmer, b. Dec. [ ], 1848 | 1 | 47 |
| Laura, m. Erie WRIGHT, Mar. 27, 1823, by Joy H. Fairchild | 1 | 101 |
| Leonora, of East Hartford, m. George SLOAN, of Tolland, Oct. 27, 1846, by Samuel Spring | 1 | 152 |
| Lois, [d. Aron & Lois], b. Mar. 28, 1770 | 1 | 15 |
| Lois, [d. Aron & Lois], b. Mar. 28, 1770 | 1 | 15 |

| | Vol. | Page |
|---|---|---|
| **FORBES, FORBS**, (cont.), | | |
| Lois, [w. Aron], d. Aug. 23, 1797 | 1 | 15 |
| Lucy, m. Levi L. **VIBERT**, b. of East Hartford, May 10, 1840, | | |
| by Samuel Spring | 1 | 132 |
| Mabel, [d. Eligah & Rebeckah], b. Nov. 3, 1781 | 1 | 22 |
| Mahlon, his w. [ ], bd. July 27, 1837, ae 62 | 1 | 78 |
| Mary, m. Ashbel **OLMSTED**, Nov. 16, 1786, by Rev. Dr. | | |
| Williams | 1 | 61 |
| Mary, d. Nov. 7, 1798, ae 84 | 1 | 63 |
| Mary Ann, of East Hartford, m. Edward L. **KENYON**, of | | |
| Hartford, Dec. 20, 1847, by Samuel Spring | 1 | 48 |
| Mary Ann, of East Hartford, m. Edward L. **KENYON**, of | | |
| Hartford, Dec. 20, 1847, by Samuel Spring | 1 | 154 |
| Mary Jane, d. Owin, farmer, ae [ ] & Julia, b. Apr. 1, 1850 | 1 | 55 |
| Moses, Capt., m. wid. Mercy **WRIGHT**, [ ], 1792, by | | |
| Rev. Dr. Williams | 1 | 62 |
| Nabby, d. [ ], 1800 | 1 | 63 |
| Olive, [d. Aaron & Lois], b. Feb. 16, 1790 | 1 | 15 |
| Oren, m. Mary **TREAT**, Nov. 15, 1821, by Joy H. Fairchild | 1 | 97 |
| Orrin, 3rd, m. Emeline **CAMP**, b. of East Hartford, Nov. 13, | | |
| 1839, by Samuel Spring | 1 | 131 |
| Phene (?), m. Jonah **WILLIAMS**, Jan. 26, 1796, by Rev. Dr. | | |
| Williams | 1 | 62 |
| Rebecca, d. Oct. 18, 1818, ae 76 | 1 | 73 |
| Russell, [s. Aaron & Lois], b. Dec. 5, 1780 | 1 | 15 |
| Russell, his child d. [ ], 1805 | 1 | 65 |
| Susan G., of East Hartford, m. J. B. **RUSSELL**, of Hartford, | | |
| Jan. 17, 1837, by Samuel Spring | 1 | 122 |
| Thomas, his w. [ ], bd. Nov. 12, 1828, ae 76 | 1 | 75 |
| Thomas, d. Mar. [ ], 1829, ae 83 | 1 | 74 |
| Thomas, bd. Mar. 18, 1829, ae 82 | 1 | 75 |
| Timothy, d. [ ], 1800, ae 58 | 1 | 63 |
| Timothy, m. Betsy **TREAT**, Nov. [ ], 1886*, by Mr. Yates | | |
| *(1806?) | 1 | 67 |
| Wells, m. Deantha D. **SPAFFORD**, b. of East Hartford, Dec. | | |
| 21, 1851, by Rev. Benjamin C. Phelps | 1 | 162 |
| ----, his child d. July [ ], 1806 | 1 | 65 |
| ----, Mr., d. [ ], 1807 | 1 | 66 |
| **FORD**, Gardiner, m. Mary **COOK**, Feb. 2, 1817, b. of Hadley, Mass. | 1 | 68 |
| Henry, wid., bd. Aug. 1, 1839, ae 40 | 1 | 78 |
| Henry F., m. Harriet **CLARK**, Mar. 30, 1817 | 1 | 68 |
| ----, his child d. [ ], 1805 | 1 | 65 |
| **FOSTER**, Caroline Elizabeth, of East Hartford, m. Charles **WRIGHT**, of | | |
| Glastenbury, Aug. 19, 1839, by Samuel Strong | 1 | 129 |
| Eldridge, m. Deborah **COTTON**, Oct. 18, 1820, by Joy H. | | |
| Fairchild | 1 | 94 |
| Ralph H., of Hartford, m. Hannah M. **SPENCER**, of East | | |
| Hartford, Oct. 16, 1839, by Samuel Spring | 1 | 130 |
| Saminda, bd. Mar. 13, 1828, ae 54 | 1 | 75 |
| William O., of Glastenbury, m. Laura M. **HILLS**, of East | | |
| Hartford, Apr. 8, 1847, by Samuel Spring | 1 | 153 |

Vol.    Page

FOWLER, Asenath, ae 46, b. Bolton, res. East Hartford, m. W[illia]m
    HALE, millwright, ae 55, b. Manchester, res. same,
    Nov. 4, 1849, by Rev. Phelps                                    1       55
    Asenath, of East Hartford, m. William HALE, of Manchester,
      Nov. 4, 1849, by Rev. Benjamin C. Phelps                     1       158
    Roderick F., m. Pamelia HILLS, Apr. 27, 1830, by V. R.
      Osbourn, V. D. M.                                            1       111
    Samuel, his w. [          ], d. Mar. [  ], 1809, ae 72          1       66
    ----, Mr., d. [          ], 1799                               1       63
FOX, Abigail, b. Aug. 22, 1768; m. Elizur McKEE, Oct. 17, 1787     1       35
    Chester, had d. [          ], b. Jan. [  ], 1849               1       51
    Cynthia, m. James PALMER, Jan. 21, 1819                       1       69
    Delia, m. Aaron WARREN, Dec. 16, 1824, by Joy H. Fairchild    1       103
    Dorithy, of East Hartford, m. S. COVIL, of Sandwich, Mass.,
      July 8, 1833, by Rev. Samuel Spring                          1       117
    Edgar M., s. Norman, millwright, ae 41, b. Sept. 12, 1850     1       59
    Eleazar, m. Susan BUCKLAND, May 17, 1821, by Joy H.
      Fairchild                                                    1       96
    Elvira, of Glastenbury, m. W[illia]m SMITH, Feb. 16, 1820     1       69
    Mary E., d. Feb. 18, 1849                                     1       53
    Mary I., m. John RISLEY, b. of Hartford, July 2, 1849, by Rev.
      S. Spring                                                    1       52
    Norman, m. Cornelia RILEY, b. of East Hartford, Jan. 9, 1839,
      by Samuel Spring                                             1       127
    Rhoda, m. Ashbel ALFORD, b. of Middletown, July 21, 1833,
      by Rev. Samuel Spring                                        1       114
    Solomon, m. Clarissa LOW, Aug. 20, 1822, by Joy H. Fairchild  1       99
    Solomon, m. Mary Ann HILLS, b. of East Hartford, Mar. 12,
      1837, by Samuel Spring                                       1       122
    Susanna, m. Joseph ISHAM, May 19, 1822, by Isaac Devinel      1       99
    ----, wid., d. July 18, 1802                                  1       64
    ----, his child d. [          ], 1804                         1       64
    ----, his child d. [          ], 1806                         1       65
    ----, his infant, d. [          ], 1808                       1       66
    ----, his child d. [          ], 1809                         1       66
    ----, his child d. [          ], 1809, ae 1 d.                1       66
FRANKLIN, Amelia, of East Hartford, m. Walter HOUSE, of
    Glastenbury, Oct. 1, 1839, by Samuel Spring                   1       130
    Elizabeth, m. Orrin FRANKLIN, b. of East Hartford, Sept. 10,
      1837, by Samuel Spring                                       1       123
    Francis, s. Jonathan F., teamster, ae 36, b. Mar. 19, 1851     1       59
    Julia Ann, m. Lorenzo D. KEENY, of Manchester, May 7,
      1834, by Samuel Spring                                       1       117
    M. E., b. East Hartford, res. same, m. C. A. TUCKER, farmer,
      ae 20, b. Maine, res. Buckfield, Mass., Aug. 29,
      1849, by Rev. S. Spring                                      1       55
    Mary, of East Hartford, m. Charles A. TUCKER, of Maine,
      Aug. 28, 1849, by Samuel Spring                              1       157
    Orrin, m. Elizabeth FRANKLIN, b. of East Hartford, Sept. 10,
      1837, by Samuel Spring                                       1       123

| | Vol. | Page |
|---|---|---|
| **FRANKLIN**, (cont.), | | |
| Russell, farmer, ae 27, of East Hartford, m. Adeline R. **HALL**, | | |
| ae 22, b. Hardwick, Vt., res. East Hartford, May 13, | | |
| 1849, by David Bradway | 1 | 52 |
| Thomas, his child bd. Nov. 1, 1828, ae 2 m. | 1 | 75 |
| Thomas C., m. Elizabeth **LOOMIS**, b. of East Hartford, Sept. | | |
| 16, 1834, by Samuel Spring | 1 | 117 |
| ----, his child d. [          ], 1806 | 1 | 65 |
| **FREEMAN**, Cynthia, colored, d. Jan. 10, 1849, ae 6 | 1 | 53 |
| Thomas, m. Harriet **LAMB**, Aug. 5, 1817 | 1 | 68 |
| **FRISBE**, Elizabeth, m. George **PRINDLE**, b. of New Haven, Sept. 2, | | |
| 1850, by Rev. Joseph Harrington, of Hartford | 1 | 159 |
| **FULLER**, Elijah, m. Hannah **CHANDLER**, Sept. 21, 1794, by Rev. Dr. | | |
| Williams | 1 | 62 |
| **GABRIEL**, George L., s. Anthony, silver smith, ae 38 & Julia, ae 43, b. | | |
| Feb. 1, 1850 | 1 | 54 |
| **GAINES, GAINS, GANES**, Albert, m. Hester **HILLS**, b. of East | | |
| Hartford, May 19, 1842, by Samuel Spring | 1 | 139 |
| Asenath, of East Hartford, m. Elizur **SMITH**, of Glastenbury, | | |
| Nov. 26, 1851, by Rev. B. C. Phelps | 1 | 161 |
| Elizabeth, seamstress, ae 22, b. East Hartford, res. Glastenbury, | | |
| m. Israel **HIGGINS**, farmer, ae 22, b. Glastenbury, | | |
| res. same, May 4, 1848, by John C. Goodrich | 1 | 48 |
| Elizabeth O., of East Hartford, m. Israel **HIGGINS**, of South | | |
| Glastenbury, May 4, 1848, by Rev. J. O. Goodridge | 1 | 155 |
| Epaphras, m. Sophia **BREWER**, Nov. 27, 1816 | 1 | 68 |
| Harriot, m. Edmund **ABBY**, Aug. 2, 1821, by Joy H. Fairchild | 1 | 96 |
| Jane M., m. David **GLEASON**, b. of East Hartford, July 2, | | |
| 1849, by [          ] | 1 | 52 |
| Jane M., of East Hartford, m. David A. C. **GLEASON**, of | | |
| Hartford, July 2, 1849, by Rev. Benjamin C. Phelps | 1 | 158 |
| Jesse, m. Caroline **BREWER**, Feb. 26, 1823, by Joy H. | | |
| Fairchild | 1 | 101 |
| Julia, m. Peter **ROGERS**, May 1, 1822, by Joy H. Fairchild | 1 | 98 |
| Lucy M., m. David **CLARK**, Dec. 9, 1824, by Joy H. Fairchild | 1 | 103 |
| Mary, m. W[illia]m W. **LARRABEE**, Nov. 27, 1817 | 1 | 68 |
| Mary A., m. Cyrus **VIBERT**, b. of East Hartford, May 11, | | |
| 1847, by Samuel Spring | 1 | 153 |
| Mary J., of East Hartford, m. Albert **BLUMENTHAL**, of | | |
| Hartford, Aug. 12, 1846, by Samuel Spring | 1 | 152 |
| Simon, d. [          ], 1814 | 1 | 66 |
| Sophia, m. W[illia]m **McROBIE**, Jan. 17, 1831, by Asa Mead | 1 | 70 |
| ----, Mr., d. [          ],1813 | 1 | 67 |
| **GALPIN**, Almon, of Washington, m. Tripheny **GOODALE**, of East | | |
| Hartford, July 24, 1839, by Rev. Lozien Pierce | 1 | 128 |
| Almon, of Washington, m. Almira **RUDGE**, of East Hartford, | | |
| Dec. 20, 1840, by Samuel Spring | 1 | 134 |
| Lucinda, m. George M. **MORRISON**, Nov. 17, 1852, by | | |
| Benjamin C. Phelps | 1 | 163 |
| **GATES**, James M., of Windham, m. Betsy **BURNHAM**, Sept. 28, 1831, | | |
| by Rev. Gurdon Robins, of East Windsor | 1 | 113 |
| **GAY**, W[illia]m, bd. Sept. 15, 1828, ae 35 (?) | 1 | 75 |

|  | Vol. | Page |
|---|---|---|
| GAYLORD, Olive L., b. June 10, 1789; m. Joseph GOODWIN, 2nd, June 25, 1836 | 1 | 44 |
| GEER, Elisha, m. Abigail L. ROBERTS, b. of East Hartford, Sept. 10, 1839, by Samuel Spring | 1 | 129 |
| Everett S., s. Elisha, painter, b. Feb. 22, 1850 | 1 | 54 |
| Nathan C., m. Julia L. BURNHAM, b. of East Hartford, Oct. 12, 1842, by Samuel Spring | 1 | 140 |
| GEHNAN, Mary A., ae 23, m. Calvin WAY, joiner, ae 34, b. Lyme, res. East Hartford, Nov. 13, 1848, by Rev. S. Spring | 1 | 52 |
| GILBERT, Mary, of Middletown, m. Wilson HILLS, of East Windsor, May 9, 1842, by Samuel Spring | 1 | 138 |
| GILLETT, GILLET, Dudley, m. Jennett SMITH, Sept. 26, 1826, by Joy H. Fairchild | 1 | 107 |
| Eli, m. Lucy GILMAN, Feb. 28, 1817 | 1 | 68 |
| Ellen E., d. Edward, ae [ ] & Anna J., b. July 26, 1848 | 1 | 46 |
| Ezra E., of Colchester, m. Mary WADSWORTH, of East Hartford, Mar. 7, 1847, by Levi Daggett, Jr. | 1 | 153 |
| Olive G., ae 25, b. S. Windsor, res. East Hartford, m. Morrison COLEMAN, harness maker, ae 26, b. Coventry, res. East Hartford, Sept. 4, 1848, by Rev. S. Spring | 1 | 52 |
| Roxey E., m. Timothy BURNHAM, b. of South Windsor, Oct. 13, 1846, by Samuel Spring | 1 | 107 |
| GILMAN, A. Erskine, s. Albert, wagon maker, ae 26, b. July 26*, 1851 *(Written over "20th") | 1 | 58 |
| A. Louise, d. Ralzman, tinner, ae 31, b. Jan. 31, 1851 | 1 | 58 |
| Albert B., of East Hartford, m. Eliza A. ANTRIM, of South Windsor, Oct. 29, 1848, by Samuel Spring | 1 | 155 |
| Ann, d. Sept. 9, 1848, ae 54 | 1 | 53 |
| Edward, m. Ann ABBEY, Sept. 25, 1817 | 1 | 68 |
| Edward H., s. Ashbel, blacksmith, ae 28 & Celia, ae 27, b. Aug. 10, 1850 | 1 | 57 |
| Elizabeth, Mrs., d. July 3, 1814, ae 88 | 1 | 67 |
| George, s. Albert B., wagon maker, ae 25 & Eliza A., ae 19, b. Oct. 8, 1849 | 1 | 54 |
| Lucy, m. Eli GILLETT, Feb. 28, 1817 | 1 | 68 |
| Mary A., m. Calvin S. WAY, b. of East Hartford, Nov. 13, 1848, by Samuel Spring | 1 | 155 |
| Oliver, bd. Feb. 15, 1834, ae 73 | 1 | 76 |
| Raphael, of Berlin, m. Maria RISLEY, of East Hartford, Jan. 17, 1830, by Rev. Timothy Benedict | 1 | 111 |
| Rebeckah, m. Eligah FORBS, Dec. 26, 1771 | 1 | 22 |
| -----, Mrs., d. [          ], 1802 | 1 | 64 |
| -----, d. [          ], 1802, ae 16 | 1 | 64 |
| -----, Mr., d. [          ], 1806 | 1 | 65 |
| -----, Mr., d. [          ], 1814 | 1 | 67 |
| GLAMSER, Hohanna, m. Frederick SCHONLAAR, b. of East Hartford, Oct. 31, 1852, by Rev. John F. Sheffield | 1 | 163 |
| GLEASON, GLESON, Chauncy, m. Deborah CHALKER, Dec. 12, 1816 | 1 | 68 |
| David, m. Jane M. GANES*, b. of East Hartford, July 2, 1849, by [          ]          *("GAINS") | 1 | 52 |

| | Vol. | Page |
|---|---|---|
| **GLEASON, GLESON**, (cont.), | | |
| David A. G., of Hartford, m. Jane M. **GANES**, of East Hartford, | | |
| July 2, 1849, by Rev. Benjamin C. Phelps | 1 | 158 |
| Elam, m. Sarah **BELDEN**, Jan. 17, 1821, by Joy H. Fairchild | 1 | 95 |
| Hanah, wid., m. Daniel **MARSH**, June 27, 1771; d. Oct. 9, | | |
| 1778 | 1 | 20 |
| Harvey, m. Sally **COLMAN**, Sept. 4, 1822, by Joy H. Fairchild | 1 | 99 |
| Moses, d. [         ], 1826 | 1 | 168 |
| **GOODALE**, Almira, m. Joel **ALVORD**, Nov. 9, 1826, by Joy H. Fairchild | 1 | 107 |
| Charles, harness maker, ae 22, b. East Hartford, res. same, m. | | |
| Mary A. **CARROLL**, ae 22, b. Ireland, res. East | | |
| Hartford, July 21, 1850 by Rev. Alderman | 1 | 56 |
| Charles J., s. Austin, farmer, ae 24 & Mary Ann, ae 23, b. Feb. | | |
| 1, 1848 | 1 | 51 |
| Eliza G., of East Hartford, m. David **BROCKWAY**, of Lime, | | |
| Dec. 1, 1833, by G. A Calhoue | 1 | 115 |
| Elizabeth F., of Glastenbury, m. Osbon O. **HILLS**, of East | | |
| Hartford, May 23, 1852, by Rev. John F. Sheffield | 1 | 162 |
| Hiram, d. Daniel & Rachael, m. Eliza **BREWER**, d. Daniel & | | |
| Mary, Nov. 17, 1830, by Asa Mead | 1 | 70 |
| Hiram, m. Eliza **BREWER**, Nov. 17, 1830, by Rev. Asa Mead | 1 | 112 |
| John L., of East Windsor, m. Betsy **TREAT**, of East Hartford, | | |
| May 1, 1822, by Rev. Elisha B. Cook | 1 | 98 |
| Maria E., ae 19, b. East Hartford, res. East Hartford, m. Horace | | |
| M. **SMITH**, painter, ae 24, b. New York, res. | | |
| Brooklyn, July 28, 1851, by S. Spring | 1 | 59 |
| Maria E., of East Hartford, m. Horace M. **SMITH**, of Brooklyn, | | |
| N. Y., July 30, 1851, by Samuel Spring | 1 | 160 |
| Rachel, m. Julius **BREWER**, Dec. 31, 1826, by Joy H. | | |
| Fairchild | 1 | 107 |
| Sally, of East Hartford, m. William H. **SIKES**, of Sheffield, Oct. | | |
| 7, 1832, by Rev. Samuel H. Biddle | 1 | 113 |
| Sarah A., ae 22, b. East Hartford, res. same, m. Henry P. | | |
| **KILBOURN**, mechanic, ae 25, b. Goshen, res. East | | |
| Hartford, Aug. [ ], 1847, by Samuel Springs | 1 | 48 |
| Sarah A., m. Henry P. **KILBOURN**, b. of East Hartford, Aug. | | |
| 26, 1847, by Samuel Spring | 1 | 153 |
| Tripheny, of East Hartford, m. Almon **GALPIN**, of Washington, | | |
| July 24, 1839, by Rev. Lozien Pierce | 1 | 128 |
| W[illia]m, cooper, d. Apr. 12, 1850, ae 78 | 1 | 57 |
| **GOODRICH**, Hellen L., of East Hartford, m. Samuel P. **ROBENSON**, of | | |
| Canterbury, Dec. 5, 1844, by Samuel Spring | 1 | 148 |
| Juliette, m. Andrew **SMITH**, b. of Glastenbury, Nov. 20, 1842, | | |
| by [       ] | 1 | 141 |
| **GOODWIN**, Abigail, w. Joseph, 2nd, d. Jan. 10, 1801, ae 21 | 1 | 63 |
| Abigail, w. Jos., d. [         ], 1801 | 1 | 63 |
| Abigail, [d. Joseph, 2nd & Eleanor], b. Oct. 5, 1805; d. Apr. 13, | | |
| 1816, ae 10 1/2 | 1 | 44 |
| Abigail, d. Jos., bp. Jan. 12, 1806; b. Oct. 5, 1805 | 1 | 67 |
| Abigail A., m. Barnabas **HASKELL**, Dec. 25, 1837 | 1 | 42 |
| Abigail A., of East Hartford, m. Barnabas **HASKELL**, of | | |
| Springfield, Mass., Dec. 25, 1837, by Samuel Spring | 1 | 125 |

GOODWIN, (cont.)                                                    Vol.    Page
Abigail Ashley, [d. Joseph, 2nd & Eleanor], b. Jan. 18, 1819; m.
   Barnabas HASKELL, [            ]                                  1      44
Anne, [d. John & Dorothy], b. [        ], 1762; d. Jan. 14,
   1780, ae 18                                                       1      43
B., his w. [        ] & child, d. [        ], 1814                   1      66
Caleb, [s. John & Dorothy], b. [         ]                          1      43
Caleb, [s. John & Sarah], b. [         ], 1712; d. Apr. 12, 1769,
   ae 57                                                            1      43
Caleb, [s. Joseph & Hannah], b. Nov. 3, 1778; d. May 24, 1830;
   ae 51 1/2, m. Harriot WILLIAMS, of Wethersfield,
   [            ]                                                    1      44
Caroline S., d. James C., farmer, ae 37, b. Jan. 10, 1851           1      58
Clairrissa, [d. Joseph & Hannah], b. Mar. 20, 1784; d. Nov. 8,
   1824, ae 40                                                      1      44
Damaris, [d. John & Sarah], b. [        ], 1699; d. Aug. [ ],
   1723, ae 24                                                      1      43
Damaras, [d. John, 2nd & Dorothy], b. [        ], 1738; d. Oct.
   18, 1773, ae 35                                                 1      43
Dolly, [d. John & Dorothy], b. [         ]; m. Benjamin
   ROBERTS, [        ]; d. Jan. 14, 1798, ae 59                     1      43
Dorothy, d. Aug. 17, 1789, ae 72                                    1      43
Edward Ozias, [s. Edward S. & Jane Treat], b. May 22, 1839          1      44
Edward S., b. Sept. 29, 1809; m. Jane Treat ROBERTS, d.
   Ozias, Sept. 24, 1835; d. Nov. 9, 1873                           1      44
Edward S., of Port Gibson, Miss., m. Jane F. ROBERTS, of
   East Hartford, Sept. 24, 1835, by Samuel Spring                  1      118
Edward Scott, [s. Joseph, 2nd & Eleanor], b. Sept. 29, 1809        1      44
Eleanor, w. Joseph, 2nd, d. Dec. 26, 1831, ae 55                    1      44
Eleanor Lord, [d. Joseph, 2nd & Eleanor], b. Jan. 13, 1812; m.
   Samuel P. ROBINSON, of Canterbury, [         ]                   1      44
Eliza E., of East Hartford, m. Edward P. CLARK, of Galena,
   Ill., Mar. 16, 1852, by Samuel Spring                            1      162
Eliza Emeline, [d. Joseph, 2nd & Eleanor], b. [         ]           1      44
Elizabeth, d. Dec. 24, 1847, ae 30                                  1      49
Elizabeth, [d. Nathaniel & Elizabeth], b. [         ]               1      43
Ellen, of East Hartford, m. Thomas L. WILLIAMS, of Boston,
   Mass., Oct. 7, 1846, by Samuel Spring                            1      152
George, his w. [         ], b. Hartford, res. East Hartford, d.
   Mar. 6, 1851, ae 62                                              1      59
George Olcott, [s. Joseph, 2nd & Eleanor], b. June 11, 1803; d.
   Aug. 28, 1831, ae 28; m. Harriet FAIRCHILD,
   [            ]                                                    1      44
Hannah, [d. Ozias], b. [         ], 1638; d. Feb. [ ], 1724, ae 86  1      43
Hannah, [d. Nathaniel & Elizabeth], b. [        ], 1685;
   d. [         ]                                                   1      43
Hannah, [d. Joseph & Hannah], b. July 4, 1781; m. John
   REYNOLDS, [         ]                                            1      44
Hannah, w. Joseph, d. July 1, 1814, ae 67                           1      44
Hannah, m. [         ] PORTER, [         ]                          1      43
Hannah, m. Dea. Moses SMITH, [         ]                            1      43
Hannah (OLMSTED), w. Jos., d. [         ], 1814                     1      67

| | Vol. | Page |
|---|---|---|
| **GOODWIN**, (cont.), | | |
| Hester, m. Abraham **WATERHOUSE**, Apr. 9, 1822, by Joy | | |
|     H. Fairchild | 1 | 98 |
| Hezekiah, [s. Joseph & Hannah], b. Sept. 21, 1789; m. Emily | | |
|     **PRATT**, [      ] | 1 | 44 |
| James Cadwell, [s. Joseph, 2nd & Eleanor], b. Sept. 4, 1815; m. | | |
|     Abigail **JUDD**, of Hartford, [     ] | 1 | 44 |
| Jane Ann, m. Francis **WOODBRIDGE**, May [  ], 1827, by Joy | | |
|     H. Fairchild | 1 | 108 |
| Jane Treat, w. Edward S., d. [       ] | 1 | 44 |
| Jedediah Ashley, [s. Joseph, 2nd & Eleanor], b. Mar. 18, 1814; | | |
|     d. May 20, 1814 | 1 | 44 |
| John, b. [      ], 1672; Dea. of East Hartford Cong. Ch., | | |
|     1748; m. Sarah [     ], [  ]; d. Feb. 6, 1757, ae | | |
|     66 | 1 | 43 |
| John, [s. Nathaniel & Sarah], b. [     ], 1672; d. [     ], | | |
|     1758, ae 86 | 1 | 43 |
| John, [s. John & Sarah], b. [     ], 1706; d. Sept. 14, 1793, | | |
|     ae 87 | 1 | 43 |
| John, 2nd, b. [     ], 1706; m. Dorothy **PITKIN**, | | |
|     [      ]; d. Sept. 14, 1793, ae 87; Chosen | | |
|     Dea. of East Hartford Ch., 1780 | 1 | 43 |
| John, [s. John, 2nd & Dorothy], b. [     ], 1741; d. | | |
|     [     ], 1784, ae 43 | 1 | 43 |
| John, m. 2nd w. wid. Mary **OLMSTED**, wid. Nicolas, | | |
|     [      ] | 1 | 43 |
| Joseph, [s. John & Sarah], b. [     ], 1711; d. Feb. 28, 1738, | | |
|     ae 27 | 1 | 43 |
| Joseph, [s. John, 2nd & Dorothy], b. May 9, 1743; d. Nov. 13, | | |
|     1809, ae 66 | 1 | 43 |
| Joseph, b. May 9, 1743; m. Hannah **ULMSTED**, June 3, 1773; | | |
|     d. Nov. 13, 1809, ae 66 | 1 | 44 |
| Joseph, [s. Joseph & Hannah], b. June 2, 1776 | 1 | 44 |
| Joseph, 2nd, b. June 2, 1776; m. Abigail **SMITH**, d. Nathaniel | | |
|     & Elizabeth, [     ] | 1 | 44 |
| Joseph, 2nd, m. 2nd w. Eleanor **OLCOTT**, d. Jedediah, of | | |
|     Bloomfield, Sept. 9, 1802 | 1 | 44 |
| Joseph, d. [     ], 1809 | 1 | 66 |
| Joseph, 2nd, m. 3rd w. Olive I **GAYLORD**, June 25, 1836 | 1 | 44 |
| Joseph Olcott, [s. Edward S. & Jane Treat], b. Apr. 16, 1843 | 1 | 44 |
| Joseph Smith, [s. Joseph, 2nd & Abigail], b. Jan. 1, 1801; d. | | |
|     Oct. 29, 1829, ae 28 3 / 4 | 1 | 44 |
| Josephine Scott, [d. Edward S. & Jane Treat], b. Oct. 13, 1841 | 1 | 44 |
| Levi, b. [     ], 1757; m. Jerusha **DRAKE**, of East | | |
|     Windsor, [     ]; d. Apr. 24, 1836, ae 78 | 1 | 43 |
| Loisa, [d. Edward S. & Jane Treat], b. Oct. 30, 1837; d. Feb. 18, | | |
|     1838, in Port Gibson, Miss. | 1 | 44 |
| Maria K., m. Henry **PITKIN**, b. of East Hartford, June 29, | | |
|     1837, by Samuel Spring | 1 | 123 |
| Mary, [d. Nathaniel & Elizabeth], b. [     ], 1690; | | |
|     d. [     ] | 1 | 43 |
| Mary, w. John, d. Mar. 2, 1760, ae 77 | 1 | 43 |
| Mary, m. Timothy **HALL**, Sept. 27, 1798 | 1 | 10 |

| GOODWIN, (cont.), | Vol. | Page |
|---|---|---|
| Mary, m. Dr. Timothy **HALL**, [ ] | 1 | 43 |
| Mary Jane, [d. Edward S. & Jane Treat], b. Sept. 26, 1836; d. | | |
| May 19, 1838, in Port Gibson, Miss. | 1 | 44 |
| Nathaniel, m. Sarah **COWLES**, d. John, of Hadley, Mass., | | |
| [ ], 1664; d. [ ], 1714 | 1 | 43 |
| Nathaniel, [s. Nathaniel & Sarah], b. [ ], 1665; | | |
| d. [ ], 1745, ae 80 | 1 | 43 |
| Nathaniel, [s. Ozias], b. [ ]; d. [ ], 1714 | 1 | 43 |
| Nathaniel, m. 2nd w. Elizabeth **PRATT**, d. Daniel, of Hartford, | | |
| [ ] | 1 | 43 |
| Ozias, d. [ ], 1683 | 1 | 43 |
| Ozias, [s. Nathaniel & Elizabeth], b. [ ], 1689; | | |
| d. [ ], 1760, ae 71 | 1 | 43 |
| Ozias, see William **GOODWIN** | 1 | 43 |
| Richard, [s. John & Sarah], b. [ ], 1719; d. Mar. 3, | | |
| 1745, ae 26 | 1 | 43 |
| Richard, [s. John, 2nd & Dorothy], b. [ ], 1753; m. Ruth | | |
| **ROBERTS**, [ ]; d. Aug. 15, 1821, ae 68 | 1 | 43 |
| Richard, m. Ruth **ROBERTS**, Feb. 6, 1784, by Rev. Dr. | | |
| Williams | 1 | 61 |
| Richard, his child d. [ ], 1797 | 1 | 63 |
| Sally, [d. Joseph & Hannah], b. Oct. 12, 1786; d. July 16, 1836, | | |
| ae 50 | 1 | 44 |
| Samuel, [s. Nathaniel & Elizabeth], b. [ ], 1682; | | |
| d. [ ], 1712, ae 30 | 1 | 43 |
| Samuel Olmsted, [s. Edward S. & Jane Treat], b. Feb. 21, 1845 | 1 | 44 |
| Sarah, [d. Nathaniel & Sarah], b. [ ], 1668; | | |
| d. [ ] | 1 | 43 |
| Sarah, w. Nathaniel, d. [ ], 1676, ae 30 | 1 | 43 |
| Sarah, 1st w. John, d. May [ ], 1735 | 1 | 43 |
| Sarah, [d. John, 2nd & Dorothy,] b. [ ], 1750; m. John | | |
| **WYLES**, [ ] | 1 | 43 |
| Thankfull, [d. John, 2nd & Dorothy], b. [ ], 1754; d. | | |
| Dec. 13, 1771, ae 17 | 1 | 43 |
| William, Elder, & brother Ozias, came from England and lived | | |
| in Cambridge, Mass., a short time, then moved to | | |
| Hartford, in 1635. William, had d. Elizabeth, who | | |
| m. John **CROW**, of Hartford, from whom descended | | |
| Daniel **WADSWORTH**, Elisha Pitkin | 1 | 43 |
| William, [s. Ozias], b. [ ], 1639; d. [ ], 1689, ae | | |
| 60 | 1 | 43 |
| William, [s. John & Sarah], b. [ ], 1709; d. Feb. 18, | | |
| 1745, ae 36 | 1 | 43 |
| William, [s. John, 2nd & Dorothy], b. [ ], 1745; d. Mar. | | |
| 20, 1785, ae 40 | 1 | 43 |
| -----, his child d. [ ], 1814, ae 9 wks. | 1 | 67 |
| **GOSLEE**, Ozias, m. Jemima **WILLIAMS**, Dec. 5, 1821, by Joy H. | | |
| Fairchild | 1 | 97 |
| **GOULD**, Benjamin, his w. [ ], bd. Apr. 11, 1834, ae 63 | 1 | 76 |
| Benjamin, bd. Apr. 1, 1843, ae 77 | 1 | 79 |
| Mary Ann, m. Thomas H. **WALES**, b. of East Hartford, Sept. | | |
| 24, 1834, by Samuel Spring | 1 | 118 |

| | Vol. | Page |
|---|---|---|
| **GOWDY**, Leonard, of Enfield, m. Clarissa A. **CULVER**, of East Hartford, Nov. 30, 1843, by Daniel Pitkin, Jr., J. P. | 1 | 144 |
| **GRADY**, Dennis, s. Pattrick, boarding, b. Mar. 29, 1849 | 1 | 51 |
| **GRAHAM**, Jane, m. Christopher **DICKEY**, b. of Glastenbury, Oct. 3, 1853, by Rev. B. C. Phelps | 1 | 166 |
| **GRANT**, Hiram, m. Susan **WILLIAMS**, Jan. 12, 1832, by Rev. Gurdon Robins, of East Windsor | 1 | 113 |
| **GRAY**, Oliver, m. Theosy **EVANS**, Dec. 17, 1821, by Isaac Divinel | 1 | 97 |
| **GREEN**, Daniel, of Manchester, m. Abby S. **HILLS**, of East Hartford, Sept. 22, 1852, by Benjamin Phelps | 1 | 163 |
| Marshall A., m. Esther **HILLS**, b. of Hartford, Sept. 1, 1838, by Samuel Spring | 1 | 126 |
| **GREENLEAF**, Jane E., m. Edward **BURR**, b. of Hartford, June 14, 1846, by Samuel Spring | 1 | 152 |
| **GRIMMANS**, Charles, of Philadelphia, Pa., m. Jane **WILCOX**, of East Hartford, Oct. 2, 1839, by Samuel Spring | 1 | 130 |
| **GRISWOLD**, Cornelia, d. Dec. 29, 1801, ae 7 m. 21 d. | 1 | 63 |
| Emily, b. Nov. 22, 1788 | TR2 | 1 |
| Emily, b. Nov. 22, 1788 | 1 | 71 |
| Esther, b. Oct. 21, 1791 | TR2 | 1 |
| Esther, b. Oct. 21, 1791 | 1 | 71 |
| Fredus H., of Barton, Miss., m. Harriet H. **FORBES**, of East Hartford, Jan. 11, 1854, by Samuel Spring | 1 | 165 |
| George Williams, b. May 23, 1794 | TR2 | 1 |
| George W[illia]m, b. May 23, 1794 | 1 | 71 |
| Julius, m. Anne **ARNOLD**, Jan. 3, 1822, by Joy H. Fairchild | 1 | 97 |
| Julius Johnson, b. Dec. 16, 1800 | TR2 | 1 |
| Julius Johnson, b. Dec. 16, 1800 | 1 | 71 |
| Lesley, b. Mar. 19, 1786 | TR2 | 1 |
| Lewey, b. Mar. 19, 1786 | 1 | 71 |
| Lovisa, m. Peter **RICHIE**, July 22, 1785, by Rev. Dr. Williams | 1 | 61 |
| Nancy, m. Tracy **BIDWELL**, b. of East Hartford, Dec. 25, 1822, by Rev. Elisha B. Cook | 1 | 101 |
| Shuball, m. Saffa **FLAGG**, May 25, 1786, by Rev. Dr. Williams | 1 | 61 |
| Shuball, m. Sarah **STANLEY**, Jan. 6, 1791, by Rev. Dr. Williams | 1 | 61 |
| Truman, of Windsor, m. Larista * A., **KEENY**, of East Hartford, Nov. 7, 1847, by Samuel Spring *(Saresta?) | 1 | 48 |
| Truman, of Windsor, m. Saresta A. **KEENEY**, of East Hartford, Nov. 7, 1847, by Samuel Spring | 1 | 154 |
| ——, Gen., his child d. [          ], 1801 | 1 | 63 |
| **GROSSMAN**, **GROSEMAN**, Eliza, m. Horace **PHILLIPS**, b. of East Hartford, Feb. 14, 1836, by Samuel Spring | 1 | 119 |
| Theodocia, m. Francis F. **BREWER**, b. of East Hartford, May [ ], 1839, by Samuel Spring | 1 | 129 |
| **GROVER**, Aner, m. Betsy **HASKELL**, Nov. 7, 1821, by Joy H. Fairchild | 1 | 97 |
| **GUERNSEY**, Lewis, m. Timothy **ANDERSON**, [          ] | 1 | 41 |
| Lewis E., m. Lucinda **BURNHAM**, Apr. 19, 1835, by Charles Remington, Elder | 1 | 118 |

|                                                                                          | Vol. | Page |
|------------------------------------------------------------------------------------------|------|------|
| **GULLIVER, GULLIVOR**, Ann, m. John M. **CHAPMAN**, Jan. 11, 1827,                      |      |      |
| by Joy H. Fairchild                                                                       | 1    | 107  |
| Betsy, m. Stephen **ROBERTS**, Dec. 7, 1820, by Joy H.                                   |      |      |
| Fairchild                                                                                 | 1    | 95   |
| Fanny, of East Hartford, m. Elisha **PORTER**, of Glastenbury,                           |      |      |
| Jan. 14, 1830, by Samuel H. Beddel                                                        | 1    | 111  |
| Tho[ma]s, m. Thankful **PORTER**, Sept. 21, 1786, by Rev. Dr.                            |      |      |
| Williams                                                                                  | 1    | 61   |
| ----, his child d. [          ], 1802                                                     | 1    | 64   |
| ----, Mrs., bd. June 29, 1830, ae 65                                                      | 1    | 76   |
| **GURLEY**, Betsey, [d. Royal & Laomi], b. June 16, 1801                                 | 1    | 1    |
| Clarissa, [d. Royal & Laomi], b. Dec. 23, 1798                                            | 1    | 1    |
| Royal, m. Laomi **ATHERTON**, [          ]                                                | 1    | 1    |
| Sallyne, [d. Royal & Laomi], b. Apr. 9, 1797                                              | 1    | 1    |
| **HAFF**, Joel, of Huntington, N. Y., m. Elizabeth **MARBLE**, of East                   |      |      |
| Hartford, Aug. 25, 1845, by Samuel Spring                                                 | 1    | 149  |
| **HALE**, Clarrasa, [d. Edmond & Lyddia], b. Aug. 8, 1797                                | 1    | 9    |
| Dorinda R., m. Charles E. **CLARK**, b. of East Hartford, June                           |      |      |
| 25, 1846, by Samuel Spring                                                                | 1    | 152  |
| Edmond, m. Lyddia **DART**, Dec. 26, 1785                                                | 1    | 9    |
| Edmond, [s. Edmond & Lyddia], b. Nov. [ ], 1786                                          | 1    | 9    |
| Eleazer, [s. Isaac], b. Oct. 2, 1778                                                      | 1    | 32   |
| Esther, [d. Isaac], b. Jan. 20, 1776                                                      | 1    | 32   |
| Henrietta, d. L. G., joiner & Rosanna, b. Nov. 16, 1849                                  | 1    | 50   |
| Henrietta, d. Sept. 27, 1850                                                              | 1    | 60   |
| Hiram, [s. Edmond & Lyddia], b. Feb. 9, 1800                                             | 1    | 9    |
| Hiram, m. Ruba **HALL**, May 1, 1821, by Rev. Elisha B. Cook                             | 1    | 96   |
| Isaac, m. [          ], 1779 (?)*          *(1770?)                                       | 1    | 32   |
| Jane Ann, m. Eleazer **BURNHAM**, b. of East Hartford, Nov. 6,                           |      |      |
| 1838, by Samuel Spring                                                                    | 1    | 127  |
| John L., of Portland, m. Ann Eliza **DICKENSON**, of Haddam,                             |      |      |
| June 11, 1854, by Rev. B. C. Phelps                                                       | 1    | 166  |
| Julia, [d. Edmond & Lyddia], b. Aug. 29, 1803                                            | 1    | 9    |
| Julia, of East Hartford, m. Thomas **JONES**, of Coventry, Oct.                          |      |      |
| 25, 1820, by Rev. Elisha B. Cook                                                          | 1    | 95   |
| Lorin, of So. Glastenbury, m. Rosanna **ENSIGN**, of East                               |      |      |
| Hartford, Dec. 31, 1844, by Samuel Spring                                                 | 1    | 146  |
| Lydia, [d. Edmond & Lyddia], b. Sept. 8, 1792                                            | 1    | 9    |
| Polly, [d. Isaac], b. July 24, 1772                                                       | 1    | 32   |
| Sally, [d. Isaac], b. Oct. 25, 1774                                                       | 1    | 32   |
| Theodosia, of East Hartford, m. Obed **KEENY**, of Glastenbury,                          |      |      |
| May 6, 1823, by Rev. Elisha B. Cook                                                       | 1    | 101  |
| William, [s. Edmond & Lyddia], b. Aug. 23, 1794                                          | 1    | 9    |
| W[illia]m, millwright, ae 55, b. Manchester, res. same, m. 2nd                           |      |      |
| w. Asenath **FOWLER**, ae 46, b. Bolton, res. East                                       |      |      |
| Hartford, Nov. 4, 1849, by Rev. Phelps                                                    | 1    | 55   |
| William, of Manchester, m. Asenath **FOWLER**, of East                                   |      |      |
| Hartford, Nov. 4, 1849, by Rev. Benjamin C. Phelps                                        | 1    | 158  |
| **HALL**, Adeline R., ae 22, b. Hardwick, Vt., res. East Hartford, m. Russell            |      |      |
| **FRANKLIN**, farmer, ae 27, of East Hartford, May                                       |      |      |
| 13, 1849, by David Bradway                                                                | 1    | 52   |

| | Vol. | Page |
|---|---|---|
| **HALL**, (cont.) | | |
| Almira, m. Eli **BARNUM**, b. of East Hartford, Apr. 17, 1834, | | |
| by Rev. Gustavus F. Davis, of Hartford | 1 | 116 |
| Almira S., ae 20, b. Blanford, Mass., res. East Hartford, m. | | |
| Henry E. **WOODRUFF**, marketing, ae 21, b. East | | |
| Hartford, res. same, June 20, 1850, by W. Clark | 1 | 56 |
| Austin, [s. Timothy & Eunice], b. July 22, 1789 | 1 | 10 |
| Calvil L., s. Lucius I., farmer, ae 31 & Caroline L., ae 25, b. | | |
| Apr. 4, 1850 | 1 | 55 |
| Eli, [s. Timothy & Eunice], b. Oct. 8, 1785 | 1 | 10 |
| Emma, [d. Timothy & Eunice], b. Sept. 18, 1787 | 1 | 10 |
| Eunice, w. Timothy, d. June 24, 1797 | 1 | 10 |
| Fedelia L., of East Hartford, m. Abner W. **DICKENSON**, of | | |
| Glastenbury, Feb. 28, 1844, by Samuel Spring | 1 | 145 |
| Luke, [s. Timothy & Eunice], b. Jan. 7, 1798 [1784?] | 1 | 10 |
| Peter V., of East Hartford, m. Louisa P. **CURTIS**, of | | |
| Glastenbury, Apr. 11, 1849, by Samuel Spring | 1 | 156 |
| Risley, [d. Daniel & Risley], b. Mar. 29, 1803 | 1 | 34 |
| Ruba, m. Hiram **HALE**, May 1, 1821, by Rev. Elisha B. Cook | 1 | 96 |
| Sally, [d. Timothy & Eunice], b. May 5, 1795 | 1 | 10 |
| Sally, m. Lyman **BRAINARD**, Nov. 29, 1820, by Joy H. | | |
| Fairchild | 1 | 95 |
| Sarah, m. W[illia]m H. **SCOVILL**, machinist, b. of East | | |
| Hartford, Jan. 4, 1851, by S. Spring | 1 | 59 |
| Sarah, of East Hartford, m. Lemuel **SCOVILLE**, of Hartford, | | |
| June 4, 1851, by Samuel Spring | 1 | 160 |
| Sophy, [d. Timothy & Eunice], b. Aug. 29, 1791; d. Apr. 12, | | |
| 1792 | 1 | 10 |
| Sophy, [d. Timothy & Eunice], b. Mar. 19, 1793 | 1 | 10 |
| Timothy, m. Eunice **HILLS**, Apr. 3, 1783 | 1 | 10 |
| Timothy, m. 2nd w. Mary **GOODWIN**, Sept. 27, 1798 | 1 | 10 |
| Timothy, Dr., m. Mary **GOODWIN**, [          ] | 1 | 43 |
| Tirzah, m. David **WELLS**, Apr. 25, 1827, by J. H. Fairchild | 1 | 108 |
| ----, Mrs., d. [          ], 1797 | 1 | 63 |
| ----, Mrs., d. Jan. [  ], 1798 | 1 | 63 |
| **HALLET**, ----, his child bd. Sept. 2, [1827] | 1 | 75 |
| **HAMILTON**, David, bd. Mar. 23, 1834, ae 42, by Russell Wildman | 1 | 76 |
| Levi, of Sheffield, Mass., m. Rebecca **HICKS**, of East Hartford, | | |
| Aug. 17, 1828, by Mr. Brace (?) | 1 | 111 |
| **HANCOCK**, Ellen, of East Hartford, m. William **MARBLE**, of Windsor, | | |
| Oct. 27, 1850, by Rev. Benjamin C. Phelps | 1 | 159 |
| Harvey G., s. Harmond, farmer, ae 46 & Mary, ae 40, b. Jan. 2, | | |
| 1848 | 1 | 46 |
| **HANMER**, Francis, m. Julia **ROBERTS**, Nov. 24, 1825, by Joy H. | | |
| Fairchild | 1 | 105 |
| Francis, m. Abigail **ROSE**, Oct. 11, 1836, by S. L. Tracy | 1 | 119 |
| Francis, power maker, ae 48 & Abigail, ae 38, had s. [          ], | | |
| s.b. July 25, 1850 | 1 | 55 |
| William, m. Caroline E. **FORBES**, b. of East Hartford, Sept. 6, | | |
| 1853, by Samuel Spring | 1 | 164 |
| **HANOVER**, Katherine, m. Seth **HOSKINS**, b. of East Hartford, Nov. 7, | | |
| 1821, by Rev. Isaac Divinel | 1 | 96 |

|  | Vol. | Page |
|---|---|---|

HARDING, Sarah, ae 21, m. W[illia]m BRYANT, painter, ae 23, b. of
  East Hartford, May 10, 1850, by S. Spring ......... 1 ... 56
  Sarah B., m. William B. BRYANT, b. of East Hartford, May
  14, 1850, by Samuel Spring ......... 1 ... 159
HARRINGTON, Edwin P., m. Electa SMITH, Nov. 11, 1824, by Joy H.
  Fairchild ......... 1 ... 103
  John, s. Daniel, power maker, ae 24, b. June 1, 1851 ......... 1 ... 59
HART, Donald, of Hartford, m. Caroline PITKIN, of Hartford, Oct. 31,
  1831, by Rev. Gustavus F. Davis, of Hartford ......... 1 ... 113
  James, m. Lucretia RISLEY, b. of East Hartford, Sept. 15,
  1845, by Samuel Spring ......... 1 ... 149
  Mary Ann, m. Adna RISLEY, b. of East Hartford, Oct. 13,
  1835, by Samuel Spring ......... 1 ... 118
HASKELL, Adeline, of East Hartford, m. Samuel E. CHAPMAN, of
  Hartford, Dec. 26, 1836, by Samuel Spring ......... 1 ... 121
  Barnabas, m. Abigail A. GOODWIN, Dec. 25, 1837 ......... 1 ... 42
  Barnabas, of Springfield, Mass., m. Abigail A. GOODWIN, of
  East Hartford, Dec. 25, 1837, by Samuel Spring ......... 1 ... 125
  Barnabas, m. Abigail Ashley GOODWIN, d. Joseph, 2nd &
  Eleanor, [          ] ......... 1 ... 44
  Betsy, m. Aner GROVER, Nov. 7, 1821, by Joy H. Fairchild ......... 1 ... 97
  Hellen Maria Texana, [d. Barnabas & Abigail A.], b. Oct. 9,
  1840, at Houston, Texas; d. Sept. 5, 1847, at Boston ......... 1 ... 42
  William Barnabas, [s. Barnabas & Abigail A.], b. Oct. 10, 1842,
  at New York City ......... 1 ... 42
HASTING, Harriet Louisa, of Hartford, m. John Nelson PORTER, of East
  Hartford, Oct. 21, 1838, by Rev. Thomas W. Giles ......... 1 ... 127
HAYDEN, Edward, m. Amelia SMITH, b. of East Hartford, May 20,
  1845, by Samuel Spring ......... 1 ... 149
  Edwin, of East Windsor, m. Huldah WILLIAMS, of East
  Hartford, June 26, 1839, by Samuel Spring ......... 1 ... 128
HAYES, Abigail, d. Aug. [ ], 1829, ae 93 ......... 1 ... 74
  Emeline, m. Hiram CLARK, May 2, 1826, by Joy H. Fairchild ......... 1 ... 105
  Lucy, m. William CLARK, Feb. 3, 1824, by Joy H. Fairchild ......... 1 ... 102
  Watson L., m. Harriet F. WARREN, b. of East Hartford, Apr.
  27, 1843, by Samuel Spring ......... 1 ... 142
  William, m. Sarah WILLIAMS, Feb. 12, 1824, by Joy H.
  Fairchild ......... 1 ... 102
  ——, his child d. Feb. 10, 1806 ......... 1 ... 65
HEATH, C., his d. [          ], bd. Oct. 2, 1830, ae 18    (Entry reads "C.
  HEATH's daughter to Roger BURNHAM") ......... 1 ... 76
  Chauncey, his w. [          ], bd. Oct. 3, 1832 ......... 1 ... 76
HICKS, Rebecca, of East Hartford, m. Levi HAMILTON, of Sheffield,
  Mass., Aug. 17, 1828, by Mr. Brace (?) ......... 1 ... 111
HIEM, Phillip, of Glastenbury, m. Rosina BINDLE, of Werlemberel,
  Germany, July 16, [Probably 1854], by C. C.
  Ashley, J. P. ......... 1 ... 166
HIGGINS, Israel, farmer, ae 22, b. Glastenbury, res. same, m. Elizabeth
  GAINES, seamstress, ae 22, b. East Hartford, res.
  Glastenbury, May 4, 1848, by John C. Goodrich ......... 1 ... 48
  Israel, of South Glastenbury, m. Elizabeth O. GAINES, of East
  Hartford, May 4, 1848, by Rev. J. O. Goodridge ......... 1 ... 155

| HILLS, HILL, (cont.), | Vol. | Page |
|---|---|---|
| Cornelia, m. Romanda COWLES, b. of East Hartford, May 5, | | |
| 1830, by V. R. Osbourn, V. D. M. | 1 | 111 |
| David, [s. Epaphras & Hannah], b. Apr. 4, 1800 | 1 | 4 |
| David, s. Elisha, d. [          ], 1804, ae 19 | 1 | 64 |
| David T., s. Abner W., mason, ae 32 & Nancy, ae 32, b. Nov. | | |
| 20, 1847 | 1 | 47 |
| Delia, [d. George & Anna], b. Dec. 22, 1797 | 1 | 15 |
| | | |
| Delia, of East Hartford, m. Sylvester WYLLYS, of Hartford, | | |
| Oct. 12, 1835, by Samuel Spring | 1 | 118 |
| Delia Ann, m. William H. RISLEY, b. of East Hartford, Apr. | | |
| 23, 1839, by Samuel Spring | 1 | 128 |
| Dolly, w. Aaron, d. Feb. 5, 1800 | 1 | 63 |
| Dorea, [d. Ashbel & Mehitable], b. July 12, 1784; d. June 14, | | |
| 1786 | 1 | 34 |
| Dorea, [d. Ashbel & Mehitable], b. Jan. 24, 1790 | 1 | 34 |
| Ebenezer, m. Ruth DEMMING, Nov. 16, 1775 | 1 | 1 |
| Ebenezer, [s. Ebenezer & Ruth], b. Aug. 19, 1776 | 1 | 1 |
| Ebenezer, had 3 children d. [          ], 1794 | 1 | 73 |
| Ebenezer, m. Elizabeth KENNEDY, Jan. 17, 1798 | 1 | 10 |
| Ebenezer, m. Elizabeth KENNEDY, Jan. 17, 1798, by Rev. Dr. | | |
| Williams | 1 | 62 |
| Ebenezer, Jr., d. July 2, 1807, ae 31 | 1 | 66 |
| Ebenezer, his s. [          ], d. Feb. 7, 1808 | 1 | 66 |
| Ebenezer, s. Ebenezer, d. Apr. 14, 1829, ae [ ] | 1 | 74 |
| Ebenezer, m. Jane HOUSE, b. of East Hartford, Apr. 16, 1837, | | |
| by Samuel Spring | 1 | 122 |
| Edward, [s. Ebenezer & Ruth], b. Nov. 31, 1784; d. Oct. 11, | | |
| 1794 | 1 | 1 |
| Edwin C., farmer, ae 31, b. East Hartford, res. same, m. | | |
| Margaret STANLEY, ae 20, b. Berlin, res. same, | | |
| Apr. 5, 1848, by Charles S. Sherman | 1 | 48 |
| Elicta, [d. Silas & Clarrisa], b. June 10, 1800 | 1 | 29 |
| Electa, m. Christopher CHAMPLIN, Apr. 10, 1827, by Joy H. | | |
| Fairchild | 1 | 107 |
| Elizur*, [s. Epaphras & Hannah], b. Dec. 29, 1782    *(Elijah?) | 1 | 4 |
| Elijah, had 2 children d. Oct. [ ], 1794 | 1 | 73 |
| Elijah, d. [          ], 1797 | 1 | 63 |
| Elijah, his child, d. [          ], 1800 | 1 | 63 |
| Elijah, his w. [          ], d. [          ], 1811 | 1 | 73 |
| Elijah, d. May 2, 1819 | 1 | 73 |
| Elizur, of East Hartford, m. Mary C. MUMFORD, of Enfield, | | |
| Jan. 1, 1838, by Samuel Spring | 1 | 125 |
| Eliphalet, m. Jerusha JUTSON, Jan. 24, 1781 | 1 | 13 |
| Eliphalet, Jr., [s. Eliphalet & Jerusha], b. Feb. 6, 1783 | 1 | 13 |
| Eliphalet, m. 2nd w. Jerusha SMITH, Feb. 6, 1789 | 1 | 13 |
| Eliphalet, d. [          ], 1801 | 1 | 63 |
| Eliphalet, d. Oct. 27, 1803, ae 42 | 1 | 64 |
| Eliza, d. Leonard & Jerusha, m. Isaac HILLS, s. Wait, Sept. [ ], | | |
| 1830, by Asa Mead | 1 | 69 |
| Eliza, m. Isaac HILLS, b. of East Hartford, Sept. 9, 1830, by | | |
| Rev. Asa Mead | 1 | 112 |

| HILLS, HILL, (cont.), | Vol. | Page |
|---|---|---|
| Elizabeth, w. Ebenezer, d. Feb. 7, 1801 | 1 | 10 |
| Elizabeth, w. Ebenezer, d. Feb. 7, 1801, ae 23 | 1 | 63 |
| Elizabeth, m. Barnaby FILLEY, Nov. 18, 1818 | 1 | 68 |
| Elizabeth A., of East Hartford, m. William HUBBARD, of | | |
| Glastenbury, Sept. 6, 1843, by Samuel Spring | 1 | 143 |
| Elizabeth A., d. Ira, joiner, ae 39 & Mary A., ae 37, b. Nov. 6, | | |
| 1848 | 1 | 50 |
| Ellen, her child d. [          ], 1807 | 1 | 65 |
| Ellen M. H., of East Hartford, m. Sherman T. STONE, of | | |
| Durham, Dec. 7, 1843, by Samuel Spring | 1 | 144 |
| Ellery, m. Jane K. TREAT, Nov. 10, 1825, by Joy H. Fairchild | 1 | 104 |
| Emily, m. Gray HOUSE, May 3, 1826, by Joy H. Fairchild | 1 | 105 |
| Emily, of East Hartford, m. T. P. CHAPMAN, of Glastenbury, | | |
| Mar. 30, 1851, by Rev. B. C. Phelps | 1 | 160 |
| Emma, m. Sylvester CLARK, Nov. 3, 1819 | 1 | 69 |
| Emma Jane, d. Ira, wagon maker, ae 42, b. Jan. 16, 1851 | 1 | 58 |
| Epaphras, m Hannah TALCOTT, Sept. 28, 1780 | 1 | 4 |
| Epaphras, [s. Epaphras & Hannah], b. Apr. 3, 1781 | 1 | 4 |
| Esther, m. Jonathan WELLS, Oct. 15, 1756; d. Feb. 9, 1795 | 1 | 17 |
| Esther, [d. Ashbel & Mehitable], b. July 9, 1775 | 1 | 34 |
| Esther, [d. Silas & Anna], b. Oct. 7, 1777 | 1 | 29 |
| Esther, m. Marshall A. GREEN, b. of Hartford, Sept. 1, 1838, | | |
| by Samuel Spring | 1 | 126 |
| Eunice, [d. Ashbel & Mehitable], b. June 8, 1773; d. Nov. 24, | | |
| 1776 | 1 | 34 |
| Eunice, [d. Ashbel & Mehitable], b. Sept. 22, 1779 | 1 | 34 |
| Eunice, m. Timothy HALL, Apr. 3, 1783; d. June 24, 1797 | 1 | 10 |
| Eunice, [d. Epaphras & Hannah], b. Feb. 7, 1798 | 1 | 4 |
| Eunice, wid. Nathaniel, d. May 23, 1807, ae 78 | 1 | 73 |
| Eunice, d. Apr. 3, 1883 (?)*, ae 38          *(Probably "1833") | 1 | 74 |
| Eveline J., of East Hartford, m. Asa WELLES, of New Haven, | | |
| June 8, 1846, by Samuel Spring | 1 | 152 |
| Fanny, [d. Epaphras & Hannah], b. July 6, 1792 | 1 | 4 |
| Fanny, [d. Ashbel & Mehitable], b. Dec. 25, 1793 | 1 | 34 |
| Francis A., of East Hartford, m. Sarah McLEAN, of | | |
| Manchester, Aug. 11, 1846, by E. L. Goodwin, J. P. | 1 | 152 |
| Frederick, s. Albert, farmer, ae 23, b. July 2, 1851 | 1 | 58 |
| George, m. Anna WARREN, Mar. 9, 1794 | 1 | 15 |
| George, m. Anne WARREN, Mar. 9, 1794, by Rev. Dr. | | |
| Williams | 1 | 62 |
| George, [s. George & Anna], b. July 4, 1796 | 1 | 15 |
| George, d. [          ], 1801 | 1 | 63 |
| George, d. [          ], 1809 | 1 | 66 |
| George, m. Sarah RICH, b. of East Hartford, June 11, 1822, by | | |
| Rev. Elisha B. Cook | 1 | 99 |
| Giles M., of East Hartford, m. Harriet CADWELL, of | | |
| Manchester, Nov. 28, 1847, by Francis Robins | 1 | 48 |
| Giles M., of East Hartford, m. Harriet CADWELL, of | | |
| Manchester, Nov. 28, 1847, by Rev. Francis L. | | |
| Robins, of Enfield | 1 | 154 |
| Hanah, [d. Silas & Anna], b. Oct. 4, 1764 | 1 | 29 |
| Hannah, [d. Epaphras & Hannah], b. Oct. 26, 1784 | 1 | 4 |

| HILLS, HILL, (cont.), | Vol. | Page |
|---|---|---|
| Hannah, b. E. Burnside, res. East Hartford, d. June 6, 1848, ae | | |
| 89 | 1 | 49 |
| Harriot, m. Martin LOW, b. of East Hartford, July 25, 1833, by | | |
| Rev. Samuel Spring | 1 | 114 |
| Harris, his w. [        ], d. Feb. [ ], 1827 | 1 | 168 |
| Harry*, [child of Silas & Anna], b. July 20, 1766      *(In | | |
| pencil "Mary") | 1 | 29 |
| Henry, of Hartford, m. Charlotte FORBES, of East Hartford, | | |
| Aug. 4, 1835, by Samuel Spring | 1 | 119 |
| Hepzibah, d. wid. Jerusha, d. Feb. 14, 1806, ae 18 | 1 | 65 |
| Hepzibah, wid. Cadwell, d. Feb. 3, 1826, ae 87 | 1 | 74 |
| Hester, m. Albert GAINES, b. of East Hartford, May 19, 1842, | | |
| by Samuel Spring | 1 | 139 |
| Hezekiah, [s. Eliphalet & Jerusha], b. Aug. 14, 1786 | 1 | 13 |
| Horrace, [s. Martin & Sally], b. Feb. 24, 1799 (?) | | |
| *(Conflicts with birth of Sally) | 1 | 14 |
| Horace H., s. Leonard & Jerusha, m. Miranda PORTER, d. Job | | |
| & Lydia, Oct. 13, 1830, by Asa Mead | 1 | 69 |
| Horace H., m. Miranda PORTER, Oct. 13, 1830, by Rev. Asa | | |
| Mead | 1 | 112 |
| Horace H., hatter, d. Nov. 30, 1847, ae 39 | 1 | 49 |
| Howard, s. Elizur, shoemaker, ae 34 & Abigail B., ae 29, b. Jan. | | |
| 17, 1848 | 1 | 46 |
| Howell, m. Jerusha FORBES, Jan. 1, 1829, by Enoch Brent | 1 | 110 |
| Huldah, w. John, d. [        ], 1809, ae 21 | 1 | 66 |
| Isaac, [s. Ashbel & Mehitable], b. Mar. 28, 1771; d. Oct. 20, | | |
| 1794 | 1 | 34 |
| Isaac, [s. Ashbel & Mehitable], b. Nov. 9, 1794 | 1 | 34 |
| Isaac, m. Elizabeth SAGE, Mar. 28, 1819 | 1 | 69 |
| Isaac, s. Wait, m. Eliza HILLS, d. Leonard & Jerusha, Sept. | | |
| [ ], 1830, by Asa Mead | 1 | 69 |
| Isaac, m. Eliza HILLS, b. of East Hartford, Sept. 9, 1830, by | | |
| Rev. Asa Mead | 1 | 112 |
| James, [s. Ashbel & Mehitable], b. Nov. 16, 1781; d. Apr. 28, | | |
| 1784 | 1 | 34 |
| James, Jr., m. Harriet M. WELLS, d. Oliver, June 10, 1841, by | | |
| [        ] | 1 | 138 |
| James Howard, s. James, shoemaker & Sarah H., b. July 14, | | |
| 1848 | 1 | 50 |
| Jane M., m. Reuben BREWER, b. of East Hartford, Sept. 10, | | |
| 1834, by Samuel Spring | 1 | 117 |
| Jane M., d. M. O., farmer & C. N., b. July 13, 1848 | 1 | 51 |
| Jemima, m. Pitkin P. HILLS, Nov. 29, 1820, by Joy H. | | |
| Fairchild | 1 | 95 |
| Jerome, s. W. R., mason & S. L., b. Apr. 15, 1848 | 1 | 51 |
| Jerusha, [d. Eliphalet & Jerusha], b. Aug. 17, 1784; d. Sept. 27, | | |
| 1794 | 1 | 13 |
| Jerusha, m. Sylvester CLARKE, May 1, 1822, by Joy H. | | |
| Fairchild | 1 | 98 |
| Joel, [s. Ebenezer & Ruth], b. July 16, 1778 | 1 | 1 |
| Joel, farmer, d. Mar. 17, 1851, ae 74 | 1 | 60 |

HILLS, HILL, (cont.),

| | Vol. | Page |
|---|---|---|
| John, [s. Silas & Anna], b. Apr. 23, 1775; d. Oct. 11, 1776 (?) | 1 | 29 |
| John, [s. Silas & Clarrisa]. b. Jan. 3, 1801 | 1 | 29 |
| John, his child d. [      ], 1809, ae 2 m. | 1 | 66 |
| John W., m. Louis RATHBURN, Apr. 14, 1822, by Isaac Devinel | 1 | 98 |
| Jonathan, [s. Eliphalet & Jerusha], b. July 1, 1788; d. Oct. 6, 1794 | 1 | 13 |
| Jonathan, [s. Eliphalet & Jerusha], b. Jan. 11, 1796 | 1 | 13 |
| Jonathan, shoemaker, d. Apr. 14, 1851, ae 65 | 1 | 60 |
| Josephine R., of East Hartford, m. Stephen R. TOBIAS, of Attica, N. Y., Sept. 2, 1851, by Rev. B. C. Phelps | 1 | 161 |
| Julia E., of East Hartford, m. Samuel T. CLYDE, of Avon, Feb. 27, 1853, by Samuel Spring | 1 | 164 |
| Laura, [d. Epaphras & Hannah], b. Sept. 8, 1789 | 1 | 4 |
| Laura, of East Hartford, m. Julius BURNHAM, of East Windsor, Dec. 15, 1841, by Rev. Cephas Brainard | 1 | 137 |
| Laura, m. Ralph ENSIGN, b. of East Hartford, Sept. 14, 1845, by Samuel Spring | 1 | 149 |
| Laura M., of East Hartford, m. William O. FOSTER, of Glastenbury, Apr. 8, 1847, by Samuel Spring | 1 | 153 |
| Leonard S., hatter, d. Feb. 25, 1850, ae 32 | 1 | 57 |
| Lois, b. July 5, 1784; m. Aron FORBES, [      ], 1796; d. Aug. 23, 1797 | 1 | 15 |
| Lorin, m. Harriet COOK, b. of East Hartford, Aug. 21, 1839, by Samuel Spring | 1 | 129 |
| Lucinda, d. Dec. [ ], 1809 | 1 | 66 |
| Lucy, b. Manchester, res. East Hartford, d. Oct. 14, 1851, ae 60 | 1 | 60 |
| Lucy A., of East Hartford, m. John F. RATHBUN, of Manchester, Sept. 7, 1843, by Samuel Spring | 1 | 143 |
| Luther, [s. Eliphalet & Jerusha], b. July 8, 1792; d. Sept. 22, 1794 | 1 | 13 |
| Lyddia, [d. Ebenezer & Ruth], b. July 26, 1780 | 1 | 1 |
| Lydia Maria, m. Newel LESTER, b. of East Hartford, Oct. 15, 1851, by Samuel Spring | 1 | 161 |
| Mabel, wid., m. Col. Jonathan WELLS, Jan. 20, 1796, by Rev. Dr. Williams | 1 | 62 |
| Mabel, m. Jonathan WELLS, Feb. 20, 1796 | 1 | 17 |
| Mabel, m. Lester COLMAN, Nov. 24, 1819 | 1 | 69 |
| Maria, m. John WHITE, Dec. 8, 1824, by Joy H. Fairchild | 1 | 103 |
| Maria A., of East Hartford, m. Henry W. CUSHING, of Hanover, Mass., Dec. 20, 1837, by Samuel Spring | 1 | 125 |
| Marianna, ae 24, b. Manchester, res. East Hartford, m. Augustus W. HILLS, mason, ae 21, b. Manchester, res. East Hartford, Nov. [ ], 1850, by D. Bradbury | 1 | 59 |
| Marianna, m. Augustus W. HILLS, b. of East Hartford, Nov. 25, 1850, by David Bradbury | 1 | 160 |
| Martha, ae 20, b. Manchester, res. East Hartford, m. Charles AMIDON, painter, ae 23, of East Hartford, Apr. 9, 1849, by David Bradway | 1 | 52 |
| Martha W., ae 20, b. Hartford, m. George W. CARY, boatmaker, ae 21, b. Mansfield, res. Hartford, June 28, 1849, by Rev. S. Spring | 1 | 52 |

| HILLS, HILL, (cont.), | Vol. | Page |
|---|---|---|
| Martha W., of East Hartford, m. G. Washington **CAREY**, of Hartford, June 28, 1849, by Samuel Spring | 1 | 157 |
| Martin, b. Oct. 3, 1769; m. Sally **BRYANT**, Mar. 9, 1798 | 1 | 14 |
| Martin, his sister, d. [         ], 1806 | 1 | 65 |
| Martin, s. Martin O., farmer, ae 36, b. July 17, 1851 | 1 | 57 |
| Martin O., m. Cornelia A. **SPENCER**, b. of East Hartford, Jan. 1, 1845, by Samuel Spring | 1 | 147 |
| Mary, m. Russell **KILBURN**, Oct. 31, 1765 | 1 | 7 |
| Mary*, [child of Silas & Anna], b. July 20, 1766 *(Arnold Copy has "Harry") | 1 | 29 |
| Mary, [d. Epaphras & Hannah], b. Mar. 3, 1787 | 1 | 4 |
| Mary, m. Shuball **HILLS**, b. of East Hartford, Aug. 20, 1832, by Enoch Brent | 1 | 113 |
| Mary, ae 24, m. W[illia]m **WILCOX**, shipmaster, ae 24, b. of East Hartford, Jan. 11, 1849, by Rev. S. Spring | 1 | 52 |
| Mary, m. William **WILCOX**, b. of East Hartford, Jan. 11, 1849, by Samuel Spring | 1 | 155 |
| Mary Ann, m. Solomon **FOX**, b. of East Hartford, Mar. 12, 1837, by Samuel Spring | 1 | 122 |
| Mary Jane, d. Feb. 27, 1849 | 1 | 53 |
| Matthew, [s. Ebenezer & Ruth], b. Oct. 21, 1792; d. Oct. 10, 1794 | 1 | 1 |
| Mindwell, m. Richard **HILLS**, Mar. 18, 1818 | 1 | 68 |
| Moses, his child d. [         ], 1809, ae 1 wk. | 1 | 66 |
| Moses, d. [         ], 1814 | 1 | 66 |
| Nancy, m. Elisha **RISLEY**, Nov. 23, 1825, by Joy H. Fairchild | 1 | 104 |
| Oen (?) F., d. Sept. 12, 1850 | 1 | 60 |
| Osbon O., of East Hartford, m. Elizabeth F. **GOODALE**, of Glastenbury, May 23, 1852, by Rev. John F. Sheffield | 1 | 162 |
| Pamelia, d. Oct. 3, 1824 | 1 | 73 |
| Pamelia, m. Roderick F. **FOWLER**, Apr. 27, 1830, by V. R. Osbourn, V. D. M. | 1 | 111 |
| Phebe L., of East Hartford, m. George T. **WILEY**, of Hartford, Apr. 9, 1846, by Samuel Spring | 1 | 151 |
| Pitkin P., m. Jemima **HILLS**, Nov. 29, 1820, by Joy H. Fairchild | 1 | 95 |
| Polly, m. David L. **BELDEN**, b. of East Hartford, Apr. 9, 1828, by Rev. Samuel H. Puddle | 1 | 109 |
| Ralph, [s. Ebenezer & Ruth], b. Jan. 15, 1788; d. Oct. 11, 1794 | 1 | 1 |
| Ralph, m. Jane **BREWER**, b. of East Hartford, Mar. 20, 1834, by Rev. Samuel Spring | 1 | 115 |
| Rebecca, m. Josiah **WHITE**, Dec. 2, 1794, by Rev. Dr. Williams | 1 | 62 |
| Richard, m. Mindwell **HILLS**, Mar. 18, 1818 | 1 | 68 |
| Russel, m. Phebe **DEMMING**, [         ], 1783 | 1 | 21 |
| Russel, [s. Russel & Phebe], b. June 2, 1786 | 1 | 21 |
| Russell, his w. [         ], d. [         ], 1797 | 1 | 63 |
| Russell, s. David, d. Feb. 10, 1813 | 1 | 67 |
| Russell, his w. [         ], d. Mar. 7, 1817, ae 55 | 1 | 73 |
| Russell, s. Ebenezer, d. Mar. 1, 1818, ae 59 | 1 | 73 |
| Ruth, [d. Silas & Anna], b. Sept. 25, 1772 | 1 | 29 |

| HILLS, HILL, (cont.), | Vol. | Page |
|---|---|---|
| Ruth, [d. Ebenezer & Ruth], b. May 26, 1790 | 1 | 1 |
| Ruth, m. Thomas LAMB, Jan. 8, 1796 | 1 | 14 |
| Ruth, w. Ebenezer, d. Aug. 8, 1802 | 1 | 64 |
| Ruth, m. Horris CHEENEY, Jan. 22, 1822, by Rev. Ebenezer | | |
|     Blake | 1 | 98 |
| Saffa, [d. Ebenezer & Ruth], b. Dec. 15, 1797 | 1 | 1 |
| Sally, [d. Ebenezer & Ruth], b. Dec. 4, 1794 | 1 | 1 |
| Sally, [d. Martin & Sally], b. Nov. 21, 1799 | | |
|     (Date conflicts with birth of Horrace) | 1 | 14 |
| Samantha, of East Hartford, m. Francis HOLLISTER, of | | |
|     Glastenbury, July 3, 1844, by Samuel Spring | 1 | 145 |
| Samuel, d. [       ], 1797 | 1 | 63 |
| Samuel, of Palmer, Mass., m. Adeline H. PITKIN, of East | | |
|     Hartford, Oct. 18, 1841, by Samuel Spring | 1 | 136 |
| Sarah, [d. Ashbel & Mehitable], b. July 16, 1767 | 1 | 34 |
| Sarah, wid., d. Dec. 15, 1806 | 1 | 65 |
| Sarah E., m. George E. ANDERSON, b. of East Hartford, Nov. | | |
|     30, 1842, by Samuel Spring | 1 | 141 |
| Sarah Marcia, d. Elizur, cordwainer, ae 36 & Abagail, ae 32, b. | | |
|     Jan. 4, 1851 | 1 | 57 |
| Shubail, [s. Ebenezer & Ruth], b. Feb. 10, 1800 | 1 | 1 |
| Shuball, m. Mary HILL, b. of East Hartford, Aug. 20, 1832, by | | |
|     Enoch Brent | 1 | 113 |
| Sidney, m. Sarah M. ROBERTS, Apr. 13, 1836, by Samuel | | |
|     Spring | 1 | 120 |
| Sydney, shoemaker, d. Apr. 27, 1848, ae 42 | 1 | 49 |
| Silas, b. Jan. 9, 1739; m. Anna HOUSE, Oct. [ ], 1761 | 1 | 29 |
| Sillus, [s. Silas & Anna], b. Aug. 30, 1769; d. Oct. 19, 1776 | 1 | 29 |
| Silas, [s. Silas & Anna], b. Sept. 1, 1779 (Conflicts with birth | | |
|     of Clarissa) | 1 | 29 |
| Silas, m. 2nd w. Clarrissa EASTON, Nov. 7, 1799 | 1 | 29 |
| Silas, tavern, d. Oct. 1, 1849, ae 67 | 1 | 56 |
| Sophia, m. Ephraim K. AVERY, Sept. 25, 1822, by Rev. Elisha | | |
|     Blake | 1 | 99 |
| Sophia W., of East Hartford, m. Albert WRISLEY, of | | |
|     Glastenbury, Nov. 16, 1842, by [       ] | 1 | 141 |
| Sophronicy, of East Hartford, m. Luther A. HOLCOMB, of | | |
|     East Granby, Nov. 21, 1837, by Samuel Spring | 1 | 124 |
| Susan, m. Henry C. BREWER, b. of East Hartford, Nov. 24, | | |
|     1836, by Samuel Spring | 1 | 121 |
| Susanna, [d. Ebenezer & Ruth], b. Oct. 9, 1782 | 1 | 1 |
| Talcott, m. Laura BREWER, Aug. 15, 1826, by Joy H. | | |
|     Fairchild | 1 | 106 |
| Theodore, s. Sibura, stonecutter, ae 25, & Mary Jane, ae 20, b. | | |
|     July 26, 1850 | 1 | 55 |
| Timothy, m. Jerusha STANLEY, Aug. 13, 1789, by Rev. Dr. | | |
|     Williams | 1 | 61 |
| Tryphena, m. Timothy BUCKLAND, Oct. 12, 1820, by Joy H. | | |
|     Fairchild | 1 | 94 |
| Wait, [s. Ashbel & Mehitable], b. Sept. 16, 1777 | 1 | 34 |
| Wait, his child d. [       ], 1800 | 1 | 63 |

HILLS, HILL, (cont.),                                                          Vol.    Page
  Walter, farmer, ae 30 & Julia, ae 24, had d. [        ], b. June
    28, 1850                                                 1       55
  William, d. Feb. 17, 1822                                            1       73
  William H., of Hartford, m. Mary Ann SMITH, of Granville,
    Mass., May 15, 1838, by Samuel Spring                    1       126
  W[illia]m H., farmer, d. Apr. 20, 1851, ae 64                        1       60
  Wilson, of East Windsor, m. Mary GILBERT, of Middletown,
    May 9, 1842, by Samuel Spring                            1       138
  ----, Mrs., d. [        ], 1803                                      1       64
  ----, his child d. [        ], 1805                                 1       65
  ----, Mrs., d. [        ], 1807                                      1       66
  ----, his child d. [        ], 1807                                 1       66
  ----, Miss, d. [        ], 1809                                     1       66
HINSDALE, Mary, m. Simeon WOOD, b. of East Hartford, Nov. 12,
    1834, by Samuel Spring                                   1       118
HOFFMAN, Edward, bd. Sept. 13, 1845, ae 47, at Hockanum                        1       80
HOLCOMB, Luther A., of East Granby, m. Sophronicy HILLS, of East
    Hartford, Nov. 21, 1837, by Samuel Spring                1       124
HOLLIS, ----, his child bd. Sept. [   ], 1830                                  1       76
HOLLISTER, HOLISTER, Aaron, [S. Josiah & Absenath], b. Apr. 30,
    1796; d. Mar. 15, 1798                                   1       18
  Absenath, [d. Josiah & Absenath], b. June 21, 1801                   1       18
  Charles Eugene, [s. Morgan & Adaline], b. Feb. 5, 1846               1       40
  Clarence, d. Sept. 12, 1850, ae [  ]                                 1       60
  Deny, [child of Josiah & Mary], b. Mar. 1, 1781                      1       18
  Elezar, twin with Hanah, s. [Josiah & Absenath], b. Mar. 9,
    1794                                                     1       18
  Esther R., of East Hartford, m. Hubbard WEBSTER, of
    Columbia, Mar. 12, 1846, by Samuel Spring                1       151
  Francis, of Glastenbury, m. Samantha HILLS, of East Hartford,
    July 3, 1844, by Samuel Spring                           1       145
  Grove, twin with Orin, s.[ Josiah & Absenath], b. Jan. 29, 1790      1       18
  Hanah, twin with Elezar, d. [Josiah & Absenath], b. Mar. 9,
    1794                                                     1       18
  Horris, [s. Josiah & Absenath], b. Nov. 5, 1791                      1       18
  Jared W., of Glastonbury, m. Harriet BISSELL, of Manchester,
    Dec. 1, 1847, by Samuel Spring                           1       48
  Jared W., of Glastonbury, m. Harriet BISSEL, of Manchester,
    Dec. 1, 1847, by Samuel Spring                           1       154
  Joseph, of Glastenbury, m. Harriet ARNOLD, of East Hartford,
    July 12, 1841, by Samuel Spring                          1       135
  Josiah, m. Mary HOUSE, Aug. 13, 1780                                 1       18
  Josiah, [s. Josiah & Mary], b. Aug. 23, 1783                         1       18
  Josiah, m. 2nd w. Absenath SWEETLAND, Apr. 10, 1787                  1       18
  Julia, of East Hartford, m. Samuel D. PORTER, of Andover,
    Nov. 15, 1837, by Samuel Spring                          1       124
  Mary, w. Josiah, d. July 13, 1786                                    1       18
  Mary, [d. Josiah & Absenath], b. Aug. 30, 1798                       1       18
  Mary E., [d. Morgan & Adaline], b. [        ]                        1       40
  Morgan, b. July 14, 1817; m. Adaline DERBY, of Glastenbury,
    July 4, 1841, in Wethersfield                            1       40
  Orin, twin with Grove, s. [Josiah & Absenath], b. Jan. 29, 1790      1       18

|  | Vol. | Page |
|---|---|---|
| **HOLLISTER, HOLISTER,** (cont.), |  |  |
| Pierpoint, [s. Josiah & Absenath], b. Jan. 7, 1788 | 1 | 18 |
| Polly, m. Chester **PITKIN**, June 23, 1820, by Rev. Elisha B. |  |  |
| Cook | 1 | 94 |
| Russell, m. Jerusha **PORTER**, Feb. 15, 1825, by Joy H. |  |  |
| Fairchild | 1 | 103 |
| Russell, of Berlin, m. Harriet **ABBEY**, of East Hartford, June |  |  |
| 26, 1837, by Samuel Spring | 1 | 123 |
| Sarah Ann, [d. Morgan & Adaline], b. Dec. 2, 1847 | 1 | 40 |
| Sarah Ann, d. Morgan, joiner, ae 31& Adaline, ae 26, b. Dec. 4, |  |  |
| 1847 | 1 | 47 |
| Wells Stoddard, [s. Morgan & Adaline], b. Aug. 18, 1844 | 1 | 40 |
| William Goodrich, [s. Morgan & Adaline], b. Jan. 10, 1843 | 1 | 40 |
| William T., of Glastenbury, m. Harriet **ABBEY**, of East |  |  |
| Hartford, Dec. 24, 1848, by Rev. J. O. Goodridge | 1 | 155 |
| W[illia]m T., mason, ae 24, b. Glastonbury, res. Windsor |  |  |
| Locks, m. Harriet **ABBEY**, ae 23, of East Hartford, |  |  |
| Dec. 28, 1848, by [        ] Goodridge | 1 | 52 |
| **HOLMSTED,** [see under **OLMSTED**] |  |  |
| **HOLTON**(?)*, Ruth Williams, m. Ralph **ENSIGN**, Oct. 14, 1824, by Joy |  |  |
| H. Fairchild        *(Written "**HOTTEN**") | 1 | 102 |
| **HOOKER,** Cynthia, m. Allen **OLCOTT**, June 11, 1792 | 1 | 30 |
| **HOSKINS,** Seth, m. Katherine **HANOVER,** b. of East Hartford, Nov. 7, |  |  |
| 1821, by Rev. Isaac Divinel | 1 | 96 |
| **HOTTEN**\*, Ruth Williams, m. Ralph **ENSIGN**, Oct. 14, 1824, by Joy H. |  |  |
| Fairchild        *(**HOLTON**?) | 1 | 102 |
| **HOUGH,** Augustus, m. Mary **LESTER**, b. of New London, Apr. 22, |  |  |
| 1837, by Samuel Spring | 1 | 123 |
| **HOUSE,** Alniarin (?), of Glastenbury, m. Harriet **FORBES**, of East |  |  |
| Hartford, Oct. 19, 1842, by Samuel Spring | 1 | 140 |
| Anna, b. Nov. 5, 1743; m. Silas **HILLS**, Oct. [ ], 1761 | 1 | 29 |
| Edward, of Glastenbury, m. Matilda **ELLIS**, of Enfield, Apr. |  |  |
| 17, 1840, by Samuel Spring | 1 | 132 |
| Elizabeth, m. Wells **COVELL**, b. of East Hartford, Dec. 31, |  |  |
| 1846, by Samuel Spring | 1 | 153 |
| Esther, b. Berlin, res. East Hartford, d. Sept. 8, 1848, ae 89 | 1 | 53 |
| Gray, m. Emily **HILLS**, May 3, 1826, by Joy H. Fairchild | 1 | 105 |
| Guy, cabinet maker, b. Glastonbury, res. East Hartford, d. Aug. |  |  |
| 27, 1848, ae [ ] | 1 | 53 |
| Harriet A., m. Porter **LESTER**, b. of East Hartford, Jan. 6, |  |  |
| 1848, by Samuel Spring | 1 | 154 |
| Harriet A., ae 21, b. East Hartford, res. same, m. Eleazer P. |  |  |
| **LESTER**, shoemaker, ae 22, b. East Hartford, res. |  |  |
| same, Jan. 7, 1848, by Samuel Springs | 1 | 48 |
| Harry, bd. Jan. 31, 1836, ae 28 | 1 | 77 |
| Harry, his wid. & d. Justice **EATON**\*, bd. Dec. 20, 1836, ae |  |  |
| 27 y.   \*(**EASTON**?) | 1 | 78 |
| Henry, m. Nancy **EASTON**, b. of East Hartford, Oct. 4, 1829, |  |  |
| by Herman Perry | 1 | 111 |
| Jane, m. Ebenezer **HILLS**, b. of East Hartford, Apr. 16, 1837, |  |  |
| by Samuel Spring | 1 | 122 |
| Julia, m. Nelson **BAGG**, b. of East Hartford, May 2, 1849, by |  |  |
| Rev. S. Spring | 1 | 52 |

| | Vol. | Page |
|---|---|---|
| **HOUSE**, (cont.), | | |
| Julia L., m. Nelson P. **BAGG**, b. of East Hartford, May 22, | | |
| 1849, by Rev. Benjamin O. Phelps | 1 | 156 |
| Mary, m. Josiah **HOLISTER**, Aug. 13, 1780; d. July 13, 1786 | 1 | 18 |
| Mehitable, b. Aug. 6, 1748; m. Ashbel **HILLS**, Oct. 8, 1766 | 1 | 34 |
| Urba, of Haddam, m. Hannah E. **McGILL**, of Manchester, Sept. | | |
| 11, 1853, by Samuel Spring | 1 | 164 |
| Walter, of Glastenbury, m. Amelia **FRANKLIN**, of East | | |
| Hartford, Oct. 1, 1839, by Samuel Spring | 1 | 130 |
| -----, Miss, d. [          ], at Westfield, Mass., bd. June 16, | | |
| 1840, ae 19 | 1 | 78 |
| **HOWARD**, Benjamin, m. Sarah **KENNEDY**, Aug. 2, 1820, by Rev. | | |
| Elisha Cushman, of Hartford | 1 | 94 |
| **HOWELL**, Benjamin, m. Rebecca **BENJAMIN**, Nov. 20, 1823, by Joy H. | | |
| Fairchild | 1 | 102 |
| **HOWLETT**, Edward D., of Hartford, m. Charlotte **BREWER**, of East | | |
| Hartford, Mar. 10, 1853, by Rufus Smith | 1 | 166 |
| Eleazer P., m. Eliza **DEMING**, b. of East Hartford, Oct. 23, | | |
| 1833, by Samuel Spring | 1 | 114 |
| Lemuel, his d. [          ], bd. Aug. 29, 1834, ae 19 y. | 1 | 76 |
| **HUBBARD**, Clarissa Ann, of East Hartford, m. Cyrus | | |
| **CHENEY**, of Hartford, Oct. 30, 1837, by Rev. Elias | | |
| C. Scott | 1 | 124 |
| Erastus, of Hartford, m. Mary Ann **PITKIN**, of East Hartford, | | |
| May 15, 1842, by Samuel Spring | 1 | 139 |
| Horace, m. Ann **BURNHAM**, May 6, 1827, by Joy H. Fairchild | 1 | 108 |
| Horace, his child bd. Nov. 15, 1833, ae 18 m. | 1 | 76 |
| Horace, paper maker, b. New Haven, res. East Hartford, d. Mar. | | |
| 16, 1848, ae 42 | 1 | 49 |
| John, m. Elizabeth L. **ROBERTS**, Oct. 20, 1825, by Joy H. | | |
| Fairchild | 1 | 104 |
| Luther, shoemaker, d. Oct. 11, 1850, ae 48 | 1 | 60 |
| Sarah D., m. Osymn **ROBERTS**, May 3, 1826, by Joy H. | | |
| Fairchild | 1 | 105 |
| William, of Glastenbury, m. Elizabeth A. **HILLS**, of East | | |
| Hartford, Sept. 6, 1843, by Samuel Spring | 1 | 143 |
| **HUDSON**, Philip Melancthon, of Hartford, m. Mary C. **AUSTIN**, of East | | |
| Hartford, Jan. 3, 1837, by Samuel Spring | 1 | 122 |
| **HUMPHREY**, Samuel, of Hartford, m. Sarah **TANDO**, of Wethersfield, | | |
| Apr. 29, 1848, by Samuel Spring | 1 | 48 |
| Samuel, of Hartford, m. Sarah **TANDO**, of Wethersfield, Apr. | | |
| 9, 1848, by Samuel Spring | 1 | 154 |
| **HUNT**, Reuben, s. b. agent, b. Vernon, res. Hartford, m. Maria | | |
| **CHALKER**, seamstress, ae 19, b. East Hartford, | | |
| res. same, May 3, 1848, by Rev. Turnbull | 1 | 48 |
| **HUNTER**, Chauncy, m. Mary **ROBERTS**, b. of Wethersfield, June 13, | | |
| 1841, by Samuel Spring | 1 | 135 |
| **HURLBURT, HURLBERT, HULBERT**, Adeline, of East Hartford, m. | | |
| Elisha **SPERRY**, of Hartford, May 8, 1823, by | | |
| Rev. Elisha B. Cook | 1 | 101 |
| Austin, his child, bd. Nov. 17, 1834, ae 1 | 1 | 76 |
| Celia, m. Henry **AMIDON**, Nov. 28, 1822, by Joy H. Fairchild | 1 | 100 |

| | Vol. | Page |
|---|---|---|
| **HURLBURT, HURLBERT, HULBERT**, (cont.), | | |
| Elizabeth C., of East Hartford, m. David **KINNE**, of Colchester, | | |
| Apr. 22, 1852, by Samuel Spring | 1 | 162 |
| Fanny, m. Elias **FARNHAM**, Sept. 16, 1824, by Joy H. | | |
| Fairchild | 1 | 103 |
| Hardin, m. Anna **RISLEY**, Aug. 1, 1816 | 1 | 68 |
| Harlan, bd. Aug. 15, 1839, ae 42 | 1 | 78 |
| Henry, s. Joseph O., teacher, ae 29, b. Feb. 13, 1851 | 1 | 58 |
| Hepsibeth, m. Michael **BURNHAM**, Sept. 21, 1819 | 1 | 69 |
| Jo, d. Nov. 21, 1802 | 1 | 64 |
| Joseph O., m. Amelia A. **HILLS**, b. of East Hartford, Oct. 30, | | |
| 1844, by Samuel Spring | 1 | 146 |
| Julia A., ae 18, b. Glastonbury, res. same, m. George P. | | |
| **BREWER**, ae 21, of East Hartford, May 1, 1849, | | |
| by Rev. Smith | 1 | 52 |
| Linus, farmer, d. [        ], ae 73 | 1 | 60 |
| Lucretia, m. Abril **COOLEY**, July 15, 1821, by Isaac Divinel | 1 | 96 |
| Luman, m. Mary **OLMSTED**, Oct. 17, 1821, by Joy H. | | |
| Fairchild | 1 | 96 |
| Luman, his s. [        ], bd. Feb. 13, 1838, ae 11 | 1 | 78 |
| Nathaniel, had three infants d. [        ], 1800, ae 30 hrs. | 1 | 63 |
| Sarah, w. Giles, d. [        ], 1803 | 1 | 64 |
| **HUTCHINS**, Jno Church, m. Eliza **WILLIAMS**, Feb. 17, 1785, by Rev. | | |
| Dr. Williams | 1 | 61 |
| **HUXFORD**, Polly L., of Marlborough, m. Henry P. **LEE**, of Colchester, | | |
| Apr. 11, 1842, by Rev. B. M. Walker | 1 | 138 |
| **INGRAHAM, INGRAM**, Caroline J., of East Hartford, m. William | | |
| **OLMSTED**, of Enfield, Oct. 27, 1837, by Samuel | | |
| Spring | 1 | 124 |
| Orrin F., of Middleburgh, N. Y., m. Maria **COWLES**, of East | | |
| Hartford, Dec. 11, 1852, by Samuel Spring | 1 | 164 |
| Oshia, m. Ann **ROBERTS**, Oct. 10, 1826, by Joy H. Fairchild | 1 | 107 |
| **ISHAM**, Joseph, m. Susanna **FOX**, May 19, 1822, by Isaac Devinel | 1 | 99 |
| -----, Mr., d. July [ ], 1827 | 1 | 168 |
| **JACKSON**, Avery, of Pittsfield, Mass., m. Sarah M. **BENJAMIN**, of | | |
| Pittsfield, Mass., Nov. 25, [1847], by Samuel | | |
| Springs | 1 | 48 |
| Avery, m. Sarah M. **BENJAMIN**, b. of Pitsfield, Mass., Nov. | | |
| 25, 1847, by Samuel Spring | 1 | 154 |
| **JAMES**, -----, her child bd. June 19, 1838 | 1 | 78 |
| **JEFFORDS**, Betsy, m. Daniel **EMMERSON**, b. of Coventry, June 28, | | |
| 1820, by Rev. Elisha B. Cook | 1 | 94 |
| **JENKINS**, Abner W., m. Mahala **MORRIS**, Oct. 6, 1822, by Isaac | | |
| Devinel | 1 | 99 |
| **JOHNSON, JONSON**, B., his child bd. Apr. 15, 1842, ae 4 | 1 | 79 |
| C. R., his child bd. Mar. 28, 1842, ae 2 | 1 | 79 |
| Georgia G., d. Henry, sea captain, ae 30 & Antonett, ae 24, b. | | |
| May 30, 1851 | 1 | 57 |
| H. W., ship master, ae 27, b. Oswego, N. Y., res. East Hartford; | | |
| m. Antoinette **KELLOGG**, ae 20, b. East Hartford, | | |
| res. same, Nov. 27, 1848 by Rev. R. Turnbull | 1 | 52 |
| Julia A., of East Hartford, m. Henry P. **SEYMOUR**, of | | |
| Hartford, July 5, 1845, by Samuel Spring | 1 | 149 |

| JOHNSON, JONSON, (cont.), | Vol. | Page |
|---|---|---|
| Richard, m. Lovina **BENT**, Nov. 11, 1821, by Rev. Isaac | | |
| Divinel | 1 | 97 |
| Rosannah, d. John, shoemaker, ae 25, b. Apr. 6, 1851 | 1 | 58 |
| Seth W., of Vernon, m. Delia **BEMONT**, of East Hartford, May | | |
| 4, 1836, by Samuel Spring | 1 | 120 |
| William B., of Hartford, m. Harriet F. **ROBERTS**, of East | | |
| Hartford, Aug. 20, 1839, by Rev. Horace Bushnal, | | |
| of Hartford | 1 | 130 |
| JONES, Anna, wid., d. Jan. 29, 1806, ae 78 | 1 | 65 |
| Asahel, m. Heppy **BIDWELL**, Mar. 4, 1819 | 1 | 69 |
| Daniel W., m. Harriet U. **PHILLIPS**, b. of Hartford, Nov. 25, | | |
| 1832, by Rev. Samuel H. Biddle | 1 | 115 |
| Daniel W., farmer, b. Hartford, res. East Hartford, d. June 8, | | |
| 1848, ae 47 | 1 | 49 |
| David, m. Lucy **ARNOLD**, b. of East Hartford, Sept. 12, | | |
| 1852 (?), by Rev. Benjamin C. Phelps | 1 | 163 |
| Edward M., s. William, mason, ae 29 & Nancy S., ae 28, b. Apr. | | |
| 29, 1850 | 1 | 55 |
| Elizabeth, of East Hartford, m. Watson **PIBBLES**, of | | |
| Glastenbury, Nov. 18, 1841, by Rev. B. M. Walker | 1 | 136 |
| Eveline, m. Harrison **CHAMBERLAIN**, Nov. 15, 1837, by | | |
| Samuel Spring | 1 | 124 |
| Hannah, d. [          ], 1797 | 1 | 63 |
| Hannah, m. John **VIBERT**, Nov. 21, 1819 | 1 | 69 |
| Isaac (?), m. Anne **FORBES**, Jan. 10, 1787, by Rev. Dr. | | |
| Williams | 1 | 61 |
| Jerusha, m. Eligah **VIBBERT**, [          ], 1796; d. [          ], | | |
| 1790 | 1 | 31 |
| Jos. P., his child bd. Jan. 24, 1825, ae 3 | 1 | 75 |
| Jos. P., his child bd. Sept. 12, 1829, ae [   ] | 1 | 75 |
| Joseph P., his d. [          ] & w. of Harrison **CHAMBERLIN**, | | |
| bd. Apr. 3, 1841, ae 29 | 1 | 79 |
| Laura, m. Persius **OLMSTED**, b. of East Hartford, Jan. 21, | | |
| 1829, by Rev. Thomas Robbins | 1 | 110 |
| Laura P., m. Samuel **KELLOGG**, Aug. 15, 1816 | 1 | 68 |
| Maria, of East Hartford, m. David F. **SMITH**, of Washington, | | |
| [          ], by Rev. Chester W. Turner | 1 | 144 |
| Maria F., m. Hezekiah **WADSWORTH**, Jan. 7, 1819 | 1 | 69 |
| Rachael, m. Stephen **COLLINS**, Oct. 7, 1823, by Joy H. | | |
| Fairchild | 1 | 102 |
| Sarah, of East Hartford, m. Nelson C. **TAYLOR**, of | | |
| Glastonbury, Dec. 28, 1844, by Rev. C. W. Turner | 1 | 146 |
| Sarah H., m. W[illia]m **KELLOGG**, Feb. 10, 1820 | 1 | 69 |
| Thomas, of Coventry, m. Julia **HALE**, of East Hartford, Oct. | | |
| 25, 1820, by Rev. Elisha B. Cook | 1 | 95 |
| Thomas A., of Hartford, m. Mary **COMSTOCK**, of East | | |
| Hartford, Aug. 24, 1851, by Samuel Spring | 1 | 161 |
| William, m. Hansey L. **BREWER**, b. of East Hartford, Nov. 25, | | |
| 1846, by Samuel Spring | 1 | 153 |
| ----, Mrs., d. Jan. 23, 1803 | 1 | 64 |
| ----, Mrs., bd. Apr. 16, 1838, ae 94 | 1 | 78 |

| KEENEY, KEENY, [see also KINNE], (cont.), | Vol. | Page |
|---|---|---|
| Elisha, m. Abigal CULIVER, Apr. 9, 1795 | 1 | 33 |
| Eliza Ann, of East Hartford, m. Francis SPENCER, of | | |
| Manchester, Feb. 22, 1844, by Samuel Spring | 1 | 144 |
| Elezabeth, [d. John & Phebe], b. Nov. 30, 1773 | 1 | 31 |
| Emeline, m. Hart PITKIN, b. of East Hartford, June 13, 1822, | | |
| by Rev. Elisha B. Cook | 1 | 99 |
| Eunice, [d. John & Phebe], b. Apr. 23, 1769 | 1 | 31 |
| Eunic[e], m. Samuel MORLEY, Sept. 5, 1790 | 1 | 8 |
| Ezekel, [s. David & Jerusha], b. Jan. 22, 1784 | 1 | 23 |
| Hubbard, m. Lydia FISH, b. of Manchester, Dec. 15, 1841, by | | |
| Rev. B. M. Walker | 1 | 137 |
| Ira, m. Betsy KEENY, b. of East Hartford, Dec. 12, 1822, by | | |
| Rev. Elisha B. Cook | 1 | 100 |
| Jacob, [s. John & Phebe], b. Dec. 26, 1762; d. Aug. [ ], 1785 | 1 | 31 |
| Jacob, [s. John & Phebe], b. Mar. 28, 1785 | 1 | 31 |
| Jerusha, [d. David & Jerusha], b. Jan. 23, 1782 | 1 | 23 |
| John, b. Feb. 17, 1742; m. Phebe SWEATLAND, [ ], | | |
| 1761; d. May 31, 1822 | 1 | 31 |
| John, [s. John & Phebe], b. Jan. 23, 1776 | 1 | 31 |
| Joseph, [s. David & Jerusha], b. Nov. 4, 1797 | 1 | 23 |
| Josiah, [s. John & Phebe], b. July 25, 1780 | 1 | 31 |
| Larista* A., of East Hartford, m. Truman GRISWOLD, of | | |
| Windsor, Nov. 7, 1847, by Samuel Spring | | |
| *(Probably "Saresta") | 1 | 48 |
| Leonard, [s. John & Phebe], b. June 20, 1790 | 1 | 31 |
| Lorenzo D., of Manchester, m. Julia Ann FRANKLIN, May 7, | | |
| 1834, by Samuel Spring | 1 | 117 |
| Malinda, m. Martin BIDWELL, b. of East Hartford, Oct. 10, | | |
| 1822, by Rev. Elisha B. Cook | 1 | 99 |
| Maria A., d. July 3, 1848, ae 17 | 1 | 49 |
| Marinda, m. Daniel WINSLOW, May 16, 1822, by Joy H. | | |
| Fairchild | 1 | 99 |
| Mervin, m. Almira WING, May 3, 1818 | 1 | 68 |
| Nathaniel, d. Jan. [ ], 1826 | 1 | 167 |
| Obed, of Glastenbury, m. Theodosia HALE, of East Hartford, | | |
| May 6, 1823, by Rev. Elisha B. Cook | 1 | 101 |
| Obediah, [s. David & Jerusha], b. Aug. 26, 1800 | 1 | 23 |
| Phebe, w. John, d. Jan. 11, 1817 | 1 | 31 |
| Rebecka, [d. David & Jerusha], b. July 28, 1788 | 1 | 23 |
| Reuben, [s. David & Jerusha], b. Apr. 15, 1793 | 1 | 23 |
| Russell, [s. Russell & Jerusha], b. Mar. 3, 1792(?) | | |
| (Date conflicts with date of marriage of parents) | 1 | 12 |
| Russell, m. Jerusha DART, [ ], 1796 | | |
| (Date conflicts with birth date of first child) | 1 | 12 |
| Sally, [d. Elisha & Abigail], b. Mar. 25, 1798 | 1 | 33 |
| Sarah, m. Benjamin BROWN, Sept. 4, 1763 | 1 | 8 |
| Sarah I., of Hartford, m. George C. SELLEW, of Brooklyn, | | |
| Oct. 10, 1850, by Samuel Spring | 1 | 159 |
| Sarah J., of Hartford, m. George C. SELLEW, of Brooklyn, | | |
| N. Y., Oct. 10, 1850, by S. Spring | 1 | 59 |
| Saresta A., of East Hartford, m. Truman GRISWOLD, of | | |
| Windsor, Nov. 7, 1847, by Samuel Spring | 1 | 154 |

|  | Vol. | Page |
|---|---|---|
| **KEENEY, KEENY**, [see also **KINNE**], (cont.), |  |  |
| W[illia]m, of East Hartford, m. Clarissa **DAVIS**, of Vernon, |  |  |
| June 24, 1821, by Rev. Isaac Divinel | 1 | 96 |
| Woodruff, [s. Russell & Jerusha], b. Feb. 15, 1803 | 1 | 12 |
| ----, Mrs., d. [        ], 1800, ae [ ] | 1 | 63 |
| ----, Mr., d. [        ], 1800 | 1 | 63 |
| **KELLOGG**, Antoinette, ae 20, b. East Hartford, res. same, m. H. W. |  |  |
| **JOHNSON**, ship master, ae 27, b. Oswego, N. Y., |  |  |
| res. East Hartford, Nov. 27, 1848, by Rev. R. |  |  |
| Turnbull | 1 | 52 |
| Caroline Bertha, d. Henry, clerk, b. Sept. 20, 1849 | 1 | 54 |
| Ebenezer, m. Abigail **OLMSTED**, Jan. 22, 1789, by Rev. Dr. |  |  |
| Williams | 1 | 61 |
| John, seafaring, ae 30, m. Maria **WADSWORTH**, ae 26, b. of |  |  |
| East Hartford, Sept. 28, 1849, by Rev. R. Turnbull | 1 | 52 |
| Lauraett, ae 21, b. East Hartford, res. same, m. John |  |  |
| **YOUNGLOVE**, merchant, ae 28, b. Brunswick, |  |  |
| N. Y., res. Cleaveland, O., Feb. 21, 1848, by Rev. R. |  |  |
| Turnbull | 1 | 52 |
| Mary Louise, d. Henry, clerk, ae 27 & Caroline, ae 26, b. May |  |  |
| 16, 1848 | 1 | 46 |
| Pauline, m. Daniel **SLOANE**, Aug. 26, 1827, by Joy H. |  |  |
| Fairchild | 1 | 108 |
| Reuben, Capt., his child bd. Feb. 4, 1845, ae 4 wks. | 1 | 80 |
| Samuel, m. Laura P. **JONES**, Aug. 15, 1816 | 1 | 68 |
| Sarah Ann, of East Hartford, m. Nathan E. **LYMAN**, of |  |  |
| Hartford, Aug. 1, 1842, by Samuel Spring | 1 | 139 |
| W[illia]m, m. Sarah H. **JONES**, Feb. 10, 1820 | 1 | 69 |
| ----, Capt., his child bd. Aug. 8, 1842, ae 11 m. | 1 | 79 |
| **KELNY**, Lucy, m. Asahel **PORTER**, June 4, 1795 | 1 | 11 |
| **KELSEY**, John, of East Hartford & Polly F.[        ], of Newport, Int. |  |  |
| Pub., Mar. 9, 1806 | 1 | 67 |
| **KENDALL, KINDALL**, Betsey, d. June 5, 1803 | 1 | 64 |
| John, his w. [        ], d. June 5, 1806 | 1 | 65 |
| Mary, d. Nov. [ ], 1805 | 1 | 73 |
| Mary, d. May [ ], 1837, ae 73 | 1 | 74 |
| Mehetable, m. Hez[ekiah] **WILSON**, June 27, 1786, by Rev. |  |  |
| Dr. Williams | 1 | 61 |
| Polly, bd. May 27, 1837 | 1 | 78 |
| **KENDRICH**, Joseph, b. Baltimore, res. same, m. Lucy Ann **WELLS**, b. |  |  |
| East Hartford, res. same, Apr. 30, 1848, by Samuel |  |  |
| Spring | 1 | 48 |
| **KENNEDY**, Almira, of East Hartford, m. Walter M. **McKEE**, of |  |  |
| Manchester, May 2, 1838, by Samuel Spring | 1 | 125 |
| Ann, m. Thomas **COOLEY**, Sept. 25, 1817 | 1 | 68 |
| Austin, his child bd. Aug. 6, 1844, ae 10 m. | 1 | 80 |
| Austin, d. Oct. 24, 1849, ae 40 | 1 | 56 |
| Catherine, of East Hartford, m. Walter **BUNCE**, of Manchester, |  |  |
| Nov. 27, 1834, by Samuel Spring | 1 | 118 |
| Clemence A., d. S. O., farmer, ae 27 & Abigail, ae 29, |  |  |
| b. May 3, 1849 | 1 | 50 |
| Electa, of East Hartford, m. Barnabas M. **COLMAN**, of |  |  |
| Newark, N. J., Sept. 1, 1834, by Samuel Spring | 1 | 116 |

| | Vol. | Page |
|---|---|---|
| **KENNEDY**, (cont.), | | |
| Eliza, m. John **ENSWORTH**, Nov. 26, 1818 | 1 | 69 |
| Elizabeth, m. Ebenezer **HILLS**, Jan. 17, 1798; d. Feb. 7, 1801 | 1 | 10 |
| Elizabeth, m. Ebenezer **HILLS**, Jan. 17, 1798, by Rev. Dr. Williams | 1 | 62 |
| George S., m. Nancy **VIBBERT**, b. of East Hartford, May 5, 1828, by Enoch Brent | 1 | 110 |
| James C., s. Austin, paper maker, ae 37, & Emily, ae 33, b. Apr. 27, 1847 | 1 | 47 |
| Jane, m. Joshua **BARBER**, May 7, 1823, by Joy H. Fairchild | 1 | 101 |
| John, farmer, d. June 20, 1848, ae 82 | 1 | 49 |
| John, of Olmsted, O., m. Esther Elizabeth **WELLS**, b. of East Hartford, [          ], by Horace Hooker | 1 | 115 |
| Kate, m. Solomon **WARREN**, Oct. 12, 1794, by Rev. Dr. Williams | 1 | 62 |
| Mary, ae 24, b. East Hartford, res. same, m. Monroe **VIBERT**, stage driver, ae 27, res. Bristol, Nov. [ ], 1847, by Samuel Springs | 1 | 48 |
| Mary, m. James M. **VIBERT**, Nov. 25, 1847, by Samuel Spring | 1 | 154 |
| Samuel, m. Sarah **OSBORN**, Oct. 15, 1818 | 1 | 68 |
| Samuel O., farmer, ae 27, b. East Hartford, res. same, m. Abigail R. **PECK**, ae 28, b. Manchester, res. East Hartford, May 3, 1848, by Samuel Springs | 1 | 48 |
| Samuel O., m. Abigail R. **PECK**, b. of East Hartford, May 3, 1848, by Samuel Spring | 1 | 155 |
| Sarah, m. Benjamin **HOWARD**, Aug. 2, 1820, by Rev. Elisha Cushman, of Hartford | 1 | 94 |
| **KENTFIELD**, John, Capt., d. [          ], 1804, ae 60 | 1 | 65 |
| **KENYON**, Edward L., of Hartford, m. Mary Ann **FORBES**, of East Hartford, Dec. 20, 1847, by Samuel Spring | 1 | 48 |
| Edward L., of Hartford, m. Mary Ann **FORBES**, of East Hartford, Dec. 20, 1847, by Samuel Spring | 1 | 154 |
| **KILBOURN, KELBOURN, KILBORN**, Alfred, d. May 22, 1806, ae 15 | 1 | 65 |
| Alfred, m. Jerusha W. **ROBERTS**, b. of East Hartford, Nov. 29, 1838, by Samuel Spring | 1 | 127 |
| Alfred, s. Alfred, farmer, ae 39 & Jerusha, ae 29, b. July 19, 1848 | 1 | 46 |
| Anne, [d. Russell & Mary], b. Jan. 24, 1767 | 1 | 7 |
| Anne, d. [          ], 1804, ae 52 | 1 | 64 |
| Ashbel, his child d. [          ], 1801 | 1 | 63 |
| Ashbel, d. June 3, 1814, ae 55 | 1 | 67 |
| Charles P., s. Henry, mechanic & Sarah Ann, b. May [ ], 1848 | 1 | 47 |
| Clarisia, [d. Russell & Mary], b. Feb. 7, 1785 | 1 | 7 |
| Emila, [child of Russell & Mary], b. Mar. 10, 1787 | 1 | 7 |
| Henry P., mechanic, ae 25, b. Goshen, res. East Hartford, m. Sarah A. **GOODALE**, ae 22, b. East Hartford, res. same, Aug. [ ], 1847, by Samuel Springs | 1 | 48 |
| Henry P., m. Sarah A **GOODALE**, b. of East Hartford, Aug. 26, 1847, by Samuel Spring | 1 | 153 |
| Hezekiah, [s. Russell & Mary], b. Oct. 29, 1790 | 1 | 7 |
| Jane E., of East Windsor, m. William Chester **COWLES**, of East Hartford, Mar. 18, 1829, by Otto S. Hoyt | 1 | 110 |
| Jeremiah, [s. Russell & Mary], b. May 10, 1780 | 1 | 7 |

| | Vol. | Page |
|---|---|---|
| **KILBOURN, KELBOURN, KILBORN,** (cont.), | | |
| Jeremiah, d. Oct. 14, 1851, ae 70 | 1 | 60 |
| Jo., had child d. at his house, [    ], 1800 | 1 | 63 |
| Maria Jane, d. Henry P., white paper maker, ae 27 & Sarah A., | | |
| ae 24, b. Feb. 5, 1850 | 1 | 55 |
| Mary, [d. Russell & Mary], b. Apr. 26, 1773 | 1 | 7 |
| Nathaniel, [s. Russell & Mary], b. June 27, 1775 | 1 | 7 |
| Nathaniel, s. [Russell & Mary], b. Sept. 14, 1777 | 1 | 7 |
| Nathaniel, his mother-in-law, bd. Jan. 8, 1834, ae 67 (d. at | | |
| Town House) | 1 | 76 |
| Patty, d. May [  ], 1798 | 1 | 63 |
| Polly, m. Enoch **KIMBALL**, Dec. 1, 1793, by Rev. Dr. | | |
| Williams | 1 | 62 |
| Russell, m. Mary **HILLS**, Oct. 31, 1765 | 1 | 7 |
| Russell, [s. Russell & Mary], b. May 26, 1769 | 1 | 7 |
| Susannah, [d. Russell & Mary] b. Mar. 31, 1782 | 1 | 7 |
| Thomas, [s. Russell & Mary], b. Apr. 27, 1771 | 1 | 7 |
| ----, Mrs., d. [    ], 1814 | 1 | 66 |
| **KILLAM**, Sarah, of East Hartford, m. Roswell **ABBY**, of Enfield, Nov. 15, | | |
| 1836, by Samuel Spring | 1 | 121 |
| **KIMBALL**, Clarence, s. E. P., farmer, b. Nov. 19, 1848 | 1 | 51 |
| E. P., his child bd. Nov. 8, 1836, ae 5 d. | 1 | 78 |
| Ebenezer P., of Petersborega, N. H., m. Elizabeth **ARNOLD**, of | | |
| East Hartford, Dec. 9, 1834, by Samuel Spring | 1 | 118 |
| Electa, m. Roswell **PITKIN**, Oct. [ ], 1801; d. Apr. 23, 1806 | 1 | 37 |
| Enoch, m. Polly **KILBOURN**, Dec. 1, 1793, by Rev. Dr. | | |
| Williams | 1 | 62 |
| Lydia L., m. Edward **BREWER**, b. of East Hartford, Jan. 1, | | |
| 1846, by Levi Daggett, Jr. | 1 | 150 |
| **KINES**, William, s. Andrew, farmer, b. Dec. 10, 1850 | 1 | 59 |
| **KING**, Alice, d. Aug. 1, 1849, ae 20 m. | 1 | 53 |
| Alpheus, farmer, ae 35, res. Springfield, Mass., & Ananila, ae | | |
| 22, had s. [    ], b. Feb. 2, 1848 | 1 | 51 |
| Austin N., of Enfield, m. Laura A. **STEEL**, of East Hartford, | | |
| Feb. 2, 1851, by David Bradbury | 1 | 106 |
| Emma L., d. George W., jeweller, b. Feb. 22, 1850 | 1 | 54 |
| George W., of Hartford, m. Julia **BURNHAM**, of East | | |
| Hartford, Oct. 5, 1842, by Samuel Spring | 1 | 140 |
| Henry, farmer, ae 32, b. S. Windsor, res. same, m. 2nd w. | | |
| Francis **FORBES**, ae 26, b. East Hartford, res. same, | | |
| Dec. 25, 1849, by S. Spring | 1 | 56 |
| Henry M., of South Windsor, m. Francis M. **FORBES**, of East | | |
| Hartford, Dec. 25, 1849, by Samuel Spring | 1 | 157 |
| Newman, blacksmith, ae 24, b. Enfield, res. same, m. Laura | | |
| **STEELE**, ae 17, b. Conn., Feb. 2, 1851, by D. | | |
| Bradbury | 1 | 59 |
| Uriah, m. Hannah **RUDGE**, b. of Hartford, June 13, 1841, by | | |
| Samuel Spring | 1 | 135 |
| **[KINGSBURY], KINGBURY, KINSBURY**, Joseph, of Coventry, m. | | |
| Amelia **REYNOLDS**, of East Hartford, Dec. 4, | | |
| 1827, by Rev. J. H. Kingsley, of Hartford | 1 | 109 |
| William, m. Susan **REYNOLDS**, Dec. 5, 1816 | 1 | 68 |

|  | Vol. | Page |
|---|---|---|
| **KINKELL**, Edward A., s. W[illia]m, gunsmith, ae 40 & Caroline, ae 35, b. Nov. 5, 1850 | 1 | 57 |
| **KINNE**, [see also **KEENEY**], David, of Colchester, m. Elizabeth C. HURLBERT, of East Hartford, Apr. 22, 1852, by Samuel Spring | 1 | 162 |
| **KNAPP**, Alfred E., of Manchester, m. Julia M. LATHROP, of East Hartford, Sept. 1, 1850, by Rev. H. B. Soule, of Hartford | 1 | 159 |
| **KNOX**, Charles, of Hartford, m. Clarissa R. ARNOLD, of East Hartford, Nov. 12, 1843, by B. R. Northrop | 1 | 144 |
| **LADD**, Emma, d. John A., wagon maker, ae 22, b. Jan. 23, 1851 | 1 | 58 |
| Ephraim, of Tolland, m. Betsy ALEXANDER, of East Windsor, Apr. 5, 1842, by Samuel Spring | 1 | 138 |
| John A., wagonmaker, ae 21, b. Haverhill, N. H., res. East Hartford, m. Eliza L. BROWN, ae 15, b. East Hartford, res. same, May 1, 1850, by S. Spring | 1 | 56 |
| John A., of Haverhill, N. H., m. Elizabeth L. BROWN, of East Hartford, May 1, 1850, by Samuel Spring | 1 | 158 |
| **LAHEY, LAHAY**, Laura, d. Thomas, burnisher, & Mary, b. Apr. 12, 1848 | 1 | 50 |
| Walter, s. Alexander, spoon maker, ae 32 & Margaret, ae 21, b. Oct. 22, 1849 | 1 | 54 |
| **LAMB**, Harriet, [d. Thomas & Ruth], b. May 19, 1801 | 1 | 14 |
| Harriet, m. Thomas FREEMAN, Aug. 5, 1817 | 1 | 68 |
| Jesse, [s. Thomas & Ruth], b. Oct. 8, 1798 | 1 | 14 |
| Thomas, b. Oct. 20, 1767; m. Ruth HILLS, Jan. 8, 1796 | 1 | 14 |
| **[LAMPHERE], LAMFIERE, LANDFEAR**, Bela, [s. David & Lucinda], b. Dec. 16, 1792 | 1 | 5 |
| David, b. June 2, 1762; m. Lucinda LORD, June 10, 1790 | 1 | 5 |
| David, & Lucinda, had infant, b. Feb. 27, 1799; d. [          ] | 1 | 5 |
| David, m. 2nd w. Doshe BISSELL, Mar. 26, 1801 | 1 | 5 |
| David, d. May [  ], 1827 | 1 | 168 |
| Harvey, [s. David & Lucinda], b. May 18, 1791 | 1 | 5 |
| Lucinda, w. David, d. Jan. 29, 1800 | 1 | 5 |
| Phila, [d. David & Lucinda], b. Oct. 31, 1795 | 1 | 5 |
| Phila, of East Hartford, m. Daniel RUSSELL, of Ellington, Mar. 5, 1822, by Rev. Elisha B. Cook | 1 | 98 |
| Rodolphus, [s. David & Lucinda], b. Nov. 2, 1794 | 1 | 5 |
| Simon, [s. David & Lucinda], b. Jan. 13, 1800 | 1 | 5 |
| Simond, m. Electa ANDROS, b. of East Hartford, Oct. 3, 1822, by Rev. Elisha B. Cook | 1 | 99 |
| **LARRABEE, LARABEE, LARRIBEE**, Louisa, b. New Haven, res. East Hartford, d. [          ], 1849 | 1 | 53 |
| Mary G., m. Wooster ALEXANDER, farmer, ae 35, b. of East Hartford, Mar. 19, 1849, by David Bradway | 1 | 52 |
| Susan A., of East Hartford, m. Edmund WILLIAMS, of Lee, Mass., Oct. 1, 1854, by Rev. Benjamin C. Phelps | 1 | 166 |
| W[illia]m W., m. Mary GAINES, Nov. 27, 1817 | 1 | 68 |
| W[illia]m W., m. Thankful ABBEY, May 4, 1819 | 1 | 69 |
| W[illia]m W., m. Amelia ROBERTS, Dec. 28, 1826, by Joy H. Fairchild | 1 | 107 |

| | Vol. | Page |
|---|---|---|
| LATHROP, Emily, m. George F. SPAFFORD, b. of East Hartford, Sept. 22, 1850, by Rev. Samuel I. Andrews, of East Windsor | 1 | 159 |
| Henry, m. Calista FORBES, b. of East Hartford, Oct. 19, 1851, by Rev. Royal Robins | 1 | 161 |
| Julia M., of East Hartford, m. Alfred E. KNAPP, of Manchester, Sept. 1, 1850, by Rev. H. B. Soule, of Hartford | 1 | 159 |
| Nancy H., Mrs., of Hartford, m. Henry C. PORTER, of East Hartford, Aug. 15, 1841, by Rev. B. M. Walker | 1 | 136 |
| LAY, Edward H., s. Horace, shoemaker, ae 28 & Charlotte, ae 23, b. Apr. 7, 1851 | 1 | 57 |
| LEE, Henry P., of Colchester, m. Polly L. HUXFORD, of Marlborough, Apr. 11, 1842, by Rev. B. M. Walker | 1 | 138 |
| James L., of Lebanon, m. Susan M. WARREN, of East Hartford, May 12, 1846, by Levi Daggett, Jr. | 1 | 151 |
| LESTER, Austin, m. Elisa WINSLOW, June 22, 1826, by Joy H. Fairchild | 1 | 106 |
| Charles, s. Porter, boat maker & Harriet, b. Oct. 6, 1848 | 1 | 50 |
| Charles H. OLMSTED, d. June 3, 1850, ae 1 1/2 (Perhaps "Charles H. OLMSTED, s. of Lester") | 1 | 57 |
| Eden, m. Thomas CAMPBELL, Oct. 27, 1832/3, by Reuben Ranson | 1 | 114 |
| Eleazer P., shoemaker, ae 22, b. East Hartford, res. same, m. Harriet A. HOUSE, ae 21, b. East Hartford, res. same, Jan. 7, 1848, by Samuel Springs | 1 | 48 |
| Elisa, m. Julius MARBLE, b. of East Hartford, May 20, 1840, by Samuel Spring | 1 | 133 |
| Henry, m. Fanny PORTER, Aug. 2, 1818 | 1 | 68 |
| Independence, s. Porter, shoemaker, ae 24, b. July 4, 1851 | 1 | 58 |
| Mary, m. Augustus HOUGH, b. of New London, Apr. 22, 1837, by Samuel Spring | 1 | 123 |
| Newel, m. Lydia Maria HILLS, b. of East Hartford, Oct. 15, 1851, by Samuel Spring | 1 | 161 |
| Porter, m. Harriet A. HOUSE, b. of East Hartford, Jan. 6, 1848, by Samuel Spring | 1 | 154 |
| Sarah, ae 39, b. East Hartford, res. same, m. Benjamin SISSON, merchant, ae 35, b. Lebanon, res. East Hartford, Feb. 27, 1848, by Samuel Spring | 1 | 48 |
| Sarah, m. Benjamin SISSONS, b. of East Hartford, Feb. 27, 1848, by Samuel Spring | 1 | 154 |
| LEWIS, David, tailor, ae 39 & Catharine, ae 33, had child b. Nov. 13, 1847 | 1 | 47 |
| David, tailor, ae 43, had d. [ ], b. Nov. 16, 1850 | 1 | 58 |
| Mary Ann, of New Haven, m. Samuel L. PITKIN, Dec. 20, 1831 | 1 | 39 |
| LIGHTFAIRTH, Mary, of Germany, m. William BUTZELL, of Glastenbury, Apr. 20, 1852, by Charles C. Ashley, J. P. | 1 | 163 |
| LONDON, -----, Mrs., bd. May 16, 1843, ae 70 | 1 | 79 |
| LOOMER, Ebenezer, of Groton, d. Nov. 18, 1835 | 1 | 77 |

|  | Vol. | Page |
|---|---|---|
| **LOOMIS, LOMIS,** Amasa, Rev. m. Fanny **PITKIN**, Aug. 30, 1819 | 1 | 69 |
| Benjamin, farmer, b. Hartford, res. East Hartford, d. Jan. 11, 1851, ae 82 | 1 | 59 |
| Daniel, m. Ann **ANDERSON**, May 2, 1833, by Erastus Doty | 1 | 113 |
| Elizabeth, m. Thomas C. **FRANKLIN**, b. of East Hartford, Sept. 16, 1834, by Samuel Spring | 1 | 117 |
| Emily, m. Noah C. **SEXTON**, Apr. 6, 1818 | 1 | 68 |
| Israiel, m. Elianer **COWLES**, Feb. 2, 1800 | 1 | 28 |
| Lovicey, [d. Israiel & Elianer], b. Nov. 2, 1800 | 1 | 28 |
| Mary Jane, of East Hartford, m. James E. **WICKHAM**, of Hartford, May 17, 1852, by Samuel Spring | 1 | 162 |
| Nancy E., m. Oliver **VIBERT**, b. of East Hartford, Apr. 25, 1841, by Samuel Spring | 1 | 135 |
| ----, Miss, d. [        ], 1804 | 1 | 64 |
| ----, Mrs., d. [        ], 1809 | 1 | 66 |
| **LORD,** Lucinda, m. David **LANDFEAR**, June 10, 1790; d. Jan. 29, 1800 | 1 | 5 |
| **LOW,** Clarissa, m. Solomon **FOX**, Aug. 20, 1822, by Joy H. Fairchild | 1 | 99 |
| Jane, m. Ira **PORTER**, b. of East Hartford, July 2, 1849, by Rev. S. Spring | 1 | 52 |
| Lucy, d. Apr. 11, 1849, ae 80 | 1 | 53 |
| Martin, m. Harriot **HILLS**, b. of East Hartford, July 25, 1833, by Rev. Samuel Spring | 1 | 114 |
| **LUCAS,** Jason W., ae 22, b. Glastenbury, res. East Hartford, m. Nancy W. **RISLEY**, ae 20, of East Hartford, Jan. [  ], 1849, by Rev. Turnbull | 1 | 52 |
| **LUTHUR,** Sally, m. Leonard **BABCOCK**, July 4, 1826, by Joy H. Fairchild | 1 | 106 |
| **LYMAN, LYAMAN,** Benjamin, [s. Benjamin], b. May 9, 1807 | 1 | 38 |
| Benjamin, Jr., d. Mar. [  ], 1826 | 1 | 167 |
| Daniel, m. Liddia Martha **BREWSTER**, Jan. 16, 1794 | 1 | 6 |
| Daniel B., of Manchester, m. Caroline **HILLS**, of East Hartford, Apr. 2, 1835, by Samuel Spring | 1 | 118 |
| Daniel Brewster, [s. Daniel & Liddia Martha], b. Jan. 26, 1800; d. [        ], 1847 | 1 | 6 |
| Diodate B., m. Elizabeth **VIBBERT**, b. of Manchester, Apr. 19, 1831, by B. F. Northrop | 1 | 112 |
| Joseph, d. Feb. 20, 1820 | 1 | 38 |
| Joseph, of Hartford, m. Maria **SPENCER**, of East Hartford, Oct. 27, 1845, by Samuel Spring | 1 | 150 |
| Joseph Wadsworth, [s. Daniel & Liddia Martha], b. Jan. 8, 1798 | 1 | 6 |
| Mabel, [d. Benjamin], b. Nov. 28, 1815 | 1 | 38 |
| Mary, [d. Benjamin], b. Jan. 26, 1813 | 1 | 38 |
| Milton, [s. Daniel & Liddia Martha], b. Nov. 15, 1795 | 1 | 6 |
| Nathan E., of Hartford, m. Sarah Ann **KELLOGG**, of East Hartford, Aug. 1, 1842, by Samuel Spring | 1 | 139 |
| **McARDLE,** Patrick, laborer, b. Ireland, res. East Hartford, m. Jane **McARDY**, Apr. 1, 1851, by S. Spring | 1 | 59 |
| Patrick, m. Jane **McARDY**, b. of East Hartford, Apr. 7, 1851, by Samuel Spring | 1 | 160 |
| **McARDY,** Jane, m. Patrick **McARDLE**, laborer, b. Ireland, res. East Hartford, Apr. 1, 1851, by S. Spring | 1 | 59 |

| | Vol. | Page |
|---|---|---|
| **McARDY**, (cont.), | | |
| Jane, m. Patrick **McARDLE**, b. of East Hartford, Apr. 7, 1851, | | |
| by Samuel Spring | 1 | 160 |
| **McCARTHY**, T., tailor, b. Ireland, res. East Hartford, d. Dec. 8, 1848, | | |
| ae 55 | 1 | 53 |
| **McDONALD**, Patrick, d. Nov. 18, 1835 | 1 | 77 |
| **McGILL**, [see also **MAGILL**], Augusta, of Manchester, m. Richard | | |
| **BROOKS**, of South Windsor, June 17, 1853, by | | |
| Samuel Spring | 1 | 164 |
| Hannah E., of Manchester, m. Urba **HOUSE**, of Haddam, Sept. | | |
| 11, 1853, by Samuel Spring | 1 | 164 |
| **McINTYRE**, Asa, of Glastenbury, m. Mary A. **O'DONALD**, of | | |
| Glastenbury, Sept. 29, 1850, by Rev. Benjamin | | |
| Phelps | 1 | 159 |
| **McKEE**, Alexander, b. Mar. 12, 1768; m. Pervis **COOPER**, July 27, 1788 | 1 | 37 |
| Anne, [d. Nathaniel & Prudence], b. July 19, 1772; | | |
| d. [ ] | 1 | 2 |
| Asahel, [s. Nathaniel & Prudence], b. Feb. 16, 1766; | | |
| d. [ ] | 1 | 2 |
| Atten (?), [child of Nathaniel & Prudence], b. Mar. 26, 1762 | 1 | 2 |
| Austin, [s. Elizur & Abigail], b. Nov. 4, 1799 | 1 | 35 |
| Chauncy, [s. Elizur & Abigail], b. Feb. 3, 1791 | 1 | 35 |
| Electa, [s. Elizur & Abigail], b. Nov. 26, 1797 | 1 | 35 |
| Eli, of Glastenbury, m. Betsy **CASE**, of East Hartford, Nov. 19, | | |
| 1821, by Rev. Elisha B. Cook | 1 | 97 |
| Elizur, b. Mar. 18, 1766; m. Abigail **FOX**, Oct. 17, 1787 | 1 | 35 |
| Esther, m. Chester **BUCKLAND**, Oct. 13, 1802; d. Dec. 9, | | |
| 1802 | 1 | 22 |
| Fanny, b. Dec. 4, 1790 | 1 | 14 |
| George, [s. Nathaniel & Prudence], b. Aug. 15, 1756; | | |
| d. [ ] | 1 | 2 |
| Jabey, [s. Nathaniel & Prudence], b. June 29, 1780; | | |
| d. [ ] | 1 | 2 |
| John, d. June [ ], 1826 | 1 | 168 |
| John, his w. [ ], d. June [ ], 1826 | 1 | 168 |
| Katy, [d. Elizur & Abigail], b. Sept. 25, 1788 | 1 | 35 |
| Mabel, m. Eligah **SKINNER**, Apr. 12, 1795 | 1 | 32 |
| Mariam, [d. Nathaniel & Prudence], b. Jan. 8, 1770 | 1 | 2 |
| McKee, s. Nathaniel & Sally, b. Jan. 26, 1781; m. [Demy* | | |
| **EVANS**, Sept. 6, 1801] *(Dency?) | 1 | 2 |
| Michael, b. May 15, 1794 | 1 | 14 |
| Mille, [d. Nathaniel & Prudence], b. Apr. 3, 1764 | 1 | 2 |
| Nathaniel, Jr., [s. Nathaniel & Prudence], b. Apr. 10, 1758; | | |
| d. [ ] | 1 | 2 |
| Prudence, [d. Nathaniel & Prudence], b. May 10, 1760 | 1 | 2 |
| Robert, d. [ ], 1826 | 1 | 168 |
| Sally, m. Alvin **PERKINS**, Feb. 20, 1825, by Elisha Cushman | 1 | 103 |
| Samuel Cooper, [s. Alexander & Pervis], b. Jan. 21, 1789 | 1 | 37 |
| Sarah, [d. Nathaniel & Prudence], b. Dec. 23, 1767 | 1 | 2 |
| Sidney, [s. Elizur & Abigail], b. Aug. 15, 1795 | 1 | 35 |
| Timothy, [s. Nathaniel & Prudence], b. July 26, 1774; | | |
| d. [ ] | 1 | 2 |

| | Vol. | Page |
|---|---|---|
| **McKEE**, (cont.), | | |
| Walter M., of Manchester, m. Almira **KENNEDY**, of East Hartford, May 2, 1838, by Samuel Spring | 1 | 125 |
| William, [s. Elizur & Abigail], b. Nov. 5, 1801 | 1 | 35 |
| **McKINLY**, James, laborer, had d. [        ], b. June 9, 1848 | 1 | 51 |
| **McKINSTREY, M'KINSTRY**, -----, Mrs. her child, d. [        ], 1802 | 1 | 64 |
| -----, Mr., d. [        ], 1814 | 1 | 66 |
| **McLEAN, McCLANE**, Alexander, m. Mary **MAKENS**, Mar. 18, 1817 | 1 | 68 |
| Alecksander, his s.[        ], d. Apr. [ ], 1826 | 1 | 167 |
| Alexsand, Jr., d. [June] [ ], 1827 | 1 | 168 |
| James, of Hartford, m. Laura **PALMER**, of East Hartford, Feb. 5, 1826, by Rev. Augustus Battes | 1 | 105 |
| John, m. Sally **BUNCE**, b. of East Hartford, July 19, 1821, by Rev. Elisha B. Cook | 1 | 96 |
| Sarah, of Manchester, m. Francis A. **HILLS**, of East Hartford, Aug. 11, 1846, by E. L. Goodwin, J. P. | 1 | 152 |
| **McROBIE**, W[illia]m, m. Sophia **GAINES**, of East Hartford, Jan. 17, 1831, by Asa Mead | 1 | 70 |
| **MAGILL**, [see also **McGILL**], Abigail, [d. John & Anna], b. Oct. 7, 1816 | 1 | 40 |
| Alanson Elmer, [s. John & Anna], b. Nov. 13, 1801 | 1 | 40 |
| Anne, [d. John & Anna], b. June 22, 1807 | 1 | 40 |
| Henry, [s. John & Anna], b. Mar. 25, 1809 | 1 | 40 |
| James, [s. John & Anna], b. Mar. 6, 1805 | 1 | 40 |
| John, m. Anna **ELMER**, Feb. 1, 1801 | 1 | 40 |
| John Westly, [s. John & Anna], b. June 13, 1815 | 1 | 40 |
| Julian, [s. John & Anna], b. Apr. 20, 1811 | 1 | 40 |
| Sophia, [d. John & Anna], b. Mar. 8, 1813 | 1 | 40 |
| Susanna, [d. John & Anna], b. Nov. 10, 1802 | 1 | 40 |
| **MAKENS, MAKEN**, Jno, d. [        ], 1797 | 1 | 63 |
| Katurah, d. Oct. 23, 1802, ae 48 | 1 | 64 |
| Mary, wid. Dea. John, d. Apr. [ ], 1804, ae 83 | 1 | 64 |
| Mary, m. Alexander **McLEAN**, Mar. 18, 1817 | 1 | 68 |
| **MALONEY**, John G., of R. I., m. Elizabeth **BROWN**, of East Hartford, June 29, 1849, by Samuel Spring | 1 | 157 |
| **MANNING**, Asa, m. Betsy **BUTLER**, Nov. 27, 1817 | 1 | 68 |
| Mary E., of East Hartford, m. Russell G. **SELLEW**, of Glastenbury, May 3, 1849, by Samuel Spring | 1 | 156 |
| William, m. Betsy **ROBERTS**, Mar. 27, 1823, by Joy H. Fairchild | 1 | 101 |
| -----, his child, bd. Oct. 27, 1831, ae 3 | 1 | 76 |
| **MAPLES**, Balinda, b. Norwich, res. East Hartford, d. July 28, 1851, ae 64 | 1 | 60 |
| **MARBLE**, Claracy, b. East Windsor, res. East Hartford, d. Feb. 27, 1850, ae 67 | 1 | 57 |
| Ebenezer G., his mother, bd. Nov. 10, 1843, ae 85 | 1 | 80 |
| Elizabeth, of East Hartford, m. Joel **HAFF**, of Huntington, N. Y., Aug. 25, 1845, by Samuel Spring | 1 | 149 |
| Ellen E., m. W[illia]m T. **MARBLE**, b. of East Hartford, Aug. 20, 1850, by B. C. Phelps | 1 | 59 |
| Julius, m. Elisa **LESTER**, b. of East Hartford, May 20, 1840, by Samuel Spring | 1 | 133 |
| Sarah, m. Janeway **BREWER**, b. of East Hartford, Feb. 7, 1833, by Rev. Samuel Spring | 1 | 113 |

| | Vol. | Page |
|---|---|---|
| **MARBLE**, (cont.), | | |
| William, of Windsor, m. Ellen **HANCOCK**, of East Hartford, Oct. 27, 1850, by Rev. Benjamin C. Phelps | 1 | 159 |
| William B., s. William B., spoonmaker, b. June 3, 1851 | 1 | 58 |
| W[illia]m T., m. Ellen E. **MARBLE**, b. of East Hartford, Aug. 20, 1850, by B. C. Phelps | 1 | 59 |
| **MARSH**, Allen, [s. Daniel & Anna], b. Mar. 9, 1762 | 1 | 20 |
| Anna, [d. Daniel & Anna], b. May 31, 1755 | 1 | 20 |
| Anna, w. Daniel, d. Mar. 29, 1770 | 1 | 20 |
| Anna, wid. Daniel (formerly wid. Anna **PITKIN**), d. May 27, 1797 | 1 | 20 |
| Betsy, [d. Daniel & Hanah], b. Feb. 28, 1777 | 1 | 20 |
| Caty, [d. Daniel & Anna], b. Mar. 15, 1763 | 1 | 20 |
| Daniel, m. Anna **MORISON**, June 2, 1752 | 1 | 20 |
| Daniel, & Anna, had s. [ ], b. Nov. 12, 1753; d. Nov. 12, 1753 | 1 | 20 |
| Daniel, m. 2nd w. wid. Hanah **GLEASON**, June 27, 1771 | 1 | 20 |
| Daniel, m. 3rd w. wid. Anna **PITKIN**, Dec. [ ], 1779 | 1 | 20 |
| Daniel, m. 4th w. Margrey **SPENCER**, July 4, 1798 | 1 | 20 |
| Daniel, m. Esther **WELLS**, Apr. 3, 1817 | 1 | 68 |
| Emely, [d. Daniel & Hanah], b. Feb. 12, 1772 | 1 | 20 |
| George, [s. Daniel & Hanah], b. Jan. 6, 1773 | 1 | 20 |
| Hannah, [d. Daniel & Hanah], b. Aug. 7, 1775 | 1 | 20 |
| Hannah, 2nd w. Daniel, d. Oct. 9, 1778 | 1 | 20 |
| Irene, [d. Daniel & Anna], b. Mar. 29, 1765; d. Mar. 27, 1790 | 1 | 20 |
| Jared, [s. Daniel & Anna], b. Sept. 20, 1757; d. Nov. 1, 1757 | 1 | 20 |
| Mary, [d. Daniel & Hanah], b. May 5, 1774 | 1 | 20 |
| Susanna, [d. Daniel & Anna], b. Oct. 9, 1752 | 1 | 20 |
| **MARSTEN**, Mary G., d. July 18, 1851, ae 6 | 1 | 59 |
| **MARTIN**, Allida, d. Rivington, hatter, ae 39 & Hannah M., ae 30, b. Sept. 25, 1847 | 1 | 47 |
| Risley, m. Jane **WADSWORTH**, b. of East Hartford, [ ], 1848, by Rev. S. Spring | 1 | 52 |
| Rivingston, his child bd. Sept. 8, 1842, ae 8 wks. | 1 | 79 |
| **MASON**, Abner, m. Betsy **BROWN**, Nov. 5, 1818 | 1 | 68 |
| **MATHER**, Elvira A., of Hydeville, Vt., m. George D. **PORTER**, of Glastenbury, Oct. 8, 1854, by Rev. Benjamin C. Phelps | 1 | 166 |
| **MATTHEWS**, Ann, m. Henry **DUNTON**, b. of East Hartford, June 27, 1841, by Samuel Spring | 1 | 135 |
| **MAY**, Franklin, s. Charles, carpenter, ae 26 & Abigail, ae 23, b. Nov. 7, 1848 | 1 | 51 |
| **MELLEN**, Olive, m. Elisha **OLMSTED**, July 4, 1824, by Joy H. Fairchild | 1 | 102 |
| **MELLORD**, Leveritt, of Vernon, m. Eunice **FORBES**, of East Hartford, May 27, 1822, by Rev. Elisha B. Cook | 1 | 99 |
| **MELVIN**, Julia Bemont, of Hartford, bd. Oct. 12, 1841, ae 25 | 1 | 79 |
| **MERRIMAN**, Eunice, b. Maine, res. East Hartford, d. Sept. 15, 1849, ae 55 | 1 | 56 |
| Joseph, m. Eliza **BEAUMONT**, b. of East Hartford, Sept. 26, 1838, at her father's house, by Rev. Henry Jackson, of Hartford | 1 | 126 |
| **MERROW**, **MERROWS**, Betsy, m. Jonathan **PRATT**, Jan. 30, 1784, by Rev. Dr. Williams | 1 | 61 |

| | Vol. | Page |
|---|---|---|
| **MERROW, MERROWS,** (cont.), | | |
| Jos. M., colored, bd. Jan. [ ], 1827, ae 23 | 1 | 75 |
| Mary, d. Oct. 4, 1804, ae 45 | 1 | 65 |
| **METCALF,** Christopher, d. Dec. 16, 1815, ae 9 | 1 | 73 |
| **MILLER,** [see also **MULLER**], Jerusha, m. Nathan **COBB,** Jan. 2, 1817 | 1 | 68 |
| Sophia, m. Allen **HILLS,** Nov. 28, 1816 | 1 | 68 |
| ----, his child d. [          ], 1800 | 1 | 63 |
| **MITCHEL,** Samuel, of Fairfield, m. Eunice **PORTER,** of East Hartford, Feb. 12, 1826, by Charles Remington | 1 | 105 |
| **MOORE, MORE,** Elisa, of New Haven, m. John **OLMSTED,** of Glastenbury, May 1, 1849, by Daniel Pitkin, Jr., J. P. | 1 | 156 |
| Esther, m. W[illia]m **WHITE,** laborer, b. Ireland, res. East Hartford, Jan. 15, 1851, by S. Spring | 1 | 59 |
| Esther, m. Rufus **WITT,** b. of Stafford, Jan. 29, 1851, by Samuel Spring | 1 | 160 |
| James A., of Tolland, m. Clarissa **COWLES,** of East Hartford, Dec. 11, 1845, by Samuel Spring | 1 | 150 |
| **MORGAN,** Michael, s. Michael, laborer, ae 30, b. July 21, 1851 | 1 | 58 |
| **MORLEY,** Betsy, [d. Samuel & Eunic[e], b. Aug. 5, 1799 | 1 | 8 |
| Champion, [child of Samuel & Eunic[e], b. Aug. 7, 1804 | 1 | 8 |
| Elvio,* [ child of Samuel & Eunic[e], b. Apr. 8, 1796 *(Perhaps "Ebio" or "Eben") | 1 | 8 |
| Jerusha, m. David **KEENY,** Nov. 30, 1781 | 1 | 23 |
| Sally, [d. Samuel & Eunic[e], b. Aug. 5, 1792 | 1 | 8 |
| Samuel, m. Eunic[e] **KEENEY,** Sept. 5, 1790 | 1 | 8 |
| **MORRAN,** Ellen, d. Michael, farmer, ae 34 & Mary, ae 23, b. May 10, 1848 | 1 | 50 |
| Michael, farmer, ae 31, b. Ireland, res. East Hartford, m. Mary **FLYNN,** ae 23, Jan. 8, 1849, by Rev. Brady | 1 | 52 |
| **MORRIS,** James, m. Martha **RISLEY,** [          ], by Rev. Dr. Williams | 1 | 61 |
| Mahala, m. Abner W. **JENKINS,** Oct. 6, 1822, by Isaac Devinel | 1 | 99 |
| **MORRISON, MORISON,** Anna, m. Daniel **MARSH,** June 2, 1752; d. Mar. 29, 1770 | 1 | 20 |
| George M., m. Lucinda **GALPIN,** Nov. 17, 1852, by Benjamin C. Phelps | 1 | 163 |
| **MORSE,** Bradford, shoemaker, ae 34 & Lydia, ae 33, had child b. Sept. 1, 1847 | 1 | 47 |
| **MORSON,** Loisa, d. Stephen, lumber merchant, b. Sept. 28, 1849 | 1 | 54 |
| **MULLER,** [see also **MILLER**], Jason, m. Hannah **CHADWICK,** Jan. 1, 1784, by Rev. Dr. Williams | 1 | 61 |
| **MUMFORD,** Mary C., of Enfield, m. Elizur **HILLS,** of East Hartford, Jan. 1, 1838, by Samuel Spring | 1 | 125 |
| **MURPHY,** Edward, s. Pattrick, powder maker, b. Oct. 20, 1848 | 1 | 51 |
| Gideon M., m. Elisa **BEMONT,** b. of East Hartford, Jan. 15, 1829, by Rev. Timothy Benedict | 1 | 110 |
| Jerome, s. Timothy, bd. Aug. 17, 1833, ae 23 | 1 | 76 |
| Timothy, his s. [          ], bd. Apr. 13, 1833, ae 7 y. | 1 | 76 |
| ----, Mr., d. [          ], 1806 | 1 | 65 |
| **NEFF,** John, m. Betsey **TARBOX,** Sept. 8, 1819 | 1 | 69 |

| | Vol. | Page |
|---|---|---|
| NELSON, Sumner W., of Cleaveland, O., m. Louisa WILLIAMS, of East Hartford, May 19, 1846, by Samuel Spring | 1 | 151 |
| NEWCOMB, Laura, m. Levi STRONG, Jr., Nov. 10, 1818 | 1 | 68 |
| -----, Miss, bd. Jan. 8, 1835, ae 73 | 1 | 77 |
| NILES, George H., b. Lowell, Mass., res. East Hartford, d. Oct. 3, 1849, ae 7 | 1 | 56 |
| Hiram, s. Levi D., lawyer, ae 34 & Mary, ae 30, b. Dec. 10, 1847 | 1 | 47 |
| Levi A., b. Hadley, res. East Hartford, d. Oct. 8, 1849, ae 5 | 1 | 56 |
| Levi D., farmer, ae 33 & Mary P., ae 26, had s. [ ], s. b. Oct. 18, 1849 | 1 | 54 |
| Sarah A., d. Jesse, lawyer, ae 37 & Roxanna, ae 31, b. Dec. 29, 1848 | 1 | 51 |
| NOBLES, Aruba, d. Oct. 1, 1848, ae 87 | 1 | 53 |
| NORTON, Anna, b. Hadley, Mass., res. East Hartford, d. Feb. 20, 1850, ae 93 | 1 | 57 |
| Elizabeth, m. James BURNS, b. of East Hartford, Oct. 3, 1837, by Samuel Spring | 1 | 124 |
| NOYES, Tempy, had s. Matthew Champlin CADWELL, b. Dec. 5, 1786; d. July [ ], 1847. Adopted s. of Matthew CADWELL | 1 | 17 |
| O'BRIAN, John, power maker, b. Ireland, res. East Hartford, d. Sept. 13, 1849, ae 27 | 1 | 56 |
| O'DONALD, Mary A., m. Asa McINTYRE, b. of Glastenbury, Sept. 29, 1850, by Rev. Benjamin Phelps | 1 | 159 |
| OLCOTT, Allen, m. Cynthia HOOKER, June 11, 1792 | 1 | 30 |
| Almira, [d. Josiah, Jr. & Mary], b. May 12, 1779 | 1 | 72 |
| Anna Hooker, [d. Allen & Cynthia], b. Apr. 26, 1797 | 1 | 30 |
| Charles, [s. Allen & Cynthia], b. Apr. 3, 1793 | 1 | 30 |
| Cynthia, [d. Allen & Cynthia], b. Aug. 4, 1799 | 1 | 30 |
| Eleanor, d. Jedediah, of Bloomfield, b. July 18, 1776; m. Joseph GOODWIN, 2nd, Sept. 9, 1802; d. Dec. 26, 1831, ae 55 | 1 | 44 |
| Jemme, [child of Josiah, Jr. & Mary], b. Mar. 13, 1781 | 1 | 72 |
| Josiah, Jr., m. Mary BABCOCK, May 27, 1778 | 1 | 72 |
| Josiah, Capt., d. Oct. 8, 1785 (This entry is listed with the children of Allen and Cynthia (HOOKER) OLCOTT) | 1 | 30 |
| Lard, & Lucretia JUDSON, b. of East Hartford, Int. Pub., Feb. 19, 1806 | 1 | 67 |
| Ruth E., m. Lot SHELDON, b. of Hartford, Jan. 6, 1842, by Samuel Spring | 1 | 138 |
| Sidney, [s. Allen & Cynthia], b. Mar. 9, 1795 | 1 | 30 |
| Sidney, d. [Mar.] [ ], 1827 | 1 | 168 |
| Walter Hooker, [s. Allen & Cynthia], b. Sept. 4, 1802 | 1 | 30 |
| OLMSTED, HOLMSTED, Aaron, Capt., d [ ], 1806, ae 54 | 1 | 65 |
| Aaron G., m. Harriet ROBERTS, b. of East Hartford, Apr. 6, 1836, by Samuel Spring | 1 | 120 |
| Abigail, m. Ebenezer KELLOGG, Jan. 22, 1789, by Rev. Dr. Williams | 1 | 61 |
| Ann, m. Solomon PHELPS, Oct. 25, 1825, by Joy H. Fairchild | 1 | 104 |
| Ann, d. May 1, 1851, ae 55 | 1 | 60 |

| | Vol. | Page |
|---|---|---|
| **OLMSTED, HOLMSTED,** (cont.), | | |
| Anna Margaret, d. Ashbel, farmer, b. July 7, 1851 | 1 | 58 |
| Antoinette A., of East Hartford, m. Samuel T. **TOWNSEND**, of | | |
| Brooklyn, N. Y., Apr. 20, 1852, by Samuel Spring | 1 | 162 |
| As[          ], his child d. [          ], 1801 | 1 | 63 |
| As[          ]l, d. [          ], 1804, ae 54 | 1 | 64 |
| Ashbel, m. Mary **FORBES**, Nov. 16, 1786, by Rev. Dr. | | |
| Williams | 1 | 61 |
| Ashbel, his child, d. Mar. 22, 1799, ae 1 1/8 | 1 | 63 |
| Ashbel, m. Delia **BELDEN**, Mar. 9, 1825, by Joy H. Fairchild | 1 | 103 |
| Ashbel, m. Emeline **STANLEY**, b. of East Hartford, Nov. 12, | | |
| 1840, by Samuel Spring | 1 | 134 |
| Caroline, d. Capt. [          ], d. July 15, 1806, ae 17 m. | 1 | 65 |
| Charles H.*, s. Lester, d. June 3, 1850, ae 1 1/2 | | |
| *(Perhaps "Charles H. Olmsted Lester") | 1 | 57 |
| Dorothy, m. Sam[ue]ll **CHURCH**, Mar. 11, 1784, by Rev. Dr. | | |
| Williams | 1 | 61 |
| Edward, m. Betsy **VIBERT**, Dec. 2, 1819 | 1 | 69 |
| Edward P., s. George H., merchant, ae 34 & Lucy A., ae 35, b. | | |
| Aug. 20, 1849 | 1 | 54 |
| Elisha, m. Olive **MELLEN**, July 4, 1824, by Joy H. Fairchild | 1 | 102 |
| Elisha, hatter, ae 22 & Harriet, had s. [          ], b. Apr. 15, | | |
| 1848, d. young | 1 | 46 |
| Elisha Sage, m. Harriet **JUDSON**, b. of East Hartford, Mar. 19, | | |
| 1845, by Samuel Spring | 1 | 148 |
| Eliza, m. Aaron **COLTON**, Apr. 5, 1787, by Rev. Dr. Williams | 1 | 61 |
| Eliza, m. Timothy **COWLES**, Apr. 26, 1787, by Rev. Dr. | | |
| Williams | 1 | 61 |
| Fanny Electa, d. Henry, farmer, b. Dec. 4, 1850 | 1 | 59 |
| Frank W[illia]m, [s. Henry, farmer], b. Nov. 15, 1844 | 1 | 46 |
| George, m. Ann **STANLEY**, Apr. 29, 1824, by Joy H. Fairchild | 1 | 102 |
| George, d. Jan. [ ], 1826 | 1 | 167 |
| George, farmer, d. Mar. 7, 1849, ae 58 | 1 | 53 |
| George, see George **HOLMSTED** | 1 | 167 |
| George H., m. Lucy A. **PHELPS**, b. of East Hartford, June 22, | | |
| 1843, by Samuel Spring | 1 | 142 |
| Giles, m. Nancy **OLMSTED**, Apr. 22, 1819 | 1 | 69 |
| Hannah, b. Jan. 13, 1747; m. Joseph **GOODWIN**, June 3, | | |
| 1773; d. July 1, 1814, ae 67 | 1 | 44 |
| Hanna, wid. Ashbel, d. Feb. 3, 1806, ae 76 | 1 | 65 |
| Hannah, w. Jonathan, d. Dec. 27, 1806, ae 89 | 1 | 65 |
| Hannah Maken, d. Capt. [          ], d. [          ], 1799, ae 4 d. | 1 | 63 |
| Hannah Pitkin, w. Thaddeus, d. Apr. 17, 1809, ae 86 y. | | |
| 7 m. 5 d. | 1 | 66 |
| Harriet M., of East Hartford, m. Elam **CHAPIN**, of Vernon, | | |
| Jan. 1, 1840, by Samuel Spring | 1 | 131 |
| James Norman, s. James, printer, ae 38 & Maria, ae 35, b. Aug. | | |
| 7, 1847 | 1 | 46 |
| Jerusha, m. John **PAGE**, Nov. 9, 1786, by Rev. Dr. Williams | 1 | 61 |
| John, of Glastenbury, m. Elisa **MOORE**, of New Haven, May | | |
| 1, 1849, by Daniel Pitkin, Jr., J. P. | 1 | 156 |
| Joseph L., silversmith, d. Sept. 7, 1848, ae 21 | 1 | 53 |
| Mable, m. George **PITKIN**, July 5, 1787, by Rev. Dr. Williams | 1 | 61 |

| | Vol. | Page |
|---|---|---|
| **OLMSTED, HOLMSTED,** (cont.), | | |
| Mary, wid. Nicolas, m. John **GOODWIN,** [          ]; | | |
| b. [          ], 1683; d. Mar. 2, 1760, ae 77 | 1 | 43 |
| Mary, w. Epaphras, d. [          ], 1803 | 1 | 64 |
| Mary, m. Luman **HURLBURT,** Oct. 17, 1821, by Joy H. | | |
| Fairchild | 1 | 96 |
| Mary, of East Hartford, m. Aaron **SWEETLAND,** of Hebron, | | |
| May 28, 1828, by Sylvester Eaton | 1 | 110 |
| Mary F., m. Austin **BURNHAM,** b. of East Hartford, Nov. 27, | | |
| 1844, by Samuel Spring | 1 | 148 |
| Nancy, m. Giles **OLMSTED,** Apr. 22, 1819 | 1 | 69 |
| Naomi, d. [          ], 1809 | 1 | 66 |
| Naomi, m. Edwin **BIRGE,** b. of East Hartford, Aug. 9, 1837, by | | |
| Samuel Spring | 1 | 123 |
| Persius, m. Laura **JONES,** b. of East Hartford, Jan. 21, 1829, | | |
| by Rev. Thomas Robbins | 1 | 110 |
| Ralph A., m. Cornelia **COWLES,** b. of East Hartford, Nov. 6, | | |
| 1838, by Samuel Spring | 1 | 127 |
| Samuel, d. Apr. 23, 1801, ae 67 | 1 | 63 |
| Samuel, m. Elizabeth **CRANE,** Mar. 13, 1825, by Joy H. | | |
| Fairchild | 1 | 104 |
| Sarah, w. Sage, d. [          ], 1803 | 1 | 64 |
| Solomon, m. Electa **TREAT,** Dec. 17, 1817 | 1 | 68 |
| Stanley P., s. Ashbel, farmer, ae 49 & Emeline, ae 35, b. Nov. 6, | | |
| 1847 | 1 | 46 |
| Thad[deus], d. [          ], 1798, ae 85 | 1 | 63 |
| William, of Enfield, m. Caroline J. **INGRAHAM,** of East | | |
| Hartford, Oct. 27, 1837, by Samuel Spring | 1 | 124 |
| -----, Capt., his child d. Sept. 6, 1801, ae 10 m. | 1 | 63 |
| ----, s.b. Apr. 15, 1848 | 1 | 49 |
| **O'NEIL, O'NEAL,** Thomas, s. Daniel, gardener, ae 36 & Margaret, ae | | |
| 31, b. July 11, 1850 | 1 | 55 |
| Thomas F., s. Michael, gardener, ae 40 & Bridget, ae 35, b. | | |
| Sept. 12, 1847 | 1 | 47 |
| **OSBORNE, OSBORN,** Elizabeth, of East Windsor, m. John **ROBERTS,** | | |
| of Grafton, N. H., Dec. 13, 1846, by Moses Elmer, | | |
| Jr., J. P. | 1 | 153 |
| Sarah, m. Samuel **KENNEDY,** Oct. 15, 1818 | 1 | 68 |
| **PACKARD,** Harriet, d. Allen, mason, ae 26, b. Nov. 18, 1850 | 1 | 58 |
| W[illia]m, bd. Oct. 31, 1835, ae 43 | 1 | 77 |
| **PAGE,** John, m. Jerusha **OLMSTED,** Nov. 9, 1786, by Rev. Dr. Williams | 1 | 61 |
| John, d. Sept. 3, 1849, ae 3 | 1 | 56 |
| **PALMER,** Ed[          ] W., d. Aug. 7, 1849, ae 17 m. | 1 | 56 |
| Edward, s. John, joiner, ae 28 & Emily, ae 25, b. Jan. 24, 1848 | 1 | 46 |
| Emily C., d. Aug. 22, 1849, ae 4 | 1 | 56 |
| James, m. Cynthia **FOX,** Jan. 21, 1819 | 1 | 69 |
| James L., of Windham, m. Mary S. **JUDSON,** of East Hartford, | | |
| Feb. 15, 1853, by Samuel Spring | 1 | 164 |
| John, carpenter, ae 32 & Emily, ae 29, had d. [          ], b. | | |
| July 27, 1851 | 1 | 57 |
| Laura, of East Hartford, m. James **McLEAN,** of Hartford, Feb. | | |
| 5, 1826, by Rev. Augustus Battes | 1 | 105 |

| | Vol. | Page |
|---|---|---|
| **PALMER**, (cont.), | | |
| Laura Ann, of East Hartford, m. Francis **COOLEY**, of | | |
| Hartford, Apr. 3, 1840, by Rev. O. E. Daggett, of | | |
| Hartford | 1 | 133 |
| Mary, m. Zacheus **PERRY**, Oct. 12, 1820, by Joy H. Fairchild | 1 | 94 |
| **PARKER**, John, m. Catherine **ARMSTRONG**, b. of East Hartford, Mar. | | |
| 29, 1840, by Samuel Spring | 1 | 132 |
| **PARMELE**, Mary, Mrs., m. Pardon **WINSLOW**, b. of East Hartford, | | |
| Sept. 26, 1841, by Rev. B. M. Walker | 1 | 136 |
| **PARSONS, PERSONS**, Emeline, m. Erastus W. **BURNHAM**, b. of East | | |
| Hartford, Feb. 8, 1833, by Rev. Samuel Spring | 1 | 117 |
| Harriet E., m. Harvey **BUEL**, Dec. 17, 1836, by Samuel Spring | 1 | 121 |
| Lydia, m. Aaron **FORBES**, Jan. 22, 1798 | 1 | 15 |
| Lydia, of Glastonbury, m. Henry **FLAVEL**, of Glastenbury, | | |
| May 22, 1849, by Rev. Benjamin O. Phelps | 1 | 156 |
| Sally, m. Samuel **PITKIN**, July 25, 1792, by Rev. Dr. Williams | 1 | 62 |
| Sarah, b. Sept. 4, 1764; m. Samuel **PITKIN**, July 25, 1792 | 1 | 3 |
| Sarah, Madam, m. Rev. Aliphalet **WILLIAMS**, June 12, 1777; | | |
| d. Jan. 23, 1800 | 1 | 9 |
| Sarah E., m. George E. **BELL**, b. of East Hartford, Mar. 30, | | |
| 1851, by S. Spring | 1 | 59 |
| Sarah H., m. George E. **BELL**, b. of East Hartford, Mar. 30, | | |
| 1851, by Samuel Spring | 1 | 160 |
| **PEASE**, Charity, of Enfield, m. Chauncy **WELLS**, of East Hartford, Jan. 6, | | |
| 1840, by Samuel Spring | 1 | 131 |
| Sarah, d. Jan. 5, 1829, ae 85 | 1 | 74 |
| **PEBBLES, PIBBLES**, Archibald, ship carpenter, b. Granville, Mass., res. | | |
| East Hartford, d. Nov. [ ], 1848 | 1 | 53 |
| Edward, of Glastenbury, m. Cornelia **JONES**, of East Hartford, | | |
| Nov. 20, 1842, by [ ] | 1 | 141 |
| Emma F., d. Edward, carpenter, ae 32 & Cornelia, ae 31, b. May | | |
| 5, 1851 | 1 | 57 |
| Maria A., d. Watson, mason, ae 30 & Elizabeth, ae 29, b. Aug. | | |
| 10, 1847 | 1 | 46 |
| Mary, d. Watson, joiner, b. Sept. 3, 1850 | 1 | 58 |
| Mary Ann, of Glastenbury, m. Ellsworth **BREWER**, of East | | |
| Hartford, Oct. 9,1842, by Rev. B. M. Walker | 1 | 140 |
| Watson, of Glastenbury, m. Elizabeth **JONES**, of East Hartford, | | |
| Nov. 18, 1841, by Rev. B. M. Walker | 1 | 136 |
| **PECK**, Abigail R., ae 28, b. Manchester, res. East Hartford, m. Samuel O. | | |
| **KENEDY**, farmer, ae 27, b. East Hartford, res. | | |
| same, May 3, 1848, by Samuel Springs | 1 | 48 |
| Abigail R., m. Samuel O. **KENNEDY**, b. of East Hartford, May | | |
| 3, 1848, by Samuel Spring | 1 | 155 |
| Clarissa, [d. Elijah & Mary], b. Nov. 1, 1779 | 1 | 6 |
| Elijah, m. Mary **WHITE**, Jan. 12, 1777 | 1 | 6 |
| Elijah, [s. Elijah & Mary], b. Apr. 6, 1785 | 1 | 6 |
| Elot, [child of Elijah & Mary], b. Sept. 4, 1787 | 1 | 6 |
| Fefe, [d. Elijah & Mary], b. Jan. 9, 1790 | 1 | 6 |
| Harvey, [s. Elijah & Mary], b. Feb. 9, 1778 | 1 | 6 |
| Jaba, [child of Elijah & Mary], b. Mar. 27, 1783 | 1 | 6 |
| Julia, of East Hartford, m. [ ] **WALTZ**, of Hartford, | | |
| Oct. 18, 1852, by Samuel Spring | 1 | 163 |

| | Vol. | Page |
|---|---|---|
| **PECK**, (cont.), | | |
| Orille, [child of Elijah & Mary], b. July 25, 1795 | 1 | 6 |
| Polly, [d. Elijah & Mary], b. Jan. 14, 1793 | 1 | 6 |
| **PELTON**, Alvin, m. Julia A. **STEWART**, June 12, 1827, by Joy H. | | |
| Fairchild | 1 | 108 |
| Ellen M., b. Cambridge, Mass., res. East Hartford, d. Oct. 11, | | |
| 1849, ae 2 | 1 | 56 |
| **PENDLETON**, Arthur, of Princeton, N. H., m. Lucinda **PITKIN**, of East | | |
| Hartford, May 4, 1836, by Samuel Spring | 1 | 120 |
| **PERKINS**, Alvin, m. Sally **McKEE**, Feb. 20, 1825, by Elisha Cushman | 1 | 103 |
| Desire, of East Hartford, m. Ira **SAVAGE**, of Chatham, Oct. 7, | | |
| 1821, by Rev. Isaac Divinel | 1 | 96 |
| -----, Mr., d. [          ], 1802 | 1 | 64 |
| -----, Mr. from Mass., bd. June 28, 1843, ae 37 | 1 | 79 |
| **PERRY**, Emely, m. Joseph **DAVIS**, b. of Hartford, Nov. 20, 1836, by S. L. | | |
| Tracy | 1 | 119 |
| Julia, m. Henry **PHELSP**, Oct. 12, 1826, by Joy H. Fairchild | 1 | 107 |
| Zacheus, m. Mary **PALMER**, Oct. 12, 1820, by Joy H. | | |
| Fairchild | 1 | 94 |
| **PETTINGILL**, Stephen, m. Angeline **HILLS**, of East Hartford, May 22, | | |
| 1836, by Samuel Spring | 1 | 120 |
| **PHELPS**, Delia, b. Hartford, res. East Hartford, d. Aug. 17, 1849, ae 59 | 1 | 56 |
| Edward, merchant, d. Nov. 2, 1849, ae 31 | 1 | 56 |
| Edward, s. Henry, succeeded his father as Sexton of North | | |
| Burying Ground | 1 | 75 |
| Eleanor, mother of Henry, bd. July 20, 1836, ae 73 y. 15 m. | 1 | 78 |
| G. S., his child d. Mar. 16, 1849, ae 6 wks. | 1 | 53 |
| George H., s. George S., merchant, ae 28 & Harriet B. or R., ae | | |
| 31, b. Feb. 3, 1849 | 1 | 50 |
| George Howell, s. George S., merchant, ae 29 & Harriet, ae 31, | | |
| b. Apr. 8, 1850 | 1 | 55 |
| George L., m. Abby **STEVENS**, b. of East Hartford, June 22, | | |
| 1845, by Samuel Spring | 1 | 149 |
| George S., m. Harriet R. **BURNHAM**, b. of East Hartford, July | | |
| 1, 1847, by Samuel Spring | 1 | 153 |
| George S., s. Henry, succeeded his brother Edward as Sexton of | | |
| North Burying Ground, Nov. 1, 1847 until Apr. [ ], | | |
| 1886 | 1 | 75 |
| Henry, m. Julia **PERRY**, Oct. 12, 1826, by Joy H. Fairchild | 1 | 107 |
| Henry, Sexton of North Burying Ground, Nov. 1, 1824; d. Apr. | | |
| 26, 1845 | 1 | 75 |
| Julia Ann, m. James **DANIELS**, b. of East Hartford, July 28, | | |
| 1846, by Samuel Spring | 1 | 152 |
| Lucy A., m. George H. **OLMSTED**, b. of East Hartford, June | | |
| 22, 1843, by Samuel Spring | 1 | 142 |
| Philo F., m. Ann L. **RISLEY**, b. of Glastenbury, Nov. 2, 1845, | | |
| by Levi Daggett, Jr. | 1 | 150 |
| Sarah Emeline, m. Daniel Merrill **SEYMOUR**, Nov. 7, 1832 | 1 | 39 |
| Solomon, m. Ann **OLMSTED**, Oct. 25, 1825, by Joy H. | | |
| Fairchild | 1 | 104 |
| W[illia]m B., b. Manchester, res. East Hartford, d. Nov. 20, | | |
| 1849, ae 1 | 1 | 56 |

|  | Vol. | Page |
|---|---|---|
| **PHILLIPS, PHILPS, PHILIPS**, Benajah, Rev., d. [          ], 1793, in | | |
| Manchester | 1 | 36 |
| George, m. Fanny **FARMER**, b. of Bolton, Nov. 27, 1820, by | | |
| Rev. Isaac Divinnell | 1 | 95 |
| Harriet U., m. Daniel W. **JONES**, b. of Hartford, Nov. 25, | | |
| 1832, by Rev. Samuel H. Biddle | 1 | 115 |
| Horace, m. Eliza **GROSSMAN**, b. of East Hartford, Feb. 14, | | |
| 1836, by Samuel Spring | 1 | 119 |
| Ralph, [s. Rev. Benajah], b. Mar. 1, 1787 | 1 | 36 |
| Sally, [d. Rev. Benajah], b. Feb. 15, 1784 | 1 | 36 |
| -----, Capt., d. [          ], 1798 | 1 | 63 |
| -----, Miss, bd. Nov. 6, 1842, ae 61 | 1 | 79 |
| **PIBBLES**, [see under **PEBBLES**] | | |
| **PIERCE**, George L., of Glastenbury, m. Abigail H. **ROBERTS**, of East | | |
| Hartford, Sept. 1, 1840, by Rev. James A. Smith, of | | |
| Glastenbury | 1 | 133 |
| **PINNEY**, Aaron, Inn keeper, ae 26 & Catherine M., ae 22, had | | |
| s. [          ], b. Dec. 16, 1848 | 1 | 50 |
| **PITKIN**, Adalaide Wells, [d. Horace & Emily], b. Dec. 2, 1815 | 1 | 38 |
| Adeline H., of East Hartford, m. Samuel **HILLS**, of Palmer, | | |
| Mass., Oct. 18, 1841, by Samuel Spring | 1 | 136 |
| Anna, wid., m. Daniel **MARSH**, Dec. [ ], 1779 | 1 | 20 |
| Ashbel, d. Oct. 8, 1802, ae 68 | 1 | 64 |
| Caroline, m. Donald **HART**, b. of Hartford, Oct. 31, 1831, by | | |
| Rev. Gustavus F. Davis, of Hartford | 1 | 113 |
| Charlotte O., m. Orrin T. **COLLINS**, b. of East Hartford, Nov. | | |
| 25, 1846, by Samuel Spring | 1 | 153 |
| Chester, m. Polly **HOLLISTER**, June 23, 1820, by Rev. Elisha | | |
| B. Cook | 1 | 94 |
| Chloe B., d. Mar. 6, 1807, ae 16 | 1 | 66 |
| Clarrisa, m. Frederic **WOODBRIDGE**, b. of East Hartford, | | |
| May 8, 1823, by Rev. Elisha B. Cook | 1 | 102 |
| Clarissa Lord, d. Edward & Clarissa, b. Oct. 7, 1824 | 1 | 38 |
| Daniel, of Norfolk, m. Eliza **PITKIN**, of East Hartford, Apr. 5, | | |
| 1831, by Rev. Samuel Spring, of Hartford | 1 | 112 |
| David, d. July 2, 1822 | 1 | 38 |
| Dorothy, b. [          ], 1717; m. John **GOODWIN**, 2nd, | | |
| [          ]; d. Aug. 17, 1789, ae 72 | 1 | 43 |
| Edward, [s. Elisha & Hannah], b. Aug. 15, 1769 | 1 | 19 |
| Edward, m. Clarrissa **ROBERTS**, June 30, 1822, by Joy H. | | |
| Fairchild | 1 | 99 |
| Edwin, physician, d. Apr. 12, 1851, ae 81 | 1 | 59 |
| Electa, w. Roswell, d. Apr. 23, 1806 | 1 | 37 |
| Electa, Mrs., d. Apr. 25, 1806, ae 26 | 1 | 65 |
| Electa, m. Simeon **BIRGE**, Sept. 22, 1819 | 1 | 38 |
| Elisha, m. Hannah **PITKIN**, July [ ], 1757; d. Mar. 11, 1819 | 1 | 19 |
| Elisha, Jr., [s. Elisha & Hannah], b. Mar. 17, 1758 | 1 | 19 |
| Elisha, certified that Farmer, d. Flora, negro, b. July [ ], 1785 | 1 | 71 |
| Elisha, d. [          ], 1802 | 1 | 64 |
| Eliza, of East Hartford, m. Daniel **PITKIN**, of Norfolk, Apr. 5, | | |
| 1831, by Rev. Samuel Spring, of Hartford | 1 | 112 |
| Elizabeth, [d. Elisha & Hannah], b. Dec. 19, 1764 | 1 | 19 |

| PITKIN, (cont.), | Vol. | Page |
|---|---|---|
| Elizabeth, m. Theodore **PITKIN** (?), Jan. 29, 1789, by Rev. Dr. | | |
| Williams | 1 | 61 |
| Elizabeth, Mrs., d. Feb. [ ], 1804 | 1 | 64 |
| Epa[ ], d. [ ], 1801, ae 68 | 1 | 63 |
| Esther, wid., d. Jan. 3, 1803 | 1 | 64 |
| Esther Woodbridge, [d. Horace & Emily], b. Dec. 25, 1817 | 1 | 38 |
| Eunice Hills, d. Jan. 22, 1802, ae 56 | 1 | 64 |
| Fanny, m. Rev. Amasa **LOOMIS**, Aug. 30, 1819 | 1 | 69 |
| Francis William, [s. Samuel & Sarah], b. May 1, 1799 | 1 | 3 |
| George, m. Mable **OLMSTED**, July 5, 1787, by Rev. Dr. | | |
| Williams | 1 | 61 |
| George, certified that Jack & Rose, negroes had child b. Mar. 2, | | |
| 1790 | 1 | 71 |
| George, Col., d. [ ], 1806, ae 77 | 1 | 65 |
| George, his child bd. Mar. 5, 1831, ae 4 | 1 | 76 |
| Hannah, m. Elisha **PITKIN**, July [ ], 1757; d. June 25, 1811 | 1 | 19 |
| Hannah, [d. Elisha & Hannah], b. June 19, 1778; d. Apr. 27, | | |
| 1781 | 1 | 19 |
| Hannah, w. Ezekiel, d. [ ], 1803 | 1 | 64 |
| Hannah, w. Elisha, d. June 25, 1811 | 1 | 19 |
| Harriet, m. Chauncy **TREAT**, Nov. 12, 1817 | 1 | 68 |
| Harris, s. Martin, d. Feb. 24, 1800 | 1 | 63 |
| Hart, m. Emeline **KEENY**, b. of East Hartford, June 13, 1822, | | |
| by Rev. Elisha B. Cook | 1 | 99 |
| Henry, m. Maria K. **GOODWIN**, b. of East Hartford, June 29, | | |
| 1837, by Samuel Spring | 1 | 123 |
| Henry Chester, [s. Roswell & Mary], b. July 4, 1807 | 1 | 37 |
| Horrace, [s. Elisha & Hannah], b. Mar. 4, 1782; d. Feb. 18, | | |
| 1801 | 1 | 19 |
| Horace, d. Feb. 18, 1801, ae 19 | 1 | 63 |
| Horace, m. Emily **WOODBRIDGE**, Dec. 21, 1814 | 1 | 38 |
| Horace Lord Kimball, [s. Roswell & Electa], b. Sept [ ], 1802; | | |
| d. Dec. 30, 1822 | 1 | 37 |
| Huldah, w. David, d. [ ], 1807, ae 44 | 1 | 65 |
| Isaac, d. [ ], 1795 | 1 | 73 |
| Jane A., of East Hartford, m. Barkes **COTENEY**, of | | |
| Collinsville, May 3, 1837, by Samuel Spring | 1 | 123 |
| Jason, d. [ ], 1814, ae 8 | 1 | 66 |
| Jerusha, of Ellington, m. Dr. William **COOLEY**, of East | | |
| Hartford, Oct. 14, 1821, by Daniel Dorchester. | | |
| Witnesses John H. **MACK** & Betsy E. **MACK** | 1 | 96 |
| Jerusha C., of East Hartford, m. Auguste D. **SCHLESINGER**, | | |
| of Naugatuck, Oct. 4, 1853, by Samuel Spring | 1 | 165 |
| Jonathan, m. Betsey **CUMMINGS**, Mar. 28, 1802, by Mr. | | |
| Yates | 1 | 67 |
| Jonathan, his child d. [ ], 1809, ae 2 wks. | 1 | 66 |
| Joseph, [s. Elisha & Hannah], b. Apr. 7, 1772 | 1 | 19 |
| Lucinda, of East Hartford, m. Arthur **PENDLETON**, of | | |
| Princeton, N. H., May 4, 1836, by Samuel Spring | 1 | 120 |
| Lucy, w. Jonathan, d. [ ], 1804 | 1 | 64 |
| Mary, m. Russell **CONE**, Dec. 13, 1787 | 1 | 3 |
| Mary, w. Roswell, d. Sept. 12, 1813 | 1 | 37 |

PITKIN, (cont.),                                                  Vol.    Page
   Mary, of East Hartford, m. John W. CRANE, M. D., of New
      York, July 15, 1839, by Rev. John A. Hempsted          1      128
   Mary Ann, of East Hartford, m. Calvin POLLARD, of
      Hartford, Apr. 20, 1834, by Samuel Spring              1      116
   Mary Ann, of East Hartford, m. Erastus HUBBARD, of
      Hartford, May 15, 1842, by Samuel Spring               1      139
   Maryann Lewis, [d. Samuel L. & Mary Ann], b. Apr. 5, 1836    1       39
   Mary T., d. Sept. 9, 1849, ae 49                             1       53
   Noah (?), d. [          ], 1826                              1      168
   Olive, d. Jonathan, d. [          ], 1806                    1       65
   Polly*, d. Sept. 22, 1799, ae 29          *(Mary)           1       63
   Priscilla, wid. d. [          ], 1809, ae 42                 1       66
   Ralph, m. Mary TREAT, Sept. 11, 1822, by Elisha Cushman      1       99
   Richard, d. May 6, 1822; Adm. Jere Horace PITKIN             1       38
   Richard Loomis, [s. Horace & Emily], b. Jan. 21, 1819        1       38
   Rosanna Knox, w. Capt. [          ], d. Apr. 23, 1806, ae 41  1      65
   Rosanna M., m. William REYNOLDS, b. of East Hartford,
      Oct. 22, 1840, by Samuel Spring                        1      133
   Roswell, [s. Elisha & Hannah], b. Oct. 7, 1774; d. Mar. 26,
      1808                                                   1       19
   Roswell, m. Electa KIMBALL, Oct. [ ], 1801                   1       37
   Roswell, m. Mary CHEENY, Oct. [ ], 1806; d. Mar. 26, 1808    1       37
   Roswell, d. [          ], 1808, ae 33                        1       66
   Roswell Kimball, [s. Roswell & Electa], b. Oct. [ ], 1805; d.
      Mar. 27, 1815                                          1       37
   Samuel, [s. Elisha & Hannah], b. May 8, 1760                 1       19
   Samuel, b. May [ ], 1760; m. Sarah PARSONS, July 25, 1792    1        3
   Samuel, m. Sally PARSONS, July 25, 1792, by Rev. Dr.
      Williams                                               1       62
   Samuel, had servant Flora, bd. Sept. 12, 1833, ae 84         1       76
   Samuel L., m. Mary Ann LEWIS, of New Haven, Dec. 20,
      1831                                                   1       39
   Samuel Leonard, [s. Samuel & Sarah], b. Apr. 1, 1703         1        3
   Sarah, m. Ja[me]s F. BALDWIN, July 30, 1818                  1       68
   Sarah Augusta, [d. Samuel L. & Mary Ann], b. Feb. 22, 1833;
      d. Sept. 30, 1835                                      1       39
   Sarah Parsons, [d. Samuel & Sarah], b. Feb. 21, 1794         1        3
   Solomon, s. [Elisha & Hannah], b. Mar. 28, 1767; d. Jan. 19,
      1793                                                   1       19
   Sophia, m. Arnold L. SPENCER, July 4, 1826, by Joy H.
      Fairchild                                              1      106
   Stephen, [s. Elisha & Hannah], b. Feb. 23, 1778 [1787?]; d.
      Aug. 11, 1817                                          1       19
   Susan E., of East Hartford, m. John THOMPSON, of
      Farmington, June 5, 1844, by Samuel Spring             1      145
   Thankful, wid., d. May 6, 1806, ae 72                        1       65
   Theodore, m. Elizabeth PITKIN, Jan. 29, 1789, by Rev. Dr.
      Williams                                               1       61
   Timothy, [s. Elisha & Hannah], b. Aug. 10, 1762; d. Dec. 19,
      1815                                                   1       19
   Walter, m. Catherine B. STANLEY, b. of East Hartford, Nov.
      5, 1835, by Samuel Spring                              1      119

| | Vol. | Page |
|---|---|---|
| **PITKIN**, (cont.), | | |
| -----, his child d. [ ], 1813 | 1 | 67 |
| **PLATT**, Henrietta, of New Haven, m. George **WICHE**, of Hartford, Apr. | | |
| 14, 1850, by Samuel Spring | 1 | 158 |
| Henrietta, ae 17, b. N. Haven, m. George **WYCHE**, tailor, | | |
| b. Germany, res. Hartford, Apr. 23, 1850, by S. | | |
| Spring | 1 | 56 |
| **POLLARD**, Calvin, of Hartford, m. Mary Ann **PITKIN**, of East Hartford, | | |
| Apr. 20, 1834, by Samuel Spring | 1 | 116 |
| **POLLY**, Henry D., of Glastenbury, m. Clarissa F. **SKINNER**, of Durham, | | |
| Dec. 21, 1851, by Rev. Benjamin C. Phelps | 1 | 162 |
| **PORTER**, Aaron, [s. [ ] & Hannah], b. [ ] | 1 | 43 |
| Asahel, m. Lucy **KELNY**, June 4, 1795 | 1 | 11 |
| Asahel, farmer, d. Nov. 23, 1848, ae 75 | 1 | 53 |
| Benjamin, d. Oct. 20, 1806, ae 76 | 1 | 65 |
| Caleb, [ s. [ ] & Hannah], b. [ ] | 1 | 43 |
| Charlott[e] L., d. Henry C., joiner, h Aug. 6, 1850 | 1 | 58 |
| Clarrisa Ann, m. Thomas L. **BANCROFT**, June 6, 1826, by | | |
| Joy H. Fairchild | 1 | 106 |
| Cornelia, of East Hartford, m. H. P. **SEXTON**, of New Haven, | | |
| June 5, 1843, by Rev. James A. Smith, of | | |
| Glastenbury | 1 | 142 |
| Damaris, [d. [ ] & Hannah], b. [ ] | 1 | 43 |
| Edwin, [s. Asahel & Lucy], b. May 11, 1796; d. Oct. 13, 1796 | 1 | 11 |
| Edwin, [s. Asahel & Lucy], b. Sept. 3, 1797 | 1 | 11 |
| Eleazer, d. Dec. 12, 1824 | 1 | 74 |
| Elisha, of Glastenbury, m. Fanny **GULLIVER**, of East | | |
| Hartford, Jan. 14, 1830, by Samuel H. Beddel | 1 | 111 |
| Elizabeth, wid. Benjamin, d. Sept. 14, 1830, ae 80 | 1 | 74 |
| Elizabeth, d. Henry C., farmer, b. Sept. [ ], 1848 | 1 | 51 |
| Elizabeth L., of East Windsor, m. Hiram **ANDERSON**, Apr. | | |
| 12, 1846, by Rev. Gurdon Robins, of Hartford | 1 | 152 |
| Emely, m. Stephen **TAYLOR**, b. of East Hartford, Sept. 10, | | |
| 1834, by Samuel Spring | 1 | 116 |
| Emiline, of East Hartford, m. Orson **SPENCER**, of Olmsted, | | |
| O., Oct. 5, 1831, by Rev. Gustavus F. Davis | 1 | 113 |
| Esther, m. Samuel F. **TICHNOR**, May 4, 1835, by Samuel | | |
| Spring | 1 | 118 |
| Eunice, of East Hartford, m. Samuel **MITCHEL**, of Fairfield, | | |
| Feb. 12, 1826, by Charles Remington | 1 | 105 |
| Fanny, m. Henry **LESTER**, Aug. 2, 1818 | 1 | 68 |
| George D., of Glastenbury, m. Elvira A. **MATHER**, of | | |
| Hydeville, Vt., Oct. 8, 1854, by Rev. Benjamin C. | | |
| Phelps | 1 | 166 |
| George F., s. John, ae 51 & Harriet, ae 39, b. Dec. 19, 1849 | 1 | 54 |
| George F., d. Sept. 30, 1850, ae 9 m. | 1 | 60 |
| Hannah, wid. John, d. May [ ], 1812 | 1 | 73 |
| Hanna, [d. [ ] & Hannah], b. [ ] | 1 | 43 |
| Henry, d. Mar. 2, 1849, ae 3 | 1 | 53 |
| Henry C., of East Hartford, m. Mrs. Nancy H. **LATHROP**, of | | |
| Hartford, Aug. 15, 1841, by Rev. B. M. Walker | 1 | 136 |
| Hepzibah, m. Royal **TREAT**, b. of East Hartford, Apr. 23, | | |
| 1834, by Samuel Spring | 1 | 116 |

| | Vol. | Page |
|---|---|---|
| **PORTER**, (cont.), | | |
| Himan B., s. John N., farmer, ae 49 & Harriet L., ae 37, b. Aug. 11, 1847 | 1 | 46 |
| Ira, m. Jane **LOW**, b. of East Hartford, July 2, 1849, by Rev. S. Spring | 1 | 52 |
| James, d. [    ], 1802, at Sea, ae 21 | 1 | 73 |
| James, s. Nathan, d. Mar. 6, 1803, at Sea, ae 19 | 1 | 64 |
| Jerusha, m. Russell **HOLISTER**, Feb. 15, 1825, by Joy H. Fairchild | 1 | 103 |
| Jerusha, d. Nov. 8, 1825, ae 45 | 1 | 73 |
| Job, d. [    ], 1799, ae 45 | 1 | 63 |
| John, m. Mary **WILLIAMS**, May 20, 1784, by Rev. Dr. Williams | 1 | 61 |
| John, 2nd, m. Anna **HILLS**, Nov. 19, 1817 | 1 | 68 |
| John, s. Jas., 2nd, d. Mar. 22, 1827, ae 69 | 1 | 74 |
| John Nelson, of East Hartford, m. Harriet Louisa **HASTING**, of Hartford, Oct. 21, 1838, by Rev. Thomas W. Giles | 1 | 127 |
| Jos[    ], d. [    ], 1801 | 1 | 63 |
| Joseph H., m. Mary **ENSIGN**, b. of East Hartford, Oct. 31, 1844, by Samuel Spring | 1 | 146 |
| Joshia, d. July 9, 1850, ae 81 | 1 | 57 |
| Laura, m. Henry **SEYMORE**, Aug. 16, 1818 | 1 | 68 |
| Lucretia L., of East Hartford, m. Henry **ABBY**, of East Windsor, May 5, 1830, by Rev. Samuel H. Biddle | 1 | 112 |
| Lucy, m. Anson **FORBES**, May 1, 1828, by Rev. Samuel Spring, of Hartford | 1 | 109 |
| Lydia, d. Nov. 15, 1825, ae 40 | 1 | 73 |
| Mabel, m. Ezra **BRAINERD**, Mar. 9, 1786 | 1 | 11 |
| Mabel, m. Ezra **BRAINARD**, Mar. 9, 1786, by Rev. Dr. Williams | 1 | 61 |
| Margaret, w. Job, d. Oct. 12, 1798, ae 45 | 1 | 63 |
| Mary, d. Feb. 21, 1795 | 1 | 73 |
| Miranda, d. Job & Lydia, m. Horace H. **HILLS**, s. Leonard & Jerusha, Oct. 13, 1831, by Asa Mead | 1 | 69 |
| Miranda, m. Horace H. **HILLS**, Oct. 13, 1830, by Rev. Asa Mead | 1 | 112 |
| Nathan, s. Ja[me]s, 2nd, d. Dec. 5, 1825, ae 77 | 1 | 73 |
| Nathan, s. Nathan, d. Feb. [ ], 1829, ae 49 | 1 | 74 |
| Pamela, [d. Asahel & Lucy], b. June 17, 1800 | 1 | 11 |
| Pamela, m. Solomon **PRATT**, Oct. 23, 1823, by Joy H. Fairchild | 1 | 102 |
| Roger, d. Dec. 3, 1797 | 1 | 63 |
| Russel, d. Oct. 20, 1850, ae 76 | 1 | 60 |
| Sally, m. Lucius **TALCOTT**, May 24, 1825, by Joy H. Fairchild | 1 | 106 |
| Samuel D., of Andover, m. Julia **HOLLISTER**, of East Hartford, Nov. 15, 1837, by Samuel Spring | 1 | 124 |
| Sarah, wid., d. Apr. 10, 1818 | 1 | 73 |
| Susanna, w. Nathan, d. Feb. [ ], 1807 | 1 | 65 |
| Thankful, m. Tho[ma]s **GULLIVER**, Sept. 21, 1786, by Rev. Dr. Williams | 1 | 61 |
| William, d. Dec. [ ], 1810 | 1 | 73 |
| -----, wid., d. [    ], 1799 | 1 | 63 |

| | Vol. | Page |
|---|---|---|
| **PORTER**, (cont.), | | |
| -----, his child d. [ ], 1803 | 1 | 64 |
| -----, Miss, d. [ ], 1807 | 1 | 66 |
| -----, m. Hannah **GOODWIN**, [ ] | 1 | 43 |
| **PRATT, PRAT**, Ame, m. Samuel **ROBERTS**, Sept. 16, 1784, by Rev. Dr. Williams | 1 | 61 |
| Arthur, s. Solomon, joiner & Amelia, b. Oct. 12, 1849 | 1 | 50 |
| Charles L., s. Algernon, merchant, ae 24 & Delia, ae 22, b. Dec. 9, 1847 | 1 | 47 |
| Dorcas, of East Hartford, m. Samuel **ELMER**, of East Windsor, Dec. 13, 1836, by Samuel Spring | 1 | 121 |
| Dorcas, d. July 17, 1848, ae 80 | 1 | 53 |
| Eli, m. [ ] **COTTON**, Apr. 21, 1819 | 1 | 69 |
| Eliab, d. [ ], 1809, ae 85 | 1 | 66 |
| Elizabeth, d. Daniel, of Hartford, m. Nathaniel **GOODWIN**, [ ] | 1 | 43 |
| Emily, m. Hezekiah **GOODWIN**, s. Joseph & Hannah, [ ] | 1 | 44 |
| Jonathan, m. Betsy **MERROW**, Jan. 30, 1784, by Rev. Dr. Williams | 1 | 61 |
| Lucy, m. Samuel **ARNOLD**, Dec. 25, 1766 | 1 | 29 |
| Lucy A., of East Hartford, m. William H. H. **DAGGETT**, of Andover, Nov. 21, 1844, by Samuel Spring | 1 | 148 |
| Martha G., of East Hartford, m. S. **BOAGE**, of New Haven, May 13, 1827, by Rev. Joel H. Linsley | 1 | 108 |
| Mary E., d. Algernon, merchant, ae 25, b. June 27, 1851 | 1 | 58 |
| Solomon, m. Pamelia **PORTER**, Oct. 23, 1823, by Joy H. Fairchild | 1 | 102 |
| **PRENTICE**, Thaddeus, Jr., of Willamantic, m. Ann L. **AYERS**, of Willimantic, N. J., Mar. 30, 1846, by Samuel Spring | 1 | 151 |
| **PRINDLE**, George, m. Elizabeth **FRISBE**, b. of New Haven, Sept. 2, 1850, by Rev. Joseph Harrington, of Hartford | 1 | 159 |
| **QUINNEY**, Mary, m. Samuel **TRAIN**, Nov. 26, 1821, by Joy H. Fairchild | 1 | 97 |
| **RAND**, Thomas, of Maine, bd. Nov. 2, 1838, ae 38 | 1 | 78 |
| **RATHBURN, RATHBUM, RATHBUN**, John F., of Manchester, m. Lucy A. **HILLS**, of East Hartford, Sept. 7, 1843, by Samuel Spring | 1 | 143 |
| Louis, m. John W. **HILLS**, Apr. 14, 1822, by Isaac Devinel | 1 | 98 |
| Saley Jones, m. Mary **BARBER**, Nov. 15, 1818 | 1 | 68 |
| **RAYMOND**, A. G., farmer, ae 30, b. Montville, res. Berlin, m. Esther B. **ROBERTS**, ae 25, b. East Hartford, res. same, Apr. [ ], 1848, by Rev. S. Spring | 1 | 52 |
| Albert C., of New Britain, m. Esther B. **ROBERTS**, of East Hartford, Apr. 10, 1849, by Samuel Spring | 1 | 156 |
| Nabby, m. Peres **COMESTOCK**, Nov. 1, 1788 | 1 | 25 |
| -----, Mrs., d. [ ], 1814 | 1 | 66 |
| **REED**, William L., s. William L., rope maker, ae 29, b. Oct. 13, 1850 | 1 | 58 |
| **REMINGTON**, Lemuel, his child bd. Nov. 25, 1840, ae 5 | 1 | 78 |
| **REVIER**, Everett, E., s. Ellsworth, farmer & Mary, b. July 18, 1849 | 1 | 51 |
| **REYNOLDS**, Amelia, of East Hartford, m. Joseph **KINSBURY**, of Coventry, Dec. 4, 1827, by Rev. J. H. Kingsley, of Hartford | 1 | 109 |

| | Vol. | Page |
|---|---|---|
| **REYNOLDS**, (cont.), | | |
| Catherine B., m. Theodore L. **WRIGHT**, b. of East Hartford, | | |
| Sept. 23, 1833, by Rev. Samuel Spring | 1 | 114 |
| Clarissa G., of East Hartford, m. Horace **SMITH**, of New York | | |
| State, Aug. 10, 1841, by Samuel Spring | 1 | 135 |
| Esther, w. Amherst, d. [ ], 1809, ae 34 | 1 | 66 |
| Hester, m. Samuel **TALCOTT**, Apr. 6, 1826, by Joy H. | | |
| Fairchild | 1 | 105 |
| John, m. Hannah **GOODWIN**, d. Joseph & Hannah, [ ] | 1 | 44 |
| Sally, m. Erastus **VORRA**, Nov. 24, 1825, by Joy H. Fairchild | 1 | 105 |
| Susan, m. William **KINGBURY**, Dec. 5, 1816 | 1 | 68 |
| William, m. Rosanna M. **PITKIN**, b. of East Hartford, Oct. 22, | | |
| 1840, by Samuel Spring | 1 | 133 |
| ----, Mr., d. [ ], 1805 | 1 | 65 |
| ----, his child d. [ ], 1814 | 1 | 66 |
| **RICH**, Sarah, m. George **HILLS**, b. of East Hartford, June 11, 1822, by | | |
| Rev. Elisha B. Cook | 1 | 99 |
| **RICHARDSON**, Frank W., s. S. D., daguerrerotypist & Louisa, b. May 8, | | |
| 1848 | 1 | 50 |
| **RICHIE**, Peter, m. Lovisa **GRISWOLD**, July 22, 1785, by Rev. Dr. | | |
| Williams | 1 | 61 |
| **RILEY**, Alice M., d. Ransom, merchant, ae 29, b. Oct. 10, 1848 | 1 | 51 |
| Cornelia, m. Norman **FOX**, b. of East Hartford, Jan. 9, 1839, by | | |
| Samuel Spring | 1 | 127 |
| Horace F., s. Horace F., grocer, b. Apr. 23, 1851 | 1 | 59 |
| Julia E., d. Ransom, merchant, ae 30, b. Oct. 4, 1850 | 1 | 59 |
| Mary I., d. H. F., carpenter, ae 27 & Mary, ae 27, b. Oct. 25, | | |
| 1849 | 1 | 54 |
| Ranson, m. Mary A. **BELDEN**, May 4, 1843, by Cephas | | |
| Brainard | 1 | 151 |
| **RIPLEY**, Henrietta, d. John & Elizabeth, late of Hartford, m. Edwin W. | | |
| **BARNARD**, of Rochester, N. Y., Mar. 7, 1831, by | | |
| Asa Mead | 1 | 70 |
| Henrietta, of Hartford, m. Edwin **BARNARD**, of Rochester, | | |
| N. Y., Mar. 7, 1831, by Rev. Asa Mead | 1 | 112 |
| **RIPNER**, Rebecca, wid., d. [ ], 1802; bd. June 27, 1802 | 1 | 64 |
| **RISING**, Darius, m. Sophia **ROBERTS**, b. of East Hartford, Mar. 31, | | |
| 1833, by Rev. Samuel Spring, of East Hartford | 1 | 114 |
| **RISLEY**, Abbey S., d. Aug. 30, 1849, ae 28 | 1 | 56 |
| Abigail, d. Sept. 25, 1850, ae 74 | 1 | 60 |
| Adna, m. Mary Ann **HART**, b. of East Hartford, Oct. 13, 1835, | | |
| by Samuel Spring | 1 | 118 |
| Albert Lester, s. Lester, shoemaker, ae 32 & Eliza C., ae 29, b. | | |
| June 11, 1850 | 1 | 55 |
| Almira, ae 26, res. Manchester, had illeg. s. Francis A. | | |
| **COWLES**, b. Jan. 15, 1849 | 1 | 54 |
| Alonzo, of Glastenbury, m. Susan C. **CHAPMAN**, of East | | |
| Hartford, June 3, 1847, by Samuel Spring | 1 | 153 |
| Ann L., m. Philo F. **PHELPS**, b. of Glastenbury, Nov. 2, 1845, | | |
| by Levi Daggett, Jr. | 1 | 150 |
| Anna, m. Hardin **HURLBURT**, Aug. 1, 1816 | 1 | 68 |
| Asa, his w. [ ], d. Jan. [ ], 1795 | 1 | 73 |
| Asa, d. May 4, 1800 | 1 | 63 |

**RISLEY, (cont.),**

| | Vol. | Page |
|---|---|---|
| Benjamin W., m. Sarah Ann **BLISS**, b. of East Hartford, Sept. | | |
| 6, 1842, by Samuel Spring | 1 | 139 |
| Benton, of East Hartford, m. Mary Ann **STEBBINS**, of | | |
| Simsbury, June 4, 1843, by Rev. B. M. Walker | 1 | 143 |
| Caleb, [s. John & Ruth], b. July 8, 1784 | 1 | 16 |
| Carolina, [d. Nathaniel & Susanna], b. July 20, 1798 | 1 | 35 |
| Charles B., boatmaker, ae 31, m. Delia A **RISLEY**, ae 20, b. of | | |
| East Hartford, Dec. 3, 1848, by [       ] Goodrich | 1 | 52 |
| Charles B., m. Delia O. **RISLEY**, [       ], by Rev. J. O. | | |
| Goodridge | 1 | 155 |
| Chauncy, of Glastenbury, m. Sophia **BREWER**, of East | | |
| Hartford, Sept. 8, 1833, by Rev. Samuel Spring | 1 | 114 |
| Chester, [s. Nathaniel & Susanna], b. Nov. 6, 1793 | 1 | 35 |
| Clare, [d. Nathaniel & Susanna], b. July 2, 1780 | 1 | 35 |
| Clara, mother of Mr. Rowell's w. [       ], bd. Oct. 21, 1841 | 1 | 79 |
| Damaras, [d. John & Ruth], b. Mar. 23, 1795 [1775?]; | | |
| d. [       ] | 1 | 16 |
| Delia, m. William **WALLACE**, b. of East Hartford, Apr. 8, | | |
| 1830, by Rev. Leonard B. Griffing | 1 | 111 |
| Delia A., ae 20, of East Hartford, m. Charles B. **RISLEY**, | | |
| boatmaker, ae 31, of East Hartford, Dec. 3, 1848, by | | |
| [       ] Goodrich | 1 | 52 |
| Delia O., m. Charles B. **RISLEY**, [       ], by Rev. J. O. | | |
| Goodridge | 1 | 155 |
| Edward, s. Seth, shoemaker, ae 34, & Mary A., ae 33, b. July 3, | | |
| 1850 | 1 | 55 |
| Eli, his child d. [       ], 1798 | 1 | 63 |
| Elisha, m. Nancy **HILLS**, Nov. 23, 1825, by Joy H. Fairchild | 1 | 104 |
| Elisha, m. Mrs. **SELLEW**, Nov. 13, 1826, by Joy H. Fairchild | 1 | 107 |
| Eliza, [d. Nathaniel & Susanna], b. Mar. 23, 1810 | 1 | 35 |
| Elizabeth P., of East Hartford, m. Andrew L. **BARROWS**, of | | |
| Hartford, Dec. 20, 1840, by Samuel Spring | 1 | 134 |
| Ellen F., d. Caleb, farmer & Jane Ann, b. Mar. 27, 1848 | 1 | 50 |
| Emeline, m. Solomon **TREAT**, b. of East Hartford, Nov. 22, | | |
| 1827, by Rev. William Lockwood | 1 | 109 |
| Erie, his child bd. June 9, 1832, ae 5 yrs. | 1 | 76 |
| Esther, [d. Nathaniel & Susanna], b. Jan. 6, 1791 | 1 | 35 |
| Eunice, [d. Nathaniel & Susanna], b. Jan. 15, 1788 | 1 | 35 |
| Ezekiel, s. Reubin, d. [       ], 1811, at Sea | 1 | 73 |
| Francis, hatter, ae 30 & Abbey S., ae 28, had child s. b. Aug. 25, | | |
| 1849 | 1 | 54 |
| Francis, farmer, b. East Hartford, res. same, m. 2nd w. Lois | | |
| **THAYER**, b. Manchester, res. same, Apr. 28, 1850, | | |
| by S. Spring | 1 | 56 |
| Francis, of East Hartford, m. Lois **THAYER**, of Manchester, | | |
| Apr. 28, 1850, by Samuel Spring | 1 | 158 |
| Francis O., s. Charles B., farmer, ae 31 & Abby D., ae 21, b. | | |
| Sept. 26, 1849 | 1 | 54 |
| George, m. Sarah **CAMP**, b. of East Hartford, Jan. 12, 1843, by | | |
| Samuel Spring | 1 | 142 |
| Hart, his child d. [       ], 1809 | 1 | 66 |
| Harvey, of Wapping, d. May [ ], 1826 | 1 | 168 |

| | Vol. | Page |
|---|---|---|
| **RISLEY**, (cont.), | | |
| Henry, silver smith, ae 22, b. Glastenbury, res. same, m. Charlott | | |
| A. **TREAT**, ae 22, b. East Hartford, Dec. 30, 1849, | | |
| by B. G. Phelps | 1 | 56 |
| Henry, of Glastenbury, m. Charlotte A. **TREAT**, of East | | |
| Hartford, Dec. 30, 1849, by Rev. Benjamin C. | | |
| Phelps | 1 | 158 |
| James, of Wethersfield, m. Maria **ROBERTS**, of East Hartford, | | |
| Nov. 22, 1836, by Rev. George May | 1 | 121 |
| Jared, d. [          ], 1809 | 1 | 66 |
| Jer[emiah], his child, d. [          ], 1802 | 1 | 64 |
| Jeremiah, d. Apr. 4, 1832 | 1 | 74 |
| Jerusha (?), d. Stephen, d. [          ], 1800, ae 10 (?) | 1 | 63 |
| Jerusha, d. Sept. 17, 1800, ae 10 | 1 | 73 |
| John, s. [John & Ruth], b. Feb. 10, 1792 | 1 | 16 |
| John, m. Ruth **ABBY**, Sept. [ ], 1793*      *(Probably "1773") | 1 | 16 |
| John, d. Feb. 4, 1810 | 1 | 73 |
| John, m. Sally **SEYMOUR**, Nov. 25, 1818 | 1 | 69 |
| John, d. Oct. [ ], 1831, ae 39 | 1 | 74 |
| John, m. Mary I. **FOX**, b. of Hartford, July 2, 1849, by Rev. S. | | |
| Spring | 1 | 52 |
| Joshua, his s. [          ], d. [          ], 1800 | 1 | 63 |
| Joshua, d. [          ], 1822 | 1 | 73 |
| Julia, d. Sept. 2, 1848, ae 11 m. | 1 | 53 |
| Lester, m. Eliza C. **DURBY**, b. of East Hartford, Aug. 7, 1840, | | |
| by Samuel Spring | 1 | 133 |
| Lorenzo, farmer, ae 23, had child b. July 11, 1851 | 1 | 57 |
| Lucinda, [d. John & Ruth], b. Sept. 10, 1780; d, [          ] | 1 | 16 |
| Lucinda, [d. John & Ruth], b. Dec. 17, 1787 | 1 | 16 |
| Lucius, of East Hartford, m. Olive **CLEVELAND**, of Hartford, | | |
| Nov. 5, 1846, by Levi Daggett, Jr. | 1 | 153 |
| Lucretia, m. James **HART**, b. of East Hartford, Sept. 15, 1845, | | |
| by Samuel Spring | 1 | 149 |
| Lucy, m. Eligah **DEMMING**, Apr. 8, 1784 | 1 | 23 |
| Lucy, m. Elizah **DEMING**, Apr. 8, 1784, by Rev. Dr. Williams | 1 | 61 |
| Maria, of East Hartford, m. Raphael **GILMAN**, of Berlin, Jan. | | |
| 17, 1830, by Rev. Timothy Benedict | 1 | 111 |
| Martha, m. James **MORRIS**, [          ], by Rev. Dr. | | |
| Williams | 1 | 61 |
| Mary, wid., d. Oct. 14, 1808 | 1 | 73 |
| Mary, of Manchester, m. Wheaton **USHER**, of Rockville, Sept. | | |
| 4, 1853, by Rev. Benjamin C. Phelps | 1 | 166 |
| Mary Elizabeth, twin with Sylvester E., d. Benton & Mary Ann, | | |
| b. May [ ], 1849 | 1 | 51 |
| Melissa, d. July 11, 1848, ae 1 1/4 | 1 | 49 |
| Moses, his child d. Oct. [ ], 1794 | 1 | 73 |
| Nancy W., ae 20, b. East Hartford, res. same, m. Jason W. | | |
| **LUCAS**, ae 22, b. Glastenbury, res. East Hartford, | | |
| Jan. [ ], 1849, by Rev. Turnbull | 1 | 52 |
| Nathaniel, s. Nathaniel, Jr., d. Apr. 17, 1808, ae 57 | 1 | 66 |
| Nathaniel, m. Susanna **CADWELL**, [          ] | 1 | 35 |
| Nathaniel Hart, [s. Nathaniel & Susanna], b. Aug. 20, 1783 | 1 | 35 |

| | Vol. | Page |
|---|---|---|
| **RISLEY**, (cont.), | | |
| Nehemiah, m. Martha **BEMONT**, June 3, 1784, by Rev. Dr. | | |
| Williams | 1 | 61 |
| Noah, m. Mary **ARNOLD**, Nov. 2, 1786, by Rev. Dr. Williams | 1 | 61 |
| Noah, d. [ ], 1800, ae 49 | 1 | 63 |
| Patty, [d. John & Ruth], b. June 4, 1790 | 1 | 16 |
| Patty, m. Moses **ENSIGN**, Jr., May 23, 1820 | 1 | 69 |
| Ralph, m. Anna **WINSLOW**, Jan. 19, 1820 | 1 | 69 |
| Ralph, farmer, d. Nov. 3, 1849, ae 51 | 1 | 56 |
| Ranson, m. Elizabeth **SMITH**, b. of Glastenbury, Dec. 12, | | |
| 1852, by Rev. Benjamin C. Phelps | 1 | 163 |
| Richard, d. Oct. 30, 1807 | 1 | 73 |
| Russell, d. Dec. 30, 1796 | 1 | 73 |
| Russell, m. Ruth **WARREN**, b. of East Hartford, Nov. 4, 1829, | | |
| by Herman Perry | 1 | 111 |
| Ruth, [d. John & Ruth], b. July 11, 1795 | 1 | 16 |
| Sally, m. Elisha **ROBERTS**, June 7, 1787, by Rev. Dr. | | |
| Williams | 1 | 61 |
| Sarah, w. Josh., d. Sept. 6, 1800 | 1 | 63 |
| Seth, m. Mary A. **WARREN**, b. of East Hartford, Sept. 25, | | |
| 1839, by Samuel Spring | 1 | 130 |
| Seth R., of Manchester, m. Mary A. **VARRA**, Nov. 3, 1842, by | | |
| Rev. Cephas Brainard | 1 | 141 |
| Sophia, m. Jacob **FILLASER**, b. of Glastenbury, Nov. 23, | | |
| 1851, by Rev. B. C. Phelps | 1 | 161 |
| Susanna, [d. Nathaniel & Susanna], b. Mar. 24, 1796 | 1 | 35 |
| Susanna, d. [ ], 1811 | 1 | 73 |
| Sylvester E., twin with Mary Elizabeth, s. Benton & Mary Ann, | | |
| b. May [ ], 1849 | 1 | 51 |
| Tryphena, m. Matthias **TREET**, Dec. 20, 1778 | 1 | 24 |
| Wealthy, m. John **BURNHAM**, Mar. 29, 1820 | 1 | 69 |
| Whiting, d. Feb. [ ], 1826 | 1 | 167 |
| W[illia]m, joiner, had child s. b. May 22, 1851 | 1 | 57 |
| William H., m Delia Ann **HILLS**, b. of East Hartford, Apr. 23, | | |
| 1839, by Samuel Spring | 1 | 128 |
| ----, wid., d. [ ], 1802 | 1 | 64 |
| ----, his child d. [ ], 1806 | 1 | 65 |
| ----, his child d. [ ], 1808 | 1 | 66 |
| ----, Mrs. of Waping, d. Feb. [ ], 1826 | 1 | 167 |
| **RIST**, [see also **RUST**], Joseph of Northbridge, Mass., m. Abby **TREAT**, | | |
| of East Hartford, Aug. 19, 1841, by Samuel Spring | 1 | 136 |
| **RITTER**, David, 2nd s. John & Hannah, of Hartford, b. Jan. 13, 1779 | TR2 | 1 |
| David, 2nd s. John & Hannah, of Hartford, b. Jan. 13, 1779 | 1 | 71 |
| Sarah, wid., d. Aug. 30, 1826, ae 83 | 1 | 74 |
| **ROBBINS**, Amos, of Hartford, m. Elizabeth **BARBER**, of Hebron, June | | |
| 23, 1844, by Samuel Spring | 1 | 145 |
| Royal, of Berlin, m. Elizabeth B. **BISSELL**, of East Hartford, | | |
| Oct. 17, 1839, by Samuel Spring | 1 | 130 |
| **ROBERTS, ROBARTS**, Abby, m. Benjamin **WICKS**, Oct. 21, 1795, by | | |
| Rev. Dr. Williams | 1 | 62 |
| Abigail H., of East Hartford, m. George L. **PIERCE**, of | | |
| Glastenbury, Sept. 1, 1840, by Rev. James A. Smith, | | |
| of Glastenbury | 1 | 133 |

| ROBERTS, ROBARTS, (cont.), | Vol. | Page |
|---|---|---|
| Abigail L., m. Elisha **GEER**, b. of East Hartford, Sept. 10, 1839, by Samuel Spring | 1 | 129 |
| Adeline, of East Hartford, m. Jerimiah W. **STRONG**, of Bolton, Sept. 28, 1841, by Rev. Cephas Brainard | 1 | 137 |
| Amelia, m. W[illia]m W. **LARABEE**, Dec. 28, 1826, by Joy H. Fairchild | 1 | 107 |
| Ann, m. Oshia **INGRAM**, Oct. 10, 1826, by Joy H. Fairchild | 1 | 107 |
| Anna, of East Hartford, m. James **BUTLER**, of Hartford, Dec. 28, 1843, by Samuel Spring | 1 | 144 |
| Ashbel, [s. Jonathan], b. Mar. 4, 1763 | 1 | 71 |
| Ashbel, his w. [      ], bd. Nov. 25, 1833, ae 70 | 1 | 76 |
| Ashbel, bd. Dec. 16, 1838, ae 76 | 1 | 78 |
| Ben, his w. [      ], d. [      ], 1798 | 1 | 63 |
| Betsy, m. William **MANNING**, Mar. 27, 1823, by Joy H. Fairchild | 1 | 101 |
| Betsy, d. Apr. 19, 1851, ae 52 | 1 | 59 |
| Clarrissa, m. Edward **PITKIN**, June 30, 1822, by Joy H. Fairchild | 1 | 99 |
| Cynthia, m. Lewis **BIDWELL**, Dec. 31, 1816 | 1 | 68 |
| Daniel, m. Mabel **EASTON**, July 8, 1794, by Rev. Dr. Williams | 1 | 62 |
| Daniel, farmer, d. Aug. 23, 1848, ae 61 | 1 | 53 |
| Delia O., of East Hartford, m. Anson **TRYON**, of Glastenbury, Aug. 2, 1843, by Samuel Spring | 1 | 143 |
| Edwin M., of East Hartford, m. Mary Ann **COWLES**, of Rathway, N. J., Sept. 17, 1844, by Samuel Spring | 1 | 145 |
| Eleanor Hills, w. Ashbel, d. Nov. [ ], 1883 (?)* *(Probably "1833) | 1 | 74 |
| Eli, [s. Jonathan], b. Nov. 2, 1767 | 1 | 71 |
| Elisha, m. Sally **RISLEY**, June 7, 1787, by Rev. Dr. Williams | 1 | 61 |
| Elisha, d. [      ], 1805 | 1 | 65 |
| Elisa M., d. Jason, farmer & Mary, b. Nov. 29, 1848 | 1 | 50 |
| Elizabeth, m. Samuel **BREWER**, b. of East Hartford, Sept. 2, 1839, by Samuel Spring | 1 | 129 |
| Elizabeth L., m. John **HUBBARD**, Oct. 20, 1825, by Joy H. Fairchild | 1 | 104 |
| Esther B., ae 25, b. East Hartford, res. same, m. A. G. **RAYMOND**, farmer, ae 30, b. Montville, res. Berlin, Apr.[ ], 1848, by Rev. S. Spring | 1 | 52 |
| Esther B., of East Hartford, m. Albert C. **RAYMOND**, of New Britain, Apr. 10, 1849, by Samuel Spring | 1 | 156 |
| Ezra, bd. Oct. 13, 1841, ae 44 | 1 | 79 |
| George, m. Lucretia **ABBY**, Mar. 19, 1822, by Joy H. Fairchild | 1 | 98 |
| George, of Hartford, m. Louisa **STEWART**, of East Hartford, Oct. 19, 1836, by Horace Hooker | 1 | 119 |
| Hannah, m. Samuel **WADSWORTH**, Dec. 12, 1805 | 1 | 38 |
| Harriet, m. Aaron G. **OLMSTED**, b. of East Hartford, Apr. 6, 1836, by Samuel Spring | 1 | 120 |
| Harriet F., of East Hartford, m. William B. **JOHNSON**, of Hartford, Aug. 20, 1839, by Rev. Horace Bushnal, of Hartford | 1 | 130 |
| Henry C., s. Jason, farmer, ae 47, b. Mar. 10, 1850 | 1 | 58 |

**ROBERTS, ROBARTS,** (cont.),

| | Vol. | Page |
|---|---|---|
| Hezikiah M., of East Hartford, m. Mary **WELDON,** of Glastenbury, [        ], by E. Edwin Hall | 1 | 145 |
| Horace, of Glastenbury, m. Elizabeth **STOUGHTON,** of East Hartford, Mar. 8, 1846, by Samuel Spring | 1 | 151 |
| Ira  T., m. Charlotte C. **COWLES,** Apr. 10, 1839, by Samuel Spring | 1 | 128 |
| Isaac, m. Anna **ENSIGN,** Apr. 2, 1817 | 1 | 68 |
| Isaac, m. Laura **COWDERY,** b. of East Hartford, Feb. 24, 1847, by Samuel Spring | 1 | 153 |
| Jane Ann, m. Joseph E. **TREAT,** Nov. 3, 1825, by Joy H. Fairchild | 1 | 104 |
| Jane F., of East Hartford, m. Edward S. **GOODWIN,** of Port Gibson, Miss., Sept. 24, 1835, by Samuel Spring | 1 | 118 |
| Jane Treat, d. Ozias, b. Dec. 10, 1811; m. Edward S. **GOODWIN,** Sept. 24, 1835; d. [        ] | 1 | 44 |
| Jason, m. Mary F. **CHAMPLIN,** b. of East Hartford, Apr. 27, 1841, by Rev. John Moore, of Hartford | 1 | 136 |
| Jerusha, w. Benjamin, d. June 3, 1806, ae 89 | 1 | 65 |
| Jerusha W., m. Alfred **KILBOURN,** b. of East Hartford, Nov. 29, 1838, by Samuel Spring | 1 | 127 |
| Jno (?), his w. [        ], d. [        ], 1804 | 1 | 64 |
| John, d. [        ], 1814 | 1 | 66 |
| John, his wid. [        ], bd. July 16, 1833, ae 80 | 1 | 76 |
| John, of Grafton, N. H., m. Elizabeth **OSBORNE,** of East Windsor, Dec. 13, 1846, by Moses Elmer, Jr., J. P. | 1 | 153 |
| Jonathan, m. [        ], Mar. 19, 1761 | 1 | 71 |
| Jonathan, [s. [Jonathan], b. Feb. 17, 1762 | 1 | 71 |
| Jos[eph], d. [        ], 1798 | 1 | 63 |
| Joseph, d. Mar. [ ], 1804, ae 79 | 1 | 64 |
| Joseph A., m. Mabel **ROBERTS,** Feb. 20, 1823, by Elisha Cushman | 1 | 101 |
| Julia, m. Francis **HANMER,** Nov. 24, 1825, by Joy H. Fairchild | 1 | 105 |
| Laura, m. Asa **ROSE,** Feb. 25, 1827, by Joy H. Fairchild | 1 | 107 |
| Lucretia, m. Dr. [        ] **COOLEY,** May 8, 1820 | 1 | 69 |
| Lucy L., of Hartford, m. Levi **WILLIAMS,** of East Hartford, Jan. 27, 1840, by Samuel Spring | 1 | 131 |
| Mabel, m. Joseph A. **ROBERTS,** Feb. 20, 1823, by Elisha Cushman | 1 | 101 |
| Maria, of East Hartford, m. James **RISLEY,** of Wethersfield, Nov. 22, 1836, by Rev. George May | 1 | 121 |
| Mariah C., d. May 18, 1850, ae 1 1/2 | 1 | 57 |
| Maria Francis, m. John **DICKIE,** b. of East Hartford, Sept. 18, 1834, by Samuel Spring | 1 | 117 |
| Martin, s. Ira T., farmer, ae 31 & Charlott C., ae 30, b. Nov. 4, 1847 | 1 | 47 |
| Mary, m. Peleg **CHAPMAN,** Apr. 1 1819 | 1 | 69 |
| Mary, m. Chauncy **HUNTER,** b. of Wethersfield, June 13, 1841, by Samuel Spring | 1 | 135 |
| Mary Ann, m. William **WOOD,** June 22, 1830, by Horace Hooker | 1 | 111 |

| ROBERTS, ROBARTS, (cont.), | Vol. | Page |
|---|---|---|
| Mary Ann, m. Horace WILLIAMS, b. of East Hartford, Mar. | | |
| 10, 1831, by Rev. Samuel Spring, of Hartford | 1 | 112 |
| Mary Jane, d. Hezekiah M., ae 64 & Mary, ae 22, b. Aug. 16, | | |
| 1848 | 1 | 50 |
| Osymn, m. Sarah D. HUBBARD, May 3, 1826, by Joy H. | | |
| Fairchild | 1 | 105 |
| Ozias, m. Nancy COMESTOCK, Mar. 26, 1823, by Joy H. | | |
| Fairchild | 1 | 101 |
| Ozias, his child bd. Dec. 20, 1834, ae 10 das. | 1 | 76 |
| Patty, w. Ozias, d. [           ], 1809, ae 21 | 1 | 66 |
| Ruth, [d. Jonathan], b. Apr. 23, 1766 | 1 | 71 |
| Ruth, m. Richard GOODWIN, Feb. 6, 1784, by Rev. Dr. | | |
| Williams | 1 | 61 |
| Ruth, m. Richard GOODWIN, [           ] | 1 | 43 |
| Samuel, m. Ame PRATT, Sept. 16, 1784, by Rev. Dr. Williams | 1 | 61 |
| Sarah M., m. Sidney HILLS, Apr. 13, 1836, by Samuel Spring | 1 | 120 |
| Sophia, m. Darius RISING, b. of East Hartford, Mar. 31, 1833, | | |
| by Rev. Samuel Spring | 1 | 114 |
| Stephen, m. Mary BURNHAM, Jan. 6, 1785, by Rev. Dr. | | |
| Williams | 1 | 61 |
| Stephen, m. Betsy GULLIVOR, Dec. 7, 1820, by Joy H. | | |
| Fairchild | 1 | 95 |
| Sylvester, m. Betsy BIDWELL, Dec. 12, 1819 | 1 | 69 |
| Thankful, m. Lemuel DEMING, Apr. 1, 1784, by Rev. Dr. | | |
| Williams | 1 | 61 |
| Timothy, m. Jemima ABEL, b. East Hartford, Oct. 31, 1832, by | | |
| Rev. Samuel Spring, of Hartford | 1 | 115 |
| W[illia]m, d. [           ], 1797, ae 50 | 1 | 63 |
| William, s. Ira T., farmer, ae 34, b. Dec. 4, 1851 | 1 | 58 |
| ROBERTSON, [see also RODERSON], -----, his child d. Nov. [ ], 1804 | 1 | 65 |
| ROBINSON, ROBENSON, Samuel P., of Canterbury, m. Hellen L. | | |
| GOODRICH, of East Hartford, Dec. 5, 1844, by | | |
| Samuel Spring | 1 | 148 |
| Samuel P., of Canterbury, m. Eleanor Lord GOODWIN, d. | | |
| Joseph, 2nd & Eleanor, [           ] | 1 | 44 |
| ROCKWELL, Alexander, of East Windsor, m. Lucy Stanley, of East | | |
| Hartford, May 22, 1834, by Samuel Spring | 1 | 117 |
| Henry W., m. Persis STRONG, b. of Hartford, Aug. 14, 1839, | | |
| by Samuel Spring | 1 | 129 |
| Roswell, m. Olive BURNHAM, Dec. 25, 1817 | 1 | 68 |
| -----, Capt., his child d. [           ], 1814 | 1 | 67 |
| RODERSON, [see also ROBERTSON], John, m. Eunice DEMING, | | |
| Mar. 21, 1802, by Mr. Yates | 1 | 67 |
| ROGERS, Hannah, m. Ezekiel KEEN, Nov. 18, 1802, by Rev. Ethan | | |
| Bromley | 1 | 36 |
| Laura, d. Independence W., engineer, b. Dec. 9, 1850 | 1 | 58 |
| Peter, m. Julia GAINES, May 1, 1822, by Joy H. Fairchild | 1 | 98 |
| Virginia Francis, d. Washington, carpenter & Laura, b. Sept. 3, | | |
| 1848, on a steamboat in the South | 1 | 50 |
| -----, wid. bd. May 25, 1836, ae 80 (by Elizabeth PITKIN) | 1 | 77 |
| RONALDSON, Arabella, m. Andrew TAIT, b. of East Hartford, June 14, | | |
| 1822, by Rev. Elisha Cook | 1 | 99 |

|                                                                          | Vol. | Page |
|--------------------------------------------------------------------------|------|------|
| ROSE, Abigail, m. Francis **HANMER**, Oct. 11, 1836, by S. L. Tracy     | 1    | 119  |
| Asa, m. Laura **ROBERTS**, Feb. 25, 1827, by Joy H. Fairchild           | 1    | 107  |
| Robert, of Norwich, m. Abigail **FORBES**, of East Hartford,            |      |      |
| Feb. 19, 1835, by Samuel Spring                                         | 1    | 118  |
| ROWELL, Lewis, of Hartford, m. Ruth **BURNHAM**, of East Hartford,      |      |      |
| Dec. 7, 1831, by Rev. G. F. Davis                                      | 1    | 113  |
| Lois, m. Joseph J. **BLISS**, b. of East Hartford, Aug. 13, 1834,       |      |      |
| by Samuel Spring                                                        | 1    | 116  |
| Lucy, of East Hartford, m. Jonathan **BOW**, of Litchfield, Jan. 1,     |      |      |
| 1822, by Joy H. Fairchild                                              | 1    | 97   |
| Paulina, m. Ira **BLISS**, Aug. 24, 1826, by Joy H. Fairchild           | 1    | 106  |
| Willard, m. Mary Ann **AMENEDON**, b. of East Hartford, Sept.           |      |      |
| 3, 1834, by Samuel Spring                                              | 1    | 116  |
| ——, his child bd. Dec. 21, 1834, ae 2 yrs.                             | 1    | 76   |
| RUDGE, Almira, of East Hartford, m. Almon **GALPIN**, of Washington,    |      |      |
| Dec. 20, 1840, by Samuel Spring                                        | 1    | 134  |
| Hannah, m. Uriah **KING**, b. of Hartford, June 13, 1841, by           |      |      |
| Samuel Spring                                                           | 1    | 135  |
| RUSSELL, Daniel, of Ellington, m. Phila **LANDFEAR**, of East Hartford, |      |      |
| Mar. 5, 1822, by Rev. Elisha B. Cook                                   | 1    | 98   |
| J. B. of Hartford, m. Susan C. **FORDED**, of East Hartford, Jan.       |      |      |
| 17, 1837, by Samuel Spring                                             | 1    | 122  |
| John, of Wethersfield, m. Elizabeth B. **CHALKER**, of East             |      |      |
| Hartford, Dec. 11, 1845, by Rev. W[illia]m Bentley                     | 1    | 150  |
| RUST, [see also **RIST**], Anne, m. Noah **RUST**, Feb. 14, 1788        | 1    | 27   |
| Anny, [d. Noah & Anne], b. Dec. 11, 1798                               | 1    | 27   |
| Betsy, [d. Noah & Anne], b. Dec. 3, 1789                               | 1    | 27   |
| Chauncy, [s. Noah & Anne], b. Dec. 17, 1791                            | 1    | 27   |
| Clarassa, [d. Noah & Anne], b. July 11, 1788                           | 1    | 27   |
| Fanny, [d. Noah & Anne], b. Feb. 20, 1801                              | 1    | 27   |
| Harriot, [d. Noah & Anne], b. June 11, 1794                            | 1    | 27   |
| Noah, m. Anne **RUST**, Feb. 14, 1788                                   | 1    | 27   |
| Noah, [s. Noah & Anne], b. Sept. 17, 1796                              | 1    | 27   |
| SAGE, Ann, m. Edwin **DEMING**, b. of East Hartford, Oct. 15, 1838, by  |      |      |
| Samuel Spring                                                           | 1    | 126  |
| Claray, d. [          ], 1807                                          | 1    | 66   |
| Elisha E., m. Olive **DEMMING**, b. of East Hartford, Sept. 7,          |      |      |
| 1841, by Samuel Spring                                                 | 1    | 136  |
| Elizabeth, m. Isaac **HILLS**, Mar. 28, 1819                            | 1    | 69   |
| Olive C., d. Elisha E., leather dealer, ae 30 & Olive, ae 29, b.        |      |      |
| Dec. 15, 1847                                                          | 1    | 47   |
| Russel, of Portland, m. Lucia **TALCOTT**, of Bolton, Sept. 8,          |      |      |
| 1850, by Rev. Benjamin C. Phelps                                      | 1    | 159  |
| SAMPSON, Salla, [d. Daniel & Elizabeth], b. Apr. 30, 1804               | 1    | 34   |
| SANBORN, Lucy, b. Lyman, N. H., res. East Hartford, d. Jan. 9, 1849,    |      |      |
| ae 24                                                                  | 1    | 53   |
| SAUNDERS, ——, Mr., d. [          ], 1802; bd. July 3, 1802             | 1    | 64   |
| SAVAGE, Ira, of Chatham, m. Desire **PERKINS**, of East Hartford, Oct. 7,|      |      |
| 1821, by Rev. Isaac Divinel                                            | 1    | 96   |
| SAWYER, Joseph, of Windham, m. Prudence **DEMING**, of East Hartford,   |      |      |
| Oct. 1, 1843, by Samuel Spring                                         | 1    | 143  |

| | Vol. | Page |
|---|---|---|

SAXTON, Asher, of Sheffield, m. Banolana WELLS, of East Hartford,
    June 26, 1822, by Rev. Elisha B. Cook    1    99
SCHLESINGER, Auguste D., of Naugatuck, m. Jerusha C. PITKIN, of
    East Hartford, Oct. 4, 1853, by Samuel Spring    1    165
SCHONLOAR, Frederick, m. Hohanna GLAMSER, b. of East Hartford,
    Oct. 31, 1852, by Rev. John F. Sheffield    1    163
SCHULTZ, Franzisku, m. Gustavus ARNOVINA, b. of Berlin, Prussia,
    July 13, 1851, by Samuel Spring    1    160
SCOTT, John B., m. Sophia ARNOLD, b. of East Hartford, July 16, 1849,
    by Rev. Benjamin C. Phelps    1    158
SCOVILLE, SCOVILL, Lemuel, of Hartford, m. Sarah HALL, of East
    Hartford, June 4, 1851, by Samuel Spring    1    160
    W[illia]m H., machinist, m. Sarah HALL, b. of East Hartford,
    Jan. 4, 1851, by S. Spring    1    59
SEAGRAVE, -----, his child bd. Jan. 11, 1833, ae 6 mos.    1    76
SEARL, Jesse, of South Hampton, Mass., m. Jane Ann STEDMAN, of
    Manchester, June 12, 1830, by B. F. Northrop    1    111
SEITZ, George, of Glastenbury, m. Francis BAIRTH, of Germany, May
    24, 1852, by Charles C. Ashley, J. P.    1    163
SELLEW, George C., of Brooklyn, N. Y., m. Sarah J. KEENY, of
    Hartford, Oct. 10, 1850, by S. Spring    1    59
    George C., of Brooklyn, N. Y., m. Sarah I. KEENEY, of
    Hartford, Oct. 10, 1850, by Samuel Spring    1    159
    Horace, of Glastenbury, m. Elisa Ann TREAT, of East
    Hartford, May 3, 1842, by Rev. James A. Smith, of
    Glastenbury    1    138
    Orrin, s. George & Dorothy, m. Susan ARNOLD, d. Elisha &
    Abigail, Oct. 19, 1830, by Asa Mead    1    70
    Orrin, m. Susan ARNOLD, Oct. 19, 1830, by Rev. Asa Mead    1    112
    Russell G., of Glastenbury, m. Mary E. MANNING, of East
    Hartford, May 3, 1849, by Samuel Spring    1    156
    -----, Mrs., m. Elisha RISLEY, Nov. 13, 1826, by Joy H.
    Fairchild    1    107
SESSIONS, Palmer, of Willimantic, m. Eunice BREWER, of East
    Hartford, May 8, 1847, by Samuel Spring    1    153
SEXTON, H. P., of New Haven, m. Cornelia PORTER, of East Hartford,
    June 5, 1843, by Rev. James A. Smith, of
    Glastenbury    1    142
    Noah C., m. Emily LOOMIS, Apr. 6, 1818    1    68
    Samuel, his w. [      ], d. [      ], 1800    1    63
SEYMOUR, SEYMORE, Catherine Merrill, [d. Daniel Merrill & Sarah
    Emeline], b. Nov. 12, 1833    1    39
    Daniel Merrill, m. Sarah Emeline PHELPS, Nov. 7, 1832    1    39
    Ellen Francis, [d. Daniel Merrill & Sarah Emeline], b. Apr. 20,
    1837    1    39
    Henry, m. Laura PORTER, Aug. 16, 1818    1    68
    Henry P., of Hartford, m. Julia A. JOHNSON, of East Hartford,
    July 5, 1845, by Samuel Spring    1    149
    Sally, m. John RISLEY, Nov. 25, 1818    1    69
SHARPER, -----, d. [      ], 1797    1    63
SHELDON, Lot, m. Ruth E. OLCOTT, b. of Hartford, Jan. 6, 1842, by
    Samuel Spring    1    138

| | Vol. | Page |
|---|---|---|
| **SHELDON**, (cont.), | | |
| W[illia]m, of Huntington, m. Francis **BUCKLAND**, of East | | |
| Hartford, Oct. 16, 1827, by Rev. Samuel Spring | 1 | 109 |
| **SHEPHERD**, Esther, d. Francis, stone cutter, ae 45, b. July 6, 1851 | 1 | 58 |
| Fanny, m. Chauncy **EASTON**, Aug. 20, 1819 | 1 | 69 |
| **SHOFFORD**, Mary Ann, m. Lyman **FILLAINE**, b. of Bolton, Sept. 6, | | |
| 1842, by Samuel Spring | 1 | 140 |
| **SIKES**, William H., of Sheffield, m. Sally **GOODALE**, of East Hartford, | | |
| Oct. 7, 1832, by Rev. Samuel H. Biddle | 1 | 113 |
| **SIMONDS, SYMONDS**, Abigail Jane, m. Norris **WINCHELL**, b. of East | | |
| Hartford, Jan. 5, 1842, by Rev. Cephas Brainard | 1 | 137 |
| Eliza, d. George, millwright, ae 31 & Mary G., ae 22, b. Aug. | | |
| 15, 1849 | 1 | 54 |
| Harriet, ae 26, m. Ages **EASTON**, farmer, ae 42, b. of East | | |
| Hartford, Sept. 21, 1848, by Rev. S. Spring | 1 | 52 |
| Harriet, m. Agis **EASTON**, b. of East Hartford, Sept. 21, 1848, | | |
| by Samuel Spring | 1 | 155 |
| Sarah H., d. Feb. 13, 1851, ae 19 | 1 | 60 |
| W[illia]m, d. [ ], 1801, ae 45 | 1 | 63 |
| **SISSON**, Benjamin, merchant, ae 35, b. Lebanon, res. East Hartford, m. | | |
| 2nd w. Sarah **LESTER**, ae 39, b. East Hartford, res. | | |
| same, Feb. 27, 1848, by Samuel Springs | 1 | 48 |
| Benjamin, m. Sarah **LESTER**, b. of East Hartford, Feb. 27, | | |
| 1848, by Samuel Spring | 1 | 154 |
| **SIZER**, Abel J., m. Hannah **TREAT**, Apr. 25, 1822, by Joy H. Fairchild | 1 | 98 |
| **SKINNER**, Caroline, m. Solomon **BIDWELL**, Aug. 5, 1818 | 1 | 68 |
| Clarissa F., of Durham, m. Henry D. **POLLY**, of Glastenbury, | | |
| Dec. 21, 1851, by Rev. Benjamin C. Phelps | 1 | 162 |
| Eli, [s. Eligah & Mabel], b. Feb. 8, 1797 | 1 | 32 |
| Eligah, m. Mabel **McKEE**, Apr. 12, 1795 | 1 | 32 |
| Horris, [s. Eligah & Mabel], b. Nov. 15, 1795 | 1 | 32 |
| Lucinda, [d. Eligah & Mabel], b. Oct. 1, 1800 | 1 | 32 |
| Mary, d. Jan. 2, 1848, ae 18 | 1 | 49 |
| Miranda, of East Hartford, m. Charles H. **BRADFORD**, of | | |
| Great Falls, N. H., Sept. 28, 1846, by Rev. H. B. | | |
| Soule, of Hartford | 1 | 152 |
| Percy, [s. Eligah & Mabel], b. July 30, 1798 | 1 | 32 |
| Rhoda, m. Timothy **CHEENY**, July 11, 1787, by B. Philps | 1 | 5 |
| **SLOANE, SLOAN**, Daniel, m. Pauline **KELLOGG**, Aug. 26, 1827, by | | |
| Joy H. Fairchild | 1 | 108 |
| George, of Tolland, m. Leonora **FORBES**, of East Hartford, | | |
| Oct. 27, 1846, by Samuel Spring | 1 | 152 |
| Lucy Ann, of Hartford, m. William **ANDROS**, of East Hartford, | | |
| Apr. 1, 1834, by Samuel Spring | 1 | 116 |
| **SMITH**, Abigail, d. Nathaniel & Elizabeth, b. [ ], 1779; m. Joseph | | |
| **GOODWIN**, 2nd, [ ]; d. Jan. 10, 1801, | | |
| ae 21 | 1 | 44 |
| Amelia, m. Edward **HAYDEN**, b. of East Hartford, May 20, | | |
| 1845, by Samuel Spring | 1 | 149 |
| Andrew, m. Mary Ann **ALVORD**, Nov. 28, 1827, by Rev. Joel | | |
| Hawes, of Hartford | 1 | 109 |
| Andrew, m. Juliette **GOODRICH**, b. of Glastenbury, Nov. 20, | | |
| 1842, by [ ] | 1 | 141 |

| SMITH, (cont.), | Vol. | Page |
|---|---|---|
| Anne, m. Ozias **WILLIAMS**, Sept. 18, 1797, by Rev. Dr. Williams | 1 | 62 |
| Augustus S., shoemaker, ae 23, b. East Hartford, res. same, m. Electa A. **SWAN**, ae 21, b. East Haddam, res. East Hartford, Apr. 12, 1848, by Nathaniel Miner | 1 | 48 |
| Charles, of Northfield, m. Catherine **WARREN**, of East Hartford, Jan. 1, 1837, by Samuel Spring | 1 | 122 |
| Charles, of Ellington, m. Cornelia C. **ARMSTRONG**, of East Hartford, May 15, 1850, at Colchester, by Rev. George W. Pendleton | 1 | 159 |
| David F., of Washington, m. Maria **JONES**, of East Hartford, [        ], by Rev. Chester W. Turner | 1 | 144 |
| Delia, d. Charles, pistol maker, ae 39 & Catharine, ae 39, b. Mar. 24, 1850 | 1 | 55 |
| E. E., had child s. b. Dec. [ ], 1848 | 1 | 53 |
| Electa, m. Edwin P. **HARRINGTON**, Nov. 11, 1824, by Joy H. Fairchild | 1 | 103 |
| Elizabeth, m. Ranson **RISLEY**, b. of Glastenbury, Dec. 12, 1852, by Rev. Benjamin C. Phelps | 1 | 163 |
| Elizur, of Glastenbury, m. Asenath **GAINES**, of East Hartford, Nov. 26, 1851, by Rev. B. C. Phelps | 1 | 161 |
| Ella L., d. Simeon, ae 48 & Laura, ae 42, b. Jan. 30, 1850 | 1 | 54 |
| Erra E., farmer, ae 27 & Mary, ae 24, had d. s.b. Dec. [ ], 1849 | 1 | 50 |
| Esther, m. James **BUTLER**, Feb. 22, 1796 | 1 | 12 |
| Estis H., of Sag Harbor, L. I., m. Charlotte **ARNOLD**, of East Hartford, May 13, 1840, by Samuel Spring | 1 | 132 |
| Ezra E., m. Mary E. **BRYANT**, b. of East Hartford, May 4, 1847, by Samuel Spring | 1 | 153 |
| Ezra Easton, s. Simeon & Sally (**HAWS**), b. Nov. 28, 1820, in Ashford, moved to East Hartford and entered the employ of his uncle W[illia]m **BIGELOW**. After uncle's death he carried on the business with his brother, W[illia]m B. He then entered the Fire Ins. business. Moved to Brookline, Mass.; d. Aug. 20, 1894 | 1 | 42a |
| George A., of Hartford, m. Jane **THURSTON**, of Hartford, Sept. 30, 1853, by Rev. John F. Sheffield | 1 | 165 |
| George W., of Suffield, m. Hannah **CASE**, of East Hartford, Jan. 26, 1841, by Samuel Spring | 1 | 134 |
| Hannah, 2nd w. Moses, d. [        ], 1799, ae 53 | 1 | 63 |
| Horace, of New York State, m. Clarissa G. **REYNOLDS**, of East Hartford, Aug. 10, 1841, by Samuel Spring | 1 | 135 |
| Horace M., painter, ae 24, b. New York, res. Brooklyn, m. Maria E. **GOODALE**, ae 19, b. East Hartford, res. East Hartford, July 28, 1851, by S. Spring | 1 | 59 |
| Horace M., of Brooklyn, N. Y., m. Maria E. **GOODALE**, of East Hartford, July 30, 1851, by Samuel Spring | 1 | 160 |
| J. Milton, of New York City, m. Electa **BREWER**, of East Hartford, Nov. 25, 1845, by Samuel Spring | 1 | 150 |
| Jedediah, of Glastenbury, m. Susan **ARNOLD**, of East Hartford, July 17, 1845, by Levi Daggett, Jr. | 1 | 149 |

| | Vol. | Page |
|---|---|---|
| **SMITH**, (cont.), | | |
| Jennett, m. Dudley **GILLET**, Sept. 26, 1826, by Joy H. | | |
| Fairchild | 1 | 107 |
| Jerusha, m. Eliphalet **HILLS**, Feb. 6, 1789 | 1 | 13 |
| Joseph P., s. Charles, farmer, ae 21, b. Mar. 12, 1848 | 1 | 51 |
| Julia, of East Haddam, m. Henry **WADSWORTH**, of East | | |
| Hartford, Jan. 2, 1845, by Rev. C. W. Turner | 1 | 146 |
| Mary Ann, of Granville, Mass., m. William H. **HILLS**, of | | |
| Hartford, May 15, 1838, by Samuel Spring | 1 | 126 |
| Moses, Dea., d. [ ], 1798, ae 67 | 1 | 63 |
| Moses, Dea., m. Hannah **GOODWIN**, [ ] | 1 | 43 |
| Reuben, his child d. Feb. 20, 1803 | 1 | 64 |
| Samuel, Capt., m. wid. Sarah **STANLEY**, Oct. 13, 1789, by | | |
| Rev. Dr. Williams | 1 | 61 |
| Samuel, Capt., d. [ ], 1800, ae 72 | 1 | 63 |
| Sarah, wid., m. Joseph **ARNOLD**, Dec. 30, 1784, by Rev. Dr. | | |
| Williams | 1 | 61 |
| Simeon, grandfather of Ezra E. **SMITH**, b. Nov. 10, 1794, was | | |
| Lieut. of Ashford Co., 1775 and Capt. of Bradley's | | |
| Battalion Wadsworth Brigade in Nov. 1776 | 1 | 42a |
| Sylvester, m. Henrietta **CADWELL**, Jan. 21, 1827, by Joy H. | | |
| Fairchild | 1 | 107 |
| W[illia]m, m. Elvira **FOX**, of Glastonbury, Feb. 16, 1820 | 1 | 69 |
| ----, Mrs., d. [ ], 1804 | 1 | 64 |
| ----, Mrs., d. [ ], 1805 | 1 | 65 |
| ----, Mrs., d. [ ], 1806 | 1 | 65 |
| **SOHALY**, Francisha, ae 20, m. Augustus **ARNERIUS**, gunsmith, ae 25, | | |
| b. Berlin, Pa., res. Hartford, July 13, 1851, by S. | | |
| Spring | 1 | 59 |
| **SPAFFORD**, Almira, of Coventry, m. Joel **FORBES**, of East Hartford, | | |
| Apr. 5, 1846, by Samuel Spring | 1 | 151 |
| Deantha D., m. Wells **FORBES**, b. of East Hartford, Dec. 21, | | |
| 1851, by Rev. Benjamin C. Phelps | 1 | 162 |
| George F., m. Emily **LATHROP**, b. of East Hartford, Sept. 22, | | |
| 1850, by Rev. Samuel I. Andrews, of East Windsor | 1 | 159 |
| Henry II., m. Harriet E. **FORBES**, Nov. 25, 1852, by Rev. John | | |
| F. Sheffield | 1 | 163 |
| **SPENCER**, Arnold L., m. Sophia **PITKIN**, July 4, 1826, by Joy H. | | |
| Fairchild | 1 | 105 |
| Caroline, of East Hartford, m. Henry **THOMPSON**, of | | |
| Rockville, Oct. 5, 1853, by Samuel Spring | 1 | 165 |
| Cornelia A., m. Martin O. **HILLS**, b. of East Hartford, Jan. 1, | | |
| 1845, by Samuel Spring | 1 | 147 |
| David G., m. Elizabeth **COMSTOCK**, b. of East Hartford, June | | |
| 29, 1842, by Samuel Spring | 1 | 139 |
| Delia C., of East Hartford, m. Edmund A. **BLISS**, of | | |
| Manchester, May 12, 1841, by Samuel Spring | 1 | 135 |
| Dorus Arnold, [d. Jared & Lucretia], b. June 6, 1789(?) | | |
| *(1799?) | 1 | 26 |
| Editha, [d. Jared & Lucretia], b. Nov. 4, 1794* *(1797?) | 1 | 26 |
| Emiline B., m. Russel W. **CADWELL**, June 7, 1831, by Rev. | | |
| Asa Mead | 1 | 112 |

| | Vol. | Page |
|---|---|---|
| **SPENCER**, (cont.), | | |
| Emiline R., d. Solomon & Phebe, m. Bissell W. **CADWELL**, s. | | |
| David & Caroline, of Hartford, June 7, 1831, by Asa | | |
| Mead | 1 | 70 |
| Francis, of Manchester, m. Eliza Ann **KEENY**, of East | | |
| Hartford, Feb. 22, 1844, by Samuel Spring | 1 | 144 |
| Frederick, his w. [ ], d. [July] [ ], 1827 | 1 | 168 |
| George, [s. George & Naomy], b. Dec. 25, 1797 | 1 | 18 |
| George, m. Naomy **BRAINERD**, [ ] | 1 | 18 |
| Hannah M., of East Hartford, m. Ralph H. **FOSTER**, of | | |
| Hartford, Oct. 16, 1839, by Samuel Spring | 1 | 130 |
| Jane, of East Hartford, m. Philander P. **TALCOTT**, of Vernon, | | |
| Nov. 26, 1846, by Samuel Spring | 1 | 153 |
| Jared, m. Lucretia **ARNOLD**, May 10, 1795 | 1 | 26 |
| Jared (?), his child d. [ ] | 1 | 64 |
| Jessy, his w. [ ], d. Feb. [ ], 1826 | 1 | 167 |
| Lucy, [d. George & Naomy], b. May 5, 1796 | 1 | 18 |
| Margrey, m. Daniel **MARSH**, July 4, 1798 | 1 | 20 |
| Margaret, wid., d. [ ], 1802 | 1 | 64 |
| Maria, of East Hartford, m. Joseph **LYMAN**, of Hartford, Oct. | | |
| 27, 1845, by Samuel Spring | 1 | 150 |
| Mary C., m. Henry W. **CUSHINGS**, b. of East Hartford, Jan. 1, | | |
| 1845, by Samuel Spring | 1 | 147 |
| Nelson, [s. George & Naomy], b. Dec. 24, 1795 | 1 | 18 |
| Olive, m. Robert **BEEBE**, b. of East Hartford, Nov. 27, 1828, | | |
| by Rev. Timothy Benedict | 1 | 110 |
| Orson, of Olmsted, O., m. Emiline **PORTER**, of East Hartford, | | |
| Oct. 5, 1831, by Rev. Gustavus F. Davis | 1 | 113 |
| Rufes, of Manchester, m. Charlotte **HILLS**, of East Hartford, | | |
| Sept. 8, 1825, by Enoch Brent | 1 | 104 |
| Sidney, of Springfield, Mass., m. Adeliza **EASTON**, of East | | |
| Hartford, Sept. 27, 1837, by Samuel Spring | 1 | 123 |
| Thomas, his w. [ ], d. June [ ], 1826 | 1 | 168 |
| William, of Hartford, m. Hannah W. **BRYANT**, of East | | |
| Hartford, Nov. 27, 1839, by Samuel Spring | 1 | 131 |
| William, of Hartford, m. Janette **BRYANT**, of East Hartford, | | |
| Sept. 6, 1842, by Samuel Spring | 1 | 139 |
| W[illia]m H., joiner, ae 27, b. Mass., res. same, m. Elizabeth | | |
| **DANIELS**, ae 17, b. Conn., Sept. 5, 1850, by D. | | |
| Bradbury | 1 | 59 |
| William H., of Warehouse Point, m. Elizabeth D. **DANIELS**, of | | |
| East Hartford, Sept. 5, 1850, by David Bradbury | 1 | 159 |
| -----, wid., d. Mar. [ ], 1804 | 1 | 64 |
| **SPERRY**, Elisha, of Hartford, m. Adeline **HURLBERT**, of East Hartford, | | |
| May 8, 1823, by Rev. Elisha B. Cook | 1 | 101 |
| **SPRAGUE**, Achsa, b. Andover, res. Coventry, d. Feb. 19, 1850, ae 49 | 1 | 57 |
| **SPRING**, Charles A., Jr., of Chicago, Ill., m. Ellen M. **SPRING**, of East | | |
| Hartford, Nov. 24, 1853, by Samuel Spring | 1 | 165 |
| Ellen M., of East Hartford, m. Charles A. **SPRING**, Jr., of | | |
| Chicago, Ill., Nov. 24, 1853, by Samuel Spring | 1 | 165 |
| **SPROUT**, Augusta, of East Hartford, m. Deodat **WOODBRIDGE**, of | | |
| Manchester, Jan. 1, 1852, by Samuel Spring | 1 | 161 |

|  | Vol. | Page |
|---|---|---|
| **STANLEY**, Ann, m. George **OLMSTED**, Apr. 29, 1824, by Joy H. | | |
| Fairchild | 1 | 102 |
| Catherine B., m. Walter **PITKIN**, b. of East Hartford, Nov. 5, | | |
| 1835, by Samuel Spring | 1 | 119 |
| Delia, m. William **TREAT**, Sept. 16, 1822, by Joy H. Fairchild | 1 | 99 |
| Emeline, m. Ashbel **OLMSTED**, b. of East Hartford, Nov. 12, | | |
| 1840, by Samuel Spring | 1 | 134 |
| Jerusha, m. Timothy **HILLS**, Aug. 13, 1789, by Rev. Dr. | | |
| Williams | 1 | 61 |
| Jon, Jr., his child d. Aug. 3, 1797 | 1 | 63 |
| Jos. S., s. Jon, d. May 6, 1799, ae 11 m. 2 d. | 1 | 63 |
| Lucy, of East Hartford, m. Alexander **ROCKWELL**, of East | | |
| Windsor, May 22, 1834, by Samuel Spring | 1 | 117 |
| Margaret, ae 20, b. Berlin, res. same, m. Edwin C. **HILLS**, | | |
| farmer, ae 31, b. East Hartford, res. same, Apr. 5, | | |
| 1848, by Charles S. Sherman | 1 | 48 |
| Sarah, wid., m. Capt. Samuel **SMITH**, Oct. 13, 1789, by Rev. | | |
| Dr. Williams | 1 | 61 |
| Sarah, m. Shuball **GRISWOLD**, Jan. 6, 1791, by Rev. Dr. | | |
| Williams | 1 | 61 |
| Sarah P., m. Giles **FORBES**, b. of East Hartford, Mar. 26, | | |
| 1839, by Samuel Spring | 1 | 127 |
| **STARKS, STARK**, Horace, m. Betsy **BIDWELL**, Apr. 2, 1828, by Rev. | | |
| Samuel Spring, of Hartford | 1 | 109 |
| -----, his w. [    ], d. June [    ], 1827 | 1 | 168 |
| **STARR**, Sarah A., d. George, spoon maker, ae 38 & Margaret, ae 42, b. | | |
| May 22, 1850 | 1 | 55 |
| **STEBBINS**, [see also **STUBENS**], Mary Ann, of Simsbury, m. Benton | | |
| **RISLEY**, of East Hartford, June 4, 1843, by Rev. B. | | |
| M. Walker | 1 | 143 |
| **STEDMAN, STEDMON**, Jane Ann, of Manchester, m. Jesse **SEARL**, of | | |
| South Hampton, Mass., June 12, 1830, by B. F. | | |
| Northrop | 1 | 111 |
| Joseph L., of Southampton, Mass., m. Maria **COTE**, of East | | |
| Hartford, Feb. 19, 1834, by Samuel Spring | 1 | 115 |
| Louisa J., of Manchester, m. David L. **BROWN**, of New | | |
| Marlboro, Mass., May 15, 1831, by Asa Mead | 1 | 70 |
| Louisa J., of Manchester, m. David L. **BROWN**, of New | | |
| Marlborough, Mass., May 15, 1831, by Rev. Asa | | |
| Mead | 1 | 112 |
| Philemon, m. Anne **CROSBY**, June 2, 1785, by Rev. Dr. | | |
| Williams | 1 | 61 |
| Ruben, d. Jan. [    ], 1826 | 1 | 167 |
| **STEELE, STEEL, STEELS**, A., had infant, d. July 31, 1851, ae 16 d. | 1 | 60 |
| Aaron, d. Feb. 15, 1802 | 1 | 64 |
| Allen, farmer, ae 45, had s. [    ], b. July 15, 1851 | 1 | 59 |
| Julia, d. Allen, farmer, ae 43 & Sarah, ae 36, b. Feb. 3, 1848 | 1 | 51 |
| Laura, ae 17, b. Conn., m. Newman **KING**, blacksmith, ae 24, | | |
| b. Enfield, res. same, Feb. 2, 1851, by D. Bradbury | 1 | 59 |
| Laura A., of East Hartford, m. Austin N. **KING**, of Enfield, Feb. | | |
| 2, 1851, by David Bradbury | 1 | 160 |
| -----, Miss, d. [      ], 1806 | 1 | 65 |

| | Vol. | Page |
|---|---|---|
| **STEELE, STEEL, STEELS**, (cont.), | | |
| ----, his child d. [ ], 1814 | 1 | 66 |
| ----, Mrs., d. [ ], 1814 | 1 | 67 |
| **STEVENS**, Abby, m. George L. **PHELPS**, b. of East Hartford, June 22, | | |
| 1845, by Samuel Spring | 1 | 149 |
| Cornelia H., m. Charles A. **ENSIGN**, b. of East Hartford, Nov. | | |
| 12, 1844, by Samuel Spring | 1 | 147 |
| Edwin, of Hartford, m. Mary **BREWER**, of East Hartford, Apr. | | |
| 8, 1840, by Samuel Spring | 1 | 132 |
| Edwin, s. Edwin, blacksmith, b. Oct. 23, 1850 | 1 | 57 |
| Orville H., of Waterbury, m. Harriet E. **ELTON**, of Hartford, | | |
| May 5, 1853, by Samuel Spring | 1 | 164 |
| Sarah Adeline, d. Edwin & Mary, b. Jan. 21, 1849 | 1 | 51 |
| **STEWART**, Allen, b. Mansfield, res. East Hartford, d. Sept. 12, 1849, | | |
| ae 73 | 1 | 56 |
| Catherine, Mrs., m. Warren **FITCH**, b. of Tolland, Sept. 26, | | |
| 1844, by Samuel Spring | 1 | 145-6 |
| Julia A., m. Alvin **PELTON**, June 12, 1827, by Joy H. | | |
| Fairchild | 1 | 108 |
| Louisa, of East Hartford, m. George **ROBERTS**, of Hartford, | | |
| Oct. 19, 1836, by Horace Hooker | 1 | 119 |
| Maria, of East Hartford, m. Samuel **WOLCOTT**, of East | | |
| Windsor, June 11, 1829, by Rev. Thomas Robbins | 1 | 110 |
| **STIMSON**, Enos, of Baltimore, Md., m. Mary A. F. **WARREN**, of East | | |
| Hartford, Nov. 7, 1853, by Samuel Spring | 1 | 165 |
| **STOCKBRIDGE**, Sarah, d. John, carpenter, b. Oct. 27, 1849 | 1 | 54 |
| **STONE**, George A., m. Caroline **FORBS**, b. of East Hartford, Apr. 28, | | |
| 1830, by Horace Hooker | 1 | 111 |
| Sherman T., of Durham, m. Ellen M. H. **HILLS**, of East | | |
| Hartford, Dec. 7, 1843, by Samuel Spring | 1 | 144 |
| **STOUGHTON**, Augustus, his w. [ ], bd., June 10, 1829, ae 43 | 1 | 75 |
| Augustus, bd. Feb. 23, 1838, ae 54 | 1 | 78 |
| Elizabeth, of East Hartford, m. Horace **ROBERTS**, of | | |
| Glastenbury, Mar. 8, 1846, by Samuel Spring | 1 | 151 |
| **STRATTON**, Asa, of Southwick, Mass., d. Nov. 18, 1835 | 1 | 77 |
| **STRONG**, Jerimiah W., of Bolton, m. Adeline **ROBERTS**, of East | | |
| Hartford, Sept. 28, 1841, by Rev. Cephas Brainard | 1 | 137 |
| Levi, Jr., m. Laura **NEWCOMB**, Nov. 10, 1818 | 1 | 68 |
| Persis, m. Henry W. **ROCKWELL**, b. of Hartford, Aug. 14, | | |
| 1839, by Samuel Spring | 1 | 129 |
| Phineas B., of Colchester, m. Sarah **WILLIAMS**, of East | | |
| Hartford, Oct. 25, 1853, by Samuel Spring | 1 | 165 |
| **STUBENS, STUBEN, STUBINS**, ----, his child d. Mar. 20, 1803 | 1 | 64 |
| ----, his child d. [ ], 1803 | 1 | 64 |
| **STUDLEY**, Alexander, of Boston, Mass., m. Francis **CUSHING**, of East | | |
| Hartford, May 11, 1846, by Samuel Spring | 1 | 151 |
| **SWAN**, Electa A., ae 21, b. East Haddam, res. East Hartford, m. Augustus | | |
| S. **SMITH**, shoemaker , ae 23, b. East Hartford, res. | | |
| same, Apr. 12, 1848, by Nathaniel Miner | 1 | 48 |
| **SWEETLAND, SWEATLAND**, Aaron, of Hebron, m. Mary | | |
| **OLMSTED**, of East Hartford, May 28, 1828, by | | |
| Sylvester Eaton | 1 | 110 |

| | Vol. | Page |
|---|---|---|
| SWEETLAND, SWEATLAND, (cont.), | | |
| Absenath, m. Josiah HOLISTER, Apr. 10, 1787 | 1 | 18 |
| Phebe, b. Oct. 8, 1745; m. John KEENY, [    ], 1761; d. Jan. | | |
| 11, 1817 | 1 | 31 |
| Sophia, m. Ward DANIELS, Feb. 13, 1823, by Isaac Devinel | 1 | 101 |
| TAFT, Pearly, b. Mar. 24, 1774, in Uxbridge, Mass., m. Cornelius | | |
| WELLS, July 11, 1799, in Uxbridge, Mass.; d. Apr. | | |
| 6, 1864 | 1 | 36 |
| TAIT, Andrew, m. Arabella RONALDSON, b. of East Hartford, June 14, | | |
| 1822, by Rev. Elisha B. Cook | 1 | 99 |
| TALCOTT, Hannah, m. Epaphras HILLS, Sept. 28, 1780 | 1 | 4 |
| Lucia, of Bolton, m. Russel SAGE, of Portland, Sept. 8, 1850, | | |
| by Rev. Benjamin C. Phelps | 1 | 159 |
| Lucius, m. Sally PORTER, May 24, 1825, by Joy H. Fairchild | 1 | 106 |
| Philander P., of Vernon, m. Jane SPENCER, of East Hartford, | | |
| Nov. 26, 1846, by Samuel Spring | 1 | 153 |
| Samuel, m. Hester REYNOLDS, Apr. 6, 1826, by Joy H. | | |
| Fairchild | 1 | 105 |
| TANDO, Sarah, of Wethersfield, m. Samuel HUMPHREY, of Hartford, | | |
| Apr. 9, 1848, by Samuel Spring | 1 | 154 |
| Sarah, of Wethersfield, m. Samuel HUMPHREY, of Hartford, | | |
| Apr. 29, 1848, by Samuel Spring | 1 | 48 |
| TARBOX, Betsey, m. John NEFF, Sept. 8, 1819 | 1 | 69 |
| TATTON, -----, laborer, colored, had child b. Aug. [ ], 1847 | 1 | 46 |
| TAYLOR, TAYLER, John, bd. May 23, 1832, ae 48 | 1 | 76 |
| Jonathan, of Warren, N. J., m. Martha WARD, of East Hartford, | | |
| Jan. 24, 1836, by Samuel Spring | 1 | 119 |
| Nelson C., of Glastenbury, m. Sarah JONES, of East Hartford, | | |
| Dec. 28, 1844, by Rev. C. W. turner | 1 | 146 |
| Norris W., of Glastenbury, m. Lucy Ann CAMP, of East | | |
| Hartford, May 19, 1844, by Rev. Warren G. Jones, | | |
| of So. Glastenbury | 1 | 145 |
| Olly (?), his child d. May [ ], 1798 | 1 | 63 |
| Stephen, m. Emely PORTER, b. of East Hartford, Sept. 10, | | |
| 1834, by Samuel Spring | 1 | 116 |
| Sybil, b. Glastenbury, res. East Hartford, d. Mar. 15, 1850, ae | | |
| 84 | 1 | 57 |
| W[illia]m, shoemaker, d. Dec. 25, 1850, ae 76 | 1 | 59 |
| THAYER, Lois, b. Manchester, res. same, m. Francis RISLEY, farmer, b. | | |
| East Hartford, res. same, Apr. 28, 1850, by S. Spring | 1 | 56 |
| Lois, of Manchester, m. Francis RISLEY, of East Hartford, Apr. | | |
| 28, 1850, by Samuel Spring | 1 | 158 |
| THOMPSON, Henry, of Rockville, m. Caroline SPENCER, of East | | |
| Hartford, Oct. 5, 1853, by Samuel Spring | 1 | 165 |
| John, of Farmington, m. Susan E. PITKIN, of East Hartford, | | |
| June 5, 1844, by Samuel Spring | 1 | 145 |
| Jonathan, m. Eunice FITCH, Apr. 24, 1789, by Rev. Dr. | | |
| Williams | 1 | 61 |
| THURSTON, Jane, m. George A. SMITH, b. of Hartford, Sept. 30, 1853, | | |
| by Rev. John F. Sheffield | 1 | 165 |
| TICHNOR, Samuel F., m. Esther, PORTER, May 4, 1835, by Samuel | | |
| Spring | 1 | 118 |
| TILLINGHAST, H. Elizabeth, d. Pardon H., bd. Nov. 19, 1839 | 1 | 78 |

|  | Vol. | Page |
|---|---|---|
| **TOBIAS**, Stephen R., of Attica, N. Y., m. Josephine R. **HILLS**, of East Hartford, Sept. 2, 1851, by Rev. B. C. Phelps | 1 | 161 |
| **TOWNSEND**, Samuel T., of Brooklyn, N. Y., m. Antoinette A. **OLMSTED**, of East Hartford, Apr. 20, 1852, by Samuel Spring | 1 | 162 |
| **TRAIN**, Samuel, m. Mary **QUINNEY**, Nov. 26, 1821, by Joy H. Fairchild | 1 | 97 |
| **TREAT, TREET**, Abby, of East Hartford, m. Joseph **RIST**, of Northbridge, Mass., Aug. 19, 1841, by Samuel Spring | 1 | 136 |
| Anna, d. July 10, 1849, ae 88 | 1 | 53 |
| Betsy, [d. Matthias & Tryphena], b. Nov. 18, 1781 | 1 | 24 |
| Betsy, of East Hartford, m. John L. **GOODALE**, of East Windsor, May 1, 1822, by Rev. Elisha B. Cook | 1 | 98 |
| Betsy, m. Timothy **FORBES**, Nov. [ ], 1886*, by Mr. Yates *(1806?) | 1 | 67 |
| Charlott A., ae 22, b. East Hartford, m. Henry **RISLEY**, silversmith, ae 22, b. Glastenbury, res. same, Dec. 30, 1849, by B. G. Phelps | 1 | 56 |
| Charlotte A., of East Hartford, m. Henry **RISLEY**, of Glastenbury, Dec. 30, 1849, by Rev. Benjamin C. Phelps | 1 | 158 |
| Chauncy, m. Harriet **PITKIN**, Nov. 12, 1817 | 1 | 68 |
| Chester, m. Esther **DRAKE**, Feb. 20, 1822, by Rev. Isaac Divinel | 1 | 98 |
| Claresy, [d. Matthias & Tryphena], b. Jan. 8, 1784 | 1 | 24 |
| Electa, m. Solomon **OLMSTED**, Dec. 17, 1817 | 1 | 68 |
| Elisha, m. Clarisa **BENTON**\*, b. of Glastonbury, Oct. 19, 1820, by Joy W. Fairchild *(In red ink, "d. of Joseph") | 1 | 94 |
| Elisa Ann, of East Hartford, m. Horace **SELLEW**, of Glastenbury, May 3, 1842, by Rev. James A. Smith, of Glastenbury | 1 | 138 |
| Franklin, s. Royal, farmer, b. Feb. 13, 1851 | 1 | 57 |
| Hannah, m. Abel J. **SIZER**, Apr. 25, 1822, by Joy H. Fairchild | 1 | 98 |
| Harry, [s. Matthias & Tryphena], b. May 8, 1798 | 1 | 24 |
| Henry, his w. [ ], d. [ ], 1826 | 1 | 168 |
| Henry, s. Julia Wells, b. Oct. 3, 1847 | 1 | 46 |
| Henry H., of Glastenbury, m. Hannah **FORBES**, of East Hartford, Mar. 19, 1845, by Samuel Spring | 1 | 148 |
| Jane K., m. Ellery **HILLS**, Nov. 10, 1825, by Joy H. Fairchild | 1 | 104 |
| Jemimee, m. Jonathan **WELLS**, Jr., Mar. 13, 1782 | 1 | 13 |
| Joseph, d. Nov. [ ], 1827 | 1 | 74 |
| Joseph E., m. Jane Ann **ROBERTS**, Nov. 3, 1825, by Joy H. Fairchild | 1 | 104 |
| Lyman, of East Hartford, m. Sarah **BILL**, of Glastenbury, Jan. 2, 1843, by Samuel Spring | 1 | 141 |
| Martha, d. Jan. 2, 1849, ae 85 | 1 | 53 |
| Mary, m. Oren **FORBES**, Nov. 15, 1821, by Joy H. Fairchild | 1 | 97 |
| Mary, m. Ralph **PITKIN**, Sept. 11, 1822, by Elisha Cushman | 1 | 99 |
| Matthias, m. Tryphena **RISLEY**, Dec. 20, 1778 | 1 | 24 |
| Matthias, [s. Matthias & Tryphena], b. July 28, 1789 | 1 | 24 |
| Matthias, d. July [ ], 1827, ae 75 | 1 | 74 |

| | Vol. | Page |
|---|---|---|
| **TREET, TREAT,** (cont.), | | |
| Matthias, m. Mrs. Sarah **WILLIAMS**, b. of East Hartford, June 11, 1840, by Rev. Lozien Peirce | 1 | 133 |
| Nancy, d. Aug. 25, 1831 | 1 | 74 |
| Olive, [d. Matthias & Tryphena], b. Oct. 29, 1786 | 1 | 24 |
| Olliver, [s. Matthias & Tryphena], b. May 1, 1795 | 1 | 24 |
| Pamelia, m. Lester **DOWDS**, Feb. 9, 1823, by Joy H. Fairchild | 1 | 101 |
| Richard, d. Nov. 4, 1823 | 1 | 74 |
| Royal, m. Hepzibah **PORTER**, b. of East Hartford, Apr. 23, 1834, by Samuel Spring | 1 | 116 |
| Sally, m. Joseph **ERWIN**, b. of East Hartford, Nov. 5, 1843, by Rev. C. W. Turner | 1 | 144 |
| Salmon, shoemaker, d. Mar. 19, 1848, ae 49 | 1 | 49 |
| Samantha, m. Chauncy **BREWER**, Feb. 10, 1825, by Joy H. Fairchild | 1 | 103 |
| Solomon, m. Emeline **RISLEY**, b. of East Hartford, Nov. 22, 1827, by Rev. William Lockwood | 1 | 109 |
| Sylvester, [s. Matthias & Tryphena], b. Sept. 8, 1792 | 1 | 24 |
| Sylvester, m. Emily **BROWN**, May 9, 1822, by Joy H. Fairchild | 1 | 98 |
| Theodore, m. Mary **WILLIAMS**, [      ], by Rev. Dr. Williams | 1 | 61 |
| Tryphena, [d. Matthias & Tryphena], b. Apr. 11, 1799 | 1 | 24 |
| Tryphenia, d. Apr. 5, 1822 | 1 | 74 |
| William, m. Delia **STANLEY**, Sept. 16, 1822, by Joy H. Fairchild | 1 | 99 |
| ----, wid., d. [      ], 1797 | 1 | 63 |
| ----, Mr., d. [      ], 1802 | 1 | 64 |
| ----, his child d. Sept. [  ], 1804 | 1 | 64 |
| ----, Mr., d. [      ], 1806 | 1 | 65 |
| ----, Mrs., d. [      ], 1814 | 1 | 67 |
| **TRENT,** Henry, d. Jan. 2, 1849, ae 6 d. | 1 | 53 |
| Martha, b. Wethersfield, res. East Hartford, d. Jan. 2, 1849, ae 85 | 1 | 53 |
| **TRICE,** John, laborer, had d. [      ], b. Feb. [  ], 1851 | 1 | 58 |
| **TRILL,** Rachel, wid., d. Aug. 31, 1801, ae 87 y. [      ] | 1 | 63 |
| **TRUMBULL,** Asaph, m. Harriet **WILLIAMS**, July 7, 1818 | 1 | 68 |
| **TRYON,** Anson, of Glastenbury, m. Delia O. **ROBERTS**, of East Hartford, Aug. 2, 1843, by Samuel Spring | 1 | 143 |
| Mary A., d. June 2, 1850, ae 20 | 1 | 57 |
| **TUCKER,** C. A., farmer, ae 20, b. Maine, res. Buckfield, Mass., m. M. E. **FRANKLIN**, b. East Hartford, res. same, Aug. 29, 1849, by Rev. S. Spring | 1 | 55 |
| Charles A., of Maine, m. Mary **FRANKLIN**, of East Hartford, Aug. 28, 1849, by Samuel Spring | 1 | 157 |
| **ULMSTED,** [see under **OLMSTED**] | | |
| **USHER,** Wheaton, of Rockville, m. Mary **RISLEY**, of Manchester, Sept. 4, 1853, by Rev. Benjamin C. Phelps | 1 | 166 |
| **VANSANT,** Mary, m. Matthew **CADWELL**, May [  ], 1761 | 1 | 17 |
| **VARRA,** Mary A., m. Seth R. **RISLEY**, of Manchester, Nov. 3, 1842, by Rev. Cephas Brainard | 1 | 141 |
| **VESTERLY,** David, b. Aug. 14, 1785 | 1 | 21 |

|  | Vol. | Page |
|---|---|---|
| VIBBERT, VIBERT, Allen, [s. Jesse & Martha], b. Jan. 26, 1801 | 1 | 26 |
| Andrew, m. Cynthia BREWER, b. of East Hartford, Oct. 25, 1846, by Samuel Spring | 1 | 152 |
| Betsy, m. Edward OLMSTED, Dec. 2, 1819 | 1 | 69 |
| Clarasa, [d. Jesse & Martha], b. Oct. 24, 1785 | 1 | 26 |
| Cynthia A., d. Andrew, farmer & Cynthia, b. Dec. 7, 1849 | 1 | 54 |
| Cyrus, m. Mary A. GAINES, b. of East Hartford, May 11, 1847, by Samuel Spring | 1 | 153 |
| Delia, m. Wooster ALEXANDER, Apr. 12, 1837, by Samuel Spring | 1 | 122 |
| Eligah, m. Jerusha JONES, [     ], 1796 | 1 | 31 |
| Eligah, m. 2nd w. Caty ABBY, [     ] | 1 | 31 |
| Eliphelet, [s. Jesse & Martha], b. Sept. 16, 1789 | 1 | 26 |
| Eliza E., d. Oliver, farmer, b. May 4, 1851 | 1 | 58 |
| Elizabeth, m. Diodate B. LYMAN, b. of Manchester, Apr. 19, 1831, by B. F. Northrop | 1 | 112 |
| Fanny, [d. Eligah & Caty], b. Dec. 23, 1800 | 1 | 31 |
| George A., s. Andrew, farmer, ae 32 & Cynthia, ae 30, b. July 30, 1848 | 1 | 46 |
| James, his w. [     ], d. May 19, 1806, ae 86 | 1 | 65 |
| James, d. Nov. 12, 1806, ae 98 | 1 | 65 |
| James M., m. Mary KENNEDY, Nov. 25, 1847, by Samuel Spring | 1 | 154 |
| Jerusha, [w. Eligah], d. [     ], 1790 | 1 | 31 |
| Jerusha, [d. Eligah & Caty], b. Oct. 2, 1799 | 1 | 31 |
| Jesse, b. Jan. 30, 1759; m. Martha ABBEY, Aug. 7, 1783 | 1 | 26 |
| Jesse, [s. Jesse & Martha], b. Mar. 3, 1784 | 1 | 26 |
| John, m. Hannah JONES, Nov. 21, 1819 | 1 | 69 |
| John, m. Emely BREWER, Nov. 29, 1820, by Joy H. Fairchild | 1 | 95 |
| John, m. Louisa BARNARD, b. of East Hartford, May 11, 1846, by Samuel Spring | 1 | 151 |
| Levi L., m. Lucy FORBES, b. of East Hartford, May 10, 1840, by Samuel Spring | 1 | 132 |
| Maria Mary, d. Cyrus, farmer & Mary, b. Aug. 23, 1849 | 1 | 50 |
| Mary, [d. Jesse & Martha], b. May 5, 1797 | 1 | 26 |
| Mary, of East Hartford, m. Charles M. CHANDLER, of Franklin, N. H., Oct. 4, 1837, by Samuel Spring | 1 | 124 |
| Monroe, stage driver, ae 24, b. East Hartford, res. Bristol, m. Mary KENNEDY, ae 24, b. East Hartford, res. same, Nov. [ ], 1847, by Samuel Spring | 1 | 48 |
| Nancy, m. George S. KENNEDY, b. of East Hartford, May 5, 1828, by Enoch Brent | 1 | 110 |
| Ollive, [d. Jesse & Martha], b. Oct. 27, 1787 | 1 | 26 |
| Oliver, m. Nancy E. LOOMIS, b. of East Hartford, Apr. 25, 1841, by Samuel Spring | 1 | 135 |
| Patte, [d. Jesse & Martha], b. Sept. 28, 1791 | 1 | 26 |
| Phene, [d. Jesse & Martha], b. Aug. 26, 1793 | 1 | 26 |
| Russel, d. [     ], 1826 | 1 | 168 |
| Stephen, [s. Jesse & Martha], b. Sept. 20, 1795; d. July 30, 1796 | 1 | 26 |
| Thomas, d. Mar. [ ], 1826 | 1 | 167 |
| -----, Mrs., d. [     ], 1813 | 1 | 67 |
| -----, wid., d. May [ ], 1826 | 1 | 168 |

|                                                                                           | Vol. | Page |
|-------------------------------------------------------------------------------------------|------|------|
| **VORRA**, Erastus, m. Sally **REYNOLDS**, Nov. 24, 1825, by Joy H. Fairchild             | 1    | 105  |
| **WADSWORTH**, Abner, bd. Feb. 1, 1829, ae 38                                             | 1    | 75   |
| Albina, of East Hartford, m. D. W. **DORMAN**, of Trenton, N. J., Dec. 29, 1851, by Rev. Benjamin C. Phelps | 1 | 162 |
| Allen, m. Jerusha **BIDWELL**, b. of East Hartford, July 11, 1820, by Joy H. Fairchild    | 1    | 94   |
| Charles W., [s. Samuel & Hannah], b. Oct. 12, 1821                                        | 1    | 38   |
| Elizabeth, [d. Samuel & Hannah], b. Oct. 29, 1807                                         | 1    | 38   |
| Emeline, [d. Samuel & Hannah], b. May 10, 1810                                            | 1    | 38   |
| George, d. [      ], 1806                                                                 | 1    | 65   |
| Henry, of East Hartford, m. Julia **SMITH**, of East Haddam, Jan. 2, 1845, by Rev. C. W. Turner | 1 | 146 |
| Hezekiah, m. Maria F. **JONES**, Jan. 7, 1819                                             | 1    | 69   |
| Hezekiah, m. Heppy **FORBES**, b. of East Hartford, Apr. 9, 1837, by Samuel Spring        | 1    | 122  |
| Jane, m. Risley **MARTIN**, b. of East Hartford, [      ], 1848, by Rev. S. Spring        | 1    | 52   |
| Maria, ae 26, m. John **KELLOG**, seafaring, ae 30, b. of East Hartford, Sept. 28, 1849, by Rev. R. Turnbull | 1 | 52 |
| Mary, of East Hartford, m. Ezra E. **GILLETT**, of Colchester, Mar. 7, 1847, by Levi Daggett, Jr. | 1 | 153 |
| Mira (?), m. Daniel **BIRGE**, Nov. 5, 1801, by Rev. Dr. Williams                         | 1    | 62   |
| Norman, of East Hartford, m. Sarah B. **WILLIAMS**, of Glastenbury, Apr. 20, 1846, by Samuel Spring | 1 | 151 |
| Olive, [d. Samuel & Hannah], b. Aug. 12, 1815                                             | 1    | 38   |
| Samuel, d. Jan. [ ], 1798, ae 52                                                          | 1    | 63   |
| Samuel, m. Hannah **ROBERTS**, Dec. 12, 1805                                              | 1    | 38   |
| Stanley, [s. Samuel & Hannah], b. Feb. 26, 1813                                           | 1    | 38   |
| ----, Mrs. d. Oct. [ ], 1804                                                              | 1    | 64   |
| ----, Mr., d. [      ], 1805, at Sea                                                      | 1    | 65   |
| ----, Mr., d. [      ], 1806, at Sea                                                      | 1    | 65   |
| **WAKEFIELD**, Amos, [s. Daniel & Anne], b. Mar. 30, 1795                                 | 1    | 33   |
| Daniel, m. Anne **KEENY**, Sept. 4, 1792                                                  | 1    | 33   |
| Fanny, [d. Daniel & Anne], b. Feb. 25, 1793                                               | 1    | 33   |
| Laura, [d. Daniel & Anne], b. Apr. 7, 1798                                                | 1    | 33   |
| **WALES**, Thomas H., m. Mary Ann **GOULD**, b. of East Hartford, Sept. 24, 1834, by Samuel Spring | 1 | 118 |
| **WALKER**, Edward N., s. Jason, spoon maker, b. Dec. 18, 1850                            | 1    | 58   |
| Jason M., d. Oct. 7, 1850, ae 2                                                           | 1    | 60   |
| **WALLACE, WALLIS**, Ann Pane, m. Osmon **CASE**, Aug. 21, 1842, by Cephas Brainard       | 1    | 139  |
| Elizabeth, d. Mar. 24, 1823, ae 95                                                        | 1    | 73   |
| W[illia]m, d. Mar. 26, 1823                                                               | 1    | 74   |
| William, his w. [ ], d. [      ], 1826                                                    | 1    | 168  |
| William, m. Delia **RISLEY**, b. of East Hartford, Apr. 8, 1830, by Rev. Leonard B. Griffing | 1 | 111 |
| W[illia]m, paper maker, b. Ireland, res. East Hartford, d. Jan. 1, 1849, ae 58           | 1    | 58   |
| **WALTZ**, ----, of Hartford, m. Julia **PECK**, of East Hartford, Oct. 18, 1852, by Samuel Spring | 1 | 163 |

| | Vol. | Page |
|---|---|---|

WARD, Martha, of East Hartford, m. Jonathan TAYLOR, of Warren,

    N. J., Jan. 24, 1836, by Samuel Spring — 1 — 119

Thomas, b. Ireland, res. East Hartford, d. Feb. 10, 1850, ae 30 — 1 — 57

W[illia]m, b. Ireland, res. East Hartford, d. Mar. 10, 1850, ae 34 — 1 — 57

WARNER, Harriet, m. Oliver J. ELLS, Oct. 25, 1818 — 1 — 68

James, m. Roselle BREWER, b. of East Hartford, Aug. 15,

    1852, by B. C. Phelps — 1 — 162

Mary, m. Ira ANDERSON, Oct. 20, 1819 — 1 — 69

WARREN, Aaron, m. Delia FOX, Dec. 16, 1824, by Joy H. Fairchild — 1 — 103

Adeline, of East Hartford, m. Ira BINGHAM, of Whiting, O.,

    Oct. 14, 1833, by Samuel Spring — 1 — 144

Anna, m. George HILLS, Mar. 9, 1794 — 1 — 15

Anne, m. George HILLS, Mar. 9, 1794, by Rev. Dr. Williams — 1 — 62

Catherine, of East Hartford, m. Charles SMITH, of Northfield,

    Jan. 1, 1837, by Samuel Spring — 1 — 122

Caty, w. Samuel, d. [    ], 1806, ae 32 — 1 — 65

Daniel, d. [    ], 1800, ae 58 — 1 — 63

David, bd. June 7, 1841, ae 40 — 1 — 79

Elisha, m. Lucretia BREWER, Dec. 28, 1786, by Rev. Dr.

    Williams — 1 — 61

Eunice, m. John COTTON, Apr. 4, 1790, by Rev. Dr. Williams — 1 — 61

Harriet F., m. Watson L. HAYES, b. of East Hartford, Apr. 27,

    1843, by Samuel Spring — 1 — 142

Jas., his child d. [    ], 1802 — 1 — 64

John N., of Glastenbury, m. Sophia CLARK, of East Hartford,

    Sept. 21, 1834, by Samuel Spring — 1 — 118

Margaret, m. James COLVIN, Feb. 4, 1824, by Joy H.

    Fairchild — 1 — 102

Mary A., m. Seth RISLEY, b. of East Hartford, Sept. 25, 1839,

    by Samuel Spring — 1 — 130

Mary A. F., of East Hartford, m. Enos STIMSON, of Baltimore,

    Md., Nov. 7, 1853, by Samuel Spring — 1 — 165

Mary E., d. Rufus, joiner, b. Sept. 13, 1847 — 1 — 46

Nathaniel, m. Sally BIDWELL, Aug. 24, 1820, by Joy H.

    Fairchild — 1 — 94

Penelope, d. July 9, 1851, ae 92 — 1 — 60

Ruth, m. Russell RISLEY, b. of East Hartford, Nov. 4, 1829,

    by Herman Perry — 1 — 111

Solomon, m. Kate KENNEDY, Oct. 12, 1794, by Rev. Dr.

    Williams — 1 — 62

Susan M., of East Hartford, m. James L. LEE, of Lebanon, May

    12, 1846, by Levi Daggett, Jr. — 1 — 151

Susannah, w. Dr. [    ]. D. May 8, 1798 — 1 — 63

W[illia]m, d. July 18, 1806 — 1 — 65

WATERHOUSE, A. A., his child bd. Sept. 28, [1827], ae 10 d. — 1 — 75

Abraham, m. Hester GOODWIN, Apr. 9, 1822, by Joy H.

    Fairchild — 1 — 98

WATERMAN, Jabez, m. Almira ARNOLD, Nov. 28, 1822, by Joy H.

    Fairchild — 1 — 100

William, m. Mary ARNOLD, Dec. 22, 1825, by Joy H.

    Fairchild — 1 — 105

| | Vol. | Page |
|---|---|---|
| **WATERMAN**, (cont.), | | |
| W[illia]m, carpenter, b. Glastonbury, res. Same, d. Dec. 12, | | |
| 49, ae 47 | 1 | 56 |
| **WAY**, Calvin, joiner, ae 34, b. Lyme, res. East Hartford, m. Mary A. | | |
| **GEHNAN**, ae 23, Nov. 13, 1848, by Rev. S. Spring | 1 | 52 |
| Calvin A., m. Mary A. **GILMAN**, b. o f East Hartford, Nov. 13, | | |
| 1848, by Samuel Spring | 1 | 155 |
| Emma, d. Calvin, joiner, ae 34 & Mary A., ae 23, b. Dec. 20, | | |
| 1849 | 1 | 54 |
| **WEBSTER**, Dudley, his sister, bd. May [ ], 1835 | 1 | 77 |
| Eldad, of Casenovia, N. Y., m. Mary **BIDWELL**, of East | | |
| Hartford, Oct. 28, 1832, by Rev. Samuel Spring, of | | |
| Hartford | 1 | 115 |
| Hubbard, of Columbia, m. Esther R. **HOLLISTER**, of East | | |
| Hartford, Mar. 12, 1846, by Samuel Spring | 1 | 151 |
| Mary, d. Charles F., sadler, ae 28, b. June 18, 1851 | 1 | 57 |
| Susannah, m. John **COUCH**, Jan. 25, 1774 | TR2 | 1 |
| Susanna, m. John **COUCH**, Jan. 25, 1774 | 1 | 71 |
| **WELDON**, Mary, of Glastenbury, m. Hezikiah M. **ROBERTS**, of East | | |
| Hartford, [ ], by E. Edwin Hall | 1 | 145 |
| **WELLES, WELLS**, Angeline, of Wethersfield, m. Erastus **CLEAVES**, of | | |
| Glastenbury, Feb. 8, 1852, by Benjamin C. Phelps | 1 | 162 |
| Anna, [d. Jonathan & Esther], b. May 9, 1761 | 1 | 17 |
| Anna W., d. Asa & Evelin, res. Glastonbury, b. Sept. 26, 1849 | 1 | 54 |
| Asa, of New Haven, m. Eveline J. **HILLS**, of East Hartford, | | |
| June 8, 1846, by Samuel Spring | 1 | 152 |
| Banolana, of East Hartford, m. Asher **SAXTON**, of Sheffield, | | |
| Mass., June 26, 1822, by Rev. Elisha B. Cook | 1 | 99 |
| Betsey, [d. Jonathan, Jr. & Jemimee], b. July 5, 1791 | 1 | 13 |
| Chauncy, of East Hartford, m. Charity **PEASE**, of Enfield, Jan. | | |
| 6, 1804, by Samuel Spring | 1 | 131 |
| Chester, [s. Jonathan, Jr. & Jemimee], b. Mar. 5, 1786 | 1 | 13 |
| Cornelius, b. Sept. 9, 1772, in Brattleborough; m. Pearly **TAFT**, | | |
| July 11, 1799, in Uxbridge, Mass.; d. Feb. 23, 1852 | 1 | 36 |
| David, [s. Jonathan & Esther], b. Oct. 7, 1763; d. Oct. 20, 1799 | 1 | 17 |
| David, d. [ ], 1799, ae 36 | 1 | 63 |
| David, m. Tirzah **HALL**, Apr. 25, 1827, by J. H. Fairchild | 1 | 108 |
| Esther, [d. Jonathan & Esther], b. Mar. 21, 1759 | 1 | 17 |
| Esther, w. Jonathan, d. Feb. 9, 1795 | 1 | 17 |
| Esther, [d. Jonathan, Jr. & Jemimee], b. Jan. 22, 1797 | 1 | 13 |
| Esther, m. Daniel **MARSH**, Apr. 3, 1817 | 1 | 68 |
| Esther Elizabeth, of East Hartford, m. John **KENNEDY**, of | | |
| Olmsted, O., [ ], by Horace Hooker | 1 | 115 |
| George, [s. Jonathan & Esther], b. Oct. 30, 1765 | 1 | 17 |
| George, m. Nancy **DOANE**, Oct. 17, 1821, by Joy H. Fairchild | 1 | 96 |
| Hannah, w. Joseph, d. [ ], 1809, ae 61 | 1 | 66 |
| Hannah Stout, [d. Cornelius & Pearly], b. June 22, 1810; d. Apr. | | |
| 14, 1864 | 1 | 36 |
| Harriet M., d. Oliver, m. James **HILLS**, Jr., June 10, 1841, by | | |
| [ ] | 1 | 138 |
| Hart, [s. Jonathan, Jr. & Jemimee], b. June 5, 1782 | 1 | 13 |
| Henry Watson, [s. Cornelius & Pearly], b. Oct. 6, 1808; d. Apr. | | |
| 13, 1846 | 1 | 36 |

| | Vol. | Page |
|---|---|---|
| WHITON, Mary, b. Feb. 10, 1807, at Ashford, Conn.; m. Sylvester G. | | |
| FARNHAM, Mar. 1, 1827, at Ashford, Conn. | 1 | 39 |
| WICHE, [see under WYCHE] | | |
| WICKHAM, James E., of Hartford, m. Mary Jane LOOMIS, of East | | |
| Hartford, May 17, 1852, by Samuel Spring | 1 | 162 |
| WICKS, Benjamin, m. Abby ROBERTS, Oct. 21, 1795, by Rev. Dr. | | |
| Williams | 1 | 62 |
| WILBER, William R., m. Wealthy DEMING, b. of Hartford, May 29, | | |
| 1836, by Samuel Spring | 1 | 121 |
| WILCOX, Jane, of East Hartford, m. Charles GRIMMANS, of | | |
| Philadelphia, Pa., Oct. 2, 1839, by Samuel Spring | 1 | 130 |
| Thurston, farmer, ae 50, b. Suffield, res. Same, m. Francis | | |
| WILLIAMS, ae 40, b. East Hartford, res. same, | | |
| May 28, 1848, by Daniel Pitkin | 1 | 48 |
| Thurston, of Suffield, m. Francis WILLIAMS, of East Hartford, | | |
| May 28, 1848, by Daniel Pitkin, Jr., J. P. | 1 | 155 |
| W[illia]m, shipmaster, ae 24, m. Mary HILLS, ae 24, b. of East | | |
| Hartford, Jan. 11, 1849, by Rev. S. Spring | 1 | 52 |
| William, m. Mary HILLS, b. of East Hartford, Jan. 11, 1849, | | |
| by Samuel Spring | 1 | 155 |
| W[illia]m, Capt., ship master, b. Stonington, res. East Hartford, | | |
| d. Nov. 6, 1849, ae 47 | 1 | 53 |
| William G., s. William, sailor, b. Nov. 3, 1849 | 1 | 54 |
| WILDMAN, [see also WILEMAN], Ep[ ], his w. [ ], bd. Mar. | | |
| 1, 1835, ae 22 | 1 | 77 |
| Russell, his child bd. Oct. 5, 1832, ae 5 | 1 | 76 |
| Russell, his w. [ ], bd. July 26, 1837, ae 36 | 1 | 78 |
| WILEMAN, [see also WILDMAN], Arthur Timothy, b. July 2, 1826 | 1 | 39 |
| Betsy, b. Aug. 18, 1824 | 1 | 39 |
| WILEY, George T., of Hartford, m. Phebe L. HILLS, of East Hartford, | | |
| Apr. 9, 1846, by Samuel Spring | 1 | 151 |
| WILKINSON, Benjamin, his w. [ ], bd. June 9, 1843, ae 26 | 1 | 79 |
| Nedabiah, d. Aug. 1, 1802, ae 56 | 1 | 64 |
| Otis, d. [ ], 1806, ae 27 | 1 | 65 |
| ----, Mrs., d. [ ], 1814 | 1 | 66 |
| WILLIAMS, Aaron, his mother, bd. June 9, 1832, ae 86 | 1 | 76 |
| Aaron G., of East Windsor, m. Cornelia L. BURNHAM, of East | | |
| Hartford, Feb. 26, 1840, by Samuel Spring | 1 | 132 |
| Aaron G., bd. Dec. 12, 1841, ae 83 | 1 | 79 |
| Abiel, d. Feb. 24, 1831, ae 48 | 1 | 74 |
| Abigail, [d. Rev. Aliphalet & Sarah], b. July 30, 1783; | | |
| d. [ ], 1867 | 1 | 9 |
| Abigail, d. May 25(?), 1806, ae 69 | 1 | 65 |
| Abigail, d. [ ], 1806 | 1 | 65 |
| Abraham, d. Sept. 3, 1807 | 1 | 73 |
| Abraham, s. David & Rachael, of East Hartford, m. Sarah L. | | |
| BURNHAM, d. Zenas, Jr. & Sarah, of East | | |
| Windsor, Apr. 7, 1831, by Asa Mead | 1 | 70 |
| Ann P., of East Hartford, m. Warren BIDWELL, of | | |
| Manchester, Sept. 9, 1841, by Rev. B. M. Walker | 1 | 136 |
| Anne, [d. Rev. Aliphalet & Mary], b. Sept. 16, 1759; d. Sept. 2, | | |
| 1810 | 1 | 9 |

| WILLIAMS, (cont.), | Vol. | Page |
|---|---|---|
| Bathsheba, m. Shuball **DRAKE**, Dec. 8, 1785, by Rev. Dr. | | |
| Williams | 1 | 61 |
| Charity, d. Dec. 17, 1823, ae 40 | 1 | 73 |
| Charlotte A., m. Edwin **FORBES**, b. of East Hartford, Mar. 8, | | |
| 1843, by Samuel Spring | 1 | 142 |
| Cornelia J., of East Hartford, m. Henry **BIDWELL**, of | | |
| Manchester, Apr. 17, 1850, by Samuel Spring | 1 | 158 |
| Daniel, d. [ ], 1811 | 1 | 73 |
| David, his child d. Mar. 24, 1806, ae 6 | 1 | 65 |
| Edmund, of Lee, Mass., m. Susan A. **LARABEE**, of East | | |
| Hartford, Oct. 1, 1854, by Rev. Benjamin C. Phelps | 1 | 166 |
| Edward, [s. Rev. Aliphalet & Mary], b. Nov. 14, 1762; d. June | | |
| 25, 1807 | 1 | 9 |
| Edward, m. Christina(?) **COTTON**, Jan. 18, 1801, by Rev. Dr. | | |
| Williams | 1 | 62 |
| Edward, d. [ ], 1807, ae 45 | 1 | 66 |
| Aliphalet, Rev. , D. D., m. Mary **WILLIAMS**, Sept. 15, 1751; | | |
| d. June 29, 1803 (Eliphalet) | 1 | 9 |
| Aliphalet, Rev., m. 2nd w. Madam Sarah **PARSONS**, June 12, | | |
| 1777 | 1 | 9 |
| Elisha, [s. Rev. Aliphalet & Mary], b. Oct. 7, 1757 | 1 | 9 |
| Eliza, m. Jno Church **HUTCHINS**, Feb. 17, 1785, by Rev. Dr. | | |
| Williams | 1 | 61 |
| Elizabeth L., m. F. W. **WHIPPLE**, b. of Glastenbury, Mar. 9, | | |
| 1851, by Rev. B. C. Phelps | 1 | 160 |
| Emerson, d. Sept. 17, 1848, ae 5 | 1 | 53 |
| Ethan, d. Apr. 18, 1813 | 1 | 73 |
| Eunice, w. Jonathan, d. Aug. 17, 1802 | 1 | 73 |
| Fanny, m. James **WILLIAMS**, Dec. 19, 1816 | 1 | 68 |
| Fanny Leonard, [d. Rev. Aliphalet & Sarah], b. May 6, 1781; d. | | |
| June 30, 1792 | 1 | 9 |
| Francis, ae 40, b. East Hartford, res. same, m. Thurston | | |
| **WILCOX**, farmer, ae 50, b. Suffield, res. same, | | |
| May 28, 1848, by Daniel Pitkin | 1 | 48 |
| Frances, of East Hartford, m. Thurston **WILCOX**, of Suffield, | | |
| May 28, 1848, by Daniel Pitkin, Jr., J. P. | 1 | 155 |
| Francis C., of East Hartford, m. Henry R. **ANDREWS**, of | | |
| Ashford, Oct. 26, 1845, by Samuel Spring | 1 | 150 |
| Hannah, wid., d. Jan. 15, 1825 | 1 | 73 |
| Harriet, m. Asaph **TRUMBULL**, July 7, 1818 | 1 | 68 |
| Harriot, of Wethersfield, m. Caleb **GOODWIN**, s. Joseph & | | |
| Hannah, [ ] | 1 | 44 |
| Horace, m. Mary Ann **ROBERTS**, b. of East Hartford, Mar. 10, | | |
| 1831, by Rev. Samuel Spring of Hartford | 1 | 112 |
| Huldah, of East Hartford, m. Edwin **HAYDEN**, of East | | |
| Windsor, June 26, 1839, by Samuel Spring | 1 | 128 |
| James, d. [ ], 1809, ae 9 | 1 | 66 |
| James, m. Fanny **WILLIAMS**, Dec. 19, 1816 | 1 | 68 |
| Jemima, m. Ozias **GOSLEE**, Dec. 5, 1821, by Joy H. Fairchild | 1 | 97 |
| Jemima, d. Dec. 10, 1821, ae 82 | 1 | 73 |
| Joel, m. Nancy **JUDSON**, Oct. 11, 1826, by Joy H. Fairchild | 1 | 107 |
| John, m. Abigail **COWLES**, Apr. 26, 1824, by Joy H. Fairchild | 1 | 102 |

| WILLIAMS, (cont.), | Vol. | Page |
|---|---|---|
| John, his child bd. Jan. 24, 1829, ae 7 m. | 1 | 75 |
| Jonah, m. Phene(?) **FORBES**, Jan. 26, 1796, by Rev. Dr. | | |
| Williams | 1 | 62 |
| Jonathan, d. [       ], 1803, at Sea | 1 | 64 |
| Jonathan, d. May [  ], 1818, ae 79 | 1 | 73 |
| Jonathan, s. Samuel L., sadler, ae 39 & Elizabeth, ae 35, b. Apr. | | |
| 25, 1848 | 1 | 46 |
| Joseph, d. Feb. 2, 1806, ae 62 | 1 | 65 |
| Joshua, d. Aug. 17, 1828, ae 90 | 1 | 74 |
| Joshua, bd. Aug. 19, 1828, ae 90 | 1 | 75 |
| Levi, his mother, bd. Nov. 24, 1831 | 1 | 76 |
| Levi, of East Hartford, m. Lucy L. **ROBERTS**, of Hartford, | | |
| Jan. 27, 1840, by Samuel Spring | 1 | 131 |
| Louisa, of East Hartford, m. Sumner W. **NELSON**, of | | |
| Cleaveland, O., May 19, 1846, by Samuel Spring | 1 | 151 |
| Lucy, wid., d. Nov. 24, 1831, ae 58 | 1 | 74 |
| Mariah A., d. Sept 22, 1849, ae 11 m. | 1 | 56 |
| Mary, m. Rev. Aliphalet **WILLIAMS**, D. D., Sept. 15, 1751; d. | | |
| June 28, 1776 | 1 | 9 |
| Mary, [d. Rev. Aliphalet & Mary], b. Sept. 15, 1765 | 1 | 9 |
| Mary, w. Rev. Aliphalet, D. D. , d. June 28, 1776 | 1 | 9 |
| Mary, m. John **PORTER**, May 20, 1784, by Rev. Dr. Williams | 1 | 61 |
| Mary, d. Apr. 19, 1809, ae 81 | 1 | 73 |
| Mary, m. Theodore **TREAT**, [            ], by Rev. Dr. Williams | 1 | 61 |
| Mary A., d. Ralph, shoemaker & Emeline, b. Dec. 3, 1848 | 1 | 50 |
| Mary Ann, d. Jonathan & Rachel, of East Hartford, m. Oliver | | |
| **JOY**, of Augusta, Me., Oct. 14, 1830, by Asa Mead | 1 | 69 |
| Mary Ann, m. Oliver **JOY**, of Maine, Oct. 14, 1830, by Rev. | | |
| Asa Mead | 1 | 112 |
| Mary Ann, d. Apr. 3, 1848, ae 41 | 1 | 49 |
| Mary C., of East Hartford, m. V. A. **BAYLEY**, of Hartford, | | |
| Nov. 10, 1840, by Samuel Spring | 1 | 134 |
| Moses, his child d. [       ], 1806 | 1 | 65 |
| Moses, his child d. Jan. [  ], 1808 | 1 | 66 |
| Moses, d. Apr. 13, 1814, ae 65, his w. [            ], d. Apr. 13, | | |
| 1814, ae 37 | 1 | 66 |
| Nancy, m. Chester **CLARK**, Jan. 28, 1819 | 1 | 69 |
| Nancy, of East Hartford, m. Thomas **DOWD**, of Hartford, June | | |
| 5, 1839, by Samuel Spring | 1 | 129 |
| Oliver, d. Mar. 29, [1824] | 1 | 74 |
| Ozias, m. Anne **SMITH**, Sept. 18, 1797, by Rev. Dr. Williams | 1 | 62 |
| Phinehas, s. W[illia]m, Jr., d. [       ], 1814, ae 45 | 1 | 66 |
| Rachael L., d. Aug. 24, 1850, ae 70 | 1 | 59 |
| Ralph, of Willington, m. Emeline **BREWER**, of East Hartford, | | |
| Jan. 1, 1838, by Samuel Spring | 1 | 125 |
| Rhoda, d. Oct. 1, 1815 | 1 | 72 |
| Roswell, s. Phinehas, d. Oct. 24, 1825, ae 30 | 1 | 73 |
| Russell, his child bd. July 23, 1831, ae 10 m. | 1 | 76 |
| Samuel L., harness maker, ae 41 & Eliza G., ae 38, had child b. | | |
| Feb. 27, 1850 | 1 | 55 |
| Sanford B., s. Aaron C., stone cutter, ae 37, b. July 28, 1851 | 1 | 58 |
| Sarah, w. Rev. Aliphalet, d. Jan. 23, 1800 | 1 | 9 |

| WILLIAMS, (cont.), | Vol. | Page |
|---|---|---|
| Sarah, w. Rev. [        ], d. [        ], 1800, ae 63 | 1 | 63 |
| Sarah, d. Apr. 18, 1819, ae 69 | 1 | 73 |
| Sarah, m. William **HAYES**, Feb. 12, 1824, by Joy H. Fairchild | 1 | 102 |
| Sarah, Mrs. M. Matthias **TREAT**, b. of East Hartford, June 11, 1840, by Rev. Lozien Peirce | 1 | 133 |
| Sarah, of East Hartford, m. Phineas B. **STRONG**, of Colchester, Oct. 25, 1853, by Samuel Spring | 1 | 165 |
| Sarah B., of Glastenbury, m. Norman **WADSWORTH**, of East Hartford, Apr. 20, 1846, by Samuel Spring | 1 | 151 |
| Solomon, [s. Rev. Aliphalet & Mary], b. July 13, 1752 | 1 | 9 |
| Solomon, Lieut., d. [        ], 1799, ae 68 | 1 | 63 |
| Susan, m. Hiram **GRANT**, Jan. 12, 1832, by Rev. Gurdon Robins, of East Windsor | 1 | 113 |
| Talcott, d. Mar. 17, 1814, ae 25 | 1 | 66 |
| Theodore, d. Oct. [ ], 1822 | 1 | 74 |
| Thomas L., of Boston, Mass., m. Ellen **GOODWIN**, of East Hartford, Oct. 7, 1846, by Samuel Spring | 1 | 152 |
| William, and his w. [        ], d. Jan. 25, 1828 | 1 | 74 |
| William, and his w. [        ], d. Jan. [ ], 1828 | 1 | 74 |
| -----, Rev. Dr., [d.] June 29, 1803, ae 77 | 1 | 64 |
| -----, Mr., d. [        ], 1803 | 1 | 64 |
| **WILSON**, Clarissa, b. Jan. 8, 1793; m. Marvin **CONE**, [        ],; d. Jan. 8, 1815 | 1 | 38 |
| Henry B., of Torringford, m. Angeline **COOK**, of Bristol, Aug. 31, 1841, by Samuel Spring | 1 | 136 |
| Hez[ekiah], m. Mehitable **KENDALL**, June 27, 1786, by Rev. Dr. Williams | 1 | 61 |
| **WINCHELL**, Lucy M. of Berlin, m. Wyllys **BRAUNSON**, of Vernon, May 19, 1829, by Rev. Thomas Robbins | 1 | 110 |
| Norris, m. Abigail Jane **SIMONDS**, b. of East Hartford, Jan. 5, 1842, by Rev. Cephas Brainard | 1 | 137 |
| **WING**, Almira, m. Mervin **KEENEY**, May 3, 1818 | 1 | 68 |
| Andrew H., m. Elizabeth **DUNHAM**, June 6, 1836, by Samuel Spring | 1 | 121 |
| Andrew H., of St. Louis, Mo., m. Emeline **BURNHAM**, of East Hartford, Sept. 30, 1841, by Samuel Spring | 1 | 136 |
| Eliza, m. Timothy **DEMING**, Nov. 22, 1825, by Joy H. Fairchild | 1 | 104 |
| Harriet, of East Hartford, m. Francis W. **COWLES**, of Manchester, Nov. 13, 1834, by Samuel Spring | 1 | 118 |
| Sabrina, m. Allen **BRAINARD**, Sept. 17, 1822, by Elisha Cushman | 1 | 99 |
| **WINSLOW**, Anna, m. Ralph **RISLEY**, Jan. 19, 1820 | 1 | 69 |
| Daniel, m. Marinda **KEENY**, May 16, 1822, by Joy H. Fairchild | 1 | 99 |
| Elisa, m. Austin **LESTER**, June 22, 1826, by Joy H. Farichild | 1 | 106 |
| Georgenan, d. Nelson, Farmer, ae 25, b. Dec. 31, 1851 | 1 | 57 |
| Mary, d. Jan. 23, 1850, ae 64 | 1 | 56 |
| Nelson, farmer, ae 22, b. East Hartford, res. same, m. Atresta **KEENY**, ae 19, b. Manchester, res. East Hartford, June 29, 1848, by B. C. Phelps | 1 | 48 |

| | Vol. | Page |
|---|---|---|
| **WINSLOW**, (cont.), | | |
| Pardon, m. Mrs. Mary **PARMELE**, b. of East Hartford, Sept. 26, 1841, by Rev. B. M. Walker | 1 | 136 |
| Sarah A., of East Hartford, m. Willis L. **BRONSON**, of Hartford, Nov. 20, 1845, by Rev. Gurdon Robins, of Hartford | 1 | 152 |
| **WITT**, Rufus, m. Esther **MORE**, b. of Stafford, Jan. 29, 1851, by Samuel Spring | 1 | 64 |
| **WOLCOTT, WOOLCOTT**, Dorcas, d. Nov. 17, 1823, ae 85 | 1 | 73 |
| Fannie, d. Henry, blacksmith, b. Apr. 9, 1850 | 1 | 55 |
| Ralph H., d. [ ], at the house of Henry **PHELPS**, bd. Jan. 19, 1834 | 1 | 76 |
| Roger, d. [ ], 1798 | 1 | 63 |
| Samuel, of East Windsor, m. Maria **STEWART**, of East Hartford, June 11, 1829, by Rev. Thomas Robbins | 1 | 110 |
| -----, Mr., his child d. Jan. 16, 1803 | 1 | 64 |
| **WOOD, WOODS**, Hiram, his child bd. Aug. 20, 1830, ae 16 . | 1 | 76 |
| Hope, d. Apr. 21, 1850, ae 74 | 1 | 57 |
| Mary, m. Eli **JUDSON**, b. of East Hartford, Sept. 27, 1843, by Samuel Spring | 1 | 143 |
| Simeon, m. Mary **HINSDALE**, b. of East Hartford, Nov. 12, 1834, by Samuel Spring | 1 | 118 |
| William, m. Mary Ann **ROBERTS**, June 22, 1830, by Horace Hooker | 1 | 111 |
| -----, Mr., d. [ ], 1802 | 1 | 64 |
| -----, of Hartford, his child, bd. July 29, 1834, ae 13 m. | 1 | 76 |
| -----, of Hartford, his child bd. Apr. 22, 1836, ae 10 y. | 1 | 78 |
| -----, his child bd. Jan. 22, 1838, ae 6 d. | 1 | 78 |
| **WOODBRIDGE**, Anne, w., Russell, d. Feb. 21, 1808, ae 90 | 1 | 60 |
| Deodat, of Manchester, m. Augusta **SPROUT**, of East Hartford, Jan. 1, 1852, by Samuel Spring | 1 | 118 |
| Electa, b. Jan. 2, 1781; m. George **CHEENY**, Oct. 18, 1798 | 1 | 4 |
| Emily, m. Horace **PITKIN**, Dec. 21, 1814 | 1 | 38 |
| Francis, m. Jane Ann **GOODWIN**, May [ ], 1827, by Joy H. Fairchild | 1 | 108 |
| Fredric, m. Clarrisa **PITKIN**, b. of East Hartford, May 8, 1823, by Rev. Elisha B. Cook | 1 | 102 |
| James, of Hartford, m. Harriet **AUSTIN**, of East Hartford, Nov. 11, 1840, by Samuel Spring | 1 | 134 |
| Russell, bd. Apr. 22, 1829, ae 82 | 1 | 75 |
| Ward, d. [ ], 1806 | 1 | 65 |
| **WOODRUFF**, Alice C., b. East Hartford, res. Glastenbury, d. Oct. 9, 1849, ae 1 | 1 | 56 |
| Candace C., b. East Windsor, res. East Hartford, d. Dec. 10, 1849, ae 50 | 1 | 56 |
| Henry E., marketing, ae 21, b. East Hartford, res. same, m. Almira S. **HALL**, ae 20, b. Blanford, Mass., res. East Hartford, June 20, 1850, by W. Clark | 1 | 56 |
| Lucy Cecile, d. Henry E., marketman, b. July 28, 1851 | 1 | 59 |
| **WOODWARD**, Alfred, book agent, ae 28, had d. [ ], b. Oct. 13, 1850 | 1 | 58 |
| Emily I., m. Peter **BROOKS**, Nov. 28, 1827, by Rev. Joel Hawes, of Hartford | 1 | 109 |

|                                                                                                          | Vol. | Page |
|----------------------------------------------------------------------------------------------------------|------|------|
| **WRIGHT**, Charles, of Glastenbury, m. Caroline Elizabeth **FOSTER**, of                                |      |      |
| East Hartford, Aug. 19, 1839, by Samuel Strong                                                           | 1    | 129  |
| Erie, m. Laura **FORBES**, Mar. 27, 1823, by Joy H. Fairchild                                            | 1    | 101  |
| Erie, his child, bd. Sept. 10, 1830, ae 6 m.                                                             | 1    | 76   |
| Griswold, of Hartford, m. Sarah **DEMING**, of East Hartford,                                            |      |      |
| Sept. 8, 1834, by Samuel Spring                                                                          | 1    | 116  |
| Harvey, of Coventry, m. Sarah **BISSELL**, of East Hartford,                                             |      |      |
| June 15, 1820, by Rev. Elisha B. Cook                                                                    | 1    | 94   |
| John, m. Tryphena **BURNHAM**, June 3, 1823, by Joy H.                                                   |      |      |
| Fairchild                                                                                                | 1    | 101  |
| Mercy, wid., m. Capt. Moses **FORBES**, [      ], 1792, by Rev.                                          |      |      |
| Dr. Williams                                                                                             | 1    | 62   |
| Theodore L., m. Catherine B. **REYNOLDS**, b. of East Hartford,                                          |      |      |
| Sept. 23, 1833, by Rev. Samuel Spring                                                                    | 1    | 114  |
| William A., s. Gibson O., farmer & Sarah, b. Sept. 3, 1847                                               | 1    | 46   |
| **WRISLEY**, Albert, of Glastenbury, m. Sophia W. **HILLS**, of East                                    |      |      |
| Hartford, Nov. 16, 1842, by [            ]                                                               | 1    | 141  |
| **WYCHE, WICHE**, George, tailor, b. Germany, res. Hartford, m. Henrietta                               |      |      |
| **PLATT**, ae 17, b. N. Haven, Apr. 23, 1850, by S.                                                     |      |      |
| Spring                                                                                                   | 1    | 56   |
| George, of Hartford, m. Henrietta **PLATT**, of New Haven, Apr.                                          |      |      |
| 14, 1850, by Samuel Spring                                                                               | 1    | 158  |
| **WYLLYS, WYLES, WYLLIS**, Ephraim, m. [            ], Nov. 8, 1792                                     | 1    | 7    |
| Ephraim, Jr., [s. Ephraim], b. July 5, 1793                                                              | 1    | 7    |
| John, [s. Ephraim], b. July 13, 1795                                                                     | 1    | 7    |
| John, m. Sarah **GOODWIN**, d. John, 2nd & Dorothy                                                      | 1    | 43   |
| Joseph, d. [      ], 1804                                                                                | 1    | 64   |
| Polly, m. Samuel **FLAGG**, Nov. 28, 1790, by Rev. Dr.                                                  |      |      |
| Williams                                                                                                 | 1    | 61   |
| Polly, [d. Ephraim], b. July 24, 1798                                                                    | 1    | 7    |
| Samuel joiner, d. July 16, 1851, ae 68                                                                   | 1    | 60   |
| Sarah, w. John, d. Sept. 21, 1809, ae 59                                                                 | 1    | 66   |
| Sylvester, of Hartford, m. Delia **HILLS**, of East Hartford, Oct.                                      |      |      |
| 12, 1835, by Samuel Spring                                                                               | 1    | 118  |
| **YANCE**, John, m. Sally **DART**, b. of East Hartford, Jan. 7, 1823, by Rev.                          |      |      |
| Elisha B. Cook                                                                                           | 1    | 101  |
| **YATES**, Levi C., joiner, ae 32, b. Haddam, res. Hartford, m. Elizabeth M.                            |      |      |
| **BURNHAM**, ae 23, b. East Hartford, res. same,                                                       |      |      |
| Nov. 12, 1850, by W. Clark                                                                               | 1    | 59   |
| Mary, w. Rev. Andrew, [      ], 1806                                                                    | 1    | 65   |
| **YORK**, -----, negro, d. [      ], 1802                                                                | 1    | 64   |
| **YOUNGLOVE**, John, merchant, ae 28, b. Brunswick, N. Y., res.                                         |      |      |
| Cleaveland, O., m. Lauraette **KELLOGG**, ae 21, b.                                                     |      |      |
| East Hartford, res. same, Feb. 21, 1848, by Rev. R.                                                      |      |      |
| Turnbull                                                                                                 | 1    | 52   |
| **NO SURNAME**                                                                                           |      |      |
| Ashbel, d. [      ], 1802                                                                                |      |      |
| Dinah, d. Jim, colored, b. Sept. [ ], 1783                                                               | 1    | 19   |
| Francis, m. James **WHITE**, negroes, of East Windsor, Aug. 15,                                         |      |      |
| 1816                                                                                                     | 1    | 68   |
| James, [s. Flora], colored, b. July [ ], 1785                                                            | 1    | 19   |
| Job, negro, d. Mar. 2, 1806                                                                              | 1    | 65   |

| | Vol. | Page |
|---|---|---|
| **NO SURNAME**, (cont.), | | |
| Leah, [d. Flora] colored, b. Sept. [ ], 1783 | 1 | 19 |
| Lill, colored, d. Flora, b. Feb. [ ], 1772 | 1 | 19 |
| Nando, [d. Flora] colored, b. Apr. [ ], 1779; d. Feb. 3, 1813 | 1 | 19 |
| Nando, negress, d. [ ], 1813 | 1 | 67 |
| Occalo, m. Peg [ ], negroes, Dec. 17, 1789, by Rev. Dr. Williams | 1 | 61 |
| Occala, negro, d. May 1, 1803 | 1 | 64 |
| Peg, m. Occalo [ ], negroes, Dec. 17, 1789, by Rev. Dr. Williams | 1 | 61 |
| Peg, negro, d. [ ], 1803 | 1 | 64 |
| Sarah, m. John **GOODWIN**, [ ]; d. May. [ ], 1735 | 1 | 43 |
| Silva, [d. Flora] colored, b. Aug. [ ], 1776; d. July [ ], 1847 | 1 | 19 |
| Tama, her negro child d. [ ], 1798 | 1 | 63 |

# EAST HAVEN VITAL RECORDS
## 1700-1852

|  | Vol. | Page |
|---|---|---|
| **ABBOT, ABBOTT**, Abygal, d. Joseph, b. Aug. 15, 1700 | TM1 | 30 |
| Marah, d. Joseph, b. Nov. 14, 1707 | TM1 | 30 |
| Mary, d. [Apr.] 6, 1783, ae 70 | DR | |
| **ALCOCK**, Abigail, w. Thomas, d. May 3, 1741, ae 58 | DR | |
| Martha, d. Apr. 24, 1728, ae 21 | DR | |
| Mary, w. Thomas, d. May 23, 1714 | DR | |
| Thomas, d. Apr. 2, 1757, ae 80 | DR | |
| **ALLEN**, Lucinda, of [East Haven], m. Theophilus **MILES**, of Derby, Sept. 29, 1802, by Rev. Nicholas Street | DR | |
| Martin, of Plymouth, m Lydia **BRADLEY**, of East Haven, Apr. 4, 1847, by Rev. Stephen Dodd | DR | |
| Martin, of Plymouth, m. Lydia **BRADLEY**, of East Haven, Apr. 4, 1847, by Stephen Dodd | TM4 | 207 |
| Thomas, s. Thomas, d. May 6, 1773, ae 2 | DR | |
| Thomas, d. [ ], 1786, ae 40 | DR | |
| ----, infant Thomas, d. [May], 4, 1775, ae 2 d. | DR | |
| **AMES**, Joseph, m. Almira **MALLORY**, Jan. 27, 1832, by Rev. John Mitchell, of Fair Haven | TM3 | 284 |
| William, m. Sarah A. **BARNES**, b. of East Haven, Nov. 4, 1840, by Rev. Stephen Dodd | DR | |
| William, m. Sarah A. **BARNES**, b. of East Haven, Nov. 4, 1840, by Stephen Dodd | TM3 | 328 |
| **ANDREWS, ANDRUS**, Abigail, wid., d. [Jan.] 31, 1837, ae 84 | DR | |
| Almena, m. Thomas **GRANNIS**, b. of East Haven, Aug. 26, 1824, by Stephen Dodd | TM3 | 169 |
| Almira, of [East Haven], m. Thomas **GRANNIS**, Aug. 26, 1824, by Rev. Stephen Dodd | DR | |
| Ame, w. Jedediah, Jr., d. Jan. 6, 1777, ae 18 | DR | |
| Ann Louisa, d. Reuel, d. [Jan.] 22, 1846, ae 16 | DR | |
| Anna, wid. Timothy, d. [Dec.] 7, 1798, ae 80 | DR | |
| Betsey P., m. Rosewell **WOODWARD**, b. of East Haven, Nov. 10, 1833, by Stephen Dodd | TM3 | 236 |
| Betsey **PARDEE**, m. Rosewell **WOODWARD**, b. of East Haven, [Nov.] 10, 1833, by Stephen Dodd | DR | |
| Celestia M., of East Haven, m. Noah W. **BRADLEY**, of New York, July 18, 1849, by Stephen Dodd | TM4 | 212 |
| Elisha, d. [Feb.] 21, 1840, ae 93 y. 2 m. | DR | |
| Eleza, d. Jared & Dorita, b. May 22, 1793 (Eliza) | TM2 | 290 |
| Eliza, m. Rev. Stephen **DODD**, pastor of Cong. ch. In East Haven, b. of East Haven, July 12, 1848, by Rev. D. William Havens | DR | |
| Eliza, m. Rev. Stephen **DODD**, b. of East Haven, July 12, 1848, by Rev. D. W[illia]m Havens | TM4 | 210 |
| Elizabeth, wid. Jedediah, d. Sept. 29, 1784, ae 60 | DR | |
| Elizabeth, of [East Haven], m. Daniel **ROWE**, Apr. 19, 1805, by Rev. Nicholas Street | DR | |

| ANDREWS, ANDRUS, (cont.), | Vol. | Page |
|---|---|---|
| Frances F., m. Mary A. HEMINGWAY, b. of East Haven, July 5, 1852, by Rev. D. W[illia]m Havens | TM4 | 218 |
| Hannah, m. Oliver BRADLEY, b. of [East Haven], May 10, 1803, by Rev. Nicholas Street | DR | |
| Jared, s. Elisha, d. Nov. 19, 1773, ae 3 | DR | |
| Jared, Jr., m. Harriet SMITH, b. of East Haven, Dec. 17, 1849, by Stephen Dodd | TM4 | 212 |
| Jedediah, d. [Jan.] 14, 1784, ae 76 | DR | |
| Jedediah, d. Oct. 2, 1799, ae 48 | DR | |
| Julia, of East Haven, m. Andrew BARNES, of North Haven, Nov. 29, 1849, by Rev. D. William Havens | DR | |
| Julia, of East Haven, m. Andrew BARNES, of North Haven, Nov. 29, 1849, by Rev. D. W[illia]m Havens | TM4 | 213 |
| Lue, m. Caleb LUDDINGTON, b. of [East Haven], Mar. 2, 1814, by Rev. Saul Clark | DR | |
| Lydia, d. Elisha, d. June 9, 1800, ae 24 | DR | |
| Lydia, of [East Haven], m. David WELLER June 20, 1802, by Rev. Nicholas Street | DR | |
| Mabel, m. Julius UPSON, b. of East Haven, [Apr.] 7, 1833, by Rev. Stephen Dodd | DR | |
| Mabel, m. Julius UPSON, Apr. 7, 1833, by Stephen Dodd | TM3 | 236 |
| Mary R., of East Haven, m. Samuel Edward LINDSLEY, of Branford, [May] 14, 1837, by Rev. Stephen Dodd | DR | |
| Mary R., of East Haven, m. Samuel C. LINDSLEY, of Branford, May 14, 1837, by Stephen Dodd | TM3 | 324 |
| Mary Roxanna, d. Ruel, d. June 15, 1837, ae 3 m. | DR | |
| Nathan, d. [      ], 1776; d. in the prison ship at New York, ae 21 | DR | |
| Nathan, d. [      ], 1798, ae 19; by a fall from a mast | DR | |
| Nathan, d. [Nov.] 26, 1828, ae 50 | DR | |
| Polle, d. Jared & Dorita, b. Feb. 13, 1795 | TM2 | 290 |
| Polly, of [East Haven], m. James FARREN, May 2, 1822, by Rev. Stephen Dodd | DR | |
| Polly, m. James FERRIN, May 2, 1822, by Stephen Dodd | TM3 | 165 |
| Samuel T., m. Sally DAVIDSON, b. of [East Haven], [Apr.] 28, 1824, by Rev. Stephen Dodd | DR | |
| Samuel T., m. Sarah DAVIDSON, Apr. 28, 1824, by Stephen Dodd | TM3 | 168 |
| Sarah, d. Feb. 16, 1818, ae 35 | DR | |
| Sarah, w. Elisha, d. [Aug.] 16, 1838, ae 87 y. 8 m. | DR | |
| Sarah W., m. Elijah BRADLEY, b. of East Haven, [Aug.] 27, 1848, by Rev. D. William Havens | DR | |
| Sarah W., m. Elijah BRADLEY, b. of East Haven, Aug. 27, 1848, by D. W[illia]m Havens | TM4 | 210 |
| Susan, of East Haven, m. Jeremiah B. DAVIDSON, Apr. 20, 1834, by Rev. Stephen Dodd | DR | |
| Susan, m. Jeremiah B. DAVIDSON, b. of East Haven, Apr. 20, 1834, by Stephen Dodd | TM3 | 281 |
| Sylvia, d. Sept. 17, 1826, ae 30 | DR | |
| Timothy, s. Elisha, d. [May] 9, 1775, ae 2 | DR | |
| Timothy, d. July 25, 1793, ae 77 | DR | |

| | Vol. | Page |
|---|---|---|
| **ANDREWS, ANDRUS,** (cont.), | | |
| Timothy, s. Samuel T., d. [Oct.] 29, 1827, ae 1 y. 2 m. | DR | |
| William, purchaser of Southend, d. Mar. 4, 1676 | DR | |
| ——, infant Jedediah & Ame, d. Jan. 6, 1777 | DR | |
| **ARNOLD,** ——, child Jehiel, d. Feb. 3, 1785, ae 2 m. | DR | |
| **ASBILL,** John, d. [      ], 1690 | DR | |
| **ATKINS,** Warren C., of Meriden, m. Louisa **BRADLEY,** of Branford, | | |
| Dec. 13, 1835, by Rev. Stephen Dodd | DR | |
| Warren C., of Meriden, m. Lavinia **BRADLEY,** of Branford, | | |
| Dec. 13, 1835, by Stephen Dodd | TM3 | 283 |
| **ATWATER,** Jeremiah, Rev. D. D., m. Mrs. Susan **BARNES,** b. of New | | |
| Haven, Dec. 2, 1834, by Stephen Dodd | TM3 | 281 |
| Mary E., of Hamden, m. Jerome **BEACH,** of North Haven, Jan. | | |
| 3, 1844, by Wyllys Hemingway, J. P. | TM4 | 203 |
| **AUGUR, AUGER, AUGOR, AWGUR,** Abraham, s. Philemon, d. [Oct.] | | |
| 30, 1801, ae 4 | DR | |
| Daniel, d. Feb. 18, 1803, ae 88 | DR | |
| Daniel, d. [Dec. ], 1824, ae 30 | DR | |
| Elizabeth, w. Daniel, d. Sept. 27, 1786, ae 65 | DR | |
| Elizabeth Emmaline, d. Rosewell, d. [Dec.] 13, 1838, ae 19 | DR | |
| Elizabeth H., of [East Haven], m. Hubbard **SCRANTON,** of | | |
| East Guilford, Apr. 25, 1811, by Rev. Saul Clark | DR | |
| Harvey, of Branford, m. Lydia **ROBINSON,** of East Haven, | | |
| Apr. 20, 1823, by Rev. Oliver Willson | TM3 | 167 |
| John, m. Elessabeth **BRADL[E]Y,** Aug. 3, 1710, by William | | |
| Malttby, J. P. | TM1 | 31 |
| John, d. [      ], 1726, ae 40 | DR | |
| John, of Saybrook, m. Orilla **HEMINWAY,** of [East Haven], | | |
| Nov. 22, 1831, by Rev. Stephen Dodd | DR | |
| John, of Saybrook, m. Orilla **HEMINWAY,** of East Haven, | | |
| Nov. 22, 1831, by Stephen Dodd | TM3 | 234 |
| Lois, d. Daniel, d. Aug. 22, 1751, ae 2 | DR | |
| Lois, d. Philemon & Tabitha, b. Sept. 20, 1782 | TM2 | 155 |
| Lovisa, w. Rosewell, d. [Oct.] 14, 1824, ae 48 | DR | |
| Marrah, d. John, b. Aug. 28, 1711 | TM1 | 31 |
| Mary, wid., d. in Madison, [Feb.] 19, 1831, ae 62 | DR | |
| Mehitabel, wid. Daniel, d. [Feb.] 29, 1824, ae 81 | DR | |
| Philemon, d. Aug. 11, 1826, ae 72 | DR | |
| Roswell, s. Philemon & Tabatha, b. Oct. 20, 1780 | TM2 | 155 |
| Rosewell, m. Mrs. Roxanna **WORKS,** b. of East Haven, May 1, | | |
| 1825, by Rev. Stephen Dodd | DR | |
| Roswell, m. Roxana **WORTS,** b. of East Haven, May 1, 1825, | | |
| by Stephen Dodd | TM3 | 169 |
| Sarah, d. Rosewell, d. Dec. 8, 1847, ae 17 | DR | |
| Tabitha, w. Philemon, d. Aug. 25, 1790, ae 33 | DR | |
| ——, infant Rosewell, d. Aug. 12, 1817 | DR | |
| **AUSTIN, ASTIN, OSTEN, OSTIN,** Abigail, d. Jonathan, d. [Oct.] 6, | | |
| 1742, ae 4 | DR | |
| Abig[a]il, d. Jonathan, [d. Oct. 6, 1742] | TM2 | 24 |
| Abigail, w. Joshua, d. Aug. 29, 1764, ae 31 | DR | |
| Abigail, w. Joshua, d. Aug. 29, 1764 | TM2 | 87 |
| Abigail, w. Joshua, d. Aug. 29, 1764 | TM2 | 158 |

| AUSTIN, ASTIN, OSTEN, OSTIN, (cont.) | Vol. | Page |
|---|---|---|
| Dani[e]l, s. Joshua, b. Jan. 5, 1762 | TM2 | 46 |
| Daniel, s. Joshua & Abigail, b. June 5, 1762 | TM2 | 46 |
| David, d. Apr. 22, 1713, ae 43 | DR | |
| Dauid, d. Apr. 22, 1713 | TM1 | 114 |
| Hannah, Mrs., of New Haven, m. Rev. Nicholas STREET, Apr. | | |
| 24, 1766, by Rev. Sam[ue]ll Bird, of New Haven | TM2 | 156 |
| John, s. John, d. Feb. 10, 1675, ae 7 | DR | |
| John, father of the East and New Haven family, d. [      ], | | |
| 1690 | DR | |
| John Pardee, s. Daniel & Sally, b. Apr. 3, 1794 | TM2 | 290 |
| Jonathan, s. Dauid, b. Apr. 27, 1708 | TM1 | 30 |
| Joshua, s. Joshua, b. Nov. 18, 1733 | TM1 | 284 |
| Joshua, m. Abig[a]il, HITCHCO[C]K, May 6, 175[ ], by Rev. | | |
| Nichlias Street | TM2 | 20 |
| Joshua, Dea., d. Mar. 29, 1760, ae 86 | DR | |
| Joshua, Dea., d. Mar. 29, 1760 | TM2 | 22 |
| Lois, d. Joshua, d. June 10, 1754 | DR | |
| Lois, d. Joshua & Abigail, b. Feb. 8, 1759 | TM2 | 46 |
| Lois, d. Joshey, b. Feb. 16, 1759 | TM2 | 46 |
| Lois, d. Joshua, d. June 10, 1763, ae 4 | DR | |
| Lois, d. Joshua & Abigail, b. June 10, 1763 | TM2 | 158 |
| Lois, d. Joshua, b. May 11, 1764 | TM2 | 46 |
| Lois, d. Joshua & Abigail, b. May 11, 1764 | TM2 | 46 |
| Lidia, d. Jonath[an], b. Sept. 17, 1740 | TM2 | 21 |
| Mary, d. John, d. Jan. 23, 1675 | DR | |
| Mary, w. John, d. Apr. 4, 1683 | DR | |
| Mary, w. John, d. Apr. 4, 1683 | DR | |
| Mary, d. John, d. Oct. 27, 1683, ae 3 | DR | |
| Mehitabel, wid. Dea. Joshua, d. [      ], 1760 | DR | |
| Polly, d. Daniel & Sally, b. June 18, 1792 | TM2 | 290 |
| Punderson, s. David, d. Feb. 21, 1743, ae 4 w. | DR | |
| Rebecca, w. David, d. Feb. 26, 1739 | DR | |
| Sally, d. Daniel & Sally, b. Jan. 9, 1805 | TM2 | 290 |
| Samuel, s. David, d. Apr. 3, 1734, ae 2 m. | DR | |
| Silence, d. Joshua, d. July [ ], 1714, ae 4 m. | DR | |
| Silence, d. Joshua, b. Feb. last day, 1714; d. July 14, [1714] | TM1 | 114 |
| Stephen, s. Stephen, d. Apr. 8, 1742, ae 7 | DR | |
| Stephen, s. Stephen, d. Feb. 18, 1744, ae 9 m. | DR | |
| Stephen, s. Daniel & Sally, b. Mar. 31, 1796 | TM2 | 290 |
| Susannah, w. Joshua, d. June 27, 1786, ae 50 | DR | |
| Susannah, w. Joshua, d. June 27, 1786 | TM2 | 158 |
| Wyllys, s. Daniel, d. July 23, 1791, ae 9 m. | DR | |
| ——, infant, John & Mary, d. Apr. 4, 1683 | DR | |
| BAILEY, Silvanus, of East Haven, m. Florilla KELSEY, of Killingworth, | | |
| Apr. 3, 1837, by Rev. Truman O. Judd, of North | | |
| Haven | TM3 | 285 |
| BAKER, Lydia, w. Joshua, d. [July] 5, 1831, ae 59; found dead on the | | |
| shore – from apoplexy | DR | |
| BALDWIN, Abigail, of [East Haven], m. Levi MOULTHROP, of New | | |
| Haven, Nov. 4, 1811, by Rev. Saul Clark | DR | |
| Anna, w. Levi, d. May 4, 1833, ae 58 | DR | |
| Eunice P., of North Branford, m. Augustus ROBINSON, of | | |
| [East Haven], Apr. 4, 1825, by Rev. Stephen Dodd | DR | |

| | Vol. | Page |
|---|---|---|
| **BALDWIN**, (cont.), | | |
| Eunice C., of North Branford, m. Augustus **ROBINSON**, of | | |
| East Haven, Apr. 4, 1825, by Stephen Dodd | TM3 | 169 |
| Henry T., of North Haven, m. Marietta **SMITH**, of East Haven, | | |
| May 10, 1837, by Stephen Dodd | TM3 | 324 |
| Israel, d. Jan. 22, 1830, ae 50 | DR | |
| Israel Augustus, of Branford, m. Abigail **CHIDSEY**, of [East | | |
| Haven], Dec. 28, 1828, by Rev. Stephen Dodd | DR | |
| Israel Augustus, of Branford, m. Abigail **CHIDSEY**, of East | | |
| Haven, Dec. 28, 1828, by Stephen Dodd | TM3 | 174 |
| Martha, m. Jared **SHEPARD**, Mar. 24, 1802, by Rev. Nicholas | | |
| Street | DR | |
| **BALL**, Alling, s. Alling, d. Sept. 21, 1689 | DR | |
| Alling, Jr., Capt., d. July [  ], 1710, ae 54 | DR | |
| Dorothy, w. Captain Alling, d. Feb. 22, 1690 | DR | |
| Elijah, of New Haven, m. Jane Ann **MALLERY**, of East | | |
| Haven, Mar. 13, 1839, by Rev. Benjamin L. Swan, | | |
| of Fair Haven | TM3 | 326 |
| Eliphalet, d. July 11, 1673, ae 23 | DR | |
| John, d. Jan. 1, 1731, ae 82 | DR | |
| Ledia, m. Jacob **HEMINGWAY**, May 3, 1711 | TM1 | 31 |
| Ledia, d. Allin[g], b. Oct. 29, 1715 | TM1 | 114 |
| Sarah, wid. Capt. Alling, Jr., d. Oct. 23, 1716, ae 57 | DR | |
| Sarah, wid. Capt. Alling, d. Oct. 23, 1716 | TM1 | 198 |
| Sarah, w. John, d. Nov. 22, 1730, ae 75 | DR | |
| **BARNES, BARNS**, Abigail, 2d. w. Nathaniel, d. [       ], 1743, ae 22 | DR | |
| Abig[a]il, w. Nathaniel, d. [Sept. 3, 1743] | TM2 | 25 |
| Abigail, w. Nathaniel, d. Oct. 27, 1782, ae 63 | DR | |
| Abiud, d. [       ], 1800, ae 19; lost at sea | DR | |
| Abraham, d. Nov. 3, 1797, ae 20 | DR | |
| Abraham, d. [May] 15, 1818, ae 71 | DR | |
| Abram Jared, s. Isaac & Lois, b. Aug. 4, 1778 | TM2 | 162 |
| Amos, s. Capt. Samuel, d. [Nov.] 30, 1797, ae 18; in West | | |
| Indies | DR | |
| Andrew, of North Haven, m. Julia **ANDREWS**, of East Haven, | | |
| Nov. 29, 1849, by Rev. D. William Havens | DR | |
| Andrew, of North Haven, m. Julia **ANDREWS**, of East Haven, | | |
| Nov. 29, 1849, by Rev. D. W[illia]m Havens | TM4 | 213 |
| Benjamin, d. [Feb.] 24, 1761, ae 68 | DR | |
| Chauncey, d. Mar. 18, 1811, ae 40 | DR | |
| Dennis, s. William, d. [Apr.] 21, 1819, ae 2 | DR | |
| Dennis, of East Haven, m. Maria **KINGSBURY**, of New | | |
| Haven, Sept. 26, 1847, by Rev. D. W[illia]m Havens | TM4 | 208 |
| Dorcas, 3d. w. Samuel, d. Mar. [  ], 1756 | DR | |
| Eli, of Southington, m. Wid. Susan **BRADLEY**, of [East | | |
| Haven], Aug. 2, 1812, by Rev. Saul Clark | DR | |
| Elizabeth, 2d. w. Samuel, d. [Sept.] 27, 1751, ae 45 | DR | |
| Elizabeth, d. Samuel, d. Sept. 9, 1772, ae 17 m. | DR | |
| Elizabeth Thompson, w. Thomas, d. [Mar.] 25, 1842; ae 19, | | |
| childbirth | DR | |
| Elmina, m. Elijah **BRADLEY**, b. of East Haven, Mar. 31, | | |
| 1833, by Rev. Stephen Dodd | DR | |

| | Vol. | Page |
|---|---|---|
| **BARNES, BARNS**, (cont.), | | |
| Elmina, m. Elijah **BRADLEY**, 3rd., b. of East Haven, Mar. 31, | | |
| 1833, by Stephen Dodd | TM3 | 235 |
| Enos, m. Abig[a]il **LUDINGTON**, Dec. 3, 1746, by Rev. Jacob | | |
| Heminway | TM2 | 20 |
| George, s. Mrs. Nancy, d. [Dec.] [ ], 1847; (in the state of Miss. | | |
| at Beloxi) | DR | |
| Grace Caroline, d. William, d. [Aug. ], 1843, ae 22 | DR | |
| Hannah, wid., d. Aug. 3, 1805, ae 84 | DR | |
| Hannah, w. Abraham, d. [Mar.] 10, 1816, ae 68 | DR | |
| Hannah C., m. Horace **THOMPSON**, b. of East Haven, May | | |
| 27, 1839, by Rev. Stephen Dodd | DR | |
| Hannah C., m. Horace **THOMPSON**, b. of East Haven, May | | |
| 27, 1839, by Stephen Dodd | TM3 | 326 |
| Harvey, 2nd, m. Charlotte M. **TUTTLE**, Dec. 4, 1849, | | |
| by B. Hart | TM4 | 213 |
| Heminway, s. Nathaniel, d. [Oct.] 7, 1795, ae 1 | DR | |
| Hepzibah, wid. Capt. Samuel, d. Jan. 26, 1834, ae 90 y. | | |
| 6 m. 12 d. | DR | |
| Hezekiah, s. Ichabod, d. [Feb.] 17, 1773, ae 5 | DR | |
| Horace, of New Haven, m. Lois **THOMPSON**, of [East | | |
| Haven], May 5, 1824, by Rev. Stephen Dodd | DR | |
| Horace, of New Haven, m. Laurinda **THOMPSON**, of East | | |
| Haven, May 5, 1824, by Stephen Dodd | TM3 | 168 |
| Huldah, of [East Haven], m. James **CHURCH**, of Haddam, Jan. | | |
| [ ], 1811, by Rev. Saul Clark | DR | |
| Huldah, wid. of [East Haven], m. Titus **SANFORD**, of New | | |
| Haven, Sept. 6, 1812, by Rev. Saul Clark | DR | |
| Huldy, d. Isaac & Lois, b. June 9, 1788 | TM2 | 162 |
| Isaac, s. Isaac, d. June 21, 1784, ae 18 m. | DR | |
| Isaac, d. [Jan.] 16, 1832, ae 82 | DR | |
| Jacob, s. Isaac & Lois, b. Nov. 19, 1785 | TM2 | 162 |
| Jacob, d. Apr. 10, 1797, ae 37 | DR | |
| James, had cousin, Leonard Russel[l], who d. [Oct.] 27, 1830, | | |
| ae 24 | DR | |
| James Davidson, s. William, d. Oct. 5, 1830, ae 19 | DR | |
| James Dennis, of East Haven, m. Maria Amelia **KINGSBURY**, | | |
| of Fair Haven, [Sept.] 26, 1847, by Rev. D. William | | |
| Havens | DR | |
| Jared, d. Sept. 2, 1795, ae 17 | DR | |
| Jeremiah, s. Samuel, d. July 22, 1783, ae 17 | DR | |
| Jeremiah, m. Mary Ann **FORBES**, [Sept.] 30, 1829, by Rev. | | |
| Stephen Dodd | DR | |
| Jeremiah, m. Mary Ann **FORBES**, b. of East Haven, Sept. 30, | | |
| 1829, by Stephen Dodd | TM3 | 231 |
| John, s. John, d. [Aug.] 21, 1773, ae 6 | DR | |
| Julia, d. Apr. 13, 1819, ae 23; died instantly | DR | |
| Lemuel, d. [Nov.] 10, 1804, ae 22 | DR | |
| Leuramah, m. Wyllys **MALLORY**, b. of [East Haven], Oct. 8, | | |
| 1821, by Rev. Stephen Dodd | DR | |
| Leuramah, m. Wyllys **MALLERY**, Oct. 18, 1821, by Stephen | | |
| Dodd | TM3 | 165 |
| Lois, wid. Isaac, d. [Oct.] 9, 1832, ae 81 y. 5 m. | DR | |

| | Vol. | Page |
|---|---|---|
| **BARNES, BARNS**, (cont.), | | |
| Loly, w. Thomas, d. [        ], 1803, ae 27 | DR | |
| Lydia, d. Solomon, [of New Haven], d. Aug. 9, [1789], ae 5; bd. | | |
| in East Haven | DR | |
| Lydia, d. Solomon, [of New Haven], d. May 11, 1791, ae 2 d.; | | |
| bd. in East Haven | DR | |
| Lydia, w. Solomon, [of New Haven], d. Sept. 16, 1803, ae 53; | | |
| bd. in East Haven | DR | |
| Marah, d. Isaac & Lois, b. Aug. 2, 1780 | TM2 | 162 |
| Mary, w. Thomas, d. [        ], 1676 | DR | |
| Mary, m. Joel **BRADLEY**, b. of [East Haven], Feb. 14, 1819, | | |
| by Rev. Stephen Dodd | DR | |
| Mary, wid. of [East Haven], m. William **HILL**, of New Haven, | | |
| Nov. 3, 1825, by Rev. Stephen Dodd | DR | |
| Mary, of East Haven, m. William **HILLS**, of New Haven, Nov. | | |
| 3, 1825, by Stephen Dodd | TM3 | 207 |
| Mary Eliza, of East Haven, m. Timothy **BRADLEY**, of | | |
| Branford, Apr. 18, 1852, by Rev. George A. Hubbell | TM4 | 216 |
| Mehitibil, d. Isaac & Lois, b. Mar. 30, 1777 | TM2 | 162 |
| Mehitabel, d. Thomas, d. Apr. 26, 1826, ae 4 | DR | |
| Mehitabel, d. [Feb.] 16, 1840, ae 49 | DR | |
| Nathaniel, Jr., & Stephen **SMITH**, had negro Bette, d. Peter & | | |
| Ginne, b. Jan. 5, 1790 | TM2 | 159 |
| Nathaniel, d. [Dec.] 10, 1798, ae 92 | DR | |
| Orilla, w. Thomas, d. Nov. 11, 1838, ae 47 | DR | |
| Rebecca, w. Samuel, d. [        ], 1739 | DR | |
| Reuel, d. Aug. 11, 1814, ae 21, at Edenton, N. C. | DR | |
| Sally, of North Haven, m. Anson **THOMPSON**, of [East | | |
| Haven], Apr. [  ], 1816, by Rev. Saul Clark | DR | |
| Samuel, Capt. , d. July 21, 1762, ae 63 | DR | |
| Samuel, d. [Dec.] 19, 1794, ae 32, at sea | DR | |
| Samuel, Capt., d. Sept 3, 1832, ae 89 y. 4 m. | DR | |
| Sarah, d. Samuel, d. [May] 12, 1783, ae 9 | DR | |
| Sarah, of [East Haven], m. Henry **SCRANTON**, of Guilford, | | |
| Dec. 2, 1822, by Rev. Stephen Dodd | DR | |
| Sarah, of East Haven, m. Henry **SCRANTON**, of Guilford, | | |
| Dec. 8, 1822, by Stephen Dodd | TM3 | 166 |
| Sarah A., m. William **AMES**, b. of East Haven, Nov. 4, 1840, | | |
| by Rev. Stephen Dodd | DR | |
| Sarah A., m. William **AMES**, b. of East Haven, Nov. 4, 1840, | | |
| by Stephen Dodd | TM3 | 328 |
| Sherman, of North Haven, m. Hulda **SMITH** of [East Haven], | | |
| [Oct.] 30, 1823, by Rev. Stephen Dodd | DR | |
| Sherman, of North Haven, m. Huldah **SMITH**, of East Haven, | | |
| Oct. 30, 1823, by Stephen Dodd | TM3 | 138 |
| Silas, m. Mary **REDFIELD**, b. of [East Haven], Mar. [  ], 1809, | | |
| by Rev. Saul Clark | DR | |
| Silas, d. [        ], 1815, ae 26; lost at sea | DR | |
| Solomon, [of New Haven], d. June 10, 1807, ae 54 | DR | |
| Susan, Mrs., m. Rev. Jeremiah **ATWATER**, D. D., b. of New | | |
| Haven, Dec. 2, 1834, by Stephen Dodd | TM3 | 281 |
| Thomas, Jr., d. [        ]1712, ae 59 | DR | |
| Thomas, s. Ichabod, d. Jan. 4, 1774, ae 4 | DR | |

| | Vol. | Page |
|---|---|---|
| **BARNES, BARNS,** (cont.), | | |
| Thomus, s. Abraham & Hanner, b. Sept. 22, 1782 | TM2 | 157 |
| Thomas, m. Orilla **HOTCHKISS,** b. of [East Haven], Oct. 16, | | |
| 1808, by Rev. Saul Clark | DR | |
| Thomas, d. [July] 20, 1840, ae 57 y. 10 m. | DR | |
| Thomas, m. Elizabeth A. **THOMPSON,** b. of East Haven, | | |
| [Nov.] 25, 1840, by Rev. Stephen Dodd | DR | |
| Thomas, m. Elisabeth A. **THOMPSON,** b. of East Haven, | | |
| Nov. 25, 1840, by Stephen Dodd | TM3 | 328 |
| William, m. Nancy **DAVIDSON,** b. of [East Haven], Mar. 11, | | |
| 1811, by Rev. Saul Clark | DR | |
| William, d. July 31, 1835, ae 53 y. 6 m. | DR | |
| -----, infant of Solomon, [of New Haven], d. Jan. 21, 1786, | | |
| ae 1 w.; bd. in East Haven | DR | |
| -----, infant of Solomon, [of New Haven], d. Sept. 1, [1791], | | |
| ae 2 d.; bd. in East Haven | DR | |
| **BARTH,** Charles, of New Haven, m. Mary Maria **DAILEY,** of | | |
| Huntington, Oct. 12, 1840, by Stephen Dodd | TM3 | 327 |
| **BARTLETT,** Julia, d. Townsend, d. [Dec.] 15, 1815, ae 14 m. | DR | |
| Nathaniel Bradley, s. Townsend & Lydia, b. Feb. 11, 1809 | TM3 | 10 |
| Townsend, m. Lydia **BRADLEY,** June 6, 1808 | TM3 | 57 |
| **BARTRAM,** Henry B., of Bridgeport, m. Elizabeth C. **BRADLEY,** of East | | |
| Haven, Apr. 6, 1849, by Rev. N. S. Richardson | DR | |
| Henry B., of Bridgeport, m. Elizabeth O. **BRADLEY,** of East | | |
| Haven, Apr. 6, 1849, by Rev. N. S. Richardson | TM4 | 211 |
| **BASSETT,** Isaac, of New Haven, m. Elizabeth **WAY,** of [East Haven], | | |
| May 1, 1808, by Rev. Saul Clark | DR | |
| Polly, of [East Haven], m. Sherlock **MANSFIELD,** of | | |
| Northford, [Sept.] 19, 1832, by Rev. Stephen Dodd | DR | |
| **BEACH,** Jerome, of North Haven, m. Mary E. **ATWATER,** of Hamden, | | |
| Jan. 3, 1844, by Wyllys Hemingway, J. P. | TM4 | 203 |
| Mary E., wid., of Branford, m. Archibal **TYLER,** of New | | |
| Hartford, N. Y., Feb. 12, 1844, by Benj[ami]n L. | | |
| Swan | TM4 | 203 |
| **BECKET,** Hannah, d. John, d. Aug. 30, 1742 | DR | |
| Hannah, d. John, d. Aug. 30, 1742 | TM2 | 24 |
| **BEECHER,** Henry, of New Haven, m. Harriet Maria **WOODWARD,** of | | |
| [East Haven], May 8, 1823, by Rev. Stephen Dodd | DR | |
| Henry, of New Haven, m. Harriet Maria **WOODWARD,** of | | |
| East Haven, May 8, 1823, by Stephen Dodd | TM3 | 167 |
| Jeremiah, of Woodbridge, m. Sally **FORBES,** of [East Haven], | | |
| June 9, 1800, by Rev. Nicholas Street | DR | |
| Josiah H., m. Susan I. **BRAY,** Aug. 18, 1847, by Burdett Hart, | | |
| in Fair Haven | TM4 | 208 |
| **BEERS,** Lydia, of North Haven, m. Gurdon **PARDEE,** of [East Haven], | | |
| [Apr.] 30, 1826, by Rev. Stephen Dodd | DR | |
| Lydia, of North Haven, m. Gurdon **PARDEE,** of East Haven, | | |
| Apr. 30, 1826, by Stephen Dodd | TM3 | 171 |
| **BEMAN,** Louisa, d. Carlisle, d. [Nov.] 26, 1829, ae 4 | DR | |
| **BEMIS,** Anson L., of Meriden, m. Henrietta **BRADLEY,** of Branford, | | |
| May 17, 1835, by Rev. Stephen Dodd | DR | |
| Anson L., of Meriden, m. Henrietta **BRADLEY,** of Branford, | | |
| May 17, 1835, by Stephen Dodd | TM3 | 282 |

|  | Vol. | Page |
|---|---|---|
| **BENEDICT**, Henry W., of New Haven, m. Sarah Eunecia | | |
| HEMINGWAY, of East Haven, Apr. 2, 1844, by | | |
| Rev. Stephen Dodd | DR | |
| Henry W., of New Haven, m. Sarah Eun[e]cia **HEMINWAY**, | | |
| of East Haven, Apr. 2, 1844, by Stephen Dodd | TM4 | 203 |
| **BENHAM**, Abigail, wid., d. Aug. 19, 1824, ae 70 | DR | |
| **BIRDSEY**, Linus, of Meriden, m. Viney Ann **MILLER**, of Fair Haven, | | |
| Apr. 15, 1846, by Rev. Harvey Miller, of Meriden | TM4 | 206 |
| **BISHOP**, Amanda, w. Elias, d. Feb. 9, 1833, ae 34 | DR | |
| Benjamin, d. [        ], 1776, ae 30 | DR | |
| Benjamin, s. Joseph, d. [Oct.] 22, 1813, ae 7 | DR | |
| Charles, had negro Harry Jamkins, b. May 15, 1788 | TM2 | 164 |
| Charles, d. Oct. 26, 1804, ae 69 | DR | |
| David, s. Joseph, d. July 12, 1775, ae 17; killed by lightning | DR | |
| Elizabeth, d. Benjamin, d. [Jan.] 21, 1773, ae 2 | DR | |
| Frederick, s. Elias, d. Oct. 7, 1842, ae 19 | DR | |
| Hannah, d. Ichabod, d. [Nov.] 5, 1795, ae 18 | DR | |
| Harriet, d. James, d. [        ], 1810, ae 2; scalded | DR | |
| Henry, s. James, d. Dec. 3, 1811, ae 10 m. | DR | |
| Ichabod, d. [Apr.] 29, 1811, ae 61 | DR | |
| James, d. Feb. 7, 1840, ae 54 | DR | |
| Joseph, d. Sept. 14, 1769, ae 64 | DR | |
| Joseph, d. [Mar.] 6, 1845, ae 68 | DR | |
| Laura, d. John, d. [July] 24, 1825, ae 9 | DR | |
| Mabel, wid. Joseph, d. July 7, 1823, ae 91 [y.] 8 m. | DR | |
| Mary, wid. Charles, d. [Oct.] 19, 1823, ae 84 | DR | |
| Mehitabel, wid. Ichabod, d. Apr. 7, 1815, ae 60 | DR | |
| Ruth, d. [Sept.] 15, 1811, ae 70; burnt | DR | |
| Stephen, s. Joseph, d. [July] 12, 1766, ae 3 | DR | |
| Stephen, s. Joseph, d. July 3, 1781, ae 14 | DR | |
| -----, infant Jared, d. May [ ], 1799 | DR | |
| -----, infant ch. Elias, d. Jan. 6, 1825, ae 10 w. | DR | |
| **BLAKESLEY**, Isaac, Lieut., d. Feb. 4, 1767, ae 63 | DR | |
| Isaac, of North Haven, m. Mercy **TUTTLE**, of [East Haven], | | |
| Oct. 29, 1810, by Rev. Saul Clark | DR | |
| **BONFOY**, Seth, of Winfield, Herkimer County, N. Y., m. Eunecia | | |
| **PARDEE**, of East Haven, June 12, 1842, by Rev. | | |
| Stephen Dodd | DR | |
| Seth, of Winfield, N. Y., m. Eunecia **PARDEE**, of East Haven, | | |
| June 12, 1842, by Stephen Dodd | TM4 | 201 |
| **BOYKIM**, Nathaniel, d. [        ], 1705 | DR | |
| **BRACKIT**, [see under **BROCKETT**] | | |
| **BRADLEY, BRADLY**, Abigail, d. Simeon, b. Jan. 6, 1762 | TM2 | 46 |
| Abigail, d. Josiah & Comfort, b. Jan. 19, 1773 | TM2 | 163 |
| Abigail, d. Josiah, d. [Sept.] 23, 1773, ae 8 m. | DR | |
| Abigail, d. Josiah & Comfort, d. Sept. 23, 1773, ae 8 m. 3 d. | TM2 | 158 |
| Abigail, d. Josiah & Comfort, b. Oct. 22, 1776 | TM2 | 163 |
| Abigail, d. Zebulon & Elisabeth, b. Sept. 27, 1798 | TM2 | 294 |
| Abigail, wid. Simeon, d. [May] 18, 1810, ae 68 | DR | |
| Abijah, d. [        ], 1779, ae 29 | DR | |
| Abraham, d. Simeon, d. [Aug.] 22, 1794, ae 14 | DR | |
| Abraham, d. [Apr.] 24, 1843, ae 48 y. 10 m. | DR | |

| BRADLEY, BRADLY, (cont.), | Vol. | Page |
|---|---|---|
| Abram, s. Simeon & Abigail, b. Aug. 20, 1780 | TM2 | 163 |
| Ada, d. [Edmon & Lydeay], b. July 9, 1788 | TM2 | 158 |
| Adah, d. Edmond, d. [Dec.] 15, 1789, ae 16 m | DR | |
| Adah, m. Isaac PARDEE, b. of [East Haven], [Mar.] 14, 1811, by Rev. Saul Clark | DR | |
| Adeline, d. Zebulon & Lois, b. June 24, 1810 | TM3 | 11 |
| Almena, w. Tyrus, d. [July] [ ], 1841 | DR | |
| Amanda, of Branford, m. Riley Smith ROWE, of East Haven, [Oct.] 26, 1842, by Rev. Stephen Dodd | DR | |
| Amanda, of Branford, m. Riley Smith ROWE, of East Haven, Oct. 26, 1842, by Stephen Dodd | TM4 | 201 |
| Ame, m. Hezekiah BRADLEY, [Sept.] 22, 1804, by Rev. Nicholas Street | DR | |
| Ame, wid., d. Mar. 12, 1847, ae 66 | DR | |
| Amma, s. Jacob & Elesebath, b. Nov. 21, 1769 | TM2 | 154 |
| Ammi, d. [Aug.] 24, 1832, ae 62 y. 8 m. | DR | |
| Amos, s. [Amos & Elisabeth], b. Aug. 24, 1798 | TM3 | 11 |
| Amos, Col., d. [Apr.] 18, 1835, ae 66 | DR | |
| Amos M., d. [July] 16, 1827, (in Cuba), ae 23 | DR | |
| Amy, see under Ame | | |
| Anna, [d. Gurdon & Mary], b. Apr 22, 1774 | TM2 | 267 |
| Anna, d. [Gurdon & Mary], b. Apr 22, 1774 | TM2 | 298 |
| Anna, twin with Anson, d. Edmond, d. Aug. 24, 1793, ae 2 m. | DR | |
| Anna, m. Gideon SMITH, b. of [East Haven], Oct. 6, 1801, by Rev. Nicholas Street | DR | |
| Anson, twin with Anna, s. Edmond, d. June 1, 1793, ae 2 w. | DR | |
| Asa, d. [ ], 1779, ae 33 | DR | |
| Asa, d. [Amos & Elisabeth], b. Mar. 24, 1803 | TM3 | 11 |
| Asa, m. Louisa STETSON, b. of New Haven, Oct. 6, 1836, by Rev. Stephen Dodd | DR | |
| Asa, 2nd., m. Louisa STILSON, b. of New Haven, Oct. 30, 1836, by Stephen Dodd | TM3 | 285 |
| Asa, 2d, [of] New Haven, d. Sept. 13, 1845, ae 42; bd. [East Haven] | DR | |
| Asahel, s. Jacob & Elisabeth, b. Apr. 23, 1778 | TM2 | 154 |
| Asahel, m. Asenath GRANNIS, Mar. 14, 1799, by Rev. Nicholas Street | DR | |
| Asahel, d. [ ], 1826, ae 58 | DR | |
| Asenath, d. Asahel 2d, d. [Oct.] 29, 1823, ae 20 | DR | |
| Asenath, w. Asahel, d. [Nov.], [ ], 1848, ae 69 | DR | |
| Aulden, s. Zebulon & Lois, b. Aug. 4, 1811 | TM3 | 11 |
| Azariah, d. Apr. 4, 1812, ae 78 | DR | |
| Betsey, d. Amos, d. Dec. 8, 1794, ae 1 | DR | |
| Betsey, of [East Haven], m. Jonathan B. HUNTL[E]Y, of Lyme, [May] 16, 1830, by Rev. Stephen Dodd | DR | |
| Betsey, of East Haven, m. Jonathan B. HUNTL[E]Y, of Lyme, May 16, 1830, by Stephen Dodd | TM3 | 232 |
| Betsey Morris, d. [Amos & Elizabeth], b. Oct. 22, 1800 | TM3 | 11 |
| Caleb, s. Wil[l]iam, b. Oct. 17, 1714 | TM1 | 114 |
| Caleb, d. [ ], 1782, ae 68 | DR | |
| Caroline Amelia, d. Samuel 2d, d. Sept. 2, 1825, ae 2 | DR | |

| | Vol. | Page |
|---|---|---|
| **BRADLEY, BRADLY**, (cont.), | | |
| Charlotte C., m. Eliada B. **MALLERY**, Sept. 8, 1851, by Rev. | | |
|     Burdett Hart, of Fair Haven | TM4 | 215 |
| Comfort, w. Josiah, d. [May] 17, 1811, ae 68 | DR | |
| Comfort, w. Josiah, d. [July] 9, 1827, ae 85 | DR | |
| Cynthia Munger, w. Jesse, d. [Dec.] 22, 1844, ae 39 y. 2 d. | DR | |
| Dan, s. Edmund, d. [Sept.] 20, 1783, ae 2 | DR | |
| Dan. s. Edmon & Lydia, b. Mar. 27, 1784 | TM2 | 158 |
| Dan, m. Ame **FORBES**, b. of [East Haven], Nov. 4, 1804, by | | |
|     Rev. Nicholas Street | DR | |
| Dana, m. Mehitabel **BRADLEY**, b. of [East Haven], Nov. 30, | | |
|     1820, by Rev. Stephen Dodd | DR | |
| Dana, m. Mihitable **BRADLEY**, of East Haven, Nov. 30, 1820, | | |
|     by Stephen Dodd | TM3 | 57 |
| Daniel, d. [Dec.] 13, 1780, ae 84 | DR | |
| Dan[i]el, d. Dec. 13, 1780 | TM2 | 87 |
| Daniel, s. Samuel d. Jan. 21, 1805, ae 1 | DR | |
| Daniel, d. Apr. 4, 1825, ae 69 | DR | |
| Desire, m. Eleazar **HEMINWAY**, Oct. 16, 1799, by Rev. | | |
|     Nicholas Street | DR | |
| Desire, d. [Nov.] 6, 1831, ae 66 | DR | |
| Eben, s. Asahel 2d, d. [Aug.] 26, 1813, ae 8 | DR | |
| Ebenezer, s. Wilyam, b. Mar. 25, 1716 | TM1 | 198 |
| Edmond, d. [Feb.] 10, 1828, ae 70 | DR | |
| Elam, of Hamden, m. Mrs. Mary **THOMPSON**, of East Haven, | | |
|     Nov. 6, 1815, by Rev. Saul Clark | DR | |
| Eli, d. Mar. 3, 1835, ae 79 | DR | |
| Elias, of Branford, m. Elizabeth **WOODWARD**, of [East | | |
|     Haven], Oct. 17, 1805, by Rev. Nicholas Street | DR | |
| Elias, s. Jared [of Branford], d. Mar. 22, 1822, ae 36; bd. in East | | |
|     Haven | DR | |
| Elijah, [of Wolcott], d. Nov. [ ], 1807, in Georgia, ae 28 | DR | |
| Elijah, m. Elmina **BARNES**, b. of East Haven, Mar. 31, 1833, | | |
|     by Rev. Stephen Dodd | DR | |
| Elijah, 3rd, m. Elmina **BARNES**, b. of East Haven, Mar. 31, | | |
|     1833, by Stephen Dodd | TM3 | 235 |
| Elijah, d. [Apr. 29, 1844, ae 84 y. 7 m. | DR | |
| Elijah, m. Sarah W. **ANDREWS**, b. of East Haven, [Aug.] 27, | | |
|     1848, by Rev. D. William Havens | DR | |
| Elijah, m. Sarah W. **ANDREWS**, b. of East Haven, Aug. 27, | | |
|     1848, by D. W[illia]m Havens | TM4 | 210 |
| Elijah Augusta, s. [Amos & Elisabeth], b. June 29, 1807 | TM3 | 11 |
| Elessabeth, m. John **AWGUR**, Aug. 3, 1710, by William | | |
|     Malttby, J. P. | TM1 | 31 |
| Elizabeth, w. Isaac, d. Jan. 3, 1713, ae 56 | DR | |
| Elesabeth, w. Icsak, d. Jan. 3, 1712/13 | TM1 | 31 |
| Elizabeth, w. Azariah, d. [Jan.] 10, 1761, ae 21 | DR | |
| Elisabeth, d. Josiah & Comfort, b. Dec. 16, 1779 | TM2 | 163 |
| Elizabeth, wid. Jacob, d. Aug. 5, 1802, ae 64 | DR | |
| Elizabeth, wid. Zebulon, d. Mar. 9, 1803, ae 87 | DR | |
| Elizabeth, [d] Daniel **BRADLEY**, 2d, m. Samuel Bradley, | | |
|     2d, July 25, 1803, by Rev. Nicholas Street | DR | |

**BRADLEY, BRADLY, (cont.),**

| | Vol. | Page |
|---|---|---|
| Elizabeth, m. John **BRADLEY**, [May] [ ], 1804, by Rev. | | |
| Nicholas Street | DR | |
| Elizabeth, d. Mar. 16, 1833, ae 67 y. 8 m. | DR | |
| Elizabeth C., of East Haven, m. Henry B. **BARTRAM**, of | | |
| Bridgeport, Apr. 6, 1849, by Rev. N. S. Richardson | DR | |
| Elizabeth O., of East Haven, m. Henry B. **BARTRAM**, of | | |
| Bridgeport, Apr. 6, 1849, by Rev. N. S. Richardson | TM4 | 211 |
| Elizabeth R., of [East Haven], m. Charles **LEWIS**, of New | | |
| Haven, Dec. 10, 1826, by Rev. Stephen Dodd | DR | |
| Elizabeth R., of East Haven, m. Charles **LEWIS**, of New | | |
| Haven, Dec. 10, 1826, by Stephen Dodd | TM3 | 172 |
| Elmina, w. Elijah, d. [Nov.] 12, 1845, ae 32 | DR | |
| Enos, d. [June] 20, 1782, ae 20; fall from masthead | DR | |
| Esther, d. [Nov.] 22, 1821, ae 23 | DR | |
| Esther, of [East Haven], m. John Chester **BRADLEY**, Mar. 18, | | |
| 1829, by Rev. Stephen Dodd | DR | |
| Esther, wid., m. Samuel **CHIDSEY**, Jr. , of East Haven, Nov. 7, | | |
| 1833, by Stephen Dodd | TM3 | 236 |
| Esther, wid. m. Samuel **CHIDSEY**, Jr. b. of East Haven, Nov. | | |
| 7, 1833, by Rev. Stephen Dodd | DR | |
| Esther, wid. Elijah, d. [Nov.] 17, 1845, ae 86 y. 3 m. | DR | |
| Eudocia, d. Daniel, d. [Aug.] 26, 1796, ae 5 | DR | |
| Eunice, wid. Daniel, d. [July] 13, 1831, ae 76 | DR | |
| George, d. [May] 16, 1833, ae 36 | DR | |
| Georgiana, d. Jesse, d. Apr. 29, 1838, ae 14 m. | DR | |
| Grace Ann, m. Henry William **SALTONSTALL**, of N. Y., | | |
| [June] 28, 1831, by Rev. Stephen Dodd | DR | |
| Grace Ann, of Branford, m. Henry William **SALTONSTALL**, | | |
| of New York, June 28, 1831, by Stephen Dodd | TM3 | 233 |
| Gurdon, Capt., d. [Nov.] 16, 1821, ae 83 | DR | |
| Hannah, wid. Isaac, d. Jan. 9, 1791, ae 66 | DR | |
| Hannah, d. Isaac, d. July 30, 1794, ae 5 | DR | |
| Hannah, d. Dec. 7, 1795, ae 36 | DR | |
| Hannah, w. Abner, d. [Sept.] 10, 1813, ae 31 | DR | |
| Hannah, of [East Haven], m. Chauncey **LINES**, of North | | |
| Haven, June 20, 1819, by Rev. Stephen Dodd | DR | |
| Harriet, d. Abner, d. [Oct.] 14, 1813, ae 1 | DR | |
| Harriet, m. Heminway **SMITH**, b. of East Haven [June] 11, | | |
| 1843, by Rev. Stephen Dodd | DR | |
| Harriet, m. Hemingway **SMITH**, b. of East Haven, June 11, | | |
| 1843, by Stephen Dodd | TM4 | 202 |
| Hemingway Holt, s. [Jesse & Lidia], b. June 6, 1792 | TM2 | 264 |
| Henrietta, m. William **HUNT**, b. of [East Haven], Nov. 11, | | |
| 1830, by Rev. Stephen Dodd | DR | |
| Henrietta, m. William Henry **HUNT**, b. of East Haven, Nov. 11, | | |
| 1830, by Stephen Dodd | TM3 | 86-87 |
| Henrietta, m. William Henry **HUNT**, b. of East Haven, Nov. 11, | | |
| 1830, by Stephen Dodd | TM3 | 233 |
| Henrietta, of Branford, m. Anson L. **BEMIS**, of Meriden, May | | |
| 17, 1835, by Rev. Stephen Dodd | DR | |
| Henrietta, of Branford, m. Anson L. **BEMIS**, of Meriden, May | | |
| 17, 1835, by Stephen Dodd | TM3 | 282 |

| | Vol. | Page |
|---|---|---|
| **BRADLEY, BRADLY,** (cont.), | | |
| Henry Bishop, s. Elijah, d. [Oct.] 16, 1845, ae 6 | DR | |
| Henry I., of Hamden, m. Marietta **SMITH,** of East Haven, May | | |
| 10, 1837, by Rev. Stephen Dodd | DR | |
| Henry Rosewell, s. Rosewell, d. Nov. 22, 1825, ae 18 | DR | |
| Hester, m. John Chester **BRADLEY,** b. of East Haven, Mar. 18, | | |
| 1829, by Stephen Dodd | TM3 | 174 |
| Hezekiah, m. Ame **BRADLEY,** [Sept.] 22, 1804, by Rev. | | |
| Nicholas Street | DR | |
| Hezekiah, d. May 20, 1807, ae 34; in West Indies | DR | |
| Horace Augustus, d. Jan. 26, 1840, ae 26 | DR | |
| Huldah, [d. Gurdon & Mary], b. June 16, 1770 | TM2 | 267 |
| Huldah, d.[ Gurdon & Mary], b. June 16, 1770 | TM2 | 298 |
| Huldah Hughes, d. Levi, d. Mar. 16, 1837, ae 24 | DR | |
| Irene, d. Simeon, b. May 6, 1760 | TM2 | 46 |
| Icsak, d. Jan. 12, 1712/13 | TM1 | 31 |
| Isaac, father of the East Haven **BRADLEY's,** d. [Jan.] 12, | | |
| 1713, ae 62 | DR | |
| Isaac, Jr., d. July 10, 1716 | DR | |
| Isaac, s. Isaac, d. July 10, 1716 | TM1 | 198 |
| Isaac, s. Samuell, b. Nov. 30, 1717 | TM1 | 198 |
| Isaac, d. [Sept.] 19, 1783, ae 65 | DR | |
| Jacob, d. [Oct.] 14, 1795, ae 61 | DR | |
| James, s. William, b. June 15, 1726 | TM1 | 245 |
| James, s. Amma, d. [Aug.] 25, 1796, ae 17 m. | DR | |
| James, m. Lydia **BRADLEY,** b. of [East Haven], May 7, 1801, | | |
| by Rev. Nicholas Street | DR | |
| James, s. Amma, d. [Sept.] 14, 1813, ae 12 | DR | |
| James, d. [Jan.] 24, 1842, ae 71 y. 8 m. | DR | |
| Jane, d. Abraham, d. June 13, 1830, ae 2 | DR | |
| Jane Adeline, d. [Amos & Elizabeth], b. Apr. 14, 1805 | TM3 | 11 |
| Jane Caroline, d. Abraham, b. [Dec.] 8, 1831, ae 15 m. | DR | |
| Jared, s. Zebulon, d. July 1, 1746, ae 2 m. | DR | |
| Jared, s. Abraham, d. May 7, 1765, ae 4 m. | DR | |
| Jared, s. Jared, [of Branford], d. June 14, 1794, ae 16; bd. in | | |
| East Haven | DR | |
| Jared, s. Amos, d. [Sept.] 13, 1796, ae 1 | DR | |
| Jared, s. Amos & Elizabeth, b. Jan. 23, 1797 | TM3 | 11 |
| Jared, [of Branford], had servant woman, d. Nov. [ ], 1803, | | |
| ae 79, [bd. in East Haven] | DR | |
| Jared, s. Asahel 2d., d. [Sept.] 30, 1813, ae 9 m. | DR | |
| Jared, s. William 2d., d. [Jan.] 11, 1826, ae 3 | DR | |
| Jared, d. June 19, 1833, ae 84 | DR | |
| Jennet, d. Samuel , 2d., d. Jan. 11, 1810, ae 2 | DR | |
| Jennet, d. Samuel, 2d., d. [Sept.] 28, 1812, ae 5 w. | DR | |
| Jeremiah, s. Josiah & Comfort, b. Aug. 11, 1766 | TM2 | 163 |
| Jeremiah, d. Apr. 23, 1789, ae 22; killed in raising the Episcopal | | |
| church | DR | |
| Jeremiah, s. [Josiah & Comfort], d. Apr. 23, 1789, | | |
| ae 22 y. 8 m. 12 d. | TM2 | 158 |
| Jeremiah, s. Zebulon & Elisabeth, b. June 6, 1800 | TM2 | 294 |
| Jesse, s. Simeon, b. July 31, 1766 | TM2 | 46 |
| Jesse, s. [Jesse & Lidia], b. Nov. 29, 1793 | TM2 | 264 |
| Jesse, d. [ ], 1796, ae 30; lost at sea | DR | |

**BRADLEY, BRADLY,** (cont.),

| | Vol. | Page |
|---|---|---|
| Jesse, d. [          ], 1810, ae 17; lost in a gale at sea | DR | |
| Jesse, m. Laura **LANFEAR**, July 4, 1845, by Rev. Stephen<br>    Dodd | DR | |
| Jesse, of East Haven, m. Laura **LANDFEAR**, of Branford, July<br>    4, 1845, by Stephen Dodd | TM4 | 204 |
| Joel, s. Simeon, b. Nov. 17, 1768 | TM2 | 46 |
| Joel, m. Mary **BARNES**, b. of [East Haven], Feb. 14, 1819, by<br>    Rev. Stephen Dodd | DR | |
| John, s. Azariah, d. Oct. 12, 1774, ae 6 m. | DR | |
| John, s. [Gurdon & Mary], b. Apr. 30, 1777 | TM2 | 267 |
| John, s. [Gurdon & Mary], b. Apr. 30, 1777 | TM2 | 298 |
| John, m. Elizabeth **BRADLEY**, [May] [   ], 1804, by Rev.<br>    Nicholas Street | DR | |
| John Chester, m. Elizabeth **BRADLEY**, of [East Haven], Mar.<br>    18, 1829, by Rev. Stephen Dodd | DR | |
| John Chester, m. Hester **BRADLEY**, b. of East Haven, Mar. 18,<br>    1829, by Stephen Dodd | TM3 | 174 |
| John Chester, d. [Aug.] 10, 1831, ae 24 | DR | |
| John S., [of New Haven], s. Jared, [of Branford], d. Oct. 8,<br>    1818, ae 30 | DR | |
| Joseph, s. William, b. July 13, 1718 | TM1 | 199 |
| Joseph, s. Jacob & Elesebath, b. May 16, 1763 | TM2 | 154 |
| Joseph, s. Daniel, d. [          ], 1782, ae 19 | DR | |
| Joseph, s. Jacob & Elesabeth, d. Sept. [  ], 1782 | TM2 | 158 |
| Joseph, s. Daniel, d. [Sept.] 24, 1789, ae 3 | DR | |
| Joseph, Capt., m. Mary Ann **WILLIAMS**, of East Haven, July<br>    28, 1832, in Hartford, by Rt. Rev. Thomas C.<br>    Brownell | DR | |
| Joseph, m. Mary Ann **WILLIAMS**, July 28, 1832, by Rev.<br>    Tho[ma]s C. Brownell, in Hartford | TM3 | 233 |
| Josiah, d. [Sept.] 30, 1827, ae 84 | DR | |
| Julia, of Branford, m. Aaron **HIGBEE**, of Wallingford, June 1,<br>    1829, by Stephen Dodd | TM3 | 231 |
| Justin, [s. Gurdon & Mary], b. May 20, 1787 | TM2 | 267 |
| Justin, s. [Gurdon & Mary], b. May 20, 1787 | TM2 | 298 |
| Justin, d. [Feb.] 16, 1814, ae 27 | DR | |
| Justin, d. Feb. 16, 1814, ae 27 y. | TM2 | 267 |
| Justin, m. Esther S. **TYLER**, b. of East Haven, Nov. 14, 1839,<br>    by Rev. Stephen Dodd | DR | |
| Justin, m. Esther **TYLER**, b. of East Haven, Nov. 14, 1839, by<br>    Stephen Dodd | TM3 | 326 |
| Justus, s. Stephen, Jr., d. Sept. 8, 1787, ae 4 | DR | |
| Justus, s. Stephen, d. Sept. 1, 1796, ae 2 | DR | |
| Kiah, s. Jacob & Elisabeth, b. July 21, 1774 | TM2 | 154 |
| Laura, m. Rosewell **CHIDSEY**, b. of [East Haven], Dec. 16,<br>    1810, by Rev. Saul Clark | DR | |
| Lavinia, of Branford, m. Warren C. **ATKINS**, of Meriden, Dec.<br>    13, 1835, by Stephen Dodd | TM3 | 283 |
| Leonard, m. Rowena **PERKINS**, b. of Fair Haven, Sept. 13,<br>    1852, by Rev. D. W[illia]m Havens | TM4 | 218 |
| Leonard F., s. wid. Abraham, d. May 27, 1846, ae 13 | DR | |
| Laverett, d. [Jan.] 23, 1848, ae 81 | DR | |

| | Vol. | Page |
|---|---|---|
| **BRADLEY, BRADLY,** (cont.), | | |
| Levi, s. Simeon & Abigail, b. Sept. 23, 1777 | TM2 | 46 |
| Levi, m. Huldah **FORBES,** b. of [East Haven], Feb. 5, 1804, by | | |
|     Rev. Nicholas Street | DR | |
| Levi, d. Oct. 8, 1846, ae 69 | DR | |
| Lois, d. Isaac & Mary, b. Jan. 15, 1783; m. Simeon | | |
|     **GOODSELL,** of Branford, May 12, 1803 | TM3 | 11 |
| Loruhanna, d. Josiah & Comfort, b. Apr. 7, 1769 | TM2 | 163 |
| Louisa, of Branford, m. Warren C. **ATKINS,** of Meriden, Dec. | | |
|     13, 1835, by Rev. Stephen Dodd | DR | |
| Louisa A., of East Haven, m. Jeremiah A. **SQUARE,** of East | | |
|     Windsor, Jan. 15, 1840, by Stephen Dodd | TM3 | 327 |
| Lowvisey, d. Jacob & Elisabeth, b. Mar. 28, 1772    (Lovisa) | TM2 | 154 |
| Lovisa, w. Joel, d. Mar. 23, 1815, ae 43 | DR | |
| Lovisa Amanda, of East Haven, m. Jeremiah A. **SQUYRE,** of | | |
|     East Windsor, Jan. 15, 1840, by Rev. Stephen Dodd | DR | |
| Lucinda, of [East Haven], m. Hezekiah L. **PARTRIDGE,** of | | |
|     North Branford, Dec. 19, 1811, by Rev. Saul Clark | DR | |
| Lucretia, d. William, d. [Oct.] 25, 1774, ae 8 | DR | |
| Lucy, of East Haven, m. Laban **PARDEE,** of New Haven, Dec. | | |
|     31, 1820, by Rev. Joseph Perry | TM3 | 164 |
| Lue, d. [Gurdon & Mary], b. Oct. 1, 1780 | TM2 | 267 |
| Lue, d. [Gurdon & Mary], b. Oct. 1, 1780 | TM2 | 298 |
| Lue, m. Doc. David **FORBES,** b. of [East Haven], Mar. 6, | | |
|     1803, by Rev. Nicholas Street | DR | |
| Lue, of East Haven, m. Laban **PARDEE,** of New Haven, Dec. | | |
|     31, 1820, by Rev. Joseph Perry | DR | |
| Luthen, s. [Amos & Elisabeth], b. Aug. 4, 1809 | TM3 | 11 |
| Luther, [of] New Haven, d. [Feb.] [ ], 1831, ae 21; bd. in East | | |
|     Haven | DR | |
| Luzerne, of East Haven, m. Jennet **BRISTOL,** of New Haven, | | |
|     Aug. 27, 1836, by Rev. Stephen Dodd | DR | |
| Luzerne, m. Jennet **BRISTOL,** b. of New Haven, Aug. 27, | | |
|     1836, by Stephen Dodd | TM3 | 285 |
| Luzerne, d. [Nov.] 23, 1843, ae 32 | DR | |
| Lydia, d. Jacob & Elesebath, b. Oct. 12, 1760 | TM2 | 154 |
| Lydia, d. [Jesse & Lidia], b. Jan. 29, 1791 | TM2 | 264 |
| Lydia, m. James **BRADLEY,** b. of [East Haven], May 7, 1801, | | |
|     by Rev. Nicholas Street | TM3 | 57 |
| Lydia, m. Townsend **BARTLETT,** June 6, 1808 | DR | |
| Lydia, wid. Azariah, b. [Oct.] 24, 1825, ae 78 | DR | |
| Lydia, wid. Edmond, d. Oct. 20, 1834, ae 73 y. 5 m. | DR | |
| Lydia, of East Haven, m. Martin **ALLEN,** of Plymouth, Apr. 4, | | |
|     1847, by Rev. Stephen Dodd | DR | |
| Lydia, of East Haven, m. Martin **ALLEN,** of Plymouth, Apr. 4, | | |
|     1847, by Stephen Dodd | TM4 | 207 |
| Lydia A., m. Willett **HEMINGWAY,** Jr., b. of East Haven, | | |
|     May 8, 1845, by Rev. Benj[ami]n L. Swan | TM4 | 204 |
| Mabel, d. Simeon, b. Dec. 16, 1763 | TM2 | 46 |
| Mabel, w. Justin, d. [Mar.] 30, 1808, ae 21; childbed | DR | |
| Mabel T., m. Justin **KIMBERLY,** b. of [East Haven], Apr. 4, | | |
|     1824, by Rev. Stephen Dodd | DR | |

| BRADLEY, BRADLY, (cont.), | Vol. | Page |
|---|---|---|
| Mabel T., m. Justus **KIMBERLY**, Apr. 4, 1824, by Stephen Dodd | TM3 | 168 |
| Marcy, d. Jan. 10, 1743/4 | TM2 | 25 |
| Maria, d. Sept. 27, 1802 | DR | |
| Maria, d. Leveret, d. [Aug.] 11, 1807, ae 6 w. | DR | |
| Maria Ann, of Branford, m. George **HOADLEY**, of New Haven, Apr. 4, 1836, by Rev. Stephen Dodd | DR | |
| Maria Ann, of Branford, m. George **HOADLEY**, of New Haven, Apr. 4, 1836, by Stephen Dodd | TM3 | 285 |
| Mary, d. [Gurdon & Mary], b. May 2, 1767 | TM2 | 267 |
| Mary, d. Gurdon & Mary, b. May 2, 1767 | TM2 | 298 |
| Mary, d. Stephen, d. [      ], 1773, ae 10 | DR | |
| Mary, d. Stephen, Jr., d. Apr. 17, 1782, ae 15 d. | DR | |
| Mary, d. William, d. Aug. 25, 1789, ae 2 | DR | |
| Mary, d. Isaac, d. June 17, 1794, ae 15 | DR | |
| Mary, w. Isaac, d. [Oct.] 6, 1813, ae 60 | DR | |
| Mary, d. Oct. 2, 1817, ae 31 | DR | |
| Mary, w. Gurdon, d. May 7, 1819, ae 75 | DR | |
| Mary, w. Gurdon, d. May 7, 1819, ae 74 y. | DR | |
| Mary, w. George, d. [Mar.] 29, 1826, ae 22 | DR | |
| Mary, w. Joel, d. [May] [ ], 1832, ae 51 y. 10 m. | DR | |
| Mary, of East Haven, m. Henry **FENN**, of Plymouth, Mar. 4, 1834, by Rev. Stephen Dodd | DR | |
| Mary, of East Haven, m. Henry **FENN**, of Plymouth, Mar. 4, 1834, by Stephen Dodd | TM3 | 281 |
| Mary, w. Levi, d. [May] 27, 1836, ae 53 | DR | |
| Mary, w. William, d. [Apr.] 31, 1844, ae 77 | DR | |
| Mary Angeline, d. Levi, d. Apr. 14, 1835, ae 27 | DR | |
| Mary Maria, w. Warren, d. [Feb.] 7, 1845, ae 29 | DR | |
| Mehitabel, w. Daniel, d. [June] 30, 1773, ae 71 | DR | |
| Mehitabel, m. Dana **BRADLEY**, b. of [East Haven], Nov. 30, 1820, by Rev. Stephen Dodd | DR | |
| Mihitable, m. Dana **BRADLEY**, Nov. 30, 1820, by Stephen Dodd | TM3 | 57 |
| Merit, s. Abner, d. Sept. 2, 1813, ae 5 | DR | |
| Mol[l]ey, d. Jacob & Elesebath, b. Nov. 24, 1765 | TM2 | 154 |
| Munson, of North Haven, m. Nabby **TUTTLE**, of [East Haven], Jan. 5, 1818, by Rev. Stephen Dodd | DR | |
| Nancy, d. [Mar.] 21, 1811, ae 27 | DR | |
| Nathaniel, d. June 5, 1798, ae 20 | DR | |
| Noah W., of New York, m. Celestia M. **ANDREWS**, of East Haven, July 18, 1849, by Stephen Dodd | TM4 | 212 |
| Olive, of [East Haven], m. Ruel **CHIDSEY**, of Branford, Feb. 3, 1805, by Rev. Nicholas Street | DR | |
| Oliver, s. Simeon & Abigail, b. Feb. 15, 1774 | TM2 | 46 |
| Oliver, s. [Jesse & Lidia], b. Feb. 19, 1796 | TM2 | 264 |
| Oliver, m. Hannah **ANDREWS**, b. of [East Haven], May 10, 1803, by Rev. Nicholas Street | DR | |
| Polly, m. Stephen **SMITH**, b. of [East Haven], Aug. 18, 1808, by Rev. Saul Clark | DR | |
| Polly, m. Samuel R. **MOULTHROP**, b. of [East Haven], Sept. 30, 1821, by Rev. Stephen Dodd | DR | |

| | Vol. | Page |
|---|---|---|
| **BRADLEY, BRADLY,** (cont.), | | |
| Polly, m. Samuel R. **MOULTHROP,** Sept. 30, 1821, by | | |
| Stephen Dodd | TM3 | 164 |
| Polly, of [East Haven], m. Henry **SEELY,** of New Haven, Oct. | | |
| 5, 1823, by Rev. Stephen Dodd | DR | |
| Polly, of East Haven, m. Henry **SEELY,** of New Haven, Oct. 5, | | |
| 1823, by Stephen Dodd | TM3 | 168 |
| Polly, w. Rosewell, d. July 29, 1826, ae 43 | DR | |
| Rebecca, wid. William, d. Jan. 26, 1797, ae 59 | DR | |
| Rosewell, d. Dec. 9, 1780, ae 25; at sea | DR | |
| Rosewell, s. William, d. [Apr.] 19, 1819, ae 20; at Martinique | DR | |
| Rosewell, d. [July] 25, 1827, ae 47 | DR | |
| Sally, m. Abijah **DAVIDSON,** b. of [East Haven], [Feb.] 17, | | |
| 1805, by Rev. Nicholas Street | DR | |
| Samuel, m. Sarah **ROBINSON,** Jan. 27, 1714/15 | TM1 | 114 |
| Samuel, d. Mar. 23, 1758, ae 72 | DR | |
| Samuel, d. [Feb.] 16, 1782, ae 32 | DR | |
| Samuel, 2d, m. Elizabeth **BRADLEY,** [d.] Daniel | | |
| **BRADLEY,** 2d, July 25, 1803, by Rev. Nicholas | | |
| Street | DR | |
| Samuel, d. [Feb.] 15, 1820, ae 45 | DR | |
| Samuel, d. June 23, 1834, ae 67 | DR | |
| Samuel, Jr., d. Sept. 14, 1843, ae 35 | DR | |
| Samuel, [s.] Stephen, m. Fanny Lavinia **ROWE,** b. of East | | |
| Haven, Oct. 11, 1846, by Stephen Dodd | TM4 | 207 |
| Samuel F., m. Sarah S. **HOLT,** b. of East Haven, July 12, 1840, | | |
| by Stephen Dodd | TM3 | 327 |
| Samuel F., m. Fanny Lavinia **ROWE,** b. of East Haven, Oct. | | |
| 11, 1846, by Rev. Stephen Dodd | DR | |
| Samuel Forbes, m. Sarah S. **HOLT,** b. of East Haven, July 12, | | |
| 1840, by Rev. Stephen Dodd | DR | |
| Samuel Thompson, s. Samuel 2d, d. Oct. 5, 1820, ae 11 w. | DR | |
| Samuel Thompson, s. Samuel, 2d, d. [Nov.] 12, 1825, ae 4 m. | DR | |
| Sarah, m. Isaac **CHIDSEY,** Jr., June 18, 1752 | TM2 | 45 |
| Sarah, w. Dan., d. Nov. 19, 1764, ae 34 | DR | |
| Sarah, d. Simeon & Abigail, b. July 8, 1771 | TM2 | 46 |
| Sarah, w. Samuel, d. Jan. 17, 1778, ae 83 | DR | |
| Sarah, wid., d. Jan. 17, 1778, in the 84th year of her age | TM2 | 110 |
| Sarah, d. Edmon & Lydeay, b. Feb. 11, 1786 | TM2 | 158 |
| Sarah, d. Daniel, d. [Sept.] 11, 1796, ae 2 | DR | |
| Sarah, m. Benjamin **PARDEE,** b. of [East Haven], Oct. 28, | | |
| 1811, by Rev. Saul Clark | DR | |
| Sarah, w. Jared, [of Branford], d. July 15, 1814, ae 66 | DR | |
| Sarah, d. [Feb.] 13, 1818, ae 46 | DR | |
| Sarah, d. [Nov.] 8, 1843, ae 23 | DR | |
| Sarah, wid., d. [Oct.] 19, 1847, ae 79 | DR | |
| Sarah, wid., Samuel Horace, d. [May] 8, 1848, ae 33 | DR | |
| Sarah, see under Sarah Bradley **WOODWARD** | DR | |
| Sarah Elizabeth, d. [Amos & Elisabeth], b. July 1, 1816 | TM3 | 11 |
| Sibel, see under Sybil | | |
| Sidney, d. [Nov.] 20, 1831, (at Savannah), ae 27 y. 7 m. | DR | |
| Simeon, d. [July] 22, 1802, ae 71 | DR | |
| Solomon, s. William, d. [ ], 1807, ae 14 | DR | |

| BRADLEY, BRADLY, (cont.), | Vol. | Page |
|---|---|---|
| Solomon, m. Emeline **LEWIS**, July 31, 1831, by Rev. John Mitchell, of Fair Haven | TM3 | 283 |
| Sophia Louisa, of Branford, m. Charles **McLEAN**, of New York, Feb. 28, 1835, by Stephen Dodd | TM3 | 282 |
| Stephen, d. Feb. 22, 1797, ae 73 | DR | |
| Stephen, d. Nov. 23, 1839, ae 80 | DR | |
| Stephen, d. Apr. 23, 1849, ae 54 | DR | |
| Susan, d. Jesse & Lidia, b. Nov. 11, 1788 | TM2 | 264 |
| Susan, m. George **THOMPSON**, b. of [East Haven], Apr. 22, 1811, by Rev. Saul Clark | DR | |
| Susan, wid. of [East Haven], m. Eli **BARNES**, of Southington, Aug. 2, 1812, by Rev. Saul Clark | DR | |
| Susannah, [twin with Willet, d. Gurdon & Mary], b. June 27, 1784 | TM2 | 267 |
| Susannah, [twin with Willit, d. Gurdon & Mary], b. June 27, 1784 | TM2 | 298 |
| Susannah, twin child Gurdon, d. July 12, 1784, ae 2 w. | DR | |
| Susannah, [twin with Willet, d. Gurdon & Mary], d. July 12, 1784, ae 15 d. | TM2 | 267 |
| Sibel, d. Jacob & Elseabath, b. May 30, 1758          (Sybil) | TM2 | 154 |
| Sibyl, d. Jacob, d. [July] 7, 1773, ae 15 | DR | |
| Sibel, d. Jacob & Elisabeth, d. July 7, 1773 | TM2 | 158 |
| Thankful, w. Stephen, d. Aug. 22, 1795, ae 72 | DR | |
| Timothy, of Branford, m. Mary Eliza **BARNES**, of East Haven, Apr. 18, 1852, by Rev. George A. Hubble | TM4 | 216 |
| Traffena, d. Zebulon & Elisabeth, b. Dec. 19, 1796 | TM2 | 265 |
| Tryfena, d. Zebulon & Elissbeth, b. Dec. 19, 1976 | TM2 | 294 |
| Tyrus, m. Almena **LUDDINGTON**, of [East Haven], [May] 27, 1824, by Rev. Stephen Dodd | DR | |
| Tyrus, m. Almena **LUDDINGTON**, May 27, 1824, by Stephen Dodd | TM3 | 169 |
| Tyrus, m. wid. Eunice **COOPER**, b. of East Haven, Sept. 20, 1846, by Rev. Stephen Dodd | DR | |
| Tyrus, m. Eunice **COOPER**, b. of East Haven, Sept. 20, 1846, by Stephen Dodd | TM4 | 206 |
| Uriel, s. Edmond, d. [Sept.] 20, 1788, ae 2 | DR | |
| Wealthy, m. Harvey **ROWE**, b. of [East Haven], [Oct.] [ ], 1810, by Rev. Saul Clark | DR | |
| Willard, d. [Jan.] 22, 1822, ae 26 | DR | |
| Willet, [twin with Susannah, s. Gurdon & Mary], b. June 27, 1784 | TM2 | 267 |
| Willit, [twin with Susannah, s. Gurdon & Mary], b. June 27, 1784 | TM2 | 298 |
| Willet, m. Susannah **MORRIS**, of [East Haven], Mar. 17, 1805, by Rev. Nicholas Street | DR | |
| Willet, d. May 15, 1811, ae 27 | DR | |
| Willet, [twin with Susannah, s. Gurdon & Mary], d. May 15, 1811, ae 27 y. | TM2 | 267 |
| Willett, m. Mary Ann **PARDEE**, b. of [East Haven], Apr. 4, 1830, by Rev. Stephen Dodd | DR | |
| Willet, m. Mary Ann **PARDEE**, b. of East Haven, Apr. 4, 1830, by Stephen Dodd | TM3 | 231 |

| | Vol. | Page |
|---|---|---|
| **BRADLEY, BRADLY**, (cont.), | | |
| William, m. Elesabeth **CHEDSEY**, Jan. 7, 1713/14 | TM1 | 114 |
| William, d. Jan. 27, 1726/7 | TM1 | 245 |
| William, d. Jan. 27, 1727 | DR | |
| William, s. Bill & Reb[e]kah, b. May 18, 1763 | TM2 | 157 |
| William, m. Lydia **SMITH**, Sept. 16, 1804, by Rev. Nicholas Street | DR | |
| William, s. Henry & gd. ch. of Stephen **SMITH**, 2d, d. Oct. 1, 1842, ae 2 | DR | |
| William Warren, s. Dana, d. [May] 19, 1828, ae 1 | DR | |
| Zebulon, s. Samuell, b. Oct. 6, 1715 | TM1 | 114 |
| Zebulon, Capt., d. Jan. 13, 1760, at New York, ae 46 | DR | |
| Zebulon, s. Josiah & Comfort, b. Sept. 16, 1774 | TM2 | 163 |
| Zebulon, d. Oct. 21, 1779, ae 26; killed in battle at sea | DR | |
| Zebulon, m. Elisabeth **GOODSELL**, May 11, 1794, by Rev. Nicholas Street | TM2 | 265 |
| Zebulon, m. wid. Lois **GOODSELL**, b. of [East Haven], Nov. 1, 1809, by Rev. Saul Clark | DR | |
| Zebulon, m. Lois **GOODSELL**, Nov. 1, 1809 | TM3 | 11 |
| Zebulon, d. [Feb.] 13, 1833, ae 58 | DR | |
| ----, s. Daniel, d. in infancy [1736] | TM2 | 23 |
| ----, infant Daniel, d. [        ], 1737 | DR | |
| ----, d. Abraham, d. July 6, 1763, ae 6 w. | DR | |
| ----, child William, d. [Nov.] 11, 1775, ae 18 m. | DR | |
| ----, twin child [of] Edward, d. July 9, 1788, ae 4 w. | DR | |
| ----, twins [of] Edmond, d. May 16, 1794, ae 2 d. | DR | |
| ----, child [of] Zebulon, d. [Nov.] 21, 1795, ae 2 m. | DR | |
| ----, infant [of] Edmond, one of the triplets, d. Mar. 13, 1800, ae 1 d. | DR | |
| ----, two of the infant triplets [of] Edmond, d. [Mar.] 30, 1800, ae 17 d., bd. together | DR | |
| ----, child [of] Edmond, d. Nov. 5, 1803 | DR | |
| ----, infant [of] Amos, d. [        ], 1813, ae 1 d. | DR | |
| ----, d. Tyrus, d. Sept. 2, 1829, ae 3 w. | DR | |
| ----, female ch. [of] Amos Jr., d. Jan. 28, 1832, ae 14 h. | DR | |
| ----, ch. [of] Jarius, d. [May] 7, 1837, ae 1 | DR | |
| ----, ch. [of] Henry, [of] Guilford, d. Apr. 12, 1843; bd. (East Haven) | DR | |
| ----, infant s. [of] Jesse, d. [Oct.] 30, 1843, ae 10 m. | DR | |
| ----, d. [of] Warren, [of] Branford, d. Jan. 9, 1845, ae 6 w. | DR | |
| ----, ch. [of] Sidney, d. [Jan.] 15, 1848 | DR | |
| ----, ch. [of] Elizur, d. [Oct.] 22, 1847, ae 7 w. | DR | |
| **BRAUGHTON**, Eliza M., of East Haven, m. Hillman W. **MILDRUM**, of Middletown, Aug. 23, 1841, by Rev. John B. Beach, of Fair Haven | TM3 | 328 |
| Eliza M., of East Haven, m. Stillman W. **WILDMAN**, of Middletown, Aug. 25, 1841, by J. B. Beach | TM4 | 202 |
| **BRAY**, Asa, Col., d. [        ], 1815, ae 60 | DR | |
| Susan I., m. Josiah H. **BEECHER**, Aug. 18, 1847, by Burdett Hart, in Fair Haven | TM4 | 208 |
| **BRINTNAL**, William, of New Haven, m. Elizabeth **THOMPSON**, May 19, 1804, by Rev. Nicholas Street | DR | |

| | | |
|---|---|---|
| **BRISTOL**, Jennet, of New Haven, m. Luzerne **BRADLEY**, of East Haven, Aug. 27, 1836, by Rev. Stephen Dodd | DR | |
| Jennet, m. Luzerne **BRADLEY**, b. of New Haven, Aug. 27, 1836, by Stephen Dodd | TM3 | 285 |
| **BRITTON**, Eunice, wid., Samuel, d. Mar. 13, 1808, ae 78 | DR | |
| Mary, d. [Dec.] 18, 1804, ae 29 | DR | |
| **BROCKETT, BRACKIT**, Delight, of East Haven, m. Horace **BUTTON**, of North Haven, [Dec.] 28, 1834, by Rev. Stephen Dodd | DR | |
| Delight, of East Haven, m. Horace **BUTTON**, of North Haven, Dec. 28, 1834, by Stephen Dodd | TM3 | 282 |
| Jane Maria, Mrs., m. Charles **LEWIS**, b. of Fair Haven, [Oct.] 6, 1845, by Rev. Stephen Dodd | DR | |
| Jane Maria, wid., m. Charles **LEWIS**, b. of Fair Haven, Oct. 6, 1845, by Stephen Dodd | TM4 | 205 |
| Lewis, of East Haven, m. Esther **STEVENS**, of Killingworth, Dec. 23, 1838, by Rev. Stephen Dodd | DR | |
| Lewis, of East Haven, m. Esther **STEVENS**, of Killingworth, Dec. 23, 1838, by Stephen Dodd | TM3 | 325 |
| Richard, d. Mar. 3, 1832, ae 63 | DR | |
| Samuel, m. Amelia **MALLORY**, b. of Fair Haven, Oct. 22, 1848, by Stephen Dodd | TM4 | 210 |
| **BROOKS**, George, of Northford, m. Sarah E. **HILL**, of East Haven, Apr. 4, 1838, by Rev. Stephen Dodd | DR | |
| George, of Northford, m. Sarah E. **HILL**, of East Haven, Apr. 4, 1838, by Stephen Dodd | TM3 | 325 |
| Maria, Mrs., of East Haven, m. Elijah **LINDSLEY**, of Branford, Aug. 7, 1837, by Rev. Stephen Dodd | DR | |
| Maria, of New Haven, m. Elijah **LINDSLEY**, of Branford, Aug. 7, 1837, by Stephen Dodds | TM3 | 324 |
| **BROTON**, Amos, d. Aug. 4, 1803, ae 31 | DR | |
| Amos, s. Amasa Mallory, d. Feb. 3, 1816, ae 3 m.   (Perhaps Amos Broton **MALLORY**) | DR | |
| Anna, d. James, d. [          ], 1776, ae 4 | DR | |
| Harriet, d. wid. Hartwell, d. [May] 18, 1828, ae 1 | DR | |
| Hartwell, d. Jan. 11, 1828, ae 30 | DR | |
| James, s. Amos, d. [Apr.] 19, 1794, ae 1 | DR | |
| James A., d. [July] 27, 1790, ae 73 | DR | |
| Nancy, d. Amos, d. [          ], 1792, ae 13 w. | DR | |
| Nancy, d. Amos, d. Oct. 22, 1796, ae 10 w. | DR | |
| Orin, d. between Sept. 18 & 25, 1819, ae 17; lost at sea | DR | |
| William, d. Jan. 18, 1823, ae 22 | DR | |
| **BROWN, BROWNE**, Almira, d. Isaac, d. [Nov.] 10, 1805, ae 10 m. | DR | |
| Aner, d. Dec. 3, 1838, ae 52 | DR | |
| Anson H., m. Rosette **SHEPARD**, b. of [East Haven], Apr. 29, 1832, by Rev. Stephen Dodd | DR | |
| Anson H., m. Rosetta **SHEPARD**, b. of East Haven, Apr. 29, 1832, by Stephen Dodd | TM3 | 324 |
| Charlotte, m. Henry **CLARK**, Jan. 10, 1832, by Rev. John Mitchell, of Fair Haven | TM3 | 284 |
| Clarissa, of East Haven, m. Jeremiah **SANFORD**, of New Haven, Sept. 10, 1821, by Stephen Dodd | TM3 | 164 |

| | Vol. | Page |
|---|---|---|
| **BROWN, BROWNE**, (cont.), | | |
| Daniel, s. Daniel, d. [Apr.] 19, 1782, ae 7 | DR | |
| Daniel, d. Oct. 9, 1788, ae 45 | DR | |
| Daniel, s. Aner, d. Sept. 4, 1810, ae 4 w. | DR | |
| Daniel, s. Issac, d. July 20, 1811, ae 5 m. | DR | |
| Eleazar, d. Sept. 21, 1768, ae 72 | DR | |
| Francis, the first of that family, d. [      ], 1668 | DR | |
| George D., of Suffield, m. Melissa **BROWN**, of Fair Haven, | | |
| Mar. 28, 1852, by Rev. D. W[illia]m Havens | TM4 | 216 |
| Hannah, d. [May] 25, 1797, ae 24 | DR | |
| Hannah, wid. d. Oct. 2, 1829, ae 79 y. 10 m. | DR | |
| Isaac, m. Sarah **HEMINWAY**, b. of [East Haven], Oct. 12, | | |
| 1800, by Rev. Nicholas Street | DR | |
| John, [d.      , 1736] | TM2 | 23 |
| John, d. [      ], 1737 | DR | |
| Marietta, d. Aner, d. [Mar.] 26, 1841, ae 22 | DR | |
| Mary, m. Wyllys **HEMINWAY**, b. of [East Haven], [Nov.] 16, | | |
| 1809, by Rev. Samuel Clark | DR | |
| Melissa, of Fair Haven, m. George D. **BROWN**, of Suffield, | | |
| Mar. 28, 1852, by Rev. D. W[illia]m Havens | TM4 | 216 |
| Nancy Jane, d. of Aner, of East Haven, m. John Miner **SMITH**, | | |
| of Derby, Dec. 18, 1839, by Rev. Benjamin L. | | |
| Swan, at Fair Haven | TM3 | 326 |
| Samuel, s. Isaac, d. Nov. 9, 1805, ae 3 | DR | |
| Samuel, s. Isaac, d. Sept. 10, 1806, ae 3 w. | DR | |
| Sarah, m. Wyllys **HEMINWAY**, b. of [East Haven], Nov. 18, | | |
| 1810, by Rev. Saul Clark | DR | |
| Sarah, w. Isaac, d. [July] 6, 1813, ae 32; childbed | DR | |
| Wyllys, s. Aner, d. [Sept.] 7, 1829, ae 2 | DR | |
| Wyllys, s. Thomas, d. Jan. 4, 1833, ae 3 m. | DR | |
| ----, ch. [of] Thomas, d. [May] 3, 1837, ae 3 w. | DR | |
| **BUCKINGHAM**, David W., of Oxford, m. Maria **POTTER**, of [East | | |
| Haven], Oct. 24, 1824, by Rev. Stephen Dodd | DR | |
| David W., of Oxford, m. Maria **POTTER**, of East Haven, Oct. | | |
| 24, 1824, by Stephen Dodd | TM3 | 169 |
| **BUEL**, Daniel T., [of] Lanesboro, Mass., d. July 29, 1848, ae 54 | DR | |
| **BUNNELL**, Elizabeth H., of East Haven, m. Samuel B. **CARTER**, of | | |
| Lasalle, Ill., Apr. 4, 1852, by Rev. D. W[illia]m | | |
| Havens | TM4 | 216 |
| Sarah An[n], of Branford, m. George **DERRICK**, of New | | |
| Haven, May 6, 1822, by Rev. Oliver Willson, of | | |
| North Haven | TM3 | 166 |
| **BURNHAM**, James, s. David & Rachel, b. Jan. 4, 1793 | TM2 | 293 |
| Martha, d. David & Rachel, b. Oct. 5, 1797 | TM2 | 293 |
| William, s. David & Rachel, b. June 11, 1795 | TM2 | 293 |
| **BURRITT**, Joseph, of Stratford, m. Asenath **CURTIS**, of [East Haven], | | |
| June [ ], 1816, by Rev. Saul Clark | DR | |
| **BUSH**, Henry, of New Haven, m. Eunice L. **SANFORD**, of New Haven, | | |
| Aug. 4, 1840, by Rev. Benj[ami]n L. Swan of Fair | | |
| Haven | TM3 | 327 |
| John A., of Madison, m. Nancy Ann **THATCHER**, of East | | |
| Haven, Apr. 5, 1842, by Rev. Stephen Dodd | DR | |

| | Vol. | Page |
|---|---|---|
| **BUSH**, (cont.), | | |
| John A., of Madison, m. Nancy A. **THA[T]CHER**, of East | | |
| Haven, Apr. 5, 1842, by Stephen Dodd | TM4 | 201 |
| **BUTLER**, Lucy, of New Haven, m. Thomas **SHEPARD**, of [East Haven], | | |
| Mar. 24, 1830, by Rev. Stephen Dodd | DR | |
| Lucy, of New Haven, m. Thomas **SHEPARD**, of East Haven, | | |
| Mar. 24, 1830, by Stephen Dodd | TM3 | 231 |
| **BUTTON**, Horace, of North Haven, m. Delight **BROCKETT**, of East | | |
| Haven, [Dec.] 28, 1834, by Rev. Stephen Dodd | DR | |
| Horace, of North Haven, m. Delight **BROCKETT**, of East | | |
| Haven, Dec. 28, 1834, by Stephen Dodd | TM3 | 282 |
| **BYINGTON**, Jane Ann, m. Albert T. **THOMPSON**, Oct. 13, 1831, by | | |
| Rev. John Mitchell, of Fair Haven | TM3 | 283 |
| **CAMP**, Sarah, [d.] Hezekiah, d. [Sept.] 10, 1743, ae 2 | DR | |
| Sary, d. Hez[ekiah], d. Sept. 10, [1743] | TM2 | 25 |
| **CANNODIS, CONNODISE**, Abigail, w. Edward, d. [Oct.] 9, 1742 | DR | |
| Abig[a]il, w. Edward, [d. Oct. 9, 1742] | TM2 | 24 |
| ----, child of Edward, [d.         , 1736] | TM2 | 23 |
| ----, child [of] Edward, d. [         ], 1737 | DR | |
| **CARNES**, Jane of Glasgow, Scotland, m. Isaac **HALL**, of West Haven, | | |
| Sept. 4, 1851, by Rev. D. W[illia]m Havens | TM4 | 217 |
| **CARTER**, Samuel B., of Lasalle, Ill., m. Elizabeth H. **BUNNELL**, of East | | |
| Haven, Apr. 4, 1852, by Rev. D. W[illia]m Havens | TM4 | 216 |
| **CEPPICK**, Sarah, m. Thomas **COUSINS**, July 18, 1852, by Rev. D. | | |
| W[illia]m Havens | TM4 | 218 |
| **CHIDSEY, CHEDSEY, CHIDEY, CHIDSEE**, Abba H., [d. Samuel & | | |
| Betsey], b. Mar. 6, 1819 | TM3 | 264 |
| Abel, s. Joseph, d. Mar. 14, 1709, ae 7 d. | DR | |
| Abygall, d. Ebenezer, b. Apr. 1, 1707 | TM1 | 30 |
| Abig[a]il, d. John, b. May 6, 1747 | TM2 | 26 |
| Abig[ai]l, d. [Isaac, Jr. & Sarah], b. Oct. 5, 1758 | TM2 | 45 |
| Abigail, w. Caleb, Jr., d. [         ], 1761, ae 62 | DR | |
| Abigail, d. John & Anne, b. Nov. 19, 1773 | TM2 | 155 |
| Abigail, of [East Haven], m. Israel Augustus **BALDWIN**, of | | |
| Branford, Dec. 28, 1828, by Rev. Stephen Dodd | DR | |
| Abigail, of East Haven, m. Israel Augustus **BALDWIN**, of | | |
| Branford, Dec. 28, 1828, by Stephen Dodd | TM3 | 174 |
| Abigail H., of East Haven, m. Seth **RUSSEL**, of North | | |
| Branford, Oct. 13, 1840, by Stephen Dodd | TM3 | 327 |
| Abigail Holt, of East Haven, m. Seth **RUSSEL**, of North | | |
| Branford, Oct. 13, 1840, by Rev. Stephen Dodd | DR | |
| Abraham, s. Abraham, b. Sept. 23, 1741 | TM2 | 21 |
| Abraham, d. [         ], 1761, ae 60 | DR | |
| Abraham, Jr., d. [Apr.] 28, 1810, ae 36 | DR | |
| Abraham, d. [Mar.] 28, 1812, ae 71 | DR | |
| Almira, [d. Samuel & Betsey], b. Apr. 22, 1813 | TM3 | 264 |
| Ama, d. Isaac, b. July 25, 1771 | TM2 | 47 |
| Anna, w. Caleb, d. Jan. 15, 1692 | DR | |
| Anna, w. John, d. June 1, 1783, ae 55 | DR | |
| Anna, [d. Samuel & Betsey], b. Oct. 26, 1807 | TM3 | 264 |
| Anna, wid. John, d. Aug. 6, 1821, ae 70 | DR | |
| Anna, of [East Haven], m. Samuel **RUSSEL**, of North | | |
| Branford, May 16, 1832, by Rev. Stephen Dodd | DR | |

| CHIDSEY, CHEDSEY, CHIDEY, CHIDSEE, (cont.), | Vol. | Page |
|---|---|---|
| Anna, of East Haven, m. Samuel F. RUSSELL, of North | | |
| Branford, May 16, 1832, by Stephen Dodd | TM3 | 234 |
| Anne, d. John & Anne, b. May 5, 1775 | TM2 | 155 |
| Anson, [of] New Haven, d. [Oct.] [ ], 1846, ae 24; bd. [East | | |
| Haven] | DR | |
| Asahel, infant [of] Abraham, d. [Mar.] 20, 1783, ae 7 d. | DR | |
| Asahel, d. Jan. 14, 1817, ae 36 | DR | |
| Azel, s. Abraham & Hannah, b. Jan. 9, 1781 | TM3 | 13 |
| Azel, s. Abraham, d. Jan. 17, 1781, ae 12; drowned | DR | |
| Bathsheba, w. Abraham, d. [ ], 1761, ae 53 | DR | |
| Betsey, [d. Samuel & Betsey], b. Mar. 23, 1815 | TM3 | 264 |
| Caleb, Dea., d. Feb. 20, 1713, ae 52 | DR | |
| Caleb, d. Feb. 20, 1712/13 | TM1 | 114 |
| Caleb, s. Caleb, b. Sept. 1, 1738 | TM2 | 26 |
| Caleb, s. Isaac, b. July 25, 1763 | TM2 | 47 |
| Caleb, d. Sept. 6, 1785, ae 89 | DR | |
| Caleb., m. Rebec[k]ah PAGE, July 17, 1792 | TM3 | 57 |
| Caleb, d. Sept. 19, 1836, ae 73 | DR | |
| Caleb, 3d., d. Jan. 1, 1761, ae 23 | DR | |
| Charlotte, d. John, d. Aug. 21, 1794, ae 18 m. | DR | |
| Charlotte, of East Haven, m. James WRIGHT, of North | | |
| Killingworth, Apr. 19, 1835, by Rev. Edward Ives | DR | |
| Charlot[t]e, of East Haven, m. Samuel WRIGHT, of North | | |
| Killingworth, Apr. 19, 1835, by E. J. Ives | TM3 | 233-4 |
| Charlot[t]e, of East Haven, m. Samuel WRIGHT, of North | | |
| Killingworth, Apr. 19, 1835, by E. J. Ives | TM3 | 283 |
| Clorinda, m. Haynes HEMINWAY, b. of [East Haven], [Feb.] | | |
| 12, 1806, by Rev. Nicholas Street | DR | |
| Daniel, s. Dea. John, d. June 4, 1667, ae 10 | DR | |
| Daniel, s. Caleb, d. [Oct.] 27, 1716, ae 21 | DR | |
| Daniell, d. Oct. 27, 1716 | TM1 | 198 |
| Daniel, s. Abraham, d. [ ], 1720, ae 1 | DR | |
| Daniel, s. Abraham, d. [ ], 1729, ae 1 | DR | |
| Daniel, s. Abraham, d. [ ], 1730, ae 6 m. | DR | |
| Daniel, s. Abraham, b. Mar. 22, 1742/3 | TM2 | 21 |
| Daniel, d. Aug. 30, 1785, ae 17 | DR | |
| Debora, d. Samuell, b. Nov. 28, 1725 | TM1 | 245 |
| Deborah, d. Isaac, b. Jan. 3, 1768 | TM2 | 47 |
| Deborah, wid. Samuel, d. June 16, 1771, ae 77 | DR | |
| Deborah, had negro, Elezander, b. Mar. 12, 1776 | TM2 | 290 |
| Deborah, d. [Aug.] 12, 1809, ae 84 | DR | |
| Desire, w. Ephraim, d. Mar. 5, 1783, ae 27; childbed | DR | |
| Desire, d. Ephraim & Desire, b. Mar. 5, 1783 | TM2 | 289 |
| Desire, d. Abraham, d. [May] 21, 1794, ae 8 | DR | |
| Desire, d. Ebenezer, d. [Oct.] 17, 1803, ae 24 | DR | |
| Desire, d. [Sept.] 4, 1813, ae 70 | DR | |
| Ebenezer, s. Ebenezer, d. June 28, 1716, ae 14 | DR | |
| Ebenezer, s. Ebenezer, d. June 28, 1716, ae about 14 y. | TM1 | 198 |
| Ebenezer, d. Sept. 26, 1726, ae 61 | DR | |
| Ebennezer, d. Sept. [ ], 1726 | TM1 | 245 |
| Ebenezer, d. July 9, 1806, ae 69 | DR | |
| Eliza, d. [Caleb & Rebec[k]ah], b. Mar. 27, 1798 | TM3 | 10 |

| CHIDSEY, CHEDSEY, CHIDEY, CHIDSEE, (cont.), | Vol. | Page |
|---|---|---|
| Eliza Ann, m. Lucius **LINDSLEY**, b. of East Haven, Nov. 4, 1841, by Rev. Stephen Dodd | DR | |
| Eliza Ann, m. Lucius **LINDSLEY**, b. of East Haven, Nov. 4, 1841, by Stephen Dodd | TM4 | 200 |
| Elizabeth, w. Dea. John, d. [        ], 1688 | DR | |
| Elizabeth, d. John, d. July 16, 1688, ae 20 | DR | |
| Elesabeth, m. William **BRADL[E]Y**, Jan. 7, 1713/14 | TM1 | 114 |
| Elizabeth, w. Caleb, Jr., & wid. of Isaac **PENFIELD**, d. Jan. 8, 1767, ae 62 | DR | |
| Elizabeth, w. Caleb, d. Jan. 8, 1767 | TM2 | 87 |
| Elizabeth, w. Ebenezer, d. [July] 9, 1803, ae 62 | DR | |
| Elizabeth, d. Samuel, d. [        ], 1826, ae 4 m. | DR | |
| Elvira, [of] North Branford, d. Jan. 23, 1847, ae 48 | DR | |
| Emily E., of East Haven, m. Laban **SMITH**, Jan. 18, 1846, by Rev. George W. Nichols | DR | |
| Emely E., m. Laban **SMITH**, b. of East Haven, Jan. 18, 1846, by Rev. George W. Nichols | TM4 | 206 |
| Epherim, s. John, b. Mar. 19, 1762 | TM2 | 26 |
| Ephraim, d. [Sept.] 26, 1832, ae 80 | DR | |
| [E]unis, d. John, b. Mar. 31, 1723 | TM1 | 245 |
| Hannah, w. Caleb. d. Dec. 25, 1703 | DR | |
| Hannah, d. Abraham, b. July 4, 1725 | TM1 | 245 |
| Hannah, d. Abraham, d. July 1, 1730 | DR | |
| Hanner, d. John & Anne, b. Jan. 18, 1771 | TM2 | 155 |
| Hannah, wid. Abraham, d. [June] 24, 1815, ae 69 | DR | |
| Hanna, [d. Samuel & Betsey], b. Apr. 23, 1821 | TM3 | 264 |
| Hannah, w. Levi, [of] Woodbury, d. Nov. 4, 1821, ae 78 | DR | |
| Hannah, of East Haven, m. Smith **HURD**, of Cumberland, Dec. 14, 1845, by Rev. Stephen Dodd | DR | |
| Hannah, of East Haven, m. Smith **HURD**, of Cumberland, Md., Dec. 14, 1845, by Stephen Dodd | TM4 | 205 |
| Hannah, wid. Ephraim, d. [Mar.] 20, 1846, ae 88 y. 5 m. | DR | |
| Harriet, [d. Samuel & Betsey], b. Jan. 31, 1804 | TM3 | 264 |
| Harriet Bradley, d. Samuel, Jr., d. [Oct.] 21, 1846, ae 5 | DR | |
| Harvey, d. Dec. 24, 1835, ae 45 | DR | |
| Horace, m. Sara A. **LANFEAR**, b. of [East Haven], Apr. 4, 1819, by Rev. Stephen Dodd | DR | |
| Isack, s. Ebenezer, b. June 3, 1710 | TM1 | 30 |
| Isaac, s. Caleb, b. Nov. 8, 1731 | TM2 | 26 |
| Isaac, Jr., m. Sarah **BRADLEY**, June 18, 1752 | TM2 | 45 |
| Isaac, s. Capt. Isaac, d. [Oct.] 23, 1779, ae 3 | DR | |
| Isaac, Capt., had servant, Andrew, d. Mar. 17, 1789, ae 28 | DR | |
| Isaac, s. Caleb & Rebecah, b. Apr. 27, 1793 | TM3 | 10 |
| Isaac, Capt., d. Aug. 12, 1793, ae 84 | DR | |
| Isaac, Capt., d. [July] 30, 1814, ae 83 | DR | |
| Isaac, d. Nov. 20, 1829, ae 68 | DR | |
| Jacob, of Foxon, d. May 25, 1831, ae 66 | DR | |
| Jacob 2d., d. [Jan.] 2, 1822, ae 43 | DR | |
| James, s. Ebenezer, d. [        ], 1726, ae 22 | DR | |
| James, s. Ebennezer, d. Sept. [ ], 1726 | TM1 | 245 |
| James, had negro Flora, b. Jan. 26, [1791] | TM2 | 236 |
| James, had servant, Flora, d. [Sept.] 29, 1805, ae 15 | DR | |

| | Vol. | Page |
|---|---|---|
| **CHIDSEY, CHEDSEY, CHIDEY, CHIDSEE**, (cont.), | | |
| James, d. [Nov.] 17, 1810, ae 65 | DR | |
| Jane A., m. John W. **GRANT**, b. of Branford, Feb. 26, 1826, by | | |
| Stephen Dodd | TM3 | 171 |
| Jared Goodsell, s. [Caleb & Rebecah], b. May 20, 1804 | TM3 | 10 |
| John, Dea. of first church at New Haven, d. Dec. 31, 1688, | | |
| ae 67 | DR | |
| John, s. Ebenezer, d. Dec. 13, 1689, ae 2 | DR | |
| John, d. [ ], 1693, ae 42 | DR | |
| John, m. Mary **FOOT**, Feb. 8, 1714/15 | TM1 | 114 |
| John, s. John, b. Sept. 15, 1720 | TM1 | 245 |
| John, m. Sarah **SHEPPARD**, Dec. 21, 1745, by Rev. Mr. | | |
| Heminway | TM2 | 20 |
| John, s. John, b. Dec. 16, 1749 | TM2 | 26 |
| John, s. John & Anne, b. Jan. 22, 1783 | TM2 | 155 |
| John, d. [Sept.] 17, 1783, ae 63 | DR | |
| John, Jr., d. Nov. [ ], 1804, ae 24 | DR | |
| John, d. [May] 6, 1816, ac 68 | DR | |
| Joseph, d. [ ], 1712, ae 57 | DR | |
| Laura, d. [Caleb & Rebecah], b. July 24, 1796 | TM3 | 10 |
| Laura, wid., d. Feb. 11, 1847, ae 53 | DR | |
| Leander, m. Julia E. **FARREN**, b. of East Haven, Sept. 5, 1852, | | |
| by Rev. D. W[illia]m Havens | TM4 | 219 |
| Levy, d. [Aug.] 4, 1825, ae 80 | DR | |
| Lois, d. Isaac, b. Sept. 25, 1765 | TM2 | 47 |
| Lorinda, [d. Samuel & Betsey], b. Oct. 5, 1805 | TM3 | 264 |
| Lorinda, of [East Haven], m. Elizur **MERRICK**, of Atwater, | | |
| Ohio, Aug. 21, 1827, by Rev. Stephen Dodd | DR | |
| Lorinda, of East Haven, m. Elizur **MERRICK**, of Atwater, | | |
| O[hio], Aug. 21, 1827, by Stephen Dodd | TM3 | 173 |
| Lucelia, of [East Haven], m. Thomas **PLANT**, of Branford, | | |
| June 8, 1831, by Rev. Stephen Dodd | DR | |
| Lucretia, d. [Caleb & Rebecah], b. Jan. 18, 1807 | TM3 | 10 |
| Lucretia, of East Haven, m. Thomas **PLANT**, of Branford, June | | |
| 8, 1831, by Stephen Dodd | TM3 | 233 |
| Lucy, w. Samuel 2d, d. July 14, 1842, ae 50 | DR | |
| Luther, s. [Caleb & Rebecah], b. Jan. 28, 1801 | TM3 | 10 |
| Lyd[i]a, d. Isaac, b. July 25, 1761 | TM2 | 47 |
| Lydia, d. Abraham, d. [Aug.] 27, 1773, ae 1 | DR | |
| Lydia, wid. Isaac, d. [Feb.] 20, 1843, ae 73 | DR | |
| Lydia B., [d. Samuel & Betsey], b. Jan. 10, 1817 | TM3 | 264 |
| Lydia B., of East Haven, m. Jerome **HARRISON**, of North | | |
| Branford, Oct. 3, 1841, by Rev. Stephen Dodd | DR | |
| Lydia B., of East Haven, m. Jerome **HARRISON**, of North | | |
| Branford, Oct. 31, 1841, by Stephen Dodd | TM4 | 200 |
| Mabel, d. Abraham, b. May 31, 1723 | TM1 | 245 |
| Mabel, w. Abraham, d. [Mar.] 8, 1734, ae 39 | DR | |
| Maria, of East Haven, m. Henry **SMITH**, Aug. 21, 1841, by | | |
| Rev. Henry Townsend | DR | |
| Mary, d. Dea. John, d. Oct. 9, 1650, ae 2 w. | DR | |
| Mary, d. Abraham, b. Oct. 2, 1727 | TM1 | 245 |
| Mary, d. Abraham, d. Mar. 5, 1735, ae 8 | DR | |
| Mary, d. Abraham, b. Oct. 25, 1735 | TM2 | 21 |

| | Vol. | Page |
|---|---|---|
| **CHIDSEY, CHEDSEY, CHIDEY, CHIDSEE**, (cont.), | | |
| Mary, d. [Abraham, d.        , 1736] | TM2 | 23 |
| Mary, w. Abraham, d. Apr. 3, 1737, ae 30 | DR | |
| Mary, d. Abraham, d. [Sept.] 11, 1743, ae 8 | DR | |
| Mary, d. Abraham, d. Sept. 11, [1743] | TM2 | 25 |
| Mary, d. Isaac, d. [Aug.] 26, 1745, ae 10 | DR | |
| Mary, d. Isaac, d. Aug. 26, 1745 | TM2 | 22 |
| Mary, d. John, b. Sept. 26, 1765 | TM2 | 47 |
| Mary, m. Phineas **CURTIS**, July 4, 1787 | TM2 | 266 |
| Mary, w. Isaac, d. [Dec.] 23, 1789, ae 77 | DR | |
| Mary, wid. Ebenezer, d. [May] 13, 1824, ae 92 | DR | |
| Mary B., of East Haven, m. James Warren **LUDDINGTON**, | | |
| [Oct.] 8, 1845, by Rev. Stephen Dodd | DR | |
| Mary B., m. Jame W. **LUD[D]INGTON**, b. of East Haven, Oct. | | |
| 8, 1845, by Stephen Dodd | TM4 | 205 |
| Matilda, d. Jacob, d. May 8, 1805, ae 3 | DR | |
| Mehitabel, wid. James, d. Mar. 26, 1828, ae 85 | DR | |
| Priscilla, wid. Ebenezer, d. [        ], 1728, ae 57 | DR | |
| Rebecca, w. Caleb, d. [Sept.] 12, 1829, ae 63 | DR | |
| Roswell, s. John, b. July 17, 1754 | TM2 | 27 |
| Rosewell, m. Laura **BRADLEY**, b. of [East Haven], Dec. 16, | | |
| 1810, by Rev. Saul Clark | DR | |
| Rosewell, d. [July] 24, 1833, ae 47 | DR | |
| Ruel, of Branford, m. Olive **BRADLEY**, of [East Haven], Feb. | | |
| 3, 1805, by Rev. Nicholas Street | DR | |
| Russell S., [s. Samuel & Betsey], b. June 4, 1802 | TM3 | 264 |
| Russel Smith, of Easton, Pa., m. Lucy Morris **STREET**, of East | | |
| Haven, Sept. 15, 1847, by Rev. D. William Havens | DR | |
| Russell Smith, of Easton, Penn., m. Lucy Morris **STREET**, of | | |
| East Haven, Sept. 15, 1847, by D. W[illia]m Havens | TM4 | 208 |
| Sally, of [East Haven], m. Jairus **PARDEE**, Nov. 17, 1819, | | |
| by Rev. Stephen Dodd | DR | |
| Sally B., [d. Samuel & Betsey], b. Dec. 15, 1800 | TM3 | 264 |
| Samuell, s. Samuell, b. Oct. 14, 1722 | TM1 | 245 |
| Samuel, d. Oct. 8, 1726, ae 28 | DR | |
| Samuell, s. [Isaac, Jr. & Sarah], b. Aug. 28, 1754 | TM2 | 45 |
| Samuel, s. Isaac, d. [Jan.] 22, 1761, ae 7 | DR | |
| Samuell, s. Isaac, d. Jan. 22, 1761 | TM2 | 22 |
| Samuel, s. John, d. Apr. 10, 1771, ae 10 | DR | |
| Samuel, s. Isaac, b. Apr. 24, 1773 | TM2 | 47 |
| Samuel, b. Apr. 24, 1773; m. Betsey **HOLT**, Jan. 26, 1800 | TM3 | 264 |
| Samuel, s. Levi, d. Nov. 12, 1777, ae 3; kicked by a horse | DR | |
| Samuel, s. Levi, d. May 2, 1783, ae 1 w. | DR | |
| Samuel, m. Betsey **HOLT**, [Jan.] 23, 1800, by Rev. Nicholas | | |
| Street | DR | |
| Samuel, Jr., [s. Samuel & Betsey], b. Jan. 2, 1810 | TM3 | 264 |
| Samuel, Jr., m. wid. Esther **BRADLEY**, b. of East Haven, Nov. | | |
| 7, 1833, by Rev. Stephen Dodd | DR | |
| Samuel, Jr., m. wid. Esther **BRADLEY**, b. of East Haven, Nov. | | |
| 7, 1833, by Stephen Dodd | TM3 | 236 |
| Samuel, 2d, m. Sarah B. **PARDEE**, b. of East Haven, Mar. | | |
| 22, 1843, by Rev. Stephen Dodd | DR | |

| | Vol. | Page |
|---|---|---|
| **CHIDSEY, CHEDSEY, CHIDEY, CHIDSEE**, (cont.), | | |
| Samuel, 2d, m. Sarah B. **PARDEE**, b. of East Haven, Mar. | | |
| 22, 1843, by Stephen Dodd | TM4 | 202 |
| Samuel Edwin, of East Haven, m. Roxanna **TYLER**, of | | |
| Branford, Aug. 17, 1851, by Rev. Collis J. Potter, of | | |
| Wolcott, Conn. | TM4 | 214 |
| Sarah, m. John **DOASEN**, July 1, 1708, by W[illia]m | | |
| Mallbie, J. P. | TM1 | 30 |
| Sarah, d. John, b. Dec. 6, 1716 | TM1 | 198 |
| Sary, d. John, b. Dec. 6, 1716 | TM1 | 199 |
| Sarah, d. [Isaac, Jr. & Sarah], b. Jan. 28, 1753 | TM2 | 45 |
| Sarah, d. John & Anne, b. Aug. 5, 1780 | TM2 | 155 |
| Sarah, d. John, d. [Oct.] 20, 1795, ae 15 | DR | |
| Sarah, wid. Caleb, d. [Dec.] 26, 1800, ae 80 | DR | |
| Sarah, w. Capt. Isaac, d. Dec. 16, 1808, ae 80 | DR | |
| Solomon, s. [Caleb & Rebecah], b. Oct. 21, 1802 | TM3 | 10 |
| Street, s. John, b. Nov. 15, 1756 | TM2 | 27 |
| Street, d. [Apr.] 20, 1777, ae 20 | DR | |
| Street, s. John & Anne, b. Sept. 8, 1778 | TM2 | 155 |
| Street, m. Fannie E. **DAVIS**, of East Haven, Sept. 4, 1842, by | | |
| Rev. George W. Nichols | DR | |
| Thankful, d. Caleb, b. May 20, 1760 | TM2 | 45 |
| -----, twins of Abraham & Mabel, d. [Mar.] 8, 1734 | DR | |
| -----infant [of] Samuel 2d., d. Apr. 13, 1828 | DR | |
| -----, ch. [of] Horace, d. [May] [ ], 1837 | DR | |
| -----, ch. [of] Street, d. [ ] [ ], 1846 | DR | |
| **CHURCH**, James, of Haddam, m. Huldah **BARNES**, of [East Haven], Jan. | | |
| [ ], 1811, by Rev. Saul Clark | DR | |
| James, d. [Nov.] 24, 1839, ae 50 | DR | |
| Jane, d. James, d. [Aug.] 16, 1825, ae 2 y. 6 m. | DR | |
| **CHURCHEL**, Zalmon, of Watertown, N. Y., m. Jerusha **LARKINS**, of | | |
| [East Haven], [Jan.] [ ], 1808, by Rev. Saul Clark | DR | |
| **CLARK**, Frances, s. Rev. Saul, d. Sept. 8, 1814, ae 10 w. | DR | |
| Francis, d. Rev. Saul & w. Samuel I. **HOPKINS**, d. [Aug.] 23, | | |
| 1841, at Carbondale, Pa., ae 25 | DR | |
| Harriet, of Granby, m. Daniel **THOMPSON**, of [East Haven], | | |
| July 26, 1829, by Rev. Stephen Dodd | DR | |
| Harriet, m. Daniel **THOMPSON**, July 26, 1829, by Stephen | | |
| Dodd | TM3 | 231 |
| Henry, m. Charlotte **BROWN**, Jan. 10, 1832, by Rev. John | | |
| Mitchell, of Fair Haven | TM3 | 284 |
| Lemuel, of Southington, m. Sophia **LANGSTON**, of [East | | |
| Haven], Dec. 15, 1808, by Rev. Saul Clark | DR | |
| Marietta, d. Rev. Saul [of] Bethany, Conn., d. Mar. 8, 1842, | | |
| ae 23; bd. [East Haven] | DR | |
| Sarah, d. [ ], 1788, ae 18 | DR | |
| Timothy, s. Rev. Saul, d. Apr. 3, 1810, ae 3 m. | DR | |
| -----, ch. [of] Kelly, d. [Apr.] 13, 1843 | DR | |
| **COLLINS, COLLING COLLINGS**, Abel, d. Mar. 29, 1773, ae 67 | DR | |
| Abiga[i]l, d. Abel, b. Aug. 15, 1744 | TM2 | 26 |
| Amos, s. Daniell, d. Jan. 1, 1724/5 | TM1 | 245 |
| Amos, s. Daniel, d. Jan. 1, 1725, ae 20 | DR | |
| Daniell, s. Danyell, b. Mar. 1, 1712/13 | TM1 | 114 |

| COLLINS, COLLING, COLLINGS, (cont.), | Vol. | Page |
|---|---|---|
| Hepsaba, d. Abel, b. July 14, 1743 | TM2 | 26 |
| Ledya, d. Danyell, b. Feb. 11, 1706; d. Apr. 22, 1707 | TM1 | 30 |
| Lydia, d. Daniel, d. Apr. 22, 1707, ae 2 m. | DR | |
| Lidia, d. Daniell, b. Dec. 4, 1710 | TM1 | 30 |
| Lydia, d. Daniel, d. Oct. 24, 1713, ae 3 | DR | |
| Ledia, d. Danyell, d. Oct. 24, 1713 | TM1 | 114 |
| Lydia, d. Daniel, d. [Oct.] 24, 1716, ae 3 | DR | |
| Marcy, d. Abel, b. Sept. 15, 1737 | TM2 | 26 |
| Nancy C., m. Isaac F. MALLORY, b. of Fair Haven, [Oct.] 18, 1840, by Rev. Stephen Dodd | DR | |
| Nancy C., m. Isaac F. MALLORY, b. of East Haven, Oct. 18, 1840, by Stephen Dodd | TM3 | 328 |
| Presilla, d. Danyel, b. Mar. 11, 1708 | TM1 | 30 |
| Rebecca, w. Abel, d. [Jan.] 18, 1767, ae 65 | DR | |
| -----, ch. [of] Abel, d. [          ], 1736 | DR | |
| -----, ch. of Abel, [d.          , 1736] | TM2 | 23 |
| COLT, Anna, w. Truman, d. Aug. 31, 1837, ae 67 | DR | |
| COOK, Orphana, w. Samuel, d. [Feb.] 25, 1780, ae 24 | DR | |
| Roswell, m. Caroline S. HICKOX, of Southington, Aug. 7, 1827, by Stephen Dodd | TM3 | 172 |
| COOPER, David, s. Levi & Thankfull, b. Nov. 13, 1778 | TM2 | 289 |
| Eunice, wid., m. Tyrus BRADLEY, b. of East Haven, Sept, 20, 1846, by Rev. Stephen Dodd | DR | |
| Eunice, m. Tyrus BRADLEY, b. of East Haven, Sept. 20, 1846, by Stephen Dodd | TM4 | 206 |
| John, d. Nov. 23, 1689 | DR | |
| Levi, s. Levi & Thankfull, b. Jan. 20, 1788 | TM2 | 289 |
| Patty, d. Levi & Thankfull, b. Nov. 24, 1776 | TM2 | 289 |
| Rebecca, d. John , d. [          ], 1668, ae 2 | DR | |
| Sarah, d. Levi & Thankfull, b. Feb. 26, 1781 | TM2 | 289 |
| Zeruah, d. Levi & Thankfull, b. Jan. 20, 1783 | TM2 | 289 |
| -----, ch. [of] Levi, d. [          ], 1804, ae 1 | DR | |
| COTTREL, Julia, d. Thomas P., d. [Aug.] 30, 1796, ae 3 | DR | |
| COUSINS, Thomas, m. Sarah CEPPECK, July 18, 1852, by Rev. D. W[illia]m Havens | TM4 | 218 |
| COWLES, Caroline, d. Edmund R., d. Aug. 30, 1845, ae 2 | DR | |
| Edmund R., of Springfield, Mass., m. Lavinia C. SMITH, of East Haven, Oct. 4, 1838, by Rev. Stephen Dodd | DR | |
| Edmond R., of Springfield, Mass., m. Lavinia C. SMITH, of East Haven, Oct. 4, 1838, by Stephen Dodd | TM3 | 325 |
| Eunicia, m. Linas COWLES, b. of Berlin, Nov. 23, 1828, by Stephen Dodd | TM3 | 174 |
| Linas, m. Eunicia COWLES, b. of Berlin, Nov. 23, 1828, by Stephen Dodd | TM3 | 174 |
| Luman, of Berlin, m. Eunecia PARDEE, of [East Haven], Jan. 1, 1812, by Rev. Saul Clark | DR | |
| Luman, of New Haven, m. Sarah A. HOLT, of East Haven, [Sept.] 21, 1845, by Rev. Stephen Dodd | DR | |
| Luman, of New Haven, m. Sarah E. HOLT, of East Haven, Sept. 21, 1845, by Stephen Dodd | TM4 | 205 |
| Marietta, d. Edmond R., [of] New Haven, d. [Oct.] [ ], 1845 | DR | |

| | Vol. | Page |
|---|---|---|
| CRANDAL, CRANDALL, Charlot[t][e] E., of New Haven, m. Herbert R. HUBBARD, of Middletown, Sept. 5, 1841, by Rev. Henry Townsend | TM3 | 328 |
| Eliza, m. Eleazer GORHAM, b. of New Haven, Feb. 7, 1831, by Stephen Dodd | TM3 | 233 |
| CRANES, Eldrige B., of Hartford, m. Sarah J. FARREN, of New Haven, July 18, 1847, by Rev. Daniel W[illia]m Havens | TM4 | 207 |
| CULVER, Andrew J., of Wallingford, m. Mary E. THOMPSON, of East Haven, Aug. 20, 1848, by Rev. D. William Havens | DR | |
| Andrew J., of Wallingford, m. Mary E. THOMPSON, of East Haven, Aug. 20, 1848, by Rev. D. W[illia]m Havens | TM4 | 210 |
| George T., d. Nov. 9, 1845, ae 18 | DR | |
| Julia Maria, d. Van Rensaleer, d. [Sept.] 28, 1840, ae 5 | DR | |
| CURTIS, CURTISS, Asenath, [d. Phineas & Mary], b. Feb. 28, 1796 | TM2 | 296 |
| Asenath, of [East Haven], m. Joseph BURRITT, of Stratford, June [ ], 1816, by Rev. Saul Clark | DR | |
| Benjamin, d. [ ], 1786, ae 21 | DR | |
| Benjamin, s. [Phineas & Mary], b. Mar. 19, 1798 | TM2 | 296 |
| Hannah, d. [Phineas & Mary], b. Mar. 17, 1790 | TM2 | 296 |
| Hannah, m. Simeon LANCRAFT, b. of [East Haven], Jan. 14, 1813, by Rev. Saul Clark | DR | |
| James R., m. Mary E. JOHNSON, of East Haven, Aug. 19, 1851, by Rev. Geo[rge] A. Hubbell | TM4 | 216 |
| John, s. [Phineas & Mary], b. Apr. 26, 1802 | TM2 | 296 |
| John, d. [Mar.] 24, 1834, ae 32 | DR | |
| Lois, of North Branford, m. Sylvester M. GRANNIS, of East Haven, Oct. 5, 1845, by Stephen Dodd | TM4 | 205 |
| Lois T., of North Branford, m. Sylvester M. GRANNIS, of East Haven, [Oct. 5], 1845, by Rev. Stephen Dodd | DR | |
| Majour, s. [Phineas & Mary], b. Dec. 20, 1800 | TM2 | 296 |
| Mary, m. Samuel THOMPSON, b. of [East Haven], July 17, 1815, by Rev. Saul Clark | DR | |
| Mercy, wid., of Southington, m. John ROWE, of [East Haven], Feb. 2, 1826, by Rev. Stephen Dodd | DR | |
| Mercy, wid., of Southington, m. John ROWE, of East Haven, Feb. 2, 1826, by Stephen Dodd | TM3 | 171 |
| Phineas, m. Mary CHIDSEY, July 4, 1787 | TM2 | 266 |
| Phineas, d. Dec. 20, 1806, ae 35 | DR | |
| Polly, d. Phineas & Mary, b. June 12, 1788 | TM2 | 296 |
| Polly, of [East Haven], m. Samuel FARREN, July 22, 1805, by Rev. Nicholas Street | DR | |
| Russel, s. [Phineas & Mary], b. Mar. 16, 1792 | TM2 | 296 |
| Sally, d. [Phineas & Mary], b. Feb. 12, 1794 | TM2 | 296 |
| Street, ch. wid. Mary, d. [Aug.] 3, 1808, ae 2 | DR | |
| Susan, d. [Phineas & Mary], b. Feb. 11, 1804 | TM2 | 296 |
| Susan, of [East Haven], m. [ ] MIX, of New Haven, Aug. 14, 1828, by Rev. Stephen Dodd | DR | |
| DAILEY, Mary Maria, of Huntington, m. Charles BARTH, of New Haven, Oct. 12, 1840, by Stephen Dodd | TM3 | 327 |
| DARROW, DAROW, DOROW, Abig[a]il, d. Ebenezer, b. July 29, 1745 | TM2 | 26 |
| Agnes, w. Albergin, d. Jan. 12, 1807, ae 30 | DR | |
| Asa, s. Ebenezer, b. May 22, 1750 | TM2 | 26 |

| DARROW, DAROW, DOROW, (cont.), | Vol. | Page |
|---|---|---|
| Diana, w. Richard, d. [Mar.] 12, 1774, ae 84 | DR | |
| Ebenezer, s. Ebenezer, b. Mar. 23, 1743 | TM2 | 26 |
| Ebenezer, s. Ebenezer, d. Oct. 1, 1749, ae 7 | DR | |
| Ebenezer, s. Ebenezer, b. Sept. 18, 1757 | TM2 | 27 |
| [E]uunis, d. Ebenezer, b. Jan. 23, 1755 | TM2 | 27 |
| Jemimah, d. Ebenezer, b. Feb. 9, 1747/8 | TM2 | 26 |
| John, s. Ritchchard, b. Jan. 13, 1712/13 | TM1 | 114 |
| John, s. Richard, b. Oct. 24, 1716 | TM1 | 199 |
| Richard, m. Sarah SHEPPARD, Aug. 7, 1710, by Abraham Braly, J. P. | TM1 | 31 |
| Richard, s. Richard, b. Aug. 30, 1711 | TM1 | 31 |
| Richard, d. [Mar.] 19, 1775, ae 94 | DR | |
| Titus, s. Ebenezer, b. Feb. 15, 1753 | TM2 | 26 |
| ----, ch. [of] Richard, d. [Dec.] 17, 1713, ae 6 m. | DR | |
| ----, ch. of Richard, d. Dec. 17, 1713 | TM1 | 114 |
| ----, ch. [of] Albergin, d. June 8, 1807, ae 1 | DR | |
| DAVENPORT, DAVENPORTE, Abigail, wid. John, Jr., d. July 20, 1717 | DR | |
| Deodate, Esq. Dea., d. Dec. 3, 1761, ae 55 | DR | |
| Hezekiah, of [East Haven], m. Philena PIERPONT, of North Haven, [May] 27, 1804, by Rev. Nicholas Street | DR | |
| John, s. John, Jr., d. [Aug.] 31, 1663, ae 7 w | DR | |
| John, Rev., of Stamford, d. Feb. 5, 1731, ae 62 | DR | |
| John, s. Roswell & Hester, b. Apr. 5, 1794 | TM3 | 13 |
| John, d. Jan. 9, 1820, ae 82 | DR | |
| Lydia, w. Capt. Deodate, d. June 18, 1758, ae 52 | DR | |
| Martha, w. Rev. John, of Stamford, d. Dec. 17, 1712 | DR | |
| Mary, w. Dea. Samuel, d. [Dec.] 21, 1803, ae 66 | DR | |
| Mercy, w. Samuel, d. July 15, 1765 | DR | |
| Phebe, wid., d. Jan. 6, 1842, ae 82 y. 6 m. | DR | |
| Rosewell, s. Deodate, d. [Sept.] 9, 1749, ae 7 | DR | |
| Samuel, Dea. d. July 9, 1810, ae 70 | DR | |
| William, s. Deodate, [d. Sept. 16, 1742] | TM2 | 24 |
| William, s. Deodate, d. [Sept.] 17, 1742, ae 8 | DR | |
| William, s. Deodate, d. [Dec.] 30, 1754, ae 10 | DR | |
| William, s. Roswell & Hester, b. Nov. 28, 1796 | TM3 | 13 |
| DAVIDSON, Abijah, m. Sally BRADLEY, b. of [East Haven], [Feb.] 17, 1805, by Rev. Nicholas Street | DR | |
| Abijah, d. May 7, 1806, ae 22 | DR | |
| Andrew, d. June 25, 1828, ae 78 | DR | |
| Elizabeth, m. Willard MALLORY, b. of East Haven, Mar. 3, 1833, by Rev. Stephen Dodd | DR | |
| Elizabeth, m. Willard MALLORY, b. of East Haven, Mar. 3, 1833, by Stephen Dodd | TM3 | 235 |
| Elizabeth, wid., d. July 1, 1840, ae 83 y. 6 m. | DR | |
| James, d. [July] 18, 1803, ae 22 | DR | |
| Jeremiah B., m. Lereumah FINCH, b. of [East Haven], Nov. 17, 1813, by Rev. Saul Clark | DR | |
| Jeremiah B., m. Susan ANDREWS, of East Haven, Apr. 20, 1834, by Rev. Stephen Dodd | DR | |
| Jeremiah B., m. Susan ANDREWS, b. of East Haven, Apr. 20, 1834, by Stephen Dodd | TM3 | 281 |
| John B., d. Nov. 12, 1828, ae 18 | DR | |

| | Vol. | Page |
|---|---|---|
| **DAVIDSON**, (cont.), | | |
| Julia, of East Haven, m. Merrit **THOMPSON**, June 30, 1846, by Rev. George W. Nichols | DR | |
| Julia, m. Merrit **THOMPSON**, June 14, 1846, by Rev. George W. Nichols | TM4 | 206 |
| Leura, m. Milton **FINCH**, b. of [East Haven], [Dec.] 28, 1814, by Rev. Saul Clark | DR | |
| Leuramah, w. Jeremiah B., d. Apr. 19, 1816, ae 24 | DR | |
| Nancy, m. William **BARNES**, b. of [East Haven], Mar. 11, 1811, by Rev. Saul Clark | DR | |
| Rachel, d. Andrew, d. Aug. 22, 1796, ae 1 | DR | |
| Sally, Mrs., m. William **WOODWARD**, b. of [East Haven], [Jan.] 15, 1812, by Rev. Saul Clark | DR | |
| Sally, m. Samuel T. **ANDREWS**, b. of [East Haven], [Apr.] 28, 1824, by Rev. Stephen Dodd | DR | |
| Sarah, m. Samuel T. **ANDREWS**, Apr. 28, 1824, by Stephen Dodd | TM3 | 168 |
| **DAVIS**, Elizur R., m. Catherin **STEPHENS**, b. of Fair Haven, Oct. 4, 1851, by Rev. D. W[illia]m Havens | TM4 | 217 |
| Fannie E., of East Haven, m. Street **CHIDSEY**, Sept. 4, 1842, by Rev. George W. Nichols | DR | |
| Frank, d. June 16, 1811, ae 30 | DR | |
| **DAWSON, DAWSUN, DOASEN**, Hannah, 2d. w. Robert, d. Jan. 30, 1714, ae 49 | DR | |
| Hannah, wid. Thomas, d. [          ], 1781, ae 82 | DR | |
| John, m. Sarah **CHEDSEY**, July 1, 1708, by W[illia]m Mallbie, J. P. | TM1 | 30 |
| John, d. Aug. 28, 1732, ae 55 | DR | |
| Joseph, s. Thomas, [d.          ], 1736, ae 2 y. | TM2 | 23 |
| Joseph, s. Thomas, d. Feb. 8, 1737, ae 2 | DR | |
| Mary, d. Thomas, d. Nov. 9, 1736, ae 10 | DR | |
| Mary, d. Thomas, [d.          ], 1736, ae 10 y. | TM2 | 23 |
| Mary, d. Thomas, d. [Feb.] 9, 1737, ae 4 | DR | |
| Mary, w. John, d. [Oct.] 11, 1742, ae 52 | DR | |
| Mary, w. John, [d. Oct. 11, 1742] | TM2 | 24 |
| Mary, m. Christopher **TUTTLE**, b. of [East Haven], May 1, 1815, by Rev. Saul Clark | DR | |
| Mehitabel, w. Thomas, d. Oct. 25, 1723 | DR | |
| Robert, s. John, b. Mar. 2, 1717/18 | TM1 | 198 |
| Robert, d. Jan. 26, 1799, ae 81 | DR | |
| Sarah, w. John, d. May 22, 1709, ae 21 | DR | |
| Sarah, w. John, d. May 22, 1709 | TM1 | 30 |
| Sary, d. Thomas, [d.          ], 1736, ae 13 y. | TM2 | 23 |
| Thankful, w. Robert, d. June 29, 1787, ae 60 | DR | |
| Thomas, d. Jan. 12, 1759, ae 72 | DR | |
| Tymothe, s. John, b. Apr. 27, 1716 | TM1 | 198 |
| Timothy, d. [May] 15, 1740, ae 24 | DR | |
| Tittus, s. John, [d. Sept. 28, 1742] | TM2 | 24 |
| Titus, s. John, d. [          ], 1742, ae 20 | DR | |
| ----, 2nd w. Robert, d. Jan. 30, 1713/14 | TM1 | 114 |
| **DAY**, William, d. Oct. 20, 1783, ae 40 | DR | |
| **DAYTON**, Joshua, of North Haven, m. Julia Ann **REDFIELD**, of [East Haven], June 7, 1821, by Rev. Stephen Dodd | DR | |

| | Vol. | Page |
|---|---|---|
| **DAYTON**, (cont.), | | |
| Joshua, of New Haven, m. Julia Ann **REDFIELD**, June 7, | | |
| 1821, by Stephen Dodd | TM3 | 164 |
| Joshua, d. Jan. 21, 1843, ae 53 | DR | |
| **DELANO**, Michael, d. [        ], 1667 | DR | |
| **DELIVERANCE**, John, d. [Dec.] 30, 1773, ae 30; d. at sea | DR | |
| **DENISON, DENYSON**, Abigail, d. James, d. Oct. 13, 1736, ae 5 | DR | |
| Abig[a]il, d. James, [d.], Oct. 13, 1736, ae 5 y. | TM2 | 23 |
| Abigail, w. Jesse, d. [Aug.] 21, 1743, ae 24 | DR | |
| Abig[a]il, w. Jesse, [d. Aug. 21, 1743] | TM2 | 25 |
| Dorothy, d. James, d. [July] 10, 1773, ae 10; bd. with James | | |
| **DENISON** | DR | |
| James, s. James, d. Jan. 2, 1663, ae 1 | DR | |
| James, d. May 8, 1719,ae 78 | DR | |
| Jam[e]s, d. May 8, 1719 | TM1 | 199 |
| James, s. James, d. [July] 10, 1773, ae 5; bd. with Dorothy | | |
| **DENISON** | DR | |
| James, d. [Sept.] 27, 1774, ae 55 | DR | |
| Jesse, d. Aug. 20, 1743, ae 25 | DR | |
| Jesse, d. Aug. 20, [1743] | TM2 | 25 |
| Jesse, d. Jan. 10, 1815, ae 69 | DR | |
| John, s. James, d. Oct. 16, 1668, ae 3 | DR | |
| John, d. [        ], 1731, ae 54 | DR | |
| Mabel, wid. Jesse, d. [Nov.] 9, 1824, ae 76 | DR | |
| Sarah, w. James, d. July 2, 1773, ae 47 | DR | |
| Sibbell, d. James, d. Oct. 18, [1743] | TM2 | 25 |
| Sibyl, d. James, d. [Oct.] 18, 1743, ae 13 | DR | |
| **DENSLOW**, John, m. Betsey **NICHOLS**, of New Haven, Mar. 25, 1821, | | |
| by Stephen Dodd | TM3 | 164 |
| **DENTON**, Jonathan, of Boston, m. Sarah **FARREN**, of [East Haven], Dec. | | |
| 27, 1815, by Rev. Saul Clark | DR | |
| **DERRICK**, George, of New Haven, m. Sarah An[n] **BUNNELL**, of | | |
| Branford, May 6, 1822, by Rev. Oliver Willson, of | | |
| North Haven | TM3 | 166 |
| **DEWEY**, Orpha, w. Solomon, d. [July] 10, 1813, ae 32 | DR | |
| Solomon, commandant at the fort, m. Maria **PARDEE**, of [East | | |
| Haven], Sept. 5, 1813, by Rev. Saul Clark | DR | |
| **DOASEN**, [see under **DAWSON**] | | |
| **DODD**, Abigail Ann, w. Rev. Stephen, d. Oct. 17, 1847, ae 74 | DR | |
| Stephen, Rev. pastor of Cong. ch. in East Haven, m. Eliza | | |
| **ANDREWS**, b. of East Haven, July 12, 1848, by | | |
| Rev. D. William Havens | DR | |
| Stephen, Rev., m. Eliza **ANDREWS**, b. of East Haven, July 12, | | |
| 1848, by Rev. D. W[illia]m Havens | TM4 | 210 |
| **DOROTHY**, Maria, of New Haven, m. William **LINDSLEY**, of [East | | |
| Haven], [Aug.] 20, 1828, by Rev. Stephen Dodd | DR | |
| Maria, of New Haven, m. William **LINDSLEY**, of East Haven, | | |
| Aug. 20, 1828, by Stephen Dodd | TM3 | 173 |
| **DOWNS**, Louisa M., m. Levi **ROWE**, Jr., b. of East Haven, Apr. 25, 1840, | | |
| by Rev. Stephen Dodd | DR | |
| Louisa, M., m. Levi **ROWE**, Jr., b. of East Haven, Apr. 25, | | |
| 1840, by Stephen Dodd | TM3 | 327 |

|                                                                                          | Vol. | Page |
|------------------------------------------------------------------------------------------|------|------|
| **DURAND**, Lucy, m. Nehemiah H. **HOIT**, Oct. 29, 1831, by Rev. John Mitchell, of Fair Haven | TM3  | 283  |
| **EDWARDS**, Polly, m. Thomas **POTTER**, July 23, 1801, by Rev. Nicholas Street          | DR   |      |
| **EELLS**, Charles A., of Milford, m. Maria **FORBES**, of East Haven, Nov. 26, 1826, by Bela Farnham, J. P. | TM3  | 172  |
| **EGGLESTON, EGELSTONE**, Abraham, d. [        ], 1793, ae 20; West Indies                 | DR   |      |
| Betsey, m. Amos **SHERMAN**, Oct. 22, 1820, by Stephen Dodd                               | TM3  | 57   |
| David, d. Sept. 11, 1812, ae 81                                                           | DR   |      |
| Elizabeth, d. [Sept.] 26, 1815, ac 70                                                     | DR   |      |
| John, d. Aug. 5, 1830, ae 62                                                              | DR   |      |
| Olive, w. John, d. Oct. 10, 1812, ae 56                                                   | DR   |      |
| Sarah, d. Zebra, d. [Dec.] 16, 1805, ae 2                                                 | DR   |      |
| **ELLIOT**, Sarah (**GOODSELL**), wid., d. Thomas **GOODSELL**, Jr. & Martha, [of North Branford], d. [        ], 1802, ae, 62 | DR   |      |
| **ELLIS**, Harriet, m. John **SMITH**, July 7, 1836, by Rev. John Mitchell, of Fair Haven | TM3  | 285  |
| **ENGLISH**, Charles L., of New Haven, m. Harriet D. **HOLT**, of East Haven, [Apr.] 20, 1848, by Rev. D. William Havens | DR   |      |
| Charles L., of New Haven, m. Harriet D. **HOLT**, of East Haven, Apr. 20, 1848, by Rev. D. W[illia]m Havens | TM4  | 209  |
| **EVERTON, EUERTON**, Daniel, s. W[illia]m & Ezebel, b. Mar. 17, 1757                     | TM2  | 165  |
| Est[h]er, d. [W[illia]m & Ezebel], b. Sept. 8, 1759                                       | TM2  | 165  |
| Est[h]er, see Ester **FORBES**                                                            | TM2  | 159  |
| Ezebel, d. [W[illia]m & Ezebel], b. Apr. 20, 1769                                         | TM2  | 165  |
| Holbruck, s. [W[illia]m & Ezebel], b. Feb. 5, 1772                                        | TM2  | 165  |
| Holbrook, d. Oct. 15, 1803, ae 22                                                         | DR   |      |
| Isabel, w. William, d. May 22, 1801, ae 67                                                | DR   |      |
| Jared, s. [W[illia]m & Ezebel], b. May 21, 1767                                           | TM2  | 165  |
| John, s. John, b. Dec. 4, 1746                                                            | TM2  | 26   |
| Mary, d. [W[illia]m & Ezebel], b. Apr. 23, 1762                                           | TM2  | 165  |
| Phebe, wid. William, d. [Oct.] 19, 1826, ae 84                                            | DR   |      |
| Will[ia]m, s. [W[illia]m & Ezebel], b. Dec. 18, 1763                                      | TM2  | 165  |
| William, d. July 3, 1813, ae 80                                                           | DR   |      |
| **FARNHAM**, Amos Wilcox, twin ch. [of] Bela, d. Dec. 27, 1802, ae 3 w.                   | DR   |      |
| Anna, w. Doc. Bela, d. Dec. 26, 1843, ae 70 y. 5 m.                                       | DR   |      |
| Bela, had twin s. Amos Wilcox, d. Dec. 27, 1802, ae 3 w.                                  | DR   |      |
| Emeline, d. Bela & Anna, b. Apr. 3, 1800                                                  | TM3  | 10   |
| Emmeline, of East Haven, m. Riley **NOTT**, of New Haven, June 20, 1836, by Rev. Stephen Dodd | DR   |      |
| Emmeline, of East Haven, m. Riley **NOTT**, of New Haven, June 20, 1836, by Stephen Dodd  | TM3  | 285  |
| Joseph Camp, s. [Bela & Anna], b. Nov. 26, 180[ ]                                         | TM3  | 10   |
| **FARREN, FERRIN, FERREN, FERRAND**, Almira, of East Haven, m. Lyman R. **FORD**, of New Haven, July 26, 1835, by Rev. Stephen Dodd | DR   |      |
| Betsey, w. John, d. Feb. 4, 1846, ae 60                                                   | DR   |      |
| Desire, wid. Zebulon, d. [June] 13, 1807, ae 64                                           | DR   |      |
| Eli, d. Aug. [ ], 1800, ae 21                                                             | DR   |      |
| Elia, m. Statira **ROWE**, Feb. 26, 1823, by Rev. Stephen Dodd                           | DR   |      |

| FARREN, FERRIN, FERREN, FERRAND, (cont.), | Vol. | Page |
|---|---|---|
| Elisabeth B., m. Hoadley E. **MONROE**, Nov. 20, 1831, by | | |
| Rev. John Mitchell, of Fair Haven | TM3 | 284 |
| Frances, d. Samuel, d. Mar. 10, 1810, ae 4 | DR | |
| Hannah, w. Abraham, d. [Oct.] 21, 1810, ae 40 | DR | |
| Harriet A., m. Edwin Ackland **WALKER**, b. of East Haven, | | |
| Jan. 30, 1841, by Rev. Stephen Dodd | DR | |
| Harriett A., m. Acklin E. **WALKER**, b. of East Haven, Jan. 30, | | |
| 1841, by Stephen Dodd | TM4 | 200 |
| Jacob, d. [Mar.] 15, 1845, ae 76 | DR | |
| James, m. Polly **ANDREWS**, of [East Haven], May 2, 1822, by | | |
| Rev. Stephen Dodd | DR | |
| James, m. Polly **ANDREWS**, May 2, 1822, by Stephen Dodd | TM3 | 165 |
| James, d. May 2, 1837, ae 42 y. 7 m. | DR | |
| Jane, d. John, [of New Haven], d. Nov. 1, [1818], ae 1 | DR | |
| Jennet, d. John, [of New Haven], d. Aug. 24, 1818, ae 1 | DR | |
| John, m. Betsey **SHEPARD**, b. of [East Haven], [Feb.] [ ], | | |
| 1804, by Rev. Nicholas Street | DR | |
| John, m. Desire **THOMPSON**, b. of East Haven, Feb. 15, | | |
| 1828, by Stephen Dodd | TM3 | 174 |
| John, 2d, m. Desire **THOMPSON**, of [East Haven], [Feb.] [ ], | | |
| 1829, by Rev. Stephen Dodd | DR | |
| John S., m. Mary **PARDEE**, Jan. 15, 1832, by Rev. John | | |
| Mitchell, of Fair Haven | TM3 | 284 |
| Julia E., m. Leander **CHIDSEY**, b. of East Haven, Sept. 15, | | |
| 1852, by Rev. D. W[illia]m Havens | TM4 | 219 |
| Lydia, w. Jacob, d. Mar. 7, 1834, ae 60 | DR | |
| Lydia Almira, of East Haven, m. Lyman R. **FORD**, of New | | |
| Haven, July 26, 1835, by Stephen Dodd | TM3 | 282 |
| Major, s. Zebulon & Desire, b. Oct. 10, 1790 | TM3 | 9 |
| Samuel, m. Polly **CURTIS**, of [East Haven], July 22, 1805, by | | |
| Rev. Nicholas Street | DR | |
| Sarah, of [East Haven], m. Jonathan **DENTON**, of Boston, Dec. | | |
| 27, 1815, by Rev. Saul Clark | DR | |
| Sarah J., of New Haven, m. Eldrige B. **CRANES**, of Hartford, | | |
| July 18, 1847, by Rev. Daniel W[illia]m Havens | TM4 | 207 |
| Sidney, s. Jacob, d. [Nov.] 30, 1807, ae 4 | DR | |
| William, m. Betsey **MALLORY**, b. of East Haven, May 10, | | |
| 1842, by Rev. Benj[ami]n L. Swan, of Fair Haven | TM4 | 201 |
| Wyllys, d. [Nov. 22], 1831, ae 23; wrecked off Jersey shore | DR | |
| Zebulon, d. Dec. 3, 1805, ae 86 | DR | |
| ——, infant [of] Abraham, d. Jan. 13, 1808, ae 2 d. | DR | |
| ——, infant [of] Abraham, d. Dec. 27, 1809, ae 4 d. | DR | |
| ——, infant [of] Samuel, [of] New Haven, d. [Feb.] 8, 1825, | | |
| ae 4 w. | DR | |
| ——, s. Samuel [of] New Haven, [Aug.] 9, 1842, ae 10; | | |
| (drowned) | DR | |
| FENN, Henry, of Plymouth, m. Mary **BRADLEY**, of East Haven, Mar. 4, | | |
| 1834, by Rev. Stephen Dodd | DR | |
| Henry, of Plymouth, m. Mary **BRADLEY**, of East Haven, Mar. | | |
| 4, 1834, by Stephen Dodd | TM3 | 281 |
| FERRAN, [see under FARREN] | | |
| FERREND, [see under FARREN] | | |

|  | Vol. | Page |
|---|---|---|
| **FIELDS**, Ezra, Capt. d. Jan. 12, 1779, ae 48 | DR | |
| Mary, wid. Capt. Ezra, d. Jan. 21, 1788, ae 55 | DR | |
| **FINCH**, Daniell, s. Daniell, b. Apr. 10, 1719 | TM1 | 245 |
| Ebenezer, s. Daniell, b. June 3, 1723 | TM1 | 245 |
| Gidian, s. Daniell, b. Feb. 21, 1720 | TM1 | 245 |
| Jonathan, d. [Aug.] 19, 1821, ae 62 | DR | |
| Lereumah, m. Jeremiah B. **DAVIDSON**, b. of [East Haven], | | |
| Nov. 17, 1813, by Rev. Saul Clark | DR | |
| Ler[e]umah, m. Elbert J. **MUNSELL**, b. of East Haven, Sept. | | |
| 22, 1833, by Rev. Stephen Dodd | DR | |
| Ler[e]umah, see also Reumah | | |
| Maria, [d.] Milton, d. [Apr.] 29, 1823, ae 4 m. | DR | |
| Merit, s. Milton, d. Feb. 12, 1820, ae 3 | DR | |
| Milton, m. Leura **DAVIDSON**, b. of [East Haven], [Dec.] 28, | | |
| 1814, by Rev. Saul Clark | DR | |
| Milton, d. Jan. 18, 1824, ae 35 | DR | |
| Orton, s. Jonathan, [of Northford], d. Jan. 6, 1799, ae 4 | DR | |
| Reumah, of East Haven, m. Alfred **MUNSELL**, of Fair Haven, | | |
| Sept. 22, 1833, by Stephen Dodd | TM3 | 326 |
| Reumah, see also Ler[e]umah | | |
| **FLAGG**, Henrietta, of [East Haven], m. Harry **HURLBUT**, of Chatham, | | |
| July 13, 1823, by Rev. Stephen Dodd | DR | |
| Henrietta, of East Haven, m. Harry **HURLBURT**, of Chatham, | | |
| July 13, 1823, by Stephen Dodd | TM3 | 167 |
| Huldah Hughes, wid. Orrin, d. Mar. 7, 1841, ae 53 | DR | |
| Sarah, of [East Haven], m. Robert B. **THROCKMORTON**, of | | |
| Lexington, Ky., [Nov.] 13, 1825, by Rev. Stephen | | |
| Dodd | DR | |
| Sarah, of East Haven, m. Robert B. **THROCKMORTON**, of | | |
| Lexington, Ky., Nov. 13, 1825, by Stephen Dodd | TM3 | 207 |
| -----, infant [of] Bethuel, d. Nov. 1, 1806, ae 1 d. | DR | |
| **FLAVEL**, Edward, s. wid., d. [Nov.] 22, 1818, ae 1 | DR | |
| **FOOTE, FOOT**, David E., of Branford, m. Marion J. **LINES**, of East | | |
| Haven, Sept. 15, 1852, by Rev. D. W[illia]m Havens | TM4 | 219 |
| I. Henry, of Fair Haven, m. Marietta **SMITH**, of East Haven, | | |
| Nov. 26, 1846, by Stephen Dodd | TM4 | 207 |
| Isaac Henry, of New Haven, m. Marietta **SMITH**, of East | | |
| Haven, Nov. 26, 1846, by Rev. Stephen Dodd | DR | |
| John, of Northford, m. wid. Almira **LINDSLEY**, of East Haven, | | |
| May 29, 1842, by Rev. Stephen Dodd | DR | |
| John, of Northford, m. wid. Almina **LINDSLEY**, of East | | |
| Haven, May 19, 1842, by Stephen Dodd | TM4 | 201 |
| Mary, m. John **CHEDSEY**, Feb. 8, 1714/15 | TM1 | 114 |
| **FORBES, FORBS, FURBS**, Almira, m. Henry **FORBES**, b. of [East | | |
| Haven], Sept. 17, 1829, by Rev. Stephen Dodd | DR | |
| Almira, m. Henry **FORBES**, b. of East Haven, Sept. 17, 1829, | | |
| by Stephen Dodd | TM3 | 231 |
| Ammasa, s. Isaac & Hannah, b. Mar. 19, 1778 | TM2 | 295 |
| Ame, m. Dan **BRADLEY**, b. of [East Haven], Nov. 4, 1804, by | | |
| Rev. Nicholas Street (Amy) | DR | |
| Ame, d. Levi & Sarah, b. Oct. 8, 1782 | TM2 | 162 |
| Anna, d. Levi & Sarah, b. Mar. 23, 1770 | TM2 | 162 |

| FORBES, FORBS, FURBS, (cont.) | Vol. | Page |
|---|---|---|
| Anna, w. John, d. [July] 26, 1795, ae 21; childbed | DR | |
| Anna, w. Isaac, d. [Mar.] 24, 1815, ae 41 | DR | |
| Anna, d. Mar. 26, 1815, ae 41 y. | TM2 | 267 |
| Anson, d. [July] [  ], 1834, ae 36 | DR | |
| Bennet, s. Parson, d. [Oct.] 17, 1826, ae 10 | DR | |
| Betsey, d. Samuel, d. [          ], 1803, ae 2 | DR | |
| Betsey, of East Haven, m. Russell HUGHES, Nov. 15, 1815, | | |
|     by Rev. Elijah G. Plumb | DR | |
| David, Doc., m. Lue BRADLEY, b. of [East Haven], Mar. 6, | | |
|     1803, by Rev. Nicholas Street | DR | |
| Edwin, s. Amasa, d. Mar. 19, 1809, ae 19 m. | DR | |
| Eleanor, w. Eli, d. May 6, 1838, ae 70 | DR | |
| Eleazar, d. [Jan.] 22, 1794, ae 20 | DR | |
| Eli, d. [Oct.] 7, 1845, ae 85 y. 11 m. | DR | |
| Elizabeth, wid. Samuel, d. Aug. 17, 1839, ae 91 | DR | |
| Esther, w. Addereno [of New Haven], d. Sept. 31, [1789], ae 30; | | |
|     bd. in East Haven | DR | |
| Est[h]er, w. Adderence & d. of W[illia]m & Ezebel EVERTON, | | |
|     d. Sept. 31, 1789 | TM2 | 159 |
| Hannah, wid. Isaac, d. Sept. 7, 1806, ae 64 | DR | |
| Harriet, d. Isaac, d. Mar. 3, 1796, ae 3 w. | DR | |
| Henry, m. Almira FORBES, b. of [East Haven], Sept. 17, 1829, | | |
|     by Rev. Stephen Dodd | DR | |
| Henry, m. Almira FORBES, b. of East Haven, Sept. 17, 1829, | | |
|     by Stephen Dodd | TM3 | 231 |
| Horace, s. John, d. Aug. 19, 1811, ae 1 | DR | |
| Hubbard, s. Parson, d. [          ], 1811, ae 6 m. | DR | |
| Huldah, m. Levi BRADLEY, b. of [East Haven], Feb. 5, 1804, | | |
|     by Rev. Nicholas Street | DR | |
| Huldah, d. Isaac, Jr., d. [July] 27, 1811, ae 4 | DR | |
| Huldah, d. Willet, d. June 4, 1813, ae 3 d. | DR | |
| Isaac, s. Samuel, b. Apr. 2, 1742 | TM2 | 294 |
| Isaac, s. Isaac & Hannah, b. Apr. 15, 1773 | TM2 | 294 |
| Isaac, had negro Cloe, d. Pink, b. June 15, 1791 | TM2 | 295 |
| Isaac, d. May 23, 1808, ae 66 | DR | |
| Isaac, d. [Nov.] 23, 1828, ae 55 | DR | |
| Isaac, d. July 21, 1845, ae 39 | DR | |
| Jared, s. [John & Anna], b. Apr. 12, 1818 | TM3 | 265 |
| Jehiel, had negro C[a]esar, s. Cork & Sibil, b. Apr. 7, 1785 | TM2 | 164 |
| Jehiel, had negro Will, s. Cork & Sibil, b. Mar. 15, 1789 | TM2 | 165 |
| Jehiel, had negro Will, s. Cork & Sibel, b. Mar. 15, 1789 | TM2 | 296 |
| Jehiel, d. Apr. 18, 1793, ae 60 | DR | |
| Jehiel, of New Haven, m. Sarah WOODWARD, of [East | | |
|     Haven], Oct. 12, 1830, by Rev. Stephen Dodd | DR | |
| Jehiel, of New Haven, m. Sarah WOODWARD, of East Haven, | | |
|     Oct. 12, 1830, by Stephen Dodd | TM3 | 232 |
| Jerome, s. Samuel 2d, d. [Sept.] [  ], 1836, ae 6 | DR | |
| John, s. Isaac & Hannah, b. Dec. 19, 1770 | TM2 | 294 |
| John, d. Feb. 21, 1837, ae 66 | DR | |
| Joseph, d. [Levi & Mary], b. Nov. 8, 1822 | TM3 | 170 |
| Justin, s. [John & Anna], b. May 25, 1815 | TM3 | 265 |
| Ledy, d. Levi & Sarah, b. Sept. 10, 1780 | TM2 | 162 |
| Leverett, s. Parsons, d. Oct. 19, 1833, ae 14 | DR | |

| | Vol. | Page |
|---|---|---|
| **FORBES, FORBS, FURBS**, (cont.), | | |
| Levi, s. Levi & Sarah, b. Mar. 14, 1785 | TM2 | 162 |
| Levi, d. Nov. 24, 1795, ae 56 | DR | |
| Levi, s. [Levi & Mary], b. Mar. 22, 1821 | TM3 | 170 |
| Leveins, s. Levi & Sarah, b. July 8, 1776 (Levins) | TM2 | 162 |
| Levins, s. Levi, d. Sept. [ ], 1794, ae 18; at sea | DR | |
| Levens Griswold, s. Levi & Mary, b. Feb. 22, 1818 | TM3 | 170 |
| Louisa, m. Abraham **THOMPSON**, [May] 28, 1837, by Rev. | | |
| Mr. Stebbins, ex. d. | DR | |
| Louisa, m. Abraham **THOMPSON**, Jr., May 28, 1837, by Rev. | | |
| Stephen W. Stebbins | TM3 | 324 |
| Lue Adeline, d. Bela, d. Dec. 24, 1822, ae 1 | DR | |
| Mabel, wid. Jehiel, d. [July] 20, 1825, ae 92 | DR | |
| Maria, of East Haven, m. Charles A. **EELLS**, of Milford, Nov. | | |
| 26, 1826, by Bela Farnham, J. P. | TM3 | 172 |
| Mary, m. John **RUSSELL**, May 23, 1717 | TM1 | 198 |
| Mary, d. [Apr.] 24, 1777, ae 70 | DR | |
| Mary, d. Isaac, Jr., d. Apr. 6, 1802, ae 2 | DR | |
| Mary, d. [Levi & Mary], b. Aug. 19, 1819 | TM3 | 170 |
| Mary Ann, m. Jeremiah **BARNES**, [Sept.] 30, 1829, by Rev. | | |
| Stephen Dodd | DR | |
| Mary Ann, m. Jeremiah **BARNES**, b. of East Haven, Sept. 30, | | |
| 1829, by Stephen Dodd | TM3 | 231 |
| Molly, d. Levi & Sarah, b. Feb. 6, 1772 | TM2 | 162 |
| Persons, s. Isaac & Hannah, b. Mar. 19, 1783 (Parsons) | TM2 | 295 |
| Parsons, d. Jan. 10, 1827, ae 44 | DR | |
| Sally, d. Isaac & Hannah, b. Mar. 7, 1767 | TM2 | 294 |
| Sally, of [East Haven], m. Jeremiah **BEECHER**, of | | |
| Woodbridge, June 9, 1800, by Rev. Nicholas Street | DR | |
| Samuel, Capt., d. [ Apr.] 20, 1757, ae 54 | DR | |
| Samuel, Capt., d. Feb. 27, 1789, ae 67 | DR | |
| Sarah, d. Levi & Sarah, b. May 20, 1774 | TM2 | 162 |
| Sarah Maria, [d.] Eli, d. Oct. 11, 1826, ae 25 | DR | |
| Sarah Tuttle, wid. Levi, d. [May] 28, 1838, ae 86 | DR | |
| Sarah Woodward, w. Jehiel, [of] New Haven, d. [Apr.] 29, | | |
| 1846, ae 57 | DR | |
| Sophia, w. Parson, d. Apr. 3, 1811, ae 28 | DR | |
| Timothy, [s.] Levi, d. Oct. 25, 1780, ae 2; scalded | DR | |
| William, s. John & Anna, b. Sept. 3, 1804 | TM3 | 265 |
| -----, ch. [of] Isaac, Jr., d. [Mar.] 14, 1797, ae 3 w. | DR | |
| -----, ch. [of] John, d.[ ], 1803, ae 2 | DR | |
| -----, ch. [of] Parson, d. Feb. 12, 1808, ae 6 w. | DR | |
| **FORD**, Benjamin, s. Benjamin & Anna, b. May 1, 1785 | TM2 | 236 |
| Benjamin, d. Jan. 6, 1787, ae 35; shot by his own gun | DR | |
| Johnson, s. Benjamin & Anna, b. Feb. 6, 1783 | TM2 | 236 |
| Lyman R., of New Haven, m. Almira **FARREN**, of East Haven, | | |
| July 26, 1835, by Rev. Stephen Dodd | DR | |
| Lyman R., of New Haven, m. Lydia Almira **FERRIN**, of East | | |
| Haven, July 26, 1835, by Stephen Dodd | TM3 | 282 |
| **FOWLER**, David Sullivan, of North Guilford, m. Charlotte **HOLT**, of | | |
| [East Haven], [May] [ ], 1832, by Rev. Stephen | | |
| Dodd | DR | |

| FOWLER, (cont.), | Vol. | Page |
|---|---|---|
| David Sullivan, of North Guilford, m. Charlotte E. **HOLT**, of | | |
| East Haven, June 20, 1832, by Stephen Dodd | TM3 | 234 |
| Edward S., of Guilford, m. Jane Elisabeth **RUSSELL**, of East | | |
| Haven, Oct. 17, 1842, by Stephen Dodd | TM4 | 201 |
| Edward Sherman, of Guilford, m. Jane Elizabeth **RUSSEL[L]**, | | |
| of East Haven, Oct. 17, 1842, by Rev. Stephen Dodd | DR | |
| -----, twin s. [of] John, d. Aug. 20, 1829, ae 2 w. | DR | |
| -----, twin d. [of] John, d. [Sept.] 9, 1829, ae 5 w. | DR | |
| FREEMAN, Violet, (b. a slave; served four successive generations of same | | |
| family), d. July 30, 1843, ae 77, at the home of | | |
| Mrs. L. Caroline **HUGHES** | DR | |
| FRISBIE, Catharine E., of East Haven, m. Russel G. **SMITH**, of Fair | | |
| Haven, Oct. 5, 1845, by Rev. Stephen Dodd | DR | |
| Catherine E., of East Haven, m. Russel G. **SMITH**, of Fair | | |
| Haven, Oct. 5, 1845, by Stephen Dodd | TM4 | 205 |
| FROST, Mary, Mrs., m. Chandler **PARDEE**, b. of [East Haven], Mar. 7, | | |
| 1813, by Rev. Saul Clark | DR | |
| Polly, of East Haven, m. Frederick William **TUTTLE**, in Christ | | |
| Ch., Jan. 1, 1810, by Rev. Bela Hubbard, D. D. | DR | |
| FULLER, Hannah, d. John, d. [May] 20, 1794, ae 2 d. | DR | |
| John, s. John, d. [Feb.] 24, 1773, ae 4 | DR | |
| John, d. Mar. 27, 1807, ae 71 | DR | |
| Lois, [d.] John, d. Mar. 8, 1773, ae 4; bd. with Sarah **FULLER** | DR | |
| Pamela, w. Levi, d. Jan. 23, 1804, ae 25; childbed | DR | |
| Sarah, [d.] John, d. Mar. 8, 1773, ae 6; bd. with Lois **FULLER** | DR | |
| GARDNER, Daniel, d. July 4, 1833, ae 19 | DR | |
| GASKILL, Elizabeth, wid. Samuel, d. Nov. 11, 1736 | DR | |
| GASSKIN, -----, Mrs., [d.          , 1736]          (GASKILL?) | TM2 | 23 |
| GATES, Eve Ely, see under Eve Ely Gates **TUTTLE** | DR | |
| Benjamin, [s.] Daniel Smith, d. [Apr.] 29, 1824, ae 4 d. | DR | |
| GAYLORD, David Penn, d. Jan. 1, 1775, ae 77 | DR | |
| GOODSELL, GOODSILL, GOODSEL, Abigail, d. Thomas, d. Aug. 4, | | |
| 1699, ae 2 | DR | |
| Abiga[i]l, d. Isaac, b. Oct. 29, 1744 | TM2 | 44 |
| Abigail, d. Dan., b. Apr. 21, 1761 | TM2 | 27 |
| Abigail, d. Samuel, d. [Dec.] 3, 1777, ae 2 m. | DR | |
| Abigail, w. Dan., d. May 10, 1792, ae 65 | DR | |
| Abigail, w. Jonathan, [of Branford], d. Apr. 17, 1821, ae 85 | DR | |
| Abigail, wid., d. Sept. 7, 1840, ae 93 y. 4 m. | DR | |
| Abigail, wid. John, d. May 4, 1843, ae 84 y. 8 m. | DR | |
| Alford, m. Sarah **LUDDINGTON**, b. of New Haven, Aug. 25, | | |
| 1824, by Stephen Dodd | TM3 | 169 |
| Ame, see under Amy | | |
| Amos, s. Dan, b. July 6, 1751 | TM2 | 26 |
| Amos, s. Dan., d. Aug. 10, 1775, ae 24 | DR | |
| Amos, s. Dan., d. Aug. 10, 1775, in the 24th year of his age | TM2 | 87 |
| Amos, [s. Edward], b. Aug. 19, 1780 | TM2 | 154 |
| Ame, [d. Edward], b. Feb. 7, 1776 | TM2 | 154 |
| Anna, d. Dan., b. Mar. 22, 1767 | TM2 | 47 |
| Bethiah, d. Jacob, b. May 1, 1764 | TM2 | 45 |
| Dan, s. Samuell, b. June 16, 1724 | TM1 | 245 |
| Dan., m. Abiga[i]l **MOULT[H]RUP**, June 30, 1748 | TM2 | 20 |

| GOODSELL, GOODSILL, GOODSEL, (cont.), | Vol. | Page |
|---|---|---|
| Dan., s. Dan., b. Mar. 28, 1754 | TM2 | 27 |
| Dan., d. [July] 29, 1795, ae 71 | DR | |
| Edward, s. Dan., b. May 8, 1749 | TM2 | 26 |
| Edward, d. Dec. 25, 1781, ae 32 | DR | |
| Edward, d. Dec. 25, 1781, in the 23rd year of his age | TM2 | 87 |
| Elisabeth, d. Jonathan, b. July 14, 1739 | TM2 | 26 |
| Elisabath, d. Isaac, b. Sept. 15, 1754 | TM2 | 44 |
| Elisabeth, d. John, b. Aug. 21, 1774 | TM2 | 27 |
| Elisabeth, m. Zebulon BRADLEY, May 11, 1794, by Rev. | | |
| Nicholas Street | TM2 | 265 |
| Elvira, d. Samuel, d. [        ], 1803, ae 7 | DR | |
| Frances Abigail, d. Jacob, d. Oct. 2, 1815, ae 10 m. | DR | |
| Grace, of [East Haven], m. George PARMELEE, of Guilford, | | |
| Mar. 18, 1832, by Rev. Stephen Dodd | DR | |
| Grace, of East Haven, m. George PARMALEE, of Guilford, | | |
| Mar. 18, 1832, by Stephen Dodd | TM3 | 234 |
| Hannah, d. Isa[a]c, b. Feb. 1, 1739/40 | TM2 | 44 |
| Hannah, d. Jacob, b. Oct. 22, 1746 | TM2 | 26 |
| Harriat, d. Simeon & Lois, b. Mar. 19, 1804 | TM3 | 11 |
| Harriet Adelaide, of New Haven, m. William H. SHIPMAN, of | | |
| Glastenbury, Feb. 12, 1826, by Stephen Dodd | TM3 | 171 |
| Isaac, s. Samuell, b. Mar. 14, 1715 | TM1 | 198 |
| Isaac, m. Elissabath PENF[I]ELD, Aug. 31, 1737, by Rev. Mr. | | |
| Hemingway. Witnesses, Samuel GOODSELL, | | |
| Mary GOODSELL, Isaac PENF[I]ELD, and | | |
| Elesabath PENF[I]ELD | TM2 | 44 |
| Isaac, s. Isaac, b. Jan. 16, 1737/8 | TM2 | 44 |
| Isabell, d. Samuell, b. Sept. 9, 1717 | TM1 | 198 |
| Isabel, d. Dan., b. Nov. 5, 1757 | TM2 | 27 |
| Jacob, s. Samuel, b. July 26, 1722 | TM1 | 199 |
| Jacob, s. Isaac, b. Feb. 17, 1763 | TM2 | 44 |
| Jacob, d. Apr. 30, 1775, ae 52; burnt, in a fish house | DR | |
| Jacob, d. Aug. 14, 1828, (New Haven), ae 50 | DR | |
| Jared, m. Abby HOLT, [June] [  ], 1806, by Rev. Nicholas | | |
| Street | DR | |
| Jeremiah, s. Jonathan, d. [Aug.] 18, 1793, ae 1 | DR | |
| Jesse, [s. Edward], b. May 21, 1771 | TM2 | 154 |
| John, s. Thomus, b. Dec. 21, 1705 | TM1 | 30 |
| John, s. John, b. Nov. 6, 177[6] | TM2 | 27 |
| John, d. [Jan.] 29, 1816, ae 68 | DR | |
| Jonathan, s. Samuell, b. June 22, 1712 | TM1 | 198 |
| Jonathan, m. E[l]isabeth TODD, Jan. 12, 1738/9, by | | |
| Rev. [        ] | TM2 | 20 |
| Josiah, s. Jonathan, d. Sept. 19, [1743] | TM2 | 25 |
| Josiah, s. Jonathan, d. [Sept.] 19, 1743, ae 18 m. | DR | |
| Josiah, s. Jonathan, d. Oct. 15, 1744, ae 9 m. | DR | |
| Josiah, s. Jonathan, [of Branford], d. Sept. [  ], [1794], ae 19; at | | |
| sea | DR | |
| Leui, s. Dan., b. Apr. 7, 1764 | TM2 | 27 |
| Levi, s. Samuel, Jr., d. July 7, 1768, ae 23 | DR | |
| Levi, s. wid. Esther LUDDINGTON, d. [Apr.] 17, 1834, | | |
| ae 6 m. | DR | |

| | Vol. | Page |
|---|---|---|
| **GOODSELL, GOODSILL, GOODSEL**, (cont.), | | |
| Lois, wid., m. Zebulon **BRADLEY**, b. of [East Haven], Nov. 1, | | |
| 1809, by Rev. Saul Clark | DR | |
| Lois, m. Zebulon **BRADLEY**, Nov. 1, 1809 | TM3 | 11 |
| Martha, [of Northford], d. Nov. 23, 1792, ae 42 | DR | |
| Martha, relict of Thomas, Jr., [of North Branford], | | |
| d. [    ] [    ], 1796, ae 96 | DR | |
| Mary, d. Samuell, b. Dec. 17, 1719 | TM1 | 199 |
| Mary, m. Sam[u]el **HOTCHKISS**, July 16, 1744 | TM2 | 20 |
| Mary, d. Isaac, b. Dec. 6, 1757 | TM2 | 44 |
| Mary, wid. Samuel d. [Dec.] 8, 1760, ae above 70 | DR | |
| Mary, wid., d. Dec. 8, 1760 | TM2 | 22 |
| Mary, [d. Edward], b. Sept. 6, 1772 | TM2 | 154 |
| Mehitabel, [d. Edward], b. Mar. 20, 1774 | TM2 | 154 |
| Penfield, s. Isaac, b. July 2, 1742 | TM2 | 44 |
| Penfield, d. Apr. 18, 1769, ae 27 | DR | |
| Penfeild, d. Apr. 18, 1769 | TM2 | 87 |
| Penfield, d. Aug. [    ], 1797, ae 24; lost at sea | DR | |
| Penfield, s. John, d. [Sept.] 25, 1799, ae 21 | DR | |
| Polly, m. Joseph **TUTTLE**, b. of [East Haven], [    ] [    ], 1816, | | |
| by Rev. Saul Clark | DR | |
| Samuell, s. Samuell, b. Oct. 30, 1710 | TM1 | 198 |
| Samuel, d. [          ], 1739, ae 54 | DR | |
| Samuel, Serg., d. May 30, 1745, ae 61 | DR | |
| Samuel, Sergt., d. May 30, 1745 | TM2 | 22 |
| Samuel, s. Isaac, b. Apr. 4, 1749 | TM2 | 44 |
| Samuel, d. Nov. 20, 1751; killed at a sawmill in Northford, | | |
| ae 41 | DR | |
| Sarah, wid. Thomas, d. Mar. 18, 1725, ae 62 | DR | |
| Sarah, wid., d. Mar. 18, 1725 | TM1 | 245 |
| Sarah, w. Jacob, d. Jan. 2, 1753, ae 25 | DR | |
| Sarah, see Sarah **ELLIOT** | | |
| Simeon, of Branford, m. Lois **BRADLEY**, of East Haven, May | | |
| 12, 1803 | TM3 | 11 |
| Thomus, d. May 10, 1713 | TM1 | 114 |
| Thomas, d. May 16, 1713, ae 67 | DR | |
| Thomas, Jr., d. Nov. 2, 1746, ae 42 | DR | |
| Thomas, s. Isaac, b. Nov. 30, 1746 | TM2 | 44 |
| Timothy, s. Isaac, b. Feb. 25, 1752 | TM2 | 44 |
| ——, s, [of] Isaac, b. July 5, 1760 | TM2 | 44 |
| ——, infant, [of] John, d. Aug. 15, 1773, ae 2d. | DR | |
| ——, infant [of] Samuel, d. [Feb.] 11, 1793, ae 6 w. | DR | |
| ——, infant [of] Jacob, d. Nov. 21, 1813, ae 4 w. | DR | |
| **GORDON**, Abby, of North Branford, m. Reuel **ROWE**, of East Haven, | | |
| July 4, 1850, by Rev. D. W[illia]m Havens | TM4 | 213 |
| **GORHAM**, Eleazer, m. Eliza **CRANDALL**, b. of New Haven, Feb. 7, | | |
| 1831, by Stephen Dodd | TM3 | 233 |
| **GRANGER**, Daniel, s. Daniel, b. Aug. 28, 1756 | TM2 | 47 |
| Daniel, d. Dec. 31, 1778, ae 22 | DR | |
| Thadeus, s. Daniel, b. Oct. 24, 1745 | TM2 | 47 |
| **GRANNIS, GRANNESS, GRANNISS**, Abigail, d. [May] 29, 1806, ae 22 | DR | |
| Almira, of East Haven, m. John **LINDSLEY**, 2d, of North | | |
| Branford, Apr. 4, 1833, by Rev. Stephen Dodd | DR | |

| GRANNIS, GRANNESS, GRANNISS, (cont.), | Vol. | Page |
|---|---|---|
| Almira, of East Haven, m. John **LINDSLEY**, 2nd, of North | | |
| Branford, Apr. 4, 1833, by Stephen Dodd | TM3 | 236 |
| Ame, d. Isaac, b. Aug. 11, 1744 | TM2 | 26 |
| Anna, m. Elias **SHEPARD**, b. of [East Haven], Feb. 3, 1813, by | | |
| Rev. Saul Clark | DR | |
| Asenath, m. Asahel **BRADLEY**, Mar. 14, 1799, by Rev. | | |
| Nicholas Street | DR | |
| Betsey, m. Stephen **SMITH**, b. of [East Haven], Jan. 11, 1815, | | |
| by Rev. Saul Clark | DR | |
| Charlotte Ann, d. Ebenezer, d. Sept. 4, 1838, ae 6 w. | DR | |
| Chloe, w. Nathaniel, of [New Haven], d. Feb. 3, 1809, ae 46; | | |
| bd. in East Haven | DR | |
| David, d. [May] 14, 1785, ae 42; drowned off Southend | DR | |
| David, d. [          ], 1803, ae 20; lost at sea | DR | |
| Desire, d. Isaac, Jr., d. [          ], 1736, ae 4 | DR | |
| Desire, d. Joseph, [d.          ], 1736, ae 4 y. | TM2 | 23 |
| Diadama, d. Isaac, b. Jan. 30, 1747/8 | TM2 | 26 |
| Edward, d. Dec. 19, 1719 | DR | |
| Elihu, d. [Feb.] 10, 1840, ae 81 | DR | |
| Elisabeth, d. Isaac, b. Oct. 22, 1741 | TM2 | 26 |
| Eunice, m. Levi **ROWE**, b. of [East Haven], Dec. 28, 1803, by | | |
| Rev. Nicholas Street | DR | |
| Eunice, w. Jared, d. July 28, 1837, ae 61 | DR | |
| Harriet, m. Justin **LUDDINGTON**, Aug. 24, 1820, by Rev. | | |
| Stephen Dodd | DR | |
| Harriet, m. Justin **LUDIN[G]TON**, Aug. 24, 1820, by Stephen | | |
| Dodd | TM3 | 57 |
| Harriet Lavinia, d. Joseph, d. Nov. 16, 1827, ae 6 m. | DR | |
| Henry H., of New Haven, m. Louisa **GRANNISS**, of East | | |
| Haven, Sept. 4, 1831, by Stephen Dodd | TM3 | 233 |
| Henry Hughes, of New Haven, m. Louisa **GRANNIS**, of [East | | |
| Haven], Sept. 4, 1831, by Rev. Stephen Dodd | DR | |
| Henry Luddington, s. Joseph, d. Dec. 17, 1845, ae 21 | DR | |
| Hezekiah, w. Isaac, d. Jan. 3, 1793, ae 79 | DR | |
| Isaac, d. [Dec.] 26, 1803, ae 36 | DR | |
| Isaac, d. [          ], 1810, ae 20; lost in a gale at sea | DR | |
| Isaac, Jr., d. Mar. 14, 1784, ae 27 | DR | |
| Jared, Jr., d. [          ], 1818, ae 19; lost at sea | DR | |
| Jared, d. [July] 23, 1845, ae 89 | DR | |
| Joseph, Jr., d. [          ], 1739, ae 35; at sea | DR | |
| Joseph, d. Feb. 7, 1812, ae 77 | DR | |
| Louisa, of [East Haven], m. Henry Hughes **GRANNIS**, of New | | |
| Haven, Sept. 4, 1831, by Rev. Stephen Dodd | DR | |
| Louisa, of East Haven, m. Henry H. **GRANNISS**, of New | | |
| Haven, Sept. 4, 1831, by Stephen Dodd | TM3 | 233 |
| Lucy, wid. Russel, Jr., d. [Dec.] 22, 1803, ae 71 | DR | |
| Lydia, wid. Russell, d. Feb. 17, 1761 | DR | |
| Lydia, wid., d. Dec. 7, 1789, ae 60 | DR | |
| Martha, w. Nathaniel, [of New Haven], d. Oct. 7, [1803], ae 47; | | |
| bd. in East Haven | DR | |
| Mary, wid. David, d. Feb. 9, 1838, ae 91 y. 4 m. | DR | |

| GRANNIS, GRANNESS, GRANNISS, (cont.), | Vol. | Page |
|---|---|---|
| Mary, wid. Russel, 3d, [of] Fair Haven, west, d. [June] 20, 1845, ae 79 y. 7 m. | DR | |
| Mehitabel, wid. Thomas, d. [Mar.] 21, 1790, ae 77 | DR | |
| Miles, s. Thomas, d. Aug. 11, 1832, ae 2 | DR | |
| Nancy, m. Hezekiah SHEPARD, b. of [East Haven], [Nov.] 28, 1813, by Rev. Saul Clark | DR | |
| Nathaniel, [of New Haven], d. June 5, 1812, ae 57 | DR | |
| Olive, w. Joseph, d. [May] 7, 1788, ae 56 | DR | |
| Polly, d. Elihu, d. Nov. 22, 1783, ae 5 | DR | |
| Polly, w. Elihu, d. Feb. 10, 1834, ae 75 | DR | |
| Russel[l], d. [July] 17, 1777, ae 50 | DR | |
| Russel[l], s. Nathaniel, [of New Haven], d. Sept. 19, 1790, ae 2; bd. in East Haven | DR | |
| Russel[l], s. Nathaniel, d. [          ], 1790, ae 2 | DR | |
| Russel[l], [of New Haven], d. June 12, 1811, ae 45 | DR | |
| Sally, m. Stephen THOMPSON, Jr., Feb. 18, 1799, by Rev. Nicholas Street | DR | |
| Sally, m. Herman MALLORY, b. of [East Haven], [Nov.] 29, 1810, by Rev. Saul Clark | DR | |
| Samuel, d. [Jan.] 18, 1837, ae 68 | DR | |
| Sarah, w. Samuel, d. July 30, 1832, ae 60 | DR | |
| Sylvester M., of East Haven, m. Lois T. CURTIS, of North Branford, [Oct. 5], 1845, by Rev. Stephen Dodd | DR | |
| Sylvester M., of East Haven, m. Lois CURTIS, of North Branford, Oct. 5, 1845, by Stephen Dodd | TM4 | 205 |
| Thomas, m. Almira ANDREWS, of [East Haven], Aug. 26, 1824, by Rev. Stephen Dodd | DR | |
| Thomas, m. Almena ANDREWS, b. of East Haven, Aug. 26, 1824, by Stephen Dodd | TM3 | 169 |
| Wealthy, m. Jesse MALLORY, b. of [East Haven], [Nov.] 27, 1813, by Rev. Saul Clark | DR | |
| -----, ch. [of] Russel, d. [Feb.] 16, 1774, ae 5 | DR | |
| -----, infant [of] Jared, d. [Jan.] 30, 1794, ae 3 d. | DR | |
| -----, infant [of] Isaac, d. [Mar.] 29, 1794, ae 3 d. | DR | |
| -----, infant [of] Jared, d. [Apr.] 12, 1801, ae 1 d. | DR | |
| -----, ch. [of] Samuel, d. [Sept.] 19, 1804, ae 5 w. | DR | |
| GRANT, John W., m. Jane A. CHIDSEY, b. of Branford, Feb. 26, 1826, by Stephen Dodd | TM3 | 171 |
| GREEN, Hannah, d. David, d. Apr. 14, 1794, ae 3 | DR | |
| GREGSON, Jane, wid. Thomas, d. June 4, 1702, ae above 80 | DR | |
| Thomas, first white settler in East Haven, d. [          ], 1647 | DR | |
| HALL, Isaac, of West Haven, m. Jane CARNES, of Glasgow, Scotland, Sept. 4, 1851, by Rev. D. W[illia]m Havens | TM4 | 217 |
| HARRISON, Jerome, of North Branford, m. Lydia B. CHIDSEY, of East Haven, Oct. 3, 1841, by Rev. Stephen Dodd | DR | |
| Jerome, of North Branford, m. Lydia B. CHIDSEY, of East Haven, Oct. 31, 1841, by Stephen Dodd | TM4 | 200 |
| Michael, d. [Aug.] 22, 1810, ae 35 | DR | |
| -----, infant -----, d.. [Sept.] 7, 1813, ae 1 d. | DR | |
| HART, Edward, s. Rev. L., [of Wolcott], d. Oct. 11, 1813, ae 1; bd. in East Haven | DR | |

| | Vol. | Page |
|---|---|---|
| **HART**, (cont.), | | |
| Harriet, wid. Rev. Lucas, d. Feb. 23, 1839, (in New Haven), ae | | |
|     53 y. 10 m.; bd. [East Haven] | DR | |
| Lucas, Rev. of Burlington, m. Harriet **MORRIS**, of [East | | |
|     Haven], [Nov.] 27, 1811, by Rev. Saul Clark | DR | |
| Lucas, Rev., [of Wolcott], d. Oct. 16, [1813], ae 29; bd. in East | | |
|     Haven | DR | |
| **HAWKINS**, David S., m. Harriet M. **HUNT**, Dec. 24, 1848, by Burdett | | |
|     Hart, in Fair Haven | TM4 | 212 |
| Joseph, d. Jan. 14, 1814, ae 52 | DR | |
| **HEMINGWAY, HEMINAWAY, HEMENWAY, HEMINWA**, | | |
|     Abiga[i]l, d. Abram, b. May 17, 1753 | TM2 | 44 |
| Abigail, w. Joseph, d. June 21, 1809, ae 56 | DR | |
| Abigail, wid. John, d. [Sept.] 24, 1834, ae 58 | DR | |
| Abijah, d. [July] 28, 1840, ae 25 | DR | |
| Abraham, s. Abraham, d. Feb. 5, 1715, ae 3 w. | DR | |
| Abraham, d. Aug. 11, 1752, ae 75; killed by lightning | DR | |
| Abraham, d. Aug. 11, 1752, ae 75 y. | TM2 | 22 |
| Abraham, Dea. [of Plymouth], d. Aug. 25, 1796, ae 69 | DR | |
| Abram, m. Marcy **TUTTEL**, Apr. 24, 1746 | TM2 | 44 |
| Abram, s. Abram, b. Apr. 10, 1751 | TM2 | 44 |
| Abram, Dea. had negro Ginne, d. Peter & Bettee, b. Jan. 5, 1770 | TM2 | 291 |
| Albert, [twin with Alfred, s. Stephen], b. Apr. 18, 1808 | TM3 | 13 |
| Alfred, [twin with Albert, s. Stephen], b. Apr. 18, 1808 | TM3 | 13 |
| Alfred, m. Mrs. Rebecca **THOMPSON**, of [East Haven], [May] | | |
|     20, 1832, by Rev. Stephen Dodd | DR | |
| Alfred, m. Rebekah **THOMPSON**, b. of East Haven, May 20, | | |
|     1832, by Stephen Dodd | TM3 | 234 |
| Almira, [d. Stephen], b. Mar. 3, 1818 | TM3 | 13 |
| Ami, d. John, b. May 25, 1743 | TM2 | 47 |
| Anna, d. Abraham, d. May 23, 1730, ae 7 | DR | |
| Anson, s. Enos, d. [    ], 1805, ae 18; drowned | DR | |
| Betsey E., m. Charles P. **KELLOGG**, Nov. 16, 1846, by | | |
|     Burdett Hart, in Fair Haven | TM4 | 207 |
| Caroline A., of East Haven, m. John G. **SMITH**, of Brooklin, | | |
|     N. Y., June 12, 1850, by Rev. D. W[illia]m Havens | TM4 | 213 |
| Chandler, s. Moses & Marthew, b. Nov. 17, 1783 | TM2 | 236 |
| Chandler, d. [Jan.] 29, 1833, ae 49 | DR | |
| Cornelia L., of East Haven, m. Edwin E. **PORTER**, of | | |
|     Brooklin, N. Y., Nov. 27, 1851, by Rev. D. | | |
|     W[illia]m Havens | TM4 | 218 |
| Daniel B., of Fair Haven, m. Louisa C. **PARDEE**, of East | | |
|     Haven, Aug. 29, 1849, by Rev. D. William Havens | DR | |
| Daniel B., of Fair Haven, m. Louisa C. **PARDEE**, of East | | |
|     Haven, Aug. 29, 1849, by Rev. D. W[illia]m Havens | TM4 | 212 |
| Desier, m. Moses **THOMSON**, b. of East Haven, Dec. 10, | | |
|     1724, by Rev. Mr. Heminway | TM1 | 245 |
| Desire, wid. Eleazer, d. [Feb.] 21, 1845, ae 66 | DR | |
| Ebe Tyler, s. Moses & Martheu, b. Dec. 18, 1791 | TM2 | 236 |
| Eben Tyler, [s.] Moses, d. Mar. 9, 1790, ae 4; kicked by a horse | DR | |
| Eben Tyler, m. Anna **SMITH**, b. of [East Haven], [Jan.] 19, | | |
|     1813, by Rev. Saul Clark | DR | |
| Edward, s. Tyler, d. Feb. 6, 1814, ae 3 m. | DR | |

| HEMINGWAY, HEMINAWAY, HEMENWAY, HEMINWA, (cont.), | Vol. | Page |
|---|---|---|
| Edward, m. Lucy M. SMITH, of East Haven, Sept. 24, 1844, | | |
| by Rev. Henry Townsend | DR | |
| Edward, m. Lucy M. SMITH, b. of East Haven, Sept. 24, 1844, | | |
| by Rev. Henry Townsend | TM4 | 204 |
| Eleazar, m. Desire BRADLEY, Oct. 16, 1799, by Rev. | | |
| Nicholas Street | DR | |
| Eleazar, d. Apr. 9, 1833, ae 60 | DR | |
| Eli, d. [Dec.] 14, 1777, ae 24; drowned | DR | |
| Elizabath, d. Abram, b. May 1, 1760 | TM2 | 44 |
| Elizabeth, w. Joseph, d. [Sept.] 28, 1785, ae 34 | DR | |
| Enos, s. Abram, b. Sept. 17, 1755 | TM2 | 44 |
| Enos, d. Mar. 4, 1845, ae 89 y. 6 m. | DR | |
| Esther, w. Stephen, d. Dec. 29, 1799, ae 27 | DR | |
| Esther, [d. Stephen], b. Dec. 3, 1801 | TM3 | 13 |
| Esther, m. Horace THOMPSON, b. of East Haven, Apr. 17, | | |
| 1822, by Rev. Oliver Willson, of North Haven | TM3 | 165 |
| Esther Elizabeth, d. Capt. John, d. [Jan.] 29, 1845, ae 17 | DR | |
| Hannah, d. John & Mary, b. Feb. 14, 1746 | TM2 | 294 |
| Hannah, d. John, b. Feb. 14, 1747 | TM2 | 47 |
| Hannah, w. Samuel, d. Feb. 17, 1787, ae 34 | DR | |
| Hannah, [d. Stephen], b. Apr. 25, 1792 | TM3 | 13 |
| Hannah, w. John, d. [Oct.] 26, 1805, ae 30 | DR | |
| Harriet, [d. Stephen], b. Apr. 5, 1811 | TM3 | 13 |
| Harve, s. Moses & Marthew, b. June 1, 1788 | TM2 | 236 |
| Harvey, m. Lydia WOODWARD, b. of [East Haven], [Mar.] | | |
| [ ], 1811, by Rev. Saul Clark | DR | |
| Haynes, m. Clorinda CHIDSEY, b. of [East Haven], [Feb.] 12, | | |
| 1806, by Rev. Nicholas Street | DR | |
| Haynes, d. [Dec.] 7, 1846, ae 64 | DR | |
| Hiram, s. [James & Elisabeth], b. Dec. 5, 1805 | TM2 | 297 |
| Hiram, s. James, d. [Sept.] 28, 1809, ae 4 | DR | |
| Huldah, wid. Jared, d. Nov. 4, 1821, ae 67 | DR | |
| Huldah, w. Abiud, [of] Southington, d. [Dec.] [ ], 1834, ae 60 | DR | |
| Isaac, s. Abraham, d. Aug. 15, 1722, ae 18 m. | DR | |
| Isaac, s. Abram, b. Feb. 22, 1747 | TM2 | 44 |
| Isaac, s. Abram, b. May 3, 1762 | TM2 | 44 |
| Jacob, m. Ledia BALL, May 3, 1711 | TM1 | 31 |
| Jacob, Rev., d. Oct. 7, 1754, ae 70 | DR | |
| Jacob, Rev., d. Oct. 7, 1754 | TM2 | 22 |
| Jacob, Col., of Virgil, Cortland County, N. Y., m. wid. Lydia | | |
| POTTER, of East Haven, Sept. 23, 1827, by Rev. | | |
| Stephen Dodd | DR | |
| Jacob, of Virgil, N. Y., m. Lydia POTTER, of East Haven, | | |
| Sept. 23, 1827, by Stephen Dodd | TM3 | 173 |
| Jeames, s. Moses & Marthew, b. June 12, 1777 | TM2 | 236 |
| James, d. May 11, 1810, ae 33 | DR | |
| Jared, s. John, b. May 17, 1749 | TM2 | 47 |
| Jared, d. [July] 11, 1782, ae 33 | DR | |
| Jared, d. July 10, 1785, ae 36 | DR | |
| Jared, m. Polly RUSSEL, b. of [East Haven], [Oct.] 9, 1801, by | | |
| Rev. Nicholas Street | DR | |
| Jennet, [d. Stephen], b. Mar. 17, 1816 | TM3 | 13 |

| | Vol. | Page |
|---|---|---|
| **HEMINGWAY, HEMINAWAY, HEMENWAY, HEMINWA**, (cont.), | | |
| Jennett, m. Asahel **THOMPSON**, b. of East Haven, Dec. 14, | | |
| 1834, by Rev. Stephen Dodd | DR | |
| Jennett, m. Asahel **THOMPSON**, b. of East Haven, Dec. 14, | | |
| 1834, by Stephen Dodd | TM3 | 282 |
| Joel, s. John, b. May 21, 1754 | TM2 | 47 |
| John, Sergt., [d. , 1736] | TM2 | 23 |
| John, Serg., d. [Feb.] 3, 1737, ae 61 | DR | |
| John, s. John, b. Aug. 6, 1739 | TM2 | 47 |
| John, had servant, Nancy d. [ ], 1743, ae 75 | DR | |
| John, had negro Nancy, d. Sept. 1, [1743] | TM2 | 25 |
| John, d. Apr. 17, 1762, ae 45 | DR | |
| John, d. Apr. 17, 1762, ae 45 | TM2 | 22 |
| John & Samuel, had negro William, s. Dick & Elles, b. June 22, | | |
| 1785; Dick, b. Jan. 10, 1764; Elles, b. Nov. 3, 1767 | TM2 | 164 |
| John, d. [Feb.] 28, 1797, ae 58 | DR | |
| John, [s. Stephen], b. May 9, 1803 | TM3 | 13 |
| John, s. John, d. [Dec.] 10, 1805, ae 4 | DR | |
| John, 4th, m. Abigail **HOLT**, b. of [East Haven], Feb. 10, 1806, | | |
| by Rev. Nicholas Street | DR | |
| John, Jr., m. Sarah **THOMPSON**, b. of [East Haven], Aug. 27, | | |
| 1818, by Rev. Stephen Dodd | DR | |
| John, d. [July] 29, 1827, ae 51 | DR | |
| John, 3rd, of East Haven, m. Mrs. Sarah **JACKSON**, of New | | |
| Haven, Sept. 2, 1851, by Rev. D. W[illia]m Havens | TM4 | 217 |
| Joseph, s. John, b. June 6, 1741 | TM2 | 47 |
| Joseph, s. John, d. Sept. 4, 1743, ae 15 m. | DR | |
| Joseph, s. John, [d. Sept. 4, 1743] | TM2 | 25 |
| Joseph, s. John, b. Mar. 14, 1745 | TM2 | 47 |
| Joseph, twin s. Joseph, d. [Aug.] 20, 1793, ae 6 | DR | |
| Joseph, d. Sept. 28, 1822, ae 77 | DR | |
| Josiah, d. [James & Elisabeth], b. June 10, 1801 | TM2 | 297 |
| Josiah, d. [Sept.] 5, 1813, ae 12 | DR | |
| Laura, d. John, d. [May] 29, 1810, ae 10 | DR | |
| Lidia, d. Jacob, b. Sept. 2, 1716 | TM1 | 198 |
| Lydia, w. Rev. Jacob, d. Mar. 6, 1738, ae 57 | DR | |
| Lyd[i]a, d. John, b. May 22, 1759 | TM2 | 47 |
| Mabel, w. Samuel, d. [Feb.] [ ], 1834, ae 55 | DR | |
| Marcey, d. Abram, b. July 5, 1757 | TM2 | 44 |
| Maria, m. Charles **WOODWARD**, b. of East Haven, Dec. 21, | | |
| 1837, by Rev. Stephen Dodd | DR | |
| Maria, m. Charles **WOODWARD**, b. of East Haven, Dec. 21, | | |
| 1837, by Rev. Stephen Dodd | TM3 | 324 |
| Martha, w. Moses, d. Sept. 25, 1801, ae 49 | DR | |
| Martha Elizabeth, d. Hervey, d. [Sept.] 8, 1813, ae 2 | DR | |
| Mary, m. Samuell **RUSSELL**, May 13, 1719 | TM1 | 199 |
| Mary, wid. John, d. [Sept.] 7, 1743, ae 71 | DR | |
| Mary, Mrs., d. [Sept. 7, 1743] | TM2 | 25 |
| Mary, d. John, b. Sept. 1, 1755 | TM2 | 47 |
| Mary, wid. John, d. [Jan.] 17, 1779, ae 58 | DR | |
| Mary, d. Moses & Marthew, b. May 22, 1779 | TM2 | 236 |
| Mary, d. Moses, d. [Feb.] 21, 1794, ae 15 | DR | |
| Mary, w. Eleazar, d. Jan. 7, 1795, ae 21; childbed | DR | |
| Mary, [d. Stephen], b. Mar. 27, 1806 | TM3 | 13 |

| HEMINGWAY, HEMINAWAY, HEMENWAY, HEMINWA, (cont.), | Vol. | Page |
|---|---|---|
| Mary, m. Jared **MALLORY**, b. of [East Haven], Jan. 30, 1828, by Rev. Stephen Dodd | DR | |
| Mary, w. Stephen, d. [Dec.] 28, 1833, ae 57 | DR | |
| | | |
| Mary A., m. Frances F. **ANDREWS**, b. of East Haven, July 5, 1852, by Rev. D. W[illia]m Havens | TM4 | 218 |
| Mary Ann, of Fair Haven, m. Alpheus **YOUNG**, of Wallingford, Oct. 26, 1847, by Rev. D. William Havens | DR | |
| Mary Ann, of Fair Haven, m. Alpheus **YOUNG**, of Wallingford, Oct. 26, 1847, by Rev. D. W[illia]m Haven | TM4 | 208 |
| Mehitabel, wid. Samuel, d. Feb. 1, 1782, ae 68 | DR | |
| Mercy, wid. Dea. Abraham, [of Plymouth], d. Jan. 20, 1812, ae 82 | DR | |
| Morris, [s. Stephen], b. Sept. 2, 1796 | TM3 | 13 |
| Moses, s. John, b. Aug. 14, 1751 | TM2 | 47 |
| Moses, d. Jan. 5, 1816, ae 54 | DR | |
| Nancy, d. Enos, d. [         ], 1785, ae 4 | DR | |
| Orilla, of [East Haven], m. John **AUGER**, of Saybrook, Nov. 22, 1831, by Rev. Stephen Dodd | DR | |
| Orilla, of East Haven, m. John **AUGER**, of Saybrook, Nov. 22, 1831, by Stephen Dodd | TM3 | 234 |
| Polly, d. James & Elisabeth, b. Oct. 8, 1798 | TM2 | 297 |
| P. Almena, m. James H. **TUTTLE**, Jan. 1, 1850, by Burdett Hart | TM4 | 213 |
| Ruel, s. Joseph, d. [Jan.] 25, 1794, ae 9 | DR | |
| Sally A., m. Hezekiah **PARMELEE**, Oct. 14, 1832, by Rev. John Mitchell, of Fair Haven | TM3 | 284 |
| Samuel, 1st, d. Sept. 1, 1711, ae about 75 | DR | |
| Samuell, d. Sept. 20, 1711 | TM1 | 31 |
| Samuel, s. Samuel, d. [Aug.] 26, 1743, ae 4 | DR | |
| Samuel, s. Samuel, d. [Aug. 26, 1743] | TM2 | 25 |
| Samuel, Dea., d. Oct. 25, 1777, ae 65 | DR | |
| Samuel, s. Enes & Sarah, b. Apr. 25, 1778 | TM2 | 47 |
| Samuel, 2d, d. [July] 25, 1802, ae 24; at Halifax | DR | |
| Samuel, s. [James & Elisabeth], b. Sept. 6, 1803 | TM2 | 297 |
| Samuel, [of North Haven], d. Aug. 21, 1821, ae 71; bd. in East Haven | DR | |
| Samuel, see John **HEMINWAY** | TM2 | 164 |
| Sarah, d. Abram, b. Feb. 11, 1749 | TM2 | 44 |
| Sarah, m. Isaac **BROWN**, b. of [East Haven], Oct. 12, 1800, by Rev. Nicholas Street | DR | |
| Sarah, wid. Samuel, [of] North Haven, d. Dec. 8, 1829, ae 79 | DR | |
| Sarah, w. Enos, d. Aug. 18, 1837, ae 79 y. 3 m. | DR | |
| Sarah, d. July 1, 1839, ae 50 | DR | |
| Sarah Eunecia, of East Haven, m. Henry W. **BENEDICT**, of New Haven, Apr. 2, 1844, by Rev. Stephen Dodd | DR | |
| Sarah Eun[e]cia, of East Haven, m. Henry W. **BENEDICT**, of New Haven, Apr. 2, 1844, by Stephen Dodd | TM4 | 203 |
| Stephen, d. Apr. 21, 1846, ae 74 y. 10 m. | DR | |

|  | Vol. | Page |
|---|---|---|
| **HEMINGWAY, HEMINAWAY, HEMENWAY, HEMINWA,** (cont.), |  |  |
| Stephen, m. Charlotte M. **TYLER,** of East Haven, Oct. 22, |  |  |
| 1848, by Rev. N. S. Richardson | DR |  |
| Stephen, m. Charlotte M. **TYLER,** b. of East Haven, Oct. 22, |  |  |
| 1848, by Rev. N. S. Richardson | TM4 | 210 |
| Willet, s. Willet, d. Sept. 4, 1810, ae 1 | DR |  |
| Willett, Jr., m. Lydia A. **BRADLEY,** b. of East Haven, May 8, |  |  |
| 1845, by Rev. Benj[ami]n L. Swan | TM4 | 204 |
| William, s. Willet, d. [Nov.] 22, 1815, ae 2 | DR |  |
| Wyllys, m. Mary **BROWN,** b. of [East Haven], [Nov.] 16, |  |  |
| 1809, by Rev. Saul Clark | DR |  |
| Wyllys, m. Sarah **BROWN,** b. of [East Haven], Nov. 18, 1810, |  |  |
| by Rev. Saul Clark | DR |  |
| -----, infant [of] Albert, d. [Sept.] [ ], 1832, ae 14 d. | DR |  |
| -----, ch. [of] Samuel, d. [Oct.] 2, 1836, ae 8 m. | DR |  |
| -----, ch. [of] Samuel, [of] New Haven, d. June 30, 1843, |  |  |
| ae 11 m. | DR |  |
| -----, w. Samuel, d. Feb. 4, 1845, ae 40 | DR |  |
| **HENMAN,** [see under **HINMAN**] |  |  |
| **HICKOX,** Caroline S., m. Roswell **COOK,** b. of Southington, Aug. 7, |  |  |
| 1827, by Stephen Dodd | TM3 | 172 |
| Darius, d. May 6, 1785, ae 26 | DR |  |
| **HIGBEE,** Aaron, of Wallingford, m. Julia **BRADLEY,** of Branford, June |  |  |
| 1, 1829, by Stephen Dodd | TM3 | 231 |
| **HIGGINS, HIGGENS, HIGENS,** Abraham, s. John, b. Feb. 26, 1747/8 | TM2 | 26 |
| Elisabeth, d. John, b. May 13, 1746 | TM2 | 26 |
| Isaac, s. John, b. Oct. 5, 1740 | TM2 | 26 |
| John, s. John, b. Mar. 10, 1742/3 | TM2 | 26 |
| Mary, wid. d. Oct. 24, 1787, ae 76 | DR |  |
| Timothy, s. John, b. Jan. 30, 1733/4 | TM2 | 26 |
| **HILL, HILLS,** Polly, w. Russel, d. Aug. 4, 1831, ae 48 | DR |  |
| Sarah E., of East Haven, m. George **BROOKS,** of Northford, |  |  |
| Apr. 4, 1838, by Rev. Stephen Dodd | DR |  |
| Sarah E., of East Haven, m. George **BROOKS,** of Northford, |  |  |
| Apr. 4, 1838, by Stephen Dodd | TM3 | 325 |
| William, of New Haven, m. wid. Mary **BARNES,** of [East |  |  |
| Haven], Nov. 3, 1825, by Rev. Stephen Dodd | DR |  |
| William, of New Haven, m. Mary **BARNES,** of East Haven, |  |  |
| Nov. 3, 1825, by Stephen Dodd | TM3 | 207 |
| **HINMAN, HENMAN,** Philemon, of Harwinton, m. Betsey |  |  |
| **LUDDINGTON,** of [East Haven], Dec. 23, 1820, |  |  |
| by Rev. Stephen Dodd | DR |  |
| Philemon, of Harwinton, m. Betsey LUD[D]IN[G]TON, of |  |  |
| East Haven, Dec. 23, 1820, by Stephen Dodd | TM3 | 57 |
| **HITCHCOCK, HICHCOK, HITCHCOK,** [see also **HICKOX**], |  |  |
| Abigail, d. Daniel, b. Apr. 25, 1734 | TM1 | 261 |
| Abig[a]il, m. Joshua **AUSTIN,** May 6, 175[ ], by Rev. |  |  |
| Nich[o]lias Street | TM2 | 20 |
| Abigail, wid. Dea. Daniel, d. [Jan.] 23, 1761, ae 53 | DR |  |
| Abiga[i]l, wid. Dea. Dani[e]l, d. Jan. 23, 1761, in the 54th year |  |  |
| of her age | TM2 | 87 |
| Abigail, d. Jacob, d. Mar. 5, 1769 | DR |  |
| Abigail, d. [Mar.] 22, 1842, ae 84 y. 8 m. | DR |  |

|  | Vol. | Page |
|---|---|---|
| **HOLBROOK, HOLEBROOK**, Lidya, d. Daniel, b. Dec. 25, 1729 | TM1 | 248 |
| Priscilla, wid. Daniel, d. [Nov.] 14, 1793, ae 86 | DR | |
| **HOLLAND**, Stephen Bishop, s. John, d. Sept. 5, 1837, ae 1 | DR | |
| **HOLT, HOLTE**, Abby, m. Jared **GOODSELL**, [June] [ ], 1806, by Rev. | | |
| Nicholas Street | DR | |
| Abygall, d. Joseph, b. Aug. 4, 1716 | TM1 | 199 |
| Abig[a]il, Mrs., [d. , 1736] | TM2 | 23 |
| Abigail, w. Joseph, d. [Feb.] 10, 1737, ae 49 | DR | |
| Abigail, m. John **HEMINWAY**, 4th, b. of [East Haven], Feb. | | |
| 10, 1806, by Rev. Nicholas Street | DR | |
| Abigail, of [East Haven], m. Anson **SMITH**, of Harwinton, Jan. | | |
| 20, 1822, by Rev. Stephen Dodd | DR | |
| Abigail, of East Haven, m. Anson **SMITH**, of Harwington, Feb. | | |
| 20, 1822, by Stephen Dodd | TM3 | 165 |
| Alford, s. Samuel & Abiga[i]l, b. Jan. 16, 1797 | TM2 | 265 |
| Alford, s. Samuel & Abigail, b. Jan. 16, 1797 | TM2 | 294 |
| Ame, d. Dan & Anne, b. Feb. 26, 1778 | TM2 | 157 |
| Anna, d. Daniel, d. [ ], 1751, ae 10 | DR | |
| Anna, w. Dan., d. Mar. 3, 1818, ae 71 | DR | |
| Anna, w. Samuel, d. [Oct.] 29, 1826, ae 80 | DR | |
| Anna, of East Haven, m. William **HULL**, of New Haven, July | | |
| 16, 1841, by Stephen Dodd | TM4 | 200 |
| Anna C., [twin with Sally A., d. Philemon & Desire], b. July 2, | | |
| 1820 | TM3 | 264 |
| Anna C., of East Haven, m. William **HULL**, of New Haven, | | |
| July 16, 1841, by Rev. Stephen Dodd | DR | |
| Anna, d. Dan & Anne, b. May 18, 1773 | Tm2 | 157 |
| Benjamin S., [s. Philemon & Desire], b. Mar. 8, 1805 | TM3 | 264 |
| Betsey, m. Samuel **CHIDSEY**, [Jan.] 26, 1800, by Rev. | | |
| Nicholas Street | DR | |
| Betsey, m. Samuel **CHIDSEY**, Jan. 23, 1800 | TM3 | 264 |
| Charlotte, of [East Haven], m. David Sullivan **FOWLER**, of | | |
| North Guilford, [May] [ ], 1832, by Rev. Stephen | | |
| Dodd | DR | |
| Charlotte E., [d. Philemon & Desire], b. Mar. 6, 1809 | TM3 | 264 |
| Charlotte E., of East Haven, m. David Sullivan **FOWLER**, of | | |
| North Guilford, June 20, 1832, by Stephen Dodd | TM3 | 234 |
| Dan, m. Anne **HITCHCOCK**, Dec. 5, 1765, by Rev. | | |
| Nic[h]oles Street | TM2 | 157 |
| Dan., [s. Philemon & Desire], b. Feb. 1, 1803 | TM2 | 264 |
| Dan, d. Jan. 31, 1829, ae 84 | DR | |
| Danyell, s. Joseph, b. Sept. 6, 1711 | TM1 | 199 |
| Daniel, d. [June] 11, 1756, ae 45 | DR | |
| Daniel, s. Dan & Anne, b. July 5, 1767 | TM2 | 157 |
| David, s. Daniel, d. [Oct.] 31, 1751, ae 7 d. | DR | |
| Desier, d. Isaac, b. Dec. 10, 1744 | TM2 | 27 |
| Ebenezer, s. Joseph & Hannah, b. June 6, 1761 | TM2 | 154 |
| Ebenezer, s. Joseph, b. July 6, 1762 | TM2 | 47 |
| Eleazer, s. Isaac, b. Aug. 1, 1752 | TM2 | 27 |
| Elizabeth, [d.] Samuel, d. [Feb.] 26, 1774, ae 5 m. | DR | |
| Hannah, d. Joseph, b. Aug. 17, 1767 | TM2 | 47 |
| Hannah, d. Josep[h] & Hannah, b. Aug. 17, 1767 | TM2 | 154 |

| HOLT, HOLTE, (cont.), | Vol. | Page |
|---|---|---|
| Hannah, w. Joseph, d. [Aug.] 25, 1794, ae 52 | DR | |
| Harriet D., [d. Philemon & Desire], b. Aug. 16, 1817 | TM3 | 264 |
| Harriet D., of East Haven, m. Charles L. **ENGLISH**, of New | | |
| Haven, [Apr.] 20, 1848, by Rev. D. William Havens | DR | |
| Harriet D., of East Haven, m. Charles L. **ENGLISH**, of New | | |
| Haven, Apr. 20, 1848, by Rev. D. W[illia]m Havens | TM4 | 209 |
| Hemenway, s. Dan & Anne, b. Feb. 26, 1772 | TM2 | 157 |
| Heminway, Capt., d. [          ], 1810, ae 38; lost in a gale at | | |
| sea | DR | |
| Heminway, d. July 4, 1827, ae 14; drowned at the lighthouse | DR | |
| Hiram, of Harwinton, m. Polly **THOMPSON**, of [East Haven], | | |
| [          ], 1816, by Rev. Saul Clark | DR | |
| Huldah, wid. Merit, d. Dec. 22, 1837, ae 39 | DR | |
| Isaac, s. Isaac, b. Jan. 1, 1743 | TM2 | 27 |
| Jacob, s. Isaac, b. Jan. 13, 1750 | TM2 | 27 |
| Jared, s. Dan & Anne, b. Feb. 3, 1783 | TM2 | 157 |
| Jared, s. Dan., [of Wolcott], d. Oct. [ ], 1803, at Cayuga, ae 21 | DR | |
| Jeremiah, s. Samuel & Abigail, b. Dec. [ ], 1798 | TM2 | 294 |
| John, d. June 16, 1733, ae 88 | DR | |
| Joseph, s. Joseph, b. Oct. 30, 1708 | TM1 | 199 |
| Joseph, s. Joseph & Hannah, b. June 5, 1773 | TM2 | 154 |
| Joseph & Stephen **SMITH**, had negro, Cloe, d. Peter & Ginne, | | |
| b. May 21, 1792 | TM2 | 159 |
| Lois, d. Isaac, b. Jan. 14, 1758 | TM2 | 27 |
| Lois, d. Dan & Anne, b. Feb. 19, 1780 | TM2 | 157 |
| Lois, of [East Haven], m. Horatio Gates **STREET**, June 21, | | |
| 1801, by Rev. Nicholas Street | DR | |
| Lydia, d. Dan & Anne, b. Aug. 25, 1770 | TM2 | 157 |
| Lydia, w. Samuel, d. [Apr.] 11, 1801, ae 55 | DR | |
| Lydia G., [d. Philemon & Desire], b. Nov. 2, 1812 | TM3 | 264 |
| Lydia G., m. James C. **WOODWARD**, b. of East Haven, Sept. | | |
| 12, 1838, by Stephen Dodd | TM3 | 325 |
| Lydia Gates, m. James C. **WOODWARD**, b. of East Haven, | | |
| Sept. 12, 1838, by Rev. Stephen Dodd | DR | |
| Marcy, d. Isaac, b. July 24, 1747 | TM2 | 27 |
| Marcy, d. Joseph & Hanna, b. Jan. 6, 1760 | TM2 | 154 |
| Marcy, see also Mercy | | |
| Mary, w. Joseph, d. June 10, 1743 | TM2 | 22 |
| Mary, w. Samuel, d. Nov. 17, 1778, ae 37 | DR | |
| Mercy, w. Joseph, d. June 10, 1743, ae 44 | DR | |
| Mercy, d. Joseph, b. Jan. 6, 1760 | TM2 | 47 |
| Mercy, 2d, wid. Samuel, see under Mercy, 2d, **HITCHCOCK** | DR | |
| Mercy, see also Marcy | | |
| Nancy, [of] New Haven, d. Feb. 2, 1828, ae 24 | DR | |
| Nickealus, s. Isaac, b. Oct. 4, 1755 | TM2 | 27 |
| Philemon, s. Dan & Anne, b. July 21, 1775 | TM2 | 157 |
| Philemon, m. Desire **SMITH**, b. of [East Haven], Apr. 3, 1802, | | |
| by Rev. Nicholas Street | DR | |
| Philemon, m. Desire **SMITH**, Apr. 8, 1802 | TM3 | 264 |
| Philemon, [s. Philemon & Desire], b. Nov. 13, 1822 | TM3 | 264 |
| Sally A., [twin with Anna C., d. Philemon & Desire], b. July 2, | | |
| 1820 | TM3 | 264 |

| | Vol. | Page |
|---|---|---|
| **HOLT, HOLTE,** (cont.) | | |
| Samuell, s. Joseph, b. July 30, 1713 | TM1 | 199 |
| Samuel, s. Samuel, d. [Sept.] 29, 1742, ae 2 | DR | |
| Samuel, s. Samuel, [d. Sept. 29, 1742] | TM2 | 24 |
| Samuel, d. [ ], 1748, ae 35; at sea | DR | |
| Samuel, m. Ann **MARTIN,** of Bethany, May 3, 1802, by Rev. | | |
| Nicholas Street | DR | |
| Samuel, Jr., d. [June] 23, 1803, ae 33 | DR | |
| Samuel, d. Feb. 10, 1831, ae 87 | DR | |
| Sarah, d. Dan & Anne, b. Nov. 25, 1768 | TM2 | 157 |
| Sarah A., of East Haven, m. Luman **COWLES,** of New Haven, | | |
| [Sept.] 21, 1845, by Rev. Stephen Dodd | DR | |
| Sarah E., of East Haven, m. Luman **COWLES,** of New Haven, | | |
| Sept. 21, 1845, by Stephen Dodd | TM4 | 205 |
| Sarah S., m. Samuel Forbes **BRADLEY,** b. of East Haven, July | | |
| 12, 1840, by Rev. Stephen Dodd | DR | |
| Sarah S., m. Samuel F. **BRADLEY,** b. of East Haven, July 12, | | |
| 1840, by Stephen Dodd | TM3 | 327 |
| Thomas, s. William, d. June 3, 1676, ae 23 | DR | |
| Thomas, s. Samuel, d. Sept. 22, 1751, ae 4 | DR | |
| -----, ch. [of] Ebenezer, d. Aug. 13, 1792, ae 1 | DR | |
| **HOPKINS,** Francis, w. Samuel I. & d. Rev. Saul **CLARK,** d. [Aug.] 23, | | |
| 1841, at Carbondale, Pa., ae 25 | DR | |
| Samuel Clark, s. [Samuel I. & Frances] d. Sept. 19, 1841, ae 2, | | |
| at Rev. Saul **CLARK's,** Bethany, Ct., & bd. [East | | |
| Haven] | DR | |
| -----, infant of Samuel I. & Francis, d. [Aug.] [ ], 1841, ae 6 w. | DR | |
| **HOSELY,** Benjamin, of Branford, m. Lois **WARD,** of East Haven, Mar. | | |
| 27, 1849, by Rev. D. William Havens | DR | |
| Benjamin A., of Branford, m. Lois **WARD,** of East Haven, Mar. | | |
| 27, 1849, by Rev. D. W[illia]m Havens | TM4 | 212 |
| Charlotte E., of Branford, m. Elisha A. **LUD[D]INGTON,** of | | |
| East Haven, Nov. 19, 1851, by Rev. D. W[illia]m | | |
| Havens | TM4 | 217 |
| **HOTCHKISS, HOTCHKIS, HODGKIS, HODGSKINS,** Abigail, d. | | |
| Samuell, b. Feb. 27, 1721/2 | TM1 | 245 |
| Abig[a]il, d. Joseph, b. May 6, 1748 | TM2 | 26 |
| Anna, m. Abraham, **PARDEE,** b. of [East Haven], June 14, | | |
| 1806, by Rev. Nicholas Street | DR | |
| Betsey, m. Samuel **TUTTLE,** Jr., Jan. 19*, 1800, by Rev. | | |
| Nicholas Street    (may be 18, typewriter strike over) | DR | |
| Daniel **BRADLEY,** s. Lyman, d. [Nov.] 14, 1825, ae 5 m. | DR | |
| Ebenezer, [of Northford], d. Oct. 7, [1774], ae 16 | DR | |
| Ellehew, s. Enos, b. Jan. 25, 1757    (Elihu) | TM2 | 27 |
| Eliza, w. Samuel R., d. [Sept.] 17, 1830, ae 28 | DR | |
| Elizabeth Amelia, d. Lyman, d. [Apr.] 15, 1825, ae 3 | DR | |
| Enos, s. Samuell, b. May 13, 1731 | TM1 | 248 |
| Esther, wid. Joseph, d. Sept. 14, 1788, ae 59 | DR | |
| Gideon, d. [Oct.] 30, 1788, ae 19 | DR | |
| Gideon, s. Asaph, d. Dec. 6, 1788, ae 3 w. | DR | |
| Grace Ann, m. Samuel C. **THOMPSON,** b. of [East Haven], | | |
| Sept. 9, 1832, by Rev. Stephen Dodd | DR | |

| HOTCHKISS, HOTCHKIS, HODGKIS, HODGSKINS, (cont.), | Vol. | Page |
|---|---|---|
| Grace Ann, m. Samuel C. **THOMPSON**, b. of East Haven, | | |
| Sept. 9, 1832, by Stephen Dodd | TM3 | 235 |
| Han[n]ah, wid., d. Jan. 9, 1712/13 | TM1 | 31 |
| Hannah, wid., d. [Jan.] 19, 1713, ae 41 | DR | |
| Heman, [of] New Haven, d. [ ] 20, 1836, ae 70 | DR | |
| Horace R., m. Charlotte A. **STREET**, Feb. 22, 1824, by | | |
| Stephen Dodd | TM3 | 168 |
| Horace Rowe, of New Haven, m. Charlotte A. **STREET**, of | | |
| [East Haven], Feb. 22, 1824, by Rev. Stephen Dodd | DR | |
| Isaac, s. Joseph, b. Dec. 10, 1753 | TM2 | 27 |
| Isaac, d. [ ], 1784, ae 30; at sea | DR | |
| James, s. Samuel, d. Feb. 19, 1707, ae 8 d. | DR | |
| Jam[e]s. s. Samuell, b. Mar. 17, 1711; d. May 10, next after his | | |
| birth | TM1 | 198 |
| James, s. Samuel, d. May 11, 1711, ae 2 m. | DR | |
| James, s. Samuel, d. Feb. 19, 1717, ae 7 w. | DR | |
| James, s. Samuel, b. Jan. 13, 1727/8 | TM1 | 248 |
| Jam[e]s, s. Samuell, b. Feb. 11, 179[ ]; d. 19th day of the same | | |
| month | TM1 | 198 |
| Joseph, s. Samuel, b. Feb. 15, 1724/5 | TM1 | 245 |
| Joseph, d. [Apr.] 27, 1776, ae 50 | DR | |
| Joseph, d. May 2, 1825, ae 68 | DR | |
| Joshua, d. Dec. 22, 1707 | DR | |
| Lucius, of New Haven, m. Maria M. **STREET**, of [East | | |
| Haven], Oct. 18, 1827, by Rev. Stephen Dodd | DR | |
| Lucius, of New Haven, m. Maria M. **STREET**, of East Haven, | | |
| Oct. 18, 1827, by Stephen Dodd | TM3 | 173 |
| Maria Street, w. Lucius, [of] New Haven, d. Sept. 1, 1833, | | |
| ae 26 | DR | |
| Mary, d. Samuell, b. Mar. 5, 1718 | TM1 | 198 |
| Mary, [of Northford], d. June 17, 1779, ae 34 | DR | |
| Orilla, m. Thomas **BARNES**, b. of [East Haven], Oct. 16, 1808, | | |
| by Rev. Saul Clark | DR | |
| Rinda, d. Asaph, d. [Dec.] 31, 1798, ae 4 | DR | |
| Sally, m. Isaac Holt **PARDEE**, b. of [East Haven], [June] 5, | | |
| 1806, by Rev. Nicholas Street | DR | |
| Samuel, Lieut., d. Jan. [ ], 1705 | DR | |
| Samuell, s. Samuell, b. June 5, 1715 | TM1 | 198 |
| Samuel, d. Dec. 22, 1740, ae 57 | DR | |
| Samuel, d. Dec. 22, 1740 | TM2 | 22 |
| Sam[u]el, m. Mary **GOODSELL**, July 16, 1744 | TM2 | 20 |
| Samuel, s. Samuel, of Northford, d. [ ], 1751, ae 5 | DR | |
| Samuel, [of Northford], d. Aug. 31, 1744, ae 59 | DR | |
| Samuel R., m. Eliza **WOODWARD**, Nov. 13, 1822, by | | |
| Stephen Dodd | TM3 | 166 |
| Samuel R., m. Cornelia C. **STREET**, of East Haven, May 5, | | |
| 1847, by Rev. Stephen Dodd | DR | |
| Samuel R., m. Cornelia C. **STREET**, b. of East Haven, May 5, | | |
| 1847, by Stephen Dodd | TM4 | 207 |
| Samuel Russel, of New Haven, m. Eliza **WOODWARD**, of | | |
| [East Haven], Oct. 13, 1822, by Rev. Stephen Dodd | DR | |
| Sarah, d. Samuell, b. May 20, 1712 | TM1 | 198 |

| | Vol. | Page |
|---|---|---|
| **HOTCHKISS, HOTCHKIS, HODGKIS, HODGSKINS**, (cont.), | | |
| Sarah, d. Samuel, of Northford, d. [Aug.] 29, 1751 | DR | |
| Temperance, wid. Joseph, d. Jan. 7, 1846, ae 85 y. 3 m. | DR | |
| ——, infant [of] Lyman, d. [June] 21, 1810 | DR | |
| **HOWD**, Hannah, w. [ ], d. [Apr.] 12, 1842, ae 51 | DR | |
| Henry C., of Wallingford, m. Catharine L. **THOMPSON**, of | | |
| East Haven, Apr. 29, 1852, by Rev. D. W[illia]m | | |
| Havens | TM4 | 218 |
| **HOWE, HOW**, Abygall, d. John, b. June 3, 179[ ] | TM1 | 31 |
| Bashua, d. John, b. June 25, 1715 | TM1 | 245 |
| Hannah, d. Nov. 7, 1775, ae 28 | DR | |
| Isaak, s. John, b. Feb. 18, 176[ ] | TM1 | 31 |
| John, d. Nov. 8, 1732, ae 65 | DR | |
| John, s. Isaac, May 22, 1734 | TM1 | 260 |
| John, d. Apr. 18, 1781, ae 45; killed at Fort Hale by British | DR | |
| Ledia, d. John, b. Dec. 19, 1711 | TM1 | 31 |
| Samuel, d. [Oct.] [ ], 1832, ae 54 | DR | |
| Thankfull, d. Isaac, b. Dec. 28, 1731 | TM1 | 260 |
| Thankful, d. Isaac, d. [ ], 1736, ae 5 | DR | |
| Thankfull, d. Isaac, [d. ], 1736, ae 5 y. | TM2 | 23 |
| **HOWEL[L]**, Desere, d. John, b. July 27, 1739 | TM2 | 21 |
| Desire, d. John, d. [Sept.] 12, 1742, ac 4 | DR | |
| Desire, d. John, d. Sept. 12, 1742 | TM2 | 24 |
| Henery, s. John, b. Apr. 10, 1737 | TM2 | 21 |
| John, d. June 23, 1744, ae 35 | DR | |
| John, d. June 23, 1744 | TM2 | 25 |
| Joseph, s. John, b. Nov. 7, 1734 | TM2 | 21 |
| Joseph, s. John, d. May 15, 1742, ae 8 | DR | |
| Joseph, s. John, b. Jan. 8, 1743/4 | TM2 | 21 |
| Samuel, s. John, b. Nov. 29, 1741 | TM2 | 21 |
| Timothy, s. John, b. Oct. 24, 1732 | TM2 | 21 |
| **[HOYT]**, [see under **HOIT**] | | |
| **HUBBARD**, Herbert R., of Middletown, m. Charlot[te] E. **CRANDAL**, of | | |
| New Haven, Sept. 5, 1841, by Rev. Henry | | |
| Townsend | TM3 | 328 |
| **HUGHES, HUSE, [HEWES]**, Aaron Atwater, s. Daniel & Sarah, b. Jan. | | |
| 20, 1797 | TM3 | 9 |
| Aaron Atwater, m. Lydia Caroline **TUTTLE**, of East Haven, | | |
| Jan. 20, 1822, by Rev. Joseph Perry | DR | |
| Aaron Atwater, d. [July] 14, 1833, ae 36 | DR | |
| Abigail Bradley, wid. Capt. **COLLINS**, d. Aug. 20, 1840, | | |
| ae 78 y. 7 m. | DR | |
| Collins, s. [Collins & Abigail], b. Jan. 24, 1798 | TM2 | 297 |
| Collins, d. [ ], 1815, ae 17; lost at sea | DR | |
| Collins, Capt. d. Sept. 30, 1818, ae 53 | DR | |
| Daniel, s. Daniel, d. Dec. 26, 1791, ae 6 m. | DR | |
| Daniel, of [East Haven], m. Rachel **SHAILOR**, of Bristol, Apr. | | |
| 5, 1818, by Rev. Stephen Dodd | DR | |
| Daniel, d. Nov. 8, 1842, ae 83 y. 4 m. | DR | |
| Henry Freeman, d. Oct. 13, 1791, ae 68 | DR | |
| Hulda, d. John & Mary, b. Feb. 25, 1787 | TM2 | 235 |
| Huldah, d. Collins & Abigail, b. June 18, 1793 | TM2 | 297 |
| Huldah, d. [Collins & Abigail], b. May 11, 1795 | TM2 | 297 |

| | Vol. | Page |
|---|---|---|
| **HUGHES, HUSE, [HEWES]**, (cont.), | | |
| Huldah, d. Capt. Collins, d. [Apr.] 4, 1812, ae 19 | DR | |
| John, s. John, d. [Oct.] 8, 1795, ae 4 | DR | |
| John, s. Capt. Collins, d. May [ ], 1816, ae 10 | DR | |
| John, d. June 1, 1846, ae 89 y. 9 m. | DR | |
| L. Caroline, Mrs., had slave Violet **FREEMAN**, who had | | |
| served four successive generations of same family & | | |
| who d. July 30, 1843, ae 77 | DR | |
| Lois, d. John & Mary, b. Sept. 12, 1782 | TM2 | 235 |
| Lucy, w. Daniel, d. June 25, 1791, ae 30 | DR | |
| Lidia, d. John & Mary, b. Aug. 17, 1779 | TM2 | 235 |
| Lydia, wid. Henry **FREEMAN**, d. Aug. 2, 1794, ae 78 | DR | |
| Mabel, w. John, d. [June] [ ], 1833, ae 76 | DR | |
| Mary, w. John, d. Dec. 7, 1804, ae 47 | DR | |
| Mary, d. John & Mary, d. Mar. 17, 1812, ae 22 | DR | |
| Nancy, of [East Haven], m. Stephen **THATCHER**, of New | | |
| Haven, Oct. 15, 1812, by Rev. Saul Clark | DR | |
| Polly, d. John & Mary, b. June 20, 1789 | TM2 | 235 |
| Rachel, wid. Daniel, d. Mar. 26, 1844, ae 71 | DR | |
| Russel, s. John & Mary, b. Nov. 6, 1784 | TM2 | 235 |
| Russell, m. Betsey **FORBES**, of East Haven, Nov. 15, 1815, by | | |
| Rev. Elijah G. Plumb | DR | |
| Russel[l], d. June 15, 1832, ae 48 | DR | |
| Sarah, of East Haven, m. William **WOODWARD**, Feb. 22, | | |
| 1807, by Rev. Bela Hubbard, D. D. | DR | |
| Sarah Ann, d. Russel, d. [Oct.] 16, 1820, ae 18 m. | DR | |
| Sarah Atwater, w. Daniel, d. [Jan.] 14, 1817, ae 60 | DR | |
| Sarah Bradley, d. [Collins & Abigail], b. June 28, 1801 | TM2 | 297 |
| Sarah Bradley, d. Collins, d. Mar. 24, 1805, ae 4 | DR | |
| Sarah Bradley, d. Collins & Abigail, d. Mar. 24, 1805 | TM2 | 159 |
| Susan, d. [Collins & Abigail], b. July 19, 1804 | TM2 | 297 |
| Susan, of East Haven, m. Wickum **MILLS**, of Brook Haven, | | |
| L. I., Oct. 29, 1825, by Rev. Tehoa Whitmore, of | | |
| Guilford | TM3 | 170 |
| **HULL**, William, of New Haven, m. Anna C. **HOLT**, of East Haven, July | | |
| 16, 1841, by Rev. Stephen Dodd | DR | |
| William, of New Haven, m. Anna **HOLT**, of East Haven, July | | |
| 16, 1841, by Stephen Dodd | TM4 | 200 |
| **HULTSE**, George, m. Annis **WEDMORE**, b. of Fair Haven, June 24, | | |
| 1832, by Rev. Stephen Dodd | DR | |
| George, m. Annis **WEDMORE**, b. of East Haven, June 24, | | |
| 1832, by Stephen Dodd | TM3 | 235 |
| George, s. George, d. Aug. 22, 1836, ae 2 y. 6 m. | DR | |
| George, s. George, d. [May] 6, 1837, ae 2 | DR | |
| **HUNT**, Charles, s. John, [of New Haven], d. Jan. 6, 1799, ae 10; bd. in | | |
| East Haven | DR | |
| Harriet M., m. David S. **HAWKINS**, Dec. 24, 1848, by Burdett | | |
| Hart, in Fair Haven | TM4 | 212 |
| Sarah, d. John, d. [ ], 1788, ae 9; kicked by a horse | DR | |
| Sarah, d. John, d. Feb. 18, 1791, ae 4 m. | DR | |
| William, m. Henrietta **BRADLEY**, b. of [East Haven], Nov. 11, | | |
| 1830, by Rev. Stephen Dodd | DR | |

| | Vol. | Page |
|---|---|---|
| **HUNT**, (cont.) | | |
| William Henry, m. Henrietta **BRADLEY**, b. of East Haven, Nov. 11, 1830, by Stephen Dodd | TM3 | 86-87 |
| William Henry, m. Henrietta **BRADLEY**, b. of East Haven, Nov. 11, 1830, by Stephen Dodd | TM3 | 233 |
| Woodward Hervey, s. John, d. Mar. 22, 1788, ae 2 m. | DR | |
| -----, grandchild of John, [of New Haven], d. June 7, 1804; bd. in East Haven | DR | |
| **HUNTER**, William, d. [ ], 1670 | DR | |
| **HUNTLY**, Jonathan B., of Lyme, m. Betsey **BRADLEY**, of [East Haven], [May] 16, 1830, by Rev. Stephen Dodd | DR | |
| Jonathan B., of Lyme, m. Betsey **BRADLEY**, of East Haven, May 16, 1830, by Stephen Dodd | TM3 | 232 |
| **HURD**, Smith, of Cumberland, Md., m. Hannah **CHIDSEY**, of East Haven, Dec. 14, 1845, by Rev. Stephen Dodd | DR | |
| Smith, of Cumberland, Md., m. Hannah **CHIDSEY**, of East Haven, Dec. 14, 1845, by Stephen Dodd | TM4 | 205 |
| **HURLBUT, HURLBURT**, George Henry, d. [Mar.] 10, 1845, ae 20; drowned | DR | |
| Harry, of Chatham, m. Henrietta **FLAGG**, of [East Haven], July 13, 1823, by Rev. Stephen Dodd | DR | |
| Harry, of Chatham, m. Henrietta **FLAGG**, of East Haven, July 13, 1823, by Stephen Dodd | TM3 | 167 |
| **IVES**, Anna Vose, d. William A., d. Jan. 23, 1844, ae 7 m. | DR | |
| Lucy, w. Elihu, d. Feb. 3, 1848, ae 67; at the Insane Retreat, Hartford, Ct. | DR | |
| William A., m. Elizabeth M. **PARDEE**, b. of East Haven, Mar. 22, 1842, by Rev. Stephen Dodd | DR | |
| William A., m. Elizabeth M. **PARDEE**, b. of East Haven, Mar. 22, 1842, by Stephen Dodd | TM4 | 200 |
| **JACKSON**, Sarah, Mrs., of New Haven, m. John **HEMINGWAY**, 3rd, of East Haven, Sept. 2, 1851, by Rev. D. W[illia]m Havens | TM4 | 217 |
| **JACOBS**, Charles, of East Haven, m. Lois **TAYLOR**, of Collinsville, Nov. 26, 1851, by Rev. D. W[illia]m Havens | TM4 | 217 |
| Margaret, d. [ ], 1798, ae 80 | DR | |
| **JENKINS**, -----, ch. [ ], d. Sept. 3, 1804, ae 1 | DR | |
| **JOCELIN**, [see under **JOSLIN**] | | |
| **JOHNSON**, Abraham, d. Sept. 23, 1844, ae 95 y. 6 m. | DR | |
| Hervey, of Meriden, m. Sarah **PARDEE**, of [East Haven], [May] 30, 1822, by Rev. Stephen Dodd | DR | |
| Hervey, of Meriden, m. Sarah **PARDEE**, of East Haven, May 30, 1822, by Stephen Dodd | TM3 | 165 |
| Mary E., m. James R. **CURTISS**, Aug. 19, 1851, by Rev. Geo[rge] A. Hubbell | TM4 | 216 |
| **JONES**, Joanna, d. [ ], 1717 | DR | |
| **JOSLIN, JOCELIN, JOSLING**, Abigall, d. Nathaniell, b. July 23, 1725 | TM1 | 245 |
| Abigail, w. Nathaniel, d. [ ], 1770, ae 70 | DR | |
| Abram, s. Nathaniell, b. Sept. 29, 1723 | TM1 | 245 |
| Anna, d. Nathaniell, b. June 29, 1729 | TM1 | 248 |
| Joseph, s. Nathaniell, b. May 31, 1726 | TM1 | 245 |
| Nathaniell, s. Nathaniell, b. Sept. 19, 1721 | TM1 | 199 |

|                                                                                                                                      | Vol. | Page |
|--------------------------------------------------------------------------------------------------------------------------------------|------|------|
| **JUD[D]**, Febe, m. Gurdin **PARDEE**, Nov. 3, 1799, by Rev. Mr. Robinson, of Southington                                           | TM2  | 266  |
| **KELLOGG**, Charles P., m. Betsey E. **HEMINWAY**, Nov. 16, 1846, by Burdett Hart, in Fair Haven                                    | TM4  | 207  |
| **KELSEY**, Florilla, of Killingworth, m. Silvanus **BAILEY**, of East Haven, Apr. 3, 1837, by Rev. Truman O. Judd, of North Haven   | TM3  | 285  |
| Mary Ann, of Clinton, m. Darius **STANNARD**, of Westbrook, Oct. 5, 1846, by Stephen Dodd                                            | TM4  | 206  |
| **KIMBERLY**, Isaac, d. [        ], 1811, ae 20                                                                                      | DR   |      |
| James Curtis, s. Justin, d. [May] 15, 1837, ae 3 y. 6 m.                                                                             | DR   |      |
| Justin, m. Mabel T. **BRADLEY**, b. of [East Haven], Apr. 4, 1824, by Rev. Stephen Dodd                                             | DR   |      |
| Justus, m. Mabel T. **BRADLEY**, Apr. 4, 1824, by Stephen Dodd                                                                      | TM3  | 168  |
| Matilda Ann, m. Edwin **MUNSELL**, Dec. 5, 1847, by Burdett Hart, in Fair Haven                                                      | TM4  | 208  |
| **KING**, Elisibath, d. G[e]orge & Elesibath, b. Sept. 14, 1785                                                                      | TM2  | 162  |
| Elisabeth, d. George & Elisabeth, b. Sept. 14, 1785                                                                                  | TM2  | 294  |
| John, s. G[e]orge & Elisibath, b. Oct. 13, 1780                                                                                      | TM2  | 162  |
| Patience, d. George, d. Jan. [   ], 1786, ae 8                                                                                       | DR   |      |
| Rebecca, d. George, d. [Jan.] 26, 1786, ae 2                                                                                         | DR   |      |
| **KINGSBURY**, Maria, of New Haven, m. Dennis **BARNES**, of East Haven, Sept. 26, 1847, by Rev. D. W[illia]m Havens                 | TM4  | 208  |
| Maria Amelia, of Fair Haven, m. James Dennis **BARNES**, of East Haven, [Sept.] 26, 1847, by Rev. D. William Havens                  | DR   |      |
| Sherman, d. July 15, 1820, ae 56                                                                                                     | DR   |      |
| **LANCRAFT, LANDCRAFT**, Amaziah, [of] New Haven, d. Oct. 1, 1836, ae 45; bd. [East Haven]                                           | DR   |      |
| George, d. Sept. 17, 1807, ae 83                                                                                                     | DR   |      |
| George, d. Dec. 16, 1840, ae 69 y. 8 m.                                                                                              | DR   |      |
| Hannah, w. Lucius, d. Jan. 12, 1848, ae 58                                                                                           | DR   |      |
| Joseph, s. George, d. Mar. 10, 1786, ae 9                                                                                            | DR   |      |
| Joseph, m. Mrs. Dorcas **SNOW**, b. of [East Haven], Dec. 24, 1812, by Rev. Saul Clark                                               | DR   |      |
| Lois, w. Thomas, d.[Sept.] 25,1829, ae 48                                                                                            | DR   |      |
| Lyman S., s. Simeon, d. Jan. 24, 1831, ae 17; killed while driving through turnpike gate, Foxon                                      | DR   |      |
| Major Thomas, s. Simeon, d. Jan. 26, 1831, ae 1                                                                                      | DR   |      |
| Mary Maria, of [East Haven], m. Lyman **POTTER**, of Hamden, June 25,1823, by Rev. Stephen Dodd                                      | DR   |      |
| Mary Maria, of East Haven, m. Lyman **POTTER**, of Hamden, June 25, 1823, by Stephen Dodd                                            | TM3  | 166  |
| Merit, s. Joseph, d. Mar. 1, 1827, ae 6                                                                                              | DR   |      |
| Nathaniel, s. Simeon, d. [July] [  ], 1834, ae 1                                                                                     | DR   |      |
| Sarah, m. Joseph **SHEPARD**, b. of East Haven, Dec. 11, 1825, by Stephen Dodd                                                       | TM3  | 207  |
| Sarah, m. Capt. Joseph **SHEPARD**, b. of [East Haven], Dec. 11, 1825, by Rev. Stephen Dodd                                          | DR   |      |
| Sarah, wid., d. [May] 29, 1827, ae 80                                                                                                | DR   |      |

| | Vol. | Page |
|---|---|---|
| **LANCRAFT, LANDCRAFT**, (cont.), | | |
| Simeon, m. Hannah **CURTIS**, b. of [East Haven], Jan. 14, | | |
| 1813, by Rev. Saul Clark | DR | |
| Thomas, s. Simeon, d. [Feb.] 9, 1829, ae 5 m. | DR | |
| Thomas, m. wid. Nancy **SHEPARD**, b. of East Haven, [Nov.] | | |
| 8, 1840, by Rev. Stephen Dodd | DR | |
| Thomas, m. Nancy **SHEPERD**, b. of East Haven, Nov. 8, 1840, | | |
| by Stephen Dodd | TM3 | 328 |
| **LANFEAR, LANDFEAR**, Laura, m. Jesse **BRADLEY**, July 4, 1845, by | | |
| Rev. Stephen Dodd | DR | |
| Laura, of Branford, m. Jesse **BRADLEY**, of East Haven, July 4, | | |
| 1845, by Stephen Dodd | TM4 | 204 |
| Maryan, d. Russel & Mehitable, b. Mar. 29, 1801 | TM3 | 9 |
| Mary Ann, of [East Haven], m. Alfred G. **MALLORY**, of New | | |
| Haven, [Apr.] 18, 1830, by Rev. Stephen Dodd | DR | |
| Mary Ann, of East Haven, m. Alfred G. **MALLORY**, of New | | |
| Haven, Apr. 18, 1830, by Stephen Dodd | TM3 | 232 |
| Nancy Lemira, of East Haven, m. Hezekiah **TUTTLE**, of New | | |
| Haven, Aug. 8, 1830, by Stephen Dodd | TM3 | 232 |
| Nancy Zemia, of [East Haven], m. Hezekiah **TUTTLE**, of New | | |
| Haven, Aug. 8, 1830, by Rev. Stephen Dodd | DR | |
| Russel, b. July 8, 1775 | TM3 | 9 |
| Russel, d. [Apr.] 25, 1840, ae 65 | DR | |
| Sally Amanda, d. Russel & Mehitable, b. July 2, 1799 | TM3 | 9 |
| Sarah A., m. Horace **CHIDSEY**, b. of [East Haven], Apr. 4, | | |
| 1819, by Rev. Stephen Dodd | DR | |
| **LANGDON**, Charles, d. Mar. 2, 1794, ae 6 | DR | |
| James Richard, s. Ozias, d. [May] 30, 1833, ae 4 w. | DR | |
| **LANGSTON**, Sophia, of [East Haven], m. Lemuel **CLARK**, of | | |
| Southington, Dec. 15, 1808, by Rev. Saul Clark | DR | |
| **LARKINS**, Jennet, d. John, d. [Oct.] 17, 1813, ae 1 | DR | |
| Jerusha, of [East Haven], m. Zalmon **CHURCHEL**, of | | |
| Watertown, N. Y., [Jan.] [ ], 1808, by Rev. Saul | | |
| Clark | DR | |
| Jerusha, w. Joshua, d. May 1, 1826, ae 73 | DR | |
| Joshua, d. Feb. 10, 1835, (in New Haven), ae 84 | DR | |
| Nancy, d. John, d. Nov. 2, 1824, ae 3 | DR | |
| **LEETE**, Miranda, m. Hezekiah **PARMELEE**, June 22, 1845, by Rev. | | |
| Stephen Dodd | DR | |
| Miranda C., m. Hezekiah **PARMELEE**, b. of East Haven, June | | |
| 22, 1845, by Stephen Dodd | TM4 | 204 |
| **LEVIT**, Keziah, m. Gideon **POTTER**, Jr., Aug. 27, 1752, by Rev. | | |
| Philemon Robbins | TM2 | 20 |
| **LEWIS**, Charles, of New Haven, m. Elizabeth R. **BRADLEY**, of [East | | |
| Haven], Dec. 10, 1826, by Rev. Stephen Dodd | DR | |
| Charles, of New Haven, m. Elizabeth R. **BRADLEY**, of East | | |
| Haven, Dec. 10, 1826, by Stephen Dodd | TM3 | 172 |
| Charles, m. Mrs. Jane Maria **BRACKET**, b. of Fair Haven, | | |
| [Oct.] 6, 1845, by Rev. Stephen Dodd | DR | |
| Charles, m. wid. Jane Maria **BROCKETT**, b. of Fair Haven, | | |
| Oct. 6, 1845, by Stephen Dodd | TM4 | 205 |
| Emeline, m. Solomon **BRADLEY**, July 31, 1831, by Rev. John | | |
| Mitchell, of Fair Haven | TM3 | 283 |

| | Vol. | Page |
|---|---|---|
| **LEWIS**, (cont.), | | |
| Sarah, of Southington, m. Rosewell **ROWE**, of [East Haven], | | |
| Aug. 14, 1825, by Rev. Stephen Dodd | DR | |
| Sarah, of Southington, m. Roswell **ROWE**, of East Haven, Aug. | | |
| 14, 1825, by [Rev.] Stephen Dodd | TM3 | 207 |
| Sarah A., m. Elbert J. **MUNSELL**, Mar. 3, 1852, by Rev. | | |
| Burdett Hart, of Fair Haven | TM4 | 215 |
| **LINDON**, John, d. [         ], 1667 | DR | |
| [         ], s. Henry, d. Sept. 8, 1660 | DR | |
| **LINDSLEY, LINSLEY**, Alfred, of Branford, m. Amarilla **MALLORY**, | | |
| of [East Haven], Nov. 25, 1816, by Rev. Saul Clark | DR | |
| Almina, wid. of East Haven, m. John **FOOT**, of Northford, May | | |
| 19, 1842, by Stephen Dodd | TM4 | 201 |
| Almira, wid., of East Haven, m. John **FOOT**, of Northford, May | | |
| 29, 1842, by Rev. Stephen Dodd | DR | |
| Charles, s. Samuel, d. [Sept.] 22, 1813, ae 2 | DR | |
| Daniel, s. Robert, d. [Mar.] 14, 1834, ae 5 m. | DR | |
| Elijah, of Branford, m. Mrs. Maria **BROOKS**, of East Haven, | | |
| Aug. 7, 1837, by Rev. Stephen Dodd | DR | |
| Elijah, of Branford, m. Maria **BROOKS**, of New Haven, Aug. | | |
| 7, 1837, by Stephen Dodds | TM3 | 324 |
| Harriet, of East Haven, m. Miles **ROWE**, of New Haven, Apr. | | |
| 5, 1848, by Rev. D. William Havens | DR | |
| Harriet, of East Haven, m. Miles **ROWE**, of New Haven, Apr. | | |
| 5, 1848, by Rev. D. W[illia]m Havens | TM4 | 209 |
| Irene B., of East Haven, m. Lyman N. **MUNROE**, of New | | |
| Haven, Apr. 5, 1848, by Rev. D. W[illia]m | | |
| Havens | TM4 | 209 |
| Irene B., of East Haven, m. Lyman N. **MUNSON**, of New | | |
| Haven, [Apr.] [  ], 1848, by Rev. D. William Havens | DR | |
| Jane, d. Samuel, d. [         ], 1813, ae 6 | DR | |
| Jane Augusta, d. Samuel, d. [May] 31, 1837, ae 17 m. | DR | |
| John, 2d, of North Branford, m. Almira **GRANNIS**, of East | | |
| Haven, Apr. 4, 1833, by Rev. Stephen Dodd | DR | |
| John, 2nd, of North Branford, m. Almira **GRANNIS**, of East | | |
| Haven, Apr. 4, 1833, by Stephen Dodd | TM3 | 236 |
| Lorana, of Branford, m. Thomas M. **SMITH**, of East Haven, | | |
| May 19, 1836, by Rev. Stephen Dodd | DR | |
| Lorana, of Branford, m. Thomas M. **SMITH**, of East Haven, | | |
| May 19, 1836, by Stephen Dodd | TM3 | 285 |
| Lucius, m. Eliza Ann **CHIDSEY**, b. of East Haven, Nov. 4, | | |
| 1841, by Rev. Stephen Dodd | DR | |
| Lucius, m. Eliza Ann **CHIDSEY**, b. of East Haven, Nov. 4, | | |
| 1841, by Stephen Dodd | TM4 | 200 |
| Robert, m. Eliza **ROWE**, Mar. 3, 1832, by John Mitchell | TM3 | 284 |
| Samuel C., of Branford, m. Mary R. **ANDREWS**, of East | | |
| Haven, May 14, 1837, by Stephen Dodd | TM3 | 324 |
| Samuel Edward, of Branford, m. Mary R. **ANDREWS**, of East | | |
| Haven, [May] 14, 1837, by Rev. Stephen Dodd | DR | |
| Sarah, d. Samuel, d. [Mar.] 29, 1823, ae 2 | DR | |
| William, of [East Haven], m. Maria **DOROTHY**, of New | | |
| Haven, [Aug.] 20, 1828, by Rev. Stephen Dodd | DR | |

| | Vol. | Page |
|---|---|---|
| **LINDSLEY, LINSLEY**, (cont.), | | |
| William, of East Haven, m. Maria **DOROTHY**, of New Haven, | | |
| Aug. 20, 1828, by Stephen Dodd | TM3 | 173 |
| -----, infant [of] William, d. May 1, 1829, ae 3 d. | DR | |
| **LINES**, Chauncey, of North Haven, m. Hannah **BRADLEY**, of [East | | |
| Haven], June 20, 1819, by Rev. Stephen Dodd | DR | |
| Lavinia Ann, d. Chauncey, d. Oct. 1, 1824, ae 4 m. | DR | |
| Marion J., of East Haven, m. David E. **FOOTE**, of Branford, | | |
| Sept. 15, 1852, by Rev. D. W[illia]m Havens | TM4 | 219 |
| **LINGE**, Benjamin, a first settler at Stoney River, d. Apr. 27, 1673 | DR | |
| **LINSLEY**, [see under **LINDSLEY**] | | |
| **LITTLE**, Elles Meriah, d. Dick & Elles, b. Sept. 11, 1799 | TM2 | 296 |
| Stille, d. Dick & Elles, b. Feb. 10, 1797 | TM2 | 296 |
| **LIXON**, Benjamin, d. Aug. 28, 1675 | DR | |
| **LUCAS**, Electa, d. [Nov.] 15, 1792, ae 18 | DR | |
| **LUDDINGTON, LUDENTON, LUDINGTON, LUDINGTUN,** | | |
| **LUDINTON**, Aaron, s. Moses, b. Apr. 19, 1739 | TM1 | 12 |
| Abygal, [twin with Rebeka], d. John, b. Aug. 8, 1707 | TM1 | 30 |
| Abig[a]il, m. Enos **BARNS**, Dec. 3, 1746, by Rev. Jacob | | |
| Heminway | TM2 | 20 |
| Abigail, wid. Eliphalet, d. Dec. 12, 1790, ae 90 | DR | |
| Abram, s. William, b. Nov. 30, 1721 | TM1 | 199 |
| Almena, of [East Haven], m. Tyrus **BRADLEY**, [May] 27, | | |
| 1824, by Rev. Stephen Dodd | DR | |
| Almena, m. Tyrus **BRADLEY**, May 27, 1824, by Stephen | | |
| Dodd | TM3 | 169 |
| Almira, m. John **TURNER**, b. of New Haven, Sept. 17, 1823, | | |
| by Stephen Dodd | TM3 | 167 |
| Ann Maria, d. Caleb, d. Dec. 11, 1825, ae 16 m. | DR | |
| Ann Maria, of East Haven, m. Edwin **RUSSEL**, [Nov.] 29, | | |
| 1849, by Rev. D. William Havens | DR | |
| Ann Maria, m. Edwin **RUSSELL**, b. of East Haven, Nov. 29, | | |
| 1849, by Rev. D. W[illia]m Havens | TM4 | 213 |
| Asa, m. Betsey **LUDDINGTON**, [Oct.] 29, 1799, by Rev. | | |
| Nicholas Street | DR | |
| Asa, d. [            ], 1811, ae 41 | DR | |
| Asa, d. Nov. 8, 1835, ae 23 | DR | |
| Betsey, m. Asa **LUDDINGTON**, [Oct.] 29, 1799, by Rev. | | |
| Nicholas Street | DR | |
| Betsey, of [East Haven], m. Philemon **HINMAN**, of Harwinton, | | |
| Dec. 23, 1820, by Rev. Stephen Dodd | DR | |
| Betsey, of East Haven, m. Philemon **HENMAN**, of Harwinton, | | |
| Dec. 23, 1820, by Stephen Dodd | TM3 | 57 |
| Caleb, s. Jesse, d. [Dec.] 12, 1788, ae 6 | DR | |
| Caleb, s. Jesse & Thankful, b. Aug. 22, 1790 | TM3 | 10 |
| Caleb, m. Lue **ANDREWS**, b. of [East Haven], Mar. 2, 1814, | | |
| by Rev. Saul Clark | DR | |
| Danyell, s. Henory, b. June 21, 1701 | TM1 | 30 |
| Daniel, s. Daniel, d. [d.            ], 1736, ae 9 y. | TM2 | 23 |
| Daniel, s. Daniel, d. [            ], 1737, ae 9 | DR | |
| Dauid, s. Moses, b. Aug. 28, 1733 | TM1 | 261 |
| Desire, wid. Samuel, d. Sept. 2, 1834, ae 79 y. 6 m. | DR | |
| Dinah, d. Henory, b. Jan. 16, 1704/5 | TM1 | 30 |

**LUDDINGTON, LUDENTON, LUDINGTON, LUDINGTUN,**

| LUDINTON, (cont.), | Vol. | Page |
|---|---|---|
| Dorcus, d. Wil[l]iam, b. July 16, 1704 | TM1 | 30 |
| Doratee, d. Wilyam, b. July 16, 1702        (Dorothy) | TM1 | 30 |
| Elam, s. Elam & Rachel, b. Nov. 2, 1777 | TM2 | 293 |
| Elam, d. Oct. 1, 1784, ae 30 | DR | |
| Eelyfalet, s. Wilyam, b. Apr. 28, 1697 | TM1 | 30 |
| Eliphalet, d. June 1, 1761, ae 63 | DR | |
| Elisha, s. Henory, b. Aug. 29, 1712 | TM1 | 31 |
| Elisha, s. Henry, d. Mar. 12, 1715, ae 7 m. | DR | |
| Elisha, s. Henory, b. Jan. 7, 1715/16 | TM1 | 114 |
| Elisha A., of East Haven, m. Charlotte E. **HOSLEY**, of | | |
| Branford, Nov. 19, 1851, by Rev. D. W[illia]m | | |
| Havens | TM4 | 217 |
| Elizabeth, d. William, d. July 28, 1707, ae 8 | DR | |
| Elesabeth, d. Wil[l]iam, d. July 28, 1707 | TM1 | 30 |
| Elesabeth, d. John, b. Sept. 25, 1710 | TM1 | 30 |
| Elizabeth, d. John, d. Dec. 13, 1713, ae 3 | DR | |
| Elesabeth, d. John, d. Dec. 13, 1713 | TM1 | 114 |
| Elesabeth, d. Wil[l]iam, Jr., b. Feb. 9, 1719/20 | TM1 | 199 |
| Elisabeth, d. John, b. June 26, 1723 | TM1 | 245 |
| Esther, wid., had s. Levi **GOODSELL**, d. [Apr.] 17, 1834, | | |
| ae 6 m. | DR | |
| [E]unis, d. Jeames, b. May 11, 1751 | TM2 | 27 |
| Eunice, m. Martheu **ROW**, Oct. 4, 1781, by Rev. Mr. Edwards | TM2 | 265 |
| Fanny, m. Matthew **ROWE**, b. of [East Haven], [Nov.] 23, | | |
| 1813, by Rev. Saul Clark | DR | |
| Han[n]ah, d. Wilyam, b. Mar. 13, 1693 | TM1 | 30 |
| Hannah, w. Daniel, d. [May] 17, 1740 | DR | |
| Hannah, d. Feb. 18, 1789, ae 68 | DR | |
| Harriet, d. July 3, 1844, ae 45 | DR | |
| Henry, d. [        ], 1676 | DR | |
| Henry, d. [        ], 1727, ae 48 | DR | |
| Henry, s. Asa, d. [Mar.] 14, 1803, ae 1 | DR | |
| Huldah, d. Feb. 13, 1811, ae 19 | DR | |
| Isaac, d. [Jan.] 10, 1782, ae 40 | DR | |
| Isaac, Jr., d. Oct. 2, 1832, ae 23 | DR | |
| Jam[e]s, s. John, b. Aug. 8, 1703 | TM1 | 30 |
| Jame W., m. Mary B. **CHIDSEY**, b. of East Haven, Oct. 8, | | |
| 1845, by Stephen Dodd | TM4 | 205 |
| James Warren, m. Mary B. **CHIDSEY**, of East Haven, [Oct.] 8, | | |
| 1845, by Rev. Stephen Dodd | DR | |
| Jared, s. Asa, d. June 6, 1803, ae 3; drowned | DR | |
| Jerusha, d. Moses, b. Aug. 23, 1735 | TM1 | 261 |
| Jesse, d. Feb. 8, 1799, ae 77 | DR | |
| Jesse, d. Jan. 1, 1841, ae 83 y. 11 m. | DR | |
| John, s. Wilyam, b. Jan. last day, 1694 | TM1 | 30 |
| John, s. John, b. Feb. 8, 1720/1 | TM1 | 245 |
| John, d. [Oct.] 30, 1726 | DR | |
| John, d. Oct. 30, 1726 | TM1 | 245 |
| John, d. [        ], 1735, ae 41 | DR | |
| John, Jr., d. [        ], 1743, ae 20 | DR | |
| John, d. [Nov.] 7, 1753, ae 58 | DR | |
| John, d. Nov. 7, 1753 | TM2 | 22 |

LUDDINGTON, LUDENTON, LUDINGTON, LUDINGTUN,

| LUDINTON, (cont.), | Vol. | Page |
|---|---|---|
| John, s. Elam & Rachel, b. May 26, 1775; d. Sept. 1, 1776 | TM2 | 293 |
| John, s. Elam, d. [ ], 1776, ae 15 m. | DR | |
| Joseph, s. William, b. Apr. 3, 1726 | TM1 | 245 |
| Jude, s. John, b. July 23, 1725 | TM1 | 245 |
| Justin, s. Jesse & Thankful, b. Aug. 22, 1796 | TM3 | 10 |
| Justin, m. Harriet **GRANNIS**, Aug. 24, 1820, by Rev. Stephen Dodd | DR | |
| Justin, m. Harriet **GRANNIS**, Aug. 24, 1820, by Stephen Dodd | TM3 | 57 |
| Levi, d. Nov. 30, 1833, ae 33 | DR | |
| Levi G., m. Esther H. **PARDEE**, of [East Haven], Oct. 12, 1828, by Rev. Stephen Dodd | DR | |
| Levi G., m. Esther H. **PARDEE**, b. of East Haven, Oct. 12, 1828, by Stephen Dodd | TM3 | 173 |
| Levi Goodsell, s. wid. Esther, d. [Apr.] 17, 1834, ae 6 m. | DR | |
| Lewsey, d. Nathaniel, b. Jan. 31, 1731/2 (Lucy) | TM1 | 248 |
| Ledia, d. Henory, b. Feb. 9, 1706/7 | TM1 | 30 |
| Lydia, wid. Matthew, d. Feb. 6, 1794, ae 82 | DR | |
| Marah, d. Wil[l]iaam, b. May last day, 1691 | TM1 | 30 |
| Mary, w. Nathaniel, d. May 7, 1758, ae 62 | DR | |
| Mary, w. William, d. Nov. 2, 1770, ae 60 | DR | |
| Mary, wid. Isaac, d. Nov. 11, 1820, ae 81 | DR | |
| Mary Jane, m. John **THOMPSON**, b. of East Haven, Dec. 29, 1843, by Rev. Stephen Dodd | DR | |
| Mary Jane, m. John **THOMPSON**, b. of East Haven, Dec. 31, 1843, by Stephen Dodd | TM4 | 202 |
| Matheu, s. William, Jr., b. Apr. 23, 1712 | TM1 | 31 |
| Mehitable, d. Elam & Rachel, b. Apr. 21, 1783 | TM2 | 293 |
| Mehitabel, w. Jesse, d. Oct. 19, 1793, ae 69 | DR | |
| Mercy, wid. William, d. Nov. 23, 1743, ae 75 | DR | |
| Mercy, wid., d. Nov. 23, 1743 | TM2 | 25 |
| Moses, s. Henory, b. Oct. 8, 1709 | TM1 | 30 |
| Naomi, d. Wil[l]iam, Jr., b. Dec. 15, 1716 | TM1 | 198 |
| Nathaniell, s. Henory, b. Apr. 20, 1708 | TM1 | 30 |
| Olive, w. Justin, d. Jan. 7, 1818, ae 20; childbed | DR | |
| Rachel, d. Elam & Rachel, b. Sept. 4, 1780 | TM2 | 293 |
| Rachel, had d. Naomi Smith, b. Mar. 3, 1787 | TM2 | 293 |
| Rebeka, [twin with Abygal], d. John, b. Aug. 8, 1707 | TM1 | 30 |
| Roxana, of [East Haven], m. Alfred **WORKS**, Aug. 12, 1819, by Rev. Stephen Dodd | DR | |
| Ruth, d. William, Jr., b. June 7, 1713 | TM1 | 198 |
| Samuell, s. William, b. Aug. 10, 1723 | TM1 | 245 |
| Samuel, d. Jan. 13, 1832, ae 90 y. 8 m. | DR | |
| Sarah, d. Henory, b. Feb. 3, 1703; d. Mar. 27, 1709 | TM1 | 30 |
| Sarah, d. Henry, d. [Mar.] 27, 1709, ae 6 | DR | |
| Sarah, d. Mar. 31, 1743, ae 29 | DR | |
| Sary, d. Mar. 31, 1743 | TM2 | 22 |
| Sarah, m. Alford **GOODSELL**, b. of New Haven, Aug. 25, 1824, by Stephen Dodd | TM3 | 169 |
| Sarah, of [East Haven], m. Reuben **TUTTLE**, of New Haven, [Oct.] 26, 1828, by Rev. Stephen Dodd | DR | |

**LUDDINGTON, LUDENTON, LUDINGTON, LUDINGTUN,**
**LUDINTON,** (cont.),                                                    Vol.    Page
   Sarah, of East Haven, m. Reuben **TUTTLE**, of New Haven,
     Oct. 26, 1828, by Stephen Dodd                    TM3     173
   Sarah, wid. Jesse, d. [Oct.] 22, 1845, ae 81 y. 9 m.           DR
   Thankful, w. Jesse, d. [Oct.] 25, 1796, ae 37                 DR
   Thankful, wid., d. Oct. 1, 1817, ae 90                        DR
   Thomas, d. May 30, 1743                                       TM2     22
   Thomas, d. May 31, 1743, ae 25; drowned                       DR
   William, the first man of this name and family, d. [        ],
     1662                                              DR
   William, s. Henory, b. Sept. 6, 1702                          TM1     30

   Willyam, m. Ann **HODGES**, Mar. 1, 1711, by John Allin     TM1     31
   William, [d.              , 1736]                             TM2     23
   William, d. [         ], 1737, ae 51                          DR
   William, m. Charlotte **PARDEE**, b. of East Haven, Aug. 19,
     1835, by Rev. Stephen Dodd                        DR
   William, m. Charlotte **PARDEE**, b. of East Haven, Aug. 29,
     1835, by Stephen Dodd                             TM3     282
   -----, infant [of] Jesse, d. [         ], 1782, ae 2 d.       DR
   -----, infant [of] Jesse, d. Dec. 9, 1784, ae 6 w.           DR
   -----, infant [of] Jesse, d. Aug. [  ], 1786, ae 1 w.        DR
   -----, infant [of] Jesse, d. Nov. 15, 1787, ae 5 d.          DR
   -----, infant [of] Levi G., d. [Aug.] 21, 1730, ae 24 d.     DR
   -----, infant ch. [of] Levi, d. [Aug.] 27, 1831, ae 2 w.     DR
   -----, ch. [of] Lewis, d. [Sept.] 20, 1836, ae 1             DR
**LUM,** Cyrus, of Monroe, m. Harriet **WILLIAMS**, of East Haven, Sept. 30,
     1835, by Rev. Edward Ives                         DR
   Cyrus, of Monroe, m. Harriet **WILLIAMS**, of East Haven,
     Sept. 30, 1835, by E. J. Ives                     TM3     233-4
   Cyrus, of Monroe, m. Harriet **WILLIAMS**, of East Haven,
     Sept. 30, 1835, by E. J. Ives                     TM3     283
**LYMAN,** Henry W., of New Haven, m. Anna A. **THOMPSON**, of East
     Haven, Nov. 25, 1850, by Rev. Henry Townsend, in
     Christ Church                                      TM4     214
**LYON,** Asahel L., of New Haven, m. Marietta Clark **SMITH**, of East
     Haven, June 11, 1843, by Rev. Stephen Dodd        DR
   Asahel L., of New Haven, m. Mari[e]tta Clark **SMITH**, of East
     Haven, June 11, 1843, by Stephen Dodd             TM4     202
**MALLORY, MALLERY, MALAREY,** Alfred G., of New Haven, m.
     Mary Ann **LANFEAR**, of [East Haven, Apr.] 18,
     1830, by Rev. Stephen Dodd                        DR
   Alfred G., of New Haven, m. Mary Ann **LANFEAR**, of East
     Haven, Apr. 18, 1830, by Stephen Dodd             TM3     232
   Almira, m. Joseph **AMES**, Jan. 27, 1832, by Rev. John
     Mitchell, of Fair Haven                            TM3     284
   Amarilla, of [East Haven], m. Alfred **LINDSLEY**, of Branford,
     Nov. 25, 1816, by Rev. Saul Clark                 DR
   Amelia, m. Samuel **BROCKETT**, b. of Fair Haven, Oct. 22,
     1848, by Stephen Dodd                             TM4     210
   Amos, s. Amos, d. [Oct.] 29, 1778, ae 2 m.                    DR
   Amos, d. [Aug.] 16, 1803, ae 45                               DR

| | Vol. | Page |
|---|---|---|
| **MALLORY, MALLERY, MALAREY,** (cont.), | | |
| Amos, d. [Oct.] 21, 1815, ae 11 | DR | |
| Amos, s. Amasa, d. Apr. 5, 1818, ae 7 w. | DR | |
| Amos Broton, s. Amasa, d. Feb. 3, 1816, ae 3 m. | DR | |
| Annis, d. [Apr.] 6, 1801, ae 22 | DR | |
| Asa, d. [Oct.] 4, 1832, ae 78 | DR | |
| Benjamin, d. Jan. 11, 1819, ae 68 | DR | |
| Betsey, m. William **FERREN**, b. of East Haven, May 10, 1842, | | |
| by Rev. Benj[ami]n L. Swan, of Fair Haven | TM4 | 201 |
| Daniel, s. Heman, d. [Sept.] 8, 1811, ae 1 w. | DR | |
| David, s. Benjamin, d. [ ], 1736, ae 2 | DR | |
| David, s. Benjamin, [d. ], 1736, ae 2 y. | TM2 | 23 |
| David, d. [ ], 1785, ae 36; drowned off Southend | DR | |
| Dorothy, w. Benjamin, d. [ ], 1742, ae 40 | DR | |
| Dorothy, w. Benjamine, [d. Sept. 19, 1742] | TM2 | 24 |
| Eleanor, wid., d. Dec. 13, 1819, ae 70 | DR | |
| Eliada B., m. Charlotte C. BRADLEY, Sept. 8, 1851, by Rev. | | |
| Burdeu Hart, of Fair Haven | TM4 | 215 |
| Elizabeth, of [East Haven], m. Isaac **MALLORY**, of New | | |
| Haven, Sept. 30, 1811, by Rev. Saul Clark | DR | |
| Emily, d. Amos, d. Sept. 7, 1783, ae 2 | DR | |
| Eunice, w. Benjamin, d. [ ], 1816, ae 65 | DR | |
| Han[n]ah, d. Josep[h], b. Sept. 1, 1709 | TM1 | 30 |
| Hannah, d. Isaac, d. July 19, 1778, ae 11 m. | DR | |
| Hannah, w. Asa, d. [ ], 1815, ae 67 | DR | |
| Hannah, wid. Jesse, d. Jan. 10, 1826, ae 63 | DR | |
| Hannah, w. Jacob, d. [Mar.] 27, 1830, ae 65 | DR | |
| Hannah Rowe, d. Wyllys, d. Dec. 1, 1828, ae 1 | DR | |
| Harvey, s. Heman, d. [July] 31, 1827, ae 15; drowned in the | | |
| river, above Grand St. Bridge, Fair Haven | DR | |
| Heman, s. Jesse & Hannah, b. Apr. 12, 1787 | TM2 | 291 |
| Heman, s. Jesse & Hannah, b. Apr. 12, 1787 | TM2 | 235 |
| Heman, m. Sally **GRANNIS**, b. of [East Haven], [Nov.] 29, | | |
| 1810, by Rev. Saul Clark | DR | |
| Heman, d. Sept. 5, 1848, ae 61 | DR | |
| Huldah, d. Asa, d. [ ], 1786, ae 2 | DR | |
| Isaac, d. [Dec.] 20, 1786, ae 55 | DR | |
| Isaac, of New Haven, m. Elizabeth **MALLORY**, of [East | | |
| Haven], Sept. 30, 1811, by Rev. Saul Clark | DR | |
| Isaac F., m. Nancy C. **COLLINS**, b. of Fair Haven, [Oct.] 18, | | |
| 1840, by Rev. Stephen Dodd | DR | |
| Isaac F., m. Nancy C. **COLLINS**, b. of East Haven, Oct. 18, | | |
| 1840, by Stephen Dodd | TM3 | 328 |
| Jacob, d. [Mar.] 13, 1834, ae 68 | DR | |
| James, s. Jesse & Hannah, b. Mar. 20, 1782 | TM2 | 291 |
| James, s. Jesse & Hannah, b. Mar. 26, 1782 | TM2 | 235 |
| James, s. James, d. [July] 31, 1827, ae 8; drowned in the river, | | |
| above Grand St. Bridge, Fair Haven | DR | |
| James, m. Polly **MALLORY**, formerly w. of Heman, b. of East | | |
| Haven, Feb. 27, 1844, by Benj[ami]n L. Swan | TM4 | 203 |
| Jane Ann, of East Haven, m. Elijah **BALL**, of New Haven, Mar. | | |
| 13, 1839, by Rev. Benjamin L. Swan, of Fair Haven | TM3 | 326 |
| Jared, d. Asa, d. [Aug.] 28, 1788, ae 10 | DR | |

| | Vol. | Page |
|---|---|---|
| **MALLORY, MALLERY, MALAREY,** (cont.), | | |
| Jared, m. Mary **HEMINWAY**, b. of [East Haven], Jan. 30, | | |
| 1828, by Rev. Stephen Dodd | DR | |
| Jesse, s. Jesse & Hannah, b. Mar. 27, 1796 | TM2 | 235 |
| Jesse, m. Wealthy **GRANNIS**, b. of [East Haven], [Nov.] 27, | | |
| 1813, by Rev. Saul Clark | DR | |
| Jesse, d. [Nov.] 27, 1825, ae 63 | DR | |
| Joanna, d. [      ], 1742, ae 33 | DR | |
| Joanner, d. Sept. 13, [1742] | TM2 | 24 |
| John, d. Apr. 5, 1777, ae 24 | DR | |
| Leuramah, w. Wyllys, d. Feb. 10, 1830, ae 25 | DR | |
| Levi, d. Mar. 14, 1799, ae 50 | DR | |
| Levi, s. James, d. [Aug.] 26, 1836, ae 2 | DR | |
| Lole, d. Jesse & Hannah, b. Oct. 3, 1784 | TM2 | 235 |
| Loly, d. Jesse & Hannah, b. Oct. 3, 1784 | TM2 | 291 |
| Mary, d. Feb. 15, 1781, ae 38 | DR | |
| Mary, wid. David, d. July 21, 1799, ae 57 | DR | |
| Mehitabel, wid. Isaac, d. [Sept.] 12, 1791, ae 57 | DR | |
| Mercy, d. Dec. [   ], 1690 | DR | |
| Mercy, d. Benjamin, d. [Sept.] 19, 1742, ae 6 | DR | |
| Nancy, wid. of Prospect, m. William **SHUTE**, Jr., of New | | |
| Haven, Dec. 21, 1851, by Rev. Stephen Dodd | TM4 | 215 |
| Polly, formerly w. of Heman, m. James **MALLORY**, b. of East | | |
| Haven, Feb. 27, 1844, by Benj[ami]n L. Swan | TM4 | 203 |
| Thankful, w. Joseph, d. [July] 30, 1773, ae 43 | DR | |
| Thomas, d. [Feb.] 15, 1691, ae 30 | DR | |
| Willard, m. Elizabeth **DAVIDSON**, b. of East Haven, Mar. 3, | | |
| 1833, by Rev. Stephen Dodd | DR | |
| Willard, m. Elizabeth **DAVIDSON**, b. of [East Haven], Mar. 3, | | |
| 1833, by Rev. Stephen Dodd | DR | |
| Willard, m. Elizabeth **DAVIDSON**, b. of East Haven, Mar. 3, | | |
| 1833, by Stephen Dodd | TM3 | 235 |
| Willis, s. Jesse & Hannah, b. Apr. 6, 1793 | TM2 | 291 |
| Wyllys, s. Jesse, d. Sept. 2, 1799, ae 6; drowned | DR | |
| Wyllys, s. Amasa, d. Aug. 3, 1812, ae 5 m. | DR | |
| Wyllys, m. Leuramah **BARNES**, b. of [East Haven], Oct. 8, | | |
| 1821, by Rev. Stephen Dodd | DR | |
| Wyllys, m. Leuramah **BARNES**, Oct. 18, 1821, by Stephen | | |
| Dodd | TM3 | 165 |
| Wyllys, s. Heman, d. [July] 31, 1827, ae 8; drowned in the river, | | |
| above Grand St. Bridge, Fair Haven | DR | |
| ----, ch. [of] Benjamine, [d. Sept. 19, 1742] | TM2 | 24 |
| ----, ch. [of] David, d. Mar. 17, 1775, ae 1 | DR | |
| ----, infant of Joseph, d. May 24, 1777, ae 3 w. | DR | |
| ----, ch. [of] Elizabeth, d. [      ], 1808, ae 1 | DR | |
| ----, infant [of] Wyllys, d. Mar. 8, 1823, ae 1 d. | DR | |
| **MALTBY,** Edward Russel, d. Apr. 7, 1842, (at Baltimore, Md.), ae 25 | DR | |
| Erastus, Rev. of Taunton, Mass., m. Almira **SMITH**, of [East | | |
| Haven, Sept.] 7, 1826, by Rev. Stephen Dodd | DR | |
| Erastus, Rev., of Taunton, Mass., m. Almira **SMITH**, of East | | |
| Haven, Sept. 7, 1826, by Stephen Dodd | TM3 | 171 |
| Isaac, m. Clarissa **PARDEE**, Feb. 7, 1832, by Rev. John | | |
| Mitchell, of Fair Haven | TM3 | 284 |

| | Vol. | Page |
|---|---|---|
| **MALTBY**, (cont.), | | |
| Jennett R., m. Lyman **WOODWARD**, b. of East Haven, Oct. 2, | | |
| 1839, by Rev. Stephen Dodd | DR | |
| Jennett R., m. Lyman **WOODWARD**, b. of East Haven, Oct. 2, | | |
| 1839, by Stephen Dodd | TM3 | 326 |
| -----, infant [of] DeGrasse, d. Aug. 1, 1808, ae 1 d. | DR | |
| **MANSFIELD**, Hannah, of Hamden, m. Hiram **ROWE**, of [East Haven], | | |
| Mar. 29, 1827, by Rev. Stephen Dodd | DR | |
| Hannah, of Hamden, m. Hiram **ROWE**, of East Haven, Mar. | | |
| 29, 1827, by Stephen Dodd | TM3 | 90-1 |
| Hannah, of Hamden, m. Hiram **ROWE**, of East Haven, Mar. | | |
| 29, 1827, by Stephen Dodd | TM3 | 172 |
| Hiram, of Northford, m. Elizabeth **RUSSEL**, of East Haven, | | |
| Nov. 16, 1836, by Rev. Stephen Dodd | DR | |
| Hirain, of Northford, m. Elisabeth **RUSSELL**, of East Haven, | | |
| Nov. 16, 1836, by Stephen Dodd | TM3 | 285 |
| Sherlock, of Northford, m. Polly **BASSETT**, of [East Haven, | | |
| Sept.] 19, 1832, by Rev. Stephen Dodd | DR | |
| Sherlock, of Northford, m. Polly **RUSSELL**, of East Haven, | | |
| Sept. 19, 1832, by Stephen Dodd | TM3 | 235 |
| **MARTIN**, Ann, of Bethany, m. Samuel **HOLT**, May 3, 1802, by Rev. | | |
| Nicholas Street | DR | |
| **MATTHEUS**, Samuel, of Bethany, m. Jane E. **ROWE**, of East Haven, | | |
| Jan. 30, 1848, by Rev. Stephen Dodd | TM4 | 209 |
| **McLEAN**, Charles, of New York, m. Sophia Louisa **BRADLEY**, of | | |
| Branford, Feb. 28, 1835, by Stephen Dodd | TM3 | 282 |
| **MERRICK**, Elizur, of Atwater, Ohio, m. Lorinda **CHIDSEY**, of [East | | |
| Haven], Aug. 21, 1827, by Rev. Stephen Dodd | DR | |
| Elizur, of Atwater, O[hio], m. Lorinda **CHIDSEY**, of East | | |
| Haven, Aug. 21, 1827, by Stephen Dodd | TM3 | 173 |
| **MERWIN**, Maria Ann, m. Naaman **PECK**, b. of Woodbridge, Sept. 13, | | |
| 1840, by Stephen Dodd | TM3 | 327 |
| **MEW**, Ann, d. Ellis, d. [    ], 1681 | DR | |
| Ann, wid. Ellis, d. Feb. [ ], 1704 | DR | |
| **MILDRUM**, Hillman W., of Middletown, m. Eliza M. **BRAUGHTON**, of | | |
| East Haven, Aug. 23, 1841, by Rev. John B. Beach, | | |
| of Fair Haven | TM3 | 328 |
| **MILES**, Lucinda, wid., d. Oct. 6, 1843, ae 80 | DR | |
| Theophilus, of Derby, m. Lucinda **ALLEN**, of [East Haven], | | |
| Sept. 29, 1802, by Rev. Nicholas Street | DR | |
| **MILLER**, Viney Ann, of Fair Haven, m. Linus **BIRDSEY**, of Meriden, | | |
| Apr. 15, 1846, by Rev. Harvey Miller, of Meriden | TM4 | 206 |
| **MILLS**, Wickum, of Brook Haven, L. I., m. Susan **HUGHES**, of East | | |
| Haven, Oct. 29, 1825, by Rev. Tehoa Whitmore, of | | |
| Guilford | TM3 | 170 |
| Wickum, d. Apr. 25, 1839, (in N. Y.), ae 35; bd. [East Haven] | DR | |
| -----, infant [of] Wickum, d. Nov. 29, 1826, ae 6 d. | DR | |
| **MIX**, [    ], of New Haven, m. Susan **CURTIS**, of [East Haven], | | |
| Aug. 14, 1828, by Rev. Stephen Dodd | DR | |
| **MONROE, MUNROE, MUNOE**, Angeline Covert, d. John, d. [Apr.] 22, | | |
| 1825, ae 5 m. | DR | |
| George Dimon, s. Edmund, d. [May] 5, 1837, ae 1 | DR | |

| | Vol. | Page |
|---|---|---|
| **MONROE, MUNROE, MUNOE,** (cont.), | | |
| Hoadley E., m. Elisabeth B. **FERREN**, Nov. 20, 1831, by Rev. | | |
| John Mitchell, of Fair Haven | TM3 | 284 |
| John, of Branford, m. Sylvia M. **WELTON**, of [East Haven], | | |
| [Jan.] 24, 1822, by Rev. Stephen Dodd | DR | |
| John, of Branford, m. Sylvia M. **WELTON**, Jan. 24, 1822, by | | |
| Stephen Dodd | TM3 | 165 |
| Lyman N., of New Haven, m. Ireen B. **LINDSLEY**, of East | | |
| Haven, Apr. 5, 1848, by Rev. D. W[illia]m Havens | TM4 | 209 |
| **MORRIS,** A., Dea., d. [Oct.] 11, 1823, ae 73 | DR | |
| Amos, had servant, Cajoe, d. [Dec.] 25, 1773, ae 45; drowned | DR | |
| Amos, m. Betsey **WOODWARD**, Dec. 20, 1778 | TM3 | 170 |
| Amos, s. Amos & Betsey, b. July 27, 1780 | TM3 | 170 |
| Amos, Jr., m. Mrs. Lois **SMITH**, b. of [East Haven], [          ], | | |
| 1816, by Rev. Saul Clark | DR | |
| Anna, w. John, d. Dec. 4, 1664 | DR | |
| Anna, wid. Eleazar, d. [Dec.] 10, 1726, ae 45 | DR | |
| Betsey, d. [Amos & Betsey], b. Nov. 2, 1781 | TM3 | 170 |
| Betsey, m. Nicholas **STREET**, b. of [East Haven], Sept. 6, | | |
| 1801, by Rev. Nicholas Street | DR | |
| Betsey, wid. Dea. Amos, d. [Oct.] 31, 1824, ae 76 | DR | |
| Charlotte, w. Amos, Jr., d. Dec. 11, 1815, ae 32 | DR | |
| Clarisia, [d. Amos & Betsey], b. July 6, 1783 | TM3 | 170 |
| Clarissa, m. Elnathan **STREET**, b. of [East Haven], Nov. 12, | | |
| 1802, by Rev. Nicholas Street | DR | |
| Eleazar, d. [          ], 1750, ae 62 | DR | |
| Elizabeth, w. John, d. [          ], 1668 | DR | |
| Elizabeth, d. Amos, d. July 25, 1760, ae 3 | DR | |
| Ephraim, twin child [of] Thomas, d. Oct. 6, 1651, ae 3 d. | DR | |
| Esther, wid. Stephen, d. Feb. 17, 1790, ae 69 | DR | |
| Hannah, w. John, d. Jan. 12, 1710, ae 59 | DR | |
| Hannah, d. Stephen, d. Aug. 6, 1750, ae 6 | DR | |
| Harriot, [d. Amos & Betsey], b. Apr. 6, 1786 | TM3 | 170 |
| Harriet, of [East Haven], m. Rev. Lucas **HART**, of Burlington, | | |
| [Nov.] 27, 1811, by Rev. Saul Clark | DR | |
| Hezekiah, s. [Amos & Betsey], b. Aug. 15, 1790; d. Oct. 31, | | |
| 1791 | TM3 | 170 |
| Hezekiah, s. Amos, Jr., d. Nov. 1, 1791, ae 18 m. | DR | |
| Jacob, s. Eleazar, d. Mar. 3, 1734, ae 4 | DR | |
| James, d. [          ], 1725, ae about 39 | DR | |
| Jeames, s. John & Desier, b. Jan. 5, 1782 | TM2 | 163 |
| James, s. John & Desire, d. Mar. 26, 1789 | TM2 | 158 |
| James, s. John, d. [Mar.] 27, 1789, ae 8 | DR | |
| John, d. Dec. 10, 1711 | DR | |
| John, d. Nov. 19, 1744, ae 60 | DR | |
| John, s. Amos, d. [Sept.] 27, 1756, ae 3 | DR | |
| John, s. John & Desier, b. Nov. 7, 1783 | TM2 | 163 |
| Joseph, d. [          ], 1712, ae 56 | DR | |
| Lois, 2d. w. Capt. Amos, d. Aug. 5, 1781, ae 48 | DR | |
| Lucy, d. [Amos & Betsey], b. Apr. 12, 1789 | TM3 | 170 |
| Lucy, of [East Haven], m. Normand **SMITH**, of Hartford, Apr. | | |
| 12, 1827, by Rev. Stephen Dodd | DR | |

| | Vol. | Page |
|---|---|---|
| **MORRIS**, (cont.), | | |
| Lucy, of East Haven, m. Normand **SMITH**, of Hartford, Apr. | | |
| 12, 1827, by Stephen Dodd | TM3 | 172 |
| Lydia, w. Dea. Amos, d. Sept. 1, 1777, ae 50 | DR | |
| Lydia, d. Amos, d. Nov. 25, 1822, ae 2 | DR | |
| Lydia C., d. [Amos & Betsey], b. June 18, 1787 | TM3 | 170 |
| Lydia C., of [East Haven], m. Dr. Benjamin **TRUMBULL**, of | | |
| Cambridge, N. Y., Mar. 22, 1817, by Rev. Saul | | |
| Clark | DR | |
| Mary, d. Ele[a]zer, [d. , 1736], ae 11 y. | TM2 | 23 |
| Mary, d. Eleazar, d. July 5, 1737, ae 11 | DR | |
| Nauncy, d. [John & Desier], b. May 28, 1789 | TM2 | 163 |
| Robert G., d. Oct. 4, 1844, ae 25 | DR | |
| Sally, d. John & Desier, b. Feb. 20, 1780 | TM2 | 163 |
| Sally, d. John & Desire, d. July 15, 1793, in the 14th year of her | | |
| age | TM2 | 158 |
| Sarah, d. John, d. July 15, 1793, ae 13 | DR | |
| Stephen, d. Oct. 28, 1775, ae 60 | DR | |
| Stephen, s. John & Desier, b. June 13, 1787 | TM2 | 163 |
| Susan, d. [Amos, & Betsey], b. Oct. 17, 1784 | TM3 | 170 |
| Susan, w. Robert, d. [Aug.] 17, 1841, ae 21 | DR | |
| Susan Louisa, d. Robert F., d. May 2, 1842, ae 13 m. | DR | |
| Susannah, of [East Haven], m. Willet **BRADLEY**, Mar. 17, | | |
| 1805, by Rev. Nicholas Street | DR | |
| Thomas, father of the **MORRIS** family, d. [July] 21, 1673 | DR | |
| Thomas, d. Apr. 17, 1726, ae 44 | DR | |
| Thomas Scott, d. Sept. 19, 1846, ae 20 | DR | |
| William, s. Stephen, d. July 5, 1761, ae 2 | DR | |
| William, s. John & Desier, b. Oct. 3, 1785 | TM2 | 163 |
| -----, ch. [of] John, d. [ ], 1669 | DR | |
| **MOULFORD** [see under **MULFORD**] | | |
| **MOULTHROP, MOLTHROP, MOULTHRUP, MOLTHROP**, | | |
| Abigail, wid. John, d. [Sept.] 3, 1743 | DR | |
| Abig[a]il, wid., [d. Sept. 3, 1743] | TM2 | 25 |
| Abiga[i]l, m. Dan **GOODSELL**, June 30, 1748 | TM2 | 20 |
| Abigail, w. Jacob, d. [July] 30, 1788, ae 26 | DR | |
| Abigail, w. Jacob, d. [July] 30, 1788, ae 26 | DR | |
| Aanne, d. Asher, b. Mar. 25, 1752 | TM2 | 27 |
| Anna, wid. Asher, d. [June] 16, 1797, ae 84 | DR | |
| Asher, s. Mathu, b. Jan. 28, 1709/10 | TM1 | 30 |
| Asher, d. Nov. 25, 1780, ae 71 | DR | |
| Asher, d. [Mar.] 29, 1832, ae 74 | DR | |
| Benjamin, s. Mathu, b. Mar. 2, 1707/8 | TM1 | 30 |
| Benjamin, s. Benjamin, b. July 20, 1735 | TM2 | 21 |
| Benjamine, [d. , 1736] | TM2 | 23 |
| Benjamin, d. [ ], 1737, ae 30 | DR | |
| Caleb, d. [Sept.] 21, 1796, ae 23 | DR | |
| Clarissa, d. Reuben, d. [Oct.] 29, 1842, ae 43 | DR | |
| Dan, d. [Jan.] 29, 1759, ae 56 | DR | |
| Daniel B., s. Reuben, [of] Boston, d. Oct. 3, 1795, ae 1; Wolcott | DR | |
| David, s. Matheu, b. Mar. 23, 1746/7 | TM2 | 26 |
| David, [of New Haven], d. [ ], 1779, ae 26; prison ship, | | |
| New York | DR | |
| David, d. Dec. 26, 1826, ae 79 y. 9 m. | DR | |

| MOULTHROP, MOLTHROP, MOULTHRUP, MOLTHROP, | Vol. | Page |
|---|---|---|
| (cont.), | | |
| Desire, d. Asher, b. Apr. 13, 1737 | TM2 | 21 |
| Desire, d. May 10, 1824, ae 31 | DR | |
| Doratee, d. Mathew, b. Dec. 1, 1712 | TM1 | 114 |
| Eli, d. [Sept.] 16, 1813, ae 61 | DR | |
| Elihu, d. [          ], 1782, ae 35 | DR | |
| Elizabeth, d. Lambert, d. May 25, 1849, ae 11 m. | DR | |
| Enoch, s. Dan, d. Feb. 2, 1737, ae 1 | DR | |
| Esther, w. Josiah, d. [May] 30, 1822, ae 58 | DR | |
| Hannah, d. Matthew, Jr., d. Jan. 2, 1662, ae 10 m. | DR | |
| Han[n]ah, d. Samuell, b. Apr. 10, 1709 | TM1 | 30 |
| Hannah, w. Matthew, d. [Dec] 28, 1781, ae 74 | DR | |
| Hannah, wid. Reuben MOULTHROP & d. Rev. Nicholas | | |
| STREET, d. June 9, 1848, ae 81 y. 3 m.; at West | | |
| Haven | DR | |
| Irene, [of North Branford], d. Mar. [ ], 1788, ae 21 | DR | |
| Isaac, s. Asher, b. Feb. 5, 1738/9 | TM2 | 21 |
| Isaac, d. May 20, 1839, ae 57 | DR | |
| Israel, s. Samuel, d. [          ], 1786, ae 7 | DR | |
| Israel, d. [Oct.] 15, 1788, ae 82 | DR | |
| Jane, wid. Matthew, d. May [ ], 1672 | DR | |
| John, Sergt., d. Feb. 14, 1712/13 | TM1 | 31 |
| John, Sergt., d. [Feb.] 14, 1713, ae 46 | DR | |
| John, d. [          ], 1727, ae 31 | DR | |
| John, s. David, d. [Feb.] 28, 1773, ae 3 | DR | |
| John, d. [          ], 1810, ae 34; lost in a gale at sea | DR | |
| Joseph, s. Joh[n], b. June 18, 170(?) | TM1 | 30 |
| Joseph, s. Matthew, d. Apr. 28, 1716, ae 17 | DR | |
| Joseph, s. Mathew, d. Apr. 28, 1716, ae about 17 y. 6 m. | TM1 | 198 |
| Joseph, s. Mathew, b. Dec. 31, 1730 | TM2 | 21 |
| Joseph, s. Joseph, d. Nov. [ ], 1793, ae 18; at sea | DR | |
| Joseph, d. Dec. 24, 1800, ae 47 | DR | |
| Josiah, d. Nov. 7, 1823, ae 70 | DR | |
| Kesiah, d. Matheu, b. Jan. 6, 1714/15 | TM1 | 114 |
| Leui, s. Asher, b. Oct. [18], 1743 | TM2 | 21 |
| Levi, of New Haven, m. Abigail BALDWIN, of [East Haven], | | |
| Nov. 4, 1811, by Rev. Saul Clark | DR | |
| Lois, [d.] wid. Lois, d. Sept. 16, 1774, ae 4 | DR | |
| Lois, wid. Solomon, d. Sept. 8, 1791, ae 45 | DR | |
| Lorana, d. [Oct.] 13, 1823, ae 45 | DR | |
| Ledia, d. Samuel, b. May 5, 1707 | TM1 | 30 |
| Lydia, wid. Dan., d. Feb. 12, 1760, ae 43 | DR | |
| Lydia, w. Josiah, d. [May] 23, 1797, ae 41; childbed | DR | |
| Lydia, w. Isaac, d. Mar. 21, 1824, ae 31 | DR | |
| Mabel, d. Mathew, b. Sept. 6, 1735 | TM2 | 21 |
| Major C., of North Haven, m. Lois ROBINSON, of East | | |
| Haven, Nov. 13, 1822, by Rev. Oliver Wilson | TM3 | 167 |
| Marah, d. Mathu, b. June 4, 1701 | TM1 | 30 |
| Marah, d. John, d. July 1, 1708 | TM1 | 30 |
| Maria, d. Reuben, [of] New Haven, d. Apr. 10, 1841, ae 43 | DR | |
| Martha, d. Mathu, b. Feb. 18, 1703 | TM1 | 30 |
| Mary, d. John, d. July 1, 1708, ae 10 | DR | |

| MOULTHROP, MOLTHROP, MOULTHRUP, MOLTHROP, (cont.), | Vol. | Page |
|---|---|---|
| Mary, m. Gideon **POTTER**, Oct. 24, 1723, by Rev. Jacob Heminway | TM2 | 20 |
| Mary, d. Matheu, d. Sept. 13, 1742 | TM2 | 24 |
| Mary, wid. Matthew 3d., d. [Aug.] 15, 1745, ae 68 | DR | |
| Mary, Mrs., d. Aug. 15, 1745 | TM2 | 22 |
| Mary, d. Asher, b. Mar. 8, 1748/9 | TM2 | 26 |
| Mary, wid. Elihu, d. [Jan.] 30, 1807, ae 61 | DR | |
| Mary, wid. Eli, d. Mar. 3, 1826, ae 77 | DR | |
| Mary, w. Asher, d. Sept. 2, 1827, ae 64 | DR | |
| Matthew, d. Dec. 22, 1668 | DR | |
| Matthew Jr., d. Feb. 1, 1691, ae 53 | DR | |
| Mathu, s. Mathu, b. Feb. 1, 1705 | TM1 | 30 |
| Matthew, 3d, d. May 12, 1740, ae 70 | DR | |
| Matthewe, d. May 12, 1740 | TM2 | 22 |
| Matthew, s. Matthew, d. [ ], 1742, ae 4 | DR | |
| Matheu, s. Matheu, d. Sept. 12, 1742 | TM2 | 24 |
| Matheu, s. Matheu, b. Nov. 9, 1743 | TM2 | 21 |
| Matthew, s. Matthew, d. Aug. 3, 1745, ae 3 | DR | |
| Matheu, s. Matheu, d. Aug. 3, 1745 | TM2 | 22 |
| Matthew, d. Apr. 28, 1748 | DR | |
| Matthew, d. [Dec.] 15, 1795, ae 90 | DR | |
| Phebe, d. Samuell, b. Aug. 29, 1712 | TM1 | 31 |
| Reuben, d. July 29, 1814, ae 51 | DR | |
| Reuben Street, s. Reuben, d. June 10, 1841, ae 33 | DR | |
| Samuel, s. Matthew, d. Oct. 14, 1677, ae 4 m. | DR | |
| Samuell, d. Jan. 30, 1712/13 | TM1 | 31 |
| Samuel, d. [Jan.] 30, 1713, ae 36 | DR | |
| Samuel, d. May 1, 1790, ae 60 | DR | |
| Samuel R., m. Polly **BRADLEY**, b. of [East Haven], Sept. 30, 1821, by Rev. Stephen Dodd | DR | |
| Samuel R., m. Polly **BRADLEY**, Sept. 30, 1821, by Stephen Dodd | TM3 | 164 |
| Sarah, d. Mathew, b. Jan. 10, 1732 | TM2 | 21 |
| Sarah, w. John, Jr., d. Nov. 3, 1734, ae 36 | DR | |
| Sarah, d. Matthew, d. [Sept.] 13, 1742, ae 10 | DR | |
| Sarah, w. Matthew 4th., d. June 2, 1745, ae 38 | DR | |
| Sarah, w. Mathew, d. June 2, 1745 | TM2 | 22 |
| Sarah, wid. Samuel, d. Oct. 1, 1819, ae 86 | DR | |
| Solomon, s. Asher, b. Oct. 3, 1745 | TM2 | 21 |
| Swayne, d. Aug. [ ], 1815, ae 24 | DR | |
| Thankfull, d. Mathew, Jr., b. Nov. 6, 1728 | TM1 | 248 |
| Thankful, d. Matthew, d. [ ], 1742, ae 14 | DR | |
| Thankfull, d. Matheu, d. Sept. 12, 1742 | TM2 | 24 |
| Thankfull, d. Asher, b. June 1, 1750 | TM2 | 26 |
| Timothy, s. Israel, d. [Sept.] 22, 1742, ae 6 | DR | |
| Timothy, s. Israel, [d. Sept. 22, 1742] | TM2 | 24 |
| William, s. Asher, b. Mar. 5, 1740/1 | TM2 | 21 |
| Wyllys, s. Isaac, d. [Feb.] 14, 1814, ae 4 m. | DR | |
| ——, ch. of Daniel, [d. , 1736] | TM2 | 23 |
| ——, ch. [of] Stephen, d. [Sept.] 27, 1773, ae 6 | DR | |
| ——, infant [of] Sarah, d. Jan. 1, 1785, ae 1 d. | DR | |
| ——, infant of Jacob & Abigail, d. [July] 30, 1788 | DR | |

| | Vol. | Page |
|---|---|---|
| **MOULTHROP, MOLTHROP, MOULTHRUP, MOLTHROP,** (cont.), | | |
| ——, twins [of] Jacob, d. [        ], 1795, ae 2 d. | DR | |
| **MULFORD, MOULFORD,** David, [s.] wid., d. Nov. 8, 1795, ae 3 | DR | |
| Mary, wid. Joel, d. Sept. 29, 1807, ae 50 | DR | |
| **MUNSELL,** Alfred, of Fair Haven, m. Reumah **FINCH,** of East Haven, Sept. 22, 1833, by Stephen Dodd | TM3 | 236 |
| Edwin, m. Matilda Ann **KIMBERLY,** Dec. 5, 1847, by Burdett Hart, in Fair Haven | TM4 | 208 |
| Elbert J., m. Lerumah **FINCH,** b. of East Haven, Sept. 22, 1833, by Rev. Stephen Dodd | DR | |
| Elbert J., m. Sarah A. **LEWIS,** Mar. 3, 1852, by Rev. Burdett Hart, of Fair Haven | TM4 | 215 |
| **MUNSON,** Lyman N., of New Haven, m. Irene B. **LINDSLEY,** of East Haven, [Apr.] [ ], 1848, by Rev. D. William Havens | DR | |
| Margaret Sophia, d. Abijah, d. July 29, 1834, ae 1 | DR | |
| Miranda, d. Seba, d. [May] 2, 1826, ae 11 | DR | |
| Seba, m. Abigail **PARDEE,** b. of [East Haven], Apr. 17, 1806, by Rev. Nicholas Street | DR | |
| Sophia Louisa, w. Capt. Abijah, d. May 15, 1847 | DR | |
| **NAILS,** Abigail, d. Henery, b. May 27, 173[5] | TM1 | 12 |
| Abram, s. Henory, b. Sept. 21, 1717 | TM1 | 198 |
| Ambros, s. Marther, b. June 19, 1749 | TM2 | 27 |
| Charl[e]s, s. Henory, b. Jan. 21, 1720 | TM1 | 199 |
| Henroy, s. Henory, b. Aug. 23, 1715 | TM1 | 114 |
| Marther, had s. Ambros, b. June 19, 1749 | TM2 | 27 |
| Pasyence, d. Henroy, b. Aug. 24, 1713 | TM1 | 114 |
| **NEWMAN, NEWMUN,** Abigail, d. [Nov.] 20, 1742 | DR | |
| Abig[a]il, [d. Nov. 20, 1742] | TM2 | 24 |
| **NICHOLS,** Betsey, of New Haven, m. John **DENSLOW,** Mar. 25, 1821, by Stephen Dodd | TM3 | 164 |
| Eliza Jane, d. Lucius, d. Sept. 14, 1830, ae 1 y. 4 m. | DR | |
| **NOTT,** Riley, of New Haven, m. Almira **WOODWARD,** of [East Haven], Mar. 13, 1823, by Rev. Stephen Dodd | DR | |
| Riley, of New Haven, m. Almira **WOODWARD,** of East Haven, Mar. 13, 1823, by Stephen Dodd | TM3 | 166 |
| Riley, of New Haven, m. Emmeline **FARNHAM,** of East Haven, June 20, 1836, by Rev. Stephen Dodd | DR | |
| Riley, of New Haven, m. Emmeline **FARNHAM,** of East Haven, June 20, 1836, by Stephen Dodd | TM3 | 285 |
| **O'NEIL, O'NEAL,** Abigail, wid. Henry, d. Apr. 1, 1786, ae 100 | DR | |
| Abraham, d. Oct. 8, 1798, ae 82 | DR | |
| Charles, d. [        ], 1774, ae 29; at sea | DR | |
| Esther, d. [Sept.] 25, 1832, ae 72 | DR | |
| James Morris, d. [Mar.] 27, 1834, ae 35 | DR | |
| Sarah, d. [July] 7, 1781, ae 20 | DR | |
| Sarah, wid. Abraham, d. Oct. 27, 1809, ae 85 | DR | |
| **OSBORN,** Lucius, d. [Feb.] 9, 1845, ae 28; (murdered, New Haven side of Quinnipiac river) | DR | |
| **OSTEN, OSTIN,** [see under **AUSTIN**] | | |
| **PAGE,** Allis, d. Samuel, b. Oct. 25, 1766 | TM2 | 47 |
| Moses, d. [Jan.] 26, 1788, ae 84 | DR | |
| Rebecah, m. Caleb **CHIDSEY,** July 17, 1792 | TM3 | 57 |

|  | Vol. | Page |
|---|---|---|
| **PALMER**, Isaac P., of Hartford, m. Nancy **SHEPARD**, of East Haven, Sept. 26, 1841, by Rev. Stephen Dodd | DR | |
| Isaac P., of Hartford, m. Nancy **SHEPHERD**, of East Haven, Sept. 26, 1841, by Stephen Dodd | TM4 | 200 |
| Timothy W., of Branford, m. Desire **SMITH**, of [East Haven], June 4, 1818, by Rev. Stephen Dodd | DR | |
| **PARDEE, PARDY**, Abigail, m. Seba **MUNSON**, b. of [East Haven], Apr. 17, 1806, by Rev. Nicholas Street | DR | |
| Abijah, m. Sarah **TODD**, of [East Haven], Jan. 14, 1824, by Rev. Stephen Dodd | DR | |
| Abijah, Jr., m. Sarah **TODD**, Jan. 14, 1824, by Stephen Dodd | TM3 | 168 |
| Abijah, d. [Sept.] 10, 1832, ae 79 y. 8 m. | DR | |
| Abijah, d. [Jan.] 26, 1843, ae 54 | DR | |
| Abraham, s. Jacob, d. [Mar.] 12, 1773, ae 1 | DR | |
| Abraham, m. Anna **HOTCHKISS**, b. of [East Haven], June 14, 1806, by Rev. Nicholas Street | DR | |
| Abraham, d. Feb. 7, 1826, ae 47 | DR | |
| Adah, w. Isaac, d. [May] 25, 1836, ae 45 | DR | |
| Alden, s. Aner **PARDEE**, res. Branford, d. [Nov.] 22, 1831, ae 24; wrecked off Jersey shore | DR | |
| Amoret, ch. [of] Benjamin, d. [Jan.] 17, 1820, ae 9 m. | DR | |
| Anor, s. Levi, b. Dec. 29, 1782 | TM2 | 45 |
| Aner, d. Apr. 21, 1845, ae 62 y. 4 m. | DR | |
| Anna, d. Abijah, d. [Jan.] 30, 1806, ae 8 | DR | |
| Benjamin, d. July 4, 1782, ae 69 | DR | |
| Benjamin, s. Jared & Rebeckah, b. June 6, 1785 | TM2 | 165 |
| Benjamin, m. Sarah **BRADLEY**, b. of [East Haven], Oct. 28, 1811, by Rev. Saul Clark | DR | |
| Benoni, d. Aug. 18, 1782, ae 25 | DR | |
| Betsey, m. Ezra **ROWE**, Jr., b. of [East Haven], [June] 5, 1806, by Rev. Nicholas Street | DR | |
| Bradley, s. Isaac, d. [Sept.] 29, 1815, ae 8 m. | DR | |
| Chandler, m. Mrs. Mary **FROST**, b. of [East Haven], Mar. 7, 1813, by Rev. Saul Clark | DR | |
| Chandler, d. Mar. 8, 1829, ae 69 | DR | |
| Charlotte, m. William **LUDDINGTON**, b. of East Haven, Aug. 19, 1835, by Rev. Stephen Dodd | DR | |
| Charlotte, m. William **LUDDINGTON**, b. of East Haven, Aug. 29, 1835, by Stephen Dodd | TM3 | 282 |
| Chester, s. Gurdon & Phebe, b. Nov. 2, 1808 | TM2 | 295 |
| Chester, d. [Apr.] 27, 1829, ae 20 | DR | |
| Clarissa, d. [Oct.] 23, 1802, ae 16 | DR | |
| Clarissa, m. Isaac **MALTBY**, Feb. 7, 1832, by Rev. John Mitchell, of Fair Haven | TM3 | 284 |
| Desire, d. [May] 22, 1785, ae 23 | DR | |
| Eliphalet, d. Sept. 3, 1723, ae 45 | DR | |
| Eliphalet, s. Eliphalet, d. Dec. 4, 1725, ae 13 | DR | |
| Eliphalet, s. Ebenezer, d. [Aug.] 15, 1752, ae 1 | DR | |
| Elizabeth, w. Joseph, d. Sept. 19, 1701 | DR | |
| Elizabeth, d. Feb. 16, 1809, ae 34 | DR | |
| Elizabeth M., m. William A. **IVES**, b. of East Haven, Mar. 22, 1842, by Rev. Stephen Dodd | DR | |

| PARDEE, PARDY, (cont.), | Vol. | Page |
|---|---|---|
| Elizabeth M., m. William A. IVES, b. of East Haven, Mar. 22, 1842, by Stephen Dodd | TM4 | 200 |
| Enos, of Northford, d. Sept. 29, 1771, ae 81 | DR | |
| Esther H., of [East Haven], m. Levi G. LUDDINGTON, Oct. 12, 1828, by Rev. Stephen Dodd | DR | |
| Esther H., m. Levi G. LUD[D]INGTON, b. of East Haven, Oct. 12, 1828, by Rev. Stephen Dodd | TM3 | 173 |
| Eunecia, d. Chandler & Lydia, b. Aug. 20, 1794 | TM3 | 9 |
| Eunecia, of [East Haven], m. Luman COWLES, of Berlin, Jan. 1, 1812, by Rev. Saul Clark | DR | |
| Eunecia, of East Haven, m. Seth BONFOY, of Winfield, Herkimer County, N. Y., June 12, 1842, by Rev. Stephen Dodd | DR | |
| Eunecia, of East Haven, m. Seth BONFOY, of Winfield, N. Y., June 12, 1842, by Stephen Dodd | TM4 | 201 |
| George, father of the East & North Haven PARDEES, d. [      ], 1700, ae 71 | DR | |
| George, Jr., d. [Nov.] 22, 1723, ae 58 | DR | |
| George, 3d., [      ], 1763, ae 73 | DR | |
| George, s. Abijah, d. Sept. 1, 1803, ae 8 | DR | |
| George, s. Isaac H., d. Nov. 7, 1819, ae 1 | DR | |
| Gurdin, s. Levi, b. [   ] 20, 1771     (Perhaps twin with Irene) | TM2 | 45 |
| Gurdin, m. Febe JUD[D], Nov. 3, 1799, by Rev. Mr. Robinson, of Southington | TM2 | 266 |
| Gurdon, s. Gurdon & Phebe, b. Sept. 30, 1815 | TM2 | 295 |
| Gurdon, of [East Haven], m. Lydia BEERS, of [North Haven, Apr.] 30, 1826, by Rev. Stephen Dodd | DR | |
| Gurdon, of East Haven, m. Lydia BEERS, of North Haven, Apr. 30, 1826, by Stephen Dodd | TM3 | 171 |
| Gurdon, d. [May] 5, 1843, ae 72 | DR | |
| Hannah, d. Eliphalet, d. Apr. 4, 1720, ae 3 | DR | |
| Hannah, d. Ebenezer, b. Mar. 28, 1728 | TM1 | 248 |
| Hannah, d. May 20, 1830, ae 83 y. 5 m. | DR | |
| Harrison, s. Benjamin, d. June 9, 1836, ae 6 | DR | |
| Henry Atwater, s. Gurdon & Phebe, b. Dec. 18, 1806 | TM2 | 295 |
| Hezekiah, d. [Sept.] 24, 1825, (in the state of Miss.), ae 32 | DR | |
| Hulda, b. Leui, b. Nov. 3, 1773 | TM2 | 45 |
| Huldah, d. Levi, d. [Nov.] 10, 1774, ae 1 | DR | |
| Hulda, d. Levi, b. Nov. 29, 1775 | TM2 | 45 |
| Irene, [d. Levi], b. [   ] 20, 1771     (Perhaps twin with Gurdon) | TM2 | 45 |
| Isaac, s. George, b. Nov. 30, 1723 | TM1 | 245 |
| Isaac, d. [Jan.] 27, 1761, ae 37 | DR | |
| Isaac, d. July 5, 1779, ae 22; killed at British invasion of East Haven | DR | |
| Isaac, m. Adah BRADLEY, b. of [East Haven, Mar.] 14, 1811, by Rev. Saul Clark | DR | |
| Isaac, m. Lydia A. SMITH, b. of East Haven, Nov. 12, 1837, by Rev. Stephen Dodd | DR | |
| Isaac, m. Lydia A. SMITH, b. of East Haven, Nov. 12, 1837, by Stephen Dodd | TM3 | 324 |
| Isaac Holt, m. Sally HOTCHKISS, b. of [East Haven, June] 5, 1806, by Rev. Nicholas Street | DR | |

| | Vol. | Page |
|---|---|---|
| **PARDEE, PARDY**, (cont.), | | |
| Isaac Holt, d. July 31, 1822, ae 41 | DR | |
| Jacob, Jr., d. [        ], 1779, ae 21 | DR | |
| Jacob, d. Aug. 10, 1807, ae 80 | DR | |
| Jairus, m. Sally **CHIDSEY**, of [East Haven], Nov. 17, 1819, by | | |
| Rev. Stephen Dodd | DR | |
| Jairus, d. Dec. 14, 1833, ae 38 | DR | |
| James, s. Ebenezer, b. Dec. 27, 1729 | TM1 | 248 |
| James, d. [        ], 1731, ae about 45 | DR | |
| Jared, d. Feb. 7, 1825, ae 76 | DR | |
| Jemima, d. Nov. 4, 1784, ae 84 | DR | |
| Jesse, d. Eliphalet, of North Haven, d. Jan. 25, 1768, ae 10 | DR | |
| John, s. George, d. June 28, 1653, ae 20 | DR | |
| John, d. [        ], 1683, ae 30 | DR | |
| John, s. Joseph, d. Oct. 27, 1689, ae 7 | DR | |
| John, d. Nov. 12, 1723 | DR | |
| John, of North Haven, d. [        ], 1761, ae 77 | DR | |
| John, d. [        ], 1796, ae 27 | DR | |
| Joseph, d. Nov. 22, 1836, ae 80 | DR | |
| Laban, of New Haven, m. Lue **BRADLEY**, of East Haven, Dec. | | |
| 31, 1820, by Rev. Joseph Perry | DR | |
| Laban, of New Haven, m. Lucy **BRADLEY**, of East Haven, | | |
| Dec. 31, 1820, by Rev. Joseph Perry | TM3 | 164 |
| Laban, of New Haven, m. Mary **THOMPSON**, of [East | | |
| Haven], June 1, 1824, by Rev. Stephen Dodd | DR | |
| Laban, of New Haven, m. Mary **THOMPSON**, of East | | |
| Haven, June 1, 1824, by Stephen Dodd | TM3 | 169 |
| Leavit, s. Leavit, d. [Nov.] 12, 1795, ae 8 | DR | |
| Levi, Dea., d. [Nov.] 21, 1813, ae 72 | DR | |
| Levi Jud[d], s. Gurdin & Febe, b. Sept. 4, 1804 | TM2 | 295 |
| Loly, d. Benjamin, Jr., d. Jan. 15, 1750 | DR | |
| Louisa C., of East Haven, m. Daniel B. **HEMINGWAY**, of Fair | | |
| Haven, Aug. 29, 1849, by Rev. D. William Havens | DR | |
| Louisa C., of East Haven, m. Daniel B. **HEMINGWAY**, of Fair | | |
| Haven, Aug. 29, 1849, by Rev. D. W[illia]m Havens | TM4 | 212 |
| Lue, w. Laban, [of New Haven], d. Oct. 14, 1821, ae 20; bd. in | | |
| East Haven | DR | |
| Lydia, d. Oct. 31, 1794, ae 64 | DR | |
| Lydia, w. Chandler, d. May 24, 1812, ae 55 | DR | |
| Lydia Fields, d. Isaac H., d. Dec. 30, 1813, ae 11 m. | DR | |
| Mariah, d. Gurdin & Febe, b. Nov. 24, 1800 | TM2 | 295 |
| Maria, of [East Haven], m. Solomon **DEWEY**, commandant at | | |
| the fort, Sept. 5, 1813, by Rev. Saul Clark | DR | |
| Maria, of [East Haven], m. William **WILLIAMS**, of New | | |
| Orleans, July 17, 1825, by Rev. Stephen Dodd | DR | |
| Maria, of East Haven, m. William **WILLIAMS**, of New | | |
| Orleans, July 17, 1825, by Stephen Dodd | TM3 | 207 |
| Mary, wid., of North Branford, d. Mar. 21, 1770 | DR | |
| Mary, d. [Oct.] 21, 1783, ae 57 | DR | |
| Mary, w. Eliphalet, [of North Haven], d. Mar. 4, 1788 | DR | |
| Mary, w. James, [of North Haven], d. Sept. 1, 1796, ae 49 | DR | |
| Mary, wid., had servant, Titus, d. May 6, 1797, ae 18 | DR | |
| Mary, d. Nov. 10, 1799, ae 82 | DR | |

| PARDEE, PARDY, (cont.), | Vol. | Page |
|---|---|---|
| Mary, w. Jacob, d. May 19, 1802, ae 68 | DR | |
| Mary, d. Aug. 8, 1809, ae 20 | DR | |
| Mary, m. John S. FARREN, Jan. 15, 1832, by Rev. John | | |
|     Mitchell, of Fair Haven | TM3 | 284 |
| Mary Ann, m. Willet BRADLEY, b. of [East Haven], Apr. 4, | | |
|     1830, by Rev. Stephen Dodd | DR | |
| Mary Ann, m. Willet BRADLEY, b. of East Haven, Apr. 4, | | |
|     1830, by Stephen Dodd | TM3 | 231 |
| Mary Frost, wid. Chandler, d. Aug. 2, 1842, ae 72 | DR | |
| Mehitabel, d. Benjamin, d. [Nov.] 12, 1774, ae 12 | DR | |
| Mahitabel, d. Levi, b. Feb. 7, 1779 | TM2 | 45 |
| Mehitabel, d. Levi, d. June 29, 1779, ae 5 m. | DR | |
| Mehitabel, d. Jared, d. [Nov.] 15, 1795, ae 5 | DR | |
| Mercy, w. George, Jr., d. [Aug.] 13, 1684 | DR | |
| Mersey, d. George, b. Jan. 10, 1724/5 | TM1 | 245 |
| Mercy, d. [May] 3, 1790, ae 60 | DR | |
| Noah, d. May 21, 1754, ae 33 | DR | |
| Noah, d. Apr. 22, 1787, ae 30 | DR | |
| Phebe, w. Gurdon, d. Jan. 1, 1822, ae 42 | DR | |
| Polly, d. Jared & Rebeckah, b. June 26, 1789 | TM2 | 165 |
| Rebecca, w. Jared, d. July 12, 1796, ae 40 | DR | |
| Reuel, s. Levi, d. [Aug.] 28, 1786, ae 10 m. | DR | |
| Reuel, s. Chandler, d. Apr. 16, 1791, ae 4 m. | DR | |
| Ruel, s. Chandler & Lydia, b. Sept. 4, 1792 | TM3 | 9 |
| Reuel, d. Nov. 6, 1825, ae 33 | DR | |
| Rosanna, wid., d. [Sept.] 27, 1844, ae 83 y. 6 m. | DR | |
| Sally, of [East Haven], m. Selah UPSON, of Wolcot[t], Sept. 3, | | |
|     1826, by Rev. Stephen Dodd | DR | |
| Sally, of East Haven, m. Selah UPSON, of Wolcott, Sept. 3, | | |
|     1826, by Stephen Dodd | TM3 | 171 |
| Samuell, s. Steuen, b. Mar. 30, 1725 | TM1 | 245 |
| Samuel H., d. June 5, 1826, ae 18 | DR | |
| Sarah, of [East Haven], m. Hervey JOHNSON, of Meriden, | | |
|     [May] 30, 1822, by Rev. Stephen Dodd | DR | |
| Sarah, of East Haven, m. Hervey JOHNSON, of Meriden, | | |
|     May 30, 1822, by Stephen Dodd | TM3 | 165 |
| Sarah, wid. Dea. Levi, d. [Dec.] 25, 1830, ae 78 | DR | |
| Sarah, w. Benjamin, d. Jan. 13, 1835, ae 47 | DR | |
| Sarah, wid. Joseph, d. [Oct.] 18, 1837, ae 76 | DR | |
| Sarah, wid. Isaac Holt, d. [Dec.] 15, 1838, ae 57 | DR | |
| Sarah B., m. Samuel CHIDSEY, 2d., b. of East Haven, Mar. | | |
|     22, 1843, by Rev. Stephen Dodd | DR | |
| Sarah B., m. Samuel CHIDSEY, 2nd., b. of East Haven, Mar. | | |
|     22, 1843, by Stephen Dodd | TM4 | 202 |
| Stephen, d. [       ], 1736, ae 40 | DR | |
| St[e]phen, [d.    , 1736] | TM2 | 23 |
| Stephen, Jr., d. [Mar.] 30, 1788, ae 63 | DR | |
| Stephen, d. Aug. 5, 1819, ae 33 | DR | |
| Stephen Brown, s. Jared & Rebeckah, b. Jan. 10, 1787 | TM2 | 165 |
| Willard, s. Isaac, d. [Oct.] 9, 1842, ae 21 | DR | |
| -----, ch. [of] Stephen, d. Dec. 3, 1775, ae 18 m. | DR | |
| -----, wid., had servant, Peggy, d. [Apr.] 7, 1783, ae 30 | DR | |

| | Vol. | Page |
|---|---|---|
| **PARDEE, PARDY,** (cont.), | | |
| ——, infant [of] Leavit, d. July 17, 1790, ae 7 d. | DR | |
| ——, infant, of Isaac Holt, d. Sept. 3, 1809, ae 1 d. | DR | |
| ——, w. Gurdon, d. Aug. 6, 1847, ae 27 | DR | |
| **PARKER,** Belinda, of Wallingford, m. Noyes **PIERPONT,** Dec. 19, | | |
| 1821, by Stephen Dodd | TM3 | 165 |
| Leman, d. between Sept. 18 & 25, 1819, ae 18; lost at sea | DR | |
| Thomas, of England, m. Harriet **SHEPARD,** of East Haven, | | |
| Sept. 18, 1834, by Rev. Stephen Dodd | DR | |
| Thomas, m. Harriett **SHEPARD,** Sept. 18, 1834, by Stephen | | |
| Dodd | TM3 | 281 |
| **PARKS,** Sarah, d. of wid., d. [Mar.] 29, 1805, ae 5 | DR | |
| **PARMELEE, PARMELY, PARMALEE, PARMERLEE,** Almira, w. | | |
| Hezekiah, d. [Apr. 27, 1844, ae 32 y. 8 m. | DR | |
| Dan., of Guilford, m. Frances **ROWE,** of [East Haven], Apr. 14, | | |
| 1823, by Rev. Stephen Dodd | DR | |
| Dan, of Guilford, m. Frances **ROWE,** of East Haven, Apr. 14, | | |
| 1823, by Stephen Dodd | TM3 | 166 |
| George, of Guilford, m. Grace **GOODSELL,** of [East Haven], | | |
| Mar. 18, 1832, by Rev. Stephen Dodd | DR | |
| George, of Guilford, m. Grace **GOODSELL,** of East Haven, | | |
| Mar. 18, 1832, by Stephen Dodd | TM3 | 234 |
| Hezekiah, m. Sally A. **HEMINGWAY,** Oct. 14, 1832, by Rev. | | |
| John Mitchell, of Fair Haven | TM3 | 284 |
| Hezekiah, m. Miranda **LEETE,** June 22, 1845, by Rev. | | |
| Stephen Dodd | DR | |
| Hezekiah, m. Miranda C. **LEETE,** b. of East Haven, June 22, | | |
| 1845, by Stephen Dodd | TM4 | 204 |
| Mary, m. Ruel **ROWE,** b. of [East Haven], [Aug.] 26, 1828, by | | |
| Rev. Stephen Dodd | DR | |
| Mary, m. Ruel **ROWE,** b. of East Haven, Aug. 26, 1828, by | | |
| Stephen Dodd | TM3 | 173 |
| **PARTRIDGE,** Hezekiah L., of North Branford, m. Lucinda **BRADLEY,** | | |
| of [East Haven], Dec. 19, 1811, by Rev. Saul Clark | DR | |
| **PATTERSON,** Edward, one of the Southend men, d. Oct. 31, 1669 | DR | |
| **PAUL,** Richard, d. [         ], 1779, ae 16 | DR | |
| **PECK,** Naaman, m. Maria Ann **MERWIN,** b. of Woodbridge, Sept. 13, | | |
| 1840, by Stephen Dodd | TM3 | 327 |
| **PENFIELD,** Elesabath, d. Isaac, b. Jan. 24, 1717 | TM1 | 198 |
| Elissabath, m. Isaac **GOODSELL,** Aug. 31, 1737, by Rev. Mr. | | |
| Hemingway. Witnesses, Samuel **GOODSELL,** | | |
| Mary **GOODSELL,** Isaac **PENF[I]ELD,** Elesabath | | |
| **PENF[I]ELD** | TM2 | 44 |
| Elizabeth, wid. Isaac & w. Caleb Chidsey, Jr., d. Jan. 8, 1767, | | |
| ae 62 | DR | |
| Hannah, w. Isaac, d. June 4, 1719, ae 27 | DR | |
| Han[n]ah, d. Isaac, b. Feb. 19, 1724 | TM1 | 245 |
| Isaac, d. [Oct.] 22, 1754, ae 70 | DR | |
| **PERKINS,** Melissa, m. Albert **ROWE,** b. of Fair Haven, Sept. 13, 1852, | | |
| by Rev. D. W[illia]m Havens | TM4 | 218 |
| Nehemiah, d. Mar. 28, 1813, ae 24 | DR | |
| Rowena, m. Leonard **BRADLEY,** b. of Fair Haven, Sept. 13, | | |
| 1852, by Rev. D. W[illia]m Havens | TM4 | 218 |

|  | Vol. | Page |
|---|---|---|
| **PIERPONT**, Noyes, m. Belinda **PARKER**, of Wallingford, Dec. 19, | | |
| 1821, by Stephen Dodd | TM3 | 165 |
| Philena, of North Haven, m. Hezekiah **DAVENPORT**, of [East] | | |
| Haven, [May] 27, 1804, by Rev. Nicholas Street | DR | |
| **PINION, PINNYAN**, Elizabeth, w. Nicholas, d. [      ], 1667 | DR | |
| Nicholas, d. Apr. [      ], 1676 | DR | |
| Thomas, d. Oct. 10, 1710 | DR | |
| Thomas, d. Oct. 10, 1710 | TM1 | 31 |
| **PLANT**, Edward, of Branford, m. Harriet **STREET**, of [East Haven], | | |
| [Sept.] 12, 1831, by Rev. Stephen Dodd | DR | |
| Edward, of Branford, m. Harriet Jennett **STREET**, of East | | |
| Haven, Sept. 12, 1831, by Stephen Dodd | TM3 | 234 |
| Evelena, d. Edward, [of] New Haven, d. [Jan.] 13, 1837, ae 3; | | |
| bd. [East Haven] | DR | |
| Thomas, of Branford, m. Lucelia **CHIDSEY**, of [East Haven], | | |
| June 8, 1831, by Rev. Stephen Dodd | DR | |
| Thomas, of Branford, m. Lucretia **CHIDSEY**, of East Haven, | | |
| June 8, 1831, by Stephen Dodd | TM3 | 233 |
| **PLUMB**, Elizabeth Isaacs, d. Rev. Elijah G., d. [Aug.] 15, 1813, ae 18 m. | DR | |
| **PORTER**, Edwin E., of Brooklin, N. Y., m. Cornelia L. **HEMINWAY**, of | | |
| East Haven, Nov. 27, 1851, by Rev. D. W[illia]m | TM4 | 218 |
| Havens | | |
| **POTTER**, Ann Maria, m. Richard **WOODWARD**, b. of East Haven, Sept. | | |
| 8, 1839, by Stephen Dodd | TM3 | 326 |
| Ann Maria, m. Richard **WOODWARD**, b. of East Haven, Sept. | | |
| 15, 1839, by Rev. Stephen Dodd | DR | |
| Anna, d. June 9, 1811, ae 19 | DR | |
| Daniel, d. Jan. 20, 1746/7 | TM2 | 22 |
| Daniel, d. Jan. 20, 1747, ae 46 | DR | |
| David, s. Gidion, b. Jan. 12, 1730/1 | TM1 | 248 |
| David, s. Gideon, b. Jan. 12, 1731/2 | TM2 | 21 |
| David, m. Mary **RIGHT**, Nov. 8, 1750, by Rev. Jacob | | |
| Heminway | TM2 | 20 |
| Desire, d. Gideon, b. May 1, 1736 | TM2 | 21 |
| Desier, d. Gidion, b. May 1, 1736 | TM1 | 248 |
| Desire, d. Gideon, d. Dec. 24, 1744, ae 9 | DR | |
| Desire, d. Gideon, d. Dec. 24, 1744 | TM2 | 22 |
| Desire, d. David, b. Jan. 25, 175[5] | TM2 | 27 |
| Dorathy, d. Gidion, b. Dec. 15, 1733; d. Nov. 11, 1736 | TM1 | 248 |
| Dorythy, d. Gideon, b. Dec. 15, 1733 | TM2 | 21 |
| Dorothy, d. Gideon, d. [Nov.] 11, 1736, ae 3 | DR | |
| Dorythy, d. Gideon, d. Nov. 11, 1736 | TM2 | 22 |
| Dorethy, d. Gideon, [d.      ], 1736, ae 3 y. | TM2 | 23 |
| Elizabeth, wid. John, Jr., d. [      ], 1715, ae 42 | DR | |
| Elisabeth, d. Joseph, b. Aug. 1, 1745 | TM2 | 26 |
| Elizabeth, w. John, 3d., d. Dec. 19, 1751, ae 78 | DR | |
| Elisabeth, wid., d. Dec 19, 1751, in the 78th y. of her age | TM2 | 22 |
| Elizabeth, d. Levi, d. Feb. 28, 1786, ae 4 m. | DR | |
| Eunice, d. Daniel, d. [      ], 1742, ae 11 | DR | |
| [E]unis, d. Daniel, d. Sept. 9, 1742 | TM2 | 24 |
| Gideon, m. Mary **MOULT[H]ROP**, Oct. 24, 1723, by Rev. | | |
| Jacob Heminway | TM2 | 20 |

| POTTER, (cont.), | Vol. | Page |
|---|---|---|
| Gidian, s. Gidian, b. Apr. 24, 1726 | TM1 | 245 |
| Gideon, s. Gideon, b. Apr. 24, 1726 | TM2 | 21 |
| Gideon, Jr., m. Keziah LEVIT, Aug. 27, 1752, by Rev. | | |
| Philemon Robbins | TM2 | 20 |
| Gideon, d. Dec. 30, 1758, ae 57 | DR | |
| Gideon, d. Mar. 19, 1767, ae 41 | DR | |
| Gideon, [s.] Gideon, d. [Sept.] 9, 1767, ae 3 | DR | |
| Hannah, d. John, d. June 13,1622, ae 6 m. | DR | |
| Hannah, w. John, d. June 15, 1675, ae 36 | DR | |
| Hannah, w. Daniel, d. [Sept.] 15, 1742 | DR | |
| Hannah, w. Daniel, d. [Sept. 15, 1742] | TM2 | 24 |
| Hosea, s. Daniel, d. [Sept.] 20, 1742, ae 7 | DR | |
| Hoseer, s. Daniel, d. [Sept. 20, 1742] | TM2 | 24 |
| Isaac, s. Enos, d. Feb. 17, 1756, ae 20 | DR | |
| Isaac, d. Feb. 17, 1756 | TM2 | 22 |
| Isaac, d. [         ], 1777, ae 18 | DR | |
| James, d. [Jan.] 11, 1815, ae 25 | DR | |
| Jered, s. Gideon, b. Sept. 25, 1742 | TM2 | 21 |
| Jerusha, d. Gideon, b. July 31, 1741 | TM2 | 21 |
| Jerusha, d. Gideon, d. Oct. 21, 1741, ae 3 m. | DR | |
| Jerusha, d. Gideon, d. Oct. 21, 1741, ae 3 m. | TM2 | 22 |
| Jesse, s. Joseph, b. May 21, 1743 | TM2 | 26 |
| John, s. John, d. Aug. 10, 1663, ae 14 m. | DR | |
| John, Serg., father of the East Haven POTTER's, d. Dec. [ ], | | |
| 1707, ae 70 | DR | |
| John, Jr., Serg., d. Mar. 12, 1713, ae 46 | DR | |
| John, Sergt., d. Mar. 12, 1712/13 | TM1 | 114 |
| John, 3d., d. Mar. 12, 1723, ae 28 | DR | |
| Joseph, d. Aug. 17, 1669 | DR | |
| Levi, s. David, b. Nov. 26, 1751 | TM2 | 26 |
| Levi, s. David, d. May 26, 1752, ae 6 m. | DR | |
| Levi, s. David, d. May 26, 1752 | TM2 | 22 |
| Levi, s. David, b. Jan. 1, 1757 | TM2 | 27 |
| Levi, s. Levi, Jr., d. [Sept.] 27, 1809, ae 6 w. | DR | |
| Levi, s. Levi, Jr., d. Aug. 2, 1813, ae 18 m. | DR | |
| Levi, Jr., d. [Aug.] 29, 1814, ae 34 | DR | |
| Levi, d. Oct. 8, 1835, ae 78 y. 9 m. | DR | |
| Lois, d. Daniel, d. Sept. 15, 1742, ae 5 | DR | |
| Lowes, d. Daniel, [d. Sept. 15, 1742] | TM2 | 24 |
| Loes, d. Gideon, Jr., b. July 15, 1756 | TM2 | 27 |
| Lydia, wid., of East Haven, m. Col. Jacob HEMINWAY, of | | |
| Virgil, Courtland County, N. Y., Sept. 23, 1827, by | | |
| Rev. Stephen Dodd | DR | |
| Lydia, of East Haven, m. Jacob HEMINGWAY, of Virgil, | | |
| N. Y., Sept. 23, 1827, by Stephen Dodd | TM3 | 173 |
| Lyman, of Hamden, m. Mary Maria LANCRAFT, of [East | | |
| Haven], June 25, 1823, by Rev. Stephen Dodd | DR | |
| Lyman, of Hamden, m. Mary Maria LANDCRAFT, of East | | |
| Haven, June 25, 1823, by Stephen Dodd | TM3 | 166 |
| Maria, of [East Haven], m. David W. BUCKINGHAM, of | | |
| Oxford, Oct. 24, 1824, by Rev. Stephen Dodd | DR | |
| Maria, of East Haven, m. David W. BUCKINGHAM, of | | |
| Oxford, Oct. 24, 1824, by Stephen Dodd | TM3 | 169 |

| POTTER, (cont.), | Vol. | Page |
|---|---|---|
| Mary, d. Gidian, b. Aug. 17, 1724 | TM1 | 245 |
| Mary, d. Gideon, b. Aug. 17, 1724 | TM2 | 21 |
| Mary, wid. Levi, Jr., d. May 4, 1817, ae 34 | DR | |
| Mercy, d. Joseph, b. Dec. 18, 1737 | TM1 | 261 |
| Samuel, s. John, d. Nov. 16, 1669, ae 1 | DR | |
| Samuel, d. Nov. 26, 1707, ae 32 | DR | |
| Samuel, d. Nov. 26, 1707 | TM1 | 30 |
| Samuel, d. [        ], 1739, ae 31 | DR | |
| Samuel, s. Levi, d. Mar. 18, 1780, ae 10 m. | DR | |
| Samuel, d. Apr. 28, 1820, ae 17 | DR | |
| Sarah, d. Enos, d. Sept. 1, 1743, ae 11 | DR | |
| Sary, d. Enos, [d. Sept. 1, 1743] | TM2 | 25 |
| Sarah, d. Enos, d. Sept. 1, 1749, ae 11 | DR | |
| Sarah, d. Oct. 7, 1810, ae 30 | DR | |
| Sarah, w. Levi, d. Sept. 12, 1835, ae 86 | DR | |
| Sibbel, see under Sybil | | |
| Stephen, s. Gideon, b. Jan. 12, 1738/9 | TM2 | 21 |
| Sibbel, d. Joseph, b. Sept. 1, 1741         (Sybil) | TM2 | 26 |
| Thankfull, d. Gidion, b. July 16, 1728 | TM1 | 245 |
| Thankfull, d. Gideon, b. July 16, 1728 | TM2 | 21 |
| Thankfull, d. Joseph, b. Aug. 26, 1739 | TM2 | 26 |
| Thankful, d. Gideon, d. [Aug.] 25, 1743, ae 15 | DR | |
| Thankfull, d. Gideon, d. Aug. 25, 1743, ae 5 y. | TM2 | 22 |
| Thankfull, d. Gideon & Mary, [d. Aug. 25, 1743] | TM2 | 25 |
| Thankfull, d. Gideon, b. Aug. 2, 1746 | TM2 | 21 |
| Thankful, d. Gideon, d. Oct. 13, 1751, ae 5 | DR | |
| Thankfull, d. Gideon & Mary, d. Oct. 13, 1751, ae 5 y. 2 m. | | |
| 11 d. | TM2 | 22 |
| Thankfull, d. Gideon, Jr. b. Nov. 10, 1753 | TM2 | 27 |
| Thankful[l], d. Gideon, d. Feb. 3, 1761, ae 8 | DR | |
| Thomas, m. Polly EDWARDS, July 23, 1801, by Rev. | | |
| Nicholas Street | DR | |
| Willard, m. Mary Ann RUSSEL, b. of East Haven, [Mar.] 24, | | |
| 1833, by Rev. Stephen Dodd | DR | |
| Willard, of Fair Haven, m. Mary Ann RUSSELL, of East | | |
| Haven, Mar. 24, 1833, by Stephen Dodd | TM3 | 235 |
| -----, infant s. [of] John, d. Dec. 21, 1670 | DR | |
| -----, ch. [of] Daniel, d. [Sept.] 9, 1742 | DR | |
| -----, ch. [of] Daniel, d. Sept. 9, 1742 | TM2 | 24 |
| -----, ch. wid. Mary, d. June 4, 1815, ae 1 | DR | |
| PRIME, Harriette E., m. Marvin TYLER, b. of East Haven, Sept. 14, | | |
| 1845, by Stephen Dodd | TM4 | 204 |
| PRIMUS, Asher, colored, d. [Aug.] 29, 1829, ae 51 | DR | |
| Stepner, d. [Mar.] 5, 1818, ae 50 | DR | |
| PRINCE, Harriet E., m. Marvin TYLER, b. of East Haven, Sept. 14, | | |
| 1845, by Rev. Stephen Dodd | DR | |
| REDFIELD, George, m. Selina STANFORD, of [East Haven], Sept. 25, | | |
| 1822, by Rev. Stephen Dodd | DR | |
| George, m. Selina SANFORD, of [East Haven], Sept. 25, | | |
| 1828, by Rev. Stephen Dodd | DR | |
| George F., m. Salina SANFORD, Sept. 25, 1822, by Stephen | | |
| Dodd | TM3 | 166 |

| | Vol. | Page |
|---|---|---|
| **REDFIELD**, (cont.), | | |
| Julia Ann, of [East Haven], m. Joshua **DAYTON**, of North | | |
| Haven, June 7, 1821, by Rev. Stephen Dodd | DR | |
| Julia Ann, m. Joshua **DAYTON**, of New Haven, June 7, 1821, | | |
| by Stephen Dodd | TM3 | 164 |
| Mary, m. Silas **BARNES**, b. of [East Haven], Mar. [ ], 1808, | | |
| by Rev. Saul Clark | DR | |
| Rhoda, wid., d. Jan. 9, 1837, ae 65 | DR | |
| Selina, w. George, d. July 10, 1825, ae 24 | DR | |
| William, d. [Oct.] 20, 1826, (N. Y.), ae 33 | DR | |
| William, d. Feb. 1, 1829, ae 60 | DR | |
| **RIGGS**, Frederic[k] F., s. Daniel, d. [Oct.] 22, 1846, ae 1 y. 9 m. | DR | |
| Joshua, of North Haven, m. Ona **ROBINSON**, of East Haven, | | |
| Nov. 19, 1826, by Jesse Brockett, J. P. | TM3 | 172 |
| **RIGHT**, [see under **WRIGHT**] | | |
| **RITTER**, David, of New Haven, m. Anne **THOMPSON**, of [East | | |
| Haven], Feb. 15, 1802, by Rev. Nicholas Street | DR | |
| **ROBERTS, ROBBERDS, ROBIRDS, ROBBORDS**, Anna, d. Thomas, | | |
| d. [Sept.] 28, 1742, ae 3 | DR | |
| Anne, d. Thomas, [d. Sept. 28, 1742] | TM2 | 24 |
| Ebenezer, s. Thomas, b. Dec. 4, 1731 | TM1 | 248 |
| Elisabeth, d. Thomas, b. Oct. 17, 1733 | TM1 | 248 |
| Elizabeth, wid. Ebenezer, d. Dec. 8, 1787, ae 60 | DR | |
| Eunice, d. Thomas, d. [Oct.] 5, 1742, ae 7 | DR | |
| [E]unis, d. Thomas, [d. Oct. 5, 1742] | TM2 | 24 |
| John, s. Thomas, b. Nov. 14, 1729 | TM1 | 248 |
| John, s. Thomas, b. June 21, 1744 | TM2 | 21 |
| Joseph, s. Thomas, b. Dec. 14, 1727 | TM1 | 248 |
| Joseph, s. Thomas, [d. , 1736], ae 9 y. | TM2 | 23 |
| Joseph, s. Thomas, d. [ ], 1737, ae 9 | DR | |
| Joseph, s. Thomas, b. Apr. 17, 1738 | TM2 | 21 |
| Mary, d. Thomas, d. [Oct.] 10, 1742, ae 5 | DR | |
| Mary, d. Thomas, [d. Oct. 10, 1742] | TM2 | 24 |
| Mary, d. [Mar.] 6, 1794, ae 77 | DR | |
| Rebecca, d. [Sept.] 9, 1796, ae 75 | DR | |
| Susanna, d. [Nov.] 7, 1791, ae 34 | DR | |
| Thomas, s. Thomas, b. Jan. 27, 1745/6 | TM2 | 21 |
| William, d. [ ], 1689 | DR | |
| William, s. Jonathan, d. July [ ], 1756, ae 2 | DR | |
| **[ROBINS], ROBINSS**, Abraham, s. Thomas, Jr., b. June 19, 1751 | TM2 | 26 |
| **ROBINSON, ROBYSON**, Andrew, s. Thomas, b. Dec. 5, 1733 | TM1 | 260 |
| Andrew, s. Thomas, d. [Oct.] 27, 1736, ae 3 | DR | |
| Andrew, Thomas, [d.] [ ], 1736, ae 3 y. | TM2 | 23 |
| Augustus, of [East Haven], m. Eunice P. **BALDWIN**, of North | | |
| Branford, Apr. 4, 1825, by Rev. Stephen Dodd | DR | |
| Augustus, of East Haven, m. Eunice C. **BALDWIN**, of North | | |
| Branford, Apr. 4, 1825, by Stephen Dodd | TM3 | 169 |
| Benjamin, s. Thomas, b. Dec. 23, 1716 | TM1 | 248 |
| Caroline L., of North Haven, m. Warren **SMITH**, of East | | |
| Haven, Apr. 21, 1844, by Rev. Davis T. Shailer | TM4 | 203 |
| Catharine, wid. Benjamin, d. Oct. 3, 1801, ae 80 | DR | |
| David, s. Thomas, Jr., b. May 23, 1756 | TM2 | 27 |
| Deney, w. Harrison, d. Nov. 3, 1831, ae 33 | DR | |

| | Vol. | Page |
|---|---|---|
| **ROBINSON, ROBYSON,** (cont.), | | |
| Desire, [twin with Uriah], d. John & Lua, b. July 6, 1787 | TM2 | 164 |
| Elyakim, s. Jacob, b. Apr. 2, 1706 | TM1 | 30 |
| Esther, d. Thomas, b. July 7, 1720 | TM1 | 248 |
| Hannah, d. Thomas, b. Sept. 9, 1731 | TM1 | 260 |
| Hannah, d. Thomas, d. [Nov.] 17, 1736, ae 5 | DR | |
| Hannah, d. Thomas, [d.           ], 1736, ae 5 y. | TM2 | 23 |
| Hannah, d. Thomas, Jr., b. Sept. 18, 1753 | TM2 | 27 |
| Harmon, d. [Oct.] [  ], 1832 | DR | |
| Lois, of East Haven, m. Major C. **MOULTHROP**, of North Haven, Nov. 13, 1822, by Rev. Oliver Willson | TM3 | 167 |
| Lydia, of East Haven, m. Harvey **AUGER**, of Branford, Apr. 20, 1823, by Rev. Oliver Willson | TM3 | 167 |
| Mary, d. John, Jr. & Lua, b. Aug. 2, 1784 | TM2 | 164 |
| Ona, of East Haven, m. Joshua **RIGGS**, of North Haven, Nov. 19, 1826, by Jesse Brockett, J. P. | TM3 | 172 |
| Rodney, d. [Mar.] 27, 1832, ae 39 | DR | |
| Samuel Rodney, b. Aug. 31, 1793 | TM3 | 12 |
| Sarah, m. Samuel **BRADLEY**, Jan. 27, 1714/15 | TM1 | 114 |
| Thomas, s. Thomas, b. Apr. 7, 1723 | TM1 | 245 |
| Thomas, d. June 9, 1766, ae 73 | DR | |
| Uriah, [twin with Desire], s. John & Lua, b. July 6, 1787 | TM2 | 164 |
| Ziba, d. Mar. [  ], 1764 | DR | |
| -----, two children [of] Thomas, d. [          ], 1745 | DR | |
| **ROSE**, Elizabeth, d. [          ], 1677 | DR | |
| **ROWE, ROW,** Abigail, w. Stephen [of New Haven], d. Sept. 16, 1813, ae 52; bd. in East Haven, afterwards removed to Union Cemetery, Fair Haven | DR | |
| Albert, s. Harvey, d. [July] 31, 1827, ae 15; drowned in the river above Grand St. Bridge, Fair Haven | DR | |
| Albert, m. Melissa **PERKINS**, b. of Fair Haven, Sept. 13, 1852, by Rev. D. W[illia]m Havens | TM4 | 218 |
| Ann Maria, of Fair Haven, m. Hamilton W. **SCRANTON**, of Madison, May 16, 1838, by Rev. Benjamin L. Swan, of Fair Haven | TM3 | 325 |
| Anna Maria, d. Daniel, d. Sept. [  ], 1815, ae 9 m. | DR | |
| Asahel, s. Stephen, d. [May] 11, 1837, ae 9 | DR | |
| Barney Nelson, s. Daniel, d. Nov 3, 1815, ae 8 | DR | |
| Daniel, s. Matthew, d. Sept. 3, 1652, ae 20 m. | DR | |
| Daniel, s. Martheu & Eunice, b. Aug. 5, 1782 | TM2 | 291 |
| Daniel, m. Elizabeth **ANDREWS**, of [East Haven], Apr. 19, 1805, by Rev. Nicholas Street | DR | |
| Daniel, s. Daniel, d. Nov. 6, 1830, ae 18 | DR | |
| Delina, d. Elijah, d. Apr. 27, 1809, ae 8 | DR | |
| Elijah, s. Ezra & Huldy, b. June 18, 1776 | TM2 | 293 |
| Eliza, m. Robert **LINSLEY**, Mar. 3, 1832, by John Mitchell | TM3 | 284 |
| Eliza Louisa, d. Matthew, d. Oct. 16, 1805, ae 2 | DR | |
| Elizabeth, d. Matthew, d. Jan. 2, 1651, ae 8 m. | DR | |
| Elisabeth, d. Ezra & Huldy, b. July 11, 1774 | TM2 | 293 |
| Elisabeth, d. Marthew & Eunice, b. May 26, 1797; d. Sept. 2, 1798 | TM2 | 292 |
| Elizabeth, d. Matthew, d. Sept. 2, 1798, ae 15 m. | DR | |
| Esther, w. John, d. Oct. 1, 1825, ae 66 | DR | |

| ROWE, ROW, (cont.), | Vol. | Page |
|---|---|---|
| Esther, d. Levi, d. Aug. 13, 1843, ae 28 | DR | |
| Esther A., m. Lucius ROWE, Apr. 7, 1852, by Rev. Burdett | | |
| Hart, of Fair Haven | TM4 | 216 |
| Eunice, d. Martheu & Eunice, b. Jan. 22, 1795 | TM2 | 291 |
| Eunice, of [East Haven], m. Thomas SANFORD, of New | | |
| Haven, Nov. 27, 1820, by Rev. Stephen Dodd | DR | |
| Eunice, of East Haven, m. Thomas SANFORD, of New | | |
| Haven, Nov. 27, 1820, by Stephen Dodd | TM3 | 57 |
| Ezra, s. [Ezra & Huldy], b. Feb. 25, 1786 | TM2 | 293 |
| Ezra, d. [Sept.] [ ], 1835, ae 83 | DR | |
| Ezra, Jr., m. Betsey PARDEE, b. of [East Haven, June] 5, | | |
| 1806, by Rev. Nicholas Street | DR | |
| Fanny, d. [Ezra & Huldy], b. Oct. 13, 1792 | TM2 | 293 |
| Fanny, of East Hartford, m. Dan PARMELY, of Guilford, Apr. | | |
| 14, 1823, by Stephen Dodd | TM3 | 166 |
| Fannie, w. Matthew, d. Apr. 12, 1844, ae 51 | DR | |
| Fanny Lavinia, m. Samuel F. BRADLEY, b. of East Haven, | | |
| Oct. 11, 1846, by Rev. Stephen Dodd | DR | |
| Fanny Lavinia, m. Samuel BRADLEY, [s.] Stephen, b. of | | |
| East Haven, Oct. 11, 1846, by Stephen Dodd | TM4 | 207 |
| Frances, of [East Haven], m. Dan PARMERLEE, of Guilford, | | |
| Apr. 14, 1823, by Rev. Stephen Dodd | DR | |
| George, m. Sarah SHEPHERD, b. of Fair Haven, Sept. 26, | | |
| 1847, by Rev. D. W[illia]m Haven | TM4 | 208 |
| George Brooks, m. Sarah SHEPARD, b. of Fair Haven, [Sept.] | | |
| [ ], 1847, by Rev. D. William Havens | DR | |
| Hannah, d. Martheu & Eunice, b. Sept. 21, 1786 | TM2 | 291 |
| Hannah, wid., John, d. Sept. 7, 1789, ae 71 | DR | |
| Hannah, w. Hiram, d. Nov. 5, 1843, ae 40 | DR | |
| Harriet, d. Harvey, d. Aug. 1, 1825, ae 2 | DR | |
| Harriet, d. Harvey, d. [Sept.] 4, 1829, ae 19 m. | DR | |
| Hervy, s. [Ezra & Huldy], b. Oct. 26, 1788    (Harvey?) | TM2 | 293 |
| Harvey, m. Wealthy BRADLEY, b. of [East Haven], [Oct.] [ ], | | |
| 1810, by Rev. Saul Clark | DR | |
| Harvey, 2d., m. Jennet WOODWARD, b. of [East Haven], May | | |
| 10, 1830, by Rev. Stephen Dodd | DR | |
| Harvey, 2nd., m. Jennet WOODWARD, b. of East Haven, May | | |
| 10, 1830, by Stephen Dodd | TM3 | 232 |
| Hiram, of [East Haven], m. Hannah MANSFIELD, of | | |
| Hamden, Mar. 29, 1827, by Rev. Stephen Dodd | DR | |
| Hiram, of East Haven, m. Hannah MANSFIELD, of | | |
| Hamden, Mar. 29, 1827, by Stephen Dodd | TM3 | 90-1 |
| Hiram, of East Haven, m. Hannah MANSFIELD, of | | |
| Hamden, Mar. 29, 1827, by Stephen Dodd | TM3 | 172 |
| Huldy, d. [Ezra & Huldy], b. July 22, 1783 | TM2 | 293 |
| Huldah, w. Ezra, d. [Aug.] 14, 1832, ae 80 y. 8 m. | DR | |
| James, s. Harvey, d. [Sept.] 16, 1835, ae 1 | DR | |
| Jane E., m. Nehemiah SMITH, Nov. 20, 1831, by Rev. John | | |
| Mitchell, of Fair Haven | TM3 | 283 |
| Jane E., of East Haven, m. Samuel MATTHEUS, of Bethany, | | |
| Jan. 30, 1848, by Rev. Stephen Dodd | TM4 | 209 |
| John, d. Jan. 11, 1789, ae 74 | DR | |

| ROWE, ROW, (cont.), | Vol. | Page |
|---|---|---|
| John, of [East Haven], m. wid. Mercy **CURTIS**, of Southington, Feb. 2, 1826, by Rev. Stephen Dodd | DR | |
| John, of East Haven, m. wid. Mercy **CURTIS**, of Southington, Feb. 2, 1826, by Stephen Dodd | TM3 | 171 |
| John, d. [Dec.] [  ], 1840, ae 86 y. 6 m. | DR | |
| Joseph, s. Matthew, d. [          ], 1659, ae 1 | DR | |
| Levi, s. [Ezra & Huldy], b. Mar. 5, 1780 | TM2 | 293 |
| Levi, m. Eunice **GRANNIS**, b. of [East Haven], Dec. 28, 1803, by Rev. Nicholas Street | DR | |
| Levi, Jr., m. Louisa M. **DOWNS**, b. of East Haven, Apr. 25, 1840, by Rev. Stephen Dodd | DR | |
| Levi, Jr., m. Louisa M. **DOWNS**, b. of East Haven, Apr. 25, 1840, by Stephen Dodd | TM3 | 327 |
| Lois, d. Stephen [of New Haven], d. Feb. 3, 1787, ae 5 w.; bd. in East Haven | DR | |
| Lois, d. Stephen [of New Haven], d. Feb. 3, 1788, ae 3 d.; bd. in East Haven | DR | |
| Lois, d. Martheu & Eunice, b. Feb. 28, 1791; d. May 10, 1791 | TM2 | 291 |
| Lois, d. Matthew, d. May 10, 1791, ae 10 w. | DR | |
| Lucius, m. Esther A. **ROWE**, Apr. 7, 1852, by Rev. Burdett Hart, of Fair Haven | TM4 | 216 |
| Mary, d. Martheu & Eunice, b. Mar. 14, 1785 | TM2 | 291 |
| Mary, of [East Haven], m. Eli **SANFORD**, of New Haven, [Nov.] 28, 1811, by Rev. Saul Clark | DR | |
| Matthew, first of that family, d. May 27, 1662 | DR | |
| Matthew, s. John, Jr., d. [Sept.] 20, 1743, ae 19 m. | DR | |
| Matheu, s. John, d. Sept. 20, [1743] | TM2 | 25 |
| Matthew, d. Dec. 29, 1750, ae 67 | DR | |
| Martheu, m. Eunice **LUDIN[G]TON**, Oct. 4, 1781, by Rev. Mr. Edwards | TM2 | 265 |
| Martheu, s. Martheu & Eunice, b. Sept. 19, 1788 | TM2 | 291 |
| Matthew, d. Feb. 23, 1813, ae 56 | DR | |
| Matthew, m. Fanny **LUDDINGTON**, b. of [East Haven, Nov.] 23, 1813, by Rev. Saul Clark | DR | |
| Miles, of New Haven, m. Harriet **LINDSLEY**, of East Haven, Apr. 5, 1848, by Rev. D. William Havens | DR | |
| Miles, of New Haven, m. Harriet **LINDSLEY**, of East Haven, Apr. 5, 1848, by Rev. D. W[illia]m Havens | TM4 | 209 |
| Rebecca, w. Matthew, d. Dec. 6, 1760, ae 76 | DR | |
| Reuel, see under Ruel | | |
| Riley Smith, of East Haven, m. Amanda **BRADLEY**, of Branford, [Oct.] 26, 1842, by Rev. Stephen Dodd | DR | |
| Riley Smith, of East Haven, m. Amanda **BRADLEY**, of Branford, Oct. 26, 1842, by Stephen Dodd | TM4 | 201 |
| Roswell, twin with Russell, s. Matthew & Eunice, b. Aug. 7, 1800 | TM2 | 292 |
| Rosewill, of East Haven, m. Sarah **LEWIS**, of Southington, Aug. 14, 1825, by Rev. Stephen Dodd | DR | |
| Roswell, of East Haven, m. Sarah **LEWIS**, of Southington, Aug. 14, 1825, by Stephen Dodd | TM3 | 207 |
| Rosewell, d. [Jan.] 7, 1833, ae 32 | DR | |

| | Vol. | Page |
|---|---|---|
| **ROWE, ROW**, (cont.), | | |
| Ruel, m. Mary **PARMELEE**, b. of [East Haven, Aug.] 26, | | |
| 1828, by Rev. Stephen Dodd | DR | |
| Ruel, m. Mary **PARMALEE**, b. of East Haven, Aug. 26, | | |
| 1828, by Stephen Dodd | TM3 | 173 |
| Reuel, of East Haven, m. Abby **GORDON**, of North Branford, | | |
| July 4, 1850, by Rev. D. W[illia]m Havens | TM4 | 213 |
| Russell, twin with Roswell, s. Matthew & Eunice, b. Aug. 7, | | |
| 1800 | TM2 | 292 |
| Russel, d. Feb. 13, 1843, ae 42 | DR | |
| Sally, wid. of East Haven, m. Charles W. **WELLINGTON**, of | | |
| Boston, Oct. 20, 1834, by Rev. Stephen Dodd | DR | |
| Samuel, s. [Ezra & Huldy], b. Apr. 8, 1778 | TM2 | 293 |
| Sarah, d. [Ezra & Huldy], b. June 26, 1790 | TM2 | 293 |
| Sarah, of East Haven, m. Charles W. **WILLINGTON**, of | | |
| Boston, Oct. 20, 1834, by Stephen Dodd | TM3 | 281 |
| Sarah, d. Stephen, [of] New Haven, d. [Feb.] 21, 1836, ae 5 | DR | |
| Statira, m. Eli **FARREN**, Feb. 26, 1823, by Rev. Stephen Dodd | DR | |
| Stephen, d. Nov. 15, 1724, ae 47 | DR | |
| Stephen, s. Martheu & Eunice, b. Mar. 22, 1792 | TM2 | 291 |
| Stephen, s. Matthew, d. June 16, 1801, ae 9; drowned | DR | |
| Stephen, [of New Haven], d. Sept. 16, 1816, ae 57; afterwards | | |
| removed to Union Cemetery, Fair Haven | DR | |
| ——, infant of Stephen, [of New Haven], d. Jan. 15, 1789, | | |
| ae 3 d.; bd. in East Haven | DR | |
| ——, infant of Stephen, [of New Haven], d. Dec. 27, [1790], | | |
| ae 3 d.; bd. in East Haven | DR | |
| ——, infant of Stephen, [of New Haven], d. Feb. 3, 1793, | | |
| ae 4 w.; bd. in East Haven | DR | |
| ——, infant of Stephen, [of New Haven], d. Dec. 18, 1800, ae 3 | | |
| w.; bd. in East Haven | DR | |
| ——, infant of Hervey, d. [June] 26, 1811, ae 3 d. | DR | |
| ——, infant of Russel, d. [Jan.] 10, 1825, ae 3 w. | DR | |
| ——, ch. of Harvey, d. Sept. 24, 1836, ae 1 | DR | |
| **RUSS**, Frederick, of Harwinton, m. Betsey **SANFORD**, of [East Haven], | | |
| Dec. 10, 1814, by Rev. Saul Clark | DR | |
| **RUSSELL, RUSSEL**, Abigail, wid. Joseph, d. Oct. 13, 1828, ae 91 y. 3 m. | DR | |
| Almira, of East Haven, m. Ralph **WARREN**, of New Haven, | | |
| [Aug.] 30, 1835, by Rev. Stephen Dodd | DR | |
| Almira, of East Haven, m. Ralph **WARREN**, of New Haven, | | |
| Aug. 30, 1835, by Stephen Dodd | TM3 | 283 |
| Almira, w. John, d. [June] 12, 1848, ae 43 | DR | |
| Betsey, d. [Dec.] 11, 1830, ae 28 | DR | |
| Calvin, m. Mary L. **SMITH**, Mar. 3, 1832, by John Mitchell | TM3 | 284 |
| Catharine, d. June 10, 1782, ae 85 | DR | |
| Catharine, d. [Jan.] 28, 1805, ae 84 | DR | |
| Edward, s. Ralph, d. Aug. 3, 1684, ae 10 | DR | |
| Edward, d. Apr. 21, 1773, ae 75 | DR | |
| Edward, Jr., d. Apr. 26, 1776, ae 47 | DR | |
| Edwin, m. Ann Maria **LUDDINGTON**, of East Haven, [Nov.] | | |
| 29, 1849, by Rev. D. William Havens | DR | |
| Edwin, m. Ann Maria **LU[D]DINGTON**, b. of East Haven, | | |
| Nov. 29, 1849, by Rev. D. W[illia]m Havens | TM4 | 213 |

| RUSSELL, RUSSEL, (cont.), | Vol. | Page |
|---|---|---|
| Elisha, s. Lidia, b. Aug. 30, 1753 | TM2 | 27 |
| Elizabeth, w. John, d. May 6, 1796, ae 22 | DR | |
| Elizabeth, of East Haven, m. Hiram MANSFIELD, of | | |
| Northford, Nov. 16, 1836, by Rev. Stephen Dodd | DR | |
| Elisabeth, of East Haven, m. Hirain MANSFIELD, of | | |
| Northford, Nov. 16, 1836, by Stephen Dodd | TM3 | 285 |
| [E]unis, m. Thomas SMITH, Mar. 11, 1742, by Rev. Jacob | | |
| Heminway | TM2 | 20 |
| Isaac Smith, s. Major, d. [Feb.] 23, 1834, ae 16 | DR | |
| Jane Elizabeth, of East Haven, m. Edward Sherman FOWLER, | | |
| of Guilford, Oct. 17, 1842, by Rev. Stephen Dodd | DR | |
| Jane Elisabeth, of East Haven, m. Edward S. FOWLER, | | |
| of Guilford, Oct. 17, 1842, by Stephen Dodd | TM4 | 201 |
| John, d. [          ], 1681 | DR | |
| John, m. Mary FURBS, May 23, 1717 | TM1 | 198 |
| John, Capt., d. Feb. 13, 1723/4 | TM1 | 245 |
| John, Capt., d. Feb. 13, 1724, ae 59 | DR | |
| John, s. John, d. Sept. 4, 1742, ae 12 | DR | |
| John, s. Lieut. John, d. Sept. 5, 1742 | TM2 | 24 |
| John, Lieut., d. [Oct.] 18, 1774, ae 80 | DR | |
| John, s. Russel & Mehitable, b. July 15, 1806 | TM3 | 9 |
| John, d. [Nov.] 9, 1842, ae 73 y. 8 m. | DR | |
| John, s. John, d. Mar. 23, 1844, ae 10 | DR | |
| Joseph, s. Joseph, d. [          ], 1687 | DR | |
| Joseph, Jr., d. [Oct.] 24, 1791, ae 19 | DR | |
| Joseph, (of Truman), d. [Jan.] 7, 1825, ae 24 y. 10 m., lost | | |
| overboard, at sea, in the Gulph Stream, on the 4th | | |
| day out. | DR | |
| Joseph, d. [Feb.] 20, 1826, ae 85 y. 7 m. | DR | |
| Leonard, d. [Oct.] 27, 1830, ae 24; (a cousin of James Barnes) | DR | |
| Lois, w. Edward, d. Mar. 6, 1816, ae 45 | DR | |
| Ledia, . Abraham UTTER, June 27, 1715          (Lydia) | TM1 | 198 |
| Lidia, d. John, b. Mar. 1, 1727 | TM1 | 248 |
| Lydia, d. [Jan.] 16, 1795, ae 68 | DR | |
| Lydia, [d.] Major, d. June 15, 1822, ae 2 | DR | |
| Mabell, d. John, b. July 14, 1706 | TM1 | 80 |
| Mable, d. John, b. May 7, 1729 | TM1 | 248 |
| Major, d. Dec. 17, 1844, ae 66 y. 5 m. | DR | |
| Mary, d. Samuel, d. Nov. 1, 1701, ae 3 | DR | |
| Mary, d. John, b. Mar. 22, 1717/18 | TM1 | 198 |
| Mary, m. Benjamin SMITH, Sr., Dec. 2, 1742, by Rev. Jacob | | |
| Heminway | TM2 | 20 |
| Mary, w. John, d. May 8, 1763, ae 66 | DR | |
| Mary, d. [          ], 1790, ae 17 | DR | |
| Mary, wid. Edward, Jr., d. [Nov.] 13, 1821, ae 90 | DR | |
| Mary Ann, m. Willard POTTER, b. of East Haven, [Mar.] 24, | | |
| 1833, by Rev. Stephen Dodd | DR | |
| Mary Ann, of East Haven, m. Willard POTTER, of Fair Haven, | | |
| Mar. 24, 1833, by Stephen Dodd | TM3 | 235 |
| Mehitabel, d. John, d. [Aug.] 20, 1742, ae 10 | DR | |
| Mehetalle, d. Lieut. John, d. Aug. 30, 1742 | TM2 | 24 |
| Mehitabel, d. John, d. Oct. 11, 1743, ae 11 | DR | |

| | Vol. | Page |
|---|---|---|
| **RUSSELL, RUSSEL**, (cont.), | | |
| Mehetabel, d. Joseph, d. Oct. 11, [1743] | TM2 | 25 |
| Mehitabel, d. Joseph, d. [Jan.] 29, 1784, ae 19 | DR | |
| Mehitabel, d. May 11, 1818, ae 73 | DR | |
| Olive, m. William **THOMPSON**, b. of [East Haven], Nov. 2, | | |
| 1828, by Rev. Stephen Dodd | DR | |
| Olive, m. William **THOMPSON**, b. of East Haven, Nov. 2, | | |
| 1828, by Stephen Dodd | TM3 | 174 |
| Polly, m. Jared **HEMINWAY**, b. of [East Haven, Oct.] 9, 1801, | | |
| by Rev. Nicholas Street | DR | |
| Polly, of East Haven, m. Sherlock **MANSFIELD**, of Northford, | | |
| Sept. 19, 1832, by Stephen Dodd | TM3 | 235 |
| Polly, w. Maj. Russel[l], d. [Jan.] 11, 1842, ae 56 | DR | |
| Rachel, d. John, b. Dec. 15, 1703 | TM1 | 30 |
| Ralph, father of the East Haven **RUSSEL's**, d. [        ], 1679 | DR | |
| Ralph, s. Samuel, d. Oct. 5, 1704, ae 14 m. | DR | |
| Samuell, m. Mary **HEMINWAY**, May 13, 1719 | TM1 | 199 |
| Samuel, d. June 26, 1724, ae 53 | DR | |
| Samuell, d. June 26, 1724 | TM1 | 245 |
| Samuel, d. July 11, 1739, ae 43 | DR | |
| Samuel, of North Branford, m. Anna **CHIDSEY**, of [East | | |
| Haven], May 16, 1832, by Rev. Stephen Dodd | DR | |
| Samuel F., of North Branford, m. Anna **CHIDSEY**, of East | | |
| Haven, May 16, 1832, by Stephen Dodd | TM3 | 234 |
| Sarah, d. Capt. John, b. Feb. 23, 1711/12 | TM1 | 114 |
| Sarah, d. John, Jr., b. Sept. 28, 1720 | TM1 | 199 |
| Sarah, w. Samuel, d. [July] 21, 1739, ae 42 | DR | |
| Seth, of North Branford, m. Abigail Holt **CHIDSEY**, of East | | |
| Haven, Oct. 13, 1840, by Rev. Stephen Dodd | DR | |
| Seth, of North Branford, m. Abigail H. **CHIDSEY**, of East | | |
| Haven, Oct. 13, 1840, by Stephen Dodd | TM3 | 327 |
| Trueman, s. Joseph, d. Feb. 5, 1775, ae 8 m. | DR | |
| Truman, d. [Dec.] 20, 1846, ae 71 y. 10 m. | DR | |
| ----, ch. [of] Samuel, d. Aug. 17, 1702 | DR | |
| ----, ch. [of] John, d. [        ], 1742, ae 9 m. | DR | |
| ----, ch. of Lieut. John, d. Sept. 5, 1742 | TM2 | 24 |
| ----, infant [of] John, d. Dec. [  ], 1798, ae 3 d. | DR | |
| **SALTONSTALL**, Henry William, of N. Y., m. Grace Ann **BRADLEY**, | | |
| [June] 28, 1831, by Rev. Stephen Dodd | DR | |
| Henry William, of New York, m. Grace Ann **BRADLEY**, of | | |
| Branford, June 28, 1831, by Stephen Dodd | TM3 | 233 |
| **SANFORD, SANTFORD**, Betsey, of [East Haven], m. Frederick **RUSS**, | | |
| of Harwinton, Dec. 10, 1814, by Rev. Saul Clark | DR | |
| Eli, of New Haven, m. Mary **ROWE**, of [East Haven, Nov.] 28, | | |
| 1811, by Rev. Saul Clark | DR | |
| Eunice L., m. Henry **BUSH**, b. of New Haven, Aug. 4, 1840, by | | |
| Rev. Benj[ami]n L. Swan, of Fair Haven | TM3 | 327 |
| Jeremiah, of New Haven, m. Clarissa **BROWN**, of East Haven, | | |
| Sept. 10, 1821, by Stephen Dodd | TM3 | 164 |
| Salina, m. George F. **REDFIELD**, Sept. 25, 1822, by Stephen | | |
| Dodd | TM3 | 166 |
| Selina, of [East Haven], m. George **REDFIELD**, Sept. 25, | | |
| 1822, by Rev. Stephen Dodd | DR | |

SANFORD, SANTFORD, (cont.),                                           Vol.    Page
  Thomas, of New Haven, m. Eunice ROWE, of [East Haven],
    Nov. 27, 1820, by Rev. Stephen Dodd                              DR
  Thomas, of New Haven, m. Eunice ROWE, of East Haven,
    Nov. 27, 1820, by Stephen Dodd                                   TM3      57
  Titus, of New Haven, m. wid. Huldah BARNES, of [East
    Haven], Sept. 6, 1812, by Rev. Saul Clark                        DR
  -----, ch. of Titus, d. [June] 10, 1800, ae 2                      DR
SCOTT, -----, ch. of Gershom, d. [Oct.] 18, 1776, ae 2               DR

SCRANTON, Hamilton W., of Madison, m. Ann Maria ROWE, of Fair
    Haven, May 16, 1838, by Rev. Benjamin L. Swan,
    of Fair Haven                                                    TM3      325
  Henry, of Guilford, m. Sarah BARNES, of [East Haven], Dec.
    2, 1822, by Rev. Stephen Dodd                                    DR
  Henry, of Guilford, m. Sarah BARNES, of East Haven, Dec.
    8, 1822, by Stephen Dodd                                         TM3      166
  Hubbard, of East Guilford, m. Elizabeth H. AUGER, of [East
    Haven], Apr. 25, 1811, by Rev. Saul Clark                        DR
  Susan Heminway, w. George H., d. Apr. 22, 1840, ae 25              DR
SEELY, Henry, of New Haven, m. Polly BRADLEY, of [East Haven,
    Oct.] 5, 1823, by Rev. Stephen Dodd                              DR
  Henry, of New Haven, m. Polly BRADLEY, of East Haven,
    Oct. 5, 1823, by Stephen Dodd                                    TM3      168
SHAILOR, Rachel, of Bristol, m. Daniel HUGHES, of [East Haven], Apr.
    5, 1818, by Rev. Stephen Dodd                                    DR
SHEPARD, SHEPHERD, SHEAPARD, SHEPPARD, Abigail, d.
    Thomas, b. June 15, 1736                                         TM1      261
  Abigail, w. Joseph, d. Jan. 3, 1796, ae 35; childbed               DR
  Abigail, wid. Samuel, d. May 3, 1838, ae 91 y. 5 m.                DR
  Abraham, d. [        ], 1800, ae 18; lost at sea                   DR
  Amos, d. [            ], 1798, ae 25; in West Indies               DR
  Amos, d. July [  ], 1833, (at a Staten Island hospital), ae 33     DR
  Amy, wid. John, 3d., d. May 17, 1813, ae 46                        DR
  Amy, wid. d. Apr. 27, 1827, ae 82 y. 9 m.                          DR
  Amy, wid. Elias, d. [Feb.] 11, 1839, ae 46                         DR
  Baldwin, of Branford, m. Nancy SMITH, of East Haven, Jan.
    24, 1838, by Rev. Stephen Dodd                                   DR
  Baldwin, of Branford, m. Nancy SMITH, of East Haven, Jan.
    24, 1838, by Stephen Dodd                                        TM3      324
  Baldwin, of Branford, m. Nancy SMITH, of East Haven, Jan.
    24, 1838, by Stephen Dodd                                        TM3      325
  Betsey, m. John FARREN, b. of [East Haven, Feb.  ], 1804, by
    Rev. Nicholas Street                                             DR
  Caroline Frances, d. Merit, d. [          ], 1841, ae 2            DR
  Charles Hezekiah, s. Capt. Joseph, d. Oct. 18, 1827, ae 1 y. 2 m.  DR
  Elias, m. Anna GRANNIS, b. of [East Haven], Feb. 3, 1813, by
    Rev. Saul Clark                                                  DR
  Elias, d. July 7, 1838, (at Savannah, Ga.), ae 50                  DR
  Elihu, of [East Haven], m. Sarah TYLER, of Branford, Jan. 25,
    1808, by Rev. Saul Clark                                         DR
  Elisabeth, d. John, b. July 20, 1734                               TM1      260
  Elizabeth, w. Samuel, d. [Apr.] 2, 1783, ae 48                     DR

| SHEPARD, SHEPHERD, SHEAPARD, SHEPPARD, (cont.), | Vol. | Page |
|---|---|---|
| Elizabeth, w. Samuel, d. Aug. 8, 1788, ae 22 | DR | |
| Elizabeth, wid. John, Jr., d. May 8, 1813, ae 67 | DR | |
| Elle, s. Thomas, b. Mar. 9, 1785 | TM2 | 154 |
| Hannah, w. Thomas, Jr., d. [Jan.] 20, 1753, ae 17 | DR | |
| Harriet, of East Haven, m. Thomas PARKER, of England, Sept. | | |
|     18, 1834, by Rev. Stephen Dodd | DR | |
| Harriett, m. Thomas PARKER, Sept. 18, 1834, by Stephen | | |
|     Dodd | TM3 | 281 |
| Henrietta, d. Stephen, Jr., d. Oct. 1, 1813, ae 5 | DR | |
| Hezekiah, m. Nancy GRANNIS, b. of [East Haven, Nov.] 28, | | |
|     1813, by Rev. Saul Clark | DR | |
| Hezekiah, d. [Sept.] [ ], 1825, (on Staten Island), ae 36 | DR | |
| Hulday, d. John, b. Nov. 25, 1755 | TM2 | 27 |
| Huldah, wid. Joseph, d. [Sept. ], 1825, ae 63 | DR | |
| Isaac, s. Thomas, d. Nov. 1, 1753, ae 15 | DR | |
| Isaac, d. Jan. 18, 1802, ae 25 | DR | |
| Jacob, s. Thomas, d. June 5, 1799, ae 7 | DR | |
| Jacob, d. [Jan.] 13, 1845, ae 30 y. 9 m. | DR | |
| Jared, s. John, d. [Jan.] 8, 1787, ae 18 | DR | |
| Jared, m. Martha BALDWIN, Mar. 24, 1802, by Rev. Nicholas | | |
|     Street | DR | |
| John, s. John, b. Feb. 19, 1736/7 | TM1 | 261 |
| John, s. John, d. [Sept.] 15, 1743, ae 12 | DR | |
| John, s. John, d. Sept. 15, [1743] | TM2 | 25 |
| John, s. John, b. Oct. 27, 1743 | TM2 | 21 |
| John, d. May 18, 1780, ae 84 | DR | |
| John, Jr., d. [Nov.] 18, 1810, ae 46 | DR | |
| John, d. [Apr.] 4, 1811, ae 68 | DR | |
| Joseph, Capt., d. Sept. [ ], 1800, ae 38; lost at sea | DR | |
| Joseph, Capt., m. Sarah LANCRAFT, b. of [East Haven], Dec. | | |
|     11, 1825, by Rev. Stephen Dodd | DR | |
| Joseph, m. Sarah LANDCRAFT, b. of East Haven, Dec. 11, | | |
|     1825, by Stephen Dodd | TM3 | 207 |
| Leui, s. John, b. Jan. 24, 1753 | TM2 | 27 |
| Lucy, w, Thomas, d. [Sept.] 5, 1834, ae 63 | DR | |
| Lydia, w. Thomas, d. [Aug.] 23, 1813, ae 67 | DR | |
| Mary, d. John, b. Sept. 13, 1731 | TM1 | 248 |
| Mary, d. John, d. [Oct.] 18, 1742, ae 12 | DR | |
| Mary, d. John, d. [Sept.] 28, 1743, ae 12 | DR | |
| Mary, d. John, d. Sept. 28, [1743] | TM2 | 25 |
| Mary, d. John, b. Sept. 30, 1746 | TM2 | 21 |
| Nancy, wid., m. Thomas LANCRAFT, b. of East Haven, | | |
|     [Nov.] 8, 1840, by Rev. Stephen Dodd | DR | |
| Nancy, m. Thomas LANDCRAFT, b. of East Haven, Nov. 8, | | |
|     1840, by Stephen Dodd | TM3 | 328 |
| Nancy, of East Haven, m. Isaac P. PALMER, of Hartford, Sept. | | |
|     26, 1841, by Rev. Stephen Dodd | DR | |
| Nancy, of East Haven, m. Isaac P. PALMER, of Hartford, Sept. | | |
|     26, 1841, by Stephen Dodd | TM4 | 200 |
| Rosette, m. Anson H. BROWN, b. of [East Haven], Apr. 29, | | |
|     1832, by Rev. Stephen Dodd | DR | |

| | Vol. | Page |
|---|---|---|
| **SHEPARD, SHEPHERD, SHEAPARD, SHEPPARD**, (cont.), | | |
| Rosetta, m. Anson H. **BROWN**, b. of East Haven, Apr. 29, | | |
| 1832, by Stephen Dodd | TM3 | 234 |
| Rosewell, d. [ ], 1800, ae 20; lost at sea | DR | |
| Samuell, s. Thomas, b. Aug. 22, 1730 | TM1 | 248 |
| Samuel, d. Feb. 1, 1805, ae 75 | DR | |
| Sarah, m. Richard **DAROW**, Aug. 7, 1710, by Abraham | | |
| Braly, J. P. | TM1 | 31 |
| Sarah, d. John, b. Mar. 11, 1728/9 | TM1 | 248 |
| Sarah, m. John **CHIDSEY**, Dec. 21, 1745, by Rev. Mr. | | |
| Heminway | TM2 | 20 |
| Sarah, w. John, d. [ ], 1761, ae 49 | DR | |
| Sarah, d. Elias, d. [ ], 1827, ae 3 | DR | |
| Sarah, w. Stephen, d. Feb. 15, 1834, ae 53 | DR | |
| Sarah, m. George Brooks **ROWE**, b. of Fair Haven, [Sept. ], | | |
| 1847, by Rev. D. William Havens | DR | |
| Sarah, m. George **ROWE**, b. of Fair Haven, Sept. 26, 1847, by | | |
| Rev. D. W[illia]m Haven | TM4 | 208 |
| Stephen, d. [Aug.] 13, 1819, ae 80 | DR | |
| Stephen, d. [Feb.] 28, 1845, ae 71 | DR | |
| Thankful, w. Thomas, d. [Sept.] 28, 1826, ae 76 | DR | |
| Thomas, father of the **SHEPARD** Family, d. [Apr.] 18, 1726 | DR | |
| Thomas, d. Apr. 18, 1726 | TM1 | 245 |
| Thomas, of [East Haven], m. Lucy **BUTLER**, of New Haven, | | |
| Mar. 24, 1830, by Rev. Stephen Dodd | DR | |
| Thomas, of East Haven, m. Lucy **BUTLER**, of New Haven, | | |
| Mar. 24, 1830, by Stephen Dodd | TM3 | 231 |
| Thomas, d. May 22, 1840, ae 82 | DR | |
| Thomas, s. of Thomas, b. Jan. 16, 1732/3 | | |
| -----, infant of Thomas, Jr., d. [ ], 1753 | DR | |
| -----, infant of Thomas, d. [ ], 1784, ae 1 d. | DR | |
| **SHERMAN**, Amos, m. Betsey **EGELSTONE**, Oct. 22, 1820, by Stephen | | |
| Dodd | TM3 | 57 |
| **SHIPMAN**, William H., of Glastenbury, m. Harriet Adelaide | | |
| **GOODSELL**, of New Haven, Feb. 12, 1826, by | | |
| Stephen Dodd | TM3 | 171 |
| **SHUTE**, William, Jr., of New Haven, m. wid. Nancy **MALLORY**, of | | |
| Prospect, Dec. 21, 1851, by Rev. Stephen Dodd | TM4 | 215 |
| **SLAUGHTER, SLAUTER**, Anne, d. David, b. Nov. 22, 1759 | TM2 | 47 |
| Martha, d. Oct. 22, 1774, ae 48 | DR | |
| Medad, d. [ ], 1780, ae 20; prison ship at New York | DR | |
| **SMITH**, Abel, s. Abel, d. May [ ], 1760, ae 18 | DR | |
| Abel, Jr., [of North Haven], d. Nov. [ ], 1789 | DR | |
| Abel, [of North Haven], d. Apr. 17, 1790, ae 79 | DR | |
| Abigail, d. Thomas, d. July 8, 1711, ae 28 | DR | |
| Abygall, d. Thomas, d. July 8, 1711 | TM1 | 31 |
| Abiga[i]l, d. Thomas, b. Feb. 3, 1747 | TM2 | 27 |
| Abigail, 2d., w. Dea. Thomas, d.[ ], 1755, ae 76 | DR | |
| Alden, m. Betsey **TYLER**, of North Branford, Aug. 5, 1833, by | | |
| Stephen Dodd | TM3 | 236 |
| Almira, of [East Haven], m. Rev. Erastus **MALTBY**, of | | |
| Taunton, Mass., [Sept.] 7, 1826, by Rev. Stephen | | |
| Dodd | DR | |

| | Vol. | Page |
|---|---|---|
| **SMITH**, (cont.), | | |
| Almira, of East Haven, m. Erastus **MALTBY**,  Rev., of | | |
| Taunton, Mass., Sept. 7, 1826, by Stephen Dodd | TM3 | 171 |
| Alvin Thompson, s. [Thomas & Desire], b. Nov. 17, 1802 | TM2 | 292 |
| Alvin Thompson, s. [Thomas & Desire], b. Nov. 17, 1802 | TM3 | 8-9 |
| Ammasa, s. Ambrose & Esther, b. Sept. 3, 1772      (Amasa) | TM2 | 155 |
| Amasa, s. Ambrose & Esther, d. Oct. 15, 1776 | TM2 | 158 |
| Amasa, s. Ambrose d. Oct. 16, 1776, ae 7 m. | DR | |
| Ambros, s. Ambros & Esther, b. Jan. 3, 1780 | TM2 | 155 |
| Ambrose, d. July 20, 1795, ae 45; lost at sea | DR | |
| Anna, w. Capt. Samuel, d. [Oct.] 19, 1743, ae 57 | DR | |
| Annah, w. Capt. Samuel, d. Oct. 19, [1743] | TM2 | 25 |
| Anna, w. Dow, Jr. [of North Branford], d. Sept. [  ], 1789, ae 42 | DR | |
| Anna, d. Samuel & Anna, b. Mar. 17, 1792 | TM3 | 9 |
| Anna, m. Eben Tyler **HEMINWAY**, b. of [East Haven, Jan.] | | |
| 19, 1813, by Rev. Saul Clark | DR | |
| Anna, wid. d. [Apr.] 30, 1845, ae 93 y. 5 m | DR | |
| Annis, w. Edward, [of] New Haven, d. Feb. 10, 1846, ae 34 | DR | |
| Anson, of Harwinton, m. Abigail **HOLT**, of [East Haven], Jan. | | |
| 20, 1822, by Rev. Stephen Dodd | DR | |
| Anson, of Harwington, m. Abigail **HOLT**, of East Haven, Feb. | | |
| 20, 1822, by Rev. Stephen Dodd | TM3 | 165 |
| Asel, s. Samuel & Anna, b. Dec. 10, 1787 | TM3 | 9 |
| Asenath, m. Charles **STOW**, b. of [East Haven, Nov.] 22, 1809, | | |
| by Rev. Saul Clark | DR | |
| Bala, s. Isaac, b. May 25, 1765 | TM2 | 45 |
| Benjamin, d. [        ], 1752, blind and insane | DR | |
| Benjamin, s. James, d. Feb. 11, 1774, ae 20 | DR | |
| Benjamin, d. Jan. 7, 1784, ae 68 | DR | |
| Benjamin, d. [Mar.] 22, 1794, ae 37 | DR | |
| Benjamin, s. Oliver, Jr., [of North Haven], d. Aug. 18, [1806], | | |
| ae 7 m. | DR | |
| Benjamin, d, [Jan.] 20, 1810, ae 27; lost at sea | DR | |
| Benjamin, Sr., m. Mary **RUSSELL**, Dec. 2, 1742, by Rev. | | |
| Jacob Heminway | TM2 | 20 |
| Caleb, [twin with Isaac], s. Isaac, b. July 15, 1770 | TM2 | 45 |
| Caleb, s. Capt. Caleb, d. [Dec.] 13, 1798, ae 4 | DR | |
| Caleb, Capt., d. [        ], 1810, ae 57; lost in a gale at sea | DR | |
| Caleb, d. [Jan.] 8, 1822, ae 51 | DR | |
| Caleb, s. William, [of] North Haven, d. [July] 22, 1841, ae 5 | DR | |
| Caleb Alfred, [s. Thomas & Desire], b. Mar. 9, 1805 | TM3 | 8-9 |
| Caleb Alfred, s. [Thomas & Desire], b. Mar. 9, 1805 | TM2 | 292 |
| Caroline B., d. Edward, [of] Hartford, d. Oct. 14, 1841, ae 1 | DR | |
| Charles W., s. Nehemiah, d. [Feb.] [  ], 1834, ae 7 w. | DR | |
| Charlotte, d. Edward R., d. [Nov.] 29, 1806, ae 8 m. | DR | |
| Charlott[e] Desire, d. [Thomas & Desire], b. June 11, 1811 | TM2 | 292 |
| Comfort, w. Dea. Stephen, d. Mar. 8, 1793, ae 66 | DR | |
| Dan, s. Stephen, [of Northford], d. Jan. 18, 1786, ae 6 | DR | |
| Dan, s. Stephen, [of Northford], d. Aug. 7, 1809, at New York, | | |
| ae 24 | DR | |
| Daniel, d. Aug. 29, 1783, ae 56 | DR | |
| Daniel, m. Mary **WOODWARD**, b. of [East Haven, July  ], | | |
| 1815, by Rev. Saul Clark | DR | |
| Daniel, [of] New Haven, d. [July] 26, 1833, ae 71 | DR | |

| | Vol. | Page |
|---|---|---|
| **SMITH**, (cont.), | | |
| Ichabod, s. John, d. [          ], 1736, ae 2 | DR | |
| Ichabod, s. John, [d.          ], 1736, ae 2y. | TM2 | 23 |
| Ichabod, s. Ambrose, d. Feb. 2, 1793, ae 3 | DR | |
| Ira, s. Isaac, b. June 2, 1763 | TM2 | 45 |
| Irene, wid. Nehemiah, d. [Jan.] 15, 1848, ae 88 | DR | |
| Isaac, s. Samuel, of Foxon, d. [Dec.] 28, 1736, ae 2 | DR | |
| Isaac, s. Samuel, [d.          ], 1736, ae 2 y. | TM2 | 23 |
| Isaac, [twin with Caleb], s. Isaac, b. July 15, 1770 | TM2 | 45 |
| Isaac, Lieut., d. [May] 20, 1790, ae 50 | DR | |
| Isaac, d. [          ], 1793, ae 30 | DR | |
| Isaac, d. [          ], 1811, ae 37; lost at sea | DR | |
| Isaac, d. Mar. 26, 1830, ae 37; found dead in Fair Haven woods | DR | |
| Isaac, s. William, [of] North Haven, d. [June] 28, 1841, ae 10 | DR | |
| Jacob, s. Patterson, d. July 19, 1745, ae 4 m. | DR | |
| Jacob, s. Thomas, b. July 7, 1749 | TM2 | 27 |
| Jacob, s. Jacob & Lois, b. Jan. 22, 1783 | TM3 | 9 |
| Jacob, d. [Nov.] 7, 1784, ae 32 | DR | |
| Jacob, d. Dec. 3, 1834, ae 53 | DR | |
| James, s. John, d. [          ], 1736, ae 7 | DR | |
| James, s. John, [d.          ], 1736, ae 7 y. | TM2 | 23 |
| James, s. John, d. May 28, 1738, ae 8 | DR | |
| James, s. Job, d. Aug. 15, 1776, ae 15 | DR | |
| James, s. Nehemiah, d. [Sept.] 23, 1785, ae 1 | DR | |
| James, Nehemiah, d. Nov. 6, 1792, ae 1 | DR | |
| James, [of North Haven], d. Apr. 20, 1803, ae 89 | DR | |
| James, d. between Sept. 18 & 25, 1819, ae 22; lost at sea | DR | |
| Jane, d. Edward R., d. Oct. 12, 1808, ae 3 w. | DR | |
| Jane E., d. Nehemiah, d. Nov. 24, 1832 | DR | |
| Jared, d. [          ], 1796, ae 24; d. at sea | DR | |
| Jared, m. Eliza **WILLIAMS**, b. of East Haven, Dec. 10, 1848, by Rev. D. William Havens | DR | |
| Jared, of East Haven, m. Eliza **WILLIAMS**, of Branford, Dec. 10, 1848, by Rev. D. W[illia]m Havens | TM4 | 212 |
| Jemima, w. Stephen, d. June 10, 1756, ae 27 | DR | |
| Job, d. May 1, 1775, ae 58 | DR | |
| John, s. Thomas, d. May 26, 1663, ae 10 w. | DR | |
| John, d. [          ], 1739, ae 71 | DR | |
| John, s. Patterson, d. Aug. 27, 1754, ae 10 | DR | |
| John, s. Thomas, [of North Haven], d. May 27, 1795, ae 22 m. | DR | |
| John, s. Nehemiah, d. [June] 30, 1797, ae 2 | DR | |
| John, s. Thomas, [of North Haven], d. Oct. 11, [1801], ae 15 | DR | |
| John, s. Nehemiah, d. [Feb.] 20, 1803, ae 2 | DR | |
| John, m. Harriet **ELLIS**, July 7, 1836, by Rev. John Mitchell, of Fair Haven | TM3 | 285 |
| John, s. Mrs. Jacob, d. [Nov.] 16, 1845, ae 23 | DR | |
| John G., of Brooklin, N. Y., m. Caroline A. **HEMINGWAY**, of East Haven, June 12, 1850, by Rev. D. W[illia]m Havens | TM4 | 213 |
| John Miner, of Derby, m. Nancy Jane **BROWN**, d. of Aner, of East Haven, Dec. 18, 1839, by Benjamin L. Swan, at Fair Haven | TM3 | 326 |
| John S., s. [Jacob & Sibyl], b. Sept. 21, 1822 | TM3 | 262 |
| Jordan, [of North Branford], d. Jan. [ ], 1800, ae 67 | DR | |

| SMITH, (cont.), | Vol. | Page |
|---|---|---|
| Joseph, d. [Oct.] 20, 1784, ae 36; at sea | DR | |
| Keziah, wid. Dow, [of North Branford], d. June 1, 1793, ae 84 | DR | |
| Laban, m. Emily E. **CHIDSEY**, of East Haven, Jan. 18, 1846, by Rev. George W. Nichols | DR | |
| Laban, m. Emely E. **CHIDSEY**, b. of East Haven, Jan. 18, 1846, by Rev. George W. Nichols | TM4 | 206 |
| Laura Anna, d. Capt. Samuel, d. Mar. 1, 1848, ae 1 y. 6 m. | DR | |
| Lavinia C., of East Haven, m. Edmund R. **COWLES**, of Springfield, Mass., Oct. 4, 1838, by Rev. Stephen Dodd | DR | |
| Lavinia C., of East Haven, m. Edmond R. **COWLES**, of Springfield, Mass., Oct. 4, 1838, by Stephen Dodd | TM3 | 325 |
| Lester, m. Louisa B. **TYLER**, b. of East Haven, May 7, 1843, by Rev. Stephen Dodd | DR | |
| Lester, m. Louis B. **TYLER**, b. of East Haven, May 7, 1843, by Stephen Dodd | TM4 | 202 |
| Levi, s. Samuel, d. Apr. 1, 1783, ae 8 m. | DR | |
| Levi, s. Samuel & Anna, b. Mar. 4, 1784 | TM3 | 9 |
| Levi, m. Desire **THOMPSON**, b. of [East Haven], June 8, 1812, by Rev. Saul Clark | DR | |
| Levi, d. [Nov.] 14, 1843, ae 59 y. 8 m. | DR | |
| Lois, w. Nehemiah, d. June 16, 1792, ae 36 | DR | |
| Lois, w. Oliver, Jr., [of North Haven] d. July 20, 1806 | DR | |
| Lois, wid. Jacob, d. Jan. 1, 1812, ae 57 | DR | |
| Lois, Mrs., m. Amos **MORRIS**, Jr., b. of [East Haven], [      ], 1816, by Rev. Saul Clark | DR | |
| Lois, m. Amma **TYLER**, b. of [East Haven, Jan.] 19, 1818, by Rev. Stephen Dodd | DR | |
| Loly, d. Ambros & Esther, b. Mar. 12, 1778 | TM2 | 155 |
| Loring, s. Job, d. [      ], 1788, ae 3 | DR | |
| Louisa B. Tyler, w. Lester, d. Dec. 4, 1846, ae 27 | DR | |
| Lucy M., of East Haven, m. Edward **HEMINGWAY**, Sept. 24, 1844, by Rev. Henry Townsend | DR | |
| Lucy M., m. Edward **HEMINGWAY**, b. of East Haven, Sept. 24, 1844, by Rev. Henry Townsend | TM4 | 204 |
| Ledia, d. William, b. Feb. 4, 1711/12 | TM1 | 31 |
| Lydia, d. Samuel, of Foxon, d. Dec. 25, 1736, ae 10 | DR | |
| Lidia, d. Samuel, [d.      ], 1736, ae 8 y. | TM2 | 23 |
| Lydia, w. Abel, d. [Dec.] 22, 1760, ae 45 | DR | |
| Lydia, d. Samuel, of Foxon, d. Aug. 9, 1767, ae 22 | DR | |
| Lydia, m. William **BRADLEY**, Sept. 16, 1804, by Rev. Nicholas Street | DR | |
| Lydia, w. Abel, [of North Haven], d. Oct. 22, 1809, ae 79 | DR | |
| Lydia, 2d w. James, [of North Haven], d. [      ], 1819, ae 93 | DR | |
| Lydia, wid., d. July 11, 1847, ae 93 y. 7 m. 13 d. | DR | |
| Lydia A., m. Isaac **PARDEE**, b. of East Haven, Nov. 12, 1837, by Rev. Stephen Dodd | DR | |
| Lydia A., m. Isaac **PARDEE**, b. of East Haven, Nov. 12, 1837, by Rev. Stephen Dodd | TM3 | 324 |
| Lyman, s. Abel, d. [      ], 1775, ae 5 | DR | |

| | Vol. | Page |
|---|---|---|
| **SMITH**, (cont.), | | |
| Marietta, of East Haven, m. Henry I. **BRADLEY**, of Hamden, May 10, 1837, by Rev. Stephen Dodd | DR | |
| Marietta, of East Haven, m. Henry T. **BALDWIN**, of North Haven, May 10, 1837, by Stephen Dodd | TM3 | 324 |
| Marietta, of East Haven, m. Isaac Henry **FOOT**, of New Haven, Nov. 26, 1846, by Rev. Stephen Dodd | DR | |
| Marietta, of East Haven, m. I. Henry **FOOTE**, of Fair Haven, Nov. 26, 1846, by Stephen Dodd | TM4 | 207 |
| Marietta Clark, of East Haven, m. Asahel L. **LYON**, of New Haven, June 11, 1843, by Rev. Stephen Dodd | DR | |
| Mari[e]tta, Clark, of East Haven, m. Asahel L. **LYON**, of New Haven, June 11, 1843, by Stephen Dodd | TM4 | 202 |
| Marina B., d. Jacob & Sibyl, b. May 26, 1817 | TM3 | 262 |
| Marvin, of Mendon, N. Y., m. Lucy **THOMPSON**, of [East Haven], Apr. 3, 1826, by Rev. Stephen Dodd | DR | |
| Marvin, of Meriden, N. Y., m. Lucy **THOMPSON**, of East Haven, Apr. 3, 1826, by Stephen Dodd | TM3 | 171 |
| Mary, d. Benjamin, Sr., b. Dec. 19, 1743 | TM2 | 21 |
| Mary, w. Samuel, of Foxon, d. Sept. 5, 1767, ae 63 | DR | |
| Mary, w. Samuel, d. [Jan.] 26, 1773, ae 28 | DR | |
| Mary, d. Sam[u]el & Anna, b. May 6, 1778 | TM3 | 9 |
| Mary, w. Ambrose, d. [Dec.] 23, 1790, ae 39; childbed | DR | |
| Mary, of [East Haven], m. Jeremiah **WOODWARD**, June 6, 1822, by Rev. Stephen Dodd | DR | |
| Mary, m. Jeremiah **WOODWARD**, b. of East Haven, June 6, 1822, by Stephen Dodd | TM3 | 165 |
| Mary, w. Laban, [of] New Haven, d. [Mar.] 18. 1834, ae 67 | DR | |
| Mary Emily, d. wid. Lydia, [of] Foxon, d. Dec. 8, 1824, ae 8 | DR | |
| Mary L., m. Calvin **RUSSELL**, Mar. 3, 1832, by John Mitchell | TM3 | 284 |
| Mercy, wid. Samuel, of Plymouth, d. [Sept.] 17, 1825, ae 68 | DR | |
| Miles, s. Ambros & Esther, b. Mar. 21, 1776 | TM2 | 155 |
| Nancy, d. Thomas & Desire, b. Aug. 20, 1813 | TM3 | 13 |
| Nancy, of East Haven, m. Baldwin **SHEPARD**, of Branford, Jan. 24, 1838, by Rev. Stephen Dodd | DR | |
| Nancy, of East Haven, m. Baldwin **SHEPARD**, of Branford, Jan. 24, 1838, by Stephen Dodd | TM3 | 324 |
| Nancy, of East Haven, m. Baldwin **SHEPARD**, of Branford, Jan. 24, 1838, by Stephen Dodd | TM3 | 325 |
| Naomi, d. Rachel Lud[d]in[g]ton, b. Mar. 3, 1787 | TM2 | 293 |
| Nehemiah, d. Oct. 17, 1803, ae 24; lost at sea | DR | |
| Nehemiah, d. [Aug.] 21, 1826, ae 76 | DR | |
| Nehemiah, m. Jane E. **ROWE**, Nov. 20, 1831, by Rev. John Mitchell, of Fair Haven | TM3 | 283 |
| Normand, of Hartford, m. Lucy **MORRIS**, of [East Haven], Apr. 12, 1827, by Rev. Stephen Dodd | DR | |
| Normand, of Hartford, m. Lucy **MORRIS**, of East Haven, Apr. 12, 1827, by Stephen Dodd | TM3 | 172 |
| Olive, w. Jude, [of North Haven], d. May 7, 1801, ae 37 | DR | |
| Oliver, [of North Haven], d. Nov. 15, 1789, ae 39 | DR | |
| Oliver, Jr., [of North Haven], d. Mar. 27, [1815], ae 35 | DR | |
| Patterson, d. Feb. 7, 1773, ae 63 | DR | |
| Polly, d. Samuel, Jr., d. Mar. 6, 1778, ae 2 | DR | |

| SMITH, (cont.),                                                                 | Vol. | Page |
|---------------------------------------------------------------------------------|------|------|
| Rachel, d. Dec. 11, 1803, ae 42                                                 | DR   |      |
| Robert, s. [Jacob & Sibyl], b. Nov. 29, 1828                                    | TM3  | 262  |
| Roger, d. [          ], 1803, ae 20; lost at sea                                | DR   |      |
| Row, s. Ambros & Esther, b. Dec. 20, 1785                                       | TM2  | 155  |
| Rowe, d. Ambrose, d. [          ], 1786, ae 1     (Probably a son)              | DR   |      |
| Russel G., of Fair Haven, m. Catharine E. **FRISBIE**, of East                  |      |      |
| Haven, Oct. 5, 1845, by Rev. Stephen Dodd                                       | DR   |      |
| Russel G., of Fair Haven, m. Catherine E. **FRISBIE**, of East                  |      |      |
| Haven, Oct. 5, 1845, by Stephen Dodd                                            | TM4  | 205  |
| Ruth, w. Jude, [of North Haven], d. Apr. 21, 1808, ae 31                        | DR   |      |
| Sally, d. [Thomas & Desire], b. Mar. 30, 1807                                   | TM2  | 292  |
| Sally, [d. Thomas & Desire], b. Mar. 30, 1807                                   | TM3  | 8-9  |
| Samuel, s. Samuel, of Foxon, d. [Dec.] 30, 1736, ae 10                          | DR   |      |
| Samuel, s. Samuel, [d.          ], 1736, ae 10 y.                               | TM2  | 23   |
| Samuel, s. Samuel, of Foxon, d. Oct. 16, 1740, ae 4                             | DR   |      |
| Samuel, s. Patterson, d. [          ], 1742                                     | DR   |      |
| Samuel, Capt. d. Jan. 6, 1765, ae 84                                            | DR   |      |
| Samuel, of Foxon, d. [          ], 1770, ae above 70                            | DR   |      |
| Samuel, d. [          ], 1776, ae 37                                            | DR   |      |
| Samuel, s. Thomas & Desire, b. Oct. 21, 1795                                    | TM2  | 292  |
| Samuel, [of] Foxon, d. [Nov.] 8, 1823, ae 75                                    | DR   |      |
| Samuel, d. [Aug.] 18, 1833, ae 83 y. 8 m.                                       | DR   |      |
| Sarah, w. Lieut. Thomas, d. Apr. 24, 1718                                       | DR   |      |
| Sarah, w. Lieut. Thomas, d. Apr. 24, 1718                                       | TM1  | 198  |
| Sarah, 2d. w. Capt. Stephen, d. Oct. 23, 1764, ae 28                            | DR   |      |
| Sarah, d. Isaac, b. Oct. 12, 1772                                               | TM2  | 45   |
| Sarah, wid. Patterson, d. [Jan.] 27, 1786, ae 67                                | DR   |      |
| Sarah, w. Jordan, [of North Branford], d. Feb. [ ], 1798, ae 56                 | DR   |      |
| Sarah, w. Thomas, [of North Haven], d. Oct. 13, 1800, ae 39                     | DR   |      |
| Sarah, d. Jan. 25, 1803, ae 22                                                  | DR   |      |
| Sarah, w. Hervey, [of North Haven], d. Sept. 27, 1818, ae 29                    | DR   |      |
| Sarah, wid. Capt. Caleb, d. Mar. 25, 1843, ae 83 y. 8 m.                        | DR   |      |
| Sarah Caroline, m. Edward Ellsworth **THOMPSON**, Dec. 12,                      |      |      |
| 1847, by Rev. D. W[illia]m Havens                                               | TM4  | 209  |
| Sarah Caroline, b. of East Haven, m. Edward Ellsworth                           |      |      |
| **THOMPSON**, Dec. 17, 1847, by Rev. D. William                                 |      |      |
| Havens                                                                          | DR   |      |
| Steuen, s. Thomas, b. Nov. 28, 1724          (Stephen)                          | TM1  | 245  |
| Stephen, Dea., had servant, Cate, d. [Mar.] 9, 1783, ae 11                      | DR   |      |
| Stephen, had negro Bette, d. Peter & Ginne, b. Jan. 5, 1790                     | TM2  | 159  |
| Stephen & Joseph Holt, had negro Cloe, d. Peter & Ginne, b.                     |      |      |
| May 21, 1792                                                                    | TM2  | 159  |
| Stephen, s. Thomas & Desire, b. Sept. 18, 1793                                  | TM2  | 292  |
| Stephen, m. Polly **BRADLEY**, b. of [East Haven], Aug. 18,                     |      |      |
| 1808, by Rev. Saul Clark                                                        | DR   |      |
| Stephen, m. Betsey **GRANNIS**, b. of [East Haven], m. Jan. 11,                 |      |      |
| 1815, by Rev. Saul Clark                                                        | DR   |      |
| Stephen, Dea., d. [Jan.] 22, 1816, ae 92                                        | DR   |      |
| Stephen, 2d, had grandchild William Bradley, s. Henry Bradley,                  |      |      |
| d. Oct. 1, 1842, ae 2                                                           | DR   |      |
| Sibyl, d. Thomas, [of North Haven], d. Oct. 4, [1795],                          |      |      |
| ae 4          (Sybil)                                                           | DR   |      |
| Thankful, w. Oliver, [of North Haven], d. Dec. 14, 1822, ae 70                  | DR   |      |

| | Vol. | Page |
|---|---|---|
| **SMITH**, (cont.), | | |
| Thomas, s. Thomas, d. Jan. 14, 1672, ae 5 m. | DR | |
| Thomas, s. Thomas, b. July 27, 1719 | TM1 | 199 |
| Thomas, Capt., father of the **SMITH** Family, d. [Nov.] 16, 1724, ae about 90 | DR | |
| Thomas, 3d, d. [ ], 1727, ae 30 | DR | |
| Thomas, m. [E]unis **RUSSELL**, Mar. 11, 1742, by Rev. Jacob Heminway | TM2 | 20 |
| Thomas, s. Thomas, b. Dec. 10, 1742 | TM2 | 21 |
| Thomas, s. Thomas, b. Dec. 10, 1742 | TM2 | 27 |
| Thomas, 4th, d. Dec. 26, 1754, ae 35 | DR | |
| Thomas, d. Dec. 26, 1754 | TM2 | 22 |
| Thomas, s. Stephen & Sarah, b. Nov. 29, 1761 | TM2 | 292 |
| Thomas, Dea., d. [ ], 1762, ae about 90 | DR | |
| Thomas, d. [ ], 1776, ae 34; burnt in a fire ship | DR | |
| Thomas, m. Desire **THOMPSON**, Oct. 16, 1792 | TM2 | 266 |
| Thomas, [of North Haven], d. Feb. 20, 1815, ae 53 | DR | |
| Thomas, d. [Sept.] 13, 1840, ae 78 y. 9 m. | DR | |
| Thomas M., of East Haven, m. Lorana **LINDSLEY**, of Branford, May 19, 1836, by Rev. Stephen Dodd | DR | |
| Thomas M., of East Haven, m. Lorana **LINSLEY**, of Branford, May 19, 1836, by Stephen Dodd | TM3 | 285 |
| Thomas Merwin, s. [Thomas & Desire], b. May 30, 1809 | TM2 | 292 |
| Thomas Mervin, [s. Thomas & Desire], b. May 30, 1809 | TM3 | 8-9 |
| Warrin, s. Thomas & Desire, b. Sept. 9, 1798 | TM2 | 292 |
| Warren, d. between Sept. 18 & 25, 1819, ae 21; lost at sea | DR | |
| Warren, of East Haven, m. Caroline L. **ROBINSON**, of North Haven, Apr. 21, 1844, by Rev. Davis T. Shailer | TM4 | 203 |
| Willard, s. Thomas & Desire, b. Aug. 12, 1800 | TM2 | 292 |
| Willard, [s. Thomas & Desire], b. Aug. 12, 1800 | TM3 | 8-9 |
| William, s. Caleb, 2d., d. Aug. 11, 1801, ae 13 m. | DR | |
| William, [of Wolcott], d. [ ], 1804, at Cayuga, ae 30 | DR | |
| William, m. Sarah **THOMPSON**, b. of East Haven, Apr. 25, 1852, by Rev. D. W[illia]m Havens | TM4 | 217 |
| ----, ch. of Samuel, d. [Nov.] 7, 1742 | DR | |
| ----, ch. of Samuel, [d. Nov. 7, 1742] | TM2 | 24 |
| ----, ch. of Patterson, d. [ ], 1742 | DR | |
| ----, infant of Joseph, d. Apr. 8, 1783, ae 4 w. | DR | |
| ----, twin ch. of Ira, d. Dec. [ ], 1786, ae 1 d. | DR | |
| ----, twin ch. of Ira, d. [Jan.] 9, 1787, ae 5 w. | DR | |
| ----, ch. of Job, d. June [ ], 1802 | DR | |
| ----, infant of Asahel, d. [Dec.] 29, 1824, ae 2 w. | DR | |
| ----, ch. of Jacob, d. [Aug.] 31, 1845, ae 2 y. 3 m. | DR | |
| **SNOW**, Dorcas, Mrs., m. Joseph **LANCRAFT**, b. of [East Haven], Dec. 24, 1812, by Rev. Saul Clark | DR | |
| Nathan, of Lebanon, m. Dorcas **WAY**, of [East Haven], Nov. 27, 1808, by Rev. Saul Clark | DR | |
| **SOMERS**, Charles, d. [Apr.] 21, 1843, ae 50 | DR | |
| John Miles, d. [Dec.] 26, 1834, ae 30 | DR | |
| **SPINKS, SPINK**, Betsey, d. Richard, d. Apr. 2, 1801, ae 7 | DR | |
| Betsey, d. [Richard & Hannah], b. Jan. 2, 1805 | TM2 | 298 |
| Hannah, d. Richard & Hannah, b. Apr. 17, 1803 | TM2 | 298 |

| | Vol. | Page |
|---|---|---|
| **SPINKS, SPINK**, (cont.), | | |
| Hannah, m. Benjamin **TYLER**, b. of Branford, July 4, 1825, by | | |
| Stephen Dodd | TM3 | 207 |
| Samuel, s. Richard & Hannah, b. Dec. 9, 1799 | TM2 | 298 |
| Samuel, m. Esther **TYLER**, July 24, 1823, by Stephen Dodd | TM3 | 167 |
| **SPRAGUE**, Hannah, d. John, b. Oct. 3, 1753 | TM2 | 27 |
| **[SQUIRE], SQUARE, SQUYRE**, Jeremiah A., of East Windsor, m. | | |
| Lovisa Amanda **BRADLEY**, of East Haven, Jan. | | |
| 15, 1840, by Rev. Stephen Dodd | DR | |
| Jeremiah A., of East Windsor, m. Louisa A. **BRADLEY**, of | | |
| East Haven, Jan. 15, 1840, by Stephen Dodd | TM3 | 327 |
| **STANFORD**, Selina, of [East Haven], m. George **REDFIELD**, Sept. 25, | | |
| 1828, by Rev. Stephen Dodd | DR | |
| **STANNARD**, Darius, of Westbrook, m. Mary Ann **KELSEY**, of Clinton, | | |
| Oct. 5, 1846, by Stephen Dodd | TM4 | 206 |
| **STANSBURY**, Samuel, d. May 24, 1822, ae 51 | DR | |
| **STEPHENS**, [see under STEVENS] | | |
| **STETSON**, Louisa, m. Asa **BRADLEY**, b. of New Haven, Oct. 6, 1836, | | |
| by Rev. Stephen Dodd | DR | |
| **STEVENS, STEPHENS, STEUENS**, Catherin, m. Elizur R. **DAVIS**, b. of | | |
| Fair Haven, Oct. 4, 1851, by Rev. D. W[illia]m | | |
| Havens | TM4 | 217 |
| Elifalet, s. Jam[e]s, b. Jan. 24, 1716/17 | TM1 | 199 |
| Esther, of Killingworth, m. Lewis **BROCKETT**, of East Haven, | | |
| Dec. 23, 1838, by Rev. Stephen Dodd | DR | |
| Esther, of Killingworth, m. Lewis **BROCKETT**, of East Haven, | | |
| Dec. 23, 1838, by Stephen Dodd | TM3 | 325 |
| Samuell, s. Jam[e]s, b. Sept. 6, 1718 | TM1 | 199 |
| **STILSON**, Louisa, m. Asa **BRADLEY**, 2nd, b. of New Haven, Oct. 30, | | |
| 1836, by Stephen Dodd | TM3 | 285 |
| **STORER**, Mary Street, w. William, [of] New Haven, d. [May] [  ], 1836, | | |
| ae 53 | DR | |
| **STOW**, Charles, m. Asenath **SMITH**, b. of [East Haven, Nov.] 22, 1809, | | |
| by Rev. Saul Clark | DR | |
| **STREET**, Anna, [of Northford], d. June 19, 1792, ae 17 | DR | |
| Benjamin, m. Maria **THOMPSON**, b. of East Haven, May 14, | | |
| 1840, by Rev. Stephen Dodd | DR | |
| Benjamin, m. Maria **THOMPSON**, b. of East Haven, May 14, | | |
| 1840, by Stephen Dodd | TM3 | 327 |
| Charlotte A., of [East Haven], m. Horace Rowe **HOTCHKISS**, | | |
| of New Haven, Feb. 22, 1824, by Rev. Stephen | | |
| Dodd | DR | |
| Charlotte A., m. Horace R. **HOTCHKISS**, Feb. 22, 1824, by | | |
| Stephen Dodd | TM3 | 168 |
| Cornelia C., of East Haven, m. Samuel R. **HOTCHKISS**, May | | |
| 5, 1847, by Rev. Stephen Dodd | DR | |
| Cornelia C., m. Samuel R. **HOTCHKISS**, b. of East Haven | | |
| May 5, 1847, by Stephen Dodd | TM4 | 207 |
| Damaris, w. Elnathan, [of Wallingford], d. May 22, 1787, ae 87 | DR | |
| Desire, d. Nicholas & Desire, b. Aug. 16, 1761 | TM2 | 156 |
| Desire, w. Rev. Nicholas, d. [Jan.] 27, 1765, ae 20 | DR | |
| Desire, [w. Rev. Nicholas], d. Jan. 27, 1765 | TM2 | 156 |
| Elnathan, s. Nicholas & Hannah, b. Feb. 16, 1774 | TM2 | 156 |

| STREET, (cont.), | Vol. | Page |
|---|---|---|
| Elnathan, [of Wallingford], d. Nov. 30, [1787?], ae 92 | DR | |
| Elnathan, m. Clarissa MORRIS, b. of [East Haven], Nov. 12, 1802, by Rev. Nicholas Street | DR | |
| Eunecia, d. Nicholas & Desire, b. Oct. 27, 1759 | TM2 | 156 |
| Francis Ann, d. [Oct.] 16, 1837, ae 27 | DR | |
| Hannah, wid. Rev. Samuel, d. [July] 19, 1730 | DR | |
| Hannah, d. [Rev.] Nicholas & Hannah, b. Mar. 8, 1767 | TM2 | 156 |
| Hannah, w. Rev. Nicholas, d. Oct. 9, 1802, ae 61 | DR | |
| Hannah, d. Rev. Nicholas, & wid. Reuben MOULTHROP, d. June 9, 1848, ae 81 y. 3 m.; at West Haven | DR | |
| Harriet, of [East Haven], m. Edward PLANT, of Branford, [Sept.] 12, 1831, by Rev. Stephen Dodd | DR | |
| Harriett Jennett, of East Haven, m. Edward PLANT, of Branford, Sept. 12, 1831, by Stephen Dodd | TM3 | 234 |
| Horatio Gates, m. Lois HOLT, of [East Haven], June 21, 1801, by Rev. Nicholas Street | DR | |
| Jane, m. Nathaniel THOMPSON, b. of [East Haven], Sept. 13, 1825, by Rev. Stephen Dodd | DR | |
| Jane C., of East Haven, m. Nathaniel F. THOMPSON, of New Haven, Sept. 13, 1825, by Stephen Dodd | TM3 | 207 |
| Jesse, [of Northford], d. Mar. 22, 1784, ae 43 | DR | |
| Justin W., d. [May] 29, 1830, ae 52 | DR | |
| Justin Washington, s. [Rev.] Nicholas & Hannah, b. Nov. 4, 1777 | TM2 | 156 |
| Lois, w. Moses A., d. July 13, 1821, ae 43 | DR | |
| Lois Marina, d. Moses A., d. Nov. 6, 1813, ae 6 | DR | |
| Lucinda, d. Nicholas & Desire, b. July 17, 1763 | TM2 | 156 |
| Lucy Morris, of East Haven, m. Russel Smith CHIDSEY, of Easton, Pa., Sept. 15, 1847, by Rev. D. William Havens | DR | |
| Lucy Morris, of East Haven, m. Russell Smith CHIDSEY, of Easton, Penn., Sept. 15, 1847, by Rev. D. W[illia]m Havens | TM4 | 208 |
| Maria M., of [East Haven], m. Lucius HOTCHKISS, of New Haven, Oct. 18, 1827, by Rev. Stephen Dodd | DR | |
| Maria M., of East Haven, m. Lucius HOTCHKISS, of New Haven, Oct. 18, 1827, by Stephen Dodd | TM3 | 173 |
| Moses A., d. Feb. 24, 1824, ae 53 | DR | |
| Moses Augustine, s. Rev. Nicholas, d. May 3, 1769, ae 14 w. | DR | |
| Moses Augustinus, s. [Rev.] Nicholas & Hannah, b. Jan. 29, [1769]; d. May 3, 1769 | TM2 | 156 |
| Moses Augustinus, 2nd, s. Nicholas & Hannah, b. Apr. 3, 1770 | TM2 | 156 |
| Nicholas, Rev., father of the STREET family, d. Apr. 22, 1674 | DR | |
| Nicholas, Rev. "ordained to his pastoral office over the Church of Christ, in East Haven, Oct. 8, 1755" | TM2 | 156 |
| Nicholas, Rev., m. Mrs. Desire THOMPSON, Dec. 6, 1758, by Rev. Dr. Dagget, of Yale College | TM2 | 156 |
| Nicholas, Rev., m. Mrs. Hannah AUSTIN, of New Haven, Apr. 24, 1766, by Rev. Sam[ue]ll Bird, of New Haven | TM2 | 156 |
| Nicholas, s. Nicholas & Hannah, b. Mar. 22, 1772 | TM2 | 156 |
| Nicholas, m. Betsey MORRIS, b. of [East Haven], Sept. 6, 1801, by Rev. Nicholas Street | DR | |

| STREET, (cont.), | Vol. | Page |
|---|---|---|
| Nicholas, Rev. d. Oct. 8, 1806, ae 76 | DR | |
| Phillip, d. Mar. 3, 1849, ae 32 | DR | |
| Polly, d. [Rev.] Nicholas & Hannah, b. Oct. 6, 1782 | TM2 | 156 |
| Samuel, Rev., of Wallingford, d. Jan. 16, 1717, in the 43 y. of his ministry, ae above 75 | DR | |
| -----, had servant, Thomas, d. May 25, 1791, ae 57 | DR | |
| STRONG, Sally, d. Feb. 21, 1842, ae 58 | DR | |
| TAINTOR, Nathaniel, d. Aug. 25, 1848, ae 65 | DR | |
| TAYLOR, TAILOR, James, d. [      ], 1695 | DR | |
| Lois, of Collinsville, m. Charles JACOBS, of East Haven, Nov. 26, 1851, by Rev. D. W[illia]m Havens | TM4 | 217 |
| THATCHER, THACHER, Elizur Hill, s. Stephen & Nancy, b. Nov. 1, 1817 | TM3 | 170 |
| John Collins, s. [Stephen & Nancy], b. Sept. 30, 1820 | TM3 | 170 |
| Maria Elizabeth, d. [Stephen & Nancy], b. May 25, 1824 | TM3 | 170 |
| Nancy A., of East Haven, m. John A. BUSH, of Madison, Apr. 5, 1842, by Stephen Dodd | TM4 | 201 |
| Nancy Aaa, d. [Stephen & Nancy], b. June 7, 1823 (Probably "Nancy Ann") | TM3 | 170 |
| Nancy Ann, of East Haven, m. John A. BUSH, of Madison, Apr. 5, 1842, by Rev. Stephen Dodd | DR | |
| Sarah Huldah, d. [Stephen & Nancy], b. July 2, 1819 | TM3 | 170 |
| Stephen, of New Haven, m. Nancy HUGHES, of [East Haven], Oct. 15, 1812, by Rev. Saul Clark | DR | |
| Stephen, Lieut., d. [Oct.] 19, 1846, ae 53 | DR | |
| THOMAS, Andrew Jackson, s. John A., d. [May] 23, 1832, ae 2 | DR | |
| Elvira, d. John A., d. May 18, 1832, ae 4 | DR | |
| Harriet, [d.] John A., d. Oct. 2, 1823, ae 7 | DR | |
| Harriet, w. John A., d. May 3, 1827, ae 30 | DR | |
| Harriet, d. John A., d. [May] 22, 1832, ae 1 | DR | |
| John A., Capt., d. [Jan.] 18, 1841, ae 69 y. 10 m. | DR | |
| Mary, d. John A., d. Sept. 25, 1831, ae 10 | DR | |
| Samuel, s. John A., d. [May] 31, 1832, ae 8 | DR | |
| THOMPSON, THOMSON, THOMSUN, Abygall, d. Samuell, b. Oct. 21, 1704 | TM1 | 30 |
| Abigail, d. Samuel, d. [Dec.] 28, 1712, ae 8 | DR | |
| Abygall, d. [Sammuell], d. Dec. 28, 1712 | TM1 | 31 |
| Abraham, s. James, d. [Sept.] 27, 1813, ae 1 | DR | |
| Abraham, m. Louisa FORBES, [May] 28, 1837, by Rev. Mr. Stebbins, ex. d. | DR | |
| Abraham, Jr., m. Louisa FORBES, May 28, 1837, by Rev. Stephen W. Stebbins | TM3 | 324 |
| Abraham, [of] Southend, d. May 6, 1848, ae 76 y. 3 m. | DR | |
| Albert T., m. Jane Ann BYINGTON, Oct. 13, 1831, by Rev. John Mitchell, of Fair Haven | TM3 | 283 |
| Amos, s. Stephen, d. [Aug.] 17, 1750, ae 5 | DR | |
| Amos, d. Sept. 24, 1817, ae 66 | DR | |
| Anna A., of East Haven, m. Henry W. LYMAN, of New Haven, Nov. 25, 1850, by Rev. Henry Townsend, in Christ Church | TM4 | 214 |
| Anne, of [East Haven], m. David RITTER, of New Haven, Feb. 15, 1802, by Rev. Nicholas Street | DR | |

| | Vol. | Page |
|---|---|---|
| **THOMPSON, THOMSON, THOMSUN,** (cont.), | | |
| Anson, of [East Haven], m. Sally **BARNES**, of North Haven, | | |
| Apr. [ ], 1816, by Rev. Saul Clark | DR | |
| Asahel, m. Jennett **HENINWAY**, b. of East Haven, Dec. 14, | | |
| 1834, by Rev. Stephen Dodd | DR | |
| Asahel, m. Jennett **HENINWAY**, b. of East Haven, Dec. 14, | | |
| 1834, by Stephen Dodd | TM3 | 282 |
| Augustus, d. [Dec.] 25, 1846, ae 66 | DR | |
| Bethia, w. John, d. [Apr.] 25, 1843, ae 39 | DR | |
| Betsey, d. Moses, d. [Sept.] 28, 1801, ae 12 | DR | |
| Caroline, d. Nathaniel F., d. Dec. 4, 1831, ae 2 | DR | |
| Catharine L., of East Haven, m. Henry C. **HOWD**, of | | |
| Wallingford, Apr. 29, 1852, by Rev. D. W[illia]m | | |
| Havens | TM4 | 218 |
| Charles, d. June 2, 1810, ae 28 | DR | |
| Daniel, of [East Haven], m. Harriet **CLARK**, of Granby, July | | |
| 26, 1829, by Rev. Stephen Dodd | DR | |
| Daniel, of East Haven, m. Harriet **CLARK**, July 26, 1829, by | | |
| Stephen Dodd | TM3 | 231 |
| Desire, Mrs., m. Rev. Nicholas **STREET**, Dec. 6, 1758, by Rev. | | |
| Dr. Dagget, of Yale College | TM2 | 156 |
| Desire, wid. Moses, d. Dec. 30, 1765, ae 58 | DR | |
| Desire, d. Samuel & Desire, b. Nov. 29, 1771 | TM2 | 292 |
| Desire, d. Timothy, d. [ ], 1774, ae 18 | DR | |
| Desire, m. Thomas **SMITH**, Oct. 16, 1792 | TM2 | 266 |
| Desire, m. Levi **SMITH**, b. of [East Haven], June 8, 1812, by | | |
| Rev. Saul Clark | DR | |
| Desire, w. Stephen d. Apr. 15, 1813, ae 30 | DR | |
| Desire, w. Samuel, d. [Dec.] 31, 1814, ae 78 | DR | |
| Desire, m. John **FERRIN**, b. of East Haven, Feb. 15, 1828, by | | |
| Stephen Dodd | TM3 | 174 |
| Desire, of [East Haven], m. John **FARREN**, 2d, [Feb ], 1829, | | |
| by Rev. Stephen Dodd | DR | |
| Desire, wid. Moses, res. New Haven, d. [Apr.] 10, 1833, ae 76; | | |
| bd. [East Haven] | DR | |
| Dorcas, w. John, d. [Oct.] 20, 1835, ae 75 y. 8 m. | DR | |
| Edward B., m. Ruth P. **WARD**, b. of East Haven, Oct. 11, | | |
| 1838, by Rev. Stephen Dodd | DR | |
| Edward B., m. Ruth P. **WARD**, b. of East Haven, Oct. 11, | | |
| 1838, by Stephen Dodd | TM3 | 325 |
| Edward Ellsworth, m. Sarah Caroline **SMITH**, Dec. 12, 1847, | | |
| by Rev. D. W[illia]m Havens | TM4 | 209 |
| Edward Ellsworth, m. Sarah Caroline **SMITH**, b. of East | | |
| Haven, Dec. 17, 1847, by Rev. D. William Havens | DR | |
| Eleanor, wid. John, the first, d. Apr. 8, 1690 | DR | |
| Elizabeth, wid. Samuel, d. [Dec.] 31, 1790, ae 80 | DR | |
| Elizabeth, m. William **BRINTNAL**, of New Haven, May 19, | | |
| 1804, by Rev. Nicholas Street | DR | |
| Elizabeth A., m. Thomas **BARNES**, b. of East Haven, [Nov.] | | |
| 25, 1840, by Rev. Stephen Dodd | DR | |
| Elisabeth A., m. Thomas **BARNES**, b. of East Haven, Nov. | | |
| 25, 1840, by Stephen Dodd | TM3 | 328 |
| Esther, d. Amos, d. Mar. 9, 1797, ae 1 | DR | |

| THOMPSON, THOMSON, THOMSUN, (cont.), | Vol. | Page |
|---|---|---|
| Esther, d. Timothy, d. July [ ], 1802, ae 2 | DR | |
| Esther, w. Timothy, d. Apr. 23, 1803, ae 74 | DR | |
| Esther, w. John, 2d, d. [July] 15, 1825, ae 25 | DR | |
| Esther, d. Timothy, d. [Sept.] 3, 1825, ae 14 | DR | |
| Eunecia, w. Timothy, d. [Aug.] 15, 1825, ae 55 | DR | |
| George, m. Susan BRADLEY, b. of [East Haven], Apr. 22, 1811, by Rev. Saul Clark | DR | |
| Hannah, w. Stephen, d. Nov. 12, 1776, ae 52 | DR | |
| Henry, s. James, d. July 2, 1831, ae 25 | DR | |
| Hezekiah, d. [July] 30, 1793, ae 21 | DR | |
| Hezekiah, s. Amos & Mary, b. Aug. 8, 1793 | TM3 | 12 |
| Hezekiah, d. Dec. 16, 1814, ae 21; in the army | DR | |
| Horace, m. Esther HEMINWAY, b. of East Haven, Apr. 17, 1822, by Rev. Oliver Willson, of North Haven | TM3 | 165 |
| Horace, m. Hannah C. BARNES, b. of East Haven, May 27, 1839, by Rev. Stephen Dodd | DR | |
| Horace, m. Hannah C. BARNES, b. of East Haven, May 27, 1839, by Stephen Dodd | TM3 | 326 |
| Huldah, d. Amos, d. Mar. 24, 1792, ae 1 | DR | |
| Isaac, s. Jared, d. Sept. 3, 1790, ae 3 | DR | |
| Isaac, d. [Feb.] 6, 1829, ae 50 | DR | |
| Jacob, d. Sept. 3, 1821, ae 29; by shipwreck | DR | |
| James, d. Dec. 1, 1777, ae 42 | DR | |
| James, s. John, d. [Mar.] 23, 1799, ae 5 | DR | |
| James, Jr., m. Leura WOODWARD, b. of [East Haven], Oct. 28, 1832, by Rev. Stephen Dodd | DR | |
| James, Jr., m. Leura WOODWARD, b. of East Haven, Oct. 28, 1832, by Rev. Stephen Dodd | TM3 | 235 |
| James 2d, Lieut. d. Aug. 14, 1838, (on board the revenue cutter Wolcott), ae 39 | DR | |
| James, s. James, Jr., d. [Mar.] 13, 1845, ae 4 m. | DR | |
| John, father of the East Haven THOMPSONS, d. Dec. 11, 1674 | DR | |
| John, Jr., Serg. d. Feb. 13, 1693 | DR | |
| John, 3d., d. Apr. 25, 1721, ae 54 | DR | |
| John, s. John, b. Oct. 21, 1721 | TM1 | 245 |
| John, Serg., d. Nov. 3, 1742, ae 51 | DR | |
| John, Sergt., [d. Nov. 3, 1742] | TM2 | 24 |
| John, d. Feb. 12, 1780, ae 26; at sea | DR | |
| John, s. John, d. [Oct.] 23, 1795, ae 12 | DR | |
| John, [of] Southend, d. [Sept.] 11, 1838, ae 85 y. 6 m. | DR | |
| John, m. Mary Jane LUDDINGTON, b. of East Haven, Dec. 29, 1843, by Rev. Stephen Dodd | DR | |
| John, m. Mary Jane LUD[D]INGTON, b. of East Haven, Dec. 31, 1843, by Stephen Dodd | TM4 | 202 |
| Joseph, s. Serg. John, d. June 29, 1728, ae 18 | DR | |
| Joseph, s. John, b. Jan. 1, 1730/1 | TM1 | 248 |
| Julia Amanda, m. William TYLER, b. of East Haven, Dec. 22, 1833, by Rev. Stephen Dodd | DR | |
| Julia Amanda, m. William TYLER, b. of East Haven, Dec. 22, 1833, by Stephen Dodd | TM3 | 236 |

| THOMPSON, THOMSON, THOMSUN, (cont.), | Vol. | Page |
|---|---|---|
| Laurinda, of East Haven, m. Horace BARNES, of New Haven, | | |
| May 5, 1824, by Stephen Dodd | TM3 | 168 |
| Leonard, s. James, d. June 15, 1831, ae 29 | DR | |
| Lois, wid. Stephen, Jr., d. [Mar.] 17, 1823, ae 70 | DR | |
| Lois, w. Joel, d. [ ], 1824, ae 59 | DR | |
| Lois, of [East Haven], m. Horace BARNES], of New Haven, | | |
| May 5, 1824, by Rev. Stephen Dodd | DR | |
| Louisa, w. Abraham, Jr., d. June 3, 1845, ae 28 | DR | |
| Lucy, of [East Haven], m. Marvin SMITH, of Mendon, N. Y., | | |
| Apr. 3, 1826, by Rev. Stephen Dodd | DR | |
| Lucy, of East Haven, m. Marvin SMITH, of Meriden, N. Y., | | |
| Apr. 3, 1826, by Stephen Dodd | TM3 | 171 |
| Lue, d. [Sept.] 8, 1833, ae 37 | DR | |
| Marah, d. Samuell, b. Apr. 30, 1709 | TM1 | 31 |
| Marcy, d. Samuel, [d. , 1736], ae 8 y. | TM2 | 23 |
| Marcy, see also Mercy | TM2 | 23 |
| Maria, m. Benjamin STREET, b. of East Haven, May 14, | | |
| 1840, by Rev. Stephen Dodd | DR | |
| Maria, m. Benjamin STREET, b. of East Haven, May 14, | | |
| 1840, by Stephen Dodd | TM3 | 327 |
| Mary, d. Samuel, [d. , 1736, ae 2 y. | TM2 | 23 |
| Mary, d. Samuel, of Foxon, d. [ ], 1737, ac 2 | DR | |
| Mary, wid. John, d. Nov. [ ], 1786, ae 85 | DR | |
| Mary, w. Amos, d. Nov. 2, 1815, ae 62 | DR | |
| Mary, Mrs. of [East Haven], m. Elam BRADLEY, of Hamden, | | |
| Nov. 6, 1815, by Rev. Saul Clark | DR | |
| Mary, wid. Samuel, d. June 2, 1817, ae 52 | DR | |
| Mary, wid. Stephen, d. Dec. 16, 1817, ae 82 | DR | |
| Mary, of [East Haven], m. Laban PARDEE, of New Haven, | | |
| June 1, 1824, by Rev. Stephen Dodd | DR | |
| Mary, of East Haven, m. Laban PARDEE, of New Haven, | | |
| June 1, 1824, by Stephen Dodd | TM3 | 169 |
| Mary E., of East Haven, m. Andrew J. CULVER, of | | |
| Wallingford, Aug. 20, 1848, by Rev. D. William | | |
| Havens | DR | |
| Mary E., of East Haven, m. Andrew J. CULVER, of | | |
| Wallingford, Aug. 20, 1848, by Rev. D. W[illia]m | | |
| Havens | TM4 | 210 |
| Mahittabel, d. Sammuell, b. Jan. 16, 1710 | TM1 | 31 |
| Mercy, d. Samuel, of Foxon, d. Mar. 12, 1737, ae 8 | DR | |
| Mercy, wid. John, d. Jan. 9, 1744, ae 77 | DR | |
| Mercy, see also Marcy | | |
| Merrit, m. Julia DAVIDSON, June 14, 1846, by Rev. George | | |
| W. Nichols | TM4 | 206 |
| Merrit, m. Julia DAVIDSON, of East Haven, June 30, 1846, by | | |
| Rev. George W. Nichols | DR | |
| Moses, m. Desier HEMINWA[Y], Dec. 10, 1724, by Rev. Mr. | | |
| Heminway, b. of East Haven | TM1 | 245 |
| Moses, s. Moses, d. [Aug.] 27, 1743, ae 17 | DR | |
| Moses, s. Moses, [d. Aug. 27, 1743] | TM2 | 25 |
| Moses, d. [Feb.] 17, 1761, ae 63 | DR | |
| Moses, d. May 15, 1804, ae 40 | DR | |

**THOMPSON, THOMSON, THOMSUN,** (cont.),                              Vol.     Page
Nancy, of [East Haven], m. William **WOODWARD**, Feb. 15,
    1829, by Rev. Stephen Dodd                     DR
Nancy, m. William **WOODWARD**, b. of East Haven, Feb. 15,
    1829, by Stephen Dodd                          TM3      174
Nathaniel, m. Jane **STREET**, b. of [East Haven], Sept. 13,
    1825, by Rev. Stephen Dodd                     DR
Nathaniel F., of New Haven, m. Jane C. **STREET**, of East
    Haven, Sept. 13, 1825, by Stephen Dodd         TM3      207
Orlando, d. [          ], 1804, ae 20; in West Indies                 DR
Orrin, m. Sarah **THOMPSON**, of East Haven, June 11, 1834,
    by Rev. Stephen Dodd                           DR
Orren m. Sarah **THOMPSON**, June 11, 1834, by Stephen
    Dodd                                           TM3      281
Polly, of [East Haven], m. Hiram **HOLT**, of Harwinton,
    [          ], 1816, by Rev. Saul Clark          DR
Priscilla, wid. Serg. John, d. [          ], 1726, ae 80              DR
Presilla, d. [          ]                                             TM1      245
Ransom, s. Stephen, d. [          ], 1795, ae 9                       DR
Rebecca, Mrs., of [East Haven], m. Alfred **HEMINWAY**,
    [May] 20, 1832, by Rev. Stephen Dodd           DR
Rebekah, m. Alfred **HEMINWAY**, b. of East Haven, May 20,
    1832, by Stephen Dodd                          TM3      234
Samuell, s. Samuell, b. June 3, 1711                                  TM1      31
Samuel, d. Dec. 25, 1712, ae 36                                       DR
Sammuell, d. Dec. 25, 1712                                           TM1      31
Samuel, d. [          ], 1717, ae 41                                  DR
Samuel, s. Samuel, d. Feb. 25, 1726, ae 6                            DR
Samuel, s. Samuel, [d.          , 1736] ae 5 y.                       TM2      23
Samuel, s. Samuel, of Foxon, d. [Feb.] 25, 1737, ae 5                DR
Samuel, d. Sept. 8, 1756, ae 46                                       DR
Samuel, s. Samuel, d. May 28, 1767, ae 24                            DR
Samuel, had negro ch., Chloe, d. [          ], 1773, ae 4            DR
Samuel, d. [Jan.] 13, 1786, ae 81                                     DR
Samuel, m. Mary **CURTIS**, b. of [East Haven], July 17, 1815,
    by Rev. Saul Clark                             DR
Samuel, d. Feb. [ ], 1817, ae 80                                     DR
Samuel C., m. Grace Ann **HOTCHKISS**, b. of [East Haven],
    Sept. 9, 1832, by Rev. Stephen Dodd            DR
Samuel C., m. Grace Ann **HOTCHKISS**, b. of East Haven,
    Sept. 9, 1832, by Stephen Dodd                 TM3      235
Samuel Curtis, s. Samuel C., [of] New Haven, d. Mar. 17, 1838,
    [in] East Haven, ae 14 m.                      DR
Sarah, d. Samuel, b. Nov. 28, 1706                                   TM1      30
Sarah, d. John, Jr., b. Jan. 17, 1718                                TM1      199
Sarah, wid. John, d. Jan. 9, 1749, ae 54                            DR
Sarah, d. Stephen, Jr., d. [May] 14, 1792, ae 2                     DR
Sarah, d. Moses, d. [Dec.] 12, 1805, ae 10                          DR
Sarah, wid. Anthony, d. [May] 17, 1806, ae 87                       DR
Sarah, m. John **HEMINWAY**, Jr., b. of [East Haven], Aug. 27,
    1818, by Rev. Stephen Dodd                     DR
Sarah, d. Abraham, d. June 3, 1821, ae 10 m.                        DR

| | Vol. | Page |
|---|---|---|
| **THOMPSON, THOMSON, THOMSUN,** (cont.), | | |
| Sarah, of East Haven, m. Orrin **THOMPSON**, June 11, 1834, | | |
| by Rev. Stephen Dodd | DR | |
| Sarah, m. Orren **THOMPSON**, June 11, 1834,by Stephen | | |
| Dodd | TM3 | 281 |
| Sarah, m. William **SMITH**, b. of East Haven, Apr. 25, 1852, by | | |
| Rev. D. W[illia]m Havens | TM4 | 217 |
| Stuen, s. John, b. Dec. 25, 1723        (Stephen) | TM1 | 245 |
| Stephen, Jr., m. Sally **GRANNIS**, Feb. 18, 1799, by Rev. | | |
| Nicholas Street | DR | |
| Stephen, Jr., d. Feb. 9, 1802, ae 40 | DR | |
| Stephen, d. Nov. 10, 1808, ae 85 | DR | |
| Sylvester, d. Aug. 5, 1810, ae 20 | DR | |
| Timothy, s. John, b. Dec. 26, 1727 | TM1 | 248 |
| Timothy, d. Nov. 26, 1807, ae 88 | DR | |
| Willet, s. Timothy, d. [Sept.] 18, 1825, ae 23 | DR | |
| William, m. Olive **RUSSEL**, b. of [East Haven], Nov. 2, 1828, | | |
| by Rev. Stephen Dodd | DR | |
| William, m. Olive **RUSSELL**, b. of East Haven, Nov. 2, 1828, | | |
| by Stephen Dodd | TM3 | 174 |
| -----, infant [of] Jared, d. May 4, 1788, ae 4 w. | DR | |
| -----, infant, [of] Timothy, d. [Jan.] 30, 1805, ae 3 d. | DR | |
| -----, ch. [of] Edward, d. [May] 4, 1837, ae 1 | DR | |
| **THROCKMORTON**, Robert B., of Lexington, Ky., m. Sarah **FLAGG**, of | | |
| [East Haven, Nov.] 13, 1825, by Rev. Stephen Dodd | DR | |
| Robert B., of Lexington, Ky., m. Sarah **FLAGG**, of | | |
| East Haven, Nov. 13, 1825, by Stephen Dodd | TM3 | 207 |
| **TODD**, Anson, d. Oct. 16, 1821, ae 18 | DR | |
| E[l]isabeth, m. Jonathan **GOODSELL**, Jan. 12, 1738/9, by | | |
| Rev. [                    ] | TM2 | 20 |
| Sarah, of [East Haven], m. Abijah **PARDEE**, Jan. 14, 1824, by | | |
| Rev. Stephen Dodd | DR | |
| Sarah, m. Abijah **PARDEE**, Jr., Jan. 14, 1824, by Stephen | | |
| Dodd | TM3 | 168 |
| -----, infant [of          ], d. [Jan.] 12, 1812, ae 3 w. | DR | |
| **TOOLEY**, Edmund, d. [          ], 1684 | DR | |
| **TOWNSEND**, Samuel, d. [Aug.] 31, 1795, ae 53 | DR | |
| Sarah, wid. Samuel, d. Feb. 17, 1801, ae 64 | DR | |
| **TRUMBULL**, Benjamin, Dr., of Cambridge, N. Y., m. Lydia C. | | |
| **MORRIS**, of [East Haven], Mar. 22, 1817, by Rev. | | |
| Saul Clark | DR | |
| **TUCKER**, -----, infant [of] Noah, d. Oct. 2, 1773, ae 1 d. | DR | |
| **TURNER**, John, m. Almira **LUDDINGTON**, b. of New Haven, Sept. 17, | | |
| 1823, by Stephen Dodd | TM3 | 167 |
| **TUTTLE, TUTTEL**, Abigail, w. Christopher, d. [Nov.] 10, 1813, ae 49 | DR | |
| Abraham, s. Stephen, d. [Sept.] 19, 1790, ae 2 | DR | |
| Amasa, s. Samuel, d. Sept. 3, 1762, ae 5 d. | DR | |
| Ame, d. Joseph, d. [Nov.] 20, 1736, ae 10 | DR | |
| Amee, d. Joseph, [d.         ], 1736, ae 10 y. | TM2 | 23 |
| Anna, d. Timothy, d. Aug. 31, 1770, ae 16 | DR | |
| Anna, w. Joel, [of Guilford], d. Oct. 2, 1775, ae 26 | DR | |
| Anna, wid. Timothy, d. Mar. 17, 1782, ae 50 | DR | |
| Bethiah, d. Samuel, d. Apr. 15, 1772, ae 14 d. | DR | |

| TUTTLE, TUTTEL, (cont.), | Vol. | Page |
|---|---|---|
| Bethiah, wid. Samuel, d. Apr. 20, 1824, ae 82 | DR | |
| Bethiah Miles, d. Samuel, d. Oct. 3, 1770, ae 7 | DR | |
| Charlotte M., m. Harvey **BARNES**, 2nd, Dec. 4, 1849, by B. Hart | TM4 | 213 |
| Christopher, m. Mary **DAWSON**, b. of [East Haven], May 1, 1815, by Rev. Saul Clark | DR | |
| Christopher, d. June 29, 1839, ae 79 y. 9 m. | DR | |
| Comfort, ch. [of] Joseph, d. [Nov.] 27, 1736, ae 5 | DR | |
| Comfort, d. Joseph, [d.          ], 1736, ae 5 y. | TM2 | 23 |
| Daniel, s. Joseph, b. Oct. 28, 1767 | TM2 | 47 |
| Daniel, d. [          ], 1793, ae 25; in West Indies | DR | |
| Daniel, d. [Aug.] 14, 1807, ae 58 | DR | |
| Desire, d. Eliphelit, b. May 5, 1743 | TM2 | 26 |
| Elizabeth, w. William, d. Dec. 30, 1684, ae 72 | DR | |
| Emily, d. Frederick W., d. [June] 30, 1832, ae 1 m. | DR | |
| Easter, d. Eliphelit, b. Feb. 19, 1746/7 | TM2 | 26 |
| Esther, d. Fred W., d. July 19, 1841, ae 22 | DR | |
| Eve Ely Gates, wid. Capt. Josiah, d. [Aug.] 18, 1838, ae 67 | DR | |
| Frederick William, m. Polly **FROST**, of East Haven, in Christ Church, Jan. 1, 1810, by Rev. Bela Hubbard, D. D. | DR | |
| Hannah, w. Thomas, d. [Oct.] 15, 1710 | DR | |
| Hezekiah, of New Haven, m. Nancy Zemia **LANFEAR**, of [East Haven], Aug. 8, 1830, by Rev. Stephen Dodd | DR | |
| Hezekiah, of New Haven, m. Nancy Lemira **LANFEAR**, of East Haven, Aug. 8, 1830, by Stephen Dodd | TM3 | 232 |
| James H., m. P. Almena **HEMINGWAY**, Jan. 1, 1850, by Burdett Hart | TM4 | 213 |
| Jennette Maria, w. Charles, d. [Jan.] 30, 1847, ae 24 | DR | |
| Joel, s. Joseph, b. Oct. 28, 1718 | TM1 | 199 |
| Joel, d. June 30, 1789, ae 71 | DR | |
| Joel, [of Guilford], d. Nov. 30, 1822, ae 76 | DR | |
| John, s. Frederick W., d. [Mar.] 13, 1826, ae 3 | DR | |
| Joseph, d. [          ], 1690, ae 62 | DR | |
| Joseph, d. [Jan.] 16, 1761, ae 68 | DR | |
| Joseph, m. Polly **GOODSELL**, b. of [East Haven,          ], 1816, by Rev. Saul Clark | DR | |
| Joseph, d. Nov. 1, 1818, ae 29 | DR | |
| Josiah, s. Joseph, b. Sept. 4, 1762 | TM2 | 47 |
| Julia, d. Joel, [of Guilford], d. Mar. 4, 1791, ae 9 m. | DR | |
| Lydia Caroline, of East Haven, m. Aaron Atwater **HUGHES**, Jan. 20, 1822, by Rev. Joseph Perry | DR | |
| Marcy, w. Capt. Joseph, d. [Sept. 6, 1743] | TM2 | 25 |
| Marcy, m. Abram **HEMINWAY**, Apr. 24, 1746 | TM2 | 44 |
| Marcy, see also Mercy | | |
| Mary, d. Joseph, Jr., b. Dec. 22, 1720 | TM1 | 199 |
| Mary, w. Joseph, d. Sept. 5, 1740 | DR | |
| Mary, d. [Eliphalet], b. Mar. 23, 1740/1    (Marginal note: "Illeg.") | TM2 | 21 |
| Mary, d. Joel, d. July 7, 1766, ae 3 | DR | |
| Mary Ann, d. Aug. 2, 1833, ae 16 | DR | |
| Mehetable, d. Eliphelit, b. Mar. 20, 1745 | TM2 | 26 |
| Mercy, w. Joseph, d. [Sept.] 6, 1743, ae 46    (Marcy) | DR | |

| | Vol. | Page |
|---|---|---|
| **TUTTLE, TUTTEL**, (cont.), | | |
| Mercy, of [East Haven], m. Isaac **BLAKESLEY**, of North | | |
| Haven, Oct. 29, 1810, by Rev. Saul Clark | DR | |
| Mercy, see also Marcy | | |
| Miles, s. Samuel, d. [Feb.] 3, 1793, ae 17; in West Indies | DR | |
| Molle, d. Joseph, b. Mar. 9, 1765 | TM2 | 47 |
| Nabby, of [East Haven], m. Munson **BRADLEY**, of North | | |
| Haven, Jan. 5, 1818, by Rev. Stephen Dodd | DR | |
| Rachel, w. Noah, d. Apr. 7, 1749, ae 46 | DR | |
| Rebecca, w. Jonathan, d. May 2, 1676 | DR | |
| Rebecca, wid. Joel, d. Jan. 7, 1806, ae 87 | DR | |
| Reuben, of New Haven, m. Sarah **LUDDINGTON**, of [East | | |
| Haven, Oct.] 26, 1828, by Rev. Stephen Dodd | DR | |
| Reuben, of New Haven, m. Sarah **LUD[D]INGTON**, of East | | |
| Haven, Oct. 26, 1828, by Stephen Dodd | TM3 | 173 |
| Samuel, Jr., m. Betsey **HOTCHKISS**, Jan. 19, 1800, by Rev. | | |
| Nicholas Street | DR | |
| Samuel, d. [May] 20, 1817, ae 78 | DR | |
| Samuel Amma, s. Samuel, d. June 18, 1773, ae 6 | DR | |
| Sarah, d. Joel, [of Guilford], d. Jan. 23, 1803, ae 23 | DR | |
| Sarah Elizabeth, d. Frederick W., d. [June] 23, 1832, ae 14 m. | DR | |
| Sarah Smith, d. Christopher, d. Sept. 11, 1805, ae 17 m. | DR | |
| Smith, s. Christopher, d. Nov. 20, 1794, ae 2 | DR | |
| Thankfull, d. Joseph, b. Sept. 3, 1709 | TM1 | 31 |
| Thomas, d. [Oct.] 19, 1710, ae 68 | DR | |
| Timothy, Jr., d. [Apr.] 19, 1777, ae 17 | DR | |
| Timothy, Capt., d. Oct. 22, 1778, ae 54 | DR | |
| -----, infant of Samuel, d. Aug. 7, 1763, ae 1 d. | DR | |
| -----, s. Samuel M., d. [    ] 26, 1836, ae 4 w. | DR | |
| **TYLER**, Amma, s. John & Mable, b. Feb. 20, 1789 | TM2 | 264 |
| Amma, m. Lois **SMITH**, b. of [East Haven, Jan.] 19, 1818, by | | |
| Rev. Stephen Dodd | DR | |
| Amma, d. [Nov.] 18, 1818, ae 28; at St. Kitts | DR | |
| Archibal, of New Hartford, N. Y., m. wid. Mary E. **BEACH**, of | | |
| Branford, Feb. 12, 1844, by Benj[ami]n L. Swan | TM4 | 203 |
| Benjamin, m. Hannah **SPINKS**, b. of Branford, July 4, 1825, by | | |
| Stephen Dodd | TM3 | 207 |
| Betsey, of North Branford, m. Alden **SMITH**, Aug. 5, 1833, by | | |
| Stephen Dodd | TM3 | 236 |
| Charlotte M., of East Haven, m. Stephen **HEMINGWAY**, Oct. | | |
| 22, 1848, by Rev. N. S. Richardson | DR | |
| Charlotte M., m. Stephen **HEMINGWAY**, b. of East Haven, | | |
| Oct. 22, 1848, by Rev. N. S. Richardson | TM4 | 210 |
| Esther, m. Samuel **SPINKS**, July 24, 1823, by Stephen Dodd | TM3 | 167 |
| Esther, m. Justin **BRADLEY**, b. of East Haven, Nov. 14, 1839, | | |
| by Stephen Dodd | TM3 | 326 |
| Esther S., m. Justin **BRADLEY**, b. of East Haven, Nov. 14, | | |
| 1839, by Rev. Stephen Dodd | DR | |
| Jerusha Loisa, d. [John & Mable], b. May 2, 1805 | TM2 | 264 |
| John, s. [John & Mable], b. June 29, 1792 | TM2 | 264 |
| John, m. Eve Ely **SMITH**, b. of [East Haven], June 30, 1814, | | |
| by Rev. Saul Clark | DR | |
| John, Jr., d. [Sept.] 3, 1827, ae 35 | DR | |

| | Vol. | Page |
|---|---|---|
| **TYLER**, (cont.), | | |
| John, d. Apr. 12, 1829, ae 69 | DR | |
| Louis B., m. Lester **SMITH**, b. of East Haven, May 7, 1843, by | | |
| Stephen Dodd | TM4 | 202 |
| Louisa B., m. Lester **SMITH**, b. of East Haven, May 7, 1843, | | |
| by Rev. Stephen Dodd | DR | |
| Mabel, wid. John, d. Aug. 15, 1841, ae 78 y. 18 m. | DR | |
| Marvin, m. Harriet E. **PRINCE**, b. of East Haven, Sept. 14, | | |
| 1845, by Rev. Stephen Dodd | DR | |
| Marvin, m. Harriette E. **PRIME**, b. of East Haven, Sept. 14, | | |
| 1845, by Stephen Dodd | TM4 | 204 |
| Roxanna, of Branford, m. Samuel Edwin **CHIDSEY**, of East | | |
| Haven, Aug. 17, 1851, by Rev. Collis J. Potter, of | | |
| Wolcott, Conn. | TM4 | 214 |
| Sarah, of Branford, m. Elihu **SHEPARD**, of [East Haven], Jan. | | |
| 25, 1808, by Rev. Saul Clark | DR | |
| William, s. [John & Mable], b. June 26, 1799 | TM2 | 264 |
| William, m. Julia Amanda **THOMPSON**, b. of East Haven, | | |
| Dec. 22, 1833, by Rev. Stephen Dodd | DR | |
| William, m. Julia Amanda **THOMPSON**, b. of East Haven, | | |
| Dec. 22, 1833, by Stephen Dodd | TM3 | 236 |
| -----, twins of John, d. June [ ], 1796, ae 1 & 2 w. | DR | |
| **UPSON**, Julius, m. Mabel **ANDREWS**, b. of East Haven, [Apr.] 7, 1833, | | |
| by Rev. Stephen Dodd | DR | |
| Julius, m. Mabel **ANDREWS**, Apr. 7, 1833, by Stephen Dodd | TM3 | 236 |
| Selah, of Wolcot, m. Sally **PARDEE**, of [East Haven], Sept. 3, | | |
| 1826, by Rev. Stephen Dodd | DR | |
| Selah, of Wolcott, m. Sally **PARDEE**, of East Haven, Sept. 3, | | |
| 1826, by Stephen Dodd | TM3 | 171 |
| -----, s. Julius, d. [Feb.] 22, 1836, ae 3 w. | DR | |
| **UTTER**, Abraham, m. Ledia **RUSSELL**, June 27, 1715 | TM1 | 198 |
| Abraham, s. Abraham, b. Mar. 7, 1716 | TM1 | 198 |
| Isaac, s. Abram, b. Feb. 22, 1724/5 | TM1 | 245 |
| Ledia, d. Abram, b. Nov. 24, 1718 | TM1 | 245 |
| Mabel, wid. d. [Apr.] 20, 1782, ae 75 | DR | |
| Samuell, s. Abram, b. Dec. 18, 1722 | TM1 | 245 |
| **VEAL**, Edward, d. Dec. 2, 1773, ae 80 | DR | |
| **VICKARS**, Edward, d. [        ], 1684 | DR | |
| **WALKER**, Acklin E., m. Harriett A. **FARREN**, b. of East Haven, Jan. 30, | | |
| 1841, by Stephen Dodd | TM4 | 200 |
| Edwin Ackland, m. Harriet A. **FARREN**, b. of East Haven, Jan. | | |
| 30, 1841, by Rev. Stephen Dodd | DR | |
| Heman, d. Sept. 27, 1842, ae 27 | DR | |
| Jerusha, w. John B., d. Nov. 18, 1848, ae 61 | DR | |
| John, s. Jeames, b. Oct. 15, 1765 | TM2 | 47 |
| John, d. June 8, 1781, ae 16; in the battle on Long Island | DR | |
| Mary, d. Jeames, b. Jan. 29, 1770 | TM2 | 47 |
| William, s. Jeames, b. Feb. 6, 1766 | TM2 | 47 |
| -----, ch. [of] Nelson, d. Apr. 14, 1834, ae 1 | DR | |
| **WANTWOOD**, Benjamin, s. Benjamin, b. Feb. 20, 1714 | TM1 | 245 |
| **WARD**, Judith, w. William, d. Feb. 7, 1836, ae 45 | DR | |
| Lois, of East Haven, m. Benjamin **HOSLEY**, of Branford, Mar. | | |
| 27, 1849, by Rev. D. William Havens | DR | |

| | Vol. | Page |
|---|---|---|
| **WARD**, (cont.), | | |
| Lois, of East Haven, m. Benjamin A. **HOSLEY**, of Branford, | | |
| Mar. 27, 1849, by Rev. D. W[illia]m Havens | TM4 | 212 |
| Ruth P., m. Edward B. **THOMPSON**, b. of East Haven, Oct. | | |
| 11, 1838, by Rev. Stephen Dodd | DR | |
| Ruth P., m. Edward B. **THOMPSON**, b. of East Haven, Oct. | | |
| 11, 1838, by Stephen Dodd | TM3 | 325 |
| **WARREN**, Ralph, of New Haven, m. Almira **RUSSEL**, of East Haven, | | |
| [Aug.] 30, 1835, by Rev. Stephen Dodd | DR | |
| Ralph, of New Haven, m. Almira **RUSSELL**, of East Haven, | | |
| Aug. 30, 1835, by Stephen Dodd | TM3 | 283 |
| **WARTS**, [see under **WORKS**] | | |
| **WASHBURN**, Abigail, d. John, d. [July] 29, 1745, ae 7 | DR | |
| **WAY**, Abigail, d. Timothy, b. Dec. 7, 1766 | TM2 | 47 |
| Abigail, w. Timothy, d. Dec. 15, 1766, ae 23 | DR | |
| Dauid, s. Dauid, b. July 25, 1723 | TM1 | 248 |
| Dorcas, d. Timothy, d. May 2, 1772, ae 2 | DR | |
| Dorcas, of [East Haven], m. Nathan **SNOW**, of Lebanon, Nov. | | |
| 27, 1808, by Rev. Saul Clark | DR | |
| Elizabeth, of [East Haven], m. Isaac **BASSETT**, of New Haven, | | |
| May 1, 1808, by Rev. Saul Clark | DR | |
| Esther, d. Dauid, b. Sept. 22, 1720 | TM1 | 248 |
| Esther, d. David, d. [Sept.] 22, 1743, ae 23 | DR | |
| Hannah, d. Dauid, b. May 6, 1727 | TM1 | 248 |
| Hannah, d. James, [d.        ], 1736, ae 1 y. | TM2 | 23 |
| Hannah, d. James, d. [        ], 1737, ae 1 | DR | |
| Hannah, w. Timothy, Jr., d. [Mar.] 7, 1794, ae 22; childbed | DR | |
| Hannah, wid. Timothy, d. [Nov.] 26, 1821, ae 65 | DR | |
| Hester, d. Da[u]id, d. Sept. 22, [1743] | TM2 | 25 |
| James, s. James, b. June 5, 1741 | TM2 | 21 |
| Marcy, d. James, [d. Sept. 20, 1742] | TM2 | 24 |
| Marcy, see also Mercy | | |
| Mary, d. Dauid, b. Mar. 28, 1722 | TM1 | 248 |
| Mary, d. James, d. [        ], 1742, ae 4 | DR | |
| May, s. Dauid, b. Feb. 13, 1724/5 | TM1 | 248 |
| Mercy, d. James, b. Aug. 30, 1728 | TM1 | 248 |
| Mercy, see also Marcy | | |
| Thomas, d. [        ], 1726 | DR | |
| Thomas, s. Dauid, b. Oct. 25, 1728 | TM1 | 248 |
| Timothy, s. James, b. Mar. 16, 1745 | TM2 | 26 |
| Timothy, d. [Jan.] 29, 1814, ae 69 | DR | |
| -----, infant [of] Timothy, Jr., d. Mar. 9, 1798, ae 1 d. | DR | |
| **WEDMORE**, Annis, m. George **HULTSE**, b. of Fair Haven, June 24, | | |
| 1832, by Rev. Stephen Dodd | DR | |
| Annis, m. George **HULTSE**, b. of East Haven, June 24, 1832, | | |
| by Stephen Dodd | TM3 | 235 |
| Charles, Capt., d. Oct. 7, 1837, ae 77 | DR | |
| Daniel, d. [        ], 1815, ae 23; lost at sea | DR | |
| Daniel, d. [Feb.      ], 1840, ae 23 | DR | |
| Lydia, w. Charles, d. July 1, 1803, ae 34 | DR | |
| Polly, wid. Capt. Charles, d. [Jan.] 30, 1846, ae 68 | DR | |
| -----, infant [of] Charles, d. Mar. 3, 1846, ae 2 m. | DR | |

| | Vol. | Page |
|---|---|---|
| WELLER, David, m. Lydia **ANDREWS**, of [East Haven], June 20, 1802, by Rev. Nicholas Street | DR | |
| WELLINGTON, Charles W., of Boston, m. wid. Sally **ROWE**, of East Haven, Oct. 20, 1834, by Rev. Stephen Dodd | DR | |
| WELTON, Eleanor, d. Noah, d. Oct. 5, 1845, ae 2 | DR | |
| Henry, d. Jan. 20, 1810, ae 36; lost at sea | DR | |
| Noah, d. [Sept.] 11, 1848 | DR | |
| Sylvia M., of [East Haven], m. John **MONROE**, of Branford, [Jan.] 24, 1822, by Rev. Stephen Dodd | DR | |
| Sylvia M., m. John **MON[R]OE**, of Branford, Jan. 24, 1822, by Stephen Dodd | TM3 | 165 |
| -----, infant [of] Henry, d. [Jan.] 29, 1806, ae 1 d. | DR | |
| -----, ch. [of] Noah, d. [Sept.] 6, 1848, ae 1 | DR | |
| -----, ch. [of] Noah, d. [Sept.] 9, 1848, ae 9 | DR | |
| WHEDON, Elizabeth, w. Thomas, d. Sept. 3, 1746 | DR | |
| Elisabeth, w. Thomas, d. Sept. 3, 1746 | TM2 | 22 |
| WILCOX, Amos, twin s. of Bela Franham, d. Dec. 27, 1802, ae 3 w. | DR | |
| WILDMAN, Stillman W., of Middletown, m. Eliza M. **BRAUGHTON**, of East Haven, Aug. 25, 1841, by J. B. Beach | TM4 | 202 |
| WILLIAMS, Charles D., d. [Nov.        ], 1843, ae 23; lost overboard from a Liverpool packet | DR | |
| Eliza, m. Jared **SMITH**, b. of East Haven, Dec. 10, 1848, by Rev. D. William Havens | DR | |
| Eliza, of Branford, m. Jared **SMITH**, of East Haven, Dec. 10, 1848, by Rev. D. W[illia]m Havens | TM4 | 212 |
| Elizabeth T., d. Ritchard W. & Elizabeth, b. July 13, 1812 | TM3 | 12 |
| Hannah S., d. Ritchard W. & Elizabeth, b. May 13, 1807 | TM3 | 12 |
| Harriet, of East Haven, m. Cyrus **LUM**, of Monroe, Sept. 30, 1835, by Rev. Edward Ives | DR | |
| Harriet, of East Haven, m. Cyrus **LUM**, of Monroe, Sept. 30, 1835, by E. J. Ives | TM3 | 233-4 |
| Harriet, of East Haven, m. Cyrus **LUM**, of Monroe, Sept. 30, 1835, by E. J. Ives | TM3 | 238 |
| Mary Ann, of East Haven, m. Capt. Joseph **BRADLEY**, July 28, 1832, in Hartford, by Rt. Rev. Thomas C. Brownell | DR | |
| Mary Ann, m. Joseph **BRADLEY**, July 28, 1832, by Rev. Tho[ma]s C. Brownwell, in Hartford | TM3 | 233 |
| William, of New Orleans, m. Maria **PARDEE**, of [East Haven], July 17, 1825, by Rev. Stephen Dodd | DR | |
| William, of New Orleans, m. Maria **PARDEE**, of East Haven, July 17, 1825, by Stephen Dodd | TM3 | 207 |
| WILLINGTON, Charles W., of Boston, m. Sally **ROWE**, of East Haven, Oct. 20, 1834, by Stephen Dodd | TM3 | 281 |
| WILSON, -----, ch. [of] Richard, d. [Dec.] 31, 1795, ae 8 | DR | |
| -----, ch. [of] Richard, d. [July] 25, 1796, ae 2 | DR | |
| WOODING, WOODDING, Jemima, d. [        ], 1712 | DR | |
| Jerima, d. [        ] | TM1 | 31 |
| WOODWARD, Almira, of [East Haven], m. Riley **NOTT**, of New Haven, Mar. 13, 1823, by Rev. Stephen Dodd | DR | |
| Almira, of East Haven, m. Riley **NOTT**, of New Haven, Mar. 13, 1823, by Stephen Dodd | TM3 | 166 |

| WOODWARD, (cont.), | Vol. | Page |
|---|---|---|
| Anna, d. Sept. 8, 1839, ae 56 | DR | |
| Betsey, m. Amos **MORRIS**, Dec. 20, 1778 | TM3 | 170 |
| Charles, m. Maria **HEMINWAY**, b. of East Haven, Dec. 21, 1837, by Rev. Stephen Dodd | DR | |
| Charles, m. Maria **HEMINWAY**, b. of East Haven, Dec. 21, 1837, by Rev. Stephen Dodd | TM3 | 324 |
| Clarissa, d. [May] 5, 1828, ae 31 | DR | |
| Eliza, of [East Haven], m. Samuel Russel **HOTCHKISS**, of New Haven, Oct. 13, 1822, by Rev. Stephen Dodd | DR | |
| Eliza, m. Samuel R. **HOTCHKISS**, Nov. 13, 1822, by Stephen Dodd | TM3 | 166 |
| Elizabeth, d. Rev. John, d. Sept. 6, 1760, ae 50 | DR | |
| Elizabeth, [of East Haven], m. Elias **BRADLEY**, of Branford, Oct. 17, 1805, by Rev. Nicholas Street | DR | |
| Harriet Maria, of [East Haven], m. Henry **BEECHER**, of New Haven, May 8, 1823, by Rev. Stephen Dodd | DR | |
| Harriet Maria, of East Haven, m. Henry **BEECHER**, of New Haven, May 8, 1823, by Stephen Dodd | TM3 | 167 |
| Hezekiah, d. May 21, 1815, ae 52 | DR | |
| Huldah, w. Rosewell, d. Jan. 9, 1773, ae 60 | DR | |
| James, s. John, d. May 26, 1791, ae 10 m. | DR | |
| James C., m. Lydia Gates **HOLT**, b. of East Haven, Sept. 12, 1838, by Rev. Stephen Dodd | DR | |
| James C., m. Lydia G. **HOLT**, b. of East Haven, Sept. 12, 1838, by Stephen Dodd | TM3 | 325 |
| James Henry, s. Richard, d. [Oct.] 30, 1846, ae 1 y. 10 m. | DR | |
| Jennet, d. Hezekiah, d. [          ], 1802, ae 8 m. | DR | |
| Jennet, m. Harvey **ROWE**, 2d, b. of [East Haven], May 10, 1830, by Rev. Stephen Dodd | DR | |
| Jennet, m. Harvey **ROWE**, 2d, b. of East Haven, May 10, 1830, by Stephen Dodd | TM3 | 232 |
| Jeremiah, d. Dec. 23, 1793, ae 22; West Indies | DR | |
| Jeremiah, m. Mary **SMITH**, of [East Haven], June 6, 1822, by Rev. Stephen Dodd | DR | |
| Jeremiah, m. Mary **SMITH**, b. of East Haven, June 6, 1822, by Stephen Dodd | TM3 | 165 |
| Jeremiah, 2d, m. Elizabeth D. **SMITH**, b. of [East Haven], Oct. 17, 1830, by Rev. Stephen Dodd | DR | |
| Jeremiah, 2d, m. Elizabeth D. **SMITH**, b. of East Haven, Oct. 17, 1830, by Stephen Dodd | TM3 | 233 |
| John, Rev. d. Feb. 14, 1746, ae 74 | DR | |
| John, d. Feb. 15, 1745/6 | TM2 | 22 |
| John, had negro Diner, d. Cate. b. Dec. 25, 1750 | TM2 | 165 |
| John, had black ch., d. July [   ], 1777, ae 1 | DR | |
| John, had servant, Guido, d. Mar. 19, 1781, ae 65 | DR | |
| John, Jr., had negro Frank, b. July 24, 1784 | TM2 | 164 |
| John, Jr., d. [          ], 1791, ae 79 | DR | |
| John, had servant, Abigail, d. [Feb.] 7, 1794, ae 78 | DR | |
| John, d. [June] 17, 1797, ae 46 | DR | |
| John, d. Nov. 2, 1810, ae 68 | DR | |
| John, d. [Aug.] 26, 1819, ae 51 | DR | |
| John, wid. Mary, d. [Nov.] 5, 1821, ae 14; accidently shot | DR | |

| | Vol. | Page |
|---|---|---|
| **WOODWARD**, (cont.), | | |
| Leura, m. James **THOMPSON**, Jr., b. of [East Haven], Oct. 28, 1832, by Rev. Stephen Dodd | DR | |
| Leura, m. James **THOMPSON**, Jr., b. of East Haven, Oct. 28, 1832, by Stephen Dodd | TM3 | 235 |
| Lydia, m. Harvey **HEMINWAY**, b. of [East Haven, Mar.    ], 1811, by Rev. Saul Clark | DR | |
| Lyman, m. Jennett R. **MALTBY**, b. of East Haven, Oct. 2, 1839, by Rev. Stephen Dodd | DR | |
| Lyman, m. Jennett R. **MALTBY**, b. of East Haven, Oct. 2, 1839, by Stephen Dodd | TM3 | 326 |
| Mary, wid. Rev. John, d. Mar. 2, 1774, ae 82 | DR | |
| Mary, wid. John, Jr., d. [Nov.] 17, 1791, ae 76 | DR | |
| Mary, m. Daniel **SMITH**, b. of [East Haven, July    ], 1815, by Rev. Saul Clark | DR | |
| Peter, d. Sept. 25, 1754, ae 58 | DR | |
| Richard, d. [July] 28, 1795, ae 80 | DR | |
| Richard, s. Hezekiah, d. [Feb.] 24, 1813, ae 3 w. | DR | |
| Richard, m. Ann Maria **POTTER**, b. of East Haven, Sept. 8, 1839, by Stephen Dodd | TM3 | 326 |
| Richard, m. Ann Maria **POTTER**, b. of East Haven, Sept. 15, 1839, by Rev. Stephen Dodd | DR | |
| Rosewell, d. Sept. 10, 1773, ae 66 | DR | |
| Rosewell, d. [Sept.] 26, 1795, ae 20 | DR | |
| Rosewell, m. Betsey Pardee **ANDREWS**, b. of East Haven, [Nov.] 10, 1833, by Rev. Stephen Dodd | DR | |
| Rosewell, m. Betsey P. **ANDREWS**, b. of East Haven, Nov. 10, 1833, by Stephen Dodd | TM3 | 236 |
| Ruth, w. John, d. Feb. 19, 1807, ae 66 | DR | |
| Ruth, d. Sept. 19, 1833, ae 36 | DR | |
| Ruth, d. Jeremiah, 2d, d. May 15, 1836, ae 2 y. 8 m. | DR | |
| Sarah, w. Rev. John, d. Oct. 20, 1720, ae 33 | DR | |
| Sarah, of [East Haven], m. Jehiel **FORBES**, of New Haven, Oct. 12, 1830, by Rev. Stephen Dodd | DR | |
| Sarah, of East Haven, m. Jehiel **FORBES**, of New Haven, Oct. 12, 1830, by Stephen Dodd | TM3 | 232 |
| Sarah Bradley, w. William, d. [Dec.] 15, 1824, ae 39 | DR | |
| Sarah Hughes, w. William, d. Apr. 12, 1808, ae 25 | DR | |
| Stephen, d. Apr. 26, 1819, ae 61 | DR | |
| Stephen Augustus, s. Stephen d. [Sept.] 24, 1813, ae 5 | DR | |
| William, d. [    ], 1761, ae 43 | DR | |
| William, m. Sarah **HUGHES**, of East Haven, Feb. 22, 1807, by Rev. Bela Hubbard, D. D. | DR | |
| William, m. Mrs. Sally **DAVIDSON**, b. of [East Haven, Jan.] 15, 1812, by Rev. Saul Clark | DR | |
| William, m. Nancy **THOMPSON**, of [East Haven], Feb. 15, 1829, by Rev. Stephen Dodd | DR | |
| William, m. Nancy **THOMPSON**, b. of East Haven, Feb. 15, 1829, by Stephen Dodd | TM3 | 174 |
| -----, Capt., had servant, Thate, d. Nov. 4, 1795, ae 70 | DR | |
| -----, infant [of] William, d. Dec. 12, 1807, ae 7 d. | DR | |

| | Vol. | Page |
|---|---|---|
| **WORKS, WORTS, WARTS**, Alford, d. between Sept. 18 & 25, 1819, | | |
| ae 26; lost at sea | DR | |
| Roxanna, Mrs., m. Rosewell **AUGER**, b. of [East Haven], May | | |
| 1, 1825, by Rev. Stephen Dodd | DR | |
| Roxana, m. Rosewell **AUGER**, b. of East Haven, May 1, | | |
| 1825, by Stephen Dodd | TM3 | 169 |
| **WORTS, WARTS**, [see under **WORKS**] | | |
| **WRIGHT, RIGHT**, Charlotte Chidsey, w. James, d. [May] 26, 1838, | | |
| ae 23 y. 10 m. | DR | |
| James, of North Killingworth, m. Charlotte **CHIDSEY**, of East | | |
| Haven, Apr. 19, 1835, by Rev. Edward Ives | DR | |
| Mary, m. David **POTTER**, Nov. 8, 1750, by Rev. Jacob | | |
| Heminway | TM2 | 20 |
| Samuel, of North Killingworth, m. Charlot[t]e **CHIDSEY**, of | | |
| East Haven, Apr. 19, 1835, by E. J. Ives | TM3 | 233-4 |
| Samuel, of North Killingworth, m. Charlot[t]e **CHIDSEY**, of | | |
| East Haven, Apr. 19, 1835, by E. J. Ives | TM3 | 283 |
| **YALE**, -----, ch. [of] Nathaniel, d. [Sept.] 10, 1798, ae 3 | DR | |
| **YOUNG**, Alpheus, of Wallingford, m. Mary Ann **HEMINWAY**, of Fair | | |
| Haven, Oct. 26, 1847, by Rev. D. William Havens | DR | |
| Alpheus, of Wallingford, m. Mary Ann **HEMINGWAY**, of Fair | | |
| Haven, Oct. 26, 1847, by Rev. D. W[illia]m Havens | TM4 | 208 |
| **NO SURNAME** | | |
| China, d. [       ], 1790, ae 35; scalded | DR | |
| Cuffee, d. May 26, 1800, ae 71 | DR | |
| Daffe, ch. of Rose, d. June 3, 1781, ae 3 | DR | |
| Elizabeth, w. George, d. Dec. 27, 1785, ae 22 | DR | |
| Esther, wid. Dea. Amorris, d. [Oct.] 4, 1813, ae 77 | DR | |
| Jane, w. James, Indian, d. Sept. 30, [1743] | TM2 | 25 |
| Jenny, d. Jan. 6, 1794, ae 70 | DR | |
| Joan, w. James, [an] Indian, d. [Sept.] 30, 1743 | DR | |
| Kism, d. Sept. 3, 1811, ae 38 | DR | |
| Nancy, servant John **HEMINWAY**, d. [       ], 1743, ae 75 | DR | |
| Nanne, d. [Feb.] 26, 1802, ae 75; perished in a snowstorm | DR | |
| Phyllis, d. Apr. 5, 1790, ae 90 | DR | |
| Susannah, d. July 12, 1787, ae 15 d. | DR | |
| Tim, s. James, [an] Indian, d. [Aug.] 24, 1743 | DR | |
| Tim, Indian s. James, d. Aug. 24, [1743] | TM2 | 25 |
| Tony, d. Aug. 20, 1778, ae 27 | DR | |
| -----, ch. of Rose, d. [June] 18, 1781, ae 5 | DR | |
| -----, ch. of Cuffee, d. May 2, 1782, ae 10 m. | DR | |
| -----, ch. of Peter & Betty, d. Dec. 20, 1782, ae 14 m. | DR | |
| -----, ch. [of] Dick, d. [       ], 1790, ae 3 m. | DR | |
| -----, ch. of Cuffee, d. [Nov.] 23, 1793, ae 2 | DR | |
| -----, ch. [of] Dick, d. Sept. 30, 1795, ae 7 | DR | |
| -----, ch. [of] Dick, d. Oct. 6, 1795, ae 3 | DR | |
| -----, ch. [of] Cuffee, d. [Mar.] 13, 1796, ae 2 m. | DR | |

# EAST LYME VITAL RECORDS
## 1839 - 1853

**BECKWITH**, (cont.),                                                                 Page

Elliot S., m. Lydia A. **HARDING**, b. of East Lyme, May 12,
    1842, by James Hepburn                                           156

Emma, m. Marvin **HUNTLEY**, b. of East Lyme, Mar. 27,
    1845, by Chester Tilden                                           158

Esther, m. Zopher **GEE**, b. of Lyme, Nov. 13, 1788                 150

Ezra W., d. Apr. 13, 1858, ae 5 m. 17 d.                            262

Genella M., d. May 15, 1858, ae 4 y. 9 m.                           262

George M., m. Janette **MANWARING**, b. of East Lyme, Feb.
    13, 1853, by George Mixter                                       162

Hellen, d. Elias S., ship carpenter, ae 27 & Lydia A., ae 27, b.
    Jan. 25, 1848                                                    2

Horace, carpenter, ae 41 & Mary, ae 41, res. Waterford, had
    child, b. May 9, 1850                                            4

John L., m. Lois H. **COMSTOCK**, b. of East Lyme, June 9,
    1839, by William Palmer, V. D. M.                                155

Joseph Miller, m. Sally **BECKWITH**, b. of Lyme, Mar. 17,
    1806                                                             152

Julia E., m. Edward **LUCE**, b. of East Lyme, Nov. 21, 1853, by
    P. G. Wightman                                                   162

Justin L., ship carpenter, ae 37 & Mary Ann, ae 38, had child b.
    Feb. 7, 1849                                                     3

Justin L., ship wright & Mary Ann, had child, b. June 20, 1851      5

Lizzie, d. Jan. 4, 1856, ae [ ]                                     260

Lorenzo, m. Charlott E. **CLARK**, b. of East Lyme, Mar. 1,
    1847, by Frederick Wightman                                      159

Lorenzo, farmer, ae 26 & Charlotte E., ae 20, had child, b. June
    17, 1848                                                         2

Louisa, m. S. Amander **BEEBE**, b. of East Lyme, Dec. 23,
    1840, by Rev. William Palmer                                     156

Lucretia, m. Thomas **GORTON**, b. of Lyme, Nov. 13, 1792          151

Lucy A., m. James R. **SPENCER**, b. of East Lyme, Oct. 17,
    1848, by P. G. Wightman                                          159

Maro, [twin with Turner], s. Horace, ship carpenter, ae 40 &
    Mary, ae 36, b. Jan. 17, 1849                                    3

Mary, d. [          ], 1856, ae 42 y.                               260

Nancy H., of East Lyme, m. James C. **ROGERS**, of New
    London, Jan. 14, 1849, by P. G. Wightman                         160

Naomi, m. Seabury **LATHAM**, b. of Lyme, Dec. 28, 1810           152

Oliver W., of Lyme, m. Adeline C. **DENISON**, of East Lyme,
    Nov. 18, 1841, by Amos D. Watrous                                156

Rebecca G., m. John M. **SMITH**, b. of East Lyme, Nov. 26,
    1844, by Chester Tilden                                          157

Richard Lamphere, m. Anna **CHAMPION**, b. of Lyme, July
    14, 1806                                                         152

Sally, m. Joseph Miller **BECKWITH**, b. of Lyme, Mar. 17,
    1806                                                             152

Sally, d. Feb. 18, 1859, ae 66 y.                                   263

Sarah Ann, of East Lyme, m. Russell L. **CHADWICK**, of
    Lyme, Nov. 3, 1840, by Rev. Frederick Wightman,
    of Haddam                                                        156

Sarah E., m. William H. **ROBBINS**, b. of Lyme, Aug. 17,
    1851, by P. G. Wightman                                          161

BECKWITH, (cont.),     Page
   Turner, [twin with Maro], s. Horace, ship carpenter, ae 40 &
      Mary, ae 36, b. Jan. 17, 1849     3
   Willard, fisherman, ae 25 & Mary, ae 24, had child b. Apr. [ ],
      1850     4
   -----, d. July 3, 1848, ae 16 d.     252
BEEBE, Betsey, of Lyme, m. Silas HUNTLEY, of Saybrook, Nov. 25,
    1804     152
   Elias, of Waterford, m. Harri[e]t MANWARING, of East
      Lyme, July 20, 1854, by Harlem Hedden     162
   Elias, d. [     ], 1856, ae 14 m.     260
   Ellen M., d. Dec. 2, 1858, ae 3 y. 10 m.     262
   Erastus, d. Feb. 21, 1848, ae 48 y.     252
   Fanny E., d. William & Maria U., b. Apr. 11, 1852     5
   Horace L., m. Mary Ann HEDDEN, Dec. 18, 1853, by Harlem
      Hedden     162
   Jane E., d. William & Maria U., b. May 17, 1850     4
   John, black-smith, ae 31 & Fanny, ae 29, res. Waterford, had d.
      [     ], b. Feb. 18, 1850     4
   John C., m. Susan HUGHES, b. of Waterford, July 4, 1844, by
      Chester Tilden     157
   John J., m. Frances C. HAYNES, b. of Waterford, Apr. 9, 1848,
      by P. G. Wightman     159
   John J., farmer, ae 28 & Frances C., ae 21, had child b. June 9,
      1849     3
   Joseph, of New London, m. Azelah SMITH, d. Josiah, of Lyme,
      Dec. 27, 1789     150
   Lemuel H., m. Nancy D. CLARK, b. of East Lyme, Jan. 31,
      1841, by William Palmer, V. D. M.     156
   Noah, m. Preserved AVERY, b. of Lyme, May 21, 1806     152
   Rebecca, d. Sept. 9, 1858, ae 74 y.     262
   S. Amander, m. Louisa BECKWITH, b. of East Lyme, Dec.
      23, 1840, by Rev. William Palmer     156
   Samuel I., of New London, m. Judith C. CHAPMAN, of Lyme,
      Aug. 15, 1849, by P. G. Wightman     160
   Sarah A., d. May 20, 1850, ae 23 y.     254
   William, m. Maria U. HARDING, Dec. 22, 1842, by Frederick
      Gridley     156
   William, farmer & Maria, had d. [     ], b. Nov [ ], 1849     3
   W[illia]m & Maria N., had child d. Feb. 4, 1858     262
   William, had child d. [     ], 1858     262
   William L., s. William & Maria U., b. Sept. 7, 1853     6
BECLHER, Joseph, late of Newport, R. I., m. Hannah WOOD, of Lyme,
    Aug. [ ], 1788     150
BIRCH, Lydia E., d. William W., farmer, ae 21, & Sally E., ae 24, b. May
    27, 1850     4
   Orrin I., m. Mary Ann MOORE, b. of East Lyme, Feb. 26,
      1843, by James Hepburn     157
   William W., m. Sally O. FOX, b. of Waterford, Oct. 1, 1848, by
      P. G. Wightman     159
BISHOP, Sherlock H., of North Haven, m. Abby T. LEE, of East Lyme,
    Dec. 26, 1839, by Frederick Gridley     155

CHAMPLIN, (cont.),                                                    Page
    Nicol F., m. Frances E. SMITH, b. of East Lyme, Sept. 16,
        1844, by Chester Tilden                                        157
CHAPMAN, Alfred W., of New London, m. Pamelia CLARK, of East
        Lyme, Feb. 7, 1841, by Frederick Gridley                       156
    Andrew J., of East Lyme, m. Ann Eliza MINER, of Colchester,
        Dec. 18, 1854, by P. G. Wightman                               162
    Anna, of Lyme, m. George SMITH, of New London, Mar. 3,
        1793                                                           151
    Charles, his s. [          ], d. Jan. 4, 1856, ae 7 y.             260
    Delia, m. Asa HALEY, Oct. 13, 1839, by Francis Darrow,
        M. G.                                                          155
    Ellen C., m. John LEE, b. of East Lyme, Dec. 18, 1854, by
        P. G. Wightman                                                 162
    Ezra, m. Phebe GEE, b. of East Lyme, Mar. 21, 1841, by Peter
        Comstock, J. P.                                                156
    Harriet, [twin with Henry], d. Solomon, farmer, ae 41 &
        Clarissa, ae 35, b. Feb. 20, 1851                                5
    Henry, [twin with Harriet], s. Solomon, farmer, ae 41 &
        Clarissa, ae 35, b. Feb. 20, 1851                                5
    John M., m. Emma L. PARTLOW, b. of East Lyme, Mar. 12,
        1848, by P. G. Wightman                                        159
    John M., his child, d. June 18, 1856, ae 1 y.                      260
    John M., & Sarah, had child, d. Feb. 17, 1858                      262
    John M., his child, d. Jan. 5, 1859, ae 2 d.                       263
    Judith C., of Lyme, m. Samuel I. BEEBE, of New London,
        Aug. 15, 1849, by P. G. Wightman                               160
    Julia, d. Feb. 6, 1851, [8 y.]                                     255
    Lucy, d. May 3. 1856, ae 24 y.                                     260
    Mariette, m. Ezera D. LATHAM, b. of East Lyme, Jan. 22,
        1844, by Frederick Gridley                                     157
    Oliver, m. Caroline BUMP, b. of Lyme, Mar. 27, 1853, by
        P. G. Wightman                                                 162
    Robert F., m. Laura Ann WATROUS, b. of East Lyme, Jan. 4,
        1846, by Chester Tilden                                        158
    Robert F., m. Lucy WATROUS, May 7, 1849, by Frederick
        Gridley                                                        160
    Sally, m. Joseph LEE, s. Benj[amin], b. of Lyme, Mar. 30, 1795     151
    Solomon, farmer, ae 39 & Clarrisa, ae 32, had child b. Sept. 25,
        1848                                                             2
    Zebulon, m. Anna LATTIMER, b. of Montville, Mar. 11, 1795          151
CHAPPELL, CHAPEL, Caroline J., of New London, m. Ebenezer M.
                RICHARDS, of East Lyme, Feb. 26, 1851, by P. G.
                Wightman                                               161
    Charles, d. June 11, 1848, ae 49 y.                                252
    Daniel, illeg. s. [          ] & Fanny CHAPPELL, seamstress,
        ae 20, b. Sept. 2, 1848                                          2
    Daniel, d. Sept. 14, 1850, ae 57 y.                                254
    Daniel, Jr., d. Sept. 18, 1850, ae 2 y.                            254
    Elizabeth H., of East Lyme, m. A. MITCHETSON, Jr., of
                Simsbury, June 5, 1848, by P. G. Wightman              159
    Fanny, seamstress, ae 20, had illeg. s. Daniel, b. Sept. 2, 1848     2

**CHAPPELL, CHAPEL**, (cont.),                    Page

    James Carrol, of Montville, m. Lucretia **LATTIMER**, of
        Montville, Dec. 29, 1791                  150

    Jeremiah, d. Aug. 26, 1849, ae 67 y.          253

    John, d. Sept. 6, 1851, ae 79 y.          255

    Mary M., d. W[illia]m, m. Collins **GORTON**, b. of Lyme, Nov.
        23, 1808         152

    Nancy D., of East Lyme, m. Amasa **LOOMIS**, of Salem, Jan. 5,
        1845, by Chester Tilden         158

    Rebecca, m. John **BOGART**, b. of East Lyme, Oct. 9, 1853, by
        Harlem Hedden         162

    Sarah M., m. Henry M. **HOLDRIDGE**, Sept. 8, 1841, by
        Frederick Gridley         156

    William, m. Rachel **LEE**, b. of New London, Oct. 3, 1793    151

**CHARLES**, -----, of Groton, m. Hannah **OCUEST**, b. Niantic Tribe
    Indians, Nov. 29, 1792         151

**CHESTER**, Joseph, of New London, m. Elizabeth **LEE**, of Lyme, Sept. 22,
    1785         150

**CLARK**, Albert H., m. Mary C. **WARREN**, Sept. 9, 1839, by Frederick
    Gridley         155

    Albert H., wagon maker & Mary, had child, b. June 6, 1849    3

    Ann Maria, d. Jeremiah, fisherman, ae 29 & Ann Maria, ae 23,
        b. Mar. 26, 1850         4

    Ann Maria, d. Mar. 29, 1850, ae 23 y.        254

    Ann Maria, d. Apr. 13, 1850, ae 21 d.        254

    Asa, d. June 12, 1857, ae 74 y.        261

    Charles, s. John, fisherman, ae 24 & Belinda, ae 23, b. Apr. [ ],
        1849         3

    Charlott[e] E., m. Lorenzo **BECKWITH**, b. of East Lyme, Mar.
        1, 1847, by Frederick Wightman       159

    Courtland, of Waterford, m. Elizabeth M. **CLARK**, of East
        Lyme, Dec. 8, 1850, by Harlan Hedden      160

    Elisha, ae 22, b. Saybrook, res. Essex, m. Harriet
        **MANWARING**, ae 19, b. Waterford, res. Essex,
        Aug. 12, 1849, by P. G. Wightman       160

    Elizabeth, of Lyme, m. Samuel **DART**, of New London, Aug.
        11, 1791         150

    Elizabeth M., of East Lyme, m. Courtland **CLARK**, of
        Waterford, Dec. 8, 1850, by Harlan Hedden     160

    Ellis M., of East Lyme, m. Winslow M. **LAMB**, of Norwich,
        Jan. 24, 1853, by P. G. Wightman      162

    Frederick L., d. Mar. 6, 1851, ae 5 y.        255

    Gurdon, ae 21, b. Salem, res. East Lyme, m. Mary
        **MAYNARD**, ae 16, b. East Lyme, res. East Lyme,
        Feb. 13, 1850, by Rev. Mr. Brown      160

    Harriet, m. Noah **LESTER**, b. of East Lyme, Dec. 19, 1842, by
        Frederick Wightman        156

    Henry A., d. Jan. 7, 1851, ae 8 y.        255

    Jane M., of Waterford, m. Reuben R. **STAPLINS**, of New
        London, Mar. 19, 1854, by P. G. Wightman     162

    Jeremiah, m. Meriah **MANWARING**, b. of East Lyme, Jan. 20,
        1847, by Frederick Wightman       159

    John, d. Aug. 14, 1858, ae 47 y.        262

CLARK, (cont.),                                                    Page
   John W., s. John P., fisherman, ae 24 & Melinda, ae 32, b. Oct.
      13, 1848                                             2
   Julia, d. Mar. 12, 1857, ae 36 y.                         261
   Julia Maria, d. John, farmer, ae 38 & Juliann, ae 34, b. June 5,
      1848                                                 2
   Lyman, Jr., fisherman, ae 25 & Lucy E., ae 21, had child, s. b.
      Sept. [ ], 1849                                      3
   Lyman, b. East Lyme, res. Little Rest, R. I., m. Jane M.
      PATTERSON, of Little Rest, R. I., June 26, 1853,
      by George Mixter                                   162
   Mary Ann, d. June 4, 1850, ae 59 y.                       254
   Nancy D., m. Lemuel H. BEEBE, b. of East Lyme, Jan. 31,
      1841, by William Palmer, V. D. M.                  156
   Nathaniel, Jr., m. Fanny JOHNSON, b. of Lyme, Sept. 23,
      1804                                               151
   Nathaniel, d. [          ], 1856, ae 78 y.                260
   Norman Sylvester, d. July 8, 1850, ae 1 y.                254
   Pamelia, of East Lyme, m. Alfred W. CHAPMAN, of New
      London, Feb. 7, 1841, by Frederick Gridley         156
   Phebe M., of East Lyme, m. Henry GARDNER, of Waterford,
      Feb. 25, 1852, by Nathan Wildman                   161
   Polly, d. [          ], 1856, ae 87 y.                    260
   Sally, m. Gibson DART, b. of Lyme, Sept. 29, 1810         152
   Samuel, m. Phebe CHADWICK, b. of Lyme, Nov. 28, 1790      150
   William, of Lyme, m. Jemina ROGERS, d. Rowland, of Lyme,
      Jan. 22, 1807                                      152
   William U., ae 19, b. Essex, res. Essex, m. Ellen W.
      MANWARING, ae 17, b. Waterford, res. Essex,
      Dec. 31, 1848, by P. G. Wightman                   159
CLASSON, John, m. Rhoda CONGDON, b. of East Lyme, June 20, 1841,
      by James Hepburn, of Chesterfield                  156
COBB, John, of Montville, m. Eunice HEWETT, of Lyme, Jan. 6, 1791    150
COLEMAN, Josiah A., m. Mary A. PHILLIPS, b. of East Lyme, Oct. 13,
      1850, by Frederick Gridley                         160
COLLINS, George W., m. Mary Ann DOUGLASS, Oct. 23, 1839, by
      Francis Darrow, M. G.                              155
COMSTOCK, Ann Cornelia, d. Feb. 1, 1848, ae 17 y. 4 m.              252
   Fanny Eliza, d. Dec. 20, 1849, ae 5 y.                    253
   Hannah, d. Feb. [ ], 1851, ae 75 y.                       255
   John J., m. Emeline L. MOORE, b. of East Lyme, Nov. 30,
      1843, by James Hepburn                             157
   Lois H., m. John L. BECKWITH, b. of East Lyme, June 9,
      1839, by William Palmer, V. D. M.                  155
   Martha, ae 30, b. Norwich, res. Waterford, m. Clark SMITH,
      ae 30, b. East Haddam, res. Waterford, Dec. 31,
      1848, by Francis Darrow                            159
   Mary E., d. W[illia]m H. H., merchant, ae 30 & Eliza Ann,
      ae 28, b. May 24, 1848                               2
   Moses W., of New London, m. Sarah Ann GRISWOLD, of
      East Lyme, Oct. 28, 1840, by Frederick Gridley     156
   Moses W., m. Phebe J. GRISWOLD, b. of East Lyme, Nov. 7,
      1847, by F. Gridley                                159

COMSTOCK, (cont.),                                                    Page
  Peter, m. Betsey S. **BECKWITH**, b. of East Lyme, Oct. 26,
    1845, by Chester Tilden                                        158
  Peter A., m. Maria **TURNER**, b. East Lyme, Mar. 9, 1840, by
    William Palmer, V. D. M.                                       156
  Sarah M., of East Lyme, m. Benjamin D. **STANTON**, of
    Waterford, Dec. 2, 1849, by P. G. Wightman                     160
  William, H. H., m. Eliza Ann **SMITH**, b. of East Lyme, Dec.
    15, 1842, by Frederick Wightman                                156
CONE, Abby H., of Colchester, m. Elias H. **BECKWITH**, of East Lyme,
    Nov. 27, 1853, by P. G. Wightman                               162
  Horace B., farmer & Lucinda his w., had child b. Dec. 27, 1847     1
  W[illia]m B., his child, d. Jan. 18, 1859, ae [ ]                   263
  William H., farmer & [      ], ae 34, had child b. May 28,
    1850                                                           4
  ——, d. Jan. 25, 1848, ae 1 m.                                       252
CONGDON, Ali, s. Henry, farmer, ae 24 & Maryette, ae 24, b. Jan. 9,
    1849                                                           3
  George W., m. Mary Ann **WATROUS**, b. of East Lyme, Sept.
    25, 1853, by P. G. Wightman                                    162
  Henry, m. Marietta **PRENTISS**, b. of East Lyme, Sept. 6, 1846,
    by P. G. Wightman                                              158
  Joel, [twin with Selina], d. May 15, 1856, ae 1 d.                  260
  Rhoda, m. John **CLASSON**, b. of East Lyme, June 20, 1841, by
    James Hepburn, of Chesterfield                                 156
  Sarah L., m. Daniel S. **WATROUS**, b. of East Lyme, Jan. 11,
    1852, by George Mixter                                         161
  Selina, [twin with Joel], d. May 15, 1856, ae 1 d.                  260
  Selina A., d. June 28, 1856, ae 17 y. 17 d.                         260
COOK, A. H., d. Mar. 7, 1858, ae 2 m.                                   262
  Selden, of Plainfield, N. Y., m. Savira **MANWARING**, of East
    Lyme, Oct. 17, 1847, by Roger Abiston                          159
CORDNER, Ephraim U., of New London, m. Mary Ann **WOODWARD**,
    of Griswold, Nov. 8, 1840, by Frederick Gridley               156
COWLES, Joel, of Ashford, m. Samantha A. **AMES**, of East Lyme, Apr.
    12, 1840, by William Palmer, V. D. M.                          156
  Joel, farmer, ae 24 & Samantha, ae 26, had child b. July 16,
    1848                                                           2
  Julia, d. [probably 1859]                                          263
CROCKER, Alonzo, d. July 9, 1850, ae 9 y.                              254
  Anson, of Waterford, m. Esther Ann **SMITH**, of East Lyme,
    June 25, 1843, by A. B. Wheeler                                157
  Anson, d. Aug. 6, 1857, ae 14 d.                                    261
  Anson, d. Sept. 2, 1857, ae 1 m. 12 d.                              261
  Chester L., d. Jan. 25, 1851, ae 5 y.                               255
  Eliza J., d. June 5, 1850, ae 28 y.                                 254
  Frances M., d. Anson, fisherman, ae 25 & Esther, ae 22, b. Nov.
    7, 1847                                                        1
  Francis M., ae 21, b. East Lyme, res. East Lyme, m. Bartlet P.
    **SAMPSON**, ae 24, b. Lyme, res. East Lyme, Oct.
    10, 1847, by Chester Tilden                                    159
  Griswold A., carpenter, ae 32 & Eliza J., ae 28, had child b.
    June 4, 1850                                                   4

CROCKER, (cont.),    Page
  John, s. Eben J., painter, ae 40 & Francis, ae 36, b. Feb. [ ],
    1848   2
  Lucinda, d. Dec. 20, 1858, ae 71 y.   262
  William M., ae 24, m. Hannah ROGERS, ae 25, b. of East
    Lyme, July 22, 1849, by C. H. Gates   160
CUMMINGS, Betsey, of East Lyme, m. Amon CHAMPION, of Lyme,
    May 14, 1843, by Frederick Gridley   157
DANIELS, Hannah, d. Feb. 18, 1849, ae 82 y.   253
  Jane L., d. Dec. 23, 1851, ae 7 m.   255
  Jasper, of New London, m. Phebe HODGE, late of Stonington,
    Feb. 15, 1789   150
  John C., m. Martha BUNNELL, b. of New London, Oct. 6,
    1839, by William Palmer, V. D. M.   155
  Naomi, m. William MORGAN, b. of New London, May 7,
    1789   150
DARROW, Emily, d. Nov. 7, 1851, ae [ ]   255
  George W., ae 23, b. Waterford, res. Waterford, m. Maria A.
    ROSE, ae 20, b. Franklin, res. Waterford, Apr. 13,
    1850, by P. G. Wightman   160
DART, Gibson, of Lyme, m. Sally CLARK, of Lyme, Sept. 29, 1810   152
  Samuel, of New London, m. Elizabeth CLARK, of Lyme, Aug.
    11, 1791   150
DAVENPORT, Oliver, d. Oct. 30, 1847, ae 29 y.   251
DAVIS, George H., d. Sept. 16, 1848, ae 2 y.   252
  James, of Waterford, m. Eunice MANWARING, of Newport,
    R. I., Dec. 29, 1844, by Chester Tilden   157
DEAN, Ellen M., d. July 14, 1858, ae 47 y. 5 m.   262
DENISON, Adeline C., of East Lyme, m. Oliver W. BECKWITH, of
    Lyme, Nov. 18, 1841, by Amos D. Watrous   156
  Elizabeth, m. Enoch LESTER, b. of East Lyme, Nov. 1, 1847,
    by Frederick Wightman   159
  John D., of East Lyme, m. Mary A. WIGHTMAN, of
    Montville, Oct. 15, 1849, by P. G. Wightman   160
  John H., m. Maryann JOHNSON, Feb. 25, 1852, by Frederick
    Gridley   161
  Juliett G., m. Chaney PRENTIS, Mar. 7, 1842, by Amos D.
    Watrous   156
  Maria, m. Sylvanus GRISWOLD, b. of Lyme, Dec. 2, 1789   150
  Mary, m. Adam MANWARING, b. of Lyme, May 26, 1785   150
  Mary, of East Lyme, m. William STAPLINS, of Waterford,
    Sept. 6, 1846, by P. G. Wightman   158
  Sarah, m. Jasper PHILLIPS, b. of East Lyme, Feb. 6, 1842, by
    Frederick Gridley   156
DICKENS, Edgar, d. Apr. 6, 1856, ae 9 m. 17 d.   260
DOOR, Deborah, of Lyme, m. Israel REYNOLDS, of Northeast Dutchess
    Co., N. Y., June 1, 1798   151
DOTON, William, d. Feb. [ ], 1848, ae 80 y.   252
DOUGLASS, Henrietta E., m. Marcus HAYNES, b. of East Lyme, Sept.
    12, 1847, by Palmer G. Wightman   159
  Josiah, of New London, m. Mary GRISWOLD, of Lyme, Aug.
    20, 1798   151

Page

GATES, Daniel C., black-smith, ae 25 & Lydia M., ae 23, had child, b.
    Apr. 14, 1851                                                 5
    Leverett, d. Sept. 26, 1858                                  262
    Philo, of Waterford, m. Elizabeth S. MANWARING, of East
        Lyme, Nov. 28, 1853, by Peter S. Mather        162
GEE, Lucinda, d. Nov. 5, 1847, ae 54 y.                     251
    Mary, m. John WAY, b. of East Lyme, Dec. 23, 1850, by D. S.
        Brainerd                                             160
    Matilda B., d. Sept. 4, 1850, ae 20 y.                   254
    Phebe, m. Ezra CHAPMAN, b. of East Lyme, Mar. 21, 1841,
        by Peter Comstock, J. P.                        156
    Sarah Ann, of East Lyme, m. Richard H. PRATT, of Essex, Jan.
        18, 1846, by Chester Tilden                 158
    Zopher, m. Esther BECKWITH, b. of Lyme, Nov. 13, 1788   150
GEEG, John S., of Essex, m. Mary A. SMITH, of East Lyme, July 30,
    1854, by P. G. Wightman                      162
GIFFORD, Ellen, d. June 10, 1856, ae 13 y.              260
GILBERT, -----, m. George B. SWANEY, b. of Lyme, [      ], 1812   152
GILLETT, GILLET, Almiran, of Windsor, m. Eunice GRISWOLD,
    2nd, of Lyme, Dec. 29, 1790                   150
    Miner H., of Lyme, m. Elizabeth T. LEE, of East Lyme, Jan.
        10, 1854, by Alpha Miller                 162
    William S., of Colchester, m. Mary E. JOHNSON, of East
        Lyme, Apr. 9, 1848, by Frederick Gridley      159
GODFREY, Joel, of Bloomfield, N. Y., m. Maria PECK, d. Mather, of
    Lyme, Sept. 20, 1810                      152
GOOLD, -----, m. Dudley SMITH, b. of Lyme, Feb. 21, 1787   150
GORTON, Collins, m. Mary M. CHAPPELL, d. W[illia]m, b. of Lyme,
    Nov. 23, 1808                               152
    Elizabeth A., m. Joseph D. HUNTLEY, b. of East Lyme, Sept.
        15, 1844, by Chester Tilden               157
    George C., d. May 27, 1848, ae 2 y.                 252
    Lucretia, wid., of Waterford, m. Joseph Denison WALES, of
        Windham, Dec. 13, 1810                 152
    Mary, m. Elisha SMITH, b. of Lyme, Dec. 26, 1808     152
    Mary, d. Apr. 6, 1856, ae 72 y.                   260
    Nooma, d. Oct. [ ], 1847, ae 95 y.      (Naomi)     251
    Orlando C., m. Fanny E. SPENCER, b. of East Lyme, Mar. 20,
        1854, by P. G. Wightman                 162
    Thomas, m. Lucretia BECKWITH, b. of Lyme, Nov. 13, 1792  151
    William G., farmer, ae 40 & Eliza R., ae 40, had child, b. July
        29, 1849                                        3
GRIDLEY, Susan E., of East Lyme, m. David P. JUDSON, of Stratford,
    Oct. 13, 1853, by Frederick Gridley         162
GRIFFING, Rebecca, m. Andrew PECK, b. of East Lyme, Sept. 2, 1850,
    by Frederick Gridley                      160
    Sarah C., m. Sylvanus GRISWOLD, b. of East Lyme, Oct. 31,
        1843, by Frederick Gridley               157
GRISWOLD, Charles, s. Sylvanus, farmer, ae 42 & Sarah, ae 30, b. Feb.
    22, 1849                                       3
    Elizabeth, m. Thomas AVERY, Mar. 12, 1845, by Frederick
        Gridley                                      158

HAYNES, (cont.),                                                             Page
   Marcus, m. Henrietta E. **DOUGLASS**, b. of East Lyme, Sept.
     12, 1847, by Palmer G. Wightman                                  159
   Mary F., d. Dec. 23, 1847, ae 5 m.                                     251
**HEDDEN**, Bartholoman H., d. Feb. 20, 1858, ae 88 y.                          262
   Mary Ann, m. Horace L. **BEEBE**, Dec. 18, 1853, by Harlem
     Hedden                                                           162
**HENRY**, Hugh, m. Betty **SISTARE**, b. of New London, Nov. 12, 1796          151
**HEWETT**, Eunice, of Lyme, m. John **COBB**, of Montville, Jan. 6, 1791       150
**HIX**, James, d. Feb. [ ], 1848, ae 65 y.                                     252
**HODGE**, Phebe, late of Stonington, m. Jasper **DANIELS**, of New London,
     Feb. 15, 1789                                                    150
**HOLDRIDGE**, Henry M., m. Sarah M. **CHAPEL**, Sept. 8, 1841, by
     Frederick Gridley                                                156
   Henry M., m. Eliza J. **KEABLES**, b. of East Lyme, May 25,
     1851, by P. G. Wightman                                          161
   Sarah M., d. Mar. 17, 1848, ae 28 y.                                   252
   William, d. Nov. 10, 1858, ae 14 y.                                    262
**HOLMES**, George R., m. Clarissa M. **FRINK**, b. of East Lyme, Mar. 6,
     1853, by P. G. Wightman                                          162
**HOLT**, Asa, m. Mary **SMITH**, d. Geo[rge], b. of New London, Apr. 7,
     1785                                                             150
**HOUGH**, Abba, of East Lyme, m. Jabez **LADD**, of Franklin, July 16,
     1848, by Frederick Wightman                                      159
   Elizabeth, m. Charles **HOWARD**, b. of East Lyme, Dec. 2,
     1840, by William Palmer, V. D. M.                                156
**HOWARD**, Charles, m. Elizabeth **HOUGH**, b. of East Lyme, Dec. 2,
     1840, by William Palmer, V. D. M.                                156
   Emma, w. Edwin, d. Sept. 20, 1858, ae 33 y.                            262
   Emma M., m. Josiah H. **MANWARING**, b. of East Lyme, Jan.
     15, 1854, by George Mixter                                       162
   Enoch N., m. Nilletta E. **BUSH**, b. of East Lyme, Nov. 27,
     1853, by Frederick Gridley                                       162
   Leander, s. Edwin, fisherman & Emma, b. Nov. [ ], 1849                   3
   Lucy, d. Apr. 5, 1849, ae 77 y.                                        263
   Lyman H., s. Edwin, fisherman, ae 28 & Emma, ae 23, b. Oct.
     13, 1847                                                           1
   Mary Elizabeth, d. July [ ], 1850, ae 1 y.                             254
**HUGHES**, Susan, m. John C. **BEEBE**, b. of Waterford, July 4, 1844, by
     Chester Tilden                                                   157
**HULL**, Mary A., d. [probably 1856], ae 59 y.                                 260
**HUNES**, Eunice H., of Plainfield, m. James **HUNTLEY**, of East Lyme,
     Oct. 30, 1842, by Frederick Wightman                             156
**HUNT**, Edward, of Newburyport, m. Esther **MORGAN**, of Lyme, Aug.
     25, 1796                                                         151
**HUNTINGTON**, Abel, of East Hampton, L. I., m. Frances **LAY**, of Lyme,
     Jan. 27, 1800                                                    151
**HUNTLEY**, Ezra R., of East Lyme, m. Harriet U. **THOMPSON**, of
     Montville, Feb. 7, 1853, by P. G. Wightman                       162
   James, of East Lyme, m. Eunice H. **HUNES**, of Plainfield, Oct.
     30, 1842, by Frederick Wightman                                  156
   John, s. Ruel B., farmer, ae 28 & Abby, ae 30, Sept. [ ], 1848          2
   John C., d. Apr. 21, 1851, ae 2 m. 15 d.                               255

LAY, (cont.),                                                                              Page
    John, of Saybrook, m. Phebe LEE, of Lyme, Jan. 11, 1784    150
    Nancy, m. John CHADWICK, b. of Lyme, Nov. 9, 1806    152
LEE, Abby T., of East Lyme, m. Sherlock H. BISHOP, of North Haven,
        Dec. 26, 1839, by Frederick Gridley    155
    Abiga[i]l, 2nd d. Elisha, of Lyme, m. Abraham GARDINER, of
        Southhold, L. I., Oct. 25, 1809    152
    Betty, m. Joseph SILL, bachelor, b. of Lyme, Mar. 11, 1800    151
    Dan, of Lyme, m. Nabby CHAMPION, of Lyme, Feb. 29,
        1784    150
    Edmund S., d. Aug. 2, 1851, ae 20 y.    255
    Eliza A., d. May 29, 1858, ae 56 y.    262
    Elizabeth, of Lyme, m. Joseph CHESTER, of New London,
        Sept. 22, 1785    150
    Elizabeth T., of East Lyme, m. Miner H. GILLETT, of Lyme,
        Jan. 10, 1854, by Alpha Miller    162
    Ellen, d. Seth S., farmer, ae 49 & Charlotte, ae 33, b. Dec. 21,
        1848    2
    Henry S., m. Elizabeth E. ROYCE, b. of East Lyme, Nov. 3,
        1850, by Oliver Brown    160
    Jason, of Lyme, m. Jane GRISWOLD, of Lyme, Feb. 18, 1793    151
    John, m. Ellen C. CHAPMAN, b. of East Lyme, Dec. 18, 1854,
        by P. G. Wightman    162
    Joseph, s. Benj[ami]n, m. Sally CHAPMAN, b. of Lyme, Mar.
        30, 1795    151
    Marietta, of East Lyme, m. Richard S. LOYD, of Cheshire,
        Eng., Nov. 2, 1851, by Frederick Gridley    161
    Nathaniel S., m. Sarah L. CAULKINS, Dec. 14, 1847, by
        Frederick Gridley    159
    Phebe, of Lyme, m. John LAY, of Saybrook, Jan. 11, 1784    150
    Rachel, m. William CHAPEL, b. of New London, Oct. 3, 1793    151
    Rhoda, of Lyme, m. John STEBBINS, of New London, Apr. [ ],
        1788    150
    Seth S., of Lyme, m. Charlotte L. WARREN, of East Lyme,
        Feb. 28, 1848, by P. G. Wightman    159
    Violet, m. Cudjo BABCOCK, b. of Lyme, b. free persons, Nov.
        8, 1798    151
    -----, Mrs., d. July 15, 1857, ae 85 y.    261
    -----, Mrs., d. May 29, 1859, ae 57 y.    263
LEECH, Hannah, wid., m. Thomas WALLACE, b. of Lyme, Dec. 30,
        1787    150
LEFFINGWELL, Marvin, minister, had child b. Mar. [ ], 1849    3
LESTER, Andrew, Jr., m. Betsey ROWLAND, d. Ezra, b. of Lyme, Feb.
        2, 1809    152
    Ann Maria, d. Dec. 17, 1858, ae 15 y.    262
    Enoch, m. Elizabeth DENISON, b. of East Lyme, Nov. 1, 1847,
        by Frederick Wightman    159
    Enoch, fisherman, ae 39 & Elizabeth, ae 25, had child b. Aug.
        [ ], 1849    3
    Erastus, m. Nancy D. FOX, b. of East Lyme, Nov. 19, 1848, by
        Frederick Wightman    159
    Erastus Benjamin, s. Erastus, fisherman, ae 26 & Mary, ae 22, b.
        Nov. 5, 1850    4

LESTER, (cont.),                                                                        Page
    Jeremiah, of Lyme, m. Nabby CHAMPION, of New London,
        June 27, 1784                                                        150
    Mary, of Lyme, m. Jeremiah TINKER, of New London, July 4,
        1790                                                                 150
    Moses, m. Mary FOX, b. of East Lyme, Dec. 26, 1844, by
        James Hepburn                                                        157
    Noah, m. Harriet CLARK, b. of East Lyme, Dec. 19, 1842, by
        Frederick Wightman                                                   156
    Stella C., d. Noah, fisherman, ae 37 & Harriet, ae 33, b. Aug.
        20, 1849                                                               3
LEVEE, Frances, m. Eliza BOLLES, b. of Waterford, [        , 1850], by
    P. G. Wightman                                                           160
LEWIS, Phebe, m. Joseph STRICKLAND, b. of Lyme, Mar. 1, 1792                              150
[L]LOYD, Richard S., of Cheshire, Eng., m. Marietta LEE, of East Lyme,
    Nov. 2, 1851, by Frederick Gridley                                       161
LOOMIS, Amasa, of Salem, m. Nancy D. CHAPPELL, of East Lyme,
    Jan. 5, 1845, by Chester Tilden                                          158
    Elijah G., of Salem, m. Mary HUNTLEY, of East Lyme, June
        16, 1853, by William A. Smith                                        162
LOVERIDGE, Annie, d. Edward, mariner, ae 31 & Ann, ae 22, b. Jan. 18,
    1848                                                                     2
    Emma E., d. Edward, mariner, ae 39 & Ann, ae 34, b. Oct. 8,
    1850                                                                     4
LUCE, Caroline M., of East Lyme, m. Charles D. ALLEN, of Tisbury,
    Mass., Dec. 23, 1846, by Frederick Wightman                              158
    Dianna, d. Nov. 11, 1848, ae 48 y.                                       252
    Edward, m. Eliza LUCE, b. of East Lyme, Oct. 1, 1848, by
        Frederick G. Wightman                                                159
    Edward, m. Julia E. BECKWITH, b. of East Lyme, Nov. 21,
        1853, by P. G. Wightman                                              162
    Eliza, m. Edward LUCE, b. of East Lyme, Oct. 1, 1848, by
        Frederick G. Wightman                                                159
    Eliza M., m. Ancil REED, b. of East Lyme, Oct. 22, 1854, by
        P. G. Wightman                                                       162
    Francis C., m. Mariann MANWARING, b. of East Lyme, Dec.
        4, 1854, by Frederick Gridley                                        162
    Frances D., m. Rebecca E. BOLLES, b. of East Lyme, Dec. 5,
        1849, by William Palmer                                              160
    Mary, d. Oct. 14, 1857, ae 56 y.                                         261
MACK, Cornelius, farmer, ae 35 & Harriet, ae 35, had child b. May 15,
    1850                                                                     4
    Cornelius B., ae 35, b. Lyme, res. East Lyme, m. Harriet
        WATROUS, ae 29, b. Lyme, res. East Lyme, Mar.
        2, 1849, by Chester Tilden                                           160
    Prudence M., d. Jonathan T., farmer, ae 46 & Jane, b. June 14,
    1850                                                                     4
MADSAN, Mary Ann, m. Thomas JOHNSON, b. of East Lyme, Aug. 15,
    1847, by Palmer G. Wightman                                              159
MAINE, Anna, d. Gershon, wagon maker, & Delia, b. Jan. 5, 1849               3
MANWARING, Adam, m. Mary DENISON, b. of Lyme, May 26, 1785                   150
    Allen W., of Waterford, m. Lydia M. WARREN, of East Lyme,
        Sept. 8, 1839, by William Palmer, V. D. M.                          155

**MANWARING**, (cont.),                                                                 Page

Allen W., caulker, ae 32 & Lydia M., ae 27, had child, b. July 7,
    1848                                                                                    2

Caroline, m. William **PARTLO**, b. of East Lyme, Jan. 8, 1854,
    by P. G. Wightman                                                                  162

Elias, d. May 15, 1857, ae 2 y. 3 m.                                                    261

Elizabeth, m. Paul **BRAMAN**, b. of New London, Nov. 26,
    1789                                                                                    150

Elizabeth A., m. Ezra C. **PARTLO**, b. of East Lyme, July 24,
    1853, by P. G. Wightman                                                            162

Elizabeth S., of East Lyme, m. Philo **GATES**, of Waterford,
    Nov. 28, 1853, by Peter S. Mather                                                  162

Ellen W., ae 17, b. Waterford, res. Essex, m. William U.
    **CLARK**, ae 19, b. Essex, res. Essex, Dec. 31, 1848,
    by P. G. Wightman                                                                  159

Eunice, of Newport, R. I., m. James **DAVIS**, of Waterford, Dec.
    29, 1844, by Chester Tilden                                                        157

Fanny W., d. Allen, caulker, ae 36 & Lydia M., ae 31, b. Sept.
    20, 1850                                                                                4

Harriet, ae 19, b. Waterford, res. Essex, m. Elisha **CLARK**, ae
    22, b. Saybrook, res. Essex, Aug. 12, 1849, by P. G.
    Wightman                                                                                160

Harri[e]t, of East Lyme, m. Elias **BEEBE**, of Waterford, July
    20, 1854, by Harlem Hedden                                                         162

Harriet W., d. Jan. 5, 1859, ae 15 y.                                                  263

Henry S., s. Daniel, fisherman, ae 37 & Mary, ae 34, b. May 19,
    1848                                                                                    2

Herbert, d. Jan. 21, 1849, ae 17 y.                                                    253

J. N., d. Sept. 12, 1857, ae 6 m.                                                      261

Janette, m. George M. **BECKWITH**, b. of East Lyme, Feb. 13,
    1853, by George Mixter                                                             162

Josiah H., m. Emma M. **HOWARD**, b. of East Lyme, Jan. 15,
    1854, by George Mixter                                                             162

Julia Ann, of Waterford, m. Joseph C. **POST**, of Westbrook,
    Apr. 9, 1843, by Gurdon T. Chappell                                                157

Julius N., had child, d. Apr. 30, 1859, ae 1 d.                                        263

Laurana, m. Samuel R. **DOWSETT**, July 29, 1849, by
    Frederick Gridley                                                                  160

Lewis Dutton, d. Feb. 22, 1849, ae 7 m.                                                253

Lucy, d. Nat, of Lyme, m. Daniel **ROGERS**, of Lebanon, Aug.
    10, 1810                                                                                152

Lydia, d. Oct. [ ], 1849, ae 73 y.                                                     253

Mariann, m. Francis C. **LUCE**, b. of East Lyme, Dec. 4, 1854,
    by Frederick Gridley                                                               162

Mary H., m. George A. **SMITH**, b. of East Lyme, Dec. 15,
    1850, by J. F. Blanchard                                                           160

Meriah, m. Jeremiah **CLARK**, b. of East Lyme, Jan. 20, 1847,
    by Frederick Wightman                                                              159

Sabra, d. July 19, 1859, ae 22 y.                                                      263

Sarah, d. Mar. 14, 1856, ae 87 y.                                                      260

Sarah, d. Dec. 27, 1858, ae 84 y.                                                      262

Sarah F., m. Perez **AUSTIN**, b. of East Lyme, Dec. 31, 1854, by
    Harlem Hedden                                                                      162

MANWARING, (cont.),    Page

Savira, of East Lyme, m. Selden **COOK**, of Plainfield, N. Y.,
Oct. 17, 1847, by Roger Abiston    159

MATHER, MATHERS, Henry, m. Mary Ann **NONSUCH**, b. of East
Lyme, Mar. 30, 1846, by Frederick Gridley    158

John, m. Hanna **PAQUENTO**, (Indians), b. of Niantic, Nov.
21, 1789    150

Lay, m. Caroline **WADE**, b. of Lyme, Sept. 20, 1792    151

Maria, d. Feb. 16, 1859, ae 24 y.    263

MAYNARD, Anson H. & Aug., had child, d. Jan. 4, 1858    262

Charles G., s. Whitman, cooper, ae 44 & Abigail, ae 39, b. Sept.
30, 1850    4

Elijah, s. Whitman, farmer & Abigail, b. Nov. [ ], 1847    1

Elijah, d. Mar. 10, 1851, ae 3 y. 9 m.    255

Frances J., m. James C. **SMITH**, b. of Greenville, Apr. 13,
1851, by George Mixter    161

Mary, ae 16, b. East Lyme, res. East Lyme, m. Gurdon
**CLARK**, ae 21, b. Salem, res. East Lyme, Feb. 13,
1850, by Rev. Mr. Brown    160

Orrin, Jr., d. July 6, 1848, ae 17 y.    252

Orrin, d. Aug. 12, 1848, ae 51 y.    252

Selden, of Lyme, m. Abby **ROGERS**, of East Lyme, Sept. 10,
1848, by Frederick Gridley    159

William H., s. William, farmer, ae 26 & Harriet, b. Aug. 11,
1850    4

William Henry, s. William, farmer, ae 26 & Harriet, ae 16, b.
Aug. 11, 1849    3

McCAULEY, Daniel, of Staten Island, N. Y., m. Isabel **PRENTIS**, of
Waterford, Oct. 12, 1848, by Frederick Wightman    159

McCONNAL, Jane, d. James, farmer, ae 26 & Esther, ae 22, b. June 8,
1849    3

McCRARY, McCRERY, Benjamin F., m. Frances C. **MOORE**, b. of
East Lyme, Dec. 1, 1850, by P. G. Wightman    160

Franklin, d. Sept. 6, 1858, ae 28 y.    262

Mary Ann, of East Lyme, m. Daniel **JACKSON**, of Stonington,
Oct. 14, 1849, by P. G. Wightman    160

MEECH, John T., of Griswold, m. Rebecca M. **WAITE**, of Lyme, Mar.
13, 1842, by Frederick Gridley    156

MILLER, Sarah A., d. Epaphroditus, farmer, ae 47 & Catharine S., ae 30,
b. Mar. 3, 1849    3

MINER, MINOR, Ann Eliza, of Colchester, m. Andrew J. **CHAPMAN**,
of East Lyme, Dec. 18, 1854, by P. G. Wightman    162

Ann H., d. Apr. 19, 1850, ae 22 y.    254

Charles B., of Wethersfield, Ill., m. Mary G. **SMITH**, of East
Lyme, Feb. 7, 1843, by Frederick Wightman    156

Elisha, m. Amy **WAY**, b. of Lyme, Feb. 3, 1785    150

Lucretia, of Montville, m. Amasa **BUSH**, of Lyme, July 11,
1803    151

Mercy, d. Apr. 4, 1851, ae 62 y.    255

Sarah, d. Elias, of Lyme, m. Samuel **SMITH**, of Waterford,
Apr. 4, 1810    152

MITCHELSON, A., Jr., of Simsbury, m. Elizabeth H. **CHAPPELL**, of
East Lyme, June 5, 1848, by P. G. Wightman    159

**PRENTISS, PRENTIS,** (cont.), Page
 Isabel, of Waterford, m. Daniel McCAULEY, of Staten Island,
  N. Y., Oct. 12, 1848, by Frederick Wightman 159
 Marietta, m. Henry CONGDON, b. of East Lyme, Sept. 6,
  1846, by P. G. Wightman 158
**REED,** Ancil, m. Eliza M. LUCE, b. of East Lyme, Oct. 22, 1854, by P. G.
  Wightman 162
 Anodora, d. Jos[eph], mariner, ae 25 & Emeline, ae 24, b. July
  24, 1851 5
**REYNOLDS,** Henry, B. L., of Lyme, m. Temperance SANDERS, of East
  Lyme, Dec. 13, 1847, by P. G. Wightman 159
 Israel, of Northeast Dutchess Co., N. Y., m. Deborah DOOR, of
  Lyme, June 1, 1798 151
 William S., of Derby, m. Delia GURLEY, of East Lyme, Jan. 1,
  1854, by P. G. Wightman 162
**RICHARDS,** Ebenezer M., of East Lyme, m. Caroline J. CHAPEL, of
  New London, Feb. 26, 1851, by P. G. Wightman 161
**ROATH,** Lucind, of East Lyme, m. Griswold C. PECK, of Lyme, Feb. 23,
  1851, by P. G. Wightman 161
**ROBBINS,** William H., m. Sarah E. BECKWITH, b. of Lyme, Aug. 17,
  1851, by P. G. Wightman 161
**ROGERS,** Abba, m. Lawrence DOWSETT, b. of Lyme, Sept. 14, 1811 152
 Abby, of East Lyme, m. Selden MAYNARD, of Lyme, Sept.
  10, 1848, by Frederick Gridley 159
 Betsey, of Lyme, m. Roswell TURNER, of Saybrook, Nov. 28,
  1805 152
 Daniel, of Lebanon, m. Lucy MANWARING, d. Nat, of Lyme,
  Aug. 10, 1810 152
 Fanny, m. Samuel CHADWICK, b. of Lyme, Nov. 10, 1810 152
 Gideon, m. Sarah R. ROYCE, b. of East Lyme, Mar. 30, 1853,
  by P. G. Wightman 162
 Hannah, ae 25, m. William M. CROCKER, ae 24, b. of East
  Lyme, July 22, 1849, by C. H. Gates 160
 Hannah, d. Dec. 8, 1857, ae [ ] 261
 Harriet U., m. William MORGAN, b. of East Lyme, Dec. 7,
  1845, by Chester Tilden 158
 Isabelle A., d. Sept. 28, 1858, ae 38 y. 262
 James C., of New London, m. Nancy H. BECKWITH, of East
  Lyme, Jan. 14, 1849, by P. G. Wightman 160
 Jemina, d. Rowland, m. William CLARK, b. of Lyme, Jan. 22,
  1807 152
 Mary, d. Mar. 8, 1858, ae 94 y. 262
 Mary A., m. Marcus M. FOX, b. of East Lyme, Sept. 3, 1854,
  by P. G. Wightman 162
 Rowland, Jr., m. Lydia H. RYAN, b. of East Lyme, July 28,
  1839, by William Palmer, V. D. M. 155
 Sally, m. Isaac BUMP, b. of Lyme, Jan. 25, 1801 151
 William, of New London, m. Adeline HAYNES, of East Lyme,
  Sept. 20, 1846, by Frederick Wightman 158
**ROICE,** [see under ROYCE]
**ROSE,** Maria A., ae 20, b. Franklin, res. Waterford, m. George W.
  DARROW, ae 23, b. Waterford, res. Waterford,
  Apr. 13, 1850, by P. G. Wightman 160

SMITH, (cont.),                                                    Page
Dudley, m. [          ] GOOLD, b. of Lyme, Feb. 21, 1787           150
Elijah W., m. Louisa J. SMITH, b. of East Lyme, Jan. 18,
   1846, by James Hepburn                          158
Elisha, m. Mary GORTON, b. of Lyme, Dec. 26, 1808                 152
Elisha, m. Sarah A. TINKER, b. of East Lyme, Dec. 11, 1842,
   by Frederick Wightman                           156
Eliza Ann, m. William H. H. COMSTOCK, b. of East Lyme,
   Dec. 15, 1842, by Frederick Wightman            156
Elizabeth, of Lyme, m. Avery HARSTON, of Mansfield, Oct.
   14, 1804                                        152
Elizabeth, d. E. W., farmer & Louisa, b. Oct. [  ], 1848           2
Elizabeth P., m. Joseph D. LATHAM, b. of East Lyme, Oct. 11,
   1854, by Frederick Gridley                      162
Emeline H., m. William F. THORP, b. of New London, June 1,
   1851, by George Mixter                          161
Esther Ann, of East Lyme, m. Anson CROCKER, of
   Waterford, June 25, 1843, by A. B. Wheeler       157
Frances E., m. Nicol F. CHAMPLIN, b. of East Lyme, Sept.
   16, 1844, by Chester Tilden                      157
George, of New London, m. Anna CHAPMAN, of Lyme, Mar.
   3, 1793, by [          ]                         151
George A., m. Mary H. MANWARING, b. of East Lyme, Dec.
   15, 1850, by J. F. Blanchard                     160
Hannah, of Waterford, m. David STRONG, of Lyme, May 24,
   1808                                             152
Hannah, d. Daniel, m. John AYER, b. of Lyme, July 27, 1808        152
Helena L., d. [          ], farmer & Mary S., b. Mar. 18, 1848     2
Horace, farmer, ae 40 & Obediance, ae 39, had child b. June 13,
   1848                                             2
James C., m. Frances J. MAYNARD, b. of Greenville, Apr. 13,
   1851, by George Mixter                          161
Jane, of Lyme, m. William STEBBINS, of Waterford, Mar. 30,
   1803                                             151
John E., d. May 23, 1849, ae 13 y.                                253
John M., m. Rebecca G. BECKWITH, b. of East Lyme, Nov.
   26, 1844, by Chester Tilden                      157
Jos[eph], s. Elijah W., farmer & Louisa, b. Apr. [  ], 1849        3
Julia P., d. William H., stone cutter, ae 28 & Louisa, ae 29, b.
   Nov. 20, 1847                                    1
Louisa J., m. Elijah W. SMITH, b. of East Lyme, Jan. 18,
   1846, by James Hepburn                          158
Margaret, of Lyme, m. Joseph STEBBINS, of New London,
   June 2, 1790                                     150
Mark, d. Nov. 8, 1858, ae 30 y.                                   262
Mary, d. Geo[rge], m. Asa HOLT, b. of New London, Apr. 7,
   1785                                             150
Mary A., of East Lyme, m. John S. GEEG, of Essex, July 30,
   1854, by P. G. Wightman                          162
Mary G., of East Lyme, m. Charles B. MINER, of Wethersfield,
   Ill., Feb. 7, 1843, by Frederick Wightman        156
Orlando Melville, s. John, farmer, ae 45 & Delia, ae 43, b. Apr.
   14, 1851                                         5

**SMITH**, (cont.),                                                    Page
    Rhoda, m. Asa **SMITH**, b. of Lyme, Jan. 16, 1794        151
    Roswell, d. Dec. 8, 1847, ae 49 y.                         251
    Samuel, of Waterford, m. Sarah **MINER**, d. Elias, of Lyme,
        Apr. 4, 1810                                         152
    Samuel, of Norwich, m. Prudence S. **MORGAN**, of Lyme, July
        10, 1842, by Frederick Wightman                      156
    Seth, Jr., m. Lydia **TUBBS**, b. of Lyme, Nov. 2, 1786    150
    Seth, d. Mar. 19, 1840                                     250
    Silas, d. Sept. 6, 1857, ae 20 y.                          261
    Simon, d. Apr. 23, 1851, ae 84 y.                          255
    William D., farmer & Jennie, had child, b. Nov. [ ], 1849    3
    William H., m. Louisa P. **STARKEY**, b. of East Lyme, Nov.
        10, 1840, by Frederick Gridley                       156
**SOBUCK**, [see under **SAWBUCK**]
**SPENCER**, Fanny E., m. Orlando C. **GORTON**, b. of East Lyme, Mar.
        20, 1854, by P. G. Wightman                          162
    James R., m. Lucy A. **BECKWITH**, b. of East Lyme, Oct. 17,
        1848, by P. G. Wightman                              159
**STANTON**, Benjamin, oil manufacturer, ae 33 & Sarah, ae 24, res.
        Waterford, had child [d.] b. Aug. 9, 1850              4
    Benjamin D., of Waterford, m. Sarah M.**COMSTOCK**, of East
        Lyme, Dec. 2, 1849, by P. G. Wightman                160
    -----, d. Aug. 7, 1851, ae 1 d.                            255
    -----, d. Aug. 9, 1851, ae 3 d.                            255
**STAPLINS**, Julia, d. Apr. 22, 1848, ae 22 y.                        252
    Reuben R., of New London, m. Jane M. **CLARK**, of Waterford,
        Mar. 19, 1854, by P. G. Wightman                     162
    William, of Waterford, m. Mary **DENISON**, of East Lyme,
        Sept. 6, 1846, by P. G. Wightman                     158
**STARKEY**, Louisa P., m. William H. **SMITH**, b. of East Lyme, Nov. 10,
    1840, by Frederick Gridley                                 156
**STEBBINS**, Eliza Eliza*, of East Lyme, m. John **KNIGHT**, of Waterford,
    Jan. 5, 1853, by P. G. Wightman
        (*So written in copy)                                162
    John, of New London, m. Rhoda **LEE**, of Lyme, Apr. [ ], 1788    150
    Joseph, of New London, m. Margaret **SMITH**, of Lyme, June 2,
        1790                                                 150
    Mary, ae 16, of East Lyme, m. Hiram **JOHNSON**, ae 25, b.
        Lyme, res. East Lyme, Jan. 1, 1850, by E. Cosby      160
    Sarah, m. Edwin J. **FORSYTH**, b. of New London, Oct. [ ],
        1848, by P. G. Wightman                              159
    William, of Waterford, m. Jane **SMITH**, of Lyme, Mar. 30,
        1803                                                 151
**STEDMAN**, John, d. Oct. 9, 1857, ae 70 y.                           261
**STODDARD**, Maria, of Eastford, m. George H. **SHELDON**, of
        Woodstock, Oct. 14, 1851, by George Mixter           161
**STRICKLAND**, Jerome, of New London, m. Hannah **PHILLIPS**, of
        Lyme, Nov. 18, 1792                                  151
    Joseph, m. Phebe **LEWIS**, b. of Lyme, Mar. 1, 1792       150
    Joseph, d. Dec. 27, 1849, ae 79 y.                         253
**STRONG**, David, of Lyme, m. Hannah **SMITH**, of Waterford, May 24,
    1808                                                       152

**STRONG,** (cont.), Page

    Sarah J., of Sag Harbor, N. Y., m. Charles B. **LATHAM**, of
East Lyme, June 26, 1853, by George Mixter — 162

**SWANEY,** George B., m. [     ] **GILBERT**, b. of Lyme, [    ],
1812 — 152

**TABER,** Cornelia, d. Oct. 6, 1847, ae 26 y. — 251

    Thomas J., farmer, ae 40 & Cornelia, ae 25, had child b. Oct. 1,
1847 — 1

    -----, child of Mrs. [    ], d. Oct. 8, 1847, ae 8 d. — 251

**TAULAQUARING,** David, of Mohegan Tribe of Indians, New London, m.
Eunice **OBID**, Niantic Tribe of Indians, Lyme, Apr.
30, 1789 — 150

**THOMPSON,** Harriet U., of Montville, m. Ezra R. **HUNTLEY**, of East
Lyme, Feb. 7, 1853, by P. G. Wightman — 162

**THORP,** William F., m. Emeline H. **SMITH**, b. of New London, June 1,
1851, by George Mixter — 161

**TILLOTSON,** Betsey, m. Joseph C. **DOWSETT**, b. of Lyme, Nov. 4,
1810 — 152

    Mary, m. William **SHIPMAN**, b. of Lyme, Apr. 13, 1794 — 151

    Sophia L., m. Jared **TURNER**, b. of East Lyme, July 25, 1852,
by George Mixter — 161

**TINKER,** Jeremiah, of New London, m. Mary **LESTER**, of Lyme, July 4,
1790 — 150

    Lucy M., d. May 17, 1848, ae 62 y. — 252

    Sarah A., m. Elisha **SMITH**, b. of East Lyme, Dec. 11, 1842,
by Frederick Wightman — 156

    William, d. Feb. 15, 1851, ae 25 y. — 255

**TUBBS,** Betty, m. Isaac **BUMP**, b. of Lyme, Feb. 23, 1794 — 151

    Hannah, of Lyme, m. Almiran **TURNER**, of Saybrook, June
15, 1807 — 152

    Job, d. Dec. 9, 1856, ae 59 y. — 260

    Lucretia, m. Ezra **CHAMPION**, b. of Lyme, Oct. 14, 1784 — 150

    Lydia, m. Seth **SMITH**, Jr., b. of Lyme, Nov. 2, 1786 — 150

**TURNER,** Almiran, of Saybrook, m. Hannah **TUBBS**, of Lyme, June 15,
1807 — 152

    Frank G., d. July 9, 1851, ae 3 y. 10 m. — 255

    Henry E., m. Marietta **FITCH**, Dec. 5, 1841, by James Hepburn — 156

    Jared, m. Sophia L. **TILLOTSON**, b. of East Lyme, July 25,
1852, by George Mixter — 161

    Maria, m. Peter A. **COMSTOCK**, b. of East Lyme, Mar. 9,
1840, by William Palmer, V. D. M. — 156

    Roswell, of Saybrook, m. Betsey **ROGERS**, of Lyme, Nov. 28,
1805 — 152

**UTLEY,** Rebecca, d. Jan. [ ], 1851, ae 88 y. — 255

**WADE,** Caroline, m. Lay **MATHER**, b. of Lyme, Sept. 20, 1792 — 151

    Sarah M., m. John **EDWARDS**, b. of New London, Mar. 14,
1847, by Palmer G. Wightman — 159

**WAITE,** Rebecca M., of Lyme, m. John T. **MEECH**, of Griswold, Mar.
13, 1842, by Frederick Gridley — 156

**WALES,** Joseph Denison, of Windham, m. Lucretia **GORTON**, wid., of
Waterford, Dec. 13, 1810 — 152

**WALLACE,** Thomas, m. Hannah **LEECH**, wid., b. of Lyme, Dec. 30,
1787 — 150

Page

WILBER, -----, Mrs., d. Sept. 16, 1848, ae [  ]                                          252
WILLIAMS, Hamlin, of Saybrook, m. Patience LATTIMER, of Lyme,
    Nov. 26, 1798                                                                    151
    Theoda, wid., m. George WILSON, b. of Lyme, Dec. 17, 1789          150
WILSON, George, m. wid. Theoda WILLIAMS, b. of Lyme, Dec. 17,
    1789                                                                             150
WOOD, Hannah, of Lyme, m. Joseph BELCHER, late of Newport, R. I.,
    Aug. [  ], 1788                                                                  150
    Julia, m. Dyer CHAMPLIN, b. of Lyme, Apr. 2, 1804                     151
WOODWARD, Betsey, m. Tabor HUNTLEY, b. of Lyme, July 28, 1811        152
    Mary Ann, of Griswold, m. Ephraim U. CORDNER, of New
    London, Nov. 8, 1840, by Frederick Gridley                          156
NO SURNAME
    -----, d. May 27, 1850, ae 4 d.                                              254
    -----, d. June 5, 1850, ae 1 d.                                              254
    -----, st. b. infant, Sept. [  ], 1850, ae 4 h.                          254